The Manichaeans of the Roman East

Nag Hammadi and Manichaean Studies

VOLUME 105

The titles published in this series are listed at *brill.com/nhms*

The Manichaeans
of the Roman East

Manichaeism in Greek Anti-Manichaica
and Roman Imperial Legislation

By

Rea Matsangou

BRILL

LEIDEN | BOSTON

Library of Congress Cataloging-in-Publication Data

Names: Matsangou, Rea, 1962– author.
Title: The Manichaeans of the Roman East : Manichaeism in Greek
 anti-Manichaica & Roman imperial legislation / by Rea Matsangou.
Description: Leiden ; Boston : Brill, [2023] | Series: Nag Hammadi and
 Manichaean studies, 0929–2470 ; volume 105 | Slight revision of the
 author's thesis (doctoral)—Leiden University, 2021. | Includes
 bibliographical references and index.
Identifiers: LCCN 2023013644 (print) | LCCN 2023013645 (ebook) | ISBN
 9789004542846 (hardback ; acid-free paper) | ISBN 9789004544222 (ebook)
Subjects: LCSH: Manichaeism—Rome. | Manichaeans—Persecutions. |
 Asceticism—History—Early church, ca. 30–600. | Rome—Religion.
Classification: LCC BT1410 .M38 2023 (print) | LCC BT1410 (ebook) | DDC
 299/.932—dc23/eng/20230522
LC record available at https://lccn.loc.gov/2023013644
LC ebook record available at https://lccn.loc.gov/2023013645

Typeface for the Latin, Greek, and Cyrillic scripts: "Brill". See and download: brill.com/brill-typeface.

ISSN 0929-2470
ISBN 978-90-04-54284-6 (hardback)
ISBN 978-90-04-54422-2 (e-book)

Copyright 2023 by Rea Matsangou. Published by Koninklijke Brill NV, Leiden, The Netherlands.
Koninklijke Brill NV incorporates the imprints Brill, Brill Nijhoff, Brill Hotei, Brill Schöningh, Brill Fink,
Brill mentis, Vandenhoeck & Ruprecht, Böhlau, V&R unipress and Wageningen Academic.
Koninklijke Brill NV reserves the right to protect this publication against unauthorized use. Requests for
re-use and/or translations must be addressed to Koninklijke Brill NV via brill.com or copyright.com.

This book is printed on acid-free paper and produced in a sustainable manner.

For Iris and Iole

φύσις κρύπτεσθαι φιλεῖ
(*Heraclitus*)

∵

Contents

Acknowledgements

This book is a slightly modified version of my Ph.D., which I defended in June 2021 at the University of Leiden. For successfully achieving this challenging yet exciting research project, first and foremost, I wholeheartedly thank my supervisor Albert de Jong (Leiden University), because he was the one who suggested I do this research, and gave me the opportunity to delve into an extremely interesting topic that took me on a journey to my favourite era, Late Antiquity. I thank him, because, knowing my academic background and interests, he rightly judged that this would be a subject that would fascinate me; because he trusted me, and with his encouragement, he made me overcome my insecurities. I also want to express my deep gratitude to my co-supervisor, Dimitris Kyrtatas (University of Thessaly), for his constant and substantial interest, his prompt response, and the feedback he has consistently given me at all stages of this project. I am very grateful to both, for their academic and personal support. Both being prominent historians of Late Antiquity, with their valuable knowledge and critical insights, guidance and useful comments, our inspirational discussions, helped to effectively complete this endeavour.

I also would like to express my gratitude to my friends, fellow researchers, and academics: Prof. Samuel Lieu (Emeritus, Macquarie University, and Bye Fellow Robinson College, Cambridge), also a prominent historian of Late Antiquity, for his whole-hearted interest, his graciousness, his always encouraging words for my research, and his support and valuable advice. Prof. Rika Benveniste (University of Thessaly), for her fruitful feedback on parts of my work, and encouragement; Dr Mattias Brand (University of Zurich), for our fruitful discussions where we exchanged our views and research findings; Petros Parthenis (PhD, University of Thessaly), for his inspired and diligent translation of some ancient Greek texts that troubled me into modern Greek; Dr Mark Locicero (University of British Columbia) for his excellency in English language editing and proofreading of my manuscript. For their interest in my research and for giving me access to their work (published and/or unpublished), I thank Prof. Johannes van Oort (Radboud University and University of Pretoria), Prof. Majella Franzmann (University of Sydney), Dr Jean-Daniel Dubois (École Pratique des Hautes Études), Prof. Nils Arne Pedersen (Aarhus University), and Afroditi Kamara (Historian-Cultural Heritage Consultant).

The academic and institutional surroundings definitely contributed greatly to the completion of this project. The meetings and symposia of the 'Late Antiquity discussion group' led by Prof. Kyrtatas (History Lab, University of Thessaly) were very inspiring. The International Association of Manichaean

Studies (IAMS), through its conferences, and the Mani in Cambridge day symposium led by Prof. Lieu, made me feel a member of the 'wider family of Manichaeologists' and gave me the opportunity to meet and discuss with leading scholars on the topic from all over the world, to present parts of my work, to test my working hypotheses, and receive useful comments and feedback. I am also indebted to all my colleagues (academic and administrative staff) from the Department of History, Archaeology, and Social Anthropology at the University of Thessaly for their support, understanding, and trust, which had a great significance for my work.

For the publication of my doctoral research as a book, I would like to express my gratitude to the members of the doctorate and examining committees who strongly encouraged me to publish my thesis. I am deeply grateful to Prof. van Oort for appreciating my work and suggesting that I publish it with Brill's Nag Hammadi and Manichaean Studies series. I also thank him for his patience and guidance during the publication process. For the final version of the text, I am grateful to Prof. Johannes van Oort and Prof. Jason BeDuhn, for their corrections, suggestions, and comments that helped me to improve the manuscript. Special thanks also go to the editors of Brill, Marjolein van Zuylen, for her always prompt, efficient, and helpful response, and to Dirk Bakker, the production editor, for his patience and the excellent and careful editing of the book in its final phase. I would also like to thank the staff of Asiatype Inc., who worked on the book typesetting.

Lastly, I am thankful to my family for their unconditional love and support and for enduring my absence by understanding the significance of this study for me. I dedicate this book to all of them, especially to my granddaughters, Iris and Iole.

Rea Matsangou
Volos, May 2023

Tables

Abbreviations and Translations

Primary Sources (Ancient Texts)

Greek Sources

Abjuration Formulas & conversion ritual

AF(s)	*Abjuration Formula(s)*
LAF	*Long Abjuration Formula*
RCM	*Ritual to be observed by those who are converted from among the Manichaeans to the pure and true faith of our Lord Jesus Christ*
SAF	*Short Abjuration Formula*

Agathias

Hist.	*Historiae*

Alexander of Lycopolis

Tract. Man.	*Tractatus de placitis Manichaeorum*

Amphilochius of Iconium

c. Haer.	*Contra haereticos*

Anastasius of Sinai

Hexaemeron	*Hexaemeron anagogicarum contemplationum libros duodecim*

Athanasius of Alexandria

[*Apoll.*]	*De incarnatione contra Apollinarium libri ii*
c. Ar.	*Orationes Contra Arianos* (*Oratio I, II, III*)
Ep. Adelph.	*Epistula ad Adelphius*
Ep. Aeg. Lib.	*Epistula ad episcopos Aegypti et Libyae*
Fug.	*Apologia de fuga sua*
H. Ar.	*Historia Arianorum*
Vit. Ant.	*Vita Antonii*

Barsanuphius

Ep.	*Epistulae*

Basil of Caesarea

Adv. Eunomium	*Adversus Eunomium*
Ep.	*Epistulae*
Hom. Hexaem.	*Homiliae in Hexaemeron*

[Basil of Caesarea]

Asceticon brev.	*Constitutiones Asceticae. Asceticon magnum sive Quaestiones* (regulae brevius tractatae)

Asceticon fus.	*Constitutiones Asceticae. Asceticon magnum sive Quaestiones* (regulae fusius tractatae)
Cosmas Indicopleustes	
Top.	*Topographia Christiana*
Cyril of Alexandria	
c. Jul.	*Contra Julianum Imperatorem*
Comm. Isaiam	*Commentarius in Isaiam*
Comm. Jo.	*Commentarii in Joannem*
Ep.	*Ad Calosyrium*
Inc.	*De incarnatione Domini*
Cyril of Jerusalem	
Catech.	*Catecheses ad illuminandos 1–18*
Cyril of Scythopolis	
Vit. Euth.	*Vita Euthymii*
Vit. Sab.	*Vita Sabae*
Didymus the Blind	
c. Manichaeos	*Contra Manichaeos*
Comm. Eccl.	*Commentarii in Ecclesiasten*
Comm. Zach.	*Commentarii in Zacchariam*
[Pseudo-Didymus]	
Trin.	*De Trinitate*
Ephrem the Syrian	
Hymni	*Hymni contra Haereses*
Epiphanius of Salamis	
Pan.	*De Haeresibus (Panarion)*
Eusebius of Caesarea	
Ep. Constantiam	*Epistula ad Constantiam Augustam*
HE	*Historia Ecclesiastica*
Vit. Const.	*Vita Constantini*
Eustathius the monk	
Ep. Tim.	*Epistula ad Timotheum scholasticum de duabus naturis adversus Severum*
Euthymius Zigabenus	
Panoplia	*Panoplia dogmatica ad Alexium Comnenum*
Evagrius the Scholastic	
HE	*Historia Ecclesiastica*
Flavius Claudius Julianus	
Ep.	*Epistulae*
Gelasius of Cyzicus	
HE	*Historia Ecclesiastica*

Georgius Cedrenus

hist. compend.   *Compendium historiarum*

Gregory of Nazianzus

Fun. oratio   *Funebris oratio in laudem Basilii Magni Caesareae in*
                       Cappadocia episcopi (orat. 43)

Gregory of Nyssa

Adv. Macedonianos   *Adversus Macedonianos de spiritu sancto*

c. Eunomium   *Contra Eunomium*

Ep. Letoium   *Epistula canonica ad Letoium*

[Hegemonius]

AA   *Acta Archelai*

Joannes Diacrinomenus

HE   *Historia Ecclesiastica*

John Chrysostom

Anom.   *De consubstantiali (= Contra Anomoeos, homilia 7)*

Hom. 1 Cor.   *Homiliae in epistulam i ad Corinthios (homiliae 1–44)*

Hom. 1 Tim.   *Homiliae in epistulam i ad Timotheum (hom. 1–18)*

Hom. 2 Cor.   *Homiliae in epistulam ii ad Corinthios (homiliae 1–30)*

Hom. 2 Cor. 4:13   *In illud: Habentes eundem spiritum*

Hom. 2 Tim.   *Homiliae in epistulam ii ad Timotheum (homiliae 1–10)*

Hom. Eph.   *Homiliae in epistulam ad Ephesios*

Hom. Gal.   *Homiliae in epistulam ad Galatas commentarius*

Hom. Gal. 2:11   *In illud: In faciem ei restiti*

Hom. Gen.$^{1-67}$ *Homiliae in Genesim (sermones 1–67)*

Hom. Gen.$^{1-9}$ *Homiliae in Genesim (sermones 1–9)*

Hom. Heb.   *Homiliae in epistulam ad Hebraeos*

Hom. Jo.   *Homiliae in Joannem (homiliae 1–88)*

Hom. Matt.   *Homiliae in Matthaeum (homiliae 1–90)*

Hom. Rom.   *Homiliae in epistulam ad Romanos (homiliae 1–32)*

Natal.   *In diem natalem*

Oppugn.   *Adversus oppugnatores vitae monasticae*

Sac.   *De sacerdotio*

Scand.   *Ad eos qui scandalizati sunt*

John of Caesarea

Adv. Manichaeos, hom. 1 *Adversus Manichaeos (hom. 1)*

Adv. Manichaeos, hom. 2 *Adversus Manichaeos (hom. 2)*

John of Damascus

c. Manichaeos   *Contra Manichaeos*

Haer.   *De haeresibus*

Julianus Arianus

comm. Job   *Commentarius in Job*

Justinian

c. monophysitas   *Contra monophysitas*

Justinus Martyr

Apol. A   *Apologia prima pro Christianis ad Antoninum Pium*

Libanius

Ep.   *Epistulae*

Macarius of Magnesia

Apocriticus   *Apocriticus seu Μονογενής*

Malalas

Chron.   *Chronographia*

Mark the Deacon

Vit. Porph.   *Vita Porphyry*

Nilus of Ankara

Ep.   *Epistulae*

Olympiodorus

Comm. Job.   *Commentarii in Job*

Peter of Sicily

Hist. ref. Man.   *Historia utilis et refutatio Manichaeorum vel
                                  Paulicianorum*

Philostorgius

HE   *Historia Ecclesiastica*

Photius

Bibl.   *Bibliotheca*

c. Manichaeos   *Contra Manichaeos*

Porphyrius

c. Christianos   *Contra Christianos*

Procopius

Hist. Arcana   *Historia Arcana*

Pseudo-Caesarius

Erotapokriseis   *Quaestiones et responsiones*

Serapion of Thmuis

c. Manichaeos   *Contra Manichaeos*

Severianus of Gabala

c. Manichaeos   *In centurionem et contra Manichaeos et Apollinaristas*

Simplicius

Comm. Man. Epict.   *In Epictetum encheiridion*

Socrates the Scholastic

HE   *Historia Ecclesiastica*

Sozomenus

HE   *Historia Ecclesiastica*

Theodoret of Cyrrhus

Ep. Sirm.	*Epistulae (Collectio Sirmondiana, epist. 1–95)*
Haer.	*Haereticarum fabularum compendium*
HE	*Historia Ecclesiastica*
Phil. hist.	*Historia Religiosa/Philotheos historia*

Theodorus Anagnostes

Epit. hist. trip.	*Epitome historiae tripartitae*
HE	*Historia ecclesiastica*

Theodorus Heracleensis vel Theodorus Mopsuestenus

Frg. Matt	*Fragmenta in Matthaeum (in catenis)*

Theodorus of Raithou

Praeparatio	*Praeparatio (= De incarnatione liber)*

Theophanes the Confessor

Chron.	*Chronographia*

Timothy the Presbyter

Recept. Haer.	*De receptione haereticorum*

Titus of Bostra

c. Manichaeos	*Contra Manichaeos*

Zacharias of Mytilene

Adv. Manichaeos	*Adversus Manichaeos*
SC	*Capita vii contra Manichaeos/Seven Chapters*

Laws

B	*Basilica*
Cod. justin.	Codex Justinianus
Cod. theod.	Codex Theodosianus
D	*Digesta*
Nov.	*Novels of Justinian*
NTh.	*Novels of Theodosius*
NVal.	*Novels of Valentinian*
Sirm.	*Sirmondian Constitutions*

Latin Sources

Augustine

c. Julianum	*Contra Julianum*
Comm. Aug.	*Commonitorium Sancti Augustini*
Conf.	*Confessiones*

Duab.	*De duabus animabus*
Faust.	*Contra Faustum Manichaeum*
Fund.	*Contra epistulam Manichaei quam vocant Fundamenti*
Haer.	*De haeresibus*
In Joannis	*In Joannis evangelium tractatus*
Mor. Manich.	*De moribus Manichaeorum*
Nat. bon.	*De natura boni contra Manichaeos*

Manichaean Texts

1 Keph.	*Kephalaia* vol. 1: *The Kephalaia of the Teacher* (Berlin *Kephalaia*)
2 Keph.	*Kephalaia* vol. 2: *The Kephalaia of the Wisdom my Lord Mani* (Dublin *Kephalaia*)
2 PsB	*Psalm-Book*, part 2
CMC	*Codex Manichaicus Coloniensis/Cologne Mani-Codex*
Hom.	*The Manichaean Homilies*
KAB	*The Kellis Agricultural Account Book*

Other Abbreviations

ACO	*Acta Conciliorum Oecumenicorum*
CP	*Cunctos Populos*
NT	New Testament
OT	Old Testament
P.Rylands 3, Gr. 469	*Catalogue of the Greek and Latin Papyri in the John Rylands Library* (Vol. 3).
PPO	Praefectus Praetorio Orientis

Secondary Sources (Journals, Encyclopedias, Series, etc.)

AHAW	Abhandlungen der Heidelberger Akademie der Wissenschaften
ANF	*Ante-Nicene Fathers.* Edited by Alexander Roberts and James Donaldson. 1885–1887. 10 vols. Repr., Peabody, MA: Hendrickson, 1994
AoF	Altorientalische Forschungen
APAW	Abhandlungen der preussischen Akademie der Wissenschaften, Philosophisch-historische Klasse 1
BJRL	*Bulletin of the John Rylands University Library of Manchester*
BSGRT	Bibliotheca Scriptorum Graecorum et Romanorum Teubneriana

BSOAS	*Bulletin of the School of Oriental and African Studies*
ByzZ	*Byzantinische Zeitschrift*
BZRGG	Beihefte zur Zeitschrift für Religions- und Geistesgeschichte
CAH	Cambridge Ancient History
CCSG	Corpus Christianorum: Series Graeca. Turnhout: Brepols, 1977–
CCSL	Corpus Christianorum: Series Latina. Turnhout: Brepols, 1953–
CCT	Corpus Christianorum in Translation
CFHBSB	Corpus Fontium Historiae Byzantinae. Series Berolinensis
CFM	Corpus Fontium Manichaeorum
ClAnt	*Classical Antiquity*
CRAI	Comptes rendus de l'Académie des Inscriptions et belles-lettres
CSCO	Corpus Scriptorum Christianorum Orientalium. Edited by Jean Baptiste Chabot et al. Paris, 1903
CSEL	Corpus Scriptorum Ecclesiasticorum Latinorum
CSHB	Corpus Scriptorum Historiae Byzantinae
DOP	*Dumbarton Oaks Papers*
EAC	Encyclopedia of Ancient Christianity
ECF	Early Church Fathers
FC	Fathers of the Church
GCS	Die griechischen christlichen Schriftsteller der ersten [drei] Jahrhunderte
GCS, N.F.	Die griechischen christlichen Schriftsteller der ersten [drei] Jahrhunderte. Neue Folge
GRBS	*Greek, Roman and Byzantine Studies*
Historia	*Historia: Zeitschrift für Alte Geschichte*
HSCP	*Harvard Studies in Classical Philology*
HTR	*Harvard Theological Review*
HTS	Harvard Theological Studies
IAMS	International Association of Manichaean Studies
JAC	*Jahrbuch für Antike und Christentum*
JAOS	*Journal of the American Oriental Society*
JECS	*Journal of Early Christian Studies*
JEH	*Journal of Ecclesiastical History*
JHS	*Journal of Hellenic Studies*
JRAS	*Journal of the Royal Asiatic Society*
JRS	*Journal of Roman Studies*
JTS	*Journal of Theological Studies*
LCC	Library of Christian Classics
LCL	The Loeb Classical Library
LFHCC	Library of Fathers of the Holy Catholic Church
LSJ	*The Online Liddell-Scott-Jones Greek-English Lexicon*

LTP	*Laval théologique et philosophique*
MS	Manichaean Studies
MTSR	*Method and Theory in the Study of Religion*
NHMS	Nag Hammadi and Manichaean Studies
NPNF	Nicene and Post-Nicene Fathers, Series 1 & 2. Edited by Philip Schaff. 1886–1889. 14 vols. Repr., Peabody, MA: Hendrickson, 1994
OCM	Oxford Classical Monographs
OCP	*Orientalia Christiana Periodica*
ODB	*Oxford Dictionary of Byzantium*
OrChrAn	Orientalia Christiana Analecta
PG	Patrologia Graeca. Edited by J.-P. Migne. 162 vols. Paris, 1857–1886
PhA	Philosophia Antiqua
PLRE	Prosopography of Late Roman Empire
PTS	Patristische Texte und Studien
RGG	*Religion in Geschichte und Gegenwart.* Edited by Hans Dieter Betz. 4th ed. Tubingen: Mohr Siebeck, 1998–2007
RGRW	Religions in the Graeco-Roman World
RIDA	*Revue internationale des droits de l'antiquité*
RPP	*Religion Past and Present: Encyclopedia of Theology and Religion.* Edited by Hans Dieter Betz et al. 14 vols. Leiden: Brill, 2007–2013
SBLTT	Society of Biblical Literature Texts and Translations
SC	Sources chrétiennes. Paris: Cerf, 1943–
SCH	Studies in Church History
SEG	Supplementum epigraphicum graecum
SHR	Studies in the History of Religions (supplements to *Numen*)
StOR	Studies in Oriental Religions
StPatr	Studia Patristica
TLG	*Thesaurus Linguae Graecae*
TS	*Theological Studies*
TU	Texte und Untersuchungen
VC	*Vigiliae Christianae*
VCS	Variorum Collected Studies (formerly Variorum Reprints)
VCSup	Supplements to Vigiliae Christianae
WGRW	Writings from the Greco-Roman World
WUNT	Wissenschaftliche Untersuchungen zum Neuen Testament
ZAC	*Zeitschrift für Antikes Christentum/Journal of Ancient Christianity*
ZDMG	*Zeitschrift der deutschen morgenländischen Gesellschaft*
ZPE	*Zeitschrift für Papyrologie und Epigraphik*
ZSS	*Zeitschrift der Savigny-Stiftung für Rechtsgeschichte*

A Note on Translations and Editions of Primary Sources and Referencing System

When English translations of ancient Greek texts are available, these are being used (see Bibliography). Where translations are modified, this is noted. Unless otherwise indicated, translations have been made by the author of this book. When a single translation, the most common is used for an ancient text, then, in the footnotes, the translator's last name and the corresponding pages are indicated. When multiple translations of ancient texts are used, publication dates are also provided. Ancient texts in a language other than Greek are provided through translations.

All citations of Cod. theod. and Cod. justin. in this book follow Mommsen's and Krueger's editions respectively. Quotations translated in English are: 1) from Coleman-Norton 1966, 3 vols, 2) Pharr 1952, 3) Frier et al. 2016, or 4) mine.

All editions of primary sources used in this book are listed in the Bibliography (Primary Sources). Quotations in ancient Greek in the footnotes are drawn from the critical editions/editions of the ancient texts, as shown in the Bibliography (Primary Sources). When a single edition is used for an ancient text, then, in the footnotes, the editor's last name (or the series name and number) and the corresponding pages are indicated. When multiple editions/publications of ancient texts are used, publication dates are also provided. Quotations in ancient Greek, with no reference to specific pages of the editions used, were accessed via *Thesaurus Linguae Graecae* (TLG) (University of California, Irvine). The help of the TGL database in locating ancient Greek texts, especially those not known in modern literature (with references to Manichaeans and Manichaeism), was substantially valuable.

The abbreviations above and the referencing system in the text and in the bibliography follow The *SBL Handbook of Style: For Biblical Studies and Related Disciplines* (2nd ed.), by B.J. Collins, B. Buller, J.F. Kutsko, P.H. Alexander, J. Eisenbraun, J.D. Ernest et al. Atlanta: SBL Press, 2014.

Introduction

And when they are about to eat bread they pray first, and tell the
bread, "I neither reaped you, nor ground you, nor pounded you, nor
put you into an oven; someone else did these things, and brought
you to me. I have been eating without guilt." And whenever [an elec-
tus] says this for himself, he tells the catechumen, "I have prayed for
you," and the catechumen withdraws.

APOLOGY TO THE BREAD[1]

∴

1 Introduction

The "Apology to the Bread" is one of the most intriguing texts we will
encounter in studying the testimonies of the Greek anti-Manichaica about
the Manichaeans of the Roman East. It is recorded only in the Greek anti-
Manichaean literature, and its original form is preserved in the earliest extant
source of the corpus (end of third cent.).[2] Despite the characteristic irony that
permeates Epiphanius' writings, this 'prayer/apology' does in fact reflect fundamental Manichaean beliefs and conducts.

The scene that it captures comes from the most important Manichaean
ritual, their sacred meal. The protagonists of the scene are the two classes
comprising the Manichaean community: the Elect (the highest echelons of
the Manichaean Church), and the catechumens or hearers (the lay believers).
The core of the prayer itself looks and could be authentic since it is compatible
with dualism, the most notable feature of the Manichaean cosmogony. At the
foundation of the Manichaean religion lies the doctrine of the two principles
(also called roots or natures), which correspond to light and darkness, good
and evil, spirit and matter. In addition, the apology reflects pivotal rules of the
community: "The mystery of the elect, with their commandments. The mystery of the catechumens their helpers, with their commandments".[3]

---

1 Epiphanius, *Pan.* 66.28 (Williams, 258). For the original text in Greek see ch.[5], 2.3.2.1.
2 P.Rylands 3, Gr. 469.
3 *1Keph.* 1.15.15–19 (Gardner 1995, 21). An analysis and interpretation of the "Apology to the
   Bread" is provided in ch.[5], 2.3.2.

Mani, the founder of Manichaeism, gave Manichaeans all the commandments, and himself established the foundations of his religion: its tenets
(recorded in a series of canonical books), a set of rituals, the organisational
structure of the religious community, and its missionary strategy.[4] Living in
the pluralistic environment of third-century Mesopotamia, the religion he
instated contains elements of many religious traditions with which he was
familiar, such as Zoroastrianism, Buddhism, Christianity, and Judaism. Mani
envisioned that his religion would surpass preceding ones by creating an
ecumenical religion that would spread and unite the world.[5] For the sake of
universality and the attraction of new adherents, Manichaeism, "facing many
different religions, cultures and languages", adapted the content of its teaching
depending on the audience "to the local peculiarities", to such an extent that
"one wonders whether a system is behind it".[6] Indeed, Manichaeism spread
very rapidly through land and sea transportation networks, first in the Greco-
Roman world (within a century) and later to the east, as far as China.[7] The
present book intends to contribute to the study of Manichaeism in the Eastern
Roman world during the fourth to sixth centuries.

2   The History of the Study of Manichaeism[8]

Manichaeism may be an ancient religion, but the study of Manichaeism is a
fairly young academic discipline. The father of Manichaean studies is considered to be Isaac de Beausobre, with his monumental and pioneering work
Histoire critique de Manichée et du Manichéisme (1734/39).[9] However, the actual

---

4   De Jong 2008, 104–05; Sala 2007, 56. On Mani and Manichaeism see also Van Oort 2002/8,
    731–41 and Van Oort 2010, 24–30.

5   *1Keph.* 151.371.5–20 (Gardner and Lieu 2004, 266): "my hope, mine: It is provided for it to
    go to the west and also for it to go to the east; and in every language they hear the voice of
    its proclamation, and it is proclaimed in all cities. In this first matter my church surpasses
    the first churches: Because the first churches were chosen according to place, according to
    city. My church, mine: It is provided for it to go out from all cities, and its good news attains
    every country".

6   Colditz 2015, 48; cf. Lieu 2016, 546.

7   In China Manichaean communities continued to exist until the seventeenth century. As
    Van Oort (2020d, 112) notes, "Even recently small communities have been discovered near
    Quanzhou on the South China Coast venerating Mani as the Buddha of Light". For more on
    these Manichaean communities see Lieu's contributions, esp. Lieu et al. 2012.

8   Among the surveys focusing on the history and progress of Manichaean studies are: Lieu
    2017, 144–58; Knuppel 2009, 179–82; Sundermann 2009; Wearring 2008, 249–61; Gardner and
    Lieu 2004, 25–45; Mirecki and BeDuhn 2001, 1–4; Mirecki and BeDuhn 1997, vii–x; Ries 1988;
    Stroumsa 2010, 113–23; Stroumsa 2000, 601–12.

9   de Beausobre 1734–1739. On de Beausobre, see Van Oort 2000b, 658–66.

starting point for the discipline came more than a century later. This is mainly due to the fact that the only sources available for the study of Manichaeism until the middle of the nineteenth century were the anti-Manichaean literature (Greek and Latin). At the same time, the interest in scholarship for heresiological accounts was relatively limited.[10] As Beausobre pointed out quite earlier, one has to be particularly critical when reading such material.

From the mid-nineteenth century onwards, a decisive shift took place in the discipline, as the sources for Manichaean studies started to increase at an exponential pace. The first step in this came with the publications of Arabic[11] and later of Syriac[12] sources on Manichaeism that previously were unknown.[13] However, a series of major discoveries of original Manichaean texts in Central Asia and Egypt truly transformed the field of Manichaean studies.

In the early twentieth century, four expeditions by German scholars (1902–1914) led to the discovery of literary and artistic remains from the Turfan oasis and Dunhuang in East Turkestan in China, a region crossed by one artery of the Silk Road. The textual findings were written in more than twenty languages and in different scripts. The publication of the Turfan material, begun in 1914, continues to the present day by a team of scholars based in Berlin, the *Turfan Research Group*.[14]

With the discovery of genuine Manichaean texts in Egypt, the rest of the twentieth century proved to be revealing for Western Manichaeism. Firstly, in the late 1920s a collection of seven codices in Coptic was found at Medinet Madi. This included: (1) the *Kephalaia of the Teacher*, (2) the *Letters* of Mani, (3) the *Synaxeis* codex (a commentary on the *Living Gospel*), (4) a historical work on the life of Mani, (5) the *Homilies*, (6) the *Psalm-book*, and (7) the *Kephalaia of the Wisdom of my Lord Mani*. Part of these texts belongs to the Berlin collection, and another part to the Chester Beatty collection in Dublin.[15]

---

10 Worth mentioning works are those of Baur (1831) and Kessler (1889).

11 *The Fihrist of al-Nadīm* (Flügel 1862; edited and translated into English by Dodge in 1970); Al-Biruni, *The chronology of Ancient Nations* (Sachau 1879).

12 The *Book of Scholia* (*Liber Scholiorum*) by Theodore bar Kônai (Pognon 1898; Scher 1910). Severus of Antioch's 123rd Homily, in the *Cathedral Homiliae*, cf. "Extrait de la CXXIII^e homélie de Sévère d'Antioche" (Kugener and Cumont 1912, 83–172); S. Ephraim's *Prose Refutations of Mani, Marcion and Bardaisan* (Mitchell 1912).

13 For the importance of a number of Arabic and Syriac testimonies, see Reeves 2011.

14 See https://turfan.bbaw.de/projekt-en/turfanbroschuere@set_language=en.html. The edited texts are published by Brepols in the publication series *Berliner Turfantexte* (BTT).

15 To date, the following texts have been edited and published: (1) the Berlin *Kephalaia* (Polotsky, Böhlig and Ibscher 1935; Funk 1999–2018); (2) recently has been published a part of the Dublin *Kephalaia* (Gardner, Beduhn and Dilley 2018); (3) the *Homilies* (Polotsky 1934; Pedersen 2006) and (4) the *Psalms* (Allberry 1938; Giversen 1986–88; Wurst 1996; Richter 1999). Cf. Robinson 2014.

Another important breakthrough for Manichaean studies was the discovery of two more Manichaean texts: the *Tebessa Codex*,[16] a Latin text found in Algeria in 1918, and the *Cologne Mani-Codex* (*CMC*), an important find from Egypt. The latter was written in Greek and bought in 1969 by the papyrus collection of the University of Cologne. It recounts Mani's autobiography and his earliest missionary journeys.[17]

The publications of these new discoveries caused an increased interest in the topic of Manichaeism. An accelerating number of studies and monographs in the field appeared throughout the twentieth century.[18] As the study of Manichaeism is an interdisciplinary topic, scholars from different disciplines (e.g. codicology, religious studies, theology, history, art, languages, patristics, etc.) oriented their research interests toward Manichaeism or even switched to Manichaean studies. Yet as Prof. Sam Lieu, a leading researcher among these 'converts' remarks, Manichaean studies were still in "a stage of infancy during the 1970s".[19]

An enormous step towards the transformation of the discipline occurred in the last decade of the twentieth century (1991 onwards) with the discovery of Manichaean texts in Coptic, Greek, and Syriac at ancient Kellis, the modern Ismant el-Kharab in the Dakhleh Oasis in Egypt. Unlike previous literary texts from Egypt, which "are still divorced from the presence of the living communities who created and used them", the new texts were found in situ.[20] A large-scale international project, the *Dakhleh Oasis Project*, continues until today to survey, excavate and record the archaeological sites of the whole Dakhleh Oasis, publishing the results of the project's fieldwork.[21]

---

16   Omont 1918 (edition princeps of the text).

17   *Codex Manichaicus Coloniensis* (Περὶ τῆς γέννης τοῦ σώματος αὐτοῦ), edited by Koenen and Römer (1988). Henrichs and Koenen 1970 & 1978; Henrichs, Henrichs and Koenen 1975.

18   Indicatively I mention some of the most important: Cumont and Kugener 1908 & 1912; Alfaric 1918; Burkitt 1925/2010; Puech 1949; Klíma 1962; Widengren 1961; Asmussen 1965; Asmussen 1969; Henrichs 1979; Tardieu 1981; Sundermann's studies on Iranian Manichaean Church history (1986, 1987). The three outstanding works of Samuel Lieu: (1) *Manichaeism in the Later Roman Empire and Medieval China* (1985; 2nd ed. rev. 1992), (2) *Manichaeism in Mesopotamia and the Roman East* (1994a), and (3) *Manichaeism in Central Asia and China* (1998a). A paper which is still regularly cited as a standard work by Manichaean scholars published in 1969 in *JRS* is Peter Brown's "The Diffusion of Manichaeism in the Roman Empire".

19   Lieu 2017, 145–46, 151.

20   Gardner and Lieu 2004, 259.

21   Worp 1995 (*Greek Papyri from Kellis I*); Gardner 1996 (*Kellis Literary texts, vol. 1*); Gardner, Alcock and Funk 1999 (*Coptic Documentary texts from Kellis, vol. 1*); Gardner 2007a (*Kellis literary text, vol. 2*); Gardner, Alcock, and Funk 2014 (*Coptic documentary texts from Kellis, vol. 2*). For more publications on Coptic, Greek, and Syriac texts from Kellis, see: http://dakhlehoasisproject.com/our-projects/.

A milestone for the starting point of Manichaean studies as an independent field was the 'First International Conference on Manichaeism' held in 1987 in Lund (Sweden), which was destined to be the first of a series of international conferences.[22] So far, ten international conferences have been organised under the aegis of IAMS with contributions on all aspects of Manichaean studies. Along with the international conferences, a series of other bi-annual gatherings of scholars, participating in theme-based symposia, are organized in the intervening years.

Apart from the publications of the two major international projects (Turfan Studies project and *Dakhleh Oasis Project*), IAMS, since 1996, runs (and partly sponsors) an international research and publication project: the *Corpus Fontium Manichaeorum* (CFM). The aim of the project is to make all the "hitherto diversely published material", available in a series.[23] CFM is divided into various subseries mainly along linguistic lines: Archaeologica et Iconographica, Arabica, Coptica, Graeca, Iranica, Latina, Sinica, Syriaca, Turcica, Biblia, Analecta Manichaica, Series Subsidia.[24]

Apart from the publications of the Manichaeologists and the projects specializing in Manichaean Studies mentioned above, there are many other scholars who have dealt with the Manichaeans in varying degrees. Equally remarkable is the tremendous increase in dedicated PhD researchers over the last five years (2013–2018). A comprehensive bibliography of Manichaean studies until 1996 was compiled by Gunner Mikkelsen in 1997.[25]

Without exaggeration, the growth that Manichaean studies has experienced over the past century remains unprecedented compared to any other field of religious studies. There is a wide variety in the forms and versions of Manichaeism, given the different eras and regions where it was practiced, and therefore its study is by nature interdisciplinary and necessitates interdependence between different scientific domains.

---

22   Rudolph 2005; Mirecki and BeDuhn 1997, viii. It was there that the idea of forming an International Association of Manichaean Studies (IAMS) was conceived. The association was founded during the second International Congress in 1989.

23   http://www.brepols.net/Pages/BrowseBySeries.aspx?TreeSeries=CFM.

24   *CFM* is solely published by Brepols. Until 2022, 26 volumes were published. Another series published by Brepols under the auspices of IAMS is the *Manichaean Studies (MAS)* series which numbers five volumes (http://www.brepols.net/Pages/BrowseBySeries.aspx ?TreeSeries=MAS). At the same time, Brill's formerly *Nag Hammadi Studies Series* was transformed into *Nag Hammadi and Manichaean Studies (NHMS)*, now also including study tools and monographs in the field of Manichaean studies (https://brill.com/view /serial/NHMS). Brepols and Brill also published selected articles of most international conferences.

25   Mikkelsen 1997.

3   Greek Anti-Manichaica (Christian and Pagan) in
        Manichaean Studies[26]

This section discusses the role that the Greek anti-Manichaean sources (both
Christian and pagan) played in the history of Manichaean scholarship. This
role was and still remains rather limited, despite the growing interest of scholars in Manichaean studies that the past century witnessed. In examining the
issue, firstly, I will highlight the reasons why the Greek corpus was neglected.
In particular I will refer to the methodological problems of the Greek corpus
which made researchers reluctant to study these sources. Then I will point out
the negative effects on several research fields that resulted due to this under-
valuation of Greek sources. Continuing on, I will review the relevant literature,
which is admittedly quite minimal. I will end this section by highlighting a
shift in the attitude of many scholars that has taken place over recent decades,
regarding the reliability and importance of the Greek corpus.

3.1   *The Critical Attitude Towards Greek Anti-Manichaica*
        (Late Nineteenth–Late Twentieth Centuries)
After the discoveries of authentic Manichaean sources during the twentieth
century, and the enthusiasm generated by these findings, scholars understand-
ably focused on the Manichaean texts. As a result, the anti-Manichaica drifted
to the margins of their interest. The general consensus of scholars was now
that the usefulness of polemical literature for Manichaeism was very limited;
their value had been "surpassed by the genuine Manichaean texts".[27]

    Especially the Greek sources were more neglected than the respective Latin
ones, since the quoted Manichaean material in the latter was more abundant.
In particular, the writings of Augustine were considered to be much more
promising sources for Manichaeism than anything in Greek, since Augustine,
before converting to Christianity, was a Manichaean hearer for nine years.[28] In
fact, the Greek anti-Manichaean (Christian) corpus is at least as voluminous as
the writings of Augustine. However, it was employed much less often, because
scholars had difficulty using these sources to answer historical questions.[29]
In particular, among the methodological difficulties highlighted by modern
scholarship are: (1) since the texts belong to the genre of heresiology their

---

26   Elements from this section have been published in a different context in Matsangou
      2017b.
27   Pedersen 2015b, 572; Lieu 1994b, 258.
28   Van Oort (2020) makes several important remarks on these so-called 'nine years' in his
      Mani and Augustine. Lieu, 1994b, 258.
29   As Berzon (2013, 41) points out, although "the study of heresy has progressed by leaps and
      bounds" "the heresiologists themselves remain largely outside the reach of reevaluation
      and rehabilitation"; cf. Cameron 2003.

information must be considered unreliable, biased, untrustworthy, and driven by a polemical agenda, (2) the historical information they provide for the reconstruction of Manichaeism (if any) is too scanty, (3) their focus is mainly on argumentative polemics rather than on Manichaean mythology, which scholars prefer,[30] and (4) Greek authors appear not to know Manichaean texts, thus, the Manichaean material quoted by them is limited, fragmentary and questionable.

Furthermore, a progressive criticism of Greek sources took place for two additional reasons. Both of these comprise core issues for my research and will be examined in the present study. First of all, most scholars believe that Greek anti-Manichaean literature as a whole is based on very few early sources (mainly the *Acta Archelai*),[31] which were recycled by later authors. As Burkitt remarks, "In Greek there are many polemics against the Manichees, but when looked at carefully it is clear that the writers are all dependent on a very few original authorities".[32] Skjærvø, summarizing Beausobre's conclusions, points out "the Acta could not possibly be original; it was probably composed, not just written down, by Hegemonius in 340, that is, over sixty years after the event it records. As all the Greek Church fathers used the *Acta* as their primary source on Mani and Manicheism, this entire tradition could not be considered original, and one therefore had to concentrate on the Oriental sources".[33] However, this is an (over)generalization that results in the outright rejection of the Greek corpus altogether. As I will argue (especially in chs.[1] and [2]), the tradition of Greek anti-Manichaica did not, in fact, begin with the *Acta Archelai* nor are all Greek sources based on it. Furthermore, even those sources which are based on the *Acta* usually provide additional information.

However, the core issue, which stands at the top of the list of methodological problems, is the meaning of the word 'Manichaean' in the sources, especially the patristic ones. Although Greek patristic literature repeatedly stressed the danger of the Manichaean threat and created an impression that Manichaeans existed everywhere, it was pointed out early on, and has since gradually become embedded in academic discourse, that patristic writings use the word *Manichaean* as a term of abuse for religious opponents of all sorts. In a series of publications, scholars have argued against taking those accusations literally. The argument was that the Church Fathers did not confront real

---

30 Stroumsa 2000, 607; Stroumsa and Stroumsa 1988, 38 fn. 5.
31 *Acta Archelai* is a pivotal anti-Manichaean source, written around the middle of the fourth century. I will discuss the *Acta Archelai* later in this chapter and more extensively in chs. [1] and [2]. Here I should just mention that Beausobre was the first who pointed out that *Acta Archelai* is a completely unreliable historical source. His critique was followed by scholars almost until the end of the twentieth century.
32 Burkitt 1925/2010, 13. See also Lieu 1994a, 107.
33 Skjærvø 2006, 12.

Manichaeans; that they had neither personal experience nor contact with them, as opposed to Augustine, who did. It has been argued that the incidents cited in Greek patristic literature and the stories about specific Manichaean individuals were either fictional (literary *topos*) or examples of slander. References to Manichaeans were therefore reinterpreted as actually targeting other religious groups.[34]

Some representative examples displaying the way scholars tend to argue will be illuminating in this regard. As R.P. Casey, the editor of Serapion of Thmuis' *Against the Manichees*, remarks in his introduction:

> His [Serapion's] method of attack resembles Titus of Bostra much more than Augustine and Alexander of Lycopolis. The latter [...] refute the heresy point by point, but Serapion and Titus launch a general attack on dualism, and develop it in detail by a series of supposititious claims and objections, which they imagine their opponents might plausibly but ineffectively advance at different stages of their arguments. This method is peculiarly confusing to the reader, who is often at a loss to know whether a real Manichaean tenet is in question or an imaginary one, invented for refutation by inference from the general premises of dualism.[35]

The same argumentation about Serapion and his knowledge of Manichaeism is reproduced stereotypically by later scholars.[36]

Along similar lines, M. Aubineau (editor and translator of Severianus of Gabala's *Contra Manichaeos et Apollinaristas*) expresses his view about all the Greek authors of the *Contra Manichaeos* works:

---

34   See Jarry 1968, 139; Stroumsa and Stroumsa 1988, 38 fn. 5: "In the Byzantine world, "Man-ichaeism" soon became a term of opprobrium, thrown at various kinds of heretics whose beliefs were not even loosely connected to Manichaeism"; Lieu 1994a, 101.

35   Casey 1931, 18. Casey's edition is the only critical edition of the full Greek text. Cf. Fitschen 1992 for a translation in German.

36   Willoughby (1932, 174) who reviewed Casey's edition reproduces his argument: "Professor Casey's study of the polemic against the Manichees convinces him that Serapion really knew very little of the system he was combating. For the sake of argument he freely invented positions the Manichees never thought of holding, in order to give himself the satisfaction of making a valiant attack on the dualism that he abhorred. Accordingly, the polemic discloses much more regarding the mind of Serapion, than it does regarding the Manichees". Cf. Lieu 1994a, 101. However, as Stroumsa (1986b, 317) stresses, "This by no means implies [...] that Serapion did not have real Manichaeans before him [...] It merely reflects the topics that were likely to appear as most threatening from the bishop's point of view".

Les traités *Contra Manichaeos* ne manquent pas, pour n'évoquer que le seul secteur grec, et il n'est guère de prédicateur chrétien qui ne décoche à l'occasion quelques flèches contre des ennemies omniprésents. Naturellement tous ces prédicateurs n'avaient pas de la secte une expérience personnelle, aussi documentée que celle d'Augustin, et leur témoignage, comparé à celui du converti d'Hippone, peut paraître parfois assez faible. Souvent, ils nous renseignent moins sur les Manichéens eux-mêmes que sur les Manichéens vus par les Chrétiens, mais un tel point de vue a son prix et relève aussi du domaine de l'historien.[37]

Decret, assessing Basil of Caesarea's knowledge of Manichaeism (although Basil's *Contra Manichaeos* is lost) states:

Toutefois, à parcourir l'œuvre de Basile, les très rares références explicites au manichéisme ne permettent pas d'affirmer que l'auteur ait eu, par ses études, ses contacts ou son ministère pastoral une connaissance directe de la secte. On ne saurait voir des indices d'une telle connaissance personnelle dans le fait qu'il s'emploie, lui aussi, à dénoncer l'hérésie: « la sottise des Manichéens », « l'abominable hérésie des Manichéens, que l'on peut appeler, sans manquer à la justice, la pourriture des Eglises ».[38]

Finally, Byard Bennett, after comparing (in several of his studies) Didymus the Blind's presentation of the Manichaean account of evil to the concept of evil as recorded in Manichaean texts (*Kephalaia* and *Psalm Book*), concludes that "Didymus had a limited knowledge of some of the principal features of the Manichaean account of evil".[39]

I will adduce some more examples where references to Manichaeans are reinterpreted by scholars "as actually targeting other religious groups" (Arians, Monophysites, Origenists, etc.).[40] Tardieu, commenting on Athanasius of Alexandria's account of the general Sebastian whom he accused of Manichaeism, concludes in a definite way:

Telle est la pièce-maîtresse du dossier sur le manichéisme de Sebastianus. Elle est totalement inconsistante. Ce n'est que de la polémique de bas

---

37 Aubineau 1983, 64.
38 Decret 1982, 1060–64, 1061–62.
39 Bennett 1997, 97; Bennett 2001a, 67.
40 For a thorough overview regarding the use of the word 'Manichaean' as a term of religious abuse, see Lieu 1994a, 101–24.

étage. L'évêque d'Alexandrie met dans le même sac ariens, manichéens, juifs, autorités civiles'. [...]

Le mot « manichéen » est un mot piège dans la littérature patristique et byzantine, et chez les auteurs orientaux. Il est regrettable que de simples croque-mitaines hérésiologiques soient pris pour argent comptant par certains historiens d'aujourd'hui.[41]

Whereas Lieu cautiously remarks on the same issue:

However, he [Sebastian] was not called a Manichaean in pagan sources and it is just possible that we are here witnessing a derogatory use of the title of the sect by Athanasius in return for the wrongs he endured at the hands of Sebastianus and his troops.[42]

In general, Lieu seems more ambivalent and reserved in his arguments regarding the use of the *Manichaean name*, when for instance he states:

However, it is just as possible that Agapius was a Christian whose belief in a strong dichotomy between flesh and spirit led to a dualistic theology which was labelled "Manichaean" by more orthodox-minded churchmen.[43]

By "Manichaeism" Procopius might have meant paganism or more probably Monophysitism.[44]

The same aspect concerning the latter source was expressed by Stroumsa:

Another such testimony, that of Procopius of Caesarea, who states that the Samaritans, having been forced to convert, preferred to become Manichees, might only reflect the use of this name as a term of opprobrium (for instance for Monophysites).[45]

Bennett, disagreeing with the editors of Didymus, who identify certain unnamed opponents of the latter with the Manichaeans, argues: "I will suggest that these passages refer not to the Manichaeans but to other groups (Valentinians, Marcionites, Platonists and Epicureans)".[46]

---

41   Tardieu 1988, 498, 500.
42   Lieu 1994a, 103.
43   Lieu 1994a, 271.
44   Lieu 1994a, 118.
45   Stroumsa 1985, 276, fn. 34.
46   Bennett 1997, 97; Bennett 2001a, 67.

Indeed, even the references of western Roman authors to the Manichaeans of the Roman East have been interpreted as targeting other religious groups. The testimony of the pagan historian Ammianus Marcellinus (who wrote in Latin) that Strategius 'Musonianus' undertook (after Constantine's command) to carry out an investigation about the Manichaeans of the eastern provinces, was interpreted by Woods as an investigation which concerned not the Manichaeans, but the Arians. As Woods concludes, Ammianus' narrative on the investigation of Manichaeans and similar sects

> [r]ather [...] is a derogatory characterization of church councils based on what Ammianus knew of them in the west by the end of the fourth century when various episcopal factions were accustomed to accuse their opponents of Manichaeism as a matter of routine.
>
> For 'Manichean' was itself a common term of religious abuse by the end of the fourth century. Various Christian factions routinely denounced their theological opponents as 'Manicheans' even when there was little or no evidence to substantiate such a charge.[47]

So, regardless of the difference in style (absolute or cautious), scholars seem to be unanimous that (any) references to Manichaeans in Greek patristic anti-Manichaica did not concern real Manichaeans. Lim, who is more suspicious of the very existence of Manichaeism as a religion, recapitulates succinctly the above trend. In his words: "In Late Antiquity, the *nomen Manichaeorum* was after all a label used [...] for marking the religious Other".[48]

Thus, while patristic texts give the impression that Manichaeans existed everywhere, modern scholarship has reduced this to the extent that in the eastern part of the Roman Empire no Manichaeans actually existed. The modern critique is not groundless; Church Fathers often correlated their religious opponents to Manichaeans. In addition, there are cases where Church Fathers themselves proclaim that they could call other heretics Manichaeans, since they had similar beliefs. This being the case, one naturally wonders whether the Manichaeans of the Roman East were actually the equivalent of the witches of the western Middle Ages. To put it differently: was the word Manichaean exclusively used as a label which could ultimately incur the death penalty for occasional opponents?

---

47 Woods 2001, 264, 259. Cf. Matsangou 2017a, 395, fn. 3. That the investigation did concern Manichaeans is not questioned by other researchers: Drijvers (1996, 532–37), Lieu (1992, 96, 121–50; 1994, 101 f.), Sundermann (2009).

48 Lim 2008, 167.

It seems not. Apart from the large amount of anti-Manichaean texts which were produced during this period, and the legislation against Manichaeans, the Manichaean presence in the Eastern Roman Empire is evidenced by both pagan and Manichaean sources. Furthermore, the fact that the word Manichaean became a label for all opponents is itself a testimony to the reality of the Manichaean presence and its missionary success. Indeed, it was the seriousness of the Manichaean 'threat' that forced Church Fathers of different eras to compare or identify all kinds of 'heretics' (e.g. Arians, Monophysites, Nestorians, Origenists) to the Manichaeans, who are presented as the worst.

Certainly, there are (anti-Manichaean) writings which were not occasioned by a 'real' Manichaean threat. Instead, their composition continues the tradition of a discussion upon a 'Manichaean' repertoire that was passed down from teacher to student.[49] On the other hand, however, overgeneralizations (such as those mentioned above) predispose future researchers not to study these sources; this in turn generates a vicious circle of cause and effect. This is because the academic discourse continues to focus 'around' the evidence on the basis of a small selection of what is actually there. This is problematic, since although the argumentation for the 'imagined Manichaeans' may apply to individual cases, it does not stand up to scrutiny when the totality of the evidence is taken into consideration.

Thus, the fact that the word *Manichaean* was indeed used as a term of abuse should not cause an interpretive myopia, suggesting that any reference to Manichaeans is interpreted through this viewpoint. Since Manichaeans did exist in the Eastern Roman Empire, it is reasonable to believe that Greek anti-Manichaica do contain reports concerning real Manichaeans. The problem is whether we can think of a method with which to distinguish between references to 'real' Manichaeans and the use of the *nomen Manichaeorum* for other, polemical, purposes.

3.2   *Resulting Effects from Undervaluing the Greek Sources*
It is worth pointing out that the Greek anti-Manichaean corpus was undervalued not only by Manichaean scholars and historians of religions but also by scholars of Patristics and of Byzantine culture. For the latter, Manichaeism is considered as a less important subject than other themes in patristic literature; for the former, Greek anti-Manichaica are considered unreliable, surpassed by the new findings, and less important than Augustine's writings.[50]

---

49   Pedersen 2004, 142. See also ch.[5], 3.2.
50   Pedersen 2004, 105; Klein 1991, 1–3.

Taken together, this attitude resulted in the lack of critical editions of Greek anti-Manichaean texts as well as in the lack of interest in studies based on this corpus. For instance, it is noteworthy that while many scholars have highlighted repeatedly the significance of Titus of Bostra,[51] a contemporary critical edition of the Greek and the Syriac text was published only in 2013 and the first translation into a modern language in 2015.[52]

Thus, in research on the Greek anti-Manichaica, a narrative slowly developed in which the Greek sources were given a place in the development of larger inquiries into Manichaean history (e.g. by Lieu and Stroumsa) but were not studied in their own right.

3.3   Review of the Relevant Literature

The first and only study (until today), examining the Greek anti-Manichaean sources *per se*, is Klein's *Die Argumentation in den griechisch-christlichen Antimanichaica* (1991). Therefore, as Pedersen suggests, it "deserves the epithet 'pioneering'".[53] Klein, recognizing the difficulty in using these sources to answer historical questions, investigated the anti-Manichaica from the perspective of the development of polemical literature, in order to categorise "the aims and methods of the polemic".[54] In his research, Klein has focused only on the main Greek Christian works which were devoted to the refutation of Manichaeism.[55] At the beginning of his work, he presents a "Patrology" of these sources, which he lists in alphabetical order. He then proceeds to a thematic survey of these sources. The themes examined include: the attack on dualism, the attack on Manichaean tradition, the apology for the Christian tradition, and the structure of the polemic.[56]

Undoubtedly, "Klein's study fills a real gap"[57] and is a contribution to both Manichaean and Patristic studies. However, his study presents some inadequacies for which it has been criticized.[58] The presentation of the sources in alphabetical rather than in chronological order, and the indiscriminate selection of his material from texts ranging from the fourth to the thirteenth century in the examination of his sub-themes, deprives the reader of the possibility to

---

51   See for example Stroumsa and Stroumsa 1988, 43; Stroumsa 1992, 338.
52   Roman et al. 2013; Roman, Schmidt, and Poirier 2015. The first edition was published by Lagarde in 1859.
53   Pedersen 2004, 105.
54   Pedersen 2004, 105–06.
55   Pedersen 2004, 105–06; Lieu 1994b, 258–59.
56   Klein 1991. Cf. Lieu 1994b, 258–59; Pedersen 2004, 105.
57   Van Oort 1993, 202.
58   Van Oort 1993, 201–203; Lieu 1994b, 258–59; Pedersen 2004, 105–06.

discern (1) the interdependence of the sources (and provenance from common sources), and (2) the development of Greek anti-Manichaean polemic argumentation over time. In addition, Klein restricts his research to a limited corpus, that of the basic anti-Manichaean Christian sources, and excludes the rest of Christian as well as the pagan (e.g. Simplicius and Alexander of Lycopolis) anti-Manichaean literature in Greek. The latter (pagan sources) would have complemented the image and would have offered Klein the ability to compare Christian to pagan argumentation on the issue. Finally, Klein's research (as Klein himself states) has not dealt with a number of questions, such as: the origin of the arguments in Christian polemics, the impact of the anti-Manichaean concern on Christian theological thought (especially in theodicy), and the Greek anti-Manichaica as a source of knowledge on Manichaeism.[59]

In addition to Klein's monograph, two more major studies were published. Both of them focus on a specific *Contra Manichaeos* work and its author. These are Bennett's (1997) *The Origin of Evil: Didymus the Blind's Contra Manichaeos*, and Pedersen's (2004) *Demonstrative Proof in Defence of God. A Study of Titus of Bostra's Contra Manichaeos*. It has to be mentioned that Pedersen's thorough study laid the groundwork for the critical edition of Titus' text and its translation. Pedersen examines a variety of questions, such as the diverse philosophical roots of the argument of Titus and his philosophical location, the question of the Manichaean sources used by Titus and whether he had access to Manichaean texts, as well as the target groups that Titus addressed. His study is considered by modern scholarship as a major contribution to both Patristics and Manichaean studies, but also to religious studies and philosophy.[60]

Yet, despite the importance of the above studies for the field, it is remarkable that so little research has been done until today. The result is that Manichaean scholars are familiar with a selection of these texts, which are 'recycled' in bibliography. However, very little is known about the Greek anti-Manichaean corpus in its own right.[61]

It is worth noting that another kind of sources suffered a similar fate to that of the Greek anti-Manichaica, the legal ones.[62] The reservations that prevented researchers from systematically using the anti-Manichaean legal sources in order to reconstruct Manichaean history (an issue discussed further in ch.[3])

---

59   Klein 1991, 3–5.
60   Klein 2007, 113–15, 115; BeDuhn 2008a, 301.
61   Pedersen 2004, 102.
62   Only one scholar, Valerio Minale, has systematically studied Roman anti-Manichaean legislation.

can be summed up in the following two arguments: (1) the promulgation of a law could be a mindless repetition, therefore laws do not necessarily reflect reality, and (2) in legislation too, the *nomen Manichaeorum* was (probably) used as a technical term, a "container where every sort of religious deviance could be thrown".[63] The result of this belief is that no single study at present examines thoroughly the entire Roman anti-Manichaean legislation, as such. There are studies either focusing on specific time periods or on individual laws,[64] or studies in which a small number of laws (usually the same) comprise part of a broader narrative (about Manichaeism in the Roman Empire) and serve as complementary evidence to other Christian, pagan, and Manichaean sources.[65]

3.4 Greek Patristic Anti-Manichaica Revisited

During the last three decades a progressive growth of the interest in the Greek-patristic anti-Manichaica can be identified. Actually, already since the 1980s some scholars have argued that the Greek sources preserve historical information; they have attempted through their writings to arouse interest, pointing out that these sources should not be ignored but be studied critically.[66]

Especially after the finds at Kellis (1990s), a research that would compare the content of these texts to the respective themes incorporated in patristic literature is considered necessary by many scholars.[67] As Lieu characteristically points out, "at least one of its [Kellis] documents deserves notice by scholars of anti-Manichaica as it is a theological hymn (The Hymn of Emanations) in Greek which calls for terminological and theological comparison with the cosmogonic teaching of Mani as presented by the Greek Fathers".[68] Pedersen, in

---

63   Minale 2012b, 176. As Minale (2012b, 190) states: "The substance of Manichaeism, an heretical dualism *par excellence*, started to appear less essential than its form: the *nomen Manichaeorum* was to include also other heterodox beliefs, without limitation of time and space, replacing the "part" with the "whole" and meaning the phenomenon of heresy in its entirety".

64   See for instance Kaden (1953, 55–68), Beskow 1988 and the rich bibliography on the issue by Minale: 2010, 2011, 2012a, 2012b, 2013, 2014, 2015, 2016a and 2016b.

65   Lieu 1994a and 1992.

66   Stroumsa 1985, 274–75; Stroumsa and Stroumsa 1988, 39–40; Stroumsa 1992, 338–39; Lieu 1994a, 133.

67   For the importance of Kellis' discoveries, see Gardner and Lieu 2004, 44–45; Pedersen 2004, 101–02. For recent finds in Kellis, see Gardner and Worp 2018, 127–42 and the publications of the *Dakhleh Oasis Project* (see Introduction, section 2, fn. 21). See also the most recent studies on the Manichaeans of Kellis, Teigen 2021 and Brand 2022.

68   Lieu 1994b, 258.

his study about Titus, also defends the importance of the *Contra Manichaeos* Greek corpus, and supports the view that the patristic argumentation could reveal patterns of evolution of both Manichaean and Christian thought; he wishes his work to become a stimulus for further research.[69]

Indeed, as the study and publication of the original Manichaean texts progresses, it turns out that the patristic writings are by no means as irrelevant and unreliable as originally believed. Gardner, in his *Mani's Letter to Marcellus: Fact and Fiction in the Acta Archelai Revisited*, claims that he found many more authentic elements in it than he had imagined in the beginning of his research. He further considers that, if the scientific community accepted his arguments, the study of anti-Manichaica would provide valuable information about Mani and Manichaeism.[70]

4   Significance, Purpose, Aim, Focus of the Study

From what has been discussed, it becomes clear that there is a knowledge gap in the field of study. Apart from Klein (1991), no single study exists that investigates the Greek anti-Manichaean sources in their own right. Moreover, as underlined, Klein's study examines a limited number of sources and focuses only on their polemical argumentation.

In the early 1990s, Klein "noted that work on the Christian anti-Manichaean literature had hardly begun".[71] More than a decade later, Pedersen (2004) remarked "Yet, scholarship on anti-Manichaean literature is still in its infancy".[72] Today, three decades after Klein's study, it is still the case that far too little attention has been paid to the genre. Several scholars during the last decades have stressed this gap in research literature. Especially after the findings at Kellis, an increasing number of outstanding scholars identified the gap and called upon researchers to investigate the Greek sources critically and in comparison with the new findings. This was the first stimulus and starting point of my research.

---

69   Pedersen 2004, 423: "A concern with *Contra Manichaeos* thus contributes to sharpening the attention to a circumstance that may never have been forgotten, but at times has been under-emphasised, namely that the history of Early Catholic theology should not merely be studied and explained as an internal development of the tradition, but should also be understood as being defined by the increasingly external relations to the surrounding pagan society and divergent Christian groups who were regarded as heretical".

70   Gardner 2007b, 46–48, esp. 47–48, 48.

71   Klein 1991, 1–3.

72   Pedersen 2004, 102.

However, apart from the shift in the scholarly attitude regarding the reliability of the Greek sources, an additional reason necessitating this inquiry is that no previous study has investigated the totality of the voluminous Greek corpus until recently; the same applies for the anti-Manichaean Roman legislation. Scholars, familiar with a relatively small number of these sources, tend to argue on a case-by-case basis, that the *nomen Manichaeorum* lacks religious associations in Byzantine literature,[73] and was used simply as a term of abuse. However, even if each one of these individual cases does not concern 'real' Manichaeans, even if not a single law or ecclesiastical document was occasioned by a 'real' Manichaean challenge, the fact that the Manichaean question occupies a very important position in both legal and ecclesiastical texts needs to be explained. This can only be done when the totality of the evidence is taken into consideration, something that has never been done so far.

Thus, my main aim in the present study is to show how this large body of literature can indeed be used to contribute to the history of Manichaeism in the Roman East. The major objective of this study is to readapt known yet neglected material into a new context in order to shine new light on the history of Manichaeism in the Roman East. This will be done by critically examining the voluminous Greek anti-Manichaean literature and by taking into account the data of new findings.

In order that this survey be conducted successfully, the knowledge of two scientific disciplines is required: Byzantine history and culture, and Manichaean studies. For the correct interpretation of the sources, one has to be well aware of the context and the content of the theological discourse of the era (patristics), as well as being informed of the new evidence and data that come to light for Manichaeism in the Eastern Roman Empire (Manichaeology). One of the reasons that Greek anti-Manichaica were overlooked by both Manichaean scholars and scholars of Byzantine culture (part of it being patristics) is that Manichaeologists know a limited amount about patristics, and scholars of patristics know little about Manichaeism.[74] By linking the two disciplines, this treatise intends to contribute to both fields of study. Firstly, it intends to be a contribution to the study of Manichaeism by promoting the knowledge of Manichaean history and thought. In turn, this knowledge may provide new perspectives for the study of early Christianity and Byzantine culture.

This research intentionally does not address Manichaean theology and Christology to a great extent. The emphasis of the investigation is on the Manichaeans, on a history about Eastern Roman Manichaeans and not on a history of the Manichaean ideas and beliefs in the Roman East. Therefore,

---

73   Lieu 1994a, 110.
74   Nagel in Pedersen 2004, ix.

I focus mainly on those Manichaean beliefs that had a visible impact on the daily life of Manichaeans.

4.1 Geographical and Chronological Scope of the Research

The geographical focus of this study is the Eastern Roman Empire. The chronological span of the study is from the fourth to the sixth century. I was led to this decision for the following reasons:

(1) The prevailing opinion in scholarship is that there is strong evidence that Manichaeans disappeared from the Roman East by the end of the sixth century, after Justinian's persecution.[75]

(2) There is an abundance of *Contra Manichaeos* works that were written during that period.

(3) The authors of this period are considered by modern research to be more reliable than the later ones who identify Paulicians and Bogomils with Manichaeans.[76]

In addition, if I expanded further than the sixth century, the volume of primary material would become unmanageable, and I would also have to explore Manichaeism's relationship with Paulicianism and Bogomilism, which in itself merits a separate dedicated study. Also, an extended chronological framework would require a different methodological approach, since the sixth century is considered a landmark for the Manichaean presence and visibility in the Roman East. In any case, the sixth century signals major historical changes and is a turning point in the history of the wider geographical area.

5 Methodological Considerations

5.1 Limitations and Research Design

The methodological problems of the Greek corpus that have been emphasised by researchers are to a great extent valid and constitute methodological difficulties also encountered in the present study. The research design of this study, as well as specific methodological tools that I discuss in this section, aim to address these problems.

In the first place, I have already stressed how important it is for accomplishing the aims of this study to examine the totality of the evidence. This and only this will allow us to trace cases where authors rely on other authors and cases where authors provide material they have freshly gathered. Such an approach

---

75   Skjærvø, 2006, 32; Gardner and Lieu 2004, 111. I will discuss this issue in ch.[8].
76   Lieu 1994a, 128–29.

will build confidence in identifying that a 'real' Manichaean 'problem' is actually there.

The methodology of the research will be the historical method, approached from a comparative perspective. The guiding axes for the examination of the primary sources will be thematic and chronological. Each chapter constitutes an autonomous thematic section with a central question and a particular corpus of sources which are examined in chronological order from the fourth to the sixth century (and beyond if necessary). The chronological order will more clearly illuminate the historical evolution of the theme investigated in each separate chapter, as well as the interdependence of the sources. Some chapters are based exclusively, or mainly, on a particular type or literary genre of primary sources. For instance, ch.[3] is based solely on Roman imperial legislation and ch.[4] mainly on anti-Manichaean treatises (i.e. works devoted entirely or partly solely to Manichaeism).

In each chapter, I attempt to develop a comparative approach for a better understanding of the question under consideration. For this purpose, I incorporate (relevant) comparative material from Latin (mainly Augustine), Syriac, and Arabic sources, in order to supplement, complement, or compare them with the Greek sources. Material also comes from genuine Manichaean texts (from within and beyond the Roman Empire), in order to respond to the research question of what can be historically verified regarding the information provided by Greek anti-Manichaean authors.[77] In ch.[3] the comparative approach is attempted by comparing the laws against Manichaeans with the laws against other heretics and minority religious groups.

Concerning the issues of reliability of the patristic sources, as I have previously mentioned, what is needed is a critical reading, meaning that the information provided should not be accepted at face value. Therefore, it is important, in analysing and interpreting sources, to investigate the authenticity of the information provided. As Bennett stresses in his study, *Didymus the Blind's Knowledge of Manichaeism*:

> Before information from an anti-Manichaean writer is used in reconstructing aspects of Manichaean belief and practice, three questions should be asked:
> (1) How much did the writer know about Manichaeism and how did he arrive at that knowledge? For example, had the writer met or debated with proponents of Manichaeism? Did the writer claim to have access to

---

77   In this effort I will also use the findings of secondary literature concerning the Syriac and Coptic Manichaean texts.

Manichaean writings or was his knowledge of Manichaeism derived from another anti-Manichaean work (or works)?

(2) Were the beliefs which the writer attributed to the Manichaeans substantially correct or did he confuse the Manichaeans' beliefs with those of other groups?

(3) Did the writer's reliance on earlier heresiological works shape how he understood and responded to Manichaean claims?[78]

In sum, the critical examination of the whole corpus in a chronological order and with a comparative approach will identify the new information and will address the issues of reliability and the interdependence of sources. Regarding the problem of the use of the *nomen Manichaeorum* as a label, this will be treated below in the section 'Defining Terms'.

5.2   *Primary Sources*

Two types of sources comprise the main corpus of the primary researched material: (1) Anti-Manichaean writings in Greek (both Christian and pagan), which constitute the bulk of the material, and (2) the Roman imperial legislation, specifically the laws against heretics, pagans and Jews (Codex Theodosianus and Codex Justinianus).

Since the period under investigation is from the fourth to the sixth century, the goal is primarily to examine all the sources dating within this period. Sources from the seventh century until the ninth or tenth centuries will only be examined to the extent that they securely refer to Manichaeans and not to Paulicians or Bogomils. Sources from after the tenth century I consider as going far beyond the timeframe of the researched period, and beyond the scope of the research questions of this study.

Apart from the Greek and legal sources, I will also use some of the Syriac, Arabic and Latin (Augustine) anti-Manichaean writings, as well as Manichaean sources, mainly the findings from Egypt. However, since the scope of this study is the examination of the Greek anti-Manichaean corpus and Roman legislation, there will be only a limited and selective use of the Manichaean sources, as well as of the anti-Manichaean East-Roman authors who wrote in Syriac and Arabic.

---

78   Bennett 2001a, 38: "Greek Christian anti-Manichaean writings have often been used as sources of information about Manichaean belief and practice, complementing and supplementing the reports found in the extant Manichaean texts. At the same time, there has been little systematic analysis of these anti-Manichaean writings, so that their value as historical sources has yet to be critically assessed".

For texts written in Greek I am using the critical editions whenever these exist.[79] Texts written in other languages than Greek (Latin, Syriac, etc.) are studied through translations.

There is a variety of literary genres of Christian sources, such as theological treatises, histories (both ecclesiastical and secular), chronographies, homilies, epistles, proceedings of debates, anathema formulas, and church canons. Some of them are entire works or chapters of works solely devoted to the refutation of Manichaeism. The rest are scattered and dispersed mentions about Manichaeism and certain Manichaean individuals, which exist throughout the whole Christian corpus.[80] In contrast to the latter group, most of the texts of the first group are rather well-known in the scholarship. Promising sources for historical information and 'real' Manichaeans are not so much the *"Against Manichaeans"* long treatises written for polemical purposes in which the discourse often is developed up to a theoretical level, but rather texts occasionally written (such as letters). Pagan anti-Manichaean works, such as the works of Alexander of Lycopolis and Simplicius, will be used since they provide information about Manichaeans from another point of view, as well as offering insight into a kind of intercultural literature that circulated in the Near East during Late Antiquity.

The majority of the lengthy anti-Manichaean works (treatises) were published during the fourth century (eleven out of thirteen).[81] Unfortunately, five of them have not survived.[82] Of the other six, one is the work of a pagan philosopher.[83] Apart from the treatises, other less theoretically inclined authors recorded their concern and worries about Manichaeans in homilies delivered to their catechumen students and flock. In these works, references and warnings about Manichaeans abound.[84] Besides those, some other authors occasionally refer to Manichaeans, with varying degrees of consistency.[85]

---

79   For more information about translations, please see the "Note on Translations and Editions of Primary Sources and Referencing System" at the beginning of this study.

80   Most of the texts of this second group were obtained through the lemma/textual search on TLG.

81   The authors of these treatises are: Alexander of Lycopolis, Serapion of Thmuis, [Hegemonius], Eusebius of Emesa, George of Laodicea, Titus of Bostra, Epiphanius of Salamis, Didymus the Blind, Heraclian of Chalcedon, Basil of Caesarea, and Diodorus of Tarsus.

82   We no longer possess the anti-Manichaean treatises of Eusebius of Emesa, George of Laodicea, Diodorus of Tarsus, Heraclian of Chalcedon, and Basil of Caesarea.

83   Alexander of Lycopolis.

84   See for example, Cyril of Jerusalem and John Chrysostom.

85   Indicatively: Amphilochius of Iconium, Athanasius of Alexandria, Basil of Caesarea, Cyril of Alexandria, Cyril of Scythopolis, Gregory of Nazianzus, Gregory of Nyssa, Julian the Neo-Arian, Libanius, Nilus of Ankara, Severianus of Gabala.

Passing into the fifth century, the picture changes: long treatises against Manichaeans are no longer produced. Moreover, texts referring to Manichaeans are much less numerous. The predominant type of literature in which we find references to Manichaeans is ascetic literature (which started by the late fourth century),[86] lives of saints,[87] *Erotapokriseis* (questions and answers), and letters written by monks or clerics with instructions on issues concerning Manichaeans.[88]

During the sixth century there is the continuation of the production of new anti-Manichaean literature originating in monastic and more provincial milieus.[89] In parallel, there is a reappearance of the kind of lengthy *Adversus Manichaeos* treatises, by two authors.[90] In addition, there are new reports by pagans criticising Manichaeism.[91]

5.3   *Defining Terms*

In this section, I will give an account of the crucial terms and the critical concepts that I employ in the book.

5.3.1   East-Roman vs. Byzantine

For reasons that serve the analysis and the discussion, I will use alternatively both terms according to the specific context and time. Generally, I opt in favour of the terms Byzantine/Byzantium: (1) for sources or events that refer to Justinian's era and beyond, and (2) for references to persons, in order to distinguish between the citizens of the eastern and western parts of the empire. In the rest of the cases, I use the term 'East-Roman'.

For the remainder of the terms, I will define their content from both an *emic* and an *etic* perspective. For the *emic* discourse, it is important to attribute the meaning to the crucial terms that the writers themselves attributed to them.[92]

---

86   Palladius; *Apophtegmata partum*; *Historia monachorum in Aegypto*.
87   Mark the Deacon, *The life of Porphyry, bishop of Gaza*.
88   Nilus of Ankara, Macarius of Magnesia.
89   See for example Cyril of Scythopolis, Eustathius the monk, Barsanuphius, Olympiodorus the deacon.
90   The one is Zacharias (later) bishop of Mytilene. To Zacharias is also attributed the composition of the *Seven Chapters* (abjuration formula). The other is John of Caesarea the theologian and cleric. According to the testimony of John of Caesarea in his *Adversus Manichaeos*, the Manichaeans, unlike the followers of Marcion, still existed in his time.
91   Simplicius, Asclepius of Tralles, Ammonius of Alexandria.
92   Cf. Cameron 2003, 471–92. See also Cameron 2008, 102–14.

5.3.2   Catholics, Catholic Church, Heretics, Heresy

5.3.2.1   *Emic Perspective*

According to the sources, Catholics are the representatives of the official church, the Catholic one. This was a constitutional institution of the Empire, identified with legality, since the decisions of Ecumenical Synods concerning dogma were embodied in state legislation. Heretics are all the others, and heresy constitutes anything opposed to the Catholic Church. Two kinds of heresies are discernible: the *old* (pre-Byzantine) and the *new*, such as Arianism, Nestorianism, Monophysitism.

Two further clarifications are considered necessary. In the first place, it is important to note that during the period under examination, Christian dogma had not yet been fully fixed, making the content of the word *Catholic* subject to continuous revision, clarification, and re-configuration. This mutability of the term *Catholic* concerns both its theological content, as well as the exponents of this content, namely the representatives of the Catholic Church. This means that depending on the time-period and location one could find representatives from the entire range of Christian parties in the bishoprics; there also were emperors who did not support what was later established as orthodoxy. So, the term 'Catholic' did not coincide with what we now call 'Orthodox' or 'Catholic' Church, but it included Arians, Monophysites etc., when they held positions of authority (locally or state-wide). Thus, from a Manichaean point of view, an Arian or a Monophysite bishop also was considered to be a *Catholic*.

Secondly, the content of the word heresy was much broader than its contemporary meaning and included concepts such as: the wrong choice, the different religious choices (especially the rival ones), the intra-Christianity parties, and the different religions (pagans and Jews). In brief, as Young concludes, answering his question "Did Epiphanius know what he meant by Heresy?" for Epiphanius the word "heresy is false religion and includes all that is outside the unity of the one, holy, catholic and orthodox Church".[93]

5.3.2.2   *Etic Perspective*

For the sake of clarity in the *etic* discourse of the study, I will employ the term *Catholic* only for the group that finally dominated the other parties. Additional reasons for this choice are: (1) this party gradually formed the majority group; (2) it had the support of the state for the longest period of time (between the fourth-sixth centuries); and (3) most of my primary sources were exponents of this party. There are alternative terms that I could have used, such as

---

93   Young 1982, 202.

'Orthodox', however the term orthodox, identified with the official church, appears later.[94]

For the rest of the parties, the terms heresy, heretics, and schismatics, will be employed conventionally. I will also keep the distinction (made by the sources) between the *old* (pre-Byzantine) and the *new* heresies, but for the latter I will adopt the term *noble* heresies, employed by Mango and Gouillard. *Noble* heresies were the result of an advanced theological discussion. Their dogma is different from the Catholic position only in sophisticated notions concerning the nature and relationships of the persons in the Holy Trinity.[95]

Recapitulating, the term *Catholic* from an *emic* perspective is identical to the official Church, while from an *etic* point of view it is identified with one of the Christian parties (not always the official church). More details on the terms heresy and heretics will be given in ch.[4].

5.3.3   Manichaeism: as a Religion

The question remains as to whether I would treat Manichaeism as a separate religious entity, or whether I would include Manichaeism within Christianity. The answer to this question depends on the clarification of the following inter-related and debated issues: a) the definition of the term *religion*, and b) the relationship between Manichaeism and Christianity, which in turn is linked with the question of the origins of Manichaeism.

5.3.3.1   *Religion*

Disagreeing with the trend in modern scholarship that it is anachronistic to use the term *religion* (θρησκεία) when referring to late antiquity (or earlier periods) because the concept is a modern one, in this study, I will use the word in the same sense we mean it today. While the word existed already since fifth century BCE (Herodotus, *Historiae* 2.37), in the primary sources used in this study the term *religion* is used systematically, indeed, most of the time with the modern meaning of the term.[96] Moreover, as has been proposed by many

---

94   See the relevant discussion in Pedersen 2004, 6.

95   Mango 1980, 94, 103. Gouillard 1965, 299–324.

96   The same view has been supported by Tolan 2014, 55–75, 58: "The concept of religion as we know it is in many ways a product of the fourth-and fifth-century Christian Roman Empire". The aspect that the concept 'religion' is a modern idea/category and for this reason we should not use it to study the distant past is dominant in modern scholarship. However, the fact that possibly in some societies the term did not exist or existed, but its use was different to the contemporary, does not mean that in these societies there was no corresponding socio-cultural category. There is a gargantuan bibliography on the issue. Below, I present indicatively the arguments developed by scholars who raise the above question in the context of the study of Manichaeism. Pedersen 2004, 8–9 and 6: "Firstly, it

modern scholars, Manichaeism is the first religion in the modern sense.[97] The
contribution of Mani and the Manichaeans to the formation of the category

---

must be underlined that in a strict sense it is anachronistic to claim that the Manichaeans
consciously understood themselves as constituting a new religion, for the good reason
that the concept of religion is a modern one. But the significance of this observation must
not be exaggerated, for if the Manichaeans distanced themselves from the Christians in
their awareness of being an independent group with a different identity, it is obvious in
a modern context to interpret this self-understanding as constituting a new 'religion'".
BeDuhn 2015b, 247, 272: "Yet its etic character, imposed at times on cultures that do not
themselves recognize a distinct 'religion' category, has been increasingly noted, often in
connection with the idea that religion is a peculiarly modern, even modernist, idea. It is
purely tautological, however, to say that the way we moderns use the term religion is a
modern invention, informed by distinctive, historically conditioned shifts in discourse
and social organization. That fact does not preclude the possibility of a pre-modern concept that anticipated the modern one by identifying the same socio-cultural entities we
would place at the center of the modern category of religion".

97   As de Jong (2008, 104–05) remarks: "What was new about Manichaeism was its designer
      status. When the prophet was executed by the king of the Iranians, on unknown charges,
      the foundations for the religion, including its canonical texts, most of its ritual life, its mis-
      sionary strategy, and the structure of its organisation, had all been laid. The well-known
      list of ten aspects in which Manichaeism was superior to the religions that had existed
      before, preserved in Iranian and Western texts, makes this absolutely clear". According to
      Sala (2007, 56), "Perhaps for the first time in history an individual deliberately devised a
      "world religion." In no other religion before did the 'founder' play such an important role.
      It was Mani himself who established the three major pillars of his religion: a complex
      set of doctrines outlined in a series of books, a clear body of rituals and a fixed orga-
      nizational structure". Yet, Sala also expresses some reservations about whether this was
      Mani's intention or was set at a later stage by his followers. As he states: "However, as we
      lack the original works of Mani, which unfortunately are extant only in a limited num-
      ber of fragments, it is impossible to assert with confidence the self-conscious creation of
      Manichaeism as a "world religion" by Mani himself. There remains the possibility that this
      image is a retro-projection of a more developed stage of Manichaeism after the demise of
      its 'founder'." Gardner (2010, 147 & 147 fn. 1), revising his previous theses, disagrees with
      the aspect that Mani designed and delivered an organized religion in the modern sense to
      his community (and that this was the first time in the history of religions). According to
      his theory (stratigraphy), the above reservation (expressed by Sala) is not just a possibil-
      ity, but what had actually happened. As he argues: "Over the last century and more, new
      discoveries and trends of scholarship have rescued the study of Manichaeism from the
      polemic of heresy, and identified it as a major world religion in its own right. It has even
      been claimed that it was the first real religion in the modern sense, in that it was (suppos-
      edly) created with its doctrines, practices, scriptures and institutions all in place. [...] As
      will be apparent here, however, I do not now believe this. Mani was not really different
      from other supposed religious 'founders' (such as Jesus), in that he saw himself within an
      established tradition where he had an especial call to interpret and present the true way.
      It was his followers, and a peculiar trajectory of development (which would in many ways
      have astonished its originator), that led to the carving out of a discrete identity called
      'Manichaeism', (similarly) 'Christianity', and so on".

religion as we understand it today is considered decisive.[98] I will return with more details regarding the use of the term *religion* during the period under investigation in ch.[4].

5.3.4   Manichaeism in Relation to Christianity
5.3.4.1   *Etic Perspective (The Question of the Origin)*
A hotly debated issue in the academic discourse, which still remains open, is the question of the origin of Manichaeism. Scholars have advanced several theories, some of them arguing for an Iranian/Zoroastrian origin, with others proposing a Christian and Judeo-Christian one. Some consider Manichaeism as the last form of Christian Gnosis, some argue that there are strong influences from Buddhism and Jainism, whereas others harmonize the above views and argue that Manichaeism borrowed and contains elements from many different religious traditions without being considered as the conceptual product of any of them exclusively.[99]

---

98   BeDuhn 2015b, 247, 272: "In what follows, I argue that Mani and his early successors in third-century Iran produced such a concept, within which they included such recognizable entities as Christianity, Mazdayasnianism, Buddhism and Jainism, as well as their own Manichaean community, in an unusually rich environment of cultural interchange and comparative awareness presaging the conditions typically associated with the modern era. [...] Mani attests the historical development in his own time from the locally-rooted traditions of the past to the new conditions of inter-cultural proselytism [...] 272: Mani was able to theorize about this change of religious landscape, as part of his crystallization of the very concept 'religion'. The role Mani and the Manichaeans seem to have played in defining the new kind of social entity we call 'religion'".

99   Initially the (pre)dominant aspect was that Manichaeans were Persians, and Manichaeism was regarded as an Iranian religion. Exponents of a Persian origin of Manichaeism were Widengren and Reitzenstein. Later, through the study of the new texts (especially the *CMC*), the Iranian origin was reassessed. The trend in scholarship thenceforth was that the origins of Manichaeism were more Judeo-Christian than Persian. For the majority of researchers the publication of the *Cologne Mani Codex* (*CMC*) has supported Brown's thesis that Manichaeism was not an Iranian religion but a religion with Judaeo-Christian origins, developed in the Judaeo-Christian milieu and that the first Manichaean missionaries in the Roman Empire were of Aramaic culture, Syrians and not Iranians; a thesis that two centuries ago Beausobre had already supported. As Brown (1969, 97), with his fascinating way of writing, states: "the history of Manichaeism is integral with the one that flourished in the ground of the Fertile Crescent, namely Syriac. [...] Whenever we meet a Syrian, we may meet a Manichee". However, during the recent decades, an increasing number of scholars argue that both hypotheses, i.e. the Zoroastrian (Persian) or the Christian origin, are the two extremes. As de Jong (2008, 92) puts it, the aspect that Manichaeism is a debased Zoroastrian religion is as uncritical, as is the aspect that Manichaeism is a variety of Christianity. In early Manichaeism there are both Christian and other "elements that unquestionably belonged to the Sasanian context. One of them, without a doubt, was geography". The gravity of notions such as "prophet, holy book and

Although the question of the origin lies beyond the aim of the current research, I must, for methodological reasons, make clear how I am treating the term Manichaeism in this study.

In contrast to Pedersen,[100] who includes Manichaeism into Christianity in his study, and agreeing with Klein,[101] who considers such a broad definition of Christianity problematic, as well as in accordance with contemporary trends in Manichaean scholarship,[102] I will treat Manichaeism as an independent religious entity. I will avoid defining it as deriving in a clean lineage from any of the earlier religious traditions (Zoroastrianism, Christianity, etc.), although it shares many elements with them.

5.3.4.2 Emic Perspective (Manichaeism in the Context of Roman Empire)

The issue of an *ab-extra* and *ab-intra* definition of Manichaeism (Manichaean exonyms and autonyms) in the context of the Roman Empire is also a debated issue.

Van Oort, criticizing Klein's distinction between 'Christians' and the 'Manichaeans', argues that "the Fathers of the Catholic Christian Church [...] considered the Manichaeans to be *Christian heretics* and themselves as orthodox Christians", stressing that we must finally accept the terminology that "both Catholic Christians and Manichaean Christians themselves" used.[103] However, as will be shown in chapter four, while Catholic Christians (and not only) called the Manichaeans heretics, did not consider them *Christian* heretics. The content of the term 'heretic' which Eastern Church Fathers attributed to the Manichaeans is not identical to its modern meaning but is much closer to the concept of the follower of a different religion/faith. So, I think

---

cultic meal" is common in Zoroastrianism, Christianity, and Manichaeism" (de Jong 2008, 105). For further discussion on the discourse of the origins of Manichaeism, cf. Gardner and Lieu 1996, 146–48; Reeves 1992; Stroumsa 2000, 612; Gardner and Lieu, 2004, 27–28; Pedersen 2004, 6; Sala 2007, 49; De Jong 2008, 104–05; Gardner 2010; BeDuhn 2015b, 274; Pettipiece 2015. Lieu 2017, 157–58; Gardner, Beduhn, Dilley 2018, 3–4.

100　Pedersen 2004, 6–9, 6: "The subject of the present study, ancient Christianity, involves both Catholic Christianity and the so-called 'heresies' (*in casu* Manichaeism). I do not therefore regard it appropriate to describe the relationship between them in terms of 'Christianity' meeting 'a foreign religion'. [...] In the present study therefore the terms Christianity/Christian/Christians etc. are used broadly, and include Manichaeism".

101　Klein 2007, 115.

102　Gardner, Beduhn and Dilley 2018, 3–4. BeDuhn 2015b, 274: "In light of this comparative project Mani initiated, it may be possible for us to put behind us once and for all vain efforts to define an 'essential' Manichaeism, deriving in a clean line of descent from either a 'Christian' or 'Mazdayasnian' heritage, or any other insular 'religious' tradition". Lieu 2017, 157–58.

103　Van Oort 1993, 202.

that scholars make a generalization and simplify the facts from the sources by arguing that Church Fathers regarded the Manichaeans as Christian heretics; however, this is the central question of ch.[4], where it will be examined thoroughly.

Lim also concludes that "we owe the sense of a distinctive Manichaean identity to the works of catholic/orthodox Christian writers", and "that people whom we have grown accustomed to calling Manichaeans mainly represented themselves as Christians".[104] However, the distinctiveness of the Manichaean identity is also highlighted in the writings of the other Christian denominations (heretics according to Catholics), as well as in pagan anti-Manichaean writings.[105]

As far as the *ab-intra* self-definition of the Manichaeans themselves is concerned, the data from Manichaean sources seem contradictory. In some cases they are self-perceived as a religious community distinct from that of the Christians,[106] while in other cases they considered themselves as Christians and their communities as assemblies of saints (i.e. a church in the Christian sense).[107] In addition, there are testimonies from other religious environments, where Manichaeans present themselves as exemplary Muslims, Buddhists, etc.[108]

In conclusion, regardless of the origin of Manichaeism, of the way Manichaeans identified themselves, of whether they expressed an alternative Christianity which the official church expelled, what is important for this study and is beyond doubt, is that Manichaeans for their contemporary Catholics, heretics, and pagans, constituted a distinctive religious group. It is on this distinctive religious group that this research focuses.

104   Lim 2008, 147.

105   The distinctiveness of Manichaean identity is not only due to the writings of Catholic-Orthodox authors but, as has been pointed out by Perczel (2004, 224) too, is also due to "the rich anti-Manichaean polemics by Christians of different confessions and also by the Neoplatonist Simplicius".

106   *1Keph.* 105: "Once again he speaks: Chris[tia]n people [...] call people who love him by hi[s name]; / and bestow his name [the name of Christ] upon their children and children's [child]/ren. [...] people who love me are c[a]lled of my name!".

107   Coyle 2004, 218, 225; Stroumsa 1986b, 308; Gardner and Lieu 2004, 35. Pedersen 2004, 12, fn. 23: "documentary texts from Ismant el-Kharab can even be interpreted to mean that the Manichaeans in ancient Kellis referred to their own congregation as the "Holy Church" (ⲧⲉⲕⲕⲗⲏⲥⲓⲁ ⲉⲧⲟⲩⲁⲃⲉ) in contrast to the "Catholic Church" (καθολικὴ ἐκκλησία)".

108   Lieu 1981a, 153–73; 1981b; 1986b; 235–75 & 260–61; 1992, 261–62 and 1998a; Stroumsa and Stroumsa 1988, 39, fn. 7; Klein 2007; Liu 1998, 182. See ch.[8], section 9.3 (Comparative evidence from other religious contexts: Islam and China).

5.3.5   Manichaeism, Manichaeans as Labels

Finally, a rather thorny methodological problem is the use of the term *Man-ichaean* as a term of abuse, which requires a critical inquiry into each sepa-rate case where the term appears in the texts. If we read these texts in their own terms, we could possibly differentiate between the literal or non-literal use of the term. In this direction, it might be useful to highlight the distinc-tion made by the writers themselves, who use three different terms: μανιχαῖος (*Manichaean*), μανιχαιόφρων, and μανιχαΐζων. Neither the μανιχαιόφρων, nor the μανιχαΐζων are Manichaeans. Μανιχαιόφρων is the Manichaean-minded individual, while μανιχαΐζων is the person whose specific views or statements on specific issues sound as if he were a Manichaean. I will adopt this distinc-tion as a heuristic tool for the *etic* discourse, although this is not an absolute criterion because the authors often use the above terms alternatively for the same person(s).

Constantly keeping in mind, throughout the whole treatise, the differenti-ated content of the terms, μανιχαῖος, μανιχαιόφρων, and μανιχαΐζων, I will exam-ine the questions I raise in each chapter (according to the following outline), aiming to illuminate some aspects of the identity (religious and social) and life of Byzantine Manichaeans.

6   Outline of the Structure and Research Questions

This book has been divided into eight themed chapters. Chapter one lays out a presentation of selected sources of Greek anti-Manichaean literature, which, apart from their significance for the study of Manichaeism in the Roman East, are particularly important for the question of the next chapter. Chapter two is entitled "The arrival and spread of Manichaeism in the Roman East" and examines the way anti-Manichaean authors show and represent the arrival and missionary efforts of Manichaeism in the Roman East. In particular, this chapter presents and compares the 'equipment' of the Manichaean mission (i.e. books, missionaries, methods and strategies), as recorded in the sources presented in the first chapter and in the earliest anti-Manichaean sources. The third chapter, "The Manichaeans in Roman imperial legislation", outlines the profile of the Manichaeans as it is depicted in the laws of the state. Initially, the position that the Manichaean question occupies in the laws is pointed out through a comparison between the attitude of the law towards Manichaeans and its attitude towards other religious groups in a series of themes (e.g. the way they are classified, the characterization of their crime, the inquisitional and prosecuting mechanisms, the penalties inflicted, etc.). The remaining part of the chapter looks at what the laws reveal and how they may have affected Manichaean daily life. Chapter four, entitled "Classifying Manichaeism", focuses on the question of the religious identity of Manichaeans by examining whether the Manichaeans were considered by their contemporaries as Christian heretics or not Christians at all (followers of a foreign religion). The approach of the survey takes into account the opinions of both Christian and pagan specialists on Manichaeism. Chapter five, "Manichaean beliefs and practices", analyses the religious and social implications of Manichaean beliefs (dualism) on Manichaean everyday behaviour and practices, as conveyed to us by anti-Manichaean authors (both Christian and pagan). For a more comprehensive and reliable picture, the testimonies of Augustine and of the Manichaean sources on the relevant issues are also examined. An important research question examined in this chapter is the extent to which the Manichaean challenge influenced the thought of theologians of eastern Christianity (especially on the issue of theodicy). Chapter six, "Manichaeism in society", questions why and to whom Manichaeism was appealing. Specifically, it attempts a sociological classification of the groups to which Manichaeism was appealing, taking into consideration the following parameters: religious profile, age, gender, and social status. The issue of the relationship between Manichaeans and other extreme Christian ascetics, a group to which Manichaeism was particularly attractive, constitutes a core issue of this chapter. Chapter seven consists of two main parts: the first explores whether Manichaean communities and churches existed, investigating the case of two major cities of the eastern part of the Empire, Jerusalem and Antioch. The second part focuses on those individuals labelled as Manichaeans by Greek anti-Manichaean authors and attempts to assess (where possible) whether they were real or imagined Manichaeans. The final chapter eight, "The dissolution of Manichaeism in the Roman East", draws upon the findings of the entire study, and investigates the question of the disappearance of Manichaeans from the Eastern Roman Empire. In this context, after examining the prevailing aspect in scholarship that the extinction of Manichaeans was the result of vigorous persecutions, and taking into account the dimensions of the phenomenon of crypto-Manichaeism, the chapter proposes that infiltration into Christianity is an alternative option for the disappearance of Manichaeism. The latter scenario, I argue, is supported by inherent features of Manichaeism as well as by comparative evidence from other religious environments and relevant testimonies about Manichaeism in the early Islamic world and medieval China.

Apart from the questions that each individual chapter addresses, there are questions that permeate the entire treatise and re-emerge steadily in all the chapters. These are: (1) the issue of interdependence and common sources of the anti-Manichaean writings, (2) the question of "real and imagined Manichaeans", (3) why Manichaeans were persecuted to such a degree, (4) the (trans)formation of the Manichaean identity during their confrontation with the official Christian Church, and also exactly because of this confrontation, and (5) the question of the silence of the sources (i.e. the fact that the Greek anti-Manichaean authors do not discuss a number of issues, concerning Manichaean organization, conduct and beliefs).

CHAPTER 1

An Introductory Presentation of Selected Sources of Greek Anti-Manichaica

1 Introduction

As the investigated Greek anti-Manichaean literature is voluminous, I selected to present here those sources that I consider most important for this study. As emphasized in the introduction, the aim of the present research is to reconstruct (aspects of) the history of Eastern Roman Manichaeism and Manichaeans and not to examine how the polemical argumentation of the anti-Manichaean authors was developed, nor the Manichaean beliefs in general, but only those beliefs that had a visible impact on everyday life.[1] Therefore, according to the above criterion, the sources that I have chosen to present in more detail in this introductory chapter are those that provide most of the historical information about Manichaeism and Manichaeans of the Roman East, thus depicting the most comprehensive picture of what Manichaeism meant for a citizen of the Roman East during the period under investigation. For the same reason, these sources are used more extensively than the other sources in this book.[2] Apart from their significance for the study of Manichaeism in the Roman East, the following sources, in addition, constitute the main body of primary material on which the next chapter is based. In this sense, the current chapter acts as an introduction to ch.[2].

The starting point of the chapter (sections 2 & 3) consists of two texts I consider principal, which belong to two different literary genres of anti-Manichaean literature: the *Acta Archelai* and the *Seven Chapters against the Manichaeans* (abjuration formula). These two sources comprise the backbone of ch.[2], because they constitute the most comprehensive sources of information for the early history and reception of Manichaeism, its fundamental constituents, and the first Manichaean missions in the Roman Empire. In

---

1 To this end, because historical information in the Greek corpus is relatively limited and scattered, it was necessary to exploit all sources, even brief references, so that through their comparative analysis, any historical information the Greek corpus provides could be drawn.

2 To note that the presentation will not be thorough, since there are critical editions devoted to each work. Apart from a brief presentation of the authors and the content of their work, emphasis will be given on: (1) the influence these texts had on posterior anti Manichaean literature and their interdependence, (2) their importance as sources for Manichaean history.

addition, both sources are of particular interest, each one for different reasons. The *Acta Archelai*, apart from being the earliest extensive testimony recording the first encounter between Christianity and Manichaeism,[3] constituted a key source for authors of the following centuries and had a huge impact on subsequent literature. "Without doubt" it was "the most popular and probably the most effective polemical work against Mani and Manichaeism in Late Antiquity".[4] The core of the *Acta*'s narrative was reproduced until the late Byzantine era, constructing a dominant image of Manichaeism, regardless of the presence of real Manichaeans in any specific time and place. On the other hand, the *Seven Chapters against the Manichaeans* is a unique source, metaphorically and literally. First, this is because it is not based on the preceding textual anti-Manichaean tradition, and because it preserves information crosschecked for its accuracy with actual Manichaean texts, which is not recorded in any other Greek polemic source. In addition, unlike the *Acta*, the *Seven Chapters* has barely attracted scholarly interest and has not been studied by Manichaean scholars, with the exception of Sam Lieu's work.[5] Later echoes of these two sources (*Acta Archelai* and abjuration formulas) in the posterior Greek anti-Manichaean corpus are presented briefly in section 4.

In the following sections of this chapter (5 & 6), I present two of the lengthy anti-Manichaean treatises; both were published during the fourth century. These are the *against Manichaeans* works of the Christian Titus, bishop of Bostra, and of the pagan philosopher Alexander of Lycopolis. In my discussion about Titus in the introduction, I have already stressed the importance of his work. For Alexander, additional information will be given in ch.[4], a significant part of which is dedicated to his work. Apart from the fact that I consider these two treatises the most important for my research, it is interesting that many scholars (as we will see below) find similarities between them or even place them in the same literary tradition, despite the different religious background of the authors.

In ch.[7] I will provide information for the authors of the homilies, namely, Cyril of Jerusalem and John the Chrysostom, to whom the chapter is mostly devoted, and in whose works many references to Manichaeans and Manichaeism are made. For the rest of the works, I will give information whenever I refer to them in the course of this treatise.

---

3 See Jason BeDuhn and Paul Mirecki, eds., *Frontiers of Faith: The Christian Encounter with Manichaeism in the Acts of Archelaus* (2007), a volume devoted to AA's encounter.

4 Lieu 2010, 165.

5 Lieu 1983, 152–218; 1994a, 203–305; 2010, 116–25, 194. For more information about Lieu's work on the sc and their importance, see ch.[1], sections 3.3.1 & 3.3.3.

2   *Acta Archelai* (*AA*) and its Echoes in Subsequent Literature

2.1   *Acta Archelai*

2.1.1   Author

The *AA* is attributed to an author named Hegemonius, who is not known from any other source. Thus, the only knowledge preserved about him comes from this text, which ascribes the authorship to him.[6]

2.1.2   Date of the *AA*'s Composition

What is certain is that the *Acts of Archelaus* (either as a tradition or as a written composition) were formed during the first half of the fourth century. The *terminus ante quem* must be 348–350 CE, since one of the *Catecheses* (6.20 ff.) of Cyril of Jerusalem provides a brief summary of part of it.[7] On the basis of internal evidence, the *terminus post quem* of the work can be put after 300 CE.[8] Some researchers have proposed a post-Nicene date for the work because of the word ὁμοούσιος in the text.[9] However, I consider that such a proposal to be unfounded, as the context in which the term is used in the *AA* has no bearing on the triadological discourse (i.e. the relationship between Father and Son in the Holy Trinity, as to their essence), which was a major theological issue discussed at the Synod of Nicaea.[10] Besides, the use of the term ὁμοούσιος, in the sense of consubstantiality, is also recorded in pre-Nicene literature.[11]

---

6   *AA* 68.5 (Vermes, 151): "I, Hegemonius, have written down this disputation which I recorded to describe for those who wish". Cf. BeDuhn and Mirecki 2007, 7. Scopello 1995, 203–04 & 2000. Klein 1991, 22.

7   We have to distinguish between the *AA* as *composition* and the *AA* as *narrative*. It seems that there was a cluster of narrative versions of *AA*. The composition that survives in the extant Latin text is one version of that tradition, but both Cyril and Epiphanius, it seems, knew it in a different version. See below in this section.

8   In *AA* 31.7 (Vermes, 85–86), Archelaus (during his debate with Mani) is said to declare, revealing the dating of the work, that "if Mani were correct (in claiming that he is the Paraclete), Jesus sent the Paraclete only after three hundred or more years". On this see Quasten 1960, 357–58. Cf. BeDuhn and Mirecki 2007, 9.

9   Quasten 1960, 357–358. Indeed, Lieu points out that "the word 'homoousios' is used in the work in a theological sense". Lieu in Vermes 2001 (Introduction), 6: "A post-Nicene date (i.e. after 325) of composition had long been suggested for the *Acta* because the word "homoousios" is used in the work in a theological sense in its date".

10   *AA* 36.7–9 (Vermes, 95–96). See also a relevant argumentation in BeDuhn and Mirecki 2007, 7.

11   For the prehistory of the term in Gnostic (and Hermetic) texts and thought (including Manichaeism) see the article of Beatrice (2002), "The Word 'Homoousios' from Hellenism to Christianity".

Taking into account that the AA constituted a basic source for Greek heresiologists, certain features allow us to attempt to narrow down the possible time-span of its composition. When the authors of the early fourth century (e.g. the philosopher Alexander of Lycopolis, the bishops Eusebius of Caesarea, and Serapion of Thmuis) were writing their anti-Manichaean works, the AA had not yet been published, for otherwise they would surely have referred to it. Alexander's work is dated circa 300 CE. The majority of researchers date the composition of the first edition of the seventh book of the *Ecclesiastical History* of Eusebius (ch. 31 about Manichaeism) quite early, before 312–313, and even before 303 CE.[12] Finally, Serapion composed his treatise *Contra Manichaeos* around 326 CE. Thus, all dates in the first half of the fourth century are likely for the AA's composition, with a higher probability for those after 326 CE.

2.1.3   Translations and Manuscripts

The work was originally written in Greek, but the entire work has survived only in Latin translations, the most important of which are preserved in the manuscripts of Montecassino 371 (eleventh–twelfth cent.) and München (early thirteenth cent.).[13]

2.1.4   Summary of the Content

The protagonist of the AA is Mani himself, who embarks on a missionary enterprise that aims to spread his religion westwards, to the Roman Empire. The story is set in two cities that are not precisely identified, but most likely were located near the border-zone between the Persian and Roman Empires. In summary, the story goes that the fame of an exceptional Christian and prominent citizen of the (unknown) Roman city of Carchar, named Marcellus, reached Mani; at this point Mani was near the Roman-Persian border fleeing persecution by the Persian king, and decides to proselytize Marcellus in order to convert the whole province to Manichaeism through him. Before meeting Marcellus himself, Mani decided to prepare the ground by sending him a letter with Turbo, who was one of the followers of his disciple Addas. In this letter, he presents himself as an apostle of Jesus and makes a first attempt to persuade

---

12   Louth 1990, 111–123. Lieu in his introduction on AA dates the composition of Eusebius' *HE* between 326 and 330. However, later (Lieu 2010, 164) he revises his opinion arguing that the first edition of Eusebius' *HE* was completed before 300 CE.

13   BeDuhn and Mirecki 2007, 7. As far as the Latin text is concerned (which is dated just before 400 CE), it is generally accepted that it was translated into Latin from Greek, see Lieu 1994a, 45 & 136–137; Gardner and Lieu 2004, 26). The München manuscript was discovered by Traube in 1903 and is the only manuscript to have preserved the full text of AA (Lieu 2010, 165).

Marcellus that his own faith was the correct one. To do this, he points out the basic doctrinal differences with Christianity: (1) the existence of two first principles (darkness-light, evil-good) instead of one, and (2) a docetic Christology. He also offered to explain in detail his doctrines to Marcellus face to face. Marcellus accepted Mani's proposal and invited him to Carchar. Meanwhile, Turbo had arrived at Carchar and was questioned by both Marcellus and the bishop of the city, Archelaus, who wished to know more about Mani and Manichaeism. Turbo briefly presented the essentials of the Manichaean faith. By the end of Turbo's narration, Mani arrived, accompanied by a large group of Elect Manichaeans and a debate between him and bishop Archelaus was held at Marcellus' house. Four eminent pagan citizens were appointed to act as the arbiters of the debate.[14]

The main topic of the debate was dualism, the belief in the two first principles/*roots*. Another subject was the challenge of the alleged 'Apostleship' of Mani and his claim that he was the Paraclete (i.e. the 'comforter', whose future coming Jesus had announced, according to John 14:16). At the end, the arbiters and the audience judged Archelaus to be the winner of the debate. Thereupon, Mani fled to a town called Diodoris (likewise unknown), where one day he began to speak and to present his teachings before the crowd. This led the local priest, Diodorus, to ask the help of bishop Archelaus; Diodorus sent him a letter in which he outlined Mani's teachings, which this time concerned only the rejection of the OT, and asked Archelaus to instruct him on how to deal with Mani. Archelaus responded immediately, trying to cover the issue as much as possible. Diodorus, after receiving and studying the letter of Archelaus, confronted Mani in a debate. The subject of that debate was the contradictions between the Old and New Testament. At some point, as it was late, the debate was interrupted and was postponed for the next morning. The next day however, Archelaus came to Diodoris and the debate was finally continued between Mani and Archelaus. The main topic of this second phase of the debate in Diodoris was the nature of Jesus (Manichaean Docetism). Although at some point Mani's argumentation seemed to be winning over the audience, eventually Archelaus became the winner of the debate. According to Hegemonius, the rest of the *AA* comprises Archelaus presenting to the congregated people his own version of Mani's 'biography' (his spiritual ancestors, his early life, his first disciples and their missions, Manichaean books, Mani's end). Ending his story, Archelaus referred to the events of the days immediately preceding the debate, when Mani was persecuted by the Persian king and took

---

14   See ch.[2], 7.3 with regard to the way debates were conducted.

shelter in 'Castellum Arabionis',[15] from where he sent the letter to Marcellus before coming to Carchar. By the end of the narration (during which Mani seems to have been present), Mani fled and returned to 'Castellum Arabionis'. Finally, he was captured and killed by the Persian king. In the two final chapters of his work, Hegemonius presents the Gnostic Basilides as the spiritual ancestor of Mani's dualism.

The contents of the AA can thus be represented in the following way:[16]

1. Marcellus' encomium (1–4).
2. Mani's epistle to Marcellus and Marcellus' response (5–6); topics of the epistle: a) the two principles (dualism), and b) the nature of Jesus (Docetism).
3. Turbo's narration (7–13); topics: Manichaean cosmogony, pantheon, anthropology, eschatology, and Manichaean behaviour and practices.
4. Advent of Mani and the preparation of the debate (14).
5. The first debate (15–33 or 42); topics: a) dualism, i.e. the two principles/roots (15–29), b) Mani's claim that he is the Paraclete, dualism, and OT (30–42).
6. From Carchar to Diodoris (43).
7. Diodorus' letter and Archelaus' response (43–51); topic: OT.
8. The second debate (52–61). Parts: a): the debate between Diodorus and Mani (52); topic: OT, b) the debate between Archelaus and Mani (53–60); topic: the nature of Jesus (Docetism), c) the end of the debate.
9. The 'biography' of Mani and of his ancestors, Mani's books, Mani's disciples and their missionary roots, Mani's end (62–66).
10. Mani's teachings as grounded on Basilides' doctrines. (67–68).

In light of the guiding question of this chapter and the following one, the contents of the AA can be divided into the following three main parts:

1. Mani's first enterprise to convert Marcellus through his epistle, and through Turbo's presentation of Manichaean beliefs.
2. The three debates conducted between Mani and local Christian clergymen.
3. The early history of Manichaeism and its spread westwards, through the 'biography' of Mani and of his ancestors.

---

15 There are various opinions on this place name. Pennacchietti's (1988) suggestion that this would be Birt Aropan has been adopted enthusiastically by many, but Luther (1999, 77–84) has collected arguments against this identification. In light of Luther's findings, it seems that this place name, too, cannot be identified with an actual place.

16 BeDuhn and Mirecki (2007, 14–15) divide the text in four parts.

The theological issues discussed during the three debates (dualism, Docetism and their refutation, as well as the rejection/defence of the OT), were further developed in all subsequent philosophical-theological anti-Manichaean treatises.

2.1.5   Historicity and Reliability of the AA

Whereas it is generally accepted that the former part of the work (as well as Mani's argumentation during the debates) draws on material from genuine Manichaean sources, the latter, biographical, part is considered to be the most unreliable and biased part of the work. Hegemonius, for the first and second parts of his report, names as his source a treatise written by the protagonist of his story, the bishop Archelaus; as source for the third part he names Sisinnius, an ex-Manichaean, as he says, who had converted to Christianity. However, this seems improbable, since it is well known and certified in Manichaean sources that Sisinnius was Mani's successor at the head of the Manichaean church. It is more likely that the author of the AA simply uses Sisinnius' name as an attempt to attribute credibility to his testimony.

Turbo's account and Mani's biography (first and third part) acquired a large popularity and were extensively used by later authors (e.g. Cyril of Jerusalem, Epiphanius of Salamis, Socrates the Scholastic, Theodoret of Cyrrhus, Theodorus Anagnostes, Photius, Peter of Sicily, etc.). These parts constituted the main source on Manichaeism for subsequent generations and shaped the representation of Mani in Christian literature, not only during the Byzantine period, but right until the twentieth century, when genuine Manichaean texts were brought to light for the first time. When these genuine Manichaean texts were found, the AA, together with the rest of the patristic anti-Manichaica (as stated in the Introduction) were almost immediately put aside as sources of information. Scholars increasingly argued that the patristic writings were unreliable and biased, and this led most of them to disregard them in their attempts to interpret Manichaean history.

Although this reaction was understandable, it had unfortunate consequences; as modern researchers observe, the AA contains a great deal of accurate information about the Manichaean religion.[17] In addition, the AA is a valuable text, not only for scholars of Manichaeism, but also for the study of early Christianity and patristics, since it sheds light on the way Christian writers perceived the interreligious contact, relation and interaction between Christianity and Manichaeism.[18]

---

17   BeDuhn and Mirecki 2007, 1–22; Gardner 2007b, 33–48; BeDuhn 2007a, 77–102 and 2007b, 131–147; Kaatz 2007, 103–118; Scopello 2000, 534 & 541–2.

18   Kaatz 2007, 103; Lim 1995, 76.

Further, since the AA constituted a basic source for Greek heresiologists, a more profound investigation of its contents is clearly necessary.[19] Since the original work in Greek is missing and only the Latin translation has survived, it is methodologically correct to co-examine the Latin version and the Greek texts that preserve parts of it.[20] Thus, the following two Greek authors (Cyril and Epiphanius) can be considered as complementary to the textual criticism and comprehension of the AA. For methodological reasons I will start with Epiphanius, although Cyril precedes him chronologically.

2.2 Epiphanius of Salamis (Fourth Century)

Epiphanius' 'Against the Manichaeans', is one of the longest chapters of his *Panarion* (Medicine Chest, 374–376/7).[21] The work preserves, and in fact reproduces almost *verbatim*, a long excerpt of the original Greek AA. To be precise, it contains Mani's epistle to Marcellus, Marcellus' response, Turbo's narration and Mani's biography (i.e. the first and the third parts of the AA). In the rest of his work, Epiphanius comments freely and rebuts each of the theses advanced by Mani during the debates. Thus, the significance of Epiphanius' work is great especially because, through the *verbatim* narration of Turbo, he provides us with a great number of divinities of the Manichaean pantheon and terms in Greek. Apart from the *Seven Chapters*, these are not recorded in any other Greek source.[22] As a source of his work, Epiphanius refers to Archelaus' book/disputation (ἀντιλογία), which means that he had a written version of the AA in his hands.[23]

Yet, the structure of the contents of Epiphanius' work differs from that followed by the AA. Epiphanius starts with Mani's biography (AA's end) and then briefly recounts the events (Mani's arrival, the debates, etc.) in chronological order. Subsequently, he refutes the Manichaean positions by quoting intermittently from Turbo's account. This 'correction' of the AA's structure seems to have been a conscious choice, for, as Epiphanius underlines, "whoever

---

19   Klein 1991, 21–24.

20   Lieu 2010, 165.

21   Cf. Lieu 1994a, 107; Lieu 2010, 168–176.

22   For the importance of Turbo's summary, see Lieu in Vermes (2001, 43–44, fn. 27). Recently, Lieu (2010, 165) revised his earlier opinion (Vermes 2001, 10) that "there is no reason to assume that Epiphanius used a different Greek version from the one rendered by the Latin *Acta*" and argued that Epiphanius probably reproduced a later Greek version of *Acta*, different from the one that was preserved in Latin translation.

23   Epiphanius, *Pan.* 66.25.2 (GCS 37:53; Williams, 252): "When the bishop Archelaus, and Marcellus, questioned Turbo about Mani's teaching, Turbo replied in the words I quote from the book" (ἅτινα ἐκ τοῦ βιβλίου παρεθέμην); Epiphanius, *Pan.* 66.32.1 (GCS 37:72; Williams, 261): "These are the passages I have quoted from the book by Archelaus that I mentioned" (Ταῦτά ἐστιν ἃ παρεθέμην ἀπὸ τοῦ Ἀρχελάου βιβλίου τοῦ προειρημένου).

embarks on a narrative must start it the best way he can, and introduce it from the very beginning".[24]

The following table compares the contents of Epiphanius' *Against the Manichaeans* with the corresponding chapters of AA:

Epiphanius	Acta
1–5 Mani's biography.	62–66
6 Letter of Mani to Marcellus.	5
7 Letter of Marcellus to Mani.	6
8–9 Arrival of Mani, Mani's teachings included in Turbo's narration.	14 & 7–13
10 The debate in Caschar (Carchar in AA).	14 & 42–43
10–11 From Caschar to Diodoris. Debate in Diodoris.	43
12 The end of Mani, the three disciples of Mani	66 & 64
13 The books of Mani.	62
14–24 Epiphanius refutes Mani's theses stated either in the debate (e.g. dualism) or in Turbo's narration (e.g. cosmogony) and refers to previous authors combating Mani.	15–42 (33?) 52–61
25–31 Turbo's narration (verbatim from the AA). The three disciples are sent to preach Mani's teachings.	7–13 & 64
32–58 Epiphanius comments and further criticizes Mani's teachings (from Turbo's narration) juxtaposing the Christian theses.	15–42 (33?) 52–61?
59–88 Epiphanius again refutes Mani's argumentation, drawing again his material from the AA, but this time he handles it more freely. He also adds his own material (date of Mani's arrival, some other books and missionaries, see next chapter).	15–42 (33?) 52–61?

Some minor discrepancies between Epiphanius' text and the AA will be discussed in chapter two. Epiphanius also informs us about the other Greek Church Fathers who had written treatises against Manichaeans. Among them is listed the now lost long treatise of George of Laodicea (a supporter of Arianism).

> Marvelously good replies to him have already been composed by great men – by Archelaus the bishop, as has been said; and, I have heard, by Origen; and by Eusebius of Caesarea and Eusebius of Emesa, Serapion

---

24   Epiphanius, *Pan.* 66.2.12–3 (Williams, 228). Epiphanius uses the same method for the whole *Panarion*, see Berzon 2016.

of Thmuis, Athanasius of Alexandria, George of Laodicea, Apollinaris of Laodicea, Titus, and many who have spoken in opposition to him.[25]

Epiphanius' clarification that he had just heard about the work of Origen strongly suggests that he knew personally the rest of the works and had possibly used some of them.[26] The fact that Epiphanius does not mention Cyril among the authors who combated the Manichaeans could be an indication that he was not aware of the content of Cyril's *Catecheses*.

2.3   Cyril of Jerusalem (Fourth Century)

Cyril compiled his *Catecheses ad Illuminandos* between 348 and 350 CE. In his sixth *Catechetical Lecture* he provides us with a brief summary of a part of the AA. It is argued that he used another more extended Greek version than the one preserved in the extant Latin translation.[27]

The AA material in the sixth *Catechetical Lecture* comes mainly from ch. 6.20 onwards, although in the earlier parts of the text there are many hints that seem to allude to Manichaeism (e.g. references to dualism). The parts of the AA from which Cyril draws information are:

(1)   *The biography*: Mani's forerunners, books, and disciples (22–24), that he was persecuted by the Persian king (25), and Mani's martyrdom (30).

(2)   *The debates*: Cyril delineates the context of the debates; that initially one debate was conducted between Archelaus and Mani (27) after which Mani fled to Diodoris(?)[28] (30). Yet, he does not mention anything else about the debates in Diodoris. Apart from the reference to Mani's claim that he was the Paraclete (25), the content of the discourse during the debate, as presented by Cyril, does not correspond to that of the AA. Initially, as a cause of this inconsistency, it was suggested that Cyril wrote the dialogue from memory and paraphrased its content. More recently, it has been argued that this mismatch is due instead to the fact that Cyril used another more extended Greek version than the extant Latin translation.[29]

---

25   Epiphanius, *Pan.* 66.21.3 (Williams, 248–49). Epiphanius consistency in presenting his records chronologically is also depicted in the order he mentions the anti-Manichaean authors.

26   Epiphanius' reference to Origen is very surprising. Origen died in 253, when Mani was already active but, we must assume, completely unknown in Egypt.

27   As Lieu remarks, with Traube's research it has become known that Cyril's source was a different more extensive version of the AA in Latin (Lieu in Vermes 2001, 8).

28   Cyril does not provide the name of this city.

29   BeDuhn, 2007b, 135. Lieu in Vermes 2001, 7–8.

(3)   *Turbo's narrative*: there are references to the Manichaean cosmogony
      (34), and to the belief of reincarnation (31). However, Cyril focuses mainly
      on Manichaean ethics and practices (32). Among the latter, Cyril refers to
      the sexual mores and practices of the Elect (33), which does not seem to
      be based on the testimony of the *AA*, at least in the extant version. This
      part of Cyril's text – "not surprisingly" – as Lieu remarks, "was heavily
      abridged" in the English translation of the Library of Fathers of the Holy
      Catholic Church (1872),[30] and this omission continued to exist in a series
      of subsequent translations (1894, 1955, 2000).[31]

2.4   Socrates the Scholastic (*Fifth Century*)

The church historian Socrates, in the first book of his *Ecclesiastical History*,
found it necessary to update the entry regarding *Manes* of Eusebius' *History*,
since as he says, Eusebius had not gone into detail concerning Mani. Socrates
wanted his readers to know "who this Manichaeus was, whence he came, and
what was the nature of his presumptuous daring".[32]

To stress the validity of the information about Manichaeans that Socrates
gives, he declares that this information is not fabricated by himself but is gathered from a book entitled *Archelaus' Disputation*. This Archelaus, Socrates adds
underlining also the reliability of his source, "disputed with Manichaeus face
to face and expounds what I wrote in his biography".[33] Specifically, Socrates'
account draws on materials from the first and third parts of the *AA* (i.e. Turbo's
narrative, Mani's epistle, and biography).

2.5   Theodoret of Cyrrhus (*Fifth Century*)

One of the sources of Theodoret's chapter on Manichaeism, in his work
Haereticarum fabularum compendium (mid-fifth century), was the *AA*. The
chapter belongs to the first of the five books of this work.[34] This book includes
all those who "invented another creator", "denied the one beginning/principle
[of the whole cosmos]", suggesting that "there were other principles which do

---

30   Lieu 2010, 166–67. LFHCC 1872, 76–77.

31   *NPNF*² 1894, translated by Gifford; Telfer 1955; Yarnold 2000. The omitted text was finally
      translated by Fox and Sheldon (Lieu 2010, 55) and by Van Oort (2016b, 432), see ch.[5],
      2.3.4 (The Ceremony of the 'Dried Fig').

32   Socrates, *HE* 1.22 (*NPNF*² 2).

33   Socrates, *HE* 1.22.13.61–65 (SC 477:206; *NPNF*² 2, altered): Ταῦτα δὲ ἡμεῖς οὐ πλάσαντες
      λέγομεν ἀλλὰ διαλόγῳ Ἀρχελάου τοῦ ἐπισκόπου Κασχάρων, μιᾶς τῶν ἐν Μεσοποταμίᾳ πόλεων,
      ἐντυχόντες συνηγάγομεν. Αὐτὸς γὰρ Ἀρχέλαος διαλεχθῆναι αὐτῷ φησιν κατὰ πρόσωπον καὶ τὰ
      προγεγραμμένα εἰς τὸν βίον αὐτοῦ ἐκτίθεται.

34   Theodoret, *Haer.* 26 (PG 83:377A8–381B31). About Theodoret's heresiological method see
      Berzon (2016, esp. 131–144).

not exist", and said "that the Lord appeared among men by illusion".[35] The book starts with the Samaritan Simon Magus, "the first inventor of these doctrines" and ends with Mani, "the Persian sorcerer [γόης]".[36]

Although not explicitly mentioned, it is from the AA (most probably from Cyril's version) that Theodoret drew his information for Manichaeism (i.e. Mani's biography, names of the first disciples, information on Manichaean ritual practices and sexual mores). However, the summary of the Manichaean cosmogony that he provides has less in common with Turbo's narratives and is rather closer to the cosmogonic myth of Basilides (as presented by Hegemonius at the end of his work) or with Severus of Antioch's and Simplicius' accounts of the Manichaean myth. As earlier authors who wrote works against Manichaeans, Theodoret names Titus of Bostra, Diodorus of Tarsus, George of Laodicea and Eusebius of Caesarea. Some researchers have argued that Theodoret, Severus of Antioch, and Titus of Bostra had a common source for Manichaean cosmogony.[37] This must then have been one of the lost anti-Manichaean works (Diodorus of Tarsus and/or George of Laodicea), which Theodoret mentions, or possibly some other genuine Manichaean source.

2.6   *Theodorus Anagnostes (Sixth Century)*

Theodorus Anagnostes, in his work entitled *Epitome historiae tripartitae* (early sixth cent.), reproduces information from the history of the proto-Manichaean Scythianus, Bodda, and of Mani (third part). He mentions as his sources the *Acts of Archelaus* and Eusebius' *Ecclesiastical History*.[38]

2.7   *Heraclian of Chalcedon (Sixth Century)*

Another author who mentions the AA (and Hegemonius for the first time) among other anti-Manichaean works, is Heraclian bishop of Chalcedon. However, this is 'second-hand information' provided by Photius, since the original work is lost.[39] His work comprised twenty books, which Photius says that he had read. As Photius states in his *Bibliotheca*, Heraclian wrote his treatise against the Manichaeans,

---

35   Theodoret, *Haer.* (PG 83:337.37–39); I have modified Cope's (1990, 76) translation here.

36   Theodoret, *Haer.* (PG 83:337C.39–41).

37   Kugener and Cumont 1912, 151–172. Bennett 2001b, 77. Pedersen 2004, 83, fn. 69. For our sources on Manichaean cosmogony, see Lieu 2010, xii–xviii.

38   Theodorus Anagnostes, *Epit. hist. trip.* 1.33 (Hansen 1995, 16–17).

39   Photius, *Bibl.* cod. 85 (65a36–65b38) (Henry 1960), (65b)5–6: "He also gives a list of those who wrote against the Manichaean impiety before him – Hegemonius, who wrote out the disputation of Archelaus against Manes". Translated by Lieu (Vermes 2001, 10–11 & Lieu 2010, 124–27, 127).

at the request of a certain Achillius, whom the author calls his faithful and beloved son. This Achillius, seeing that the Manichaean heresy was growing, begged that it might be publicly refuted, and this work was written [...] This most pious Heraclian flourished in [...].[40]

The rest of the text, unfortunately, is not preserved, so it is difficult to specify when the work was written. Yet, current researchers date it around 500 CE.[41] The other anti-Manichaean authors mentioned by Heraclian are: Titus of Bostra, George of Laodicea, Serapion of Thmuis, and Diodorus of Tarsus.

3　　Abjuration Formulas (AFs): The *Seven Chapters* (SC)

It is at the time when Heraclian of Chalcedon wrote his treatise (500 CE. in all probability), that the composition of the *Seven Chapters* is dated.[42] This was a time during which the spread of Manichaeism had taken on such dimensions that it alarmed both the state and the ecclesiastical authorities.

The *Seven Chapters* belong to the literary genre known as abjuration formulas (AFs). It is commonly accepted that AFs and *Anathemas* are of particular value as historical sources.[43] In comparison to other available anti-heretical sources, AFs are more reliable and provide us with a great deal of accurate information about the persecuted heresies. As Beskow characteristically says, for the case of the AFs against Manichaeism:

> The anti-Manichaean documents produced by those authorities which wanted to repress the community of Mani are a most valuable complement to Manichaean source-material. More than the purely theological treatises against Manichaeism [...] they give us information about the actual situation of the Manichaean communities in the Roman (or Byzantine) Empire before their actual extinction, and contain details not to be found in the Manichaean documents themselves. The abjuration formulae from Byzantine times comprise such an anti-Manichaean source of information.[44]

40　　Photius, *Bibl.* cod. 85 (65a/b).

41　　Pedersen 2004, 67, 79 and 138 fn. 73. On the dating of Heraclian, see also Alfaric 1918, 66, 100; Henry 1960, 9 fn. 1; Sfameni Gasparro 2000, 549.

42　　Lieu 1994a, 225.

43　　Lieu 1994a, 217; Badenas 2002, 97.

44　　Beskow 1988, 1.

These texts were part of a ritual of abjuration.[45] The 'heretic' had to condemn the doctrine and the worship of his former faith during a public renunciation ceremony. The ritual consisted of two stages. First, the converted anathematized his former heretical religious beliefs in the hearing of all (εἰς ἐπήχοον πάντων).[46] At the end of the ceremony, he had to sign a written statement of the anathemas, which the *chartophylax* kept in the ecclesiastical archives.[47] This procedure is clearly illustrated in the introduction of the following Latin anathema formula: "these are the chapters of Saint Augustine which those who are suspected of being Manichaeans should read out in public and sign".[48]

3.1 Form of Abjuration Formulas

Because of their use in this ritual setting, the AFs soon became standardized. Already existing AFs (or parts of those) often formed the basis for the AFs of later sects. Thus, the Manichaean AFs were used for the anathematization of Paulicians and Bogomils.[49] However, it seems that standard AFs were not used for all kind of heretics. The renunciations in the heresiological collections of the Vienna and Turin manuscripts, which were studied in an important work by Eleuteri and Rigo are classified into two major categories: (1) the ancient AFs (Le formule d'abiura più antiche), and (2) the more recent AFs (Le formule d'abiura più recenti). In the first group are included the short and long *antimanichea* and *antiebraica*, as well as the formulas for the Athingani and the Muslims. The second group comprises the AFs for the converted Armenians, Jacobites, and Bogomils.[50] The AFs "have come down to us mainly in manuscripts of Byzantine euchologies".[51]

---

45 Badenas 2002, 97–106.
46 Eleuteri and Rigo 1993, 19.
47 Badenas 2002, 99. Gouillard 1967, 301–303. More details on this ritual will be given in ch.[8], section 5.
48 *Prosperi anathematismi et fidei catholicae professio*, PL 65.23 in Adam 1954, 90–93; Lieu 1994a, 210; Lieu 2010, 104–9. Cf. Lieu 1986a, 459–62.
49 Badenas 2002, 97–106.
50 Eleuteri and Rigo 1993, 5. Texts included in the collection: The earliest abjuration formulas. 1) *How heretics who present themselves to the Holy and Apostolic Church of God should be received*; 2) The *Diataxis* of the patriarch Methodius,, 3) The "shorter" Anti-Manichaean formula, 4) The *Ritual for the Manichaeans who convert to the pure and true faith of us Christians*, 5) The "longer" Anti-Manichaean formula, 6) the "shorter" Anti-Jewish formula, 7) The *Logos* of Gregory Asbestas, metropolitan of Nicea, 8) The "longer" Anti-Jewish formula, 9) The Formula for the Athinganoi, and 10) The formula for the Muslims. The more recent abjuration formulas: 1) The formula for the Armenians, 2) The formula for the Jacobites and 3) The formula for the Bogomils.
51 Lieu 1994a, 212.

3.2   *Date*

The AFs against Manichaeans are considered to be the most ancient. Indeed, according to Lieu, some form of anathemas existed since Cyril's time. As he argues, "although there was no mention yet of set abjuration formulas, it appears that catechumens who had formerly been Manichaeans had to renounce Mani publicly before they could be baptized".[52] However, the latter remains an assumption since it is not explicitly recorded in Cyril's text.

3.3   *The Greek Abjuration Formulas Against Manichaeans*

There are three (surviving) anti-Manichaean *formulas* in Greek. Two of them have been known in scholarship since the seventeenth century, and are those included in the Vienna collection: the short and the long AFs.[53] The former is dated before the seventh century, perhaps even during the fifth or sixth centuries, since it contains no reference to Paulicians. The majority of scholars support the view that it was written sometime in the mid-fifth century.[54] The latter is dated in the ninth or tenth[55] centuries, because "it combines twenty-seven Anathemas against Manichaeism with ten Anathemas more specifically directed against Paulicianism".[56] The third is our source, the *Seven Chapters*. According to Lieu, both the *Long* and the *Short Formulas* have the *Seven Chapters* as a common source.[57] The question of the interdependence of the three AFs will be discussed in the following sections and in ch.[2].

3.3.1   The *Seven Chapters* (SC)

The SC has been known to scholarship since the late twentieth century, thanks to Marcel Richard. It was first published in 1977 in a volume containing the works of John of Caesarea, edited by Richard. Subsequently, it was republished by Lieu, first in 1983, with a translation of the text in English and full commentary (revised and updated in Lieu 1994a), and then in 2010 (Lieu's translation

---

52   Lieu 1992, 132.

53   About the editions of SAF and LAF and their content, cf. Lieu (1994a, 212–19); Eleuteri and Rigo 1993, 39–42; Adam 1954, 93–103.

54   Lieu 1994a, 215; Eleuteri and Rigo 1993, 40 cite Ficker (*Sammlung*, p. 445); Astruc *et al.* 1970, 187, fn. 10; Klein 1991, 16; Adam 1954, 93.

55   Eleuteri and Rigo (1993, 41) cite Ficker (*Sammlung*, p. 446); Adam 1954, 97; Lieu 1994a, 217.

56   Lieu 1994a, 214.

57   Lieu 1994a, 218–19: "The Manichaean part of the *Long Formula* and the entire *Short Formula* have clearly a common source. [...] There are some minor differences [...]. [...] However, the similarities, reinforced by exact verbal parallels, are so overwhelming that both Formulas must be derived from the exact source, either directly or indirectly".

revised by Fox and with a complementary commentary by Lieu).[58] As Lieu points out, "The *Seven Chapters* is a particularly valuable source because of its comprehensive coverage of the history as well as the doctrine of the sect and preserves a host of proper names and *termini technici* in Greek not attested in any other anti-Manichaean text in Greek or Latin".[59]

3.3.1.1 Authorship

Although the text is anonymous, Richard suggested that Zacharias of Mytilene (or Rhetor, or Scholasticus, c. 465 – after 536) was its author, because in the prologue of another work of Zacharias, the *Antirrhesis*, it is stated that he himself was also the author of seven chapters/anathemas against Manichaeism.[60] It is interesting to note that Zacharias, during Anastasius' reign, before becoming an orthodox and bishop of Mytilene, had been a Monophysite church historian. He was a supporter of Anastasius' policy and the biographer of Severus of Antioch; both Anastasius and Severus were labelled as Manichaeans by their opponents.

3.3.1.2 Date

The exact date of composition remains uncertain, but it is likely that it preceded the *Antirrhesis* (sixth century).[61] In any case, the absence of anathemas against the Paulicians "suggests a pre-seventh century date".[62]

3.3.1.3 Sources

The work, as evident from the introduction of the *sc*, was based on "various works of theirs (i.e. Manichaeans) and from those composed against them by the teachers of the Holy Catholic Church of God".[63] Judging from the accuracy of Zacharias' information, he must have had real access to the Manichaean books.[64] As far as his anti-Manichaean sources are concerned, it seems that he

---

58   Richard 1977, xxxii–xxxix; Lieu 1983, 152–218; 1994, 203–305; 2010, 116–25, 194.
59   Lieu 2010, 194.
60   Richard 1977, XXXII. Lieu 2010, 194.
61   *Antirrhesis* must have been written between 527 and 536 (Zacharias' ordination date as a bishop of Mytilene) because, as stated in the prologue of the work, Zacharias wrote it when he was still *scholasticus*, under Justinian. Cf. Eleuteri and Rigo 1993, 41.
62   Lieu 1994a, 223.
63   *sc* pr. (Lieu 1994a, 223): Κεφάλαια ἑπτὰ σὺν ἀναθεματισμοῖς [...] συνηγμένα ἐκ διαφόρων αὐτῶν βιβλίων καὶ ἐξ ὧν κατ᾽ αὐτῶν συνεγράψαντο οἱ τῆς ἁγίας τοῦ θεοῦ καθολικῆς ἐκκλησίας διδάσκαλοι.
64   Lieu 1994a, 223.

had borrowed material from the *AA*,[65] and probably from sources that did not survive, such as works of Diodorus of Tarsus and Heraclian of Chalcedon.[66]

3.3.1.4   *Content*

Through the anathemas, the *SC* provides us with valuable information, such as the names of Mani's students, parents, books, the divinities of the Manichaean pantheon, the grades of the Manichaean hierarchy, the community rituals and feasts. Most of these are not found in the *AA* tradition, yet are accurate and confirmed by the Manichaean sources.

The table below shows the contents of the *SC*:

Chapter	Content
1st Ch.	The converted Manichaean had to anathematize dualism.
2nd Ch.	He then anathematized Mani, Mani's claim to be the Paraclete, his parentage, his forerunners and teachers, his disciples, his books and the Manichaean hierarchy. The lists of disciples, books, and hierarchical grades record information not provided by other Greek sources but securely attested in the Manichaean sources.
3rd Ch.	The anathematization of Mani's cosmogonic myth and of the whole Manichaean Pantheon. Here, a valuable list of the names of the Manichaean deities with the Greek forms is provided.[a]
4th Ch.	The anathematization of those who reject the OT and the anathematization of Manichaean Christology.
5th Ch.	The anathematization of Manichaean Christology and of the claim of Mani to be the Paraclete.
6th Ch.	The anathematization of Manichaean anthropology. Mainly of the Manichaean claim of consubstantiality of human souls with God and the belief in metempsychosis.
7th Ch.	The anathematization of the Manichaean ethics which mainly concern certain Manichaean beliefs and religious and social practices.

a   Tardieu 1980, 340–341.

3.3.2   The Other Two Abjuration Formulas

As Lieu argues, especially the *Long formula* (*LAF*) "derived almost all its information on Manichaeism" from the *SC*; the "borrowings are verbatim", and the

---

65   Lieu 1994a, 224–225.
66   Lieu 1994a, 225.

"verbal parallels are so striking".[67] The *Short formula* (*SAF*) too, derives its information mainly from the *SC*. However, the *LAF* also preserves information from the tradition of the *AA* (probably through Photius and Peter of Sicily), which is not recorded in the *SC* (e.g. Cubricus, Terebinthus). Lieu points out that the text of the *SC* is "closer to the true Manichaean position" than that of the later versions, which were further embellished, something which is worth noting for the present study.[68]

3.3.3   The Importance and Reliability of the *Seven Chapters*

Samuel Lieu is the only scholar who elaborated a full commentary on the text of Richard's edition, providing also a translation in English.[69] As he observes, "The value of this new material does not seem to have been fully realized".[70] For the value and importance of the text, it is better to let Lieu himself speak:

> Abbé Richard has laid before us an exciting and important document [...] The excellence of its information is enhanced by the fact that it was composed in Greek as we do not have an abundance of accurate sources on Manichaeism in that language, especially on Manichaean cosmogony. The new text has preserved the Greek forms of many important Manichaean technical terms which cannot be found elsewhere except for those which had been excerpted into the later Byzantine formulas. To the compilers of these later texts we owe much for preserving some of the excellent material from the *Seven Chapters* for us. However, their late date and the fact that much of the *Long Formula* is directed against Paulicians have hitherto cast a dark shadow on their usefulness to the study of the early history of Manichaeism. It is gratifying therefore to know that much of the excellent material pertaining to genuine Manichaeism goes back to a sixth century source which we now have in our possession. We owe a great debt to the late Abbé Marcel Richard for making a preliminary publication of this fascinating text in his edition of the works of John of Caesarea. Had he not done so we may have had to wait for many years before it is rediscovered.[71]

There are many open questions concerning the *SC*. From which Manichaean works does the author draw his information? Was he the only one, among the

---

67   Lieu 1994a, 225–26.
68   Lieu 1994a, 227.
69   Lieu 1983, 1994a & 2010.
70   Lieu 1994a, 231, fn. 153.
71   Lieu 1994a, 233.

many Greek anti-Manichaean authors, who had access to these sources? In any case, it appears that he had access to sources which the authors of the *Acta* tradition did not have (or did not use). Was he the only one? Or were there others before him whose works were lost, such as Diodorus of Tarsus and Heraclian of Chalcedon? A further question is how the posterior tradition of the sc is recorded in the literature thereafter (apart from the later abjuration formulas). As I will argue in the next section, the first authors who used the sc are Photius and Peter of Sicily, who probably derived their information from their contemporaneous LAF. The sc does not rely on a previous tradition, nor did it create a new one; it was not exploited by authors of the sixth century who wrote works against Manichaeans. How can this be interpreted?

4   Later Echoes of the *Acta Archelai* and the Abjuration Formulas

4.1   *Photius (Ninth Century)*

Photius, in his work *Contra Manichaeos*, mainly attacks the Paulicians whom he considers to be neo-Manichaeans. He traces the origins of Paulicianism to the Manichaean heresy, and therefore considers it appropriate to briefly present it. He declares that his sources for this presentation are the accounts of Cyril of Jerusalem, Epiphanius of Salamis, Titus of Bostra, Serapion of Thmuis, Alexander of Lycopolis and Heraclian of Chalcedon.[72] He does not mention the AA, but he draws much information from the AA's narrative (as it is reproduced by Cyril and Epiphanius), which he then enriches with information from the abjuration formulas.[73] On the contrary, in his other work, the *Bibliotheca*, Photius refers firstly to the AA as one of the sources of Heraclian.[74]

4.2   *Peter of Sicily (Ninth Century)*

Peter of Sicily mainly used Cyril in his *Historia utilis et refutatio Manichaeorum vel Paulicianorum*,[75] reproducing the AA story and mentioning his source.

---

72   Photius, *c. Manichaeos* 37.19–28, p. 131.

73   Contents drawn from AA (38–49 & 53): from the third part, Mani's biography, i.e. the story of the proto-Manichaean Scythianus etc., Mani's persecution by the Persian king, Mani's claim that he is the Paraclete, and Mani's end. From the second part, the debates. Archelaus, Carchar, debates, and Diodoris, appear in two parts of the work (46–49 & 53). Contents drawn from abjuration formulas (49–52): Sisinnius as Mani's successor, and extra names of Mani's disciples and expositors. Contents apart from AA and abjuration formulas: that Mani had twelve disciples.

74   Photius, *Bibl.* 85 (65b) 5–6.

75   Peter of Sicily, *Hist. ref. Man.* Papachryssanthou 1970, 7–67. Astruc et al. 1970, 7–67.

A long part of the work is quoted almost *verbatim* from Cyril. Like Photius, Peter also complements the information from the AA with material drawn from the AFs.[76] He also mentions the anti-Manichaean writings of Socrates the Scholastic (78–81) and Epiphanius (82–83).

4.3 SUDA *Lexicon (Tenth Century)*

The main source of the entry on Mani in the *Suda Lexicon* is the biography of Mani as recorded in the AA, although the compiler does not mention it. Instead, he refers to Theodorus of Raithou as one of those combating Manichaeans.[77]

5 Alexander of Lycopolis' *Contra Manichaei opiniones disputatio*

5.1 *Author & Work*

Alexander a pagan philosopher from Lycopolis of Egypt became famous thanks to his treatise *Against the Doctrines of Mani*, the only surviving of his works, which he composed around 300 CE. Alexander's work is the unique pagan and the oldest anti-Manichaean treatise. Because his work combated Manichaeism, a strong competitor to Christianity during the fourth century (when most anti-Manichaean treatises were composed by Christian authors), Alexander was considered by later writers to be a Christian, indeed a Christian bishop. Photius, in his list of known authors of anti-Manichaean works, mentions him as the bishop of the city of Lycōn (Λύκων).[78] Alexander's 'Christianization' is the main reason why his work survived and was included in Migne's *Patrologia*

---

76 Peter of Sicily, *Hist. ref. Man.* chs. 46–83, i.e. 37 from the 189 chapters in total; verbatim quotation from Cyril are chs. 46–77: "Ἤδη δὲ λοιπὸν καὶ τῶν ὑπομνηματικῶν ἱστοριῶν ἀπάρξασθαι καιρός ἐστιν. Ἀπάρξομαι δ᾿ οὕτως τά τε παρὰ τοῦ μακαρίου Κυρίλλου ἐν ταῖς κατηχήσεσιν ῥηθέντα προθεὶς καὶ τὰ παρ᾿ ἡμῶν ἀρτίως διαγνωσθέντα ὑποθείς, ὡς ἂν ἄρα οἰκειοτέρα ἡ σκέψις γενήσεται. [...] Ἐξήγηται δὲ αὐτοῦ καὶ ὑπομνηματισταὶ γεγόνασιν Ἱέραξ καὶ Ἡρακλείδης καὶ Ἀφθόνιος. Ὑπῆρχον δὲ αὐτῷ καὶ ἕτεροι μαθηταὶ τρεῖς Ἀγάπιος ὁ τὴν Ἑπτάλογον συντάξας, καὶ Ζαρούας καὶ Γαβριάβιος.

77 *Suda Lexicon*, entry 147.1–23; entry 147.30: περὶ οὗ καὶ Θεόδωρος ὁ τῆς Ῥαϊθοῦ πρεσβύτερός φησι. Theodorus of Raithou (sixth-seventh cent.) in his work *Praeparatio* devoted a paragraph to Mani's beliefs (see ch.[4], 2.2).

78 Photius, *c. Manichaeos* 37.19–28, p. 131: Καὶ ταῦτα μὲν ἐπὶ τοσοῦτον, εἰ δέ τισι φίλον καὶ ἄνωθέν ποθεν ἰδεῖν αὐτῶν τὴν δυσσέβειαν, καὶ τὰ πρῶτα σπέρματα ὅθεν κατεβλήθη, Κύριλλός τε αὐτοῖς, ὁ τὰ τῆς Ἱερᾶς πόλεως ἐγκεχειρισμένος πηδάλια, τῆς ἱστορίας καθηγήσεται, καὶ ὁ πολὺς ἐν θαύμασιν Ἐπιφάνιος, ναὶ δὴ καὶ τῶν τὰς ἐκκλησιαστικὰς ἱστορίας ἀναταξαμένων οὐκ ὀλίγοι, Τίτος τε ὁ Βοστρηνῶν ἐπίσκοπος καὶ Σαραπίων ὁ τῆς Θμούεως, ὅ τε τῆς πόλεως Λύκων Ἀλέξανδρος τοὺς ἀρχιερατικοὺς ἐγκεχειρισμένος νόμους, ἐπὶ δὲ τοῖς εἰρημένοις καὶ ὁ τούτων πάντων κατὰ κράτος μάλιστα θριαμβεύσας τε καὶ διελέγξας τὴν προκειμένην ἀσέβειαν Ἡρακλειανός, ὁ Καλχηδόνος ἐπίσκοπος, ἐν εἴκοσι βιβλίοις τοὺς κατὰ τῆς ἀποστασίας ἀγῶνας καταβαλλόμενος, καὶ πλεῖστοι

Graeca.[79] A further reason why authors of antiquity passed Alexander off as a Christian, is that, although he was a pagan, as his argumentation reveals, was particularly sympathetic to Christianity. It is interesting that, for the same reason, the question of Alexander's supposed Christian identity has been raised again in the academic discourse by modern scholars. First, Riggi argued that Alexander was a crypto-Christian, and recently Edwards supported the view that he was a Christian.[80] However, the fact that Alexander's entire refutation of Manichaeism is based exclusively on Greek philosophy and not at all on the Christian scriptures makes the thesis supporting Alexander's new Christianization weak. Furthermore, Alexander in his work speaks as a representative of the Greek culture and philosophical tradition, in which he places himself. This is an additional argument in favour of his pagan origin.[81]

According to Mansfeld, "we may consider Alexander as a professional philosopher", although it is not easy to decide "where, exactly, as a philosopher, Alexander himself may have stood".[82] And this is because, although Alexander was a Neoplatonist, he also had important differences with classical Neo-Platonist positions. His view of 'matter', which he considered an outgrowth of the First Principle instead of seeing it as an evil first principle itself, makes him stand "rather lonely in the Platonic tradition".[83] "Perhaps", as Van Oort argues, "it is best to characterize him [Alexander] as a pre-Plotinian Neoplatonist".[84] As the Platonic and Manichaean views of matter are very close to each other, in order to combat Manichaean dualism, Alexander does not hesitate to put himself at odds with the entire Platonic tradition.

To this day we have only one critical edition of the text, dating from the nineteenth century: the one of Brinkmann, on which the translation of Van der Horst & Mansfeld was based. An older translation is that of Hawkins, which, however, was based on an antiquated version of the text.[85]

ἕτεροι· πλὴν καὶ νῦν ὁ λόγος, οὐκ ἀσύμφορον τοῦτο λογιζόμενος, κατ᾽ ἐπιδρομήν τινα τῶν εἰς γνῶσιν ἐχόντων τὸ ἀπαραίτητον διελεύσεται.

79   See Van der Horst & Mansfeld 1974, 6. Stroumsa 1992, 338. Lieu 2010, 162.

80   Riggi 1969 in Van der Horst & Mansfeld 1974, 3. Edwards 2015, 138–42 & 152–57. See more on this in ch.[4], section 3, fn. 161.

81   For example, referring to the Greek mythology and poetry, Alexander says, 'our own tradition', 'our poetry' (Alexander, *Tract. Man.* 5), cf. ch. [4], section 3.

82   Van der Horst & Mansfeld 1974, 6–7. For Alexander's philosophical position in detail, see Van der Horst & Mansfeld 1974, 6–47.

83   Stroumsa 1992, 340. For Alexander's views on matter, see Van der Horst & Mansfeld 1974, 19–23.

84   Van Oort 2013, 282.

85   Hawkins' translation (1869) in a volume of the Ante-Nicene Christian Library.

Regarding Alexander's sources, there has been disagreement among researchers as to whether Alexander derives his information from Manichaean sources (e.g. Mani's disciples), or his account is based on an earlier Neoplatonic interpretation of Mani's system.[86]

5.2   Structure & Content of the Work

The work consists of twenty-six small chapters. Alexander, in his first four chapters, gives a brief account of Mani and the main Manichaean tenets. In the rest of his work (chs. 5–26) refutes Manichaeism by providing additional information about Manichaean doctrines and attitudes. Main axes of his argumentation for the refutation of the Manichaean system consist of the irrational character and the contradictions of the following Manichaean doctrines: dualism, Manichaean cosmogony, nature and status of matter, creed about the sun and the moon, the creation of man, Manichaean Christology, and eschatology. Alexander also criticizes harshly and comments on Manichaean asceticism and ritual practices.

5.3   Impact

Serapion of Thmuis and Titus of Bostra were probably aware of Alexander's treatise, although they did not mention it, nor anything in their works indicates direct dependence.[87] Nevertheless, as has been pointed out by researchers, there are many parallels between Titus' and Alexander's treatises. Strangely, Photius, is the first and only one who explicitly lists Alexander among the known anti-Manichaean authors. Perhaps his absence from the lists of earlier authors is due to his pagan origin.

5.4   Alexander's Treatise as a Source for Manichaeism & Manichaean History

Alexander's treatise is undoubtably a very important early witness of both the spread of Manichaeism in Roman territory, and of the success of the Manichaean mission among the pagan population of the empire. However, the value of the treatise as a source for Manichaeism was undermined by the disagreement of the researchers on the question regarding the origin of Alexander's sources and in specific by the opinion that Alexander's source was a Neoplatonic summary rather than rooted in Manichaeism. Yet as Van der Horst observes, this academic debate concerned the four first chapters, and

---

86   Van der Horst & Mansfeld 1974, 2, fn. 3. Cf. Widengren 1985.
87   Stroumsa 1992, 338.

not the entire treatise.[88] In fact, as he remarks, the whole research, until the time of the translation, drew only from the first chapters (2–4). Thus, the goal of the translation in English, as Van der Horst and Mansfeld state in their introduction, was (1) to enable researchers to study the entire treatise, and 2) to stimulate a new critical edition. Yet for some strange reason, none of the above happened, and the use of the treatise in Manichaean studies was essentially limited to the first four chapters.

It must therefore be emphasized that the importance of Alexander's entire treatise for the reconstruction of the history of the Manichaeans of the Roman East is great because, it captures a more 'original', if I may say so, version of Manichaeism, before its admixture with the local cultural elements and before the term 'Manichaean', apart from its literal content, became a term of abuse. In addition, studying the entire treatise, one finds a wealth of information about the behaviour, daily life, and attitude of Manichaeans, which is complementary to the information from Christian literature on similar subjects.

6   Titus of Bostra's *Contra Manichaeos*

6.1   *Author*
Titus was bishop of the city of Bostra, capital of Petraea Arabia, under a number of emperors (Constantius II, Julian, Jovian and Valens). Sozomenus includes him among the most outstanding of the very learned men and authors of the time of Constantius II.[89] However, the information we have about his life is scarce. We know that under Julian he faced problems with the pagan population of the city. In a letter in 362 Julian urged the citizens of Bostra to "drive out" their bishop.[90] From Julian's letter we also learn the religious composition of the city, that the Christians were equal in number to the pagans, and that the relationship between them was strained. In 363 Titus participated in the Council of Antioch and signed the synodal *Acta* that recognized the 'homoousion' doctrine and ratified the Nicene Creed. However, Titus did not play

---

88   Van der Horst & Mansfeld 1974, 2–3.

89   Sozomenus, *HE* 3.14.41–42 (GCS 50): ... ἀνδρῶν μὲν οὖν πέρι, οἳ τότε ἐν εὐσεβείᾳ καὶ ἐκκλησιαστικῷ θεσμῷ ἐφιλοσόφουν, τάδε ἔγνων ὡς συνέγραψα. ὑπερφυῶς δὲ πολλοὶ καὶ μάλα ἐλλόγιμοι κατὰ τὸν αὐτὸν χρόνον ἐν ταῖς ἐκκλησίαις διέπρεπον. ἐπισημότατοι δὲ ἐν τούτοις ἐγένοντο Εὐσέβιος ὁ τὴν Ἐμέσης ἱερωσύνην ἐπιτροπεύσας καὶ Τίτος ὁ Βόστρης καὶ Σαραπίων ὁ Θμούεως, Βασίλειός τε ὁ Ἀγκύρας καὶ Εὐδόξιος ὁ Γερμανικείας καὶ Ἀκάκιος ὁ Καισαρείας καὶ Κύριλλος, ὃς τὸν Ἱεροσολύμων θρόνον ἐπετρόπευσε. σύμβολα δὲ τῆς αὐτῶν παιδείας συνεγράψαντο καὶ καταλελοίπασι πολλά τε καὶ λόγου ἄξια. Cf. Pedersen 2004, 66–67 and CCSG 82, XV.

90   Flavius Claudius Julianus, *Ep. 114*: Ἰουλιανὸς Βοστρηνοῖς. See also Sozomenus, *HE* 5.15.11–12.

a decisive role in the ecclesiastical disputes of the fourth century for the formation of the doctrine. He gained his fame thanks to his work against the Manichaeans, the most extensive and "comprehensive Christian theological refutation of Manichaeism", which has been preserved.[91] According to Jerome, Titus died during the reign of Valens, so between 28 March 364 and 9 August 378.[92]

Titus belonged to the circle of the Antiochian School, which emphasized and defended man's free will and moral responsibility. That is why his perspective on anthropology is optimistic, and this is reflected in his interpretation of the Paradise myth.[93] Although he was not a professional philosopher, his work demonstrates that he could excellently handle and use philosophical concepts as tools to refute Manichaeism.[94]

6.2   The Work

6.2.1   Date of Composition

In 377, Titus' *Contra Manichaeos* had been already written, because Epiphanius refers to it in his *Panarion*, which he composed between 374 and 377. Important for determining the *terminus post quem* is an internal reference by Titus to an earthquake which has been identified by scholars as the earthquake that destroyed Nicomedia and Nicaea on the second of December, 362.[95] Furthermore, if Jerome's information is accurate that it was written under Julian and Jovian, i.e. between 361 and 364, the *terminus ante quem* is the time of Jovian's death, February 17, 364.[96] So, the possible time-span for the composition of the work can be narrowed down between December 362 and February 364.[97] Soon, before 411, the entire work had been translated into Syriac.[98]

---

91   CCT 21, 15; CCSG 82, XVI.

92   Pedersen 2004, 126.

93   See Pedersen (2004) pp. 143–144 and pp. 320–365 ('Titus of Bostra's Interpretation of the Paradise Narrative').

94   About Titus' philosophical position, see Pedersen 2004, 255–319 and CCT 21, 15–16.

95   Titus of Bostra, *c. Manichaeos*, 2.28.1–3. Regarding this earthquake, see also Ammianus Marcellinus (*Res Gestae*, 22.13.5). Cf. CCT 21, 14–15; Pedersen 126–127.

96   Cf. Pedersen 2004, 125–127; CCT 21, 14–15.

97   Cf. CCT 21, 14–15. However, Pedersen (1, 126–27) states "It is possible, though, that Jerome was being imprecise and that *Contra Manichaeos* was not finally concluded and published until a few years after Emperor Jovian's death".

98   Lieu 2010, 167; Pedersen 2004, 68 & 112–13; CCT 21, 18, 41. According to Klein (1991, 41), the Syriac translation was made between the years 378–383.

6.2.2   Structure, Addressees, & Summary of the Content

The work consists of four books. Its structure is twofold. The first two books are aimed at pagans and their argumentation is based on 'common notions' (κοιναὶ ἔννοιαι). The second two are addressing Christians and are based on the Bible. Addressing these two groups, Titus, as a Christian, seeks to ally Christians and pagans against Manichaeans, projecting a cultural gap between their shared Greco-Roman culture and Manichaean irrationalism.[99]

The *hypothesis* of each book, as Titus himself briefly states at the beginning of his work, is as follows: The first book refutes the basic Manichaean doctrines (i.e. the doctrine of two opposing principles, Manichaean cosmogony, and eschatology) stressing that they are alien to 'common notions'. In the second book, on the occasion of the classic Manichaean question about the origin of evil, Titus makes it clear that there is no evil in essence, therefore not even an evil principle opposed to God. Titus argues that it is not because of some eternal (ἀνάρχου) and opposed to God evil, which in fact does not exist, that man sins; none of the beings is essentially evil. The book also accentuates the role of divine providence, showing that there is no necessity in supposing a second principle opposed to God. In the third book, Titus defends the divine inspiration and provenance of the OT which the Manichaeans reject; Titus argues that everything there agrees with the New Testament and that, on this side also, there is no need to suppose some second principle, opposed to God. Lastly, in the fourth book, he protects the NT from the fragmentary use and interpretation made by the Manichaeans. As Titus says, the Manichaeans have never had any association with its text; and it is in vain that they falsify (ἐκβιάζονται) certain parts of it in order to establish their impiety.[100]

6.2.3   Manuscripts, Critical Editions & Modern Translations

The Greek original has not survived in its entirety. In the manuscripts available so far, the entire first two books are preserved, the third up to chapter 30.5, and from the fourth book only some fragmentary passages are preserved (91, 97, 99–101). For this reason, the importance of the Syriac translation which preserves the complete text is very great.[101] For the critical editions of the text, and the first translation in modern language I have referred to the introduction.[102]

---

99   Pedersen 2004, 166–171.

100   Titus of Bostra, *c. Manichaeos*, hyp. 1–4.

101   On the problematic situation of the surviving Greek original text, see CCSG 82, XX; CCT 21, 17–18; Pedersen 2004, 109–119.

102   See Introduction, section 3.3.

6.3   *Sources*

6.3.1   Manichaean

Researchers are unanimous in that Titus' *Contra Manichaeos* draws from Manichaean texts.[103] Titus himself, as will be shown in the next chapter, refers to some titles of Manichaean books without, however, being clear if he had these books at his disposal or if he relied on second hand information. Various Manichaean books have been suggested from time to time by scholars as candidate sources for the Manichaean material that Titus uses. Others are Mani's own works (such as *The Book of Mysteries*, the *Book of Giants*, the *Gospel*) and others works of his students (*Kephalaia*, Adda's writings). The question of Titus' sources has been raised since antiquity. As Heraclian of Chalcedon argues, Titus with his work combated Adda's books, and not – as he mistakenly thought – those of Mani.[104]

Pedersen in his work gives a thorough account and assessment of the history of research on the question of Titus' Manichaean sources which in turn is directly related to the consequent question of the value of his work as a source of knowledge on Manichaeism.[105] However, the editors of the recent translation in French point out that before proceeding with any assumptions about the Manichaean sources of Titus, first, the genuine Manichaean material in his work must be identified. This task is not always easy, as this material is often incorporated into Titus' argumentation, making it difficult to distinguish where the one stops and the other begins. This material must then be examined in comparison with the so far found Manichaean texts.[106] The difficulty of the above endeavour has been demonstrated in Pettipiece's recent work on the inventory of the 'Manichaean Citations' used by Titus.[107]

6.3.2   Anti-Manichaean

It is probable that Titus knew and had drawn material from earlier anti-Manichaean works (Eusebius, *Acta Archelai*, Serapion of Thmuis, and Cyril). However, since he does not mention his sources, it is difficult to decide whether he depends on any of them. Pedersen found no evidence that Titus made use of Serapion's *Contra Manichaeos* but considers "probable that [he] knew of *Acta Archelai* and to a limited degree drew on it".[108] He also does not rule out

---

103   CCT 21, 42–43.
104   Pedersen 2004, 185.
105   Pedersen (2004), see especially pp. 78–88 and his chapter 6, 177–254, esp. pp. 186–205.
106   CCT 21, 43, 45, 85.
107   Poirier and Pettipiece 2017. Pedersen 2019, 463–471.
108   Pedersen 2004, 132, 146, 152, 156.

the possibility that Titus use Eusebius' *Ecclesiastical History* and *Chronicon*, yet not without reservation.[109]

Regarding the interpretation of the paradise narrative (3.13–29), Pedersen considers that both Titus and Theodore Mopsuestias the interpretation of whom has much in common with Titus are based on a common lost Antiochene anti-Manichaean work, probably that of George of Laodicea.[110]

Moreover, as was said above, it is argued that Titus of Bostra (in his first book), Theodoret of Cyrrhus, Severus of Antioch and according to some scholars Alexander of Lycopolis too had used a common source for Manichaean cosmogony.[111] Finally, similarities have also been pointed out between the anti-Manichaean polemic in Titus and the Neo-Platonic philosopher Simplicius.[112]

6.3.3   Correlation with Alexander's Work

Interestingly, many researchers point out the existence of analogies between the work of Titus and Alexander. Beyond the similarities in argumentation, the use of common sources for Manichaean presentation is also considered possible.[113] The latter, of course, does not mean "direct borrowing" of Titus from Alexander.[114] One could argue that both works, as they are addressed

---

109   Pedersen 2004, 152.

110   See Pedersen's (2004) chapters eight and nine. As Pedersen concludes (2004, 423): "Even though Theodore did not himself devote any particular attention to the battle against Manichaeism, I suggest that his interpretations on this point derive from earlier Antiochene anti-Manichaeism, just as I make the case that ultimately there must be a common source behind these interpretations and that of Titus; this source could be George of Laodicea's lost anti-Manichaean work." Pedersen 2004, 79. Kugener and Cumont 1912, 159.

111   Kugener and Cumont 1912, 151–172, 162. See also Pedersen 2004, 79–86. Bennett (2001b, 77), however, concluded after examining one of the parallels on Manichaean cosmogony between Titus, Severus, and Theodoret (namely the Manichaean division of primordial space into four quarters) that there are other authors too who give similar information. Titus of Bostra, *Contra Manichaeos* 1.11 (CCSG 82:25): Αὖθις τὸ μεσημβρινὸν μέρος τῇ κακίᾳ διδόντες ὡς ὄναρ τῆς δημιουργίας διαγράφουσι. Ποῦ γὰρ ἦν μεσημβρία πρὸ μεσημβρίας.

112   Pedersen 2004, 67.

113   As we read in Pedersen (2004), Alfaric believed that Alexander of Lycopolis had also used this source that Titus, Theodoret and Severus had used (p. 80) [...] Schaeder underlined "the similarity between" Titus' "and Alexander's account of Manichaeism" (p. 81) [...] "Reitzenstein believed that the Manichaean sources for both Titus and Alexander of Lycopolis belonged to the same transmission nucleus" (p. 81) [...] Baur underlined how Titus gave almost the same picture of Manichaeism as an abstract thought-system of concepts as Alexander of Lycopolis.

114   Stroumsa 1992, 338: "I could not find in his work, however, any indication to suggest a direct borrowing from Alexander". Stroumsa 1992, 140–141, 340.

to philosophically educated circles, belong to these anti-Manichaean works which according to Bauer's classification replace mythological elements with philosophical abstract concepts.[115] Moreover, both works criticize the literalness of the Manichaean myth, identify the same implications of dualism in social life, and criticize with the same rationale the Manichaean attitudes.

Summarizing his analysis of Titus' sources, Pedersen concludes that Titus "drew on some of the Manichaeans' own texts and on previous Christian heresiology, including earlier anti-Manichaean literature, as well as perhaps pagan philosophical works."[116]

6.4   *Impact*

A number of writers mention Titus among their lists of authors who combated the Manichaeans and wrote anti-Manichaean works. These, in chronological order, are: Epiphanius, who is the first to mention him,[117] Theodoret of Cyrrhus,[118] Heraclian of Chalcedon,[119] and Photius.[120] However, apart from the fact that Titus' work is in the lists of several later writers, it is difficult to decide whether and how much it was used by them.[121]

---

115 Pedersen 2004, 88. According to Baur, there are two kinds of anti-Manichaean texts: Those that present the mythological character of Manichaeism, and those that replace the mythological elements with philosophical abstract concepts. The two ends of the above classification are the AA and Alexander's treatise. In-between, he places Augustine (closer to AA) and Titus (closer to Alexander). For this classification of Baur, see Pedersen 2004, 75. See also Pedersen 2004, 186.

116 Pedersen 2004, 420.

117 Epiphanius *Pan.* 66.21.3. Cumont and Kugener (1912, 157–59) examined in parallel both texts and showed that Epiphanius used Titus' work. Cf. Pedersen 2004, 67.

118 Theodoret of Cyrrhus (*Haer.* 83.381) names Titus of Bostra, Diodorus of Tarsus, George of Laodicea and Eusebius of Caesarea, as authors of anti-Manichaean texts.

119 Heraclian of Chalcedon apud Photius, *Bibl.* cod. 85 (65a/b). The other anti-Manichaean authors mentioned by Heraclian are: George of Laodicea, Serapion of Thmuis, and Diodorus of Tarsus.

120 Photius, *c. Manichaeos* 37.19–28, p. 131. Photius mentions as his sources the accounts of Cyril of Jerusalem, Epiphanius of Salamis, Titus of Bostra, Serapion of Thmuis, Alexander of Lycopolis and Heraclian of Chalcedon. Cf. Pedersen 2004, 68. John of Damascus, quotes Titus in his *Sacra Parallela*. See "Les extraits des Sacra Parallela attribués à Jean Damascene" in CCSG 82, CXI–CLV.

121 Pedersen 2004, 66–67: "It is still not possible at present to draw a clear picture of Titus's importance for posterity. [...] Several writers from his immediate posterity name Titus". Pedersen adds Jerome to the list, see p. 66, fn. 2. According to CCSG (*82*, XX), Titus of Bostra's work had a very limited circulation: "En tout cas une chose est sûre: la tradition directe montre que le Contre les manichéens de Titus de Bostra n'a connu qu'une diffusion très limitée. Une telle situation s'explique sans doute par les dimensions mêmes de l'ouvrage, par une langue et un style assez rébarbatifs, et par le fait que les oeuvres

6.5   *Titus' Contra Manichaeos as a Source for Manichaeism*
& Manichaean History

The anti-Manichaean work of Titus is the only evidence for the existence of Manichaeans in the city of Bostra. Both the size of the treatise and its translation into Syriac within a short period of time (in 411), reflects the rapid spread and success of Manichaean propaganda in the Roman territories of the East.[122] Stroumsa believes it to be the most important anti-Manichaean work in Greek. It may not give us specific names of deities, or of the students of Mani, it may not refer to events, but it does give us a lot of information about behaviour, practices, life attitude, and rules of conduct that govern the daily life of East Roman Manichaeans. These Manichaean commandments, in turn, are the result of specific Manichaean doctrines.

In addition, as I will show in the next chapter, there are references to specific titles of Mani's books, and references to anonymous Manichaean works, as well as rich Manichaean material, which Titus uses to present and refute the main Manichaean positions and doctrines. But further research is needed until it is possible to identify this rich material with specific Manichaean works. The *Contra Manichaeos* of Titus is one of the Greek Manichaean works that certainly still has a lot to give us.

---

       polémiques risquent toujours de sombrer dans l'oubli, une fois disparue l'hérésie ou l'erreur qu'elles prétendaient réfuter." Different opinion has been expressed by Stroumsa (1992, 338) who states: "Mainly through Epiphanius of Salamis, who not only refers to it but also makes generous use of its argumentation, Titus's work was to have the most profound impact on later Christian literature *adversus Manichaeos*."

122   CCT 21, 16. Cf. ch. 2.

CHAPTER 2

The Arrival and Spread of Manichaeism in the Roman East

> Manichaeans ... have but recently advanced or sprung forth ... from their native homes among the Persians ... and have settled in this part of the world ... disturbing the tranquillity of the peoples and causing the gravest injuries to the civic communities.
>
> RESCRIPT OF DIOCLETIAN[1]

∴

> This sect is widely reported and is talked of in many parts of the world, and as I said, owes its worldwide spread to a man named Mani.
>
> EPIPHANIUS OF SALAMIS[2]

∴

1 Introduction

After introducing the most important sources for this research and tracing their remnants in the Greek anti-Manichaean corpus, this chapter examines how the anti-Manichaean writers portrayed Mani and outlined the arrival and efforts of the first Manichaean missionaries on Roman soil. In particular, the issues that will be discussed in this chapter are: (1) the portrait of Mani and of Manichaeism, (2) the books of the Manichaean canon, (3) the grades of the Manichaean hierarchy, (4) the first Manichaean missionaries and their mission, (5) the ways Manichaeans diffused into Roman territories and, finally, (6) the methods and strategies (epistles, debates, etc.) used by Manichaean

---

1 *Mosaicarum et Romanarum Legum Collatio* 15.3 in Hyamson 1913, 130–33 (trans. in Gardner and Lieu 2004, 117–18).
2 Epiphanius, *Pan.* 66.1.3 (Williams, 227). For the original text in Greek see section 6 in this chapter.

missionaries. In specific, this chapter discusses the setting of the debates, whereas the themes disputed during these debates (dualism, the Manichaean pantheon, cosmogony, anthropogony/logy and ethics) will be examined in ch.[5].

By building my analysis on the axes of the two principal texts (the AA and the AFs) and their later echo, I will investigate and compare the presentation of the abovementioned topics mainly in the sources I presented in the first chapter, as well as in the earliest anti-Manichaean sources. The comparative approach used in this chapter aims to reconstruct a picture of Manichaeism and Manichaean mission by drawing upon all extant sources which complement each other. Thus, the interdependence of the sources will emerge, their differences will be pointed out, and their case-by-case reliability will be assessed. Moreover, the aforementioned Greek anti-Manichaean sources will be examined in light of the genuine Manichaean sources and complemented by the Latin, Syriac and Arabic whenever relevant material exists.

2   The First Reports about Mani and Manichaean Missionaries

2.1   *Portrait of Mani and of Manichaeism Before the Acta*
2.1.1   Zosimus of Panopolis
Zosimus of Panopolis (third-fourth cent.) was an Egyptian alchemist, recognized by his contemporaries "as one of the greatest representatives of Greek alchemy", who "enjoyed immense prestige by his successors who quoted him on every occasion".[3] Researchers have associated an enigma set by Zosimus in one of his works with Mani. As Zosimus states, in his treatise entitled *On the Letter Omega*, the imitator and rival daemon (ἀντίμιμος δαίμων/antimimos daimōn), who calls himself son of God (λέγων ἑαυτὸν υἱὸν θεοῦ), before his advent, dispatched a precursor from Persia (πρόδρομον ἀπὸ τῆς Περσίδος), who, through his fictitious and deceptive speeches (μυθοπλάνους λόγους), attempted to mislead men, instructing them to believe in destiny (εἱμαρμένην). Rather than naming the Persian precursor of the imitator daemon, Zosimus challenges his readers to guess his name by giving them the following riddle: his name consists of nine letters, two of which comprise a diphthong as is the case of the term 'destiny'/'εἱμαρμένη'.[4]

---

3   Mertens (1995/2002), xi.
4   Zosimus of Panopolis, *On the letter omega*, §14 (Mertens, 1–10, 7–8): Εἰσὶ δὲ τὰ στοιχεῖα τοῦ ὀνόματος αὐτοῦ ἐννέα, τῆς διφθόγγου σῳζομένης, κατὰ τὸν τῆς εἱμαρμένης ὅρον. See also Jackson's (1978) edition and translation *Zosimos of Panopolis. On the letter omega*. Stroumsa (1984, 142–43) investigating the origins of the myth, suggests that the figure of *antimimos daimōn* in Zosimus' test is a transformation of (another form for) the Gnostic *leader of the archons* into

This has generally been taken as a reference to Mani's name in its Greek form (i.e. Manichaios: Μανιχαῖος), a reading that fulfils the conditions of the number of letters and the diphthong (αι). Additional facts supporting this interpretation are: (1) the text says that this person comes from Persia. Both Greek and Latin authors of the era emphasized Mani's Persian origin; (2) Mani claimed that he was the Paraclete, something that fits with the text which says that the imitator daemon will introduce himself as the son of God (the Paraclete was to be sent by the son of God); and (3) anti-Manichaean literature presents Mani as believing in destiny, as does Zosimus' mysterious figure.[5]

2.1.2   Rescript of Diocletian

One of the first Roman testimonies which records the arrival of Manichaeism in the Roman teritorry is the famous rescript of Diocletian.[6]

During one of his visits to Alexandria, Diocletian sent this letter to Julian, the Proconsul of Africa, in response to a petition of the latter. The year is missing from the text, and from among the proposed possible dates (287, 297, 302 and 307) the majority of scholars now consider the year 302 (31 March) as the most likely. That is, just a year before the great persecution against the Christians broke out.[7] The discussion surrounding the authenticity of the rescript is gargantuan; however, the dominant interpretation in the current academic discourse favours its authenticity.[8] The letter is preserved in the *Collatio* or *Lex Dei*, which reports that it originates from the seventh book of the *Codex Gregorianus* under the heading of "Sorcerers and Manichaeans".[9] The text runs as follows:

---

the false Son of God par excellence. Interestingly, he remarks that "the idea of imitation is also associated with the King of Darkness and with Sakla in Manichaean contexts".

5   See Mertens 1995/2002, 106–09, fn. 93.

6   *Mosaicarum et Romanarum Legum Collatio* 15.3 (*De maleficis et Manichaeis*) (Hyamson 1913, 130–33); cf. Adam 1954, 82–84; Gardner and Lieu 2004, 116–18; Lieu 2010, 40–41, 163. For a definition and the system of rescripts, see Tony Honoré 1979, 52–56, 52: "Rescripts were not legislative. Though very occasionally they purport to derogate from existing law by granting an indulgence, they never purport to change it. They simply declare what the law is. Nor do they have the force of a judgment, or any other executive force", and Corcoran 1996, 43–122, esp. 48–49: "a subscriptio or private rescript can be called a lex, but is only authoritative for a particular case, being neither precedential nor innovative. [...] Rescripts do not legislate. They do not seek to change the law. Rather they seek to make an authoritative, or even definitive, exposition of what the law already is".

7   Coleman-Norton 1966, 334; Corcoran 1996, 135. Lieu and Gardner 2004, 116–118. Lieu 2010, 163. Edwards 2015, 141.

8   The authenticity of the rescript has been supported by many eminent legal historians. Yet, there are still other historians who challenge it. Concerning the question of authenticity, see Minale 2013, 17–128. Seston 1940, 345–54; Schwartz 1913, 50f. According to Lieu (2010, 163): "The authenticity of the rescript [...] is without doubt".

9   Adam 1954, 82; Baviera et al. 1940.

The Emperors Diocletian and Maximianus (and Constantius) and
Maximianus (i.e. Galerius) to Julianus, Proconsul of Africa. Well-beloved
Julianus:
(1) Excessive leisure sometimes incites ill-conditioned people to trans-
gress the limits of nature, and persuades them to introduce empty and
scandalous kinds of superstitious doctrine, so that many others are lured
on to acknowledge the authority of their erroneous notions. (2) However,
the immortal gods, in their providence, have thought fit to ordain that
the principles of virtue and truth should, by the counsel and delibera-
tions of many good, great and wise men, be approved and established
in their integrity. These principles it is not right to oppose or resist, nor
ought the ancient religion be subjected to the censure of a new creed.
It is indeed highly criminal to discuss doctrines once and for all settled
and defined by our forefathers, and which have their recognised place
and course in our system. (3) Wherefore we are resolutely determined to
punish the stubborn depravity of these worthless people. (4) As regards
the Manichaeans, concerning whom your carefulness has reported
to our serenity, who, in opposition to the older creeds, set up new and
unheard-of sects, purposing in their wickedness to cast out the doctrines
vouchsafed to us by divine favour in older times, we have heard that they
have but recently advanced or sprung forth, like strange and monstrous
portents, from their native homes among the Persians – a nation hostile
to us – and have settled in this part of the world, where they are perpe-
trating many evil deeds, disturbing the tranquillity of the peoples and
causing the gravest injuries to the civic communities; and there is danger
that, in process of time, they will endeavour, as is their usual practice, to
infect the innocent, orderly and tranquil Roman people, as well as the
whole of our empire, with the damnable customs and perverse laws of the
Persians as with the poison of a malignant serpent. (5) And since all that
your prudence has set out in detail in your report of their religion shows
that what our laws regard as their misdeeds are clearly the offspring of a
fantastic and lying imagination [...] we have appointed pains and punishments due and fitting for these people. (6) We order that the authors and
leaders of these sects be subjected to severe punishment, and, together
with their abominable writings, burnt in the flames. We direct that their
followers, if they continue recalcitrant, shall suffer capital punishment,
and their goods be forfeited to the imperial treasury. (7) And if those who
have gone over to that hitherto unheard-of, scandalous and wholly infamous creed, or to that of the Persians, are persons who hold public office,
or are of any rank or of superior social status, you will see to it that their

estates are confiscated and the offenders sent to the (quarry) at Phaeno or the mines at Proconnesus. (8) And in order that this plague of iniquity shall be completely extirpated from this our most happy age, let your devotion hasten to carry out our orders and commands.

Given at Alexandria, 31 March.[10]

2.1.2.1   Diocletian's Fears

Three key issues are highlighted by the rescript:

(1)   *The Persian origin*: The rescript depicts Manichaeism as a foreign religion, indeed, as a religion which comes from Persia, the arch-enemy of Rome at that time. The Persian origin of Manichaeism is emphatically stressed, as is the idea that Persia is "a nation hostile" to the Roman Empire. The projected imagery is that of a "malignant serpent" which has "advanced or sprung forth" from Persia and "settled in this part of the world [Roman Empire]", which threatens to infect the Roman citizens with its poison.

(2)   *The vice of the new Perso-Manichaean religion threatens the virtue of the ancient Roman religion*: The entire rhetoric of the rescript seeks to highlight the superiority of Roman laws, principles, mores ("ancient Roman virtue"), by contrasting them with the respective Manichaean ones: identified as those of the Persians ("new Persian vice").[11] The Manichaeans with their laws (perverse), doctrines (erroneous, superstitious, scandalous and wholly infamous creed), customs (damnable), and misdeeds (the offspring of a fantastic and lying imagination) disturb "the innocent, orderly and tranquil Roman people", "causing the gravest injuries to the civic communities". The question could be posed as to why Diocletian had such a problem with the Manichaeans, while he does not seem to be troubled by oriental mystery cults or Mithraism, which were also believed to have come from Persia?[12] The answer to this question relies on the third thematic axis upon which the rescript of Diocletian focuses.

(3)   *The Manichaean religion aimed to substitute the ancient Roman religion*: A more careful reading of the rescript brings to light that the Manichaeans, as opposed "to the older creeds", and apart from "importing 'Persian customs'" aimed to substitute the "ancient religion" (i.e. the "approved and established" ... "principles of virtue and truth", "the doctrines vouchsafed

---

10   The above translation is from *Collatio Mosaicarum* 15.3, ed. and trans. by Hyamson (1913), 130–33, revised by Lieu in Gardner and Lieu 2004, 116–18 (for a further revised translation, see Lieu 2010, 40–41).

11   Corcoran 1996, 136. Cf. Corcoran 2015, 75–76.

12   Cf. Lieu 1992, 122–23.

to us [Rome] by divine favour in older times") for "new and unheard-of sects [creed]". For Diocletian, the latter probably meant that the Manichaeans, like the Christians and Jews, demanded exclusivity from their followers.[13] This undermined the moral welfare and the security of the Empire. As Diocletian makes clear from the beginning of his rescript "It is indeed highly criminal to discuss doctrines once and for all settled and defined by our forefathers, and which have their recognised place and course in our system".

As Lieu comments, "an air of patriotic conservatism [...] permeates Diocletian's rescript".[14] According to the Roman political thought of the era, substituting "new gods for old" meant that people would be persuaded "to accept different laws and customs (ἀλλοτριονομεῖν)" which, in turn, was interconnected with the outbreak of "conspiracies and rebellions which would be injurious to the empire".[15] Since the rescript mentions that there already were many who had been "lured on to acknowledge the authority of" the principles of this unheard-of religion, Diocletian's fear, was (in his words) that "there is danger that, in process of time, they [Manichaeans] will endeavour, as is their usual practice, to infect ... the whole of our empire". In order to prevent this Manichaean tactic and extirpate "this plague of iniquity", Diocletian enacted very harsh sentences for Manichaeans and ordered Julian (acknowledging his devotion) to hasten their enforcement.[16]

2.1.2.2   Diocletian's Fears: Real or Imagined?

Lieu, commenting on the rescript, argues that Diocletian's fears were "more imaginary than real" since he seems to ignore "that the Manichaeans who flocked into the Roman Empire at the turn of the third century" were persecuted by Persian rulers, so it is unlikely that (at the same time) they were Persian secret agents.[17]

However, the latter is not mentioned explicitly in the rescript. The emphasis is on the corruption of the Roman morals from Persian customs, something that in the long run was believed to undermine the security of the empire. Further, from a Roman perspective, the fact that Manichaeans were

---

13   Lieu 1992, 123, 146; Edwards 2015, 141. On the sense of exclusiveness/exclusivity cf. Baker-Brian 2011, 31, 53; Franzmann 2017, 76–81.

14   Lieu 1992, 123. Cf. Colleman-Norton 1966, 1:333.

15   Lieu 1992, 123.

16   According to the rescript, the leaders, with their books, had to be burnt; their adherents who would not recant were also put to death. I shall return to the issue of punishments in the next chapter (section 3.3).

17   Lieu 1992, 122.

persecuted by some Persian kings did not mean that Manichaeism ceased to be considered as a Persian religion. This is especially the case since there were other Persian kings who had patronized Mani; it was known (at least to one Greek anti-Manichaean author) that Mani was a member of the entourage of Shapur I.[18] Worth noting is that during the reign of Narses (293–302), the policy of persecutions ceased. Dignas (following Frye) correlates this change of Persian policy with Diocletian's rescript, arguing that the former took place in order "to secure the support of Manichaeans in the Roman Empire", so that they could "be used in the battle against Rome".[19] In any case, judging from the subsequent literature and legislation, it seems that Diocletian's fears regarding the corruption of the entire empire by Manichaean practices were shared by Christian emperors of the following centuries. The Manichaeans continued for many years to be considered as the most dangerous corrupters of Roman citizens.

As expressed directly in the rescript, Diocletian derives his information about the Manichaean "religion" from Julian's detailed report: "Well-beloved Julianus [...]. As regards the Manichaeans, concerning whom your carefulness has reported to our serenity [...]. And since all that your prudence has set out in detail in your report of their religion [...]". Yet, apart from the abusive characterizations (superstitious, scandalous, and wholly infamous), the rescript does not record the misdeeds and the doctrines themselves which Julian apparently reported in detail to Diocletian. The content of Julian's report remains unknown.

However, as is also illustrated in the rescript, Diocletian also seems to "have heard" about Manichaeans and their recent arrival in Roman territories from elsewhere.[20] It seems that the arrival and spread of Manichaeans became a general issue at that time in Egypt; roughly contemporary with Diocletian's rescript and Zosimus' enigma are two other sources written by Egyptian authors.

---

18   See below, Alexander of Lycopolis, *Tract. Man.* 2.5–12.

19   Both Dignas and Frye date the rescript in 297. Dignas and Winter 2007, 27–28: "However, it is remarkable that persecutions of the Manichaeans ceased in Persia after 297 in order that their support could be used in the battle against Rome". Frye 1983, 131: "The religious policy of persecution of the Manichaeans, for one thing, changed to toleration under Narseh. This change may have been induced by Narseh's desire to secure the support of Manichaeans in the Roman empire, for in 297 in Alexandria Diocletian issued an edict against the propaganda of the Manichaeans".

20   "As regards the Manichaeans, concerning whom your carefulness has reported to our serenity, we have heard that they have but recently advanced or sprung forth". See also Corcoran 1996, 136.

2.1.3   Alexander of Lycopolis

One of them is the work of the philosopher Alexander of Lycopolis, the only extant treatise against Manichaeans by a pagan author. In the beginning of his work, Alexander introduces Mani and Manichaeism stating, "Manichaeus himself is said to have lived during the reign of Valerianus [253–260 CE] and to have accompanied Shapur the Persian king [240–272/3 CE] during his military campaigns" against Rome,[21] something that the *magoi* (Zoroastrian priests) also used to do with the previous Persian kings.[22] Alexander first characterizes Manichaeism as 'newfangledness' (καινοτομία) which "has but recently come to the fore". As he emphasizes, this Manichaean 'novelty', together with its astonishing doctrines, surpasses in vice any previous false doctrine (κακοδο-ξία). The lack of norms, of laws, and of theoretical precision renders the moral progress of people unachievable.[23]

2.1.4   Theonas (?)

The other Egyptian source is an anonymous epistle against the Manichaeans. The letter is probably the earliest anti-Manichaean testimony at our disposal and is preserved in an excerpt that currently belongs to the John Rylands Library. Roberts, the editor of the first critical edition and translation of the text, dates the epistle to the end of third century (275–300 CE); as its most likely author, Roberts proposes the bishop of Alexandria, Theonas (282–300 CE).[24] The target and main concern of the author were the 'blasphemous' beliefs and prayers of the Manichaeans, their 'abominable' practices during their ritual

---

21   Alexander of Lycopolis, *Tract. Man.* 2.5–12 (Brinkmann, 4; Van der Horst and Mansfeld, 52): [Μάνης] ὥσπερ ὁ λεγόμενος Μανιχαῖος, ὃς Πέρσης μέν τίς ἐστιν τὸ γένος, [...] αὐτὸς δὲ ἐπὶ Οὐαλεριανοῦ μὲν γεγονέναι λέγεται, συστρατεῦσαι Σαπώρῳ τῷ Πέρσῃ. *1Keph.* 16.1: I a[pp]eared before Shapur the king. [...] He gave me permission to journey in [... / ... pr]eaching the word of life. I even spent some year[s / ...] him in the retinue; many years in (16) Pers[i]a, in the country of the Parthians, up to Adiabene, and / the bor[de]rs of the provinces of the kingdom of the Romans. Cf. Lieu 1992, 78. Pettipiece 2014, 37.

22   As de Jong (1997, 455–56) states, highlighting the important position that the Persian priesthood had in the ancient world, the magoi "accompany the Persian armies on the move and direct the decisions on religious matters in war situations. They [...] act as advisers to the kings [...]".

23   Alexander of Lycopolis, *Tract. Man.* 2.5–8 (Brinkmann, 4; Van der Horst and Mansfeld, 51) & 1.25–28: κατά γε τὴν ἐμὴν δόξαν πάντας ὑπερβαλὼν τῷ θαυμάσια λέγειν· καὶ οὐ πάλαι μὲν ἐπεπόλασεν ἡ τούτου καινοτομία; λόγον ἀκριβείας οὐκ ἐφικνουμένων [...] κανόνος δὲ οὐδενὸς ὑπόντος οὐδὲ νόμων.

24   Roberts 1938, in P.Rylands 3, Gr. 469, 11, pp. 38–46. Gardner and Lieu 2004, 114–15. See Lieu 2010, 36–37 for a revised English translation and Roberts 1938, 38–46, for the Greek text (42–43).

meetings, their challenge of established institutions such as marriage, and the moral consequences of all these for the Roman citizens.

> Again the Manich[aea]ns speak [falsely against marriage ...] [...] And the Manichaeans manifestly wor[ship the creation ...] [...] they require their [of the Manichaean elect women] menstrual blood for the abominations of their madness.[25]

As Roberts suggests, this was a circular letter (encyclical); that is, it was not addressed to a particular recipient but was "circulated by him [the bishop] to the churches in his diocese". Indeed, Roberts argues that Diocletian's rescript "might well have been endorsed" by the content of this epistle. If both the Christian church and Roman state "recognized the danger with which the religion of Mani threatened them, we might well expect them to take simultaneous action".[26]

2.1.5   Eusebius of Caesarea

Thus, the first reports (of East-Roman authors) on Mani and Manichaeans, as well as the first long treatises against them come from Egypt.[27] However, not much later, a Manichaean presence is testified in Syria and Palestine. One of the earliest testimonies within Roman Palestine is that of the church historian Eusebius. The seventh book of his *Ecclesiastical History*, in which he presents Manichaeism, probably dates back quite early, around 312.[28]

Eusebius uses two landmark events to date the arrival and spread of Manichaeism in Roman territories, which converge to 269 CE. These are: (1) the time of the condemnation of Paul of Samosata in the synod of Antioch (269), for as

---

25   P.Rylands 3, Gr. 469 (Roberts 1938, 42; Lieu 2010, 36–37): αὐτοὶ πάλειν οἱ Μανιχ[εῖ]ϲ κατα[ψεύδονται τοῦ γάμου ...] [...] καὶ οἱ Μανιχῖϲ δηλονότι προσκυ[νοῦσι τὴν κτίϲιν] [...] διὰ τὸ δηλονότι χρῄζειν αὐτοὺϲ τοῦ ἀπὸ τῆϲ ἀφέδρου αἵματοϲ αὐτῶν εἰϲ τὰ τῆϲ μανίαϲ μυϲάγματα.

26   Roberts 1938, 38–39. As Lieu (2010, 161) remarks, the bishop's fears are absolutely justified since Manichaeans had a very bad reputation, due to their antisocial and 'immoral' activities during their secret meetings. Thus, the Alexandrian bishop Theonas, through his circular letter, wished to make clear to both Christians and pagans, especially to the pagan authorities, that the Manichaeans had no relationship with the Catholic Church.

27   The Egyptians Serapion of Thmuis (ca 326) and Athanasius of Alexandria (338–372) are also among the earliest anti-Manichaean authors.

28   See ch.[1], section 2.1.2 (Date of the AA's Composition).

Eusebius states, it was at that very moment that the Manichaean error began;[29] and (2) the year that Felix assumed the papal throne of Rome (269–274 CE).[30]

His representation of Manichaeism goes as follows:

> At that time also the madman, named after his devil-inspired heresy, was taking as his armour distortion of logic; for the devil, that is Satan himself, the adversary of God, had put the man forward for the destruction of many. His very speech and manners proclaimed him a barbarian in mode of life, and, being by nature devilish and insane, he suited his endeavours thereto and attempted to pose as Christ: at one time giving out that he was the Paraclete and the Holy Spirit Himself, conceited fool that he was, as well as mad; at another time choosing, as Christ did, twelve disciples as associates in his newfangled system. In short, he stitched together false and godless doctrines that he had collected from the countless, long extinct, godless heresies, and infected our empire with, as it were, a deadly virus that came from the land of the Persians; and from him the profane name of Manichaean is still commonly on men's lips to this day. So then such is the character of this falsely-called knowledge, which came into being at the time that has been indicated.[31]

Eusebius' brief presentation of Manichaeism echoes the language, style, and content of the decree of Diocletian, issued a few years earlier. Mani "a barbarian in mode of life (speech and manners)", being a vehicle of "the adversary of God", Satan, "came from the land of the Persians" and wiping off "his

---

29   Eusebius, *HE* 7.pin.1.38–39 (LCL 265:134–35): Ὅπως ὁ Παῦλος ἀπελεγχθεὶς ἐξεκηρύχθη [...] τῆς τῶν Μανιχαίων ἑτεροδόξου διαστροφῆς ἄρτι τότε ἀρξαμένης.

30   Eusebius, *HE* 7.30.23–31.4 (LCL 265:226–27): Ῥώμης ἐπίσκοπον Διονύσιον [...] διαδέχεται Φῆλιξ. Ἐν τούτῳ καὶ ὁ μανεὶς τὰς φρένας ἐπώνυμός τε τῆς δαιμονώσης αἱρέσεως....

31   Eusebius, *HE* 7.31 (slightly altered translation of Oulton LCL 265: 226–27 & Lieu 2010, 43): Ἐν τούτῳ καὶ ὁ μανεὶς τὰς φρένας ἐπώνυμός τε τῆς δαιμονώσης αἱρέσεως τὴν τοῦ λογισμοῦ παρατροπὴν καθωπλίζετο, τοῦ δαίμονος, αὐτοῦ δὴ τοῦ θεομάχου σατανᾶ, ἐπὶ λύμῃ πολλῶν τὸν ἄνδρα προβεβλημένου. βάρβαρος δῆτα τὸν βίον αὐτῷ λόγῳ καὶ τρόπῳ τήν τε φύσιν δαιμονικός τις ὢν καὶ μανιώδης, ἀκόλουθα τούτοις ἐγχειρῶν, Χριστὸν αὐτὸν μορφάζεσθαι ἐπειρᾶτο, τοτὲ μὲν τὸν παράκλητον καὶ αὐτὸ τὸ πνεῦμα τὸ ἅγιον αὐτὸς ἑαυτὸν ἀνακηρύττων καὶ τυφούμενός γε ἐπὶ τῇ μανίᾳ, τοτὲ δέ, οἷα Χριστός, μαθητὰς δώδεκα κοινωνοὺς τῆς καινοτομίας αἱρούμενος· δόγματά γε μὴν ψευδῆ καὶ ἄθεα ἐκ μυρίων τῶν πρόπαλαι ἀπεσβηκότων ἀθέων αἱρέσεων συμπεφορημένα καττύσας, ἐκ τῆς Περσῶν ἐπὶ τὴν καθ' ἡμᾶς οἰκουμένην ὥσπερ τινὰ θανατηφόρον ἰὸν ἐξωμόρξατο, ἀφ' οὗ δὴ τὸ Μανιχαίων δυσσεβὲς ὄνομα τοῖς πολλοῖς εἰς ἔτι νῦν ἐπιπολάζει. τοιαύτη μὲν οὖν ἡ καὶ τῆσδε τῆς ψευδωνύμου γνώσεως ὑπόθεσις, κατὰ τοὺς δεδηλωμένους ὑποφυείσης χρόνους.

newfangled system" on the Roman empire, infected people as with "a deadly virus/poison".

Although the authors of the sources examined so far come from different cultural backgrounds,[32] despite their differences, they have many things in common in their portrayal of Mani and their representation of Manichaeism and its arrival. These are:

1) The emphasis on the *Persian origin* of Mani and Manichaeism, in Zosimus, Rescript of Diocletian, Alexander, Eusebius,

2) *Perso-Manichaean vice misleading* Roman citizens in Zosimus, Theonas, Rescript of Diocletian, Alexander, Eusebius,

3) The *Manichaean newfangledness* (καινοτομία): the Manichaean beliefs, practices, and values are in complete contrast to the established values, the traditional codes of ethics, and the laws of the Roman Empire. Diocletian, Alexander, and Eusebius characterize Manichaeism as 'newfangledness'. Manichaeism is a 'newfangledness' either because it opposes the ancient religion and values (Diocletian), or because "the novelty of his doctrines" makes any "progress in virtue" "complicated and ineffectual" (Alexander), or because Mani's system is a synthesis of all the false, long extinct, doctrines (Rescript of Diocletian, Alexander, Eusebius), and

4) *Manichaeism's spread westwards* threatens the integrity of Roman citizens and Roman Empire, in Rescript of Diocletian, Alexander, Eusebius.

In addition, the language and the imagery that the above authors employ also have a lot in common.

1) *The daemon/Antichrist sends a forerunner*: Mani is presented as the forerunner of the imitator daemon/Satan/anti-Christ (Zosimus, Eusebius). The imagery of the precursor of a royal figure was a common topos. The avant-courier is a person who would come in advance to herald the arrival of an important visitor and prepare people's hearts for his coming.

2) Manichaeism is depicted as a malignant Persian serpent or a virus (plague of iniquity), which with its poison infects the citizens of Roman Empire (Rescript of Diocletian, Eusebius).

---

32 The "different cultural background" has been challenged by Edwards (2015, 138–42 & 152–57) who argues that both Zosimus and Alexander were Christians. The authenticity of Diocletian's rescript was also questioned and the possibility that in its present form it is a Christian reworking cannot be ruled out.

TABLE 1   Synoptic table of the pre-*Acta* sources (portrait of Mani and of Manichaeism)

	Zosimus	Rescript of Diocletian	Alexander	Eusebius
The imitator daemon	the mimic daemon ... claiming that he is the son of God			Mani "attempted to imitate Christ: at one time giving out that he was the Paraclete and the Holy Spirit Himself"
The mimic daemon sends a forerunner	But before the mimic, the zealot, dares these things he first dispatches his own fore-runner ... leading men			"the devil, that is Satan himself ... had put the man forward for the destruction of many"
The Persian Serpent poison/ virus/plague		– Perso-Manichaean laws and customs "infect ... Roman people" as "the poison of a malignant serpent". – Manichaeism as a "plague of iniquity"		– Manichaeism "infected our empire [as] a deadly poison/virus"
The Persian origin	dispatches his own forerunner from Persia	– "they have but recently advanced or sprung forth ... from their native homes among the Persians – a nation hostile to us" – "the damnable customs and perverse laws of the Persians" – "those who have gone over to that ... creed ... of the Persians"	– "Manichaeus, a Persian by birth" – "Manichaeus himself is said ... to have accom-panied Shapur the Persian king during his mili-tary campaigns"	Mani "came from the land of the Persians"

TABLE 1   Synoptic table of the pre-*Acta* sources (portrait of Mani and of Manichaeism) (*cont.*)

	Zosimus	Rescript of Diocletian	Alexander	Eusebius
Perso-Manichaean vice misleading men	telling deceptive, fabulous tales and leading men on about Fate.	– "scandalous kinds of superstitious doctrine, so that many others are lured" – "perpetrating many evil deeds, disturbing the tranquillity of the peoples and causing the gravest injuries to the civic communities, with the damnable customs and perverse laws of the Persians" "their misdeeds are clearly the offspring of a fantastic and lying imagination"	– Manichaeism as harmful and "hopelessly complicated and ineffectual thing" – Mani's "astonishing doctrines" the lack of "norms or laws" and of "theoretical precision" rendered "moral disposition" unattainable – "Ethical instruction declined and grew dim"	-Mani "was taking as his armour mental delusion" – Mani's "speech and manners proclaimed him a barbarian in mode of life"
The Manichaean newfangledness		ancient religion vs a new creed – "highly criminal to discuss doctrines once and for all settled and defined by our forefathers" – "Manichaeans ... who, in opposition to the older creeds, set up new and unheard-of sects, purposing in their wickedness to cast out the doctrines vouchsafed to us by divine favour in older times"	– Mani's "astonishing doctrines, in my opinion, far surpass those of all the others. This newfangledness of his has but recently come to the fore"	– Mani "stitched together false and godless doctrines that he had collected from the countless, long extinct, godless heresies" "in his newfangled system"

TABLE 1 Synoptic table of the pre-*Acta* sources (portrait of Mani and of Manichaeism) *(cont.)*

	Zosimus	Rescript of Diocletian	Alexander	Eusebius
	Manichaeism's spread westwards	– Manichaeans "have but recently advanced or sprung forth ... from [Persia]... and have settled in this part of the world"	– Manichaeism "has but recently come to the fore".	– "the profane name of Manichaean is still commonly on men's lips to this day"

2.2 *Portrait of Mani and of Manichaeism in the Acta and Its Echo*

These thematic axes or constituents of Mani's representation by earlier authors (Persian origin, Perso-Manichaean vice, Manichaean newfangledness versus established tradition) are also characteristic of the *AA*, and are scattered throughout the whole work (introduction, debates, and letters). However, the classic portrait that became highly influential in later anti-Manichaean discourse is the biography (caricature) of Mani that bishop Archelaus recounted before the congregated audience, after the debates at Diodoris (*AA* 62–65).

2.2.1 Mani's Biography

Archelaus begins his account promising to reveal everything about Mani: "I shall declare to you the lineage and deeds of that man who has recently thrust himself upon us from the province of Persia ... Moreover I shall set out very clearly the origin of his doctrine".[33] Below follows a free and concise summary of the biography.

"The originator and founder of this sect" was not Mani, but a certain Scythianus (a Saracen in race) who had lived "in the time of the apostles". This is the one who introduced dualism, which he had "inherited from Pythagoras", but worsened it, introducing "enmities between the two unbegotten beings". Scythianus "married a woman prisoner from the upper Thebaid" and lived with her in Egypt, where he excelled in the "wisdom of the Egyptians", as he was very talented. He acquired a certain disciple named Terebinthus, "who wrote four books for him". However, in a trip he made to Judea, in order to meet all those who had a reputation as learned and famous teachers, he suddenly lost his life (*AA* 62). Terebinthus, after his death, went to Babylonia, where he was renamed

---

33   *AA* 62.1 (Vermes, 140). All quotes in the following summary are from *AA* 62–65 (Vermes, 140–47).

Buddha, and constructed "a remarkable story about himself"; he claimed that "he had been born from a virgin" and brought up "by an angel on the mountains". Although the priests of Mithras "accused him of falsehood", he continued his teachings about the creation of the world, the reincarnations, "and still more evil things". However, he "acquired not a single disciple there apart from" an old woman, a widow with whom he lived. "Finally early one morning" during a kind of a religious "ceremony or magic" which he performed on "a high roof top", he was "thrust beneath the ground" by a spirit and died (AA 63). All his inheritance, with the four books, passed to "the old woman", who obtained a boy of about seven years of age, called Corbicius, to serve her. "At once she gave him his freedom" and instructed him in reading and writing. When this boy "had reached the age of twelve, the old woman died" and left to him all her possessions, and among other things were "those four books that Scythianus had written". Corbicius then was renamed Manes[34] and "moved home to the middle of the city where the king of the Persians dwelt" (Seleucia-Ctesiphon). When he "had reached nearly sixty years of age", he had acquired great erudition in all the branches of learning ("he had become learned") "surpassing anyone else". He acquired also three disciples: Thomas, Addas, and Hermas. Then he copied the four books, inserting into them his own material; moreover, "he attached his own name to the books, deleting the name of the former writer, as if he alone had written them all by himself". Then he sent two of his disciples to preach the doctrines he had formed in various cities and villages into the "upper regions of that ... province", in order to attract more followers. After his disciples departed, the king's son got sick, and the king "issued an edict" offering a large reward to anyone who would heal his son. "Manes presented himself in person before the king, claiming that he would cure the boy", but "the boy died in his hands, or rather was killed off". Then the king imprisoned Mani and hunted down his two disciples, who "although fugitives", continued to preach (AA 64). When they returned to Manes (who was in prison), they told him the sufferings they went through "in each separate place". Mani counselled them to fear nothing, and sent them to districts where there were Christians, and after giving them a small amount of money, ordered them to acquire all the books of Christian Scriptures, and bring them back to him. When the books were brought to him in prison, Mani began to seek out all the statements which supported the idea of a dualism. Then, by rejecting some things and altering others in the Christian Scriptures, as well as adding the name of Christ, he advanced his own doctrines from the Christian scriptures. "He pretended to adopt that name" so that the people in the cities hearing the name of Christ,

---

34   The spelling of Mani's name in AA. AA 64.3 (Vermes, 144).

did not harass his disciples. In addition, misinterpreting the Scripture, as he "had not read carefully that the Paraclete had already come", at the time of the apostles, Mani claimed that he himself might be that Paraclete. "So having put together" these impious inventions, he sent "his disciples ... to proclaim these fictions and errors with all boldness, and to make these false and novel words known in every quarter". The king of Persia learned this and wanted to punish him, but he "bribed the guards" and fled, ending up in the 'castle of Arabion', from where he sent the letter to Marcellus by "means of" Turbo. Archelaus finished his story informing the audience that "the king ordered that Manes be hunted and arrested wherever he should be found", and that he was still "sought (by the king of the Persians) right up to the present day" (AA 65). Here ends Archelaus' account.

As Hegemonius continues, Archelaus' narrative stirred up the rage of the crowd, who wanted to deliver Mani to the Persian king. Mani fled and went back to the Arabion fortress. But later, the Persian king arrested him, and ordered him to be flayed and hung his skin (infused with drugs) in front of the gate of the city, while his flesh was ordered to be given to the birds. Hegemonius explains that when Archelaus learned of this latest news he added it to his book, "so as to make it known to everybody" (AA 66.4).

(1) *The Persian origin*: As can be noted in the biography, Mani's Persian origin is repeatedly stressed. Archelaus states from the outset of his story that Mani "has recently thrust himself upon us from the province of Persia".[35] Subsequently, Mani is presented as making strategic moves to get the support of the Persian king: (a) he moved out from Babylon "to the middle of the city [Ctesiphon], where dwelt the king of the Persians";[36] (b) "He changed his name and called himself Manes [Mani] instead of Corbicius" preferring the "inflection given in the Persian language";[37] and (c) he presented himself as a skilful therapist promising to heal/cure the son of the king (irrespective of the result). Apart from Mani's Persian origin, the text also emphasizes the relationship of his ancestors and disciples with Persia. Mani's predecessor Terebinthus also resided in Babylonia, which as Archelaus explains, "is at present a province inhabited by Persians".[38] Even Basilides, whom Hegemonius presents as Mani's spiritual ancestor and an agent of dualism, is portrayed by Hegemonius as

---

35   AA 62 (Vermes, 140).
36   AA 63.3 (Vermes, 142).
37   AA 64.3 (Vermes, 144). This comment of AA's author is ironic, since it is commonly believed that 'Mani' was an Aramaic name/title (indicated also by Epiphanius (66.1), see fn. 67), whereas there are reasons to believe that behind 'Corbicius' there might have been a genuine Iranian name (something like Kirbagig = virtuous).
38   AA 63.1 (Vermes, 142).

"a preacher" "among the Persians".[39] The Persian origin of Manichaeism is repeatedly stressed not only in the biography, but also from the very beginning of the work. Whatever is "beyond the river Stranga",[40] from where both Mani and Turbo came, is "into the territory of Persia". Marcellus' reputation crossed the border of the river Stranga, and spread into the Persian territories where Mani lived.[41] During his trip on the way to Carchar, Turbo stayed in "the wayside inns that Marcellus in his great hospitality had established, upon being asked by the innkeepers where he came from, who he was or who had sent him, he would say 'I am from Mesopotamia, but I come here from Persia, and was sent by Manichaeus the teacher of the Christians'".[42] Archelaus finishing his first representation of Mani at the point when the latter arrived to Carchar, comments: "his appearance was like that of an old Persian magician or warlord".[43] Here the magician's attribute is added to highlight the Persian origin. Terebinthus is also presented as practicing magical ceremonies. Also, the story of Scythianus and his wife echoes the history of Simon Magus, which is the most iconic heresiological motif, and to whom all heresies are often said to go back.[44]

It is important to underline here that all of the emphasis that Manichaeism came from Persia (i.e. the Sasanian Empire), is historically correct. That the heresiologists (in their polemical agenda) exploited this fact in order to stress the 'otherness' of Manichaeism, does not render the word 'Persia(n)' just a mere label.

During the debates, Archelaus does not miss any opportunity to call Mani a Persian: "You barbarian Persian [...]. You barbarian priest and conspirator with Mithras".[45] The Persian origin of Mani 'guarantees' the unreliability of his words. It is repeated even where it is unnecessary. In Mani's assertion that "I am, in truth, the paraclete who was predicted by Jesus would be sent",[46] Archelaus said: "And how are we to believe that Manes, who comes from Persia,

---

39   AA 67.4 (Vermes, 149). This is totally unfounded, as is the idea that Basilides would have been the one who introduced dualism, see Lieu in Vermes 2001, 149, fn. 329.
40   Lieu in Vermes 2001, 18. There are several proposals by scholars regarding the identification of the river Stranga, yet the general consensus is that we don't know which river this is.
41   AA 4.1 (Vermes, 39).
42   AA 15.1 (Vermes, 40).
43   AA 14.3 (Vermes, 58).
44   Mirecki 2007, 149.
45   AA 40.5 & 40.7 (Vermes, 105).
46   AA 15.3 (Vermes, 59).

really is the Paraclete, as he says that he is?"[47] And he adds: "I would rather call him a parasite than the paraclete".[48]

That Mani dares to say that he is the Paraclete, is first reported by Eusebius,[49] and is not neglected by subsequent writers, whether they reproduce the AA or not.[50] Manichaean sources sometimes identify Mani as the Paraclete and sometimes as his envoy.[51]

(2) *Perso-Manichaean vice* (*values, beliefs & practices*) *misleading men/ Roman citizens*: Mani is paralleled to a "barbarian or tyrant, attempting to invade people who are living under the justice of laws".[52] It is impressive how the words of Archelaus recall Diocletian's rescript: "the Manichaeans [...] will endeavour to infect the innocent, orderly and tranquil Roman people". The same is reflected in the following extracts:

AA	Diocletian's rescript
54.3 ... Even indeed when you were assaulting us and causing us injury, and disparaging our ancestral traditions, and when you wanted to slay the souls of men that were well founded and preserved with conscientious care[a]	causing the gravest injuries cast out the doctrines vouchsafed to us by divine favour in older times

a   AA 54.3 (Vermes, 127).

47   AA 39.4 (Vermes, 102–03).
48   AA 25.3 (Vermes, 75).
49   Eusebius, *HE* 7.31 (LCL 265: 227).
50   Socrates, *HE* 1.22. *SC*, 2 (Lieu 2010, 117; 1994, 236): "I anathematize Manes who is also Manichaeus, who dared to call himself the Paraclete and Apostle of Jesus Christ, in order that he might deceive those whom he encountered".
51   For the identification of Mani with Paraclete in Manichaean sources, see: *CMC* 17, 46, 63, 70; *1Keph.* 1,14.5–20 & 16.29–30; *2PsB* 3,21, 9–11, 33,17, 102,29–30. For the relevant bibliography on the issue see indicatively: Lieu (Vermes, 59, fn. 82); Van Oort 2004, 139–57; Pettipiece 2008, 422; Brand 2019, 146, 158, 207–08 (Paraclete mentioned in the Kellis letters). As Gardner and Lieu (2004, 18) point out, "It is notable that in the personal letters of believers from fourth-century Kellis, Mani is quoted not by name but 'as the *Paraclete* has said'". One of the Manichaean psalms (*2PsB*, 9.3–11.32, Psalm 223) also praises Mani as 'the Spirit of truth that comes from the Father" and exhorts Manichaean believers to worship him: "This is the knowledge of Mani, let us worship him and bless him. Blessed is he every one that believes in him [...] Glory and victory to our lord Mani, the Spirit of truth that comes from the Father, who has unveiled for us, the beginning, the middle and the end".
52   AA 40.2 (Vermes, 104).

(3) *The Manichaean newfangledness*: Eusebius' idea of newfangledness (i.e. that Mani's system is a synthesis of all the false doctrines and is plagiarized) is illustrated and developed in detail in the biography. Mani "is not the first author of this kind of doctrine, nor the only one" (*AA* 62.2). Apart from being a copyist and collector of the "countless, long extinct" false doctrines, Mani is also a copyist of the Christian Scriptures. However, he does not understand and distorts them (*AA* 32.5 & 44.5), aiming to find evidence in them to support his dualism (*AA* 65.4). In the debates, Mani appears to ground his argumentation on a distorted interpretation of Christian scriptures. Mani gives thirty-eight Biblical quotations in the first debate and fourteen in the second.[53]

In their correspondence before the debates in Diodoris, the bishop Archelaus and presbyter Diodorus refer to Mani between themselves, and indicate the mark of Mani's religious identity:

> On a particular day Manes had gathered a crowd and was haranguing them, and as the people stood around was propounding to them various foreign notions alien to the inherited tradition, showing no fear whatsoever of anything that could be made to block him.[54]
>
> Diodorus: a certain man called Manes has arrived in this area, who professes that he completes the doctrine of the New Testament. Indeed, there were some parts of what he was saying which belonged to our faith, but some of his assertions were a long way distant from those that have come down to us in the tradition of our fathers. For he interpreted certain things in a strange way, and added to them from his own views, which seemed to me extremely outlandish and lacking in faith.[55]
>
> Archelaus: the same fellow, who some days ago had come to me and wanted to propagate another form of knowledge, different from that which is apostolic and accepted by the Church.[56]

Mani's disciples undertook the task "to teach in the various cities" these "foreign notions alien to the inherited tradition". They "never ceased inculcating from place to place this alien doctrine inspired by the Antichrist".[57]

(4) *The daemon/Antichrist sends a forerunner*: The *AA* also presents Mani as a vehicle of the Antichrist in order to prepare the latter's arrival:

---

53   BeDuhn 2007a, 83.
54   *AA* 43.5 (Vermes, 111).
55   *AA* 44.1–2 (Vermes, 111).
56   *AA* 46.2 (Vermes, 115).
57   *AA* 64.9 (Vermes, 146).

[...] for a prediction was written about you [Mani]; [...] 2. You are the vessel of the Antichrist; [...] For it is just as when some barbarian or tyrant, attempting to invade people who are living under the justice of laws, first sent ahead someone as it were destined for death ... for he himself was afraid [...] the Antichrist send you.[58]

The imagery of the *AA*'s Antichrist who "sent ahead someone[else] ... for he himself was afraid" recalls Zosimus' *antimimos daimōn*.[59] As far as Manichaeism's spread westwards is concerned, the whole of the *AA* records this first encounter between Manichaeism and Christianity. Hegemonius places the arrival of Mani and Manichaeism a few years later than Eusebius, that is, during the reign of emperor Probus (276–282 CE).[60]

2.2.2   The Afterlife of Mani's Biography in the *Acta* Tradition

2.2.2.1   *Cyril of Jerusalem*

Cyril is the first author who draws on information from the *AA*'s tradition. Before proceeding to the Manichaean practices, he depicts the portrait of Mani. He provides a very brief and concise but faithful version of Mani's biography from the *AA*, as well as adding his own comments here and there.[61] According to Cyril, Mani began his missionary activities under the reign of emperor Probus (as in the *AA*). He emphasizes how recent the sect is by saying that it "is just seventy years standing", and goes on to underline that "there are to this day men who have seen him [Mani] with their own eyes".[62] Cyril states that Mani chose this name because it means the mighty speaker in Persian.[63]

2.2.2.2   *Epiphanius of Salamis*

Epiphanius, in two of his works, gives the following dates for the arrival of Mani and Manichaeism. According to *De mensuris et ponderibus*, Mani "ascended from Persia" to Caschar of Mesopotamia in 262 (i.e. the ninth year of the reign of Valerian and Gallienus), where he debated with the bishop of the city, Archelaus.[64] According to the *Panarion*, where Epiphanius reproduces the

---

58   *AA* 40.2 (Vermes, 104–105).
59   See 2.1.1 in this chapter. About the relationship between Antichrist and the "demon who mimics", see Stroumsa 1984, 142–43.
60   *AA* 31.8 & 32.1 (Vermes, 86).
61   Cyril, *Cath.* 6.22–26, Mani's end in 6.30, and Mani's disciples in 6.31.
62   Cyril, *Cath.* 6.20.
63   Cyril, *Cath.* 6.24. The source of this information is unknown, but it is incorrect.
64   Epiphanius, *De mensuris et ponderibus*, lines 548–550. The same date is given by Photius in *Contra Manichaeos* (p. 139).

biography of the *AA*, the Manichaean heresy was brought to Eleutheroupolis, Epiphanius' city of birth, in 273, through a Manichaean missionary named Ἀκούας.

> They began to preach to the world at that time, and brought a great evil on the world after the ⟨sect⟩ of Sabellius. For they arose in the time of the emperor Aurelian, about the fourth year of his reign.[65]

Epiphanius begins the biography of Mani stating that "Mani was from Persia". According to him, the reason why Mani chose this name is that it means a vessel/pot in Babylonian.[66] Then he continues with the biography, going back to Mani's ancestors. Epiphanius' biography of Mani does not differ in content from that of the *AA*, but he recounts it in his own way; he enriches it with comments, and adds his own bitter touches. The few points in which Epiphanius' version of Mani's biography is different from the *AA* are: (1) Apart from Mani, Terebinthus is also a slave of Scythianus, (2) Scythianus' wife is not a slave but a prostitute from Hypsele (whom Scythianus took from the brothel), (3) Scythianus too is portrayed as practicing magic[67] and as having exactly the same end as Terebinthus,[68] (4) Mani sent his disciples to find the Christian Scriptures before going to prison,[69] whereas in the *AA* he did this while he was in prison.[70]

Further, Epiphanius gives some additional information regarding Scythianus' commercial activity and about Mani's disciples and books, which I will examine in the following sections of the chapter.

---

65   Epiphanius, *Pan.* 66.1.2 (Williams, 226–27).
66   Epiphanius, *Pan.* 66.1.4–5 (GCS 37:14–15): Μάνης δὲ οὗτος ἀπὸ τῆς τῶν Περσῶν ὡρμᾶτο γῆς. Κούβρικος μὲν τὸ πρῶτον καλούμενος, ἐπονομάσας δὲ ἑαυτῷ τοῦ Μάνη ὄνομα, [...] καὶ ὡς μὲν αὐτὸς ᾤετο, κατὰ τὴν τῶν Βαβυλωνίων γλῶτταν δῆθεν σκεῦος ἑαυτῷ τὸ ὄνομα ἐπέθετο· τὸ γὰρ Μάνη ἀπὸ τῆς Βαβυλωνίας εἰς τὴν Ἑλληνίδα μεταφερόμενον σκεῦος ὑποφαίνει τοὔνομα. In contrast to Cyril, Epiphanius is correct in saying that Mani's name in Aramaic means vessel. For the name and other terms and titles of Mani, see Shapira 1999.
67   Epiphanius, *Pan.* 66.3.7–8 (GCS 37:19): ἐπετήδευσε δι' ὧν εἶχε μαγικῶν βιβλίων – καὶ γὰρ καὶ γόης ἦν.
68   Epiphanius, *Pan.* 66.3.8–9 (GCS 37:19): ἐπὶ δώματος ⟨γὰρ⟩ ἀνελθὼν καὶ ἐπιτηδεύσας, ὅμως οὐδὲν ἰσχύσας, ἀλλὰ καταπεσὼν ἐκ τοῦ δώματος, τέλει τοῦ βίου ἐχρήσατο.
69   Epiphanius, *Pan.*, 66.5.1–4 (Williams, 232): "5,1 Thus Mani, or Cubricus, remained ⟨in⟩ confinement, [...]. 5,4 Giving his disciples money, he sent them to Jerusalem. (5) (But he had done this before his imprisonment ...)".
70   *AA* 65.2: "But he urged them to fear nothing ... Now at last, while languishing in prison, he ordered that the books of the law of the Christians be obtained".

Brief versions of the biography of Mani are reproduced by subsequent authors, who echo the AA, such as Socrates the Scholastic, Theodoret of Cyrrhus, Theodorus Anagnostes, etc. That Manichaeism was a recent heresy is pointed out (apart from Cyril) by the following authors: Epiphanius ("For the sect is not an ancient one"), Socrates, according to whom "the Manichaean religion (θρησκεία) sprang up a few years before Constantine", and Theodoret ("First exponent of these doctrines was Simon Magus and the last was Mani, the magician, the Persian").[71]

2.2.3 Some Remarks Concerning Mani's Portrait

As I have noted in ch.[1], scholars initially considered the 'biography' to be the most unreliable part of the AA; it was seen as a caricature of Mani's 'biography', in fact, an anti-legend with its anti-heroes. Indeed, the purpose of the AA was not a historical one. Hegemonius' discrediting tactic aimed to humiliate and obliterate his opponent, Mani, something which runs throughout the whole text.[72] By emphasizing the foreign (Persian) character of Manichaeism, Mani's credibility and skills of persuasion are being challenged. The often-repeated wordplay with Mani's name (first introduced by Eusebius) has the same effect: his name written in Greek as *Maneis* means to 'be mad'.[73] Nevertheless, an increasing number of researchers argue that even the 'biography' preserves some historical information about Mani and early Manichaean history. As Scopello argues, Mani's biography is a synthesis of fiction and history, in which one could find true events from Mani's life, but chronologically and locally misplaced.[74] In particular, Scopello supports the view that, although Mani's predecessors Scythianus and Terebinthus are two legendary figures, the events attributed to them could be hints to those from Mani's life. So, through the presentation of three biographies, we could acquire a quite sufficient idea about Mani's life. As she characteristically says, Scythianus' conflict with the Jews could actually have been Mani's clash with the community of Baptists. Similarly, Terebinthus' renaming to Boudda reminds us of Mani's title (Mani-Buddas)

---

71   Epiphanius, *Pan.* 66.12.4 (GCS 37:33): οὐκ ἔστι γὰρ ἀρχαΐζουσα ἡ αἵρεσις; Socrates, *HE* 1.22.15 (SC 477:206): "Ὅπως μὲν οὖν μικρὸν ἔμπροσθεν τῶν Κωνσταντίνου χρόνων ἡ Μανιχαίων παρεφύη θρησκεία; Theodoret of Cyrrhus, *Haer.* (PG 83:337): Τούτων δὲ τῶν δογμάτων πρῶτος μὲν εὑρε- τὴς Σίμων ὁ μάγος ὁ Σαμαρείτης, ἔσχατος δὲ Μάνης ὁ γόης ὁ Πέρσης. Theodorus Anagnostes (*Epit. hist. trip.* 1.33) places the beginning of the Manichaean heresy, quite early, during the episcopacy of Denys of Alexandria (247/8–264/5). Photius (*c. Manichaeos*, ch. 53), agree- ing with Alexander and Epiphanius, dates the arrival of Mani in Carchar during the reign of Valerian (253–260) and Gallienus (253–268).

72   Coyle 2007a, 23–32; Coyle 2007b, 67. Kaatz 2007, 103.

73   *AA* 59.10 (Vermes, 137: "you madman"). Van Oort 2000a, 459. Coyle 2004, 222.

74   Scopello 1995, 215–225, 220.

in some eastern sources. Lastly, as Scopello notes, the information given by the AA and Epiphanius, that Mani moved from Babylon to Seleucia-Ctesiphon when embarking on his new career as a religious leader is confirmed in the CMC. Mani, after his break with the Baptists, crossed over a bridge in order to reach the cities (πόλεις); this refered to the twin cities Seleucia-Ctesiphon.[75]

In the same fashion, BeDuhn and Mirecki point out that there are many parallels between Mani's biography in the AA and reports on "Mani's missions and death recovered in both Coptic and Middle Iranian Manichaean literature". Some of the most notable are: the name Corbicius recalls the Iranian title *kirbakkar* which means virtuous; the death age of Mani was actually around 60, as is recorded in the AA (64.4); that Mani sent his disciples on missions (AA 64.4, 64.6) and received back their missionary reports; that Mani prepared the texts for their missionary use (AA 65.1–6); the identification of Mani with the Paraclete (AA 65.6); Mani's "activities as a healer to the royal court (AA 64.7) and the association of his disfavor at court with a death in the royal family (AA 64.8, 66.3); his imprisonment in heavy chains (AA 64.9), and the flaying of his body and its display at the gates of the capital (AA 66.3)". The two authors conclude: "Hegemonius' reliance on Manichaean sources – either directly or mediated by another polemicist – seems clear".[76] In addition, accurate information recorded in this text is: the reference to the fundamental principle of Manichaeism (i.e. 'the two unbegotten beings'), the belief in reincarnation, the importance attributed by Manichaeans to missionary activities, and likely the rooftop ritual performed by Terebinthus.[77]

Further, the aforementioned thematic axes of the sources 'before the *Acta*' discussed above are emphasized by all subsequent authors.[78] The emphasis

---

75   Scopello 1995, 214, 220, 224 & 234. CMC 111,1–7 (Koenen and Römer 1988, 78): ἔφ[η δὲ πρός]αὐτούς· "ἐγὼ αὐτὸν ἐ[θεα]σάμην ἐπὶ τῆς γεφύρ[ας] περῶν εἰς τὰς πόλεις." Παττίκιος δὲ ὡς ἤκο[υ]σεν ἐχάρη καὶ ἐξέβη [ἐ]λευσόμενος πρός με εἰς Κτησιφῶντος. Althougt Scopello's argument might be interesting, I would like to stress that it can not be argued that AA's information is 'historically correct', as if it described actual things that actually happened during Mani's life. The argument should, and can be, however, that in the AA we find reflections of actual Manichaean narratives of the life of the prophet.

76   BeDuhn and Mirecki 2007, 1–22, 21.

77   On this ritual see Mirecki 2007, 149–155; Spät 2004, 8–11.

78   The *virus/infection* rhetoric/imagery is continued: Epiphanius (*Pan.* 66.1.1, GCS 37:13–14): the Manichaean missionary Akouas "ἐν τῇ Ἐλευθεροπόλει ἐνέγκαντα ταύτην τὴν τοῦ δηλητηρίου τούτου πραγματείαν". As Cyril (*Catech* 6.20; Reischl and Rupp 1848, 184) warns his disciples the Manichaeans "ὄφεις γάρ εἰσι γεννήματα ἐχιδνῶν ... τὸν ἰὸν φυλάσσου". *Newfangledness* and *plagiarism* are foundumental in Mani's system: For Cyril, the innovation of Manichaeism was that it surpassed everyone in the copy-paste of all evil doctrines. Cyril, *Catech.* 6.20 (Reischl and Rupp 1848, 182, 184): Καὶ μίσει μὲν πάντας αἱρετικοὺς, ἐξαιρέτως δὲ τὸν τῆς μανίας ἐπώνυμον [...] τῆς κακίας ἐργάτην, τὸ δοχεῖον παντὸς ῥύπου, τὸν πάσης

on the Persian origin of Mani continues in subsequent authors, irrespectively
of whether they reproduced the *AA* or not. Augustine also describes the heresy
of his youth as a Persian mistake.[79]

3   The Manichaean Books in Greek Anti-Manichaica

3.1   *The Manichaean Canon*

Manichaeans attributed great importance to their books, and for this reason
Manichaeism is characterized as a religion of the book *par excellence*.[80] A
distinctive feature of Mani's biography in the *AA* is the story about the books
of Manichaeism and that these were the result of a repeated plagiarism. The
author of the books and inspirer of the Manichaean doctrines is not Mani himself, but Scythianus (or even Basilides). Mani simply appropriated and modified Scythianus' books, introducing into them his own material and his own
signature, presenting them as if he had composed them all by himself.

> When he [Mani] had reached the age of twelve, the old woman died
> and bequeathed to him all her goods, and alongside the other remnants
> also those four books that Scythianus had written, each containing a few

αἱρέσεως βόρβορον ὑποδεξάμενον. Φιλοτιμούμενος γὰρ ἐν κακοῖς ἐξαίρετος γενέσθαι, τὰ πάντων
λαβών, καὶ μίαν αἵρεσιν πεπληρωμένην βλασφημιῶν καὶ πάσης παρανομίας συστησάμενος [...]
κλέπτης γάρ ἐστιν ἀλλοτρίων κακῶν, ἐξιδιοποιούμενος τὰ κακά. Cyril, *Catech.* 16.9: Μάνης ὁ
τὰ τῶν αἱρέσεων πασῶν κακὰ συνειληφώς. καὶ οὗτος τελευταῖος βόθρος ἀπωλείας τυγχάνων,
τὰ πάντων συλλέξας. Epiphanius *Pan.* 66.4.1 (GCS 37:21–22; Williams 231): "everyone who
heard Mani's teaching was annoyed, and rejected it for its novelty, shocking stories, and
empty imposture" (καὶ ὡς οὐδεὶς αὐτῷ ἐπείθετο, ἀλλὰ ἀκούοντες Μανιχαίου διδασκαλίαν ἐδυ-
σφόρουν μὲν καὶ ἐξενολεκτοῦντο πάντες ἐπὶ τῇ καινοτομίᾳ καὶ δεινῇ μυθοποιίᾳ καὶ κενῇ ἀπάτῃ).
Socrates, *HE* (SC 477:202, 204): Κούβρικος καὶ ἐπὶ τὰ Περσῶν μέρη χωρήσας μετονομάζει μὲν
ἑαυτὸν Μάνην, τὰ δὲ τοῦ Βούδδα ἤτοι Τερεβίνθου βιβλία ὡς οἰκεῖα τοῖς ὑπ' αὐτοῦ πλανηθεῖσιν
ἐξέδωκεν [...] τὴν Ἐμπεδοκλέους καὶ Πυθαγόρου δόξαν εἰς τὸν χριστιανισμὸν παρεισήγαγεν [...]
εἱμαρμένην εἰσάγων τὸ ἐφ' ἡμῖν ἀναιρεῖ, καὶ μετενσωματώσιν δογματίζει, [...] καὶ ἑαυτὸν ὀνο-
μάζει παράκλητον, ἅπερ πάντα ἀλλότρια τῆς ὀρθοδόξου ἐκκλησίας καθέστηκεν. Apart from
the *Acta* tradition, Mark the Deacon, *Vit. Porph.* 86 (Lieu 2010, 98–99): καὶ οἱ Μανιχαῖοι,
ἐκ διαφόρων δογμάτων ἀντλήσαντες, ἀπετέλεσαν τὴν αὐτῶν κακοδοξίαν, μᾶλλον δὲ ἐκ διαφόρων ἑρπετῶν τὸν ἰὸν συναγαγόντες καὶ μίξαντες, θανατηφόρον φάρμακον κατεσκεύασαν πρὸς
ἀναίρεσιν ἀνθρωπίνων ψυχῶν. Pseudo-Athanasius (ca 360), *Sermo contra omnes haereses*
(PG 28:501–524, 513): Εἴπωμεν καὶ πρὸς τοὺς ἀσεβεστάτους Μανιχαίους, τοὺς τρυγιοὺς τῶν
κακῶν.

79   Augustine, *Faust.* 28.2–4.
80   For Manichaeism as a religion of the book (par excellence), see: Gardner and Lieu 2004,
      111; Stroumsa 2004, 648; Tardieu 2008/1981, 33; About the importance that books and the
      art of book writing had in Manichaean tradition, see Brand 2019, 293–25.

lines. [...] when that boy had reached nearly sixty years of age, he had become learned in the doctrine that exists in those parts [...] yet he studied more diligently the things contained in those four books. [...] Then he took those books and copied them, not without inserting into them many other things of his own [...] moreover he attached his own name to the books, deleting the name of the former writer, as if he alone had written them all by himself.[81]

However, according to the AA, Mani did not stop at this first stage of 'copy-pasting', but proceeded to 'selective plagiarism'; he picked over the Christian Scriptures to find the arguments or passages by which he could further support the notion of dualism. To this end, he sent his students to collect the Christian Scriptures.

> [...] while languishing in prison, he ordered that the books of the law of the Christians be obtained.[82]
>
> To cut a long story short, they obtained all the books of our Scriptures, and delivered them to Manes residing in prison. This astute individual received the books and began to look in our writings for passages in support of his dualism – or rather, not his, but Scythianus', who had propounded this doctrine much earlier. He also tried to advance his own assertions from our books [...] by attacking some statements in them, and altering others.[83]

Perhaps, this ridicule of Mani by the heresiologists (i.e. to describe him as an expert in plagiarism) was not accidental, but combated the Manichaean claim that one of the ten advantages that made their religion superior to others was that its holy Scriptures were written down and delivered to the Manichaean community by its founder, Mani himself.[84] Mani is presented to proclaim in the *Kephalaia*

---

81 *AA* 64.2–4 (Vermes, 144). The respective text in Epiphanius *Pan.* is 66.2.9, 3.12, 5.7 & 8 (Williams, 229–232).

82 *AA* 65.2. Epiphanius (66.5.3, Williams, 232), in his version, mentions in detail the titles of "the books of the law of the Christians": "I mean ⟨the⟩ Christian books, the Law and Prophets, the Gospels, and the Apostles"; briefly: OT and NT.

83 *AA* 65.4–5 (Vermes, 146–47).

84 Or vice-versa, i.e. the *ten advantages* tradition was created in response to the heresiological ridicule?

My church surpasses in the wisdom and ... which I have unveiled for you in it. This (immeasurable) wisdom I have written in the holy books, in the great *Gospel* and the other writings; so that it will not be changed after me. Also, the way that I have written it in the books: (This) also is how I have commanded it to be depicted. Indeed, all the (apostles), my brethren who came prior to me: (They did not write) their wisdom in books the way that I, I have written it. (Nor) did they depict their wisdom in the *Picture* (*-Book*) the way (that I, I have) depicted it. My church surpasses (in this other matter also), for its primacy to the first churches.[85]

This was the second in the list of the ten advantages. Due to the fact that the Manichaean community had a canon of its own constitutional books from the very beginning, Manichaeism is considered by many scholars as the first 'religion', in the modern sense.[86] In that same list, the fourth advantage seems to confirm one of the chief accusations of the AA against the Manichaeans: that the Manichaeans had appropriated Christian and other writings. The text reads:

The writings, wisdom, revelations, parables, psalms of all the first churches have been collected in every place. They have come down to my church. They have added to the wisdom that I have revealed ... and have become great wisdom.[87]

The technique in both sources (Manichaean *Kephalaia* and anti-Manichaean AA) is the same. What differentiates the two testimonies is their diverging points of view. In the polemical framework of the AA, this practice constitutes plagiarism and a distortion of the meaning of Christian (Holy) Scriptures. In the *Kephalaia* case, it is one of the ten advantages of the Manichaean religion, as it collects the wisdom of all previous religions. Mani's revelation as crystallised in his books comprises a synthesis of all previous wisdom. As Mani declares, "the measure of all wisdom" is recorded in his books. "Everything that has occ[urred], / and [th]at will oc[cu]r is written in them!"[88]

---

85   *1Keph.* 151, 371.20–30 (the ten advantages: 370.16–375.15) in Gardner and Lieu 2004, 265–68, 266 (no 91). Cf. Gardner and Lieu 2004, 151.

86   See Introduction, section 5.3.3.

87   *1Keph.* 151, 372.10–20 (Gardner and Lieu 2004, 266).

88   *1Keph.* intr.5.25–30. (Gardner 1995, 12).

Lists of the titles of the books of the Manichaean canon are recorded in several Manichaean sources. Their number varies between five and eight books. In the introduction of the *Kephalaia*, Mani himself gives us the titles of his books, which are seven in number:

> I have written them in my books of light: in *The Great Gospel* and *Treasury of the Life*; in *the Treatise* (Gr: Pragmateia); in *The One of the Mysteries*; in *The Writing*, which I wrote on account of the Parthians; and also all my *Epistles*; in *The Psalms* and *The Prayers*.[89]

The list is slightly different in the Manichaean *Homilies*, where in place of 'the Writing [...] of the Parthians' we find the *Book of the Giants*.[90] In addition, here, apart from the seven titles, the Picture-Book is listed.

> The Gospel and The Treasury of the Life, The Treatise and The Book of the Mysteries, The Book of the Giants and The Epistles, The Psalms and the Prayers of my lord, his Picture (-Book) and his apo(caly)pses, his parables and his mysteries.[91]

The *Gospel* or *The Living Gospel*, as the whole title is (sometimes also mentioned as the *Great Living Gospel*), heads both the lists.[92] As reflected by later Manichaean sources, the canon of the seven Scriptures and "the one drawing" (i.e. the *Picture-Book*), continued to be in use until much later. According to the *Compendium of Manichaean Doctrines* (731 CE), the canon for the Chinese Manichaeans under the Tang Dynasty was as follows:

> [1] the great *yinglun* (from Gr. *evangelion*), interpreted 'book of wisdom which thoroughly understands the roots and origins of the entire doctrines' (i.e. *The Great Living Gospel*); [2] [...] 'the sacred book of the treasure of pure life' (i.e. *The Treasure of Life*); [3] [...] 'the sacred book of discipline', also called 'the sacred book of healing' (i.e. *The Epistles*); [4]

---

89   *1Keph.* intr.5.21–25 (Gardner 1995, 11; Gardner and Lieu 2004, 153).

90   Tardieu 2008, 45: "In the preamble to the Kephalaia, the compiler has Mani enumerate the books of the canon of the Manichaean church, established after his death. There Mani includes Giants, describing it as 'the book I wrote at the request of the Parthians'".

91   *Hom.* 25.1–6 (Gardner and Lieu 2004, 152, fn. 1: "ascribed to Koustaios, who may well have acted as Mani's scribe").

92   Tardieu 2008, 35.

[...] 'the sacred book of secret law' (i.e. *The Mysteries*);[93] [5] [...] 'book of instruction which testifies the past' (i.e. *The Pragmateia*); [6] [...] 'book of the strong heroes' (i.e. *The Book of the Giants*); [7] [...] 'book of praises and wishes (vows)' (i.e. *The Psalms and Prayers*); [8] [...] 'the drawing of the two great principles' (i.e. *The Picture-book* or *Eikon*).

The seven great scriptures and the (one) drawing mentioned above, Mani [...] (he himself) transmitted (them) to the five grades (of believers).[94]

The *Compendium* is certainly a much later source. Moreover, it does not come from the context of the Roman Empire. Nevertheless, sources such as the *Compendium* "do illustrate the unity and longevity Mani's canon achieved for Manichaeism".[95]

3.2   The Manichaean Books in the Acta Archelai

The *AA* inaugurates the most frequently cited tradition in anti-Manichaica for the titles of the Manichaean Scriptures, which was reproduced by subsequent Christian heresiologists.

He [Scythianus] had a particular disciple [Terebinthus], who wrote four books for him, one of which he called the book of *Mysteries*, another that of the *Capitula*, the third the *Gospel*, and the last book of all he called the *Thesaurus*.[96]

The 'tetrateuch', as Tardieu names the four books, which was "represented by Christian heresiologists, Syriac, Greek, and Latin alike, as forming the Manichaean canon, has no foundation in the Manichaean sources".[97] Out of the four books of the *AA* tradition, three are canonical. These are: 1) the *book*

93 According to later Greek sources (*SAF*, *LAF*, Photius and Peter of Sicily), the book of Mysteries refuted the Law and the Prophets, Cf. Bennett 2001a, 47.

94 *Compendium of Manichaean doctrines in Chinese* in Gardner and Lieu 2004, 155–56.

95 Gardner and Lieu 2004, 154. As Tardieu (2008, 49) points out, "the presence of the same canon in the *Compendium* indicates that the decision of the founding Babylonian church continued to be respected by Chinese Manichaeans under the T'ang Dynasty [...] Further, the list in the *Compendium* follows exactly the one given in the final section of the Coptic Homilies".

96 *AA* 62.6 (Vermes, 141). Epiphanius, *Pan.* 66.2.9.

97 Tardieu 2008, 49.

of Mysteries,[98] 2) the *Gospel*,[99] and 3) the *Thesaurus*.[100] The *Kephalaia*, which Manichaeans valued highly, was in fact the work of Mani's disciples. Indeed, after emphasizing the importance of his own writings and listing his books, Mani urged his disciples to record (and preserve) his oral teachings, sermons, lessons. This also provides a justification for considering the *Kephalaia* as a sub-canonical text.[101]

---

98   The book of Mysteries was one of the canonical books. Lieu 1994a, 269: "A list of its chapter headings [eighteen] is known from the *Fihrist* of al-Nadim [pp. 797–98]. [...] It seems that an important part of the work is a discussion (or even a refutation) of Bardaisan's teaching, especially on the soul. Bardaisan himself according to Ephraim was also the author of a *Book of Mysteries*". Gardner and Lieu 2004, 155; Tardieu 2008, 38–41. For further information about the books, see Lieu in Vermes 2001, 141–42, fn. 309–12.

99   The Gospel is a "much cited canonical work of Mani" (Lieu in Vermes, 141). Lieu 1994a, 269: "We possess an extract of it in Greek in the *CMC* 66.4–70.10"; Lieu 2010, 147–48. Tardieu 2008, 35–36. Reeves 2011, 94–98. About a reconstruction of the Living Gospel and its content, see Mohammad Shokri-Foumeshi 2015, 2017 & 2018. The Gospel in Manichaean sources: *CMC* 66.4–70.10. According to *Kephalaia* (355.4–25), "*The Great Living Gospel* is the gift of the *Ambassador*" (Gardner and Lieu 2004, 154). 2PsB 139.56–59 (Psalmoi Sarakōtōn): "His Great Gospel (εὐαγγέλιον): His New Testament (διαθήκη): The Manna of the skies. The inheritance (κληρονομία) of ...". About the Gospel in the *Compendium* see section 3.1 (The Manichaean Canon) in this chapter. About the Gospel in Islamic sources, see Shokri-Foumeshi & Farhoudi 2014.

100   Tardieu 2008, 38, 37: "the Treasure was the first systematic exposition of Manichaean theology", "Three fragments have come down to us indirectly through later authors": (1) al-Biruni, *Tahqiq*, (2) Augustine, *Nat. bon.* 44 (The Third Messenger exploits "the 'deadly unclean lust' congenital to hostile bodies in the heavens in order to cause them to release the living elements they contain") and (3) Augustine, *Fel.* [2.5]. See also Lieu in Vermes 2001, 142; Lieu 1994a, 269; Lieu 2010, 149: "The longer citation from the *De Natura Boni* suggests that it contains, *inter alia*, a detailed account of Mani's cosmogonic myth, including the infamous scene known as the Seduction of the Archons". Reeves 2011, 108–109, 109: "the book [Thesaurus] must have included a narrative presentation of the fundamental Manichaean cosmogonic myths".

101   Gardner 1995, 10: "Mani then asserts his revelation of total wisdom in his canonical scriptures. However, he also stresses his oral teaching; and urges his followers to write down what he has taught them. [...] In consequence, Mani again admonishes his disciples to remember and write down his teachings". Gardner and Lieu 2004, 153 & 152 fn. 1: "Mani then [after listing his books] urges his disciples also to preserve all his occasional discourses" [Kephalaia], "Kephalaiac literature was necessarily sub-canonical, since by its nature it was the recording of Mani's sermons, lessons, occasional parables and such like". The two works: (1) the *Kephalaia of the Teacher* (Berlin) & (2) The *Kephalaia of the Wisdom of my Lord Mani* (Dublin) constitute one collection (Gardner, BeDuhn and Dilley 2018, 1). Lieu in Vermes, 141. Pettipiece 2005, 247–260. See Funk (1997, 143–59) about the "Reconstruction of the Manichaean Kephalaia". See also Lieu (2010, xii) about the great importance that Manichaeans attributed to some non-canonical books and works of Mani's disciples, such as the *Kephalaia* and the Historical work (part of *CMC*).

[Yet], now [I will] entrust to you [.../...] The world has not permitted me to write down [.../...] to me all of it; and if you, my childr[en and my discip]/les, write all my wisdom [.../...] the questions that you have asked me [...]and the explanations that I have made clea[r to you from t/im]e to time; the homilies, the lessons, that I have proclaimed with the teache[rs / to] the leaders, together with the elect and the catechume [ns; / and] the ones that I have uttered to free men and free women; [... / ...] all of them, that I have proclaimed from time to time! Th[eyJ are [not] writt[en. Y]ou must remember them and write th[em; ga]ther them i[n / differ]ent places; because much is the wisdom that I ha[ve ut]tered [to y/ou].[102]

So they did, and a new group of books, the sub-canonical Manichaean literature, was formed. Thus, the AA tradition combines three Manichaean canonical books with one of the greatest sub-canonical books of the community, the *Kephalaia*. Tardieu names the sub-canonical literature as the Manichaean Patrology, since it was written by Mani's disciples and not by himself.[103] However, this "had a problematic element in view of Mani's critique of such practices in prior churches".[104] A further problem, is "the flimsy survival of Mani's scriptures themselves". "The seven works" and "the *Picture* (*-Book*) [...] are in very large part lost". So, we know very little about their content. Although we have a minimal amount of texts directly attributed to Mani, it is remarkable that we have "thousands of pages of text, written by [his] followers [...] including large amounts of kephalaic material".[105] This fact seems quite ironic in light of Mani's certainty that his recorded wisdom would remain forever unchanged.[106]

Of course, this enormous lacuna, to a certain extent, could have been recovered by the *Contra Manichaeos* works, as is usually the case with the anti-heretical literature. However, in the research conducted until now the prevailing interpretation is that we have very few exact parallels or citations from the genuine Manichaean texts in the anti-Manichaica (especially the Greek). Yet there are studies supporting the view that some Christian authors must have had the authentic works of Mani at their disposal. Thus, an additional question to be examined below, apart from the reproduction of the AA's canon in the subsequent tradition, is whether East-Roman authors had access

---

102   Gardner 1995, 12.
103   Tardieu 2008, 50.
104   Gardner and Lieu 2004, 152, fn. 1.
105   Gardner and Lieu 2004, 152. See Pedersen 2015a (284–88) for fragments possibly originating from Mani's *Book of Giants*.
106   Cf. Pettipiece 2005, 250, fn. 10.

to the writings of Mani and, if so, what additional information they provide us about the Manichaean books.

3.3   Before the Acta

The only reference of Alexander of Lycopolis to the Manichaean books is that the Manichaean doctrines and teachings rely upon their scriptures, old and new.

> [Manichaeans] using their old and new scriptures (which they believe to be divinely inspired) as underpinnings, they express their private doctrines as a conclusion drawn from these, and they are of the opinion that such conclusions admit of a refutation if, and only if, it happens that something is said or done by them which does not follow from these scriptures.[107]

What does Alexander mean by "their old and new scriptures (τὰς παρ᾽ αὐτοῖς γραφὰς παλαιάς τε καὶ νέας)"? Initially one thinks that he is referring to the Christian OT and NT. However, this interpretation is problematic because the Manichaeans did not see the OT as divinely inspired, and Alexander knew that very well. One interpretation could be that Alexander meant the books attributed to Mani as old scriptures, whereas the new ones were those attributed to his students (*Kephalaia*, etc.).

The anonymous author of Rylands 469 (bishop Theonas?) states that what he says in his letter is a concise citation of what he has read in a Manichaean document (ἔγγραφον), which fell into his hands.[108] What kind of document could this be? The meaning of the word ἔγγραφον is that of an official document, a scriptural writing, or even a Scripture. So, it is not unlikely that this was one of the books of the Manichaean canon. Unfortunately, nothing more can be said, as the author's previous reference to his source is also missing ("As I said before"/"Ταῦτα ὡς προεῖπον").[109]

---

107   Alexander of Lycopolis, *Tract. Man.* 5 (Brinkmann, 8–9; Van der Horst and Mansfeld, 58–59): ἕρμαιόν τε ἀληθῶς ἐστιν τὸ τῶν ἁπλῶς λεγομένων φιλοσοφεῖν, οἳ τὰς παρ᾽ αὐτοῖς γραφὰς παλαιάς τε καὶ νέας ὑποστησάμενοι – θεοπνεύστους εἶναι ὑποτιθέμενοι – τὰς σφῶν αὐτῶν δόξας ἐντεῦθεν περαίνουσιν καὶ ἐλέγχεσθαι μόνον τηνικαῦτα δοκοῦσιν, ἐάν τι μὴ ταύταις ἀκόλουθον ἢ λέγεσθαι ἢ πράττεσθαι ὑπ᾽ αὐτῶν συμβαίνῃ.

108   P.Rylands 3, Gr. 469.12–42 (Roberts, 42–43; Lieu 2010, 36–37): ταῦτα, ὡς προεῖπον ἐν συντόμῳ παρεθέμην ἀπὸ τοῦ παρεμπεσόντος ἐγγράφου τῆς μανίας τῶν Μανιχέων. Cf. Gardner and Lieu 2004, 115.

109   Roberts 1938, 45, fn. 30.

3.4   The Acta's Echo

3.4.1   Cyril of Jerusalem

Cyril (6.22–24) repeats the tradition of the four books of Scythianus coming into Mani's possession through Terebinthus; he emphasizes from the outset that Mani is not their author, since "he is a thief and appropriator of other men's evils" (κλέπτης γάρ ἐστιν ἀλλοτρίων κακῶν, ἐξιδιοποιούμενος τὰ κακά) (6.21). The order of the books in his list is different from that in the *AA*: *Gospel*, *Kephalaia*, *Book of Mysteries* and *Thesaurus*.

> Scythianus […] composed four books, one called the *Gospel*, yet, though bearing this title is not an account of the acts of Christ; and another called *Kephalaia*; and a third called the *Book of Mysteries*; and a fourth, which Manichaeans are carrying around lastly, called the *Thesaurus*.[110]

The information, emphasized by Cyril, that Mani's disciples carried their prophet's book during their missionary endeavours is accurate and attested by Manichaean sources.[111] Besides, according to Hegemonius, Mani himself arrived in Carchar for the debate, carrying "a Babylonian book under his left arm".[112] Cyril's account additionally reveals that the Manichaean missionaries of his region (Jerusalem) were circulating their recent acquisition, the *Thesaurus*, probably for the first time in the area. Further, apart from the above books, Cyril warns his flock not to read the Gospel of Thomas, "for it is not the work of one of the Twelve Apostles, but of one of the three evil disciples of Mani".[113]

The same information is reproduced by Photius, Peter of Sicily, and the *Long Abjuration Formula* (*LAF*). Peter of Sicily, whose source is Cyril, slightly altered his words and admonished the faithful not to read the Gospel of Thomas because it was written by one of the "twelve evil disciples of the Antichrist Mani".[114] Cyril, also in his fourth Catechesis, attributes the authorship of the Gospel of Thomas[115] to the Manichaean Thomas:

---

110   Cyril, *Catech.* 6.22 (Reischl and Rupp 1848, 184, 186): [Σκυθιανός] τέσσαρας βίβλους συνέταξε, μίαν καλουμένην Εὐαγγέλιον, οὐ Χριστοῦ πράξεις περιέχουσαν, ἀλλ᾽ ἁπλῶς μόνον τὴν προσηγο-ρίαν· καὶ μίαν ἄλλην καλουμένην Κεφαλαίων· καὶ μίαν τρίτην, Μυστηρίων· καὶ τετάρτην ἣν, νῦν περιφέρουσι, Θησαυρόν.

111   See also Scopello 1995, 227–28.

112   *AA* 14.3 (Vermes, 58).

113   Cyril, *Catech.* 6.31.

114   Peter of Sicily, *Hist. ref. Man.* 68.31.

115   See, Quispel 1957, 189–207. The apocryphal Gospel of Thomas was a collection of logia attributed to Jesus, very similar to those of the synoptical tradition, yet extended with many additions. Except for the Manichaeans, the Gospel of Thomas was used by Gnostics and Naassenes. Cf. Falkenberg 2021, 98–127.

The Manichaeans also wrote a *Gospel of Thomas*, which being tinged with the fragrance of the evangelic name, corrupts the souls of the simple-minded.[116]

What we know is that another apocryphon bearing the name of Thomas, *The Acts of Thomas*, was a favourite text of Mani and of Manichaeans. Further, among the Psalms of the Coptic Manichaean *Psalm-Book* are listed the "Psalms of Thomas" which, according to Lieu, may have been written by a Manichaean disciple named Thomas.[117] However, Poirier suggested to read the word 'Thom' instead as a Greek rendering of the Aramaic word Tauma, which means 'twin'.[118] In any case, it seems that, as Tardieu argues, "the legend of Thomas" played a definite role and "determined Mani's career".[119]

Cyril, from the beginning of his account, states that he will present only a part of what he knows about the Manichaean beliefs and practices, because no time would be long enough for giving a full account (ὅλον γὰρ αὐτοῦ τὸν βόρβορον, οὐδ' ὁ πᾶς αἰὼν κατ' ἀξίαν διηγήσεται) (6.21). At the end of his narrative, Cyril makes it clear to his readers that he had read the Manichaean books, explaining that he had to do this for the safety of his flock. He had to read them for himself because he disbelieved those who informed him of what was written in the Manichaean books.

> These are written in the books of the Manichaeans. These we have read, disbelieving those who affirmed them. For your safety, we have inquired into their depravity.[120]

Cyril, wanting to anticipate any reservation towards the credibility of his testimony, reassures that he has read the things he discusses in the Manichaean books. If this statement is true, which books did he read? Probably the *Thesaurus*, since according to him, that was the book that the Manichaean missionaries in his area circulated during his days. What we know about the content of the *Treasure of Life* (*Thesaurus*) has come down to us through Augustine. The main topic of the *Thesaurus* was dualism, in particular the

---

116   Cyril, *Catech.* 4.36.
117   2*PsB* 203–227. Lieu 1994a, 264.
118   Poirier 2001, 9–28. The psalms are referenced as Psalms of Thom, which has been taken to be an abbreviation for Thomas – something that would be most unusual.
119   Tardieu 2008, 31–32.
120   Cyril, *Catech.* 6.34.16–19 (Reischl and Rupp 1848, 204): Ταῦτα γέγραπται ἐν ταῖς τῶν Μανιχαίων βίβλοις. Ταῦτα ἡμεῖς ἀνεγνώκαμεν, ἀπιστοῦντες τοῖς λέγουσιν. Ὑπὲρ γὰρ τῆς ὑμετέρας ἀσφαλείας, τὴν ἐκείνων ἀπώλειαν ἐπολυπραγμονήσαμεν.

Manichaean cosmogonic myth which included the *Seduction of the Archons*.[121] At the moment, it is sufficient to say that the small number of Manichaean beliefs and practices that Cyril recounts echo the *Seduction of the Archons*, another indicator in favour of the hypothesis that he had read the *Thesaurus*.

3.4.2   Epiphanius of Salamis

Epiphanius' work (Against Manichaeans), which is the most faithful reproduction of the *AA*, reiterates the well-known story of the four books of Scythianus, enumerating them in the same order as the *AA*.

> Scythianus, whose mind was blind about these things, took his cue from Pythagoras and held such beliefs, and composed four books of his own. He called one the *Book of the Mysteries* the second the *Book of the Kephalaia*, the third the *Gospel* and the fourth the *Treasury*.[122]

From Scythianus the books passed to Terebinthus, and so on.[123] Further on, Epiphanius, in a part of his text which is not grounded in the *AA*, provides us with a second list of books, which he says were written by Mani himself.

> Now then, the savage Mani begins his teaching, speaking and writing in his work on faith. For he issued various books, one composed of ⟨twenty-two sections⟩ to match ⟨the⟩ twenty-two letters of the Syriac alphabet. Most Persians use the Syrian letters besides ⟨the⟩ Persian, just as, with us, many nations use the Greek letters even though nearly every nation has its own. But others pride themselves on the oldest dialect of Syriac, if you please, and the Palmyrene – it and its letters. But there are twenty-two of them, and the book is thus divided into twenty-two sections. He calls this book the Mysteries of Manichaeus, and another one the Treasury. And he makes a show of other books he has stitched together, the Lesser Treasury, as one is called, and another on astrology. Manichaeans have no shortage of this sort of jugglery; they have astrology for a handy subject of boasting, and phylacteries – I mean amulets – and certain other incantations and spells.[124]

---

121 See fn. 101 in this chapter; cf. Tardieu 2008, 37; Lieu 2010, 149; Gardner and Lieu 2004, 159–160 & 187–191 (*De Haeresibus* 46).

122 Epiphanius, *Pan*. 66.2.9 (Williams, 229, slightly altered).

123 Epiphanius *Pan*. 66.3.12.

124 Epiphanius, *Pan*. 66.13.2–7 (GCS 37:34–36; Williams, 240): ὅθεν δὴ ἄρχεται διδάσκειν τε καὶ γράφειν καὶ λέγειν ὁ χαλεπώτατος Μάνης ἐν τῷ περὶ πίστεως αὐτοῦ λόγῳ. βίβλους γὰρ οὗτος διαφόρους ἐξέθετο, μίαν μὲν ἰσάριθμον ⟨τῶν⟩ εἴκοσι δύο στοιχείων τῶν κατὰ τὴν τῶν

As one notes, Epiphanius in this second list of books restates which were the three canonical books of Mani but omits the *Kephalaia*. He explicitly names the *Book of Mysteries* and the *Thesaurus*, while the first book he mentions (which he seems to identify with the *Book of Mysteries*), was the *Gospel*; it was 'composed of twenty-two sections' in order to correspond to the Syrian alphabet. Epiphanius is the only Greek source that gives this information. We now know, as Shokri-Foumeshi recently said, "from both Manichaean and non-Manichaean writings [...] that Mani's *Gospel* was divided into twenty-two chapters [...] corresponding to the twenty-two letters of the Syriac/Manichaean alphabet".[125] According to a canon list embedded in the Medinet Madi *Psalm-Book*, "there are two and twenty compounds in his anti-dote: His *Great Gospel*, the good tidings of all them that are of the light".[126] In a Middle Persian Turfan fragment, we read: "He teaches (the chapter) *Aleph* of the *Gospel*; he teaches (the chapter) *Tau* of the *Gospel*, the *Gospel* of the twenty-two wondrous things".[127] Epiphanius, in explaining why a Persian by race (Mani) composed his books in Syriac, gives the very significant information that most Persians, apart from their own language, used the Syriac, just as many other nations used the Greek koinē together with their own ethnic language. Thus, the fact that the Manichaean books were written in Syriac does not prove the Syrian origin of the first Manichaean missionaries, as was argued by some modern scholars.[128]

Σύρων στοιχείωσιν δι᾽ ἀλφαβήτων συγκειμένην – χρῶνται γὰρ οἱ πλεῖστοι τῶν Περσῶν μετὰ ⟨τὰ⟩ Περσικὰ στοιχεῖα καὶ τοῖς Σύρων γράμμασι, ὥσπερ παρ᾽ ἡμῖν πολλὰ ἔθνη τοῖς Ἑλληνικοῖς κέχρηνται, καίτοι γε ὄντων σχεδὸν κατὰ ἔθνος ἰδίων γραμμάτων. [...] εἴκοσι δύο δὲ ταῦτα ὑπάρχει διόπερ καὶ ἡ αὐτὴ βίβλος εἰς εἴκοσι δύο τμήματα λόγων τέτμηται. – ταύτῃ δὲ ἐπιτίθησιν ὄνομα Μανιχαίου Μυστήρια, ἑτέρα δὲ Θησαυρός. Καὶ ἄλλας δὴ βίβλους καττύσας φαντάζεται, τὸν μικρὸν δὴ Θησαυρὸν οὕτω καλούμενον, ἄλλην δὲ τὴν περὶ ἀστρολογίας. Οὐ γὰρ ἀποδέουσι τῆς τοιαύτης περιεργίας, ἀλλὰ μᾶλλον αὐτοῖς ἐν προχείρῳ καυχήματος πρόκειται ἀστρονομία καὶ φυλακτήρια, φημὶ δὲ τὰ περίαπτα, καὶ ἄλλαι τινὲς ἐπῳδαὶ καὶ μαγγανεῖαι.

125 Shokri-Foumeshi 2018, 45, 45–47. Cf. Lieu 1994a, 269 & 2010, 147; Tardieu 2008, 35. Epiphanius here seems to confuse the *Gospel* with the *Book of Mysteries* which as we know had eighteen chapters. Cf. Kugener & Cumont (1912), 157.

126 *2PsB* 46.20–22. Cf. Gardner and Lieu 2004, 164.

127 Shokri-Foumeshi 2018, 45. "Thanks to W. Sundermann, the Parthian fragment M 5510 could well shed light on the subject. This very interesting document, [...] undoubtedly speaks about the division of the *Living Gospel* into twenty-two chapters". Al-Biruni (*Chronology*, Sachau 1879, 190) also states that Mani "arranged [his Gospel] according to the twenty-two letters of the alphabet".

128 Cf. Lieu 1998b, 211; Burkitt 1925, 111–19. On "the Manichaean's use of Syriac language", see Pedersen and Larsen 2013.

The second list of Epiphanius also refers to a second *Thesaurus*, the *Lesser* one. Some scholars suggested that the *Lesser Thesaurus* was a summary of *The Treasury of Life*, while others supported the view that it was a supplement of the latter.[129] Then, Epiphanius appears to quote from the beginning of one of Mani's books:

> This is how Mani begins his book: There were God and matter, light and darkness, good and evil, all in direct opposition to each other, so that neither side has anything in common with the other.

Could this quotation by Epiphanius be an extract from Mani's Gospel? As he comments,

> And this is the scum's prologue; he begins his mischief there. And broadly speaking, that is the book, which contains certain bad propositions of this sort, the difficulty of which, and the contradiction at the very outset between the words and their aim, must be understood.[130]

According to Williams, Titus of Bostra (1.5) records a text with relevant content "as a summary of Mani's teaching".[131] Concerning the Gospel of Thomas, mentioned by Cyril, Epiphanius does not make any reference. Williams implies that there is an indirect reference to the following verse of Epiphanius, addressed to Mani: "Unless you play the fool by writing yourself and palming off some forged books in the names of saints [i.e. the Acts of Thomas]. Tell us where you come from, you with your primordial principle of evil!"[132] However, it seems unlikely that it would refer to a specific text.

3.4.3   Severianus of Gabala
Severianus of Gabala begins his presentation of the Manichaean beliefs saying the following, which could be interpreted as a reference to the Manichaean *Thesaurus*: "So, the faithful brings forth his faith from the good treasure, but

---

129   Pedersen 2004, 178, fn. 3.

130   Epiphanius, *Pan.* 66.14.1–2 (GCS 37:36; Williams, 240): ἄρχεται γοῦν ἐν τῇ αὐτοῦ βίβλῳ λέγειν ὁ αὐτὸς Μάνης· "ᵒἮν θεὸς καὶ ὕλη, φῶς καὶ σκότος, ἀγαθὸν καὶ κακόν, τοῖς πᾶσιν ἄκρως ἐναντία, ὡς κατὰ μηδὲν ἐπικοινωνεῖν θάτερον θατέρῳ." καὶ οὗτος μέν ἐστιν ὁ πρόλογος τοῦ ἀγύρτου. As Shokri-Foumeshi and Farhoudi (2014, 53) state, according to Islamic sources, "some of the more important subject matters of Mani's Gospel were the Land of the Light and of the Darkness, the Mixture and process of the *liberatio* of the Aeons".

131   Williams 2013, 240, fn. 79.

132   Epiphanius, *Pan.* 66.59.7–10 (Williams, 284).

the heretic utters his infidelity from the evil treasure".[133] Although Severianus does not say it explicitly, it is reasonable to assume that he purposefully uses the well-known evangelical maxim (from Matt 12:35 and Luke 6:45, which was a common literary wordplay used by many heresiologists), in order to hint at the homonymous Manichaean book. This is also the way the AA begins: "The true 'thesaurus' or rather the disputation held in Carchar, a city in Mesopotamia, by the bishop Archelaus against Manes" (AA 1.1). As Lieu comments, the "true 'thesaurus'", here, is used in contradistinction to the "false 'thesaurus' – the title of a canonical work of Mani".[134]

3.4.4   Nilus of Ankara

Nilus was the abbot of a monastery near Ankara. He states that the Manichaeans call their books mysteries and treasuries of goods things, giving the impression that he is referring to more than one *Thesaurus*. This recalls Epiphanius' list, with both the *Thesaurus*, and the *Lesser Thesaurus*.[135]

3.4.5   Socrates the Scholastic

Socrates repeats the AA's story and lists the four books of Scythianus, which he organizes in an order of his own.

> 5. Then he composes four books, one he entitled The Mysteries, another Gospel, Treasure is the third and a fourth the Kephalaia. [...] 8. Hence the postulates of these books are Christian in voice, but pagan in ideas/beliefs.[136]

The same order is followed by Theodorus Anagnostes, in his *Epitome Historiae tripartitae.*[137]

Later sources that recycle the AA tradition are the ninth century writers Peter of Sicily[138] and Photius,[139] who mention the four books according to the sequence of their source, Cyril. After describing briefly each book, they add

---

133   Severianus of Gabala, *c. Manichaeos* 15.

134   Lieu in Vermes, 35.

135   Nilus of Ankara, *Ep. 117* (to Evandrius): Οὔτω καὶ Μανιχαῖοι μυστήρια καὶ θησαυρῶν ἀγαθῶν ἀποκαλοῦσι τὰ βιβλία τῆς δυσσεβείας, καὶ τῆς παρανομίας. About the authenticity of Nilus' letters see Cameron 1976b.

136   Socrates, *HE* 1.22.5 & 8 (SC 477:204): Τῶν βιβλίων τοίνυν τούτων αἱ ὑποθέσεις χριστιανίζουσι μὲν τῇ φωνῇ, τοῖς δὲ δόγμασιν ἑλληνίζουσιν.

137   Theodorus Anagnostes, *Epit. hist. trip.* 1.33.6–8.

138   Peter of Sicily, *Hist. ref. Man.*, 48.1–5 (p. 25). Peter also reproduces Cyril's information that Manichaeans carry around *Thesausus of Life.*

139   Photius, *c. Manichaeos* 38.3–7 (p. 133).

their own abusive comments. In parallel, their contemporary chronographer, Georgius Monachus, followed the enumeration established by Socrates (without comments).[140] The order of Socrates was also followed by later sources such as the *Suda Lexicon* (tenth cent.), Constantinus VII Porphyrogenitus (tenth cent.) and the chronographer Georgius Cedrenus (eleventh-twelfth cent.).[141]

3.5   *Titus of Bostra and Heraclian of Chalcedon*

Two notable cases, each of particular interest and both distinct from the rest of anti-Manichaean literature concerning the Manichaean books, come from Titus of Bostra and Heraclian of Chalcedon.

3.5.1   Titus of Bostra

In his first book, Titus presents the Manichaean cosmogony, declaring that Mani's books are written in the Syriac language.[142] Furthermore, part of his first book describes how the primordial mixture of the two primal principles took place according to Mani's system; Titus seems to refer to a particular Manichaean book from which he quotes, pointing out that "this is exactly what they say in their book".[143] At the end of the same book (1.41–42), Titus mentions something that I have not encountered again in any other Greek source: "While here on earth matter is occupied with the captive light", God in the meanwhile, "is sitting filling up the abyss from which matter comes with earth/soil". So, according to Mani, "God sits and carries eternally masses of soil, with which he gradually fills in some depths".[144] A similar imagery exists in one of the Manichaean Psalms:

> When the Holy Spirit came he revealed to us the way of truth and taught us that there are two natures, that of light and that of darkness, separate one from the other from the beginning. [...] The sun and moon he founded, he set them on high, to purify the soul. Daily they take up the

---

140   Georgius Monachus, *Chronicon (lib. 1–4)* p. 468. 12–14; *Chronicon breve* (lib. 1–6) (redactio recentior), v. 110 p. 556 lines 10–14.

141   *Suda Lexicon*, entry 147 lines 10–12. Constantinus VII Porphyrogenitus, *De virtutibus et vitiis*, v. 1 p. 141 lines 13–15. Georgius Cedrenus, *Compendium historiarum* 1: 455.20–22.

142   Titus of Bostra, *c. Manichaeos*, 1.17.

143   Titus of Bostra, *c. Manichaeos*, 1.21 (CCSG 82:49): Ὅτε τοίνυν, αὐτῇ λέξει φησὶν ἡ παρ' αὐτοῖς βίβλος.

144   Titus of Bostra, *c. Manichaeos*, 1.42 (CCSG 82:95): Πρὸς δὲ τούτοις ἅπασι, θαυμάσιον αὐτοῦ δὴ κἀκεῖνο, ἔνθα φησὶν ὡς τῆς κακίας ἐνταυθοῖ ἀσχολουμένης, εἴτ' οὖν δεδεμένης, θεὸς ἐν τῷ μεταξὺ τὸ βάθος ἀναπληροῖ χώματι, ὅθεν ἀνέκυψεν ἡ ὕλη [...] Κάθηται δὲ θεὸς κατὰ τὸν μανέντα δι' αἰῶνος μεταφέρων χώματα καὶ κατὰ βραχὺ προσχωννύων βάθη τινά. Parts of the translated text come from Pedersen 2004, 23, 187.

refined part to the heights, but the dregs however they scrape down to the abyss, what is mixed they convey above and below.[145]

According to al-Nadim, a similar concept is also developed in a chapter of the *Book of Mysteries*, entitled "The Three Trenches" (ch. 14).[146] As Tardieu argues, "this section is concerned to develop a point of cosmology. The trenches [...] designate a series of pits (varying between three and seven in number) dug around the world, into which the demonic waste of the firmaments is poured (see *Keph.* 43, 45)".[147]

In his third book, the topic of which is the Manichaean rejection of the OT, Titus refers to a specific chapter of a Manichaean book that he seems to have at his disposal. This book apparently criticized *Genesis* and *Exodus*. As Titus states, this Kephalaion was named, either by Mani himself or by one of his disciples, '*Concerning the first human moulding*'. Titus then quotes excerpts from the book, clarifying that what follows is a verbatim quotation from this Kephalaion.[148]

Finally, in his fourth book, Titus states that Mani babbled endlessly in his lengthy hymns and letters, which, apart from revealing that he knew them as Mani's works, implies that he had access to their content.[149]

---

145   *2PsB* 9.3–11.32 (Psalm 223). Cf. Gardner and Lieu 2004, 176 (The community sing 'the knowledge of Mani'). The same scenery in *1Keph.* 1.15.1–19 (Gardner 1995, 20): "He unveiled to me [...] the myster[y] of the dep[ths] and the heights. [...] the mystery of the light and the darkness [...] Aft[erwards], he unveiled to me also: How the light [...] the darkness, through their mingling this universe was set up [...] the way that the ships were constructed; [to enable the go]ds of light to be in them, to purity the li[ght from] creation. Conversely, the dregs and the eff[lue]nt [... to the] abyss".

146   Al-Nadim, *Fihrist* 2: 9 (Dodge, 798).

147   Tardieu 2008, 40. *1Keph.* 43.45 in Gardner 1995, 117: "The dark were finally poured into three pits that he had constructed. However, a remnant of each remains upon earth, dark qualities that mar the light".

148   Titus of Bostra, *c. Manichaeos* 3. 4.1–5.19 (CCSG 82:247): Φησὶ δὲ πρὸς λέξιν αὐτὴν ἐκεῖνος, ἢ ἕτερός τις τῶν ἀπ᾽ ἐκείνου, ἐπιγράψας τὸ κεφάλαιον Περὶ τῆς ἀνθρωπίνης πρωτοπλαστίας. For the rest of the text and about the content of this chapter (according to Titus) see ch.[5], 3.1.1. It has been argued by some scholars that Titus' quotation comes from the Manichaean *Kephalaia*; indeed, Böhlig identified it with *1Keph.* 55.68 entitled: *Concerning the Fashion/ing of Adam* (Gardner 1995, 141). Cf. Pedersen 2004, 82–83. See also Pedersen (2004, 35 and esp. 189–199) for an extensive discussion of Titus' sources in this chapter.

149   Titus of Bostra, *c. Manichaeos* 4.44.21. The Hymns (Psalms and Prayers?) and the epistles (of a great importance for the Manichaeans) were among Mani's canonical works. Al-Nadim in his *Fihrist* (2: 9, Dodge, 799–800) provides a list of titles of seventy-six letters, some written by Mani and others by his disciples and successors. Cf. Lieu 1994a, 271; Pedersen 2004, 55 & 204; CCT 21, 363–64.

et il écrit dans ses livres des psaumes sans fin et, à partir d'eux et à leur sujet, il allonge par de très inutiles détails des lettres démesurées.[150]

3.5.1.1   The Question of Accessibility to the Manichaean Books[151]

As Titus states (in 3.9), the Manichaeans were instructed by Mani to hide their books and not to give them to those who wanted to read them. The reason they did this was to prevent anyone from being able to check and prove the mistakes of their scripts.

> They say, indeed, that his nonsenses are many and very extensive. And his followers have taken care to keep his books hidden and never show them to those who want [to read] them, obviously as if by his order, since he would no longer have the courage to talk about his fabrications if [his fraud] had already been uncovered. Because lying likes to be hidden, to deceive shamelessly and to pierce the souls [of people], in contrast to the truth, which is overtly spoken. They do keep secret [his texts] because they are ashamed of those who will be able to judge these texts before they fall victim to their mischief.[152]

Titus repeats his conviction that the Manichaeans kept their book in secret two more times (1.17 & 3.80, both preserved only in the Syriac text). However, as some scholars argue, this may be a heresiological topos.[153]

> 1.17: For he has concealed his books and has placed them in darkness because he feared the refutation which would be (made) against them on the basis of [lit. from] them.[154]

---

150   Titus of Bostra, c. Manichaeos 4.44 (CCT 21, 418–19).

151   See Pedersen (2004, 195–272) about "The Manichaean texts used by Titus of Bostra".

152   Titus of Bostra, c. Manichaeos 3.9.1–10 (CCSG 82:255): Πολλὰς μὲν δὴ φασι καὶ λίαν ἀπλέ-
       τους εἶναι τὰς ἐκείνου φλυαρίας. Κρύπτειν δὲ τούτου τὰς βίβλους ἐσπουδάκασιν οἱ ἐξ αὐτοῦ καὶ
       μηδαμῶς εἰς μέσον προστιθέναι τοῖς βουλομένοις, δῆλον ὡς ὑπ' ἐκείνου προστεταγμένοι, σαφῶς
       ἐντεῦθεν ἐλεγχομένου ἐφ' οἷς γε ἐπενόησε παρρησιάσασθαι μὴ τολμῶντος. Φιλεῖ γὰρ τὸ μὲν ψεῦ-
       δος λανθάνειν καὶ ἀνεπαισχύντως ἀπατᾶν καὶ εἰς ψυχὰς ὑποδύεσθαι, ἡ δὲ ἀλήθεια θαρραλέως
       ἀναφανδὸν κηρύττεσθαι. Οἱ δὲ κρύπτουσιν, αἰσχυνόμενοι τοὺς πρὶν ἁλῶναι τῆς σφῶν αὐτῶν γοη-
       τείας κρίνειν μέλλοντας τὰ γεγραμμένα.

153   Cf. Pedersen (2004, 35, 49 and 204 fn. 62). Brand (2019, 320–25) challenges the predomi-
       nant view in recent scholarship that the Manichaean Elect concealed the canonical
       books (or that access was restricted) of the sect from their catechumens and outsiders.

154   Pedersen 2004, 204 fn. 62.

3.80: [...] ils cachent leurs livres et ne les donnent pas a ceux qui peuvent Ies examiner et reprouver les inepties de leur folie.[155]

Nevertheless, despite the Manichaean secrecy, a later Titus' statement might be interpreted in a way that leaves space that he might have had access to the so-called *Thesaurus*.[156]

3.5.2 Heraclian of Chalcedon

From Photius' *Bibliotheca*, we know that the bishop of Chalcedon, Heraclian (ca. 500), had written an anti-Manichaean work comprising twenty books, which Photius had read. This work refuted "the [book] that the Manichaeans call the *Gospel* and *the Book of the Giants* and the *Treasures*".[157]

To refute them, it is presupposed that he knew them. "*The Gospel* is without doubt the same as *The Living Gospel*; Heraclian himself writes the full title a little further on, when he mentions Diodore".[158] We note that while Photius mentions one *Thesaurus* in his own list, reproducing the AA, here he speaks of *Treasures* in the plural, confirming the testimony of Epiphanius and Nilus of Ankara that there were more than one *Treasure*. In addition, Photius' testimony "also shows that Heraclian used the so-called *Little Treasury*".[159] It is also important to underline here that, for the first time, a Greek source is referring to the *Book of the Giants*, a book that, according to Photius, Heraclian knew.

Moreover, Photius' text states that Heraclian listed all previous authors who combated Manichaeans through their treatises, namely Hegemonius, Titus of Bostra, George of Laodicea, Serapion of Thmuis, and Diodore of Tarsus. According to Heraclian (through Photius' voice) two of the above authors, namely Titus of Bostra and Diodorus of Tarsus, while they thought they were fighting Mani's books, in fact refuted Adda's writings. Concerning the case of Titus, the observation is quite general and does not refer to any particular book. On the other hand, in the case of Diodorus Heraclian speaks of specific books.

---

155 CCT 21, 316–17, 377.
156 Titus of Bostra, *c. Manichaeos*, 3.9.10–17 (CCSG 82:255): Ἡμεῖς ὅλως, εἰ καὶ τὸν λεγόμενον αὐτοῦ τῆς μανίας θησαυρὸν εἰλήφειμεν εἰς χεῖρας, πάντως ἂν τοῖς γε ὀλίγοις καὶ ἀναγκαίοις τὴν ἀπολογίαν προσαγαγόντες, ληρεῖν ἀπέραντα διὰ τῶν ἄλλων φλυαριῶν αὐτὸν οὐκ ἂν ἐκωλύσαμεν. Δῆλον γὰρ ὡς τὰ μείζω καὶ περιφανῆ πανταχοῦ τῶν κινουμένων, λόγου τυγχάνοντα, ἐξ ἀνάγκης ἑαυτοῖς καὶ τὰ ἐλάττω συνυπάγει. Cf. Pedersen 2004, 204.
157 Photius, *Bibl.*, cod. 85, p. 65a–b (9,37–10,38). 65a.37–65b.1–3 (PG 103): Ἀνεγνώσθη Ἡρακλειανοῦ ἐπισκόπου Καλχηδόνος κατὰ Μανιχαίων ἐν βιβλίοις κ'. [...] Ἀνατρέπει δὲ τὸ παρὰ τοῖς Μανιχαίοις καλούμενον εὐαγγέλιον καὶ τὴν Γιγάντειον βίβλον καὶ τοὺς Θησαυρούς. Pedersen 2004, 178 & 138; Lieu 1994a, 108; Vermes 2001, 10.
158 Pedersen 2004, 178.
159 Pedersen 2004, 178.

As Heraclian says, Diodorus, in his first seven (out of 25) books, thought he was defying Mani's Gospel, whereas he was combating the *Modion* of Adda.[160]

3.6   *Abjuration Formulas*
3.6.1   The *Seven Chapters*

In the introduction to the sc, prior to the first anathema, the editor of the text informs us that his sources are various Manichaean books, as well as the refutations "composed against them by the teachers of the Holy and Catholic Church".

> Below are seven chapters together with suitable anathemas against the most godless Manichaeans and their foul and abominable heresy, compiled from various books of theirs and from those composed against them by the teachers of the Holy and Catholic Church of God – chapters showing how those who wish to repent with their whole soul and their whole heart must anathematize their former heresy and give full satisfaction to us Christians.[161]

Since the information given by the author of the sc is accurate and unique in the patristic literature, his claim is of particular importance, and we have every reason to believe that he really had access to the Manichaean books. Other authors who declare something similar are Cyril and Titus of Bostra.

In the second anathema, the converted Manichaean had to anathematize "all the Manichaean books" (πάσας τὰς μανιχαϊκὰς βίβλους), in addition to Mani, his forerunners, his disciples, and the hierarchy of the Manichaean community.

> I anathematize all the Manichaean books, the one which they call *Treasure* and their dead and death bearing Gospel which they in their error call *Living Gospel*, they by doing so having mortified themselves apart from God, and that which they call the *Book of the Secrets* and that of the *Mysteries* and that of the *Recollections* and that which refutes the Law and the holy Moses and the other prophets composed by Adda and Adeimantos, and the so-called *Heptalogue* of Agapius and Agapius

---

160   Photius, *Bibl.*, cod. 85, 65b.4–16. Cf. Lieu 1992, 91.

161   sc intr. (lines 1–8) (Lieu 1994a, 234 & 2010, 116–17): Κεφάλαια ἑπτὰ σὺν ἀναθεματισμοῖς προσφόροις κατὰ τῶν ἀθεωτάτων Μανιχαίων καὶ τῆς μιαρᾶς αὐτῶν καὶ θεοστυγοῦς αἱρέσεως, συνηγμένα ἐκ διαφόρων αὐτῶν βιβλίων καὶ ἐξ ὧν κατ᾽ αὐτῶν συνεγράψαντο οἱ τῆς ἁγίας τοῦ θεοῦ καθολικῆς ἐκκλησίας διδάσκαλοι, καὶ παριστῶντα πῶς δεῖ τούτους ἐξ ὅλης ψυχῆς καὶ ἐξ ὅλης καρδίας μετανοεῖν βουλομένους ἀναθεματίζειν τὴν γενομένην αὐτῶν αἵρεσιν καὶ ἡμᾶς τοὺς Χριστιανοὺς πληροφορεῖν.

himself and every book of theirs together with the *Epistles* of the most godless Manichaeus and every so-called *prayer* of theirs – as being full of sorcery and paying homage to the Devil their father.[162]

In the above list of the *sc*, five out of the seven canonical books of Mani are mentioned, namely: *Thesaurus* (Θησαυρὸν), *Living Gospel* (Ζῶν εὐαγγέλιον), *Book of Mysteries* (βίβλον τῶν Μυστηρίων), the *Epistles of Mani* (τῶν ἐπιστολῶν τοῦ ... Μανιχαίου), and the Manichaean *Prayers* (καὶ πᾶσαν εὐχὴν αὐτῶν). Two books of the canon are omitted: *The Treatise* (*Pragmateia*) and *The Book of the Giants* (quoted solely by Heraclian). However, according to the Manichaean sources, these two books, along with *the Book of Mysteries*, could count as one. In *Kephalaion* 148 it is expressly declared that "these three writings form only a single one".[163] As Tardieu argues, commenting on it (*Keph.* 148), "by placing the three books concerned with the exposition of mythology together in this way, the Manichaean sources themselves show that the primitive and authentic heptateuch can *also* be considered as a pentateuch. This view is confirmed by the testimony of the Manichaean Felix".[164] It is true that earlier authors did refer to all of the five canonical books mentioned in the *Seven Chapters*, but none of them has mentioned all of them together.

Some remarks are necessary here concerning the four new books in the list of the *Seven Chapters*:

1) The *Book of Secrets* (βίβλον τῶν Ἀποκρύφων) which is presented "as distinct from the *Book of Mysteries*" is unattested in Manichaean sources.[165] It is also mentioned by the LAF (fifth in order), but by no other source.

2) It has been argued that the *Book of Recollections* probably recorded Mani's biography and the early history of Manichaeism. It was found in Medinet Madi but has been very poorly preserved. It has been suggested that the

---

162   *sc*, ch. 2 (lines 40–51) (Lieu 2010, 118–19): Ἀναθεματίζω πάσας τὰς μανιχαϊκὰς βίβλους, τὸν λεγόμενον παρ' αὐτοῖς Θησαυρὸν καὶ τὸ νεκρὸν καὶ θανατηφόρον αὐτῶν Εὐαγγέλιον, ὃ ἐκεῖνοι πλανώμενοι Ζῶν εὐαγγέλιον ἀποκαλοῦσι, νεκρωθέντες ἐντεῦθεν ἤδη ἀπὸ θεοῦ, καὶ τὴν παρ' αὐτοῖς ὀνομαζομένην βίβλον τῶν Ἀποκρύφων καὶ τὴν τῶν Μυστηρίων καὶ τὴν τῶν Ἀπομνημονευμάτων καὶ τὴν κατὰ τοῦ νόμου καὶ τοῦ ἁγίου Μωϋσέως καὶ τῶν ἄλλων προφητῶν Ἀδδᾶ καὶ Ἀδειμάντου συγγραφήν, καὶ τὴν λεγομένην Ἑπτάλογον Ἀγαπίου καὶ αὐτὸν Ἀγάπιον καὶ πᾶσαν αὐτῶν βίβλον μετὰ καὶ τῶν ἐπιστολῶν τοῦ ἀθεωτάτου Μανιχαίου καὶ πᾶσαν εὐχὴν αὐτῶν λεγομένην, οἷα γοη-τείας οὖσαν ἀνάπλεω καὶ τὸν διάβολον, τὸν αὐτῶν πατέρα, θεραπεύουσαν.

163   *1Keph.* 148, see Tardieu 2008, 49.

164   Tardieu 2008, 49: "Felix ... during his debate with Augustine in December 404 referred to the five *auctores* (*Contra felicem*, I, 14)-that is, to the totality of Mani's works, classified as a pentateuch for reasons of theological concordance, as the very title of *Keph.* 148 makes clear: 'On the Five Books insofar as They Belong to the Five Fathers'".

165   Lieu 1994a, 269.

CMC could have been the first part of the *Book of Recollections* in Greek, but there is no evidence for this.[166]

3) The writing of Adda and Adeimantos, which was directed against the Jewish Law and prophets, is a work based on the *Antitheses* of Marcion; it combats the OT with a parallel juxtaposition of corresponding passages in the OT and NT to prove the contradiction between the two testaments.[167] As said above, according to Heraclian, both Titus of Bostra and Diodorus of Tarsus combated Adda's writings.[168]

4) Lastly, both Agapius and his work *Heptalogue* (Ἑπτάλογον Ἀγαπίου), which is anathematized as a Manichaean work, are unattested in Manichaean sources. I will further examine the case of Agapius and his work in ch.[7], section 3.6.[169]

At the beginning of the second anathema, there is a reference to the *Zaradean prayers*, which Mani allegedly had composed in honour of Zoroaster. As far as I know, we still do not know whether such a Manichaean work existed.[170]

> I anathematize Manes [...] and Zarades, whom he [...] also calls [...] the Sun and therefore compiled the Zaradean prayers for the successors of his own (i.e. Manes') error.[171]

Other references to the Manichaean books, specifically to their magical works, are found in the third anathema. The converted Manichaean, after anathematizing in detail the whole Manichaean pantheon, concluded:

> I anathematize all these myths and condemn them [...] and to put it simply, (I anathematize) whatever is contained in the Manichaean books, especially their magical works.[172]

---

166   Lieu 1994a, 270.

167   Lieu 1994a, 270. This work was refuted by Augustine. About Augustine's text see Van den Berg 2010 and Baker-Brian 2006.

168   Photius, *Bibl.*, cod. 85, 65.b 4–20.

169   Lieu 1994a, 270–71, 123.

170   Further about the Zaradean prayers see Lieu 1994a, 261. Cf. Dilley 2015, 134. On Zoroastrian motifs in the Manichaean texts see also Sundermann, 2008.

171   *SC*, ch. 2 (lines 27–33) (Lieu 2010, 116–19): Ἀναθεματίζω Μάνην [...] καὶ Ζαραδήν, [...] ὃν καὶ ἥλιον ἀποκαλεῖ, ὥστε καὶ Ζαραδίας εὐχὰς συνθεῖναι τοῖς διαδόχοις τῆς αὐτοῦ πλάνης.

172   *SC*, ch. 3 (lines 81–82, 85–87) (Lieu 2010, 118–19): Τοὺς μύθους τούτους ἅπαντας ἀναθεματίζω καὶ καταθεματίζω [...] καὶ ἁπλῶς εἰπεῖν ὅσα ταῖς μανιχαϊκαῖς, μᾶλλον δὲ ταῖς γοητευτικαῖς αὐτῶν περιέχεται βίβλοις.

In the last, seventh, chapter/anathema is anathematized a book entitled *Theosophy*, which equates Judaism, Hellenism, Christianity, and Manichaeism. It was written by a certain Aristocritus whose motive was "to make all men Manichaeans".

> I anathematize in the same way that most atheistic book of Aristocritus which he entitled *Theosophy*, through which he tries to demonstrate that Judaism, Hellenism, Christianity and Manichaeism are one and the same doctrine, with no other ulterior motive than to make all men Manichaeans, as far as he can.[173]

However, "we do not now possess a work entitled *Theosophy* by Aristocritus"; moreover, there is no other reference anywhere else linking such a book to Manichaeism.[174]

3.6.2 *Long* and *Short Abjuration Formulas*

The list of the books in the LAF is exactly the same as that in the SC, while the list in the SAF is different. According to the latter, the books composed by Mani himself were five, namely the *Living Gospel*, the *Treasure of Life*, the *Collection of Letters*, the *Book of Mysteries*, and the *Treatise of the Giants*.

> Anathema to Mani otherwise known as Manichaeus and Cubricus and to his doctrines and all that is expounded or composed by him and those who have been persuaded by him and, as I have said before, the five books which are impiously set forth by him. He entitled them: the *Living Gospel* (which in actual fact causes death), the *Treasure of Life* (which truly is the treasure of death). And I anathematize (his) *The Collection of Letters* and the *(Book) of Mysteries* which is intended by them for the overturning of the Law and the holy Prophets,[175] and the *Treatise of the Giants* and the

---

173   SC, ch. 7 (lines 222–227) (Lieu 2010, 124–25): ἀναθεματίζω κατὰ τὸν ὅμοιον τρόπον καὶ τὴν ἀθεωτάτην βίβλον Ἀριστοκρίτου, ἣν ἐκεῖνος Θεοσοφίαν ἐπέγραψεν, δι᾽ ἧς πειρᾶται δεικνύναι τὸν Ἰουδαϊσμὸν καὶ τὸν Ἑλληνισμὸν καὶ τὸν Χριστιανισμὸν καὶ τὸν Μανιχαϊσμὸν ἓν εἶναι καὶ τὸ αὐτὸ δόγμα.

174   About Aristocritus, see Lieu 1994a, 295–96.

175   Both the SAF and the LAF state that the *Book of Mysteries* refuted the Law and the Prophets. Cf. Bennett, 2001a, 47. Incidentally (?), according to the *Compendium of Manichaean doctrines* the *Mysteries* (4th book in the list) is characterized as 'the sacred book of secret law' (Haloun and Henning 1952, 194).

so-called Heptalogus of Agapios and Agapios himself and every book of
theirs and every prayer uttered by them, especially the sorcery.[176]

The *SAF* is the second Greek source (after Heraclian) that mentions the
Treatise of the Giants. Instead of τὴν Τῶν γιγάντων πραγματείαν, Goar's text gives
τὴν τῶν πάντων πραγματείαν. According to Lieu this is a misreading "and appears
to be a crasis of the titles of two Manichaean works, *The Book of the Giants*
and *Treatise (Pragmateia)*".[177] It is strange that the latter (*Pragmateia*) is not
mentioned as a book of the Manichaean canon by any other Greek source,
since according to Tardieu, "the picturesque aspect of its accounts of the birth
of the gods and of men furnished heresiologists with a great many piquant and
comical details, well suited to confound and ridicule the disciples of a teller of
such tales".[178] It is also worth noting, that while the *SAF* refers to a book (?) of
prayers (πᾶσαν εὐχὴν),[179] it does not include it among Mani's writings. Another
source that gives the titles of the Manichaean books is Timothy the Presbyter
(late sixth-early seventh century). Timothy starts his list with the books of the
SAF, including the prayers, and listing them with almost the same order. Then,
he adds some of those previously mentioned works (*Heptalogue* of Agapius,
Kephalaia, *Gospel of Thomas*), as well some new titles. He also states that these
books are the innovation of Mani's followers.[180]

3.6.3   Some Remarks from the Comparison of the Abjuration Formulas
As we can observe in table (2), the main source of Timothy's *De receptione haereticorum* was the *SAF* while the source of the compiler of the *LAF* was the *SC*.
Among the many similarities between the *SAF* and Timothy, it is characteristic
that in both texts "the title of the *Epistles* is given as the 'Collected Letters'

---

176   *SAF* (e cod. Barb. gr. 336, sec. 148) (*SAF* in Lieu 2010, 132–33, slightly altered): Ἀνάθεμα
        Μάνεντι ἤτοι Μανιχαίῳ τῷ κα(ὶ) Κουβρίκῳ καὶ τοῖς δόγμασιν αὐτοῦ καὶ πᾶσι(ν) τοῖς ἐκτεθεῖσι
        καὶ συγγραφε(ῖ)σι(ν) παρ' αὐτοῦ καὶ πᾶσι(ν) τοῖς π(ε)ιθομένοις αὐτῷ καὶ τοῖς, ὡς προεῖπον,
        παρ' αὐτοῦ ἀσεβῶς ἐκτεθε(ῖ)σι(ν) πέντε βίβλοις, ἃ καὶ ἐκάλεσεν οὗτος τὸ ζῶν εὐαγγέλιον, ὅπερ
        νεκροποιεῖ, καὶ τὸν θησαυρὸν τῆς ζωῆς, ὅπερ ἐστί(ν) θησαυρὸς θανάτου, καὶ ⟨τὴν⟩ τῶν ἐπιστο-
        λῶν ὁμάδα, καὶ τὴν τῶν μυστηρίων, ἥτις ἐστί(ν) πρὸς τὴν ἐπιτηδευθεῖσαν αὐτοῖς ἀνατροπὴν τοῦ
        νόμου καὶ τῶν ἁγίων προφητῶν, καὶ τὴν τῶν γιγάντων πραγματείαν, καὶ τὴν λεγομένην ἑπτά-
        λογον Ἀγαπίου, καὶ αὐτὸν Ἀγάπιον καὶ πᾶσαν αὐτῶ⟨ν⟩ βίβλον, καὶ πᾶσαν εὐχὴν παρ' αὐτῶ⟨ν⟩
        λεγομένην, μᾶλλον δὲ γοητ(ε)ίαν.
177   Lieu 1994a, 230.
178   Tardieu 2008, 42–43.
179   If "πᾶσαν εὐχὴν" refers to the book of Prayers.
180   Timothy the Presbyter, *Recept. Haer.* (PG 86ᴬ:12–73; 20–24, 21): Οἱ δ' ἀπ' αὐτοῦ θεοστυγεῖς
        Μανιχαῖοι καινοτομοῦσιν ἑαυτοῖς δαιμονιώδη βιβλία ἅπερ εἰσὶ τάδε. The term 'innovation' in
        Late Antiquity had a negative content. Cf. Athanassiadi 2018, 145.

(τῶν ἐπιστολῶν ὁμάδα)".[181] As Lieu notes, "the similarity between the list of Mani's writings in the *Short Formula* and the one provided by Timothy requires further investigation as does the question of the source of the differences between the *Short Formula* and the other two formulas".[182] However, as both Timothy and (mainly) the *LAF* are later sources that draw information from the *SAF* and the *SC* respectively, the similarities are to be expected. What I think is worth investigating are the deviations (and their cause) between the two earlier sources (i.e. the *SC* and *SAF*). I will deal with this question at the end of next section.

TABLE 2   The Manichaean canon in the abjuration formulas tradition

Kephalaia (Intr.) 5,22–25/Homilies 25.1–6/Chinese Compendium	Seven chapters	Short abjuration formula	Long abjuration formula	Timothy[a]
The Great Gospel (1) The Gospel (1) The great yinglun (= Evangelion): 'book of wisdom which thoroughly understands the roots and origins of the entire doctrines' (1)	(2) The Living Gospel τὸ νεκρὸν καὶ θανα- τηφόρον αὐτῶν Εὐαγγέλιον, ὃ ἐκεῖνοι πλανώμενοι Ζῶν εὐαγγέλιον ἀποκαλοῦσι	(1) The Living Gospel τὸ Ζῶν εὐαγ- γέλιον, ὅπερ νεκροποιεῖ	(2) The death-bearing Gospel τὸ νεκροποιόν αὐτῷ εὐαγγέλιον, ὅπερ Ζῶν καλοῦσι	(1) The Living Gospel Τὸ Ζῶν Εὐαγγέλιον
The Treasury of Life (2) The Treasury of Life (2) 'the sacred book of the treasure of pure life' (2)	(1) The Treasure Θησαυρὸν	(2) The Treasure of Life τὸν Θησαυρὸν τῆς ζωῆς, ὅπερ ἐστὶν θησαυρὸς θανάτου	(3) The Treasure of Life Θησαυρὸν ζωῆς	(2) The Treasure of Life Ὁ Θησαυρὸς τῆς ζωῆς

a   Timothy's list provides, additionally, the following titles: The *Kephalaia* (7), The *Gospel of Thomas* (9), The *Gospel of Philip* (10), The *Acts of the Apostle Andrew* (11), The *Fifteenth Epistles to the Laodiceans* (12), The so called *Infancy of the Lord* (13).

181   Lieu 1994a, 271 & 230.
182   Lieu 1994a, 230.

TABLE 2   The Manichaean canon in the abjuration formulas tradition (*cont.*)

Kephalaia (Intr.) 5,22–25/Homilies 25.1–6/Chinese Compendium	Seven chapters	Short abjuration formula	Long abjuration formula	Timothy
the Pragmateia (3) the Pragmateia (3) 'book of instruction which testifies the past' (5)	–	–	–	–
the Book of the Mysteries (4) the Book of the Mysteries (4) 'the sacred book of secret law' (4)	(4) The (Book) of Mysteries [βίβλον] τὴν τῶν Μυστηρίων	(4) The (Book) of Mysteries (described as an anti-O.T. work) τὴν Τῶν μυστηρίων	(4) The (Book) of Mysteries Μυστηρίων βίβλον	(4) The (Book) of Mysteries Ἡ τῶν Μυστηρίων
the scripture I have written for the Parthians (5)[b] The Book of the Giants (5) The 'book of the strong heroes' (6)	–	(5) The Treatise (Book) of the Giants τὴν Τῶν γιγάντων πραγματείαν	–	(8) The Treatise (Book) of the Giants Ἡ τῶν Γιγάντων πραγματεία
the Epistles (6) the Epistles (6) 'the sacred book of discipline or of healing' (3)	(8) The Epistles of Mani τῶν ἐπιστολῶν τοῦ ... Μανιχαίου	(3) The collected letters Τῶν ἐπιστολῶν ὁμάδα	(1) The Book of Epistles τὸ τῶν ἐπιστολῶν αὐτοῦ βιβλίον	(3) The collected letters Ἡ τῶν ἐπιστο- λῶν ὁμάς
Psalms and Praises (7) The Psalms and The Prayers (7) 'book of praises and wishes (vows)' (7)	(9) Prayers πᾶσαν εὐχήν... λεγομένην, ... γοητείας	(7) Prayers πᾶσαν εὐχήν ... λεγομένην, μᾶλ- λον δὲ Γοητείαν	(9) Prayers πᾶσαν εὐχήν, μᾶλλον δὲ γοητείαν	(6) The (Book) of Prayers Ἡ τῶν Εὐχῶν

---

b   In this first canonical list (*1Keph.* (Intr.) 5.22–26) it appears that *The (Book of the) Giants* is called 'the writing for the Parthians' (Gardner and Lieu 2004, 153).

TABLE 2 The Manichaean canon in the abjuration formulas tradition (*cont.*)

Kephalaia (Intr.) 5,22–25/Homilies 25.1–6/Chinese Compendium	Seven chapters	Short abjuration formula	Long abjuration formula	Timothy
'the drawing of the two great principles' (Picture-book or Eikon) (8)	–	–	–	-
The Book of as-Saburaqan, containing the chapters 'The dissolution of the Hearers', 'The dissolution of the Elect', and 'The dissolution of life'-CMC?	(3) The Book of Secrets Βίβλον τῶν Ἀποκρύφων?		(5) The (Book) of Secrets τὴν τῶν Ἀποκρύφων?	
	5) The (Book) of Recollections τὴν τῶν Ἀπομνημονευμάτων		(6) The (Book) of Recollections τὴν τῶν Ἀπομνημονευμάτων	
	(6) The anti-OT work of Addas and Adminatus Ἀδδᾶ καὶ Ἀδειμάντου συγγραφήν		(7) The anti-OT work of Addas and Adminatus Ἀδδᾶ καὶ Ἀδειμάντου	
	(7) The Heptalogue of Agapius Ἑπτάλογον Ἀγαπίου	(6) The Heptalogue of Agapius Ἑπτάλογον Ἀγαπίου	(8) The Heptalogue of Agapius Ἑπτάλογον Ἀγαπίου	(5) The Heptalogue of Alogius Ἡ Ἑπτάλογος Ἀλογίου

4   The Manichaean Hierarchy

4.1   *The Structure of Manichaean Hierarchy – Institution*
The most important distinction among the members of the Manichaean community was, of course, its division into the two classes, the catechumens and the Elect. Some of the latter constituted the Manichaean ministry and administration by assuming additional offices and tasks (e.g. priestly, missionary, educational, etc.).

The only Greek anti-Manichaean source that records the whole hierarchical structure of the Manichaean church in detail is the *sc*. The second chapter of the formula, where the converted ex-Manichaean anathematized Mani, his forerunners, his disciples, and his books, concludes with the following words:

> I anathematize them all and curse them together with their leaders, and their teachers and bishops and presbyters and elect (ones) and hearers with their souls and bodies and their impious tradition.[183]

The titles of the six Manichaean hierarchical grades (i.e. *archegos*/leader, teacher, bishop, presbyter, elect, and hearer), given by the *sc* in Greek, are well attested both in Manichaean and anti-Manichaean (Syriac, Arabic and Latin) literature.[184] Furthermore, Augustine informs us about the number of the members in each grade: (1) there was one leader at a time, (2) the number of the Manichaean teachers was 12 and remained stable from the time of Mani until his days, and (3) there were 72 bishops. He also provides information on the relationships between lower and higher grades in the hierarchy. The leader had to belong to the class of teachers, and therefore was the thirteenth teacher. The 72 bishops were consecrated and received orders from the teachers and in turn, they ordained the presbyters of the sect.[185] These grades are attested in Arabic sources, which also provide brief details about the basic qualitative

---

183   *sc*, ch. 2.51–55 (Lieu 1994a, 238 & 2010, 118–19 slightly altered): Ἅπαντας τούτους ἀναθεμα
τίζω καὶ καταθεματίζω σὺν ἀρχηγοῖς αὐτῶν καὶ διδασκάλοις καὶ ἐπισκόποις καὶ πρεσβυτέροις
καὶ ἐκλεκτοῖς αὐτῶν καὶ ἀκροαταῖς μετὰ τῶν ψυχῶν αὐτῶν καὶ σωμάτων καὶ τῆς ἀθέου αὐτῶν
παραδόσεως. The same text is reproduced in *LAF* 3 (PG 100:1466/D/8A, Lieu 2010, 140).
Apart from minor changes in grammatical forms of words, interestingly, the anathema
refers separately to male and female Elect: ἀναθεματίζω καὶ καταθεματίζω [...] ἐκλεκτοὺς
καὶ ἐκλεκτάς.

184   Lieu 1994a, 272. Cf. BeDuhn, 1995b (PhD), 76–93; BeDuhn 2000b, 30. For the office of
Teacher in fourth-century Egypt see Gardner 2006.

185   Augustine, *Haer.* 46.16 (Lieu 2010, 91; Gardner and Lieu 2004, 190–91): "The Manichaeans
keep this number even today. For they have twelve of their elect whom they call 'masters',
and a thirteenth who is their chief, but seventy-two bishops who receive their orders from

feature of each class. Thus, according to al-Nadim, the five grades represent the five essences/qualities of God:

> the teachers, who are the offspring of intellect; the deacons, who are the offspring of knowledge; the priests, (who are) the offspring of intelligence; the Elect, (who are) the offspring of what is invisible; and the catechumens, (who are) the offspring of sagacity.[186]

More importantly, the Manichaean *hierarchical* rank structure is well attested by Manichaean texts. Indeed, according to the Coptic Kephalaion, entitled "On the ten advantages of the Manichaean religion", its organizational structure is one of the key advantages that will allow Mani's religion to remain indestructible over the years:

> Older religions (remained in order) as long as there were holy leaders in it; [...] However, my religion will remain firm through the living (... tea)chers, the bishops, the elect and the hearers;[187]

Mani himself appears to have introduced the dual structure of the community and to have established the upper tiers of its hierarchy. In an Iranian Manichaean text, apart from the number of teachers (12) and bishops (72), we find that the number of presbyters was 360. At the top of the hierarchical pyramid is found the 'Chef de l' Église':

> [...] à l'entière cinq-...-Église: à son Altesse le Chef de l'Église, les 12 Docteurs, les 72 Évêques, les 360 Anciens, les Dendars élus et justes, et les pieux Auditeurs.[188]

This hierarchical structure remained in force until much later, as is shown by Manichaean sources found in Central Asia and China, such as the *Compendium*

───────────

the 'masters', and any number of priests who are ordained by the bishops. The bishops also have deacons. The rest are called merely the Elect".

186 Al-Nadim, *Fihrist* in Reeves 2011, 209–210. Cf. Van Tongerloo 1982, 274–75: "Les docteurs (...), fils de la clémence (...); les évêques (...), fils de connaissance (...); les anciens (...), fils de l'intelligence (...); les elus (litt. les justes: (...), fils du secret (...); les auditeurs (...), fils de la perspicacité (...)."

187 *1Keph.* 151.370.16–375.15 in Gardner and Lieu 2004, 109. BeDuhn 1995b, 28: "Puech considered the well-organized structure of the Manichaean Church one of its principal strongpoints in terms of success and survival".

188 Van Tongerloo 1982, 276.

of the Doctrines and Styles of Mani the Buddha of Light (eighth cent.). Here again (article four) a brief description of the task of each class is provided. The twelve teachers are characterized as the "trustee of the Law and teacher of the Way"; the seventy-two bishops as "attendant of the Law"; the three hundred and sixty presbyters as the "principal of the hall of law"; the elect as "all immaculately good men" and the auditors as "all purely faithful listeners".[189]

In another Chinese Manichaean hymn, the *Hymnaire*, the Manichaean believers firstly invoke and praise "the universal venerable Lord Mani", as the "Wise Light [...] and the awakening Sun, Who came from that great Light-realm into this world [...] Who selected the twelve great Mu-she [teachers], The seventy-two Fu-tuo-tan [bishops], The Doctrine-receivers who dwell in the Hall of Law, The clean and pure good Masses, and the Hearers".[190]

As one observes, the numerical structure 1-12-72-360 "of the central Manichaean administration" was widespread and in force in all the Manichaean communities regardless of time and place.[191] Further, as is evident, this structure is reminiscent of the corresponding organization of the Christian Church.[192] Therefore, it is surprising that it is not recorded by any other Greek anti-Manichaean source. Regarding Mani's successors in the office of the Manichaean leadership of the Manichaean church, our sources cite the first two, namely Sisinnius, and Innaios. The name of Sisinnius (*archegos* after Mani's death) is found in both the *AA* and *AF* tradition, while that of Innaios is recorded only by the *SC* (and the *LAF*), yet, without mentioning his office.[193] According to several researchers, the seat of the Manichaean leader (*archegos*) was located at Seleucia-Ctesiphon "until at least the end of the eighth century",[194]

189   Haloun and Henning 1952, 188–212, 195. See also Lieu 1981a, 157, 161.

190   *Mo-ni Chiao Hsia Pu Tsan.* "The Lower (Second?) Section of the Manichaean Hymns" (in Giles 1943, trans. by Tsui Chi), 188. Cf. Van Tongerloo 1982, 275.

191   BeDuhn 1995b, 77: "The 1-12-72 structure of the central Manichaean administration was known to all Manichaeans, from North Africa to China". The stable structure of the higher Manichaean hierarchy strengthened the perception of the unity of the Manichaean church and mission, despite the diversity of local traditions, see Lim 1989, 231–50.

192   Lieu 1994a, 168–69: "The organisation of the Manichaean Church, with its twelve apostles and seventy-two bishops, also closely parallels that of the Christian Church"; Tongerloo 1982, 281: "the title (épithète) 'bishop' (évêque), "a été influencé par l'Église chrétienne". On the question of the origin (Christian tradition or astronomy) of the scheme 1-12-72-360, see Leurini 2009, 169–79; Leurini 2013, 141; Leurini 2017.

193   I will discuss both of them in the next subsection.

194   Lieu 2010, XX: "After the death of Mani, the first *archegos* was Sisinnios but he too suffered martyrdom and was succeeded by Innaios. Subsequent *archegoi* remained in Ctesiphon until the centre of the archdiocese was moved to the outskirts of Baghdad in the Islamic period. Later (c.908 CE) the seat of the *archegos* was moved to Chorasan in Central Asia as the religion attracted increasing numbers of followers on the Silk Road". Gardner and Lieu 2004, 24: "Until the tenth century the Twin-Cities (al-Mada'in) remained the seat of the

something that our sources apparently did not know. Otherwise, the lack of any comment linking the Byzantine Manichaeans with the headquarters of their religion would indeed be strange. Concerning the other grades of the Manichaean hierarchy, there are only few and scattered references to individual ranks (i.e. teachers, bishops, and presbyters) in the literature.[195]

5   First Manichaean Missionaries in Greek Anti-Manichaica

5.1   *Before the Acta*

Alexander of Lycopolis is the oldest and the only Greek anti-Manichaean source before the *AA* that records the names of the first Manichaean missionaries and expositors of Mani's teaching in his area, Egypt. He strongly emphasizes the intimate relationship between them and Mani. These are Papos and Thomas and others after them.

> This newfangledness of his has but recently come to the fore. The first expounder of his doctrines to visit us was a man called Papos, after whom came Thomas, and again some others after both of these. [...] So, our knowledge concerning his doctrines came to us from those who know him intimately.[196]

Concerning Papos, his name is attested in Manichaean sources, where he is presented as belonging to a circle of students around Mani.[197] The case of Thomas will be examined in the next sub-chapter, since his name appears again in the *AA* tradition.

---

archegos or *imam*. Ecclesiastical authority was mediated downwards via twelve teachers (*magister*), thence to the bishops (*episcopus*), then the elders (*presbyter*), and so to the general body of the elect and hearers". Lieu 1994a, 104–105: "From An-Nadim's testimony, we know that the seat remained there until at least the end of the 8th century. "In the time of Abu Ja'far al-Mansur (754–775), a Manichaean from Africa, Abu Hilal al-Dayhuri became the Imam (i.e. archegos) of the sect at al-Madain (formerly Seleucia-Ctesiphon) – the traditional seat of the supreme head of the Manichaean church". BeDuhn 1995b, 28: "At its headquarters in "Babylon" (no doubt Seleucia-Ctesiphon) resided the Manichaean "pope" [...] This leader consecrated the twelve teachers, who in turn ...".

195   I will examine all these references in ch.[7], 3.

196   Alexander of Lycopolis, *Tract. Man.* 1–2 (Brinkmann, 4; Van der Horst and Mansfeld, 52 altered): οὐ πάλαι μὲν ἐπεπόλασεν ἡ τούτου καινοτομία – πρῶτός γέ τις Πάπος τοὔνομα πρὸς ἡμᾶς ἐγένετο τῆς τοῦ ἀνδρὸς δόξης ἐξηγητὴς καὶ μετὰ τοῦτον Θωμᾶς καί τινες ἕτεροι μετ' αὐτοὺς [...] Τοιάδε οὖν τις φήμη τῆς ἐκείνου δόξης ἀπὸ τῶν γνωρίμων τοῦ ἀνδρὸς ἀφίκετο πρὸς ἡμᾶς.

197   Lieu 1994a, 265. In the Coptic 2*PsB* 34.12, Pappos appears in a list of Manichaean saints.

5.2   *The Acta and Its Echoes. The Trio: Addas, Thomas, and Hermas*

5.2.1   The *AA* and Epiphanius

The *AA* tradition always cites three Manichaean missionaries together: Addas, Thomas, and Hermas. That the inner circle of Mani's disciples consisted of three students is also attested by the *CMC*. However, in that source, the names of Mani's three original disciples are Simeon, Abizachaeus, and Patticius.[198] Both Hegemonius and Epiphanius, in Mani's biography and Turbo's account, inform us about how the aforementioned students of Mani embarked upon their missionary career. The three of them appear together in three different parts of the texts: twice at the end of Mani's biography and once in Turbo's account. The first reference to the three in Mani's biography concerns their election as students of Mani.

> So when that boy [Mani] had reached nearly sixty years of age [...] also acquired three disciples whose names are as follows: Thomas, Addas, and Hermas.[199]

In Epiphanius' version, it appears that while Mani was in prison, he had formed a group of students who visited him and who, according to Epiphanius, were 22 in number. Of these, he chose three, "with the intention of sending them to Judaea" to find the Christian books.

> Thus Mani, or Cubricus, remained ⟨in⟩ confinement, visited by his own disciples. For by now the scum had gathered a band, as it were, already about twenty-two, whom he called disciples. He chose three of these, one named Thomas, and Hermeias, and Addas, with the intention ⟨of sending them to Judaea⟩. For he had heard of the sacred books to be found in Judaea and the world over – I mean ⟨the⟩ Christian books, the Law and Prophets, the Gospels, and the Apostles.[200]

The second reference in the biography and the reference in Turbo's account concern the dispatch of the three by Mani for missionary action. According to Mani's biography in the *AA*:

---

198   According to *CMC* 106.7–23 (Koenen and Römer, 74): Παττίκι[ο]ς πρῶτός σου τῆς ἐκλο[γ]ῆς γενήσεται καὶ συνα[κο]λουθήσει σοι. [τότε] τοίνυν παρεγένον[⟨τό⟩ μοι] νεανίαι δύο ἐκ τῶν [βαπ]τιστῶν, οἳ καὶ πλη[σιόχω]ροί μου ὑπῆρχον, [Συμεὼ]ν καὶ Ἀβιζαχίας.[ἦλθον δὲ] πρός ἐμὲ συνε[λευσόμεν]οι εἰς πάντα τό[πον· καὶ παρ]ῆσά[ν μοι]συνερ[γοὶ ὅπου ἐπορεύθη]μεν.

199   *AA* 64.4 (Vermes, 144).

200   Epiphanius, *Pan.* 66.5.1–3 (Williams, 232).

Next he decided to send his disciples with the things he had written in the books to the upper regions of that same province, and among the scattered cities and villages, in order to obtain some other people to follow him. Thomas decided to take the regions of Egypt, Addas those of Scythia, while only Hermas chose to remain with Manes.[201]

According to Epiphanius' version of Mani's biography:

> After he had died like that and had left his disciples whom we have mentioned, Addas, Thomas and Hermeias – he had sent them⟩ out before he was punished as we described – (4) Hermeias went⟩ to Egypt. [...] (5) Addas, however, went north and Thomas to Judaea, and the doctrine has gained in strength to this day by their efforts.[202]

The mission of the three students is also the subject of the third reference at the end of Turbo's account. According to it, Mani delivered his teachings to those three disciples and "ordered them to go to the three areas of the world".

> AA: Addas obtained the regions of the East, Thomas received the lands of the Syrians, and Hermas set out for Egypt. Right down today they remain there in order to preach this faith.[203]
>
> Epiphanius: Mani imparted this entire teaching to his three disciples and told each of them to make his way to his own area: Addas was assigned the east, Syria fell to Thomas, but the other, Hermeias, journeyed to Egypt. And they are there to this day for the purpose of establishing the teaching of this religion.[204]

We note the following discrepancies in the above texts:

(1)   The acquisition of the three disciples in the AA is placed prior to the imprisonment of Mani, whereas in Epiphanius it takes place while Mani was in prison.

(2)   Different missionary destinations: While the missionary destinations given by the AA and Epiphanius are the same in Turbo's narration, they differ in Mani's biography. What seems odd, however, is that the

---

201   AA 64.6 (Vermes, 144–45).
202   Epiphanius, Pan. 66.12.3–5 (Williams, 239).
203   AA 13.4 (Vermes, 58).
204   Epiphanius, Pan. 66.31.8 (Williams, 261).

destinations of the three missionaries in both the *AA* and Epiphanius are different between Mani's biography and Turbo's account. The following table delineates the different versions of Mani's disciples' apostleship:

	Addas	Thomas	Hermas
Acta 64, biography	Scythia	Egypt	remain with Manes
Epiphanius 12, biography	North	Judaea	Egypt
Acta 13.4, Turbo	East	Syria	Egypt
Epiphanius 31, Turbo	East	Syria	Egypt

Scopello also raises the question as to how to explain this difference.[205] In any case, what can be said is that the three missionaries departed from Seleucia-Ctesiphon (or somewhere else in the Sasanian Empire) and moved northwards towards the Roman Empire, "to the upper regions of that same province, and among the scattered cities and villages, in order to obtain [followers]" (*AA* 64.6). Despite the highlighted differences, what is important to note here, is "how far beyond Iran Manichaeism had spread at that time".[206]

5.2.2　　Cyril of Jerusalem
Cyril, in contrast to the *AA* and Epiphanius, just mentions the names of the three disciples (Baddas instead of Addas), at the end of Mani's biography. Also, he does not give any comments about their mission: "Mani had three disciples, Thomas and Baddas and Hermas".[207]

5.2.3　　Theodoret of Cyrrhus
The next writer who reproduces the trio of the *AA* and their mission is Theodoret, who seems to adopt his own version for the destinations.

> At first, Manes had three students, Aldas, and Thomas and Hermas. And he sent Aldas as a missionary to the Syrians and Thomas to the Indians.[208]

205　Scopello 1995, 228.
206　Tardieu 1986: http://www.iranicaonline.org/articles/archelaus-author.
207　Cyril, *Catech.* 6.31 (Reischl and Rupp 1848, 198): Τούτου μαθηταὶ τρεῖς γεγόνασι, Θωμᾶς καὶ Βαδδᾶς καὶ Ἑρμᾶς.
208　Theodoret of Cyrrhus, *Haer.* (PG 83:380.54–55). Apparently, Theodoret confuses the Manichaean with the Christian Thomas, who was believed (wrongly, it seems) to have gone to India.

At this point, it would be worth examining what genuine Manichaean sources have to tell about these three missionaries.

5.2.4 The *Acta's* Tradition Missionaries in Manichaean Sources
5.2.4.1 *Addas*

Among the three disciples of Mani named in the AA tradition, Addas is the best testified in both the anti-Manichaean and Manichaean sources (eastern and western).[209] In general, Addas is considered to be the most important name in Manichaean missions. According to a Syriac testimony "he was [...] sent by Mani to establish Manichaean communities", both in the East, (to Karkā de Bēt Selōk in Bēt Garmai, i.e. in modern Kirkuk), coinciding with the AA's testimony, and in the West, in the Roman Empire.[210]

> They went to the Roman Empire [...]. Hereafter the Lord sent three scribes, the *Gospel* and two other writings to Adda (Addai). He gave the order: "Do not take it farther, but stay there like a merchant who collects a treasure!" Adda laboured very hard in these areas, founded many monasteries, chose many Elect and Hearers, composed writings and made wisdom his weapon.[211]

In the *Acta*, Addas is also presented as Turbo's instructor,[212] while according to Epiphanius, Turbo was a disciple of Mani.[213] According to a third version

---

209   CMC 165 (Koenen and Römer, 112): πάλιν [..... ....] α αβε[..... ....] Ἀδδἀ[ν..... ....] ἄνδρα[..... ....]. *2PsB* 34. Lieu in Vermes 2001, 39 fn. 10. Cf. Sfameni Gasparro's (2000, 546–559) "Addas-Adimantus".

210   *The Acts of the Martyrs of Karkā de Bēt Selōk* in Lieu 1994a, 263: Addas "also appears in a Chinese Manichaean text as a model disciple of Mani".

211   Asmussen 1975, 21: "The Coming of the Apostle into the Countries." "They went to the Roman empire (and) saw many doctrinal disputes with the religions. Many Elect and Hearers were chosen. [...] Patēg was there for one year. [...] He opposed the 'dogmas' with these (writings), (and) in everything he acquitted himself well. He subdued and enchained the 'dogmas'. He came as far as Alexandria. He chose Nafshā for the Religion. Many wonders and miracles were wrought in those lands. The Religion of the Apostle was advanced in the Roman Empire". Gardner and Lieu 2004, 111.

212   AA 4.3 (Vermes, 39–40): "He summoned one of the disciples of Addas called Turbo, who had been instructed by Addas, gave him the letter and told him to go and deliver it to Marcellus".

213   Epiphanius, *Pan.* 66.25.1 (Williams, 252): "But next I appropriately insert Mani's doctrine word for word as Turbo himself revealed it, one of Mani's disciples whom I mentioned earlier"; 66.5.12 (Williams, 233): "But he sent him a letter from the boundary of the river Stranga, from a place called Fort Arabio, by Turbo, one of his disciples, and this is what it said".

of the text (in Latin) preserved in the Codex Bobiensis, Turbo and Addas were one and the same person.[214] It is well known that Addas was a prolific writer. As said, according to Heraclian, both of the works against Manichaeans written by Titus of Bostra and Diodorus of Tarsus actually refuted Adda's writings and not Mani's.[215] Adda's book, *Antitheses*, has been suggested as one of Hegemonius' sources, in specific, for the report of Diodorus to Archelaus (*AA* 44–45).[216]

5.2.4.2   *Thomas*

Thomas, according to the accounts of Hegemonius and Epiphanius, was sent by Mani to Syria and/or Judea and/or Egypt. Alexander of Lycopolis also testified to this mission to Egypt, and he writes that Thomas was the second Manichaean missionary who came to Egypt after Papos. According to Cyril, this Manichaean Thomas was also the author of a Gospel of Thomas. As Lieu argues, "this same Thomas may have also been the author of the 'Psalms of Thomas'".[217] However, since no Manichaean source mentions that Mani had a disciple named Thomas, some researchers have questioned the *AA*'s testimony. An argument against these reservations and in favour of the *AA*'s credibility is that more reliable sources, such as the pagan philosopher Alexander and the author of the *Seven Chapters*, give the same testimony as the heresiologists of the *AA*'s tradition.[218]

5.2.4.3   *Hermas*

If the lack of testimonies in Manichaean sources casts doubt as to whether Thomas was a student of Mani, things are even more complicated in the case of Hermas, since even his name is entirely unknown in Manichaean literature. However, some shcolars have suggested that 'Hermas' could be just a Hellenized version of the name of Mar Ammō, who was an outstanding disciple of Mani and founder of the Manichaean religion in the East.[219]

According to the story of the *AA*, Hermas was either sent to spread the Manichaean religion to Egypt or he preferred to stay with Mani. However, according to the Manichaean sources, it was Ozeos and not Hermas who stayed with Mani during his last moments.[220] Interesting in this regard is Epiphanius'

---

214   Tardieu 2008, 64.
215   Photius, *Bibl.*, cod. 85, 65.b 4–20. Lieu 1994a, 263. Lieu 1992, 91.
216   BeDuhn 2007b, 131–147.
217   Lieu 1994a, 264.
218   Lieu 1994a, 264. Church and Stroumsa 1980, 47–55.
219   Lieu in Vermes 2001, 144, fn. 320. Lieu 1994a, 263.
220   Lieu in Vermes 2001, 145, fn. 323.

claim, that he himself knew "people who had met this Hermeias" in Egypt and "described him to" Epiphanius.[221] This testimony recalls Cyril's claim that he also knew people who had seen Mani with their own eyes.[222]

5.2.4.4   Turbo and Sisinnius

Turbo, who plays such an important role in the AA, is not referred to by any Manichaean source either. According to the AA, Turbo converted to Christianity and was ordained by the bishop Archelaus as a deacon.[223] Apart from the trio and Turbo, other references to Manichaean students, we have, pertain to Sisinnius in the AA and Akouas in Epiphanius. Both the Manichaean and anti-Manichaean sources testify that Sisinnius was a disciple and successor of Mani in the leadership (*archegos*) of the Manichaean Church.[224] In the AA, Sisinnius is mentioned by Archelaus as the source of Mani's biography. Archelaus, at the end of the second debate, confesses to his audience that his source of Mani's biography is Sisinnius, one of Mani's twenty-two ex-companions in Carchar, whom he could call upon to attest his words, since he converted to Christianity, as Turbo had also done.

> But now I beseech you to listen to me in silence as I wish to speak very briefly, to enable you to learn who he is that has arrived, and where he comes from and what he is like. A certain Sisinnius, one of his comrades, has given me this information, and I am prepared to call him to testify to what I shall state, if you desire. But not even he will prevent me saying what I am saying in Manes' presence, for the man I have named has become a believer in our doctrine, just as another called Turbo when staying with me.[225]

As Klein remarks, the AA presented Sisinnius as one of Mani's retinue, without any allusion to the important role he had in the Manichaean mission.[226] Needless to say, Hegemonius' claim that his sources (for Mani's doctrines and

---

221   Epiphanius, *Pan.* 66.12.4 (Williams, 239). About Thomas' mission in Egypt see also Lieu in Vermes 2001, 145 fn. 322 & 58, fn. 79.
222   Cyril, *Cath.* 6.20.
223   AA 43.4 (Vermes, 111): "His servant Turbo was handed over to Archelaus by Marcellus, and when Archelaus had ordained him deacon, he remained in Marcellus' household".
224   Tardieu 1991, 3–8. Cf. Augustine, *Fund.* 25–26.
225   AA 61.3–4 (Vermes 139–40).
226   Klein 1991, 21. Cf. Lieu 1994a, 262. Sisinnius was Mani's successor and a martyr (Lieu in Vermes 2001, 139–140, fn. 306). Scopello (2000, 541; 1995, 203–234, 211) considers plausible that Turbo had been a Manichaean convert.

biography) were two converted Manichaeans (Turbo and Sisinnius respectively), clearly serves his anti-Manichaean propaganda. What better way to achieve his goals than to present the main follower of Mani (Sisinnius) as a convert to Christianity? Besides, if Sisinnius had actually converted, Hegemonius certainly would not have failed to refer to his status, for such information would have made Archelaus' testimony more reliable. Epiphanius' text makes no such reference to Sisinnius. This omission is an indication that Epiphanius had used another Greek version of the AA.

5.2.4.5   Akouas (Acvas)

Epiphanius begins his work with the Manichaean 'veteran' from Mesopotamia, Akouas. As he says, this Akouas brought the Manichaean heresy to Eleutheropolis of Palestine, Epiphanius' city of birth, in the fourth year of the reign of Aurelian (273), shortly after the heresy of Sabellius. Indeed, according to Epiphanius, Manichaeans (in his region) were also called *Akouanites*, after Akouas' name.

> The Manichaeans ⟨are⟩ also called Acvanites after a veteran from Mesopotamia named Acvas who practiced the profession of the pernicious Mani at Eleutheropolis.[227]

Epiphanius is the only Greek source that mentions the name Akouas.[228] Some scholars have proposed that this Akouas could have been Mār Zaku, one of Mani's early students and a leading missionary (d. ca. 301).[229] Williams does not rule out the possibility of him being a local Manichaean missionary at Eleutheropolis.[230] From the word 'veteran', de Stoop concluded that Manichaeism like the mysteries of Mithras, would have appealed to the military classes and especially to those at the frontiers with Persia.[231] However, according to Lieu, the prohibition of taking one's life, which was very strict in Manichaeism, makes it very improbable that Manichaeism attracted soldiers.[232] Besides, according to Tardieu the word veteran could also mean

---

227   Epiphanius, *Pan.*, 66.1.1 (Williams, 226).
228   John of Damascus (*Haer.* 66.1; PTS 22:37), much later (7th–8th cent.), reproduces Epiphanius' information that the Manichaeans are also called Akonites: Μανιχαῖοι, οἱ καὶ Ἀκονῖται. Οὗτοι Μάνη τοῦ Πέρσου μαθηταί.
229   Burkitt 1925, 3; Henning 1977; Lieu 1994a, 53–4, 265; Lieu 1981b, 28; Williams 2013, 226, fn. 2. Cf. Stroumsa 1985, 275; Dubois 2003, 281.
230   Williams 2013, 226, fn. 2.
231   de Stoop 1909, 57–58.
232   Lieu 1994a, 53–4.

'ascetic' or 'monk', (i.e. 'veteran of faith'), or could alternatively be a title of a highly posed person in the hierarchy of the Manichaean community.[233]

In a similar fashion, Theodoret of Cyrrhus employed the military terms ταξι-άρχης and λοχαγός. According to him, Mani, for the missionary purpose of his religion, appointed commanders (ταξιάρχαις) and centurions (λοχαγοῖς) who would become the ministers of his doctrines.[234] Thus, interpreting the term 'veteran' as 'the high-ranking missionary', it is not unlikely that the veteran mentioned by Epiphanius was Mār Zaku, who brought the Manichaean heresy to Palestine. The fact that the Manichaeans of Epiphanius' region were called after his name denotes his leading position in the Manichaean hierarchy. Besides, Epiphanius' dating of Akouas' arrival fits well with what is known for Mār Zaku, who was one of the "Manichaean missionaries of the second wave sent to the Roman Empire",[235] after Mani's death. Furthermore, this interpretation is strengthened by the following reasons: first because the spelling and the phonetic pronounciation of the two names are very similar (Akuas/Zaku); secondly, because Epihanius' description of Akouas in military terms matches the description of Mār Zaku in the Manichaean texts. Some titles, among the many in the *Elegy on the Death of Mar Zako* that reflect the great honour attributed to this prominent missionary of the early Manichaean Church, are the following: "Battle-stirrer who left (his) army", "Greatest Caravan-leader", "terror seized the troop, and the military column was confused", "Great Giant", "Hero", etc.[236]

5.3 Abjuration Formulas, Photius, and Peter of Sicily

5.3.1 The Seven Chapters

The SC are surprising for the accuracy of their information, as attested by comparison to the Manichaean sources. In the second anathema the converted Manichaean had to anathematize Mani's first disciples together with his predecessors and ancestors.

> 2. [...] (I anathematize) Sisinios who he says appeared with a body in much the same fashion before him among the Persians. I anathematize the disciples of Mani, Addas and Adeimantos, Thomas, Zarouas and Gabriabios and Paapis, Baraies and Salmaios and Innaios and the rest,

---

233 Tardieu 1979, 253.

234 Theodoret, *Haer.* (PG 83.381.20–24): Τοιοῦτο τοῦ Μάνεντος τὸ τέλος, ταῦτα τῆς δυσσεβοῦς αἱρέσεως τὰ κεφάλαια. [...] Τοιαῦτα [...] ἐνήχησε δόγματα, τοιούτοις ἐχρήσατο λοχαγοῖς καὶ ταξιάρχαις, κατὰ τῆς ἀληθείας παραταττόμενος.

235 Stroumsa 1985, 275.

236 References to Mar Zako/Zaku in a Manichaean Parthian text (M 6, Parthian, MM III pp. 865–867, Cat. p. 2) cited in Asmussen 1975, 31–32.

and Pattikios, the father of Mani as being a liar and a father of the lie
and Karosa his mother and Hierax, the historian of Manichaean atheism
[...] (1 anathematize) [...] and the so-called *Heptalogue* of Agapius and
Agapius himself.[237]

As one can note from the names of Mani's disciples in the AA tradition, in
the SC appear only those testified in the Manichaean sources (i.e. of Addas
and Thomas), while Hermas and Turbo are omitted. Further, another testified name that reappears is Paapis, who is identified with Alexander's Papos.
Thus, the compiler of the SC brings back onto the lists a name forgotten in
the Greek anti-Manichaean literature for about two centuries. The name of
Zarouas, which seems to be a new name on the list, is considered by Kessler as
an altered form of Epiphanius' Akouas,[238] who in all probability (as said above)
was Mār Zaku. This list, therefore, collects all those names mentioned by the
previous authors which appear in the Manichaean sources. Moreover, apart
from them, the SC also records another four new names, which appear for the
first time in Greek anti-Manichaica, and which are also attested in genuine
Manichaean sources. These are: Gabriabios (Γαβριάβιον), Baraies (Βαραίην),
Salmaios (Σαλμαῖον), and Innaios (Ἰνναῖον). The author of the SC seems to correct the inaccuracies of previous authors and to complement them. The only
inaccuracy in his disciples' list concerns Sisinnius. Although he is mentioned,
his name precedes the list of students and strangely is presented as Mani's predecessor, despite the fact that he was Mani's student and his successor in the
leadership of the Manichaean religion.

Another name which appears for the first time in Greek anti-Manichaica
is that of Adeimantos. In the whole text it appears three times (twice in the
second anathema and one in the fourth) and is always placed next to Addas.
The first time that the two names appear in the second anathema, they head
the list of Mani's disciples. The second time, they are presented as the author/s
of the Manichaean book which refutes the *Law*, Moses, and the other prophets.

---

237   SC, ch. 2 (Lieu 1994a, 236, 238, 252 & Lieu 2010, 116, 118–19, slightly altered): Ἀναθεματίζω
      ... καὶ τὸν Σισίνιον, ὃν μετὰ σώματός φησι φανῆναι κατὰ τὸν ὅμοιον τρόπον πρὸ αὐτοῦ παρὰ
      Πέρσαις. Ἀναθεματίζω τοὺς Μανιχαίου μαθητάς, Ἀδδὰν καὶ Ἀδείμαντον, Θωμᾶν, Ζαρούαν καὶ
      Γαβριάβιον καὶ Πάαπιν, Βαραίην καὶ Σαλμαῖον καὶ Ἰνναῖον καὶ τοὺς λοιπούς, καὶ Παττίκιον τὸν
      πατέρα τοῦ Μανιχαίου, οἷα ψεύστην καὶ τοῦ ψεύδους πατέρα, καὶ Καρῶσαν τὴν αὐτοῦ μητέρα
      καὶ τὸν συγγραφέα τῆς μανιχαϊκῆς ἀθεΐας Ἱέρακα. [...] Ἀναθεματίζω [...] καὶ τὴν λεγομένην
      Ἑπτάλογον Ἀγαπίου καὶ αὐτὸν Ἀγάπιον.
238   Kessler 1889, 364, fn. 3, cited in Lieu 1994a, 265.

I anathematize the disciples of Mani, Addas and Adeimantos ...
I anathematize [...] that [book] which refutes the Law and the holy Moses
and the other prophets composed by Adda and Adeimantos.[239]

In both cases above, the author of the *sc* does not make it clear whether Addas
and Adeimantos were one or two different persons; whereas, in the fourth
anathema, where the two names reappear together, he is clearly referring to
them as two separate persons.

even if Manichaeus and his disciples Addas and Adeimantos, who along
with the Hellenes (i.e. pagans) and Jews do not believe in the mystery of
the holy incarnation, explode with fury![240]

However, many modern scholars support the view that Addas and Adeimantos
are one and the same person.[241] The same opinion was also held by Augustine.[242]
   With regard to the new names, Gabriabios, Baraies, Salmaios and Innaios,
no further information is provided. The latter three also exist in the *cmc* and
in other Manichaean sources. The Manichaean *Psalm-Book* records Gabriab,
Salmaios and Innaios among others.[243] In the *cmc*, Baraies the Teacher
(Βαρ(α)ίης ὁ διδάσκαλος) is "the source of several extracts on Mani's early life";[244]
Salmaios, who apart from the *cmc* also appears in Coptic sources, has the epithet of the Ascetic (Σαλμαῖος ὁ ἀσκητής);[245] and Innaios, indeed, became the
archegos after Sisinnius' martyrdom.[246] As far as Gabriabios (Gabryab) is concerned, we know from Manichaean texts that he was a missionary active in the
area of Erevan in Armenia.[247]

239 *sc*, ch. 2 (Lieu 1994a, 236; 2010, 118–19): Ἀναθεματίζω [...] καὶ τὴν κατὰ τοῦ νόμου καὶ τοῦ
      ἁγίου Μωϋσέως καὶ τῶν ἄλλων προφητῶν Ἀδδᾶ καὶ Ἀδειμάντου συγγραφήν.
240 *sc*, ch. 4 (Lieu 1994a, 242; 2010, 120–21): κἂν διαρρήγνυνται ὁ Μανιχαῖος καὶ οἱ τούτου μαθη-
      ταί, Ἀδδᾶς καὶ Ἀδείμαντος, σὺν Ἕλλησι καὶ Ἰουδαίοις ἀπιστοῦντες τῷ μυστηρίῳ τῆς θείας
      ἐνανθρωπήσεως.
241 Lieu 1994a, 263–64. Van den Berg (2010, esp. 19–20), following Prosper Alfaric and
      Tubach argues that Adeimantos is an epithet for Addas which in Greek means fearless.
      Baker-Brian 2006.
242 Augustine (*Contra Adimantum*) in Baker-Brian 2006, 63–80, 66–67.
243 *2PsB* 34.10–13 (rest names: Sisinnius, Pappos, Ozeos and Addas). About the aforemen-
      tioned missionaries, cf. Lieu 1994a, 265–266, 262.
244 *cmc* 14.4–26.5; 44.9–72.7; 79.13–23. Cf. Lieu 1994a, 266.
245 *cmc* 5.14 Cf. Lieu 1994a, 266.
246 Lieu 1994a, 266.
247 About Gabryab's missionary activity, see Lieu 1994a, 31–32; Lieu 1992, 105–07. Lieu 1994a,
      265: "An early disciple of Mani. In a Sogdian Turfan fragment [...] we find Mār Gabryab
      achieving missionary success at the city of ryβ'n (probably Erevan in Armenia)".

Lastly, Hierax, who is referred to as the historian of the Manichaean atheism, clearly did not belong to the first disciples of Mani and surely was a figure of a later era. Besides, his name is not included in the list of Mani's students but follows the reference to the names of Mani's parents. The name Hierax is also mentioned by the later abjuration formulas, as well as by Photius and Peter of Sicily. Both the cases of Hierax and Agapius will be examined further in ch.[7].

5.3.2 Short Abjuration Formula

The SAF records only five names of Mani's disciples, and all of them also are attested in Manichaean sources.

> Furthermore I anathematize both Sisinios, the successor of this Mani and Adda the Adimantus (τὸν καὶ Ἀδείμαντον), whom this same impious Mani sent to different regions. In addition to this, I anathematize and curse together with all those stated above, Hierax and Heracleides and Aphthonius, the expositors and commentators of this lawless and profane Mani, and Thomas and Zarouas and Gabriabios.[248]

The first two names on the list are the two most important missionaries whose role in the spread of Manichaeism in the Roman Empire was decisive. These are Sisinnius and Addas. Further, Sisinnius, in the SAF's list, assumes his proper role, that is, the successor of Mani. Addas' name appears again along with Adeimanthos. However, as opposed to the SC, for the author of the SAF it was clear that the two names concerned one and the same person. This person was Addas, otherwise known as Adeimantos, whom Mani sent for missionary action to various regions. The latter, moreover, is in agreement with the picture we previously formed that Addas acted both eastwards and westwards (Roman Empire). In the next paragraph of the SAF, after the names of the expositors and commentators of the Manichaean writings (Hierax, Heracleides, and Aphthonius), the names of Thomas, Zarouas, and Gabriabios are mentioned without any comment.

---

248   SAF in *Euchologium* (e cod. Barb. Gr. 336) sec. 148 (SAF in Lieu 2010, 132–33): "Ἔτι ἀναθε-
μᾰτίζω καὶ τὸν Σισίννιον τὸν διάδοχον τοῦ αὐτοῦ Μάνεντος, καὶ Ἀδδᾶν τὸν καὶ Ἀδ(ε)ίμαντον ὃν
ἀπέστειλεν ὁ αὐτὸς δυσσεβὴς Μάνης εἰς διάφορα κλίματα. Πρὸς δὲ τούτοις ἀναθεματίζω καὶ
καταθεματίζω σὺν τοῖς προγεγραμμένοις πᾶσιν· Ἱέρακα καὶ Ἡρακλείδην καὶ Ἀφθόνιον τοὺς ἐξη-
γητὰς καὶ ὑπομνηματιστὰς τοῦ αὐτοῦ ἀνόμου καὶ βεβήλου Μάνεντος, καὶ Θωμᾶν καὶ Ζαρούαν
καὶ Γαβριάβιον. Goar's edition instead of Ἀδδᾶν has Ἄδδαντον.

In conclusion, the compiler of the SAF names five Manichaean missionaries (Sisinnius, Addas, Thomas, Zarouas, and Gabryab), all of which are found in SC, and three of which in the AA. For the first time in the Greek literature Sisinnius is restored in his actual role, that of the leader of the sect. However, he omits four of the names provided by the SC (i.e. Paapis/Papos, Baraies, Salmaios, and Innaios).

5.3.3   Peter of Sicily and Photius

Peter of Sicily, in his list of the first Manichaean missionaries, seems to combine information from the SAF and Cyril. However, he seems to ignore the SC, as he also does not mention any of the following four disciples listed there: Paapis, Baraies, Salmaios, and Innaios.

> The disciples of the antichrist Mani were twelve in number; Sisinnios his successor, and Thomas who composed a Manichaean Gospel named after him, Bouddas and Hermas, Adantos and Adēmantos, whom he sent to various regions to teach his error. The commentators and expositors of his writings were Hierax and Heracleides and Aphthonius. There were also three other disciples Agapius who composed the Heptalogue and Zarouas and Gabriabios.[249]

Photius provides exactly the same names and in the same order. Only his comments differ slightly, not in terms of their content but in terms of language.[250]

5.3.4   *Long Abjuration Formula*

The LAF based the part of the anathemas against Manichaeans on the SC and returned to their place the four disciples omitted by the SAF (i.e. Paapis, Salmaios, Innaios, and Baraies), as well as by Peter and Photius.

> (1468 B) I anathematize Patekios (Patticius), the father of the Mani, as being a liar and a father of the lie and his mother Karossa and Hierax and Heracleides and Aphthonius, the commentators and expositors of

---

249 Peter of Sicily, *Hist. ref. Man.* 67.
250 Photius, *c. Manichaeos*, 50: Μαθηταὶ μέντοι τοῦ δυσωνύμου Μάνεντος γεγόνασι δώδεκα· Σισίνιος ὁ καὶ τὸ ἀξίωμα αὐτοῦ τῆς δυσσεβοῦς διδασκαλίας ἀναδεξάμενος, καὶ Θωμᾶς ὁ τὸ κατ' αὐτὸν ὀνομαζόμενον συνταξάμενος Εὐαγγέλιον, Βούδας τε καὶ Ἑρμᾶς καὶ Ἀδάμαντος καὶ Ἀδείμαντος, ὃν καὶ διαφόροις διέπεμψε κλίμασι τῆς πλάνης καὶ τῆς ἀποστασίας αὐτῶν κήρυκα. Ἐξήγηται δὲ αὐτοῦ καὶ οἷον ὑπομνηματισταὶ γεγόνασιν Ἱέραξ τε καὶ Ἡρακλείδης καὶ Ἀφθόνιος. Ἠριθμοῦντο δὲ τῷ χορῷ τῶν μαθητευθέντων αὐτῷ καὶ Ἀγάπιος ὁ τὴν Ἑπτάλογον καλουμένην συντάξας καὶ Ζαρούας καὶ Γαυριάβιος.

his writings, and all his remaining disciples, Sisinnios the successor of his
madness, Thomas who composed the Gospel named after him, Bouddas,
Hermas, Adas, Adeimantus, Zarouas, Gabriabius, Agapius, Hilarius,
Olympius, Aristokritus, Salmaius, Innaius, Paapis, Baraias ...[251]

The *LAF*, which is the most recent *AF*, combines the traditions of the *AA* and
of the previous *AFs*. Among the names of all the previous traditions, which
are just listed in a series without comments, are added two new ones: those
of Hilarius and of Olympius. The seventh anathema of the *SC* anathemizes
two supposed offshoots of Manichaeism. These are the Hilarians and the
Olympians about whom we know nothing and who probably were "groups
labelled as Manichaeans".[252] The compiler of the *LAF* considered it appropriate to include their leaders in his list of Mani's students. After them, the list
continues with the names of the Paulicians.

In conclusion, what is important to note is that the information of the *SC* is
not reproduced by subsequent authors, until the *LAF*. Various questions arise.
If the editor of the *SAF* had as his source the *SC* (as Lieu argues) why did he
omit the names of Salmaios, Innaios, Paapis, and Baraies? As it seems, the *SC*
were neither based on a previous textual tradition, nor did they create their
own. For some strange reason, Greek authors seem to have ignored them for
at least three centuries. An answer to this could be that their use was purely
sacramental. The document was not intended to be circulated as a piece of
literature. Its purpose was to be used in an actual situation, namely in the conversion of real Manichaeans. Further, it is possible that the *SC* was not the text
of the anathema that was read in public ("εἰς ἐπήκοον πάντων"), but a more
extensive written version of it, which the converted Manichaean had to sign,
and which the *chartophylax* kept in the ecclesiastical archives.[253] The same
applies for the *SAF*. In brief, my suggestion regarding the interrelation of the
two *AFs* is that the *SC* and the *SAF* are two contemporary and independent
documents. It is plausible to assume that other *AFs* with varied content were
in use too.

---

251   Lieu 2010, 141.
252   Lieu 1994a, 232.
253   As is stated in *SAF*: This is "How those who came into the Holy Church of God from the
        Manichaeans should abjure in writing" (Lieu 2010, 130–31). As stated, according to the
        SC, the converted Manichaean at the end of the anathemas had to sign that he is truly
        converted (Lieu 2010, 124–25). See ch.[1], section 3.

5.4 *The (Fluctuating) Number of Mani's First Disciples (3, 12, 22, 7)*

Alexander names two Manichaean missionaries and states that many others followed after them. Some of the sources refer to the first twelve teachers in the history of Manichaeism, the disciples of Mani, and highlight that Mani himself established this grade. Eusebius was the first one to introduce the tradition of the twelve disciples of Mani: "Mani chose twelve students as participants of his innovation".[254] The tradition of the twelve is reproduced by Theodoret,[255] Photius,[256] Peter of Sicily,[257] and *Suda Lexicon*.[258] What is mostly criticized by anti-Manichaean authors is that Mani elected twelve disciples in imitation of Christ and his twelve apostles.[259] The same information is also given by Augustine.[260] Further, the number twelve is also confirmed by some Manichaean sources.[261]

The authors of the AA tradition do not make any reference to twelve disciples. There, the basic number is three. Further, the number twenty-two also seems to have had a specific gravity in relation to the disciples, both in the AA and in Epiphanius. Epiphanius speaks about twenty-two disciples who were visiting Mani in prison, out of whom Mani elected the three. This could have derived from the AA's testimony that twenty-two young Elect men and women accompanied Mani to his first debate.[262] Cyril limits the number to three, and says that Thomas was one of these three evil disciples of Mani; Peter, whose source was Cyril, harmonizes Cyril's testimony with the tradition of the twelve and states that Thomas was one of the twelve students of Mani. Theodoret also combines the two traditions by saying that Mani originally had three disciples, and then stating that Mani chose twelve disciples like Jesus.[263]

---

254   Eusebius, *HE* 7.31 (LCL 265:226–27): μαθητὰς δώδεκα κοινωνοὺς τῆς καινοτομίας αἱρούμενος.
255   Theodoret of Cyrrhus, *Haer.* (PG 83.381).
256   Photius, *c. Manichaeos*, 50: Μαθηταὶ μέντοι τοῦ δυσωνύμου Μάνεντος γεγόνασι δώδεκα.
257   Peter of Sicily, *Hist. ref. Man.*, 67: Μαθηταὶ δὲ τούτου τοῦ ἀντιχρίστου Μάνεντος γεγόνασι δώδεκα.
258   *Suda Lexicon*, entry 147.
259   Theodoret, *Haer.* (PG 83.381.8–10): "Mani imitating Christ elected twelve disciples" (Οὗτος δυοκαίδεκα μαθητὰς κατὰ τὸν Κυριακὸν ποιησάμενος τύπον); *Suda Lexicon*, entry 147: Μάνης οὗτος ὁ τρισκατάρατος ἐπὶ Αὐρηλιανοῦ βασιλέως ἐφάνη, Χριστὸν ἑαυτὸν καὶ πνεῦμα ἅγιον φανταζόμενος· μαθητὰς ιβ′ ὡς ἂν ὁ Χριστὸς ἐπαγόμενος.
260   Augustine, *Haer.* 46.8. Cf. Lieu 1994a, 168–69, 262.
261   Sundermann (1974, 135) in Lieu 1994a, 262. BeDuhn and Mirecki 2007, 19.
262   Epiphanius, *Pan.*, 5.1 (Williams, 232).
263   Theodoret, *Haer.* (PG 83.380, l. 54 & 381, l. 8).

Lastly, unique testimony in anti-Manichaica is Turbo's statement that the first group of Elect around Mani did not exceed seven in number.[264] As BeDuhn and Mirecki comment, this is probably a misrepresentation or a simple factual error, since it does "not serve any definite polemical purpose or set up any future line of polemic later in the document".[265]

The listed disciples of Mani in the abjuration formulas, which do not give a specific number, are respectively: eight or nine in the SC, five in the SAF (Ἀδδάν, τον καὶ Ἀδείμαντον as one person), and sixteen in the LAF (Ἀδδάν, τον καὶ Ἀδείμαντον as two persons).

6   The Ways of Diffusion

The texts under examination record the dynamic that the Manichaean spread already had achieved in the fourth century. According to Epiphanius, at the time he was writing his *Panarion*, Manichaeism was already a legendary widespread heresy, "widely reported and ... talked of in many parts of the world" and, as Epiphanius underlines, owed "its worldwide spread to a man named Mani".[266] About ten years earlier (364), Libanius, the famous rhetor from Antioch, reported in a letter addressed to Priscianus, the governor of Palaestina Prima, that the Manichaeans were "found in many places of the world but everywhere they ... [were] only few in number".[267]

It has been argued that Manichaeism was spread westwards through the trade routes, in specific the Silk Road(s), firstly in urban centres, and later in rural areas. It also has been claimed that the popularity of pilgrimages during the fourth century could have reinforced that diffusion. Two distinct trade routes were suggested as possible channels of Manichaean penetration into the Roman Empire: a) a land route, through Palmyra and Sinai, and b) a maritime route, through the Red Sea ports to Berenice and subsequently overland to the Nile Valley, via the Nile, and up to the Nile Delta.[268]

---

264   *AA* 11.4 (Vermes, 56): "He also instructed only his elect, who are not more than seven in number, that when they have stopped eating they should pray and put on their head olive oil. ...". The same is found in Epiphanius *Pan.* 66.30.3.

265   BeDuhn and Mirecki 2007, 19. Yet, see BeDuhn 2013, 279: "Seven angels shall be engendered by the fasting of each one of the Elect; and not only the Elect, but the Catechumens engender them on the Lord's Day (kyriakē)".

266   Epiphanius, *Pan.* 66.1.3. (GCS 37:14; Williams, 227): ἔστι δὲ ἡ αἵρεσις αὕτη πολυθρύλητος καὶ ἐν πολλοῖς μέρεσι τῆς γῆς φημιζομένη, ἐκ Μάνη τινός, ὡς ἔφην, λαβοῦσα τὸ πλατυνθῆναι ἐν μέρεσι τῆς γῆς.

267   Libanius, *Ep.* 1253.

268   Lieu 1994a, 28–30, 37, 92, 105; Lieu 1992, 97–106, 119; Van Lindt 1992, 227.

TABLE 3 First Manichaean missionaries in Greek Anti-Manichaica

Alexander ca 300 CE	Acta 300/350 CE Theodoret 5th cent.	Cyril 348/50 CE	Epiphanius ca 374/7 CE	Seven Chapters 5th or 6th cent.	Short abjuration formula 5th or 6th or 7th cent.	Peter Sic. 9th century	Photius 9th century	Long abjuration formula 9th or 10th century	Manichaean sources
	(1) Addas (AA) / (1) Aldas (Theod.) Ἀλδάς (Theod.)	(2) Baddas Βαδδάς	(1) Addas Ἀδδάς	(1) Addas and Adeimantos Ἀδδάς καὶ Ἀδείμαντος	(2) Addas the Adimantus Ἀδδάν τον καὶ Ἀδείμαντον	(3) Adantos and Adēmantos Ἄδαντος καὶ Ἀδήμαντος	(5) Adamantos and Adeimantos Ἀδάμαντος καὶ Ἀδείμαντος	(5) Adas, Adeimantos Ἀδάς, Ἀδείμαντος	Adda (2PsB)
						(3) Bouddas Βουδδᾶς[a]	(3) Bouddas Βούδας	(3) Boudas Βούδας	
(2) Thomas Θωμᾶς	(2) Thomas (AA) / (2) Θωμᾶς (Theod.)	(1) Thomas Θωμᾶς	(2) Thomas Θωμᾶς	(2) Thomas Θωμᾶς	(3) Thomas Θωμᾶς	(2) Thomas Θωμᾶς	(2) Thomas Θωμᾶς	(2) Thomas Θωμᾶς	
	(3) Hermas (AA) / (3) Ἑρμᾶς (Theod.)	(3) Hermas Ἑρμᾶς	(3) Hermeias Ἑρμείας			(4) Hermas Ἑρμᾶς	(4) Hermas Ἑρμᾶς	(4) Hermas Ἑρμᾶς	Mār Ammo?
			Akouas Ἀχούας	(3) Zarouas Ζαρούας	(4) Zarouas Ζαρούας	(5)/(10) Zarouas Ζαρούας	(5)/(10) Zarouas Ζαρούας	(6) Zarouas Ζαρούας	Mār Zaku?

a Bouddas in Photius and Peter of Sicily is Addas. See also, Baudrillart, et al. (1912, 512).

TABLE 3   First Manichaean missionaries in Greek Anti-Manichaica (*cont.*)

Alexander ca 300 CE	Acta 300/350 CE Theodoret 5th cent.	Cyril 348/50 CE	Epiphanius ca 374/7 CE	*Seven Chapters* 5th or 6th cent.	*Short abjuration formula* 5th or 6th or 7th cent.	Peter Sic. 9th century	Photius 9th century	*Long abjuration formula* 9th or 10th century	Manichaean sources
	Turbo (disciple of Addas or Addas?) (AA)								
	Sisinnius (one of Mani's comrades) (AA)			Sisinnios Σισίνιος	(1) Sisinnios Σισίννιον	(1) Sisinnios Σισίννιος	(1) Sisinios Σισίνιος	(1) Sisinnios Σισίννιον	Sisin Σισίννιος (2PsB)
				(4) Cabriabios Γαβριάβιος	(5) Cabriabios Γαβριάβος	(6)/(11) Cabriabios Γαβριάβιος	(6)/(11) Cabriabios Γαυριάβιος	(7) Cabriabios Γαβριάβιος	Gabryab Γαβριάβ
(1) Papos Πάπος				(5) Paapis Πάαπις				(14) Paapis Πάαπις	Pappos (2PsB)
				(6) Baraies Βαραίης				(15) Baraias Βαραίας	Baraies Βαραίης the Teacher (CMC)

TABLE 3 First Manichaean missionaries in Greek Anti-Manichaica (cont.)

Alexander ca 300 CE	Acta 300/350 CE Theodoret 5th cent.	Cyril 348/50 CE	Epiphanius ca 374/7 CE	Seven Chapters 5th or 6th cent.	Short abjuration formula 5th or 6th or 7th cent.	Peter Sic. 9th century	Photius 9th century	Long abjuration formula 9th or 10th century	Manichaean sources
				(7) Salmaios Σαλμαῖος				(12) Salmaios Σαλμαῖος	Salmaios Σαλμαῖος the Ascetic (CMC) & (2PsB)
				(8) Innaios Ἰινναῖος				(13) Innaios Ἰινναῖος	Innaios Ἰινναῖος (2PsB) & (CMC)b

b Other names of Manichaean first disciples mentioned in CMC are: Abiesous (Ἀβιησοῦς) the Teacher, Sitaios (Σιταῖος) the elder of their council, Sabbaios (Σαββαῖος) the Baptist, Timothy (Τιμόθεος), Symeōn (Συμεών), Koustaios (Κουσταῖος) the son of the treasure of Life, Ana (Ἀνά) the brother of Zacheas (Ζαχέου) the disciple, Abizachias (Ἀβιζαχίας). Ozeos is mentioned in the Psalm Book.

As mentioned above, Scythianus' and Terebinthus' activities may reflect Mani's own activity.[269] Following the same rationale, some scholars suggest that under Mani's mask in the *AA*, could be Adda.[270] Besides the above assumptions, what seems certain is that the routes recorded in the sources we examined reflect the ways that the Manichaean mission spread westwards. According to the *AA* tradition, the missionary itineraries of Mani's first disciples (the trio) in Syria, Judaea, and Egypt reflect the spread of Manichaean missionaries in the Roman Empire by the land route. The same applies to the Akouas mentioned by Epiphanius, who reached Eleutheropolis in Syria-Palaestina through Mesopotamia.[271] On the other hand, the itineraries of the proto-Manichaean Scythianus reflect the Manichaean spread westwards through the maritime route.

Epiphanius, in his version of Mani's biography, records in detail the itinerary that the merchant Scythianus used to follow for his mercantile activities, which coincides with the above maritime route of the Manichaean spread. Thus, starting from Epiphanius, we could map out the lines of early Manichaean diffusion. As Epiphanius narrates, Scythianus was brought up in Saracene (Arabia), where he had a profound Greek education. He "made continual business trips" due to his commercial activity. He was merchandising goods from India, which he transported through the ports of the Red Sea (Aelon, Castrum in Clysma, and Berenice) to Thebais, and he distributed them to the whole land of Egypt, up to Pelusium, via the Nile.

> Scythianus had been taught the language and literature of the Greeks there, and had become proficient in their futile worldly doctrines. But he made continual business trips to India, and did a great deal of trading. And so he acquired worldly goods and as he traveled through the Thebaid – there are various harbors on the Red Sea, at the different gateways to the Roman realm. One of these is at Aelan – Aelon [...] Another harbor is at Castrum in Clysma, and another is the northernmost, at a place called Bernice. Goods are brought to the Thebaid by way of this port called Bernice, and the various kinds of merchandise from India are either distributed there in the Thebaid or to Alexandria by way of the river Chrysorroes – I mean the Nile, which is called Gihon in the scriptures – and to all of Egypt as far as Pelusium. And this is how merchants from

---

269 Scopello 1995, 215–225.
270 BeDuhn 2007a, 82.
271 Epiphanius, *Pan.* 66.1.1.

India who reach the other lands by sea make trading voyages to the Roman Empire.[272]

As Lieu argues, the above itinerary "could not have been invented by Epiphanius". On the contrary, it "fits exceedingly well with our knowledge of the diffusion of early Manichaeism".[273] There, in the Thebaid, was also located Hypsele, the town where Scythianus met his wife and decided to live with her.[274]

> To begin with, then, Scythianus was puffed up by his great wealth, and his possessions of spices and other goods from India. And in traveling over the Thebaid to a town called Hypsele, he found a woman there who was extremely depraved though of evident beauty, and made a deep impression on his stupidity. Taking her from the brothel – she was a prostitute – he grew fond of the woman and set her free, and she became his wife.[275]

It is important to underline that Hypsele is very close to Lycopolis (ca. 7 km), one of the first cities which the Manichaean missionaries visited according to Alexander's testimony. In addition, most of the extant Manichaean texts in Coptic were written in the dialect that was spoken in the area of Hypsele at that time.[276]

272　Epiphanius, *Pan.* 66.1.8–12 (GCS 37:16–17; Williams, 227–28): [...] οὗτος ὁ Σκυθιανὸς ἐν τοῖς προειρημένοις τόποις παιδευθεὶς τὴν Ἑλλήνων γλῶσσαν καὶ τὴν τῶν γραμμάτων αὐτῶν παιδείαν δεινός τε γέγονε περὶ τὰ μάταια τοῦ κόσμου φρονήματα. ἀεὶ δὲ στελλόμενος τὴν πορείαν ἐπὶ τὴν τῶν Ἰνδῶν χώραν πραγματείας χάριν πολλὴν ἐμπορίαν ἐποιεῖτο. ὅθεν πολλὰ κτησάμενος ἐν τῷ κόσμῳ καὶ διὰ τῆς Θηβαΐδος διιών, ὅρμοι γὰρ τῆς ἐρυθρᾶς θαλάσσης διάφοροι, ἐπὶ τὰ στόμια τῆς Ῥωμανίας διακεκριμένοι, ὁ μὲν εἷς ἐπὶ τὴν Αἰλᾶν, [...] ὁ δὲ ἕτερος ὅρμος ἐπὶ τὸ Κάστρον τοῦ Κλύσματος, ἄλλος δὲ ἀνωτάτω ἐπὶ τὴν Βερνίκην καλουμένην, δι' ἧς Βερνίκης καλουμένης ἐπὶ τὴν Θηβαΐδα φέρονται, καὶ τὰ ἀπὸ τῆς Ἰνδικῆς ἐρχόμενα εἴδη ἐκεῖσε τῇ Θηβαΐδι διαχύνεται ἢ ἐπὶ τὴν Ἀλεξανδρέων διὰ τοῦ Χρυσορρόα ποταμοῦ, Νείλου δέ φημι, τοῦ καὶ Γεὼν ἐν ταῖς γραφαῖς λεγομένου, καὶ ἐπὶ πᾶσαν τῶν Αἰγυπτίων γῆν καὶ ἐπὶ τὸ Πηλούσιον φέρεται· καὶ οὕτως εἰς τὰς ἄλλας πατρίδας διὰ θαλάσσης διερχόμενοι οἱ ἀπὸ τῆς Ἰνδικῆς ἐπὶ τὴν Ῥωμανίαν ἐμπορεύονται.

273　Lieu (Vermes, 2001, 8–9) considers very likely that Epiphanius "drew material from Manichaean missionary history".

274　AA 62.4 (Vermes, 14): "This Scythianus came from the race of the Saracens, and married a woman prisoner from the upper Thebaid, who persuaded him to live in Egypt rather than in the desert".

275　Epiphanius, *Pan.* 66.2.3–4 (GCS 37:17; Williams, 228): ἐν ἀρχῇ τοίνυν οὗτος ὁ Σκυθιανὸς πλούτῳ πολλῷ ἐπαρθεὶς καὶ κτήμασιν ἡδυσμάτων καὶ τοῖς ἄλλοις τοῖς ἀπὸ τῆς Ἰνδίας καὶ ἐλθὼν περὶ τὴν Θηβαΐδα εἰς Ὑψηλὴν πόλιν οὕτω καλουμένην, εὑρὼν ἐκεῖ γύναιον ἐξωλέστατον καὶ κάλλει σώματος πρόοπτον ἐκπλῆξάν τε αὐτοῦ τὴν ἀσυνεσίαν, ἀνελόμενός τε τοῦτο ἀπὸ τοῦ στέγους (ἕστηκε γὰρ ἡ τοιαύτη ἐν τῇ πολυκοίνῳ ἀσεμνότητι) ἐπεκαθέσθη τῷ γυναίῳ καὶ ἐλευθερώσας αὐτὸ συνήφθη αὐτῷ πρὸς γάμον.

276　Lieu 1994a, 92. For Hypsele: next to Lycopolis, see Steven Armstrong 2004.

Some further remarks regarding the spatio-temporal dispersion of Manichaeism throughout the East-Roman Empire (fourth-sixth cent.) will be presented, following the production of the anti-Manichaean literature. As said (in the Introduction), passing from the fourth into the fifth century, it is possible to note a change in the produced anti-Manichaean literary genre.[277] This seems to reflect a shift of the Manichaean 'problem' from the metropolises to smaller provincial towns, or even to monasteries. The truth is that this period also coincides with a more general shift of social life from towns to villages.[278] However, one cannot exclude the possibility that this shift reflects the impact of the penalty of exile from the cities, a religious policy against Manichaeans; this was inaugurated since 389 in the Roman legislation and gradually intensified in the long run (at least until 450).[279] This does not mean that there were no Manichaeans in the cities. Indeed, their existence is implied by the continuous repetition of the exile penalties in the laws. As Theodoret of Cyrrhus complains in a letter addressed to the imperial officer Nomus, while it was prohibited to him by a decree (449) to visit other cities, these cities were open not only to Arians and Eunomians but also to the Manichaeans, Marcionites, Valentinians, Montanists, Greeks (pagans), and Jews.[280] Theodoret is the only one from the church historians of the fifth century (the Theodosian trio) who refers to his contemporary Manichaeans. The other two, Socrates the Scholastic and Sozomenus, mainly record episodes that took place in the fourth century.[281] The production of new lengthy *Adversus Manichaeos* treatises and of pagan reports (e.g. Simplicius' testimony about his discussion in Athens with a Manichaean teacher) during the sixth century suggests that Manichaeans reappeared in the cities.[282] There are also many reports of historians (both ecclesiastical and secular) and chronographers who record episodes and incidents that happened during their days which involved Manichaeans (real or imagined). Generally, the impression is that in the sixth century, there is a comeback, or a re-emergence of Manichaeans in the cities and metropolises.

---

277   Introduction section 5.2.

278   See Mango 1980, 83 ff.

279   I will discuss in detail this issue in the next chapter.

280   Theodoret, *Epist. Sirm. 1–95, ep.* 81. Nomus was an influential officer of Theodosius II, being "Magister Officiorum" in 443, consul in 445, and patrician in 449, and was a friend of Dioscorus. He opposed Theodoret and was instrumental in procuring the decree which confined the bishop to his diocese in 449.

281   Socrates, *HE*, books 1, 2, 5, 6 & 7. Sozomenus, *HE* 7.1 & 8.12.

282   Simplicius, *Comm. Man. Epict.*

7 Manichaean Missionary Methods and Strategies

7.1 Epistles

Apart from their books, which, as we have seen, the Manichaeans carried under their arms, another literary weapon in their quiver born from their missionary endeavours was their letters. The fact that the Manichaeans attributed great importance to their letters is testified by the inclusion of Mani's letters in the Manichaean canon. Such a letter, recorded in the *AA*, could have been the one that Mani is said to have written to Marcellus.[283] What do we know about it?

Mani sent his epistle to Marcellus via Turbo, from the fortress Arabion where he fled after his persecution by the Persian king. The purpose of his epistle was to convert Marcellus to Manichaeism and through him the whole province. Key themes in the epistle are dualism and Docetism. While Mani's letter to Marcellus claimed that they had discussed the same topics in a previous talk (ὡς προείπομεν),[284] in the epistle-response of Marcellus, it seems as if Marcellus had heard of Mani for the first time: "Marcellus, a man of standing, to Manichaeus who has made himself known by means of his letter, greetings".[285] From the introductory greetings in Mani's letter, we are informed that a group of his disciples (Electi and Electae) was in touch with him, and was visiting him at jail: "Manichaeus, apostle of Jesus Christ, and all the saints and virgins with me, to Marcellus his very dear son".[286]

It is important to note from the outset that, although it is attested that Mani used to send letters to eminent citizens urging them to convert, at least until today, nothing parallel to this letter has been found among the Manichaean sources.[287] The only relevant evidence is al-Nadims' testimony, that one of Mani's letter was entitled "To Kaskar", which could have been the place where

---

283   *AA* 5–6 (Vermes 40–43). On "Mani's Epistles and Manichaean Letter-Writing", see Gardner 2013, 291–314. On "the earliest Manichaean letter from Egypt", see Gardner, Nobbs, and Choat 2000, 118–24. The Byzantines were aware of the importance the epistles of Mani had for the Manichaean mission. By attributing to Mani epistles supposedly written by himself, they turned the Manichaean missionary means into their own literary weapon in the frame of their polemic against the μανιχαιόφρονες and μανιχαΐζοντες. Cf. Eustathius Monachus, *Ep. Tim. 3 & 30*.

284   *AA* 5.3 & Epiphanius, *Pan.* 66.6.5.

285   *AA* 4.2. Epiphanius, *Pan.* 66.7.5 (GCS 37:28): Μάρκελλος ἀνὴρ ἐπίσημος Μανιχαίῳ τῷ διὰ τῆς ἐπιστολῆς δηλουμένῳ χαίρειν.

286   *AA* 5.1. (Vermes 41). The same text in Epiphanius, *Pan.* 66.6.1 (GCS 37:25–26): Μανιχαῖος ἀπόστολος Ἰησοῦ Χριστοῦ καὶ οἱ σὺν ἐμοὶ πάντες ἅγιοι καὶ παρθένοι Μαρκέλλῳ τέκνῳ ἀγαπητῷ. The words 'Ἅγιοι καὶ παρθένοι' are conceived as 'electi and electae', as in *Hom.* 22.6, see Lieu in Vermes (2001, 41 fn. 15).

287   Gardner 2007b, 35.

our story is unfolding.[288] Initially, the letter was considered as fictional, as was Marcellus' response to it. Researchers thought that it was a contrived device, and argued that, apart from the introduction of the letter and especially the expression "may the Right Hand of Light preserve you from the present evil age" (ἡ δεξιὰ τοῦ φωτὸς διατηρήσῃ σε),[289] which is typically Manichaean, the rest of the letter does not resemble authentic Manichaean letters.[290] However, academic opinion concerning the authenticity of the above letter has shifted recently.

Gardner, in his "Mani's Letter to Marcellus: Fact and Fiction in the Acta Archelai Revisited" compared the epistle's structure, aim, terminology, biblical quotations, and doctrine, to authentic Manichaean letters. He concluded that "The 'letter to Marcellus' is not an entirely fictional creation of the author of the *AA*", and that the writer (Hegemonius) not only composed it using genuine Manichaean letters that he had at his disposition as a model, but was probably also holding an authentic letter of Mani.[291]

BeDuhn agrees with Gardner that the epistle is genuine, and building on his argument suggests that the letter is part of a longer authentic letter of Mani, the rest of which was used by Hegemonius for the construction of the debates. This hypothesis is based on his remark that the two main issues briefly mentioned in the epistle are extensively developed in the debates. As BeDuhn argues, if the words of Archelaus and the judges are removed from the debates, the continuing and coherent argumentation of Mani is revealed.[292] So, it is quite possible that Hegemonius' source was one letter of Mani in which he exposed the two basic subjects that Manichaean missionaries – recruited in the Roman territories – used to discuss, namely the two principles and Jesus' nature.[293]

According to BeDuhn, the only part of the *AA* that draws material from another source is the epistle that Diodoros sent to Archelaus. The main topic of this letter is the contradiction between the Old and the New Testament. BeDuhn, after examining the biblical references cited in this letter, concluded

---

288   Al-Nadim, *Fihrist* 2.9 (Dodge 799). Al-Nadim provides us a list with the titles of Mani's letters. Gardner 2007b, 35.

289   The rest of the letter: "[...] Grace, mercy, and peace from God the Father and our Lord Jesus Christ; and may the Right Hand of Light preserve you from the present evil age and from its disasters and from the snares of the evil one. Amen" (*AA* 5.1, Vermes, 41); Epiphanius, *Pan.* 66.6.1.

290   Lieu in Vermes 2001, 41, fn. 14; cf. Lieu 1994a, 150–51.

291   Gardner 2007b, 33–48, 47.

292   BeDuhn 2007a, 83–84.

293   BeDuhn 2007a, 77.

that Hegemonius' source was another genuine Manichaean source, probably Adda's *Antitheses*.[294]

7.2   Door-to-Door Visits (Canvassing)

As Archelaus states in the *Acta*, Mani used to visit private places and entered the houses, pressuring and asking people to convert to Manichaeism. He succeded to convert some of them, but others he questioned, and some others he begged.

> So how can this man stand here, urging and asking everyone to become a Manichaean, going round and entering houses, seeking to deceive souls that are burdened with sins? This is not just our own feeling; rather we should bring the situation into the open and compare it, if you are willing, with the perfect Paraclete. For you can see that sometimes he causes people to repent, at others he asks questions, and frequently he uses entreaty.[295]

However, in Marcellus' case, Mani appeared more prudent. He was vacillating between two methods of action: either to visit Marcellus directly, or to send him an epistle first. He chose the second option as the more sensible one. According to Hegemonius, Mani was afraid lest his unexpected visit would become harmful.[296]

According to an anonymous author of the fourth century, the 'door to door' practice was one of the dearest methods of the Manichaean missionaries.

> Although this would fit all heretics, as they (all) inveigle themselves into houses and charm women with persuasive and crafty words so that through them they might deceive the men ... it matches the Manichaeans above all others ... they seek out women, who always want to hear something for sheer novelty, and persuade them through what they like to hear to do foul and illicit things.[297]

---

294   BeDuhn 2007a, 84.
295   *AA* 42.8–9 (Vermes, 108–09).
296   *AA* 4.2 (Vermes, 39).
297   Ambrosiaster, *ep. ad Tim.* in Gardner and Lieu 2004, 119.

7.3   *The Debates*

7.3.1   Introduction

7.3.1.1   *The Culture and Historicity of the Debates*

The central theme of the AA, which constitutes its major part, is the three debates that were conducted between Mani and local clergymen in Carchar and Diodoris. Accordingly, an important part of the academic discourse about the AA concerns the investigation of the question of the historicity of these debates. Were they real or imagined? Further, were debates, indeed, a method that the Manichaean missionaries used to employ or is this historically unattested?

The (re)presentation of public disputations in the AA as one method of Manichaean propaganda is historically consistent.[298] It is generally accepted, that from the end of the third century to the end of the fourth century, public debates between Christians and Manichaeans, or other religious 'deviant' groups, were in fashion.[299] This reflects a multicultural environment of religious freedom and tolerance, which gradually faded out by the end of the fourth century with the establishment of Christianity as the official religion of the Empire. The new order of things entailed that minority groups, including the Manichaeans, "could no longer compete as equals in the religious market of late antiquity".[300] A characteristic example that eloquently reflects this change is that by the late fifth to early sixth century Christians did not need to debate with Manichaeans anymore. It was sufficient to ask all those suspected of heresy to sign a written abjuration formula in which they had to anathematize their previous faith.[301] Apart from the debates in the AA, there are three more debates in Byzantine literature, which were conducted by three eponymous Manichaeans from different eras: Aphthonius, Julia, and Photinus, from the fourth, fifth and sixth centuries respectively.[302]

7.3.1.2   *The Testimony of the Manichaean Sources*

The fact that Manichaeans and Christians confronted each other in public debates is also testified by Manichaean sources. "They went to the Roman Empire (and) saw many doctrinal disputes with the religions [...] Adda laboured very hard in these areas [...] chose many Elect and Hearers, composed writings and made wisdom his weapon. He opposed the 'dogmas' with these [...]

---

298   Lieu in Vermes 2001, 24.
299   Pettipiece 2005, 256. Lim 1995, 70–108.
300   Lim 1995, 104.
301   Lim 1995, 103–04.
302   I will briefly refer to these debates in the next sections, and in more detail in ch.[6], 2.3 and ch.[7], 3.3 and 3.10.

The Religion of the Apostle was advanced in the Roman Empire".[303] So, even if the specific debates were imagined, they could provide us with valuable information on the real thing. It is important to note that both Manichaean and anti-Manichaean literature record the same motifs. The difference between these types of sources is their point of view. For instance, in the Manichaean sources, the Manichaean missionaries always triumph in the debates,[304] while in the anti-Manichaean sources they are always defeated and fleeing.[305] However, despite the hagiographic or libellous character of these texts, as well as their precariousness as historical sources, the two types of sources complement each other. To contemporary researchers they offer important evidence for the history of Manichaeism. If we remove the part of fiction, the two kinds of literature are in agreement with regard to the ways of diffusion, the names of the Manichaean missionaries, as well as with the Manichaean missionary methods and strategies.

7.3.1.3 The Aim of the Debates

We have always to keep in mind that the period we are discussing was a transitional era, during which the passage from the ancient Roman cults to Christianity took place. Christianity was not yet the official religion of the State. The final Christian dogma that clearly distinguished 'orthodoxy' from 'heresy' had not yet been formulated. There were several groups claiming to represent the truth of the Christian teaching. Among these, the Manichaeans presented themselves as the authentic Christian Church, whilst for them all the others were heretic.[306] So, the aim of those debates, for which Christians and Manichaeans were competing, as Lim puts it, was "the hearts and minds of the pagan elites".[307] During the debates, both parties could count their forces and estimate their effectiveness in persuading people, something that was important for their missionary organization and strategies. Thus, public disputations serviced as a religious strategy for social acceptance and 'legalization'.

---

303 Asmussen 1975, 21 (The Coming of the Apostle into the Countries); Gardner and Lieu 2004, 111.

304 Gardner and Lieu 2004, 111–12.

305 AA 15–33 & 54–60. Mark the Deacon, Vit. Porph. 87–91. See also the episode with the Manichaean who was challenged by Corpes to trial by fire in Historia Monachorum in Aegypto 10.30–35. Cf. Gardner and Lieu 2004, 121. The following narration of Palladius (Lausaic History 37.8) belongs to the same literary genre, which captures the missionary success of Christianity over Manichaeism. As Palladius narrates, the holy man Sarapion the Sindonite (pretending to be a servant) managed to convert to Christianity a prominent citizen of Sparta, and all his family.

306 See Pettipiece 2005, 247–260. BeDuhn 2007a, 77–102. Cf. BeDuhn 2015a, 31–53.

307 Lim 1995, 78.

7.3.1.4   *Who Provoked the Debates?*

An often-posed question is whether it was the Manichaeans or the local author-ities who provoked the debates.[308] Were public disputes a distinctive weapon of Manichaean strategy and propaganda, or is this unattested? Were they in fact forced to participate in such debates due to their opponents' challenges?

According to Augustine, the Manichaeans declared that "no one [had] to believe until the truth had first been discussed and then explained".[309] The debates offered a perfect setting in which Manichaeans could manifest their knowledge. For this reason, even if they did not provoke the debates them-selves, they did not avoid them when challenged.[310] As recorded in the debates of the AA, the Manichaeans were experts in refuting other doctrines, and in bringing to light the contradictions of Christian doctrine. The inconsistency between the Old and New Testament is a common topic of all the AA debates, especially of the second one.[311] Works such as the *Antithesis* of Marcion and the *Modion* of Addas served this task. This method, according to Augustine, was very clever, because technically it was much easier to refute others than to support their arguments.[312] Another subject dear to Manichaeans and dis-cussed extensively during the first debate was the "whence evil" question, which the Manichaeans considered as their strong point.[313]

7.3.2   Historicity of the Specific Debates

Concerning the historicity of the specific debates, it has been argued that they are fictional fabrications. However, even in that case, since it is testified that debates between Christians and Manichaeans were actually conducted, even fictional stories may reflect facts. Kaatz, in commenting on the historicity of the

---

308   According to Lim (1995, 86, 103), it was not the Manichaeans but the local Catholic bish-ops who provoked those debates, in order to estimate Manichaeans' missionary influence upon their flock and populace.

309   Augustine, *De utilitate credendi* 1.2 (Vermes, 24).

310   Lieu in Vermes 2001, 26. Lim 1995, 86: "However, though Manichaeans did not generally ini-tiate public debates as part of a grand missionary strategy, they rarely avoided public con-tests with opponents less ready for such encounters. A Manichaean missionary-teacher could not afford to be seen backing down from a contest, however contrived and fraught with peril".

311   This is well-attested Manichaean method. See Lieu in Vermes 2001, 25.

312   Augustine, *De utilitate credendi* 1.2 (Vermes, 26, fn. 98).

313   As Lim (1995, 103) states, "the use of formal public disputation as part of the Manichaean missionary effort is almost unattested. Instead, we find an emphasis on aporetic dis-putation using such questions as "Whence evil?" Their purpose was not to draw listen-ers into debate, though this sometimes happened, but to allow them to appreciate the Manichaean kerygma as the solution to real theological problems."

first debate, emphasizes that even if the debate never took place, the author is well informed about the argumentation used by the Manichaeans. The biblical verses, which the author puts in Mani's mouth (Matt 7:18, John 8:44, and 1 John 5:19) "have a number of parallels" in Manichaean and anti-Manichaean literature.[314] According to BeDuhn, there are three possible alternative suggestions: (1) the debate is entirely fictional, based on plausible argumentation with dualistic and docetic elements, (2) the debate took place, but (as is supported by some scholars) Adda or Sisinnius was the real protagonist and not Mani, and (3) Mani's words in the debate originate from an authentic Manichaean source, the writer of which could be Mani himself.[315] BeDuhn, after comparing the biblical quotations and argumentation of Mani in the *Acta* to those of genuine Manichaean texts, proposed that, while the narrative framework of the debate (time, location, and characters) could be Hegemonius' contrivance, the content of the discussion (biblical quotation and Mani's argumentation) is genuine and probably comes from an authentic epistle of Mani. Hegemonius segmented this text and created the imaginary framework of the two debates (first and third). In that way, he had the opportunity to refute Mani's theses word for word.[316] Likewise, Epiphanius puts an argument in the mouth of Mani that accords well with the well-known Manichaean hatred of Judaism. According to him, Mani referred to the conquest of Palestine by the Jews after the Exodus and argued against the injustice and partiality of the Jewish God towards other nations: "He spoiled the Egyptians, expelled the Amorites and Girgashites and the other nations, and gave their land to the children of Israel; he who says 'You shall not covet' how did he gave them other people's property?"[317]

In any case, independently of whether or not the debate actually happened, even if Marcellus, Archelaus and Turbo did not exist, the author of the *AA* creates a fiction in order to narrate facts: the Manichaeans were there, actively missionizing, threatening the newly established Christian communities. Under the same rationale, the subsequent reproduction of the *AA* could be

---

314 Kaatz 2007, 117–18.

315 BeDuhn 2007a, 77–102.

316 BeDuhn 2007b, 131. This, as said, was also Epiphanius' method of refutation of Mani's doctrines: ἅτινα κατὰ λέξιν διελεῖν καὶ τὰ πρὸς ἀντίθεσιν πάντων αὐτῶν γράψαι (*Pan.* 66.21.2, GCS 37:48; cf. Williams 248: "⟨... I intend⟩ to analyze them phrase by phrase, and set down the arguments against them all").

317 Epiphanius, *Pan.* 66.83 (GCS 37:124; Williams, 310, modified): ἐσκύλευσε μὲν τοὺς Αἰγυπτίους, ἐξέβαλε δὲ Ἀμορραίους καὶ Γεργεσαίους καὶ τὰ ἄλλα ἔθνη, καὶ ἔδωκε τὴν γῆν αὐτῶν τοῖς υἱοῖς Ἰσραήλ· ὁ λέγων 'μὴ ἐπιθυμήσῃς' πῶς ἔδωκεν αὐτοῖς τὰ ἀλλότρια; On Manichaean anti-Judaism see BeDuhn 2021.

an indication that, for the later authors who echoed the *AA*, the Manichaean threat was still present.

In addition, as I will present below, the *AA* provides us with useful information about the protocol during these debates, such as that the debates took place either in public or in private houses; that when the debate took place in a private place there were invitations; that the Christians were represented by their bishop or local clerics, while the Manichaeans were represented by a group of Elect; that there were referees who judged the debate's outcome; that these judges were pagan for impartiality; that the proceedings of the debates were recorded and edited, etc.

7.3.3   Locations of the Two Debates in the *Acta*
7.3.3.1   *Carchar (Kashkar – Carrhae – Karka)*
According to the majority of researchers, the debate was fictional. If we consider this scenario to be the most likely, the question to answer is not where the debate took place, but where Hegemonius locates it.

According to the *AA*, the first debate took place in Mesopotamia, on Roman soil, in a city near the Persian-Roman frontier, named Carchar,[318] or Caschar (Κασχάρη) according to both Epiphanius[319] and Socrates the Scholastic.[320] Some researchers assume that these Greek writers located the place of the debate in the Persian city Kashkar/Kaskar in the Characene-Mesene area of southern Mesopotamia because of the form of the name of the city (i.e. 'Κασχάρη'). The suggestion that the debate was located in Kashkar/Kaskar has been supported by at least one scholar.[321] However, this scenario is unlikely, since in the story line of the *AA* it is clear that *Carchar* was located on Roman soil. Archelaus speaks of his place as a place not held by the Persians, thus

---

318   *AA* 1.1 (Vermes, 35). About the venue of the debate see Lieu (1994, 140–46) and Lieu in Vermes 2001, 16–23. BeDuhn and Mirecki 2007, 9.

319   Epiphanius *Pan.* 66.5.10 & 66.10.2 (GCS 37:25, 31): Μαρκέλλου τοὔνομα, κατοικοῦντος ἐν Κασχάρῃ πόλει τῆς Μεσοποταμίας [...] συζήτησιν δημοσίᾳ ἐν αὐτῇ τῇ Κασχάρῃ, ⟨Μάρκελλός τε καὶ Ἀρχέλαος⟩. In *Pan.* 66.11.1 (GCS 37:32), the form ʽΚαλχάρων': ἔρχεται εἰς κώμην τινὰ τῆς Καλχάρων. Epiphanius, *De mensuris et ponderibus* 551.48–50: Ἀρχέλαον τὸν ἐπίσκοπον Κασχάρων τῆς Μεσοποταμίας [...] Διοδωρίδα κώμην τῆς Κασχάρων περιοικίδος.

320   Socrates, *HE* 1.22.13 (SC 477: 206): Ἀρχελάου τοῦ ἐπισκόπου Κασχάρων, μιᾶς τῶν ἐν Μεσοποταμίᾳ πόλεων. Whereas Photius (c. *Manichaeos* 135.46.3 & 139.53.5) gives the version with the 'ρ' instead of 'σ': Ὁ δὲ τῶν Καρχάρων ἐπίσκοπος, Ἀρχέλαος [...] εἰς Διωρίδα Καρχάρων κώμην.

321   This scholar was Kessler (see Lieu in Vermes 2001, 16–17). As BeDuhn (2007a, 86–87) comments, "in that occasion Marcellus could have probably been the leader of the community of the Christian refugees who king Shapur brought as war captives (250–60 CE)". Cf. BeDuhn and Mirecki 2007, 10.

excluding the scenario of Kashkar.[322] Beyond that, I consider that interpreting Epiphanius' use of 'Κασχάρη' to mean the Persian city of Kashkar in southern Mesopotamia is not consistent with his wording in *De mensuris et ponderibus*. The latter supports the view that Epiphanius located 'Κασχάρη' in northern Mesopotamia: Mani *"ascended* from Persia to Caschar of Mesopotamia".[323]

According to another proposal, Carchar could have been a city in the region of Osrhoene in northern Mesopotamia, near the border between Persia and the Roman Empire, specifically Carrhae (=Harran), known as a centre of paganism.[324] In favour of this view are the testimonies of the Syrian authors (Afrahaṭ and Ephrem) "about infiltration of Manichaeism into Osrhoene in the early years of the fourth century".[325]

Lastly, it has been claimed, that since the word 'carchar' is similar to the Syriac word *karka* that means 'town', it could be any other city across the border except Harran, because the *Acta*'s framework suggests a town with a strong Christian community and not at all a centre of paganism.[326]

That Carchar was a Roman city is the first claim in the document. The second claim is that the city was near the borderline that was formed by the river Stranga. The geographical information provided in the AA supporting these two claims is abundant. "Marcellus' reputation was being spread abroad [...] had even crossed the river Stranga" and brought his name into the territory of Persia.[327] The crowd in Diodoris "wanted to [...] hand Mani ... over to the powers of the barbarians [Persians] who were their neighbours beyond the river Stranga".[328] Thus, a crucial point of reference for the identification of the city is the identification of the river Stranga which, according to the AA,

---

322   AA 63.1 (Vermes, 142).

323   Epiphanius, *De mensuris et ponderibus* 547–550: ἀνέβη Μάνης ἀπὸ τῆς Περσίδος [...] πρὸς Ἀρχέλαον τὸν ἐπίσκοπον Κασχάρων τῆς Μεσοποταμίας. The ascent of Mani in northen Mesopotamia is also illustrated by the wording of Photius (c. *Manichaeos* 39.53.3–5: φυλακὴν διαφυγών – οὐδὲν γὰρ κωλύει διελθεῖν ἃ τῆς ἱστορίας ὁ δρόμος παρῆλθεν ἄνωθεν – καὶ κατὰ Μεσοποταμίαν γεγονώς. Less clear is the wording in Cyril, *Catech.* 6.27 (Mani "escapes from the prison, and *come* (ἔρχεται) to Mesopotamia"), and in Theodoret of Cyrrhus, *Haer.* (PG 83:381): "Mani *arrived* (ἀφίκετο) in the middle of the rivers (εἰς τὴν μέσην ... τῶν ποταμῶν) [Tigris and Euphrates]".

324   Fiey 1968 (*Assyrie chrétienne*). See also Tardieu 1986. Lieu in Vermes 2001, 17–18. BeDuhn and Mirecki 2007, 10–11: "Some researchers have proposed that Carrhae stands behind the Latin text's "Carchar." The idea was already put forward by the AA's first editor, Zacagni, in 1698, and has been favorably repeated by, among others, Fiey and Pennacchietti".

325   Tardieu 1986 (Archelaus): http://www.iranicaonline.org/articles/archelaus-author.

326   Lieu 1994a, 45. BeDuhn and Mirecki 2007, 10–11. Lieu in Vermes 2001, 21.

327   AA 4.1 (Vermes 39).

328   AA 66.1 (Vermes 147–48).

was the boundary between the two empires. Notable is that from the Greek sources reproducing the *AA*, only Epiphanius refers to the name Stranga.[329]

The above scenarios (i.e. of Harran or of any city along the border in Osrhoene), presuppose that the river Stranga is identified with the Khabur, which is supported by many scholars. However, the Khabur did not mark the Roman frontier with Persia, neither at the time of the *AA*'s narrative nor in Hegemonius' time.[330] In addition, the name 'Stranga' is extremely rarely encountered in Greek sources. It is, in fact, restricted to two clusters of tradition: the *AA* (only in Epiphanius' text) and the Alexander Romance.[331] In the latter, the name Stranga is given to the river Tigris. So, if Hegemonius used the name Stranga to refer to the Tigris, then Kaschar/Carchar could be identified with "Hatra [...] or Singara, or even Nisibis".[332] Yet, all of these are just scenarios; the research conducted so far suggests that the identification of the river Stranga (and therefore of Carchar) is extremely difficult. Both the anachronisms that exist in the *AA*, and the continuous shifting of the borders between Mani's and Hegemonius' era, render Hegemonius' information unreliable and his sense of geography problematic.[333] Moreover, the consensus among scholars that the events in the *AA* are fictitious further explains this confusion of the text (*AA*).

7.3.3.2   *Diodoris*

As far as Diodoris is concerned, it must have been located nearby Carchar. According to the *AA*, "Manes [...] reached a village far distant from the city, which was called Diodoris".[334] According to Epiphanius, after Mani was crushed by Archelaus at the first debate, he "withdrew and came to a village [κώμην] ⟨in the neighborhood⟩ of Caschar [τῆς Καλχάρων] called Diodoris".[335] Cyril describes this κώμη as 'insignificant' (εὐτελεστάτην) and adds that Archelaus went there on foot as a good shepherd in order to find Mani, which suggests that the two

---

329   Epiphanius, *Pan.* 66.5.11.

330   BeDuhn and Mirecki 2007, 12.

331   The *Alexander Romance* by Ps.-Callisthenes is a legendary version of the history of Alexander the Great composed in Greek and dated ca. 200 CE (translated into Latin ca. 300 CE) Cf. Nawotka, 2017; BeDuhn and Mirecki 2007, 12–13 fn. 33. Epiphanius, *Pan.* 66.5.12 (GCS 37:25): ... γράφει δὲ αὐτῷ ἐπιστολὴν διὰ Τύρβωνος τινὸς τῶν αὐτοῦ μαθητῶν ἀπὸ τοῦ πέρατος τοῦ Στράγγα ποταμοῦ, ἀπὸ καστέλλου Ἀραβίωνος οὕτω καλουμένου ...

332   BeDuhn and Mirecki 2007, 13.

333   Cf. BeDuhn and Mirecki 2007, 12–14.

334   *AA* 43.3 (Vermes, 111). Lieu in Vermes (111, fn. 229): "There is no town or village by that name in Mesopotamia in the Late Roman period".

335   Epiphanius, *Pan.* 66.31–32 (Williams 238).

locations were close to one another.[336] In ancient Greek, the word κώμη, apart from small town/village, also can mean neighbourhood/ward/quarter of a city. Therefore, it is likely that Diodoris was a district of Carchar, a poor one, in contrast to the area where Marcellus' house was located.

7.3.3.3   The 'Usual Place for the Debates'

The debates usually took place in public places, such as public squares, church courtyards, and monasteries. According to our texts, the first debate was held at the house of the eminent citizen of Carchar, Marcellus (AA 14), and the second at the central square of Diodoris. The debate at Marcellus' house, although it occurred in a private place, should have been an event that involved a large part of the town.[337] The huge house of Marcellus was full of people who were invited to attend the debate.[338] Among them were all the upper layers of the city.

To return to the question about who was provoking the debates, the first debate in Marcellus' house was organized and held by Mani's opponents, whilst Mani initially tried to convert Marcellus through his epistles. Coyle, agreeing with Lim, points out that it was not Mani who came to confront Archelaus. Manichaeans did not start the debates; their opponents started them in order to counteract the Manichaeans' successful propaganda and proselytizing activity.[339] However, this does not apply to the second debate. Things at Diodoris, at least initially, were more spontaneous. One particular day, Mani gathered the crowd around him and talked to them for a long time in the usual place for the debates, something that forced Diodorus to clash with him after having been advised by Archelaus.[340] Late in the evening, because it became dark, Diodorus/Trypho asked that the debate would stop and be continued next morning.[341] Very early next morning, Mani went to the centre of the κώμη. When the crowd gathered, "once again" he "began publicly to challenge Diodorus to engage with him in a debate".[342]

---

336   Cyril, Catech., 6.30 (Reischl and Rupp 1848, 196): Ἀρχέλαος [...] ἀκούσας τὴν φυγὴν, εὐθέως δρομαῖος [...].

337   Lim 1995, 77.

338   AA 14.6 (Vermes, 59).

339   Coyle 2007b, 70.

340   AA 43.5, 52.1 & 52.3 (Vermes, 111, 124 & 126, respectively).

341   AA 52.9 (Vermes, 125).

342   AA 53.1–2 (Vermes, 125). Epiphanius, Pan. 66.1.4–6.

7.3.4   The Participants

In the first debate, apart from the debaters (Mani and bishop Archelaus) and Marcellus, there were four outstanding persons who would act as chair and would judge the outcome of the debate. These were pagans for reasons of impartiality.[343] "Bishop Archelaus [...] debated with him [Mani] before philosophers as judges, bringing together a Gentile audience, lest if Christians judged, the judges might be considered partial".[344] In the beginning of the *Acta*, Hegemonius just mentions their names, Manippus, Aegialeus, Claudius, and Cleobulus, stating that they would act as judges.[345] Further on, after Turbo's narration, just before the beginning of the debate, Hegemonius clarifies that the four judges were chosen by Marcellus "amongst them who were Gentiles by religion", and informs us about their professions. Manippus was "very learned in grammar and the skill of rhetoric". Aegialeus was "a very distinguished physician and [was] supremely knowledgeable in literature". Claudius and Cleobulus were brothers and "excellent rhetoricians".[346] Epiphanius' version slightly differs in the professions and names he gives for the first judge. For him both Marcellus and Archelaus chose the four judges.

⟨Marcellus and Archelaus⟩ [...] had previously chosen a man named Marsipus, and Claudius, and Aegeleus and Cleobulus as judges of their disputation. One was a pagan philosopher, one a professor of medicine, another, a professional teacher of grammar, and the other a sophist.[347]

As Coyle comments, "these four judges (who, though given individual names, never act as individuals) have been chosen for this encounter in order to project the illusion of impartiality. They are clearly pagan, [...] but it is also clear early in the debate whose side they are on".[348] As Lim comments, "that pagans presided in this public debate between two who were emphatically not pagan, and that these *iudices* rendered their opinion in a communal voice throughout the dialogue, are particularly noteworthy aspects of this narrative".[349] The

---

343   *AA* 53.9 (Vermes, 127): "I request you only, as I said earlier, to be impartial judges, and to give the true honour and the prize to the one who speaks the truth".

344   Cyril, *Cathech.* 6.27.1–5 (Reischl and Rupp 1848, 190; LFHCC 73, altered): [...] Ἀρχέλαος ἐπίσκοπος. Καὶ ἐπὶ φιλοσόφων κριτῶν ἐλέγξας, ἀκροατήριον Ἑλληνικὸν συστησάμενος, ἵνα μὴ χριστιανῶν κρινάντων δοκῶσιν οἱ κριταὶ χαρίζεσθαι.

345   *AA* 1.1 (Vermes, 35).

346   *AA* 14.5–6 (Vermes, 59).

347   Epiphanius, *Pan.* 66.10.3 (Williams, 237–38).

348   Coyle 2007a, 26.

349   Lim 1995, 77–78, 87.

pagans that attended the debate in Gaza, between the Manichaean Julia and the bishop Porphyry, are also adumbrated in the same fashion.[350] In Lim's words, "As in the Acta Archelai, the pagans in the *Vita* constituted the silent partner in this confrontation between a Christian and a Manichaean".[351]

Apart from the protagonists and the judges, the AA states that Mani was accompanied by twenty-two young *Electi* and *Electae*,[352] while Epiphanius (E66.10) speaks of a retinue of men of unknown number.[353] It seems that it was a common Manichaean practice for the leader of the debate to be accompanied by young Elect. From the life of Porphyrius of Gaza, we learn that at the debate in Gaza, the Manichaean Julia was accompanied by "two men and two women. All four of them were young and good-looking, but very pale".[354] It seems that dress codes were important in Manichaean propaganda. Impressive is the vivid and detailed description of Mani's appearance given in the *Acta*, which gives the reader the impression that he has seen a portrait of Mani.

> When he saw Manes, Marcellus was first astonished at the garments he was wearing. For he wore a kind of shoe which is generally known commonly as the 'trisolium', and a multi-coloured cloak, of a somewhat ethereal appearance, while in his hand he held a very strong staff made of ebony-wood. He carried a Babylonian book under his left arm, and he had covered his legs with trousers of different colours, one of them scarlet, the other coloured leek-green. His appearance was like that of an old Persian magician or warlord.[355]

For researchers, Hegemonius' intention was to ridicule Mani. However, Diodorus in his epistle to Archelaus presents Mani as showing no fear and being self-confident, something mirrored in his appearance: "the man is extremely forceful both in what he says and what he does, as is also clear in his appearance and in his dress".[356] As Brown put it, "The arrival in the forum of a

---

350   Mark the Deacon, *Vit. Porph.* 91.
351   Lim 1995, 87.
352   AA 14.2 (Vermes, 58).
353   Epiphanius, *Pan.* 66.10.1 (GCS 37:31; Williams, 237): ἰδοὺ ὁ Μάνης παρεγένετο μεθ' ὧν εἶχε μεθ' ἑαυτοῦ ἀνδρῶν. On the contrary, for Epiphanius, the disciples that visited Mani at the jail (in Persia) were twenty-two, three of whom were chosen for his missionary plans to the Roman West.
354   Mark the Deacon, *Vit. Porph.* 88 (Lieu 2010, 98–99): Τῇ δὲ ἐπαύριον παραγίνεται [...] ἔχουσα μεθ' ἑαυτῆς ἄνδρας δύο καὶ τοσαύτας γυναῖκας· ἦσαν δὲ νεώτεροι καὶ εὐειδεῖς, ὠχροὶ δὲ πάντες, ἡ δὲ Ἰουλία ἦν προβεβηκυῖα".
355   AA 14 (Vermes, 58).
356   AA 44.4 (Vermes, 111).

group of pale men and women, clasping mysterious volumes and dressed with ostentatious barbarity, was a sight to be seen".[357]

When all those invited to attend the debate gathered and absolute silence had been established, the judges sat above all the rest and the floor was given to Mani.[358] In the debate in Diodoris, as it was spontaneous, there were neither judges nor invited people. Judges and audience were the congregated crowd. Additionally, there is no reference to Mani's retinue.

7.3.5   The Audience

According to Hegemonius, the house of Marcellus, though huge, was full of all those invited to attend the first debate. It is worth noting that at the second debate in Diodoris, among the audience also were all those who came with Archelaus "from his province and from other neighbouring areas".[359] This transfer of followers from other nearby locations reminds us of contemporary electoral speeches of politicians, or football games. The audience at both locations is presented by Hegemonius as acting emotionally. At times they celebrated, became aggressive, or deeply moved. Indeed, to Hegemonius' eyes, the audience in Diodoris was particularly vulnerable to the Manichaean danger. During the third debate, for a moment, when Mani had finished his speech, "the crowds were deeply moved, as if the words held an account of the truth and Archelaus had nothing to oppose to them. This was indicated by the uproar that had arisen amongst them".[360] However, at the end of both debates, when Archelaus was declared as winner, the crowd wanted to attack and lynch Mani.[361] In general, the Manichaean answer to the question of the origin of evil was more convincing and consoling than the respective Christian answer. In specific, for those cities on the frontiers, where life was troublesome and 'evil' existed in the everyday routine of people being taken captive from both sides of the borders, the Manichaean approach provided the Manichaean missionary argumentation with an extra advantage.

7.3.6   The Proceedings of the Debates

It is to be noted that minutes of the confrontations were taken. The proceedings of the debates were recorded by the stenographers and could be used as a simplified, popularized guide on how to confront Manichaeans or other

---

357   Brown 1969, 100–101.
358   *AA* 14.6 (Vermes, 59).
359   *AA* 61.2 (Vermes, 139).
360   *AA* 56.1 (Vermes, 130).
361   *AA* 66.1 (Vermes, 147–48). As Lim (1995, 78) remarks, "here we glimpse one possible role of a partisan audience, namely, to impose firm closure on a debate".

'heretics'.[362] The practice of stenographers, who recorded the confrontation verbatim, was first introduced in the debate between Paul of Samosata and Malchion. This practice gave the opportunity to control the inconsistencies of the opponents and therefore made it much easier to refute their arguments.[363] In the debate in Gaza, after the permission of bishop Porphyrius, the deacon Cornelius, who knew the "signs of Ennomos", undertook the task to record the debate assisted by two instigators (Mark the Deacon and Baruchas). As these minutes were too lengthy, Mark the Deacon proposed to write them down in a separate work, which unfortunately did not survive.[364]

Irrespective of the historicity of the debates in the AA, the following state-ment that Archelaus (or Hegemonius) is presented to claim, after the end of the first debate, reveals the importance attributed to the keeping of minutes.

> [...] since this disputation should be recorded and written down [...]
> [I] have trusted in the good will of my readers that they will pardon me,
> if my narration shall sound at all naïve or colloquial. For my only purpose
> is this, that an awareness of what took place should not elude any serious
> enquirer.[365]

The grand success the AA had among "enquirers" of later centuries, until the late Byzantine era (and afterwards), makes it hard to resist the temptation to comment on how well he (Archelaus or/and Hegemonius) achieved his purpose!

8   Conclusions

After the comparative examination of the sources, we can summarize the most important points of analysis and make some concluding remarks.

Regarding the representation of Mani and of Manichaeism, despite the different cultural background of the authors and the different literary genre of the sources, we have seen that they use the same language and imagery to represent the arrival of Manichaeism in the Roman Empire. The basic

---

362   Coyle 2007b, 76.

363   Lieu in Vermes 2001, 24. See also Lim 1995, 78.

364   Mark the Deacon, *Vit. Porph.* 88 (Lieu 2010, 98–99): "τὰ Ἐννόμου σημεῖα". The 'signs of Ennomos' is a reference to the system of stenography, which was probably named like-wise after the Neo-Arian Eunomius, who was a skilled tachygrapher and teacher of tachygraphy in Constantinople. See entry "Byzantium" in *ODB*, 746.

365   *AA* 43.3 (Vermes, 110–11).

common features which they underline are: (1) the Persian origin of Mani and Manichaeism, (2) that the Perso-Manichaean beliefs and practices misled Roman citizens, (3) that Manichaeism is a 'novelty' seeking to replace traditional (pagan and Christian) institutions/values, and (4) that Manichaeism's spread westwards threatens the integrity of Roman citizens and of the whole of the Roman Empire.

These thematic axes are also basic structural elements of the *Acta*, and are emphasized by all subsequent authors, irrespectively of whether they reproduced the *AA* or not. Mani's biography in the *AA* was the most extended portrait of Mani and subsequently influential. Of this work, it has been highlighted that despite being considered as the most unreliable part of the *AA*, it in fact reflects true events of Mani's life. Both Epiphanius and Cyril give additional information, not recorded in the rest of the *AA* tradition, such as about Mani's disciples, books, commercial activity and itineraries of proto-Manichaeans, as well as their rituals. The trace of the *AA* in later sources is limited to a brief presentation of Mani and of Manichaeism that draws from the core of the *AA*'s biography: the time Mani appeared, the time of his arrival in the Roman Empire, that he confronted Archelaus in debates, the names of his students and their mission, the titles of the Manichaean books. There is a divergence among the sources regarding the time of Mani's arrival. Epiphanius' dating is more realistic. He dates Mani's missionary activity during the reign of Valerian and Gallienus (253–268), as Alexander also did. He also dates the arrival of the second wave of Manichaean missionaries in Palestine in the time of the emperor Aurelian (270–275), just before Mani's death. According to our sources, Manichaeism had already spread throughout the Roman Empire since the mid-fourth century.

Regarding the question of the titles of the Manichaean Scriptures, the *AA* recorded the titles of three out of the seven canonical books (*Gospel*, *Mysteries* and *Thesaurus*) and one of the sub-canonical tradition, the *Kephalaia*, a work of Mani's students. Epiphanius and Cyril provide some additional information which denotes a provenance from different sources (another version of the *AA*?) or first-hand information. Especially important because it is unique and accurate is Epiphanius' testimony that Mani's Gospel comprised twenty-two chapters which corresponded to the Syriac alphabet. Combining Cyril's testimony that Manichaean missionaries were carrying around copies of the *Thesaurus*, with the fact that the latter was the most cited book not only in the *AA*'s tradition but also by individual writers (Titus, Severianus, Nilus of Ankara), it appears that the *Thesaurus* was the most well-known and widespread Manichaean book in the Roman East.

Of particular interest is Titus' testimony, who knew that Mani's books were written in the Syriac language. He names as titles of Mani's books, the *Thesaurus*, *Prayers*, and *Epistles*; from the quotation he gives, it seems that he had access to other genuine Manichaean books too (*Mysteries*, *Kephalaia*, *Homilies*?). Heraclian and the sᴀғ are the only sources that refer to the book of *Giants*.

The sᴄ and sᴀғ (contemporary works?) together give the most accurate information regarding the titles of the Manichaean canonical books. The sᴄ gives us the titles of five out of the seven canonical books of Mani (*Thesaurus*, *Living Gospel*, *Book of Mysteries*, the *Epistles of Mani*, and the Manichaean *Prayers*). Indeed, the above pentateuch can be expanded into a heptateuch, given that the *Treatise*, the *Book of the Giants*, along with the *Book of Mysteries* could count as one, according to Manichaean sources. Similarly, the sᴀғ states that the canonical books are five (it gives six titles but does not include the *Prayers* in the canon), while among the five canonical works includes the *Book/Treatise of the Giants*.

Regarding the question of accessibility, Theonas, Cyril, Titus, and the compiler of the sᴄ explicitly declared that they had access to and read Manichaean books, whereas in the case of Epiphanius and Heraclian this is only implied. The *Treasure* is the only book which at least Cyril explicitly states that he had read (this is probable for Titus too). The question of the canon's secrecy (i.e. that the access to Manichaean canonical books was restricted), is raised only by Titus.

With regard to the question of the names of the first Manichaean missionaries, the sᴄ again gives the most accurate information. Seven out of the nine names it gives are testified in genuine Manichaean sources. For the remaining two (Thomas and Zarouas), there are sound arguments in favour of their Manichaeanness. On the other hand, from the ᴀᴀ's trio only one (Addas) is testified. The ᴀᴀ also refers to Sisinnius, however ignoring, as it seems, his role in the Manichaean leadership. The value of the sᴀғ lies in the fact that, for the first time in Greek literature, Sisinnius assumes his proper role as the successor of Mani. The sᴄ is the only Greek anti-Manichaean source that records the six grades of the Manichaean hierarchy in detail.

Concerning the similarities/differences between the sᴄ, sᴀғ, and ʟᴀғ the following comments can be made: The fact that the sᴄ neither derives from earlier/previous literature nor leaves its footprint in posterior tradition until the ʟᴀғ is probably due to its sacramental use: the conversion ceremony of real Manichaeans. Logically, many of such ᴀғs would have been stored in the *chartophylakeion* (Archives) of the several dioceses. One of them could have been the *SAF*. It is reasonable to assume that, although the basic structure of these formulas was standardized, there would have been (minor) deviations in their content.

The Manichaean missionary methods recorded in the *AA* (the conversion of important persons, the use of letters, the debates) are also testified by Manichaean texts. Indeed, it has been argued that the *AA* probably contains genuine Manichaean documents, such as the 'letter to Marcellus' which could have been an authentic letter of Mani. The debates of the *AA*, although they are considered fictitious, preserve accurate information concerning the protocol of the debates and Mani's statements during the debates. I will examine the latter together with the Manichaean cosmogony narrated by Turbo in ch.[5].

CHAPTER 3

The Manichaeans in Roman Imperial Legislation

... and Manichaeans, who have attained to the lowest villainy of crimes, nowhere on Roman soil should have the right of assembly and of prayer.

CODEX THEODOSIANUS[1]

•••

We decree that those who have embraced the pernicious error of the Manichaeans shall have no freedom or permission to reside anywhere in Our Empire. If any appear (to do so) or are discovered, they shall by subjected to capital punishment

CODEX JUSTINIANUS[2]

∵

1   Introduction

The previous chapter investigated the ways in which Greek anti-Manichaica (both pagan and Christian) outlined and reproduced the first encounter with Manichaeism and the first Manichaean missions in the Roman Empire. This chapter will survey the representation of Manichaeism and Manichaeans in Roman imperial legislation. The aim of the first two sections of the chapter (3.2 and 3.3) is to outline the profile of the Manichaeans as depicted in the laws and in how this compares with the corresponding profile of other religious groups. As far as I know, there has not been any other research examining all anti-Manichaean laws of the period (fourth to sixth centuries) using a comparative approach. The comparison will reveal the gravity that the Manichaean question had for the state, as well as attempt to shed light on the reasons why Manichaeism was the most persecuted heresy. Questions that will be examined through the comparative perspective are: What was the spatio-temporal geography of the sect? With which other religious groups does the law classify

---

1   Cod. theod. 16.5.65, 428 CE (Coleman-Norton, 643).
2   Cod. justin. 1.5.11, 487 or 510 CE (Frier et al., 201).

© REA MATSANGOU, 2023 | DOI:10.1163/9789004544222_005

the Manichaeans? Were all Manichaeans persecuted (Elect, catechumens, men and women)? Why were Manichaeans persecuted that much? Was the 'topos' of the persecution their beliefs and teachings or their practices? What was the nature of the Manichaean crime as revealed through the prosecuting process, the inquisitional mechanism and the penalties imposed? A core question that runs through section 3.3 is whether the state considered Manichaeans as Christian heretics or as a religious group outside of Christianity. A further goal of this section is to point out the changes in the religious policy of the state during the period under investigation.

Section 3.4 attempts a reconstruction of aspects of the Manichaean daily life as these were captured through the provisions of the laws (prohibition of certain practices, restriction of rights and privileges, etc). Based on the dialectical relationship between law and social reality, the central question of this section is twofold. What does the law reveal and how does it affect the following aspects of Manichaean everyday life: (1) the existence of Manichaean communities, (2) the existence and ownership status of Manichaean assembly places, (3) the social networks supporting or denouncing Manichaeans, (4) the family relationships and Manichaean social profile.

1.1   The Sources and Their Limitation

The main sources of this chapter are the anti-Manichaean laws recorded in the following statutory legislation:

Laws compiled under the reign of Theodosius II (408–450): (1) The *Theodosian Code* (hereafter Cod. theod.), in specific book sixteen, which refers to religion and especially chapter five (16.5), which is entitled *De Haereticis*. (2) The relevant *Sirmondian Constitutions* (against heretics) which are preparatory texts of the laws and for this reason more extensive, preserving a great deal of valuable information. (3) The relevant *Novels* (against heretics), which are laws issued after the compilation of the code (i.e. from 438 to 450).

Laws compiled under the reign of Justinian I (527–565): (1) The *Justinian Code* (hereinafter *Cod. justin.*), in specific, chapter five from the first book, entitled, *De haereticis et Manichaeis et Samaritis*. (2) Justinian's *Novels*.

There is an ongoing academic debate concerning the reliability of the legal codes and their use as historical sources. Basic questions that have been raised by scholars are: (1) questions of authenticity, (2) questions of representativeness, and (3) the problem of mindless reiteration of laws, which calls into question the dialectic relationship between law and social reality.

1.2   Questions of Authenticity (Cod. Theod. and Cod. Justin.)

Are the laws that were included in the codes (Cod. theod. and Cod. justin.) the authentic texts (i.e. transcribed exactly as they had been issued in the first place), or were they paraphrased versions? In other words, did the compilers of the codes have access to the original laws, or did they use other paraphrased versions? In case they had access, did they alter the original text paraphrasing its content?

On this specific point, Honoré argues, "from Theodosius I (379) onwards, the compilers of the code (Cod. theod.) were able to draw increasingly on the authentic archives of the prefectures and imperial bureaus".[3] Moreover, it is generally accepted, that, although almost all the constitutions in the Cod. theod. are abbreviations of those originally issued, they generally remain "faithful to the original versions of the laws in terms of their content although not in terms of language".[4] The language of the law especially in the religion chapters has a different style from the rest of the legislation, a theological nuance, which denotes the Church's influence.[5] Indeed, as Linder points out, "Book 16 of the Code enjoyed the unique status of having been accepted by the Church as an authoritative source of canon law".[6] In this sense book sixteen (as probably other similar ones) could have been 'edited' by churchmen.

In the case of the Cod. justin., comparing the laws which exist in both codes (Cod. theod. and Cod. justin., i.e. the laws issued by Arcadius and Theodosius II), we can note that some modifications and alterations (additions, omissions or interpolations) were made, in order to adapt them to the contemporary social context.[7]

1.3 Questions of Representativeness (Cod. Theod. and Cod. Justin.)

How representative are the constitutions included in the codes? Did the compilers include all the issued laws in the codes? This question, in turn, raises two

---

3 Honoré 1986, 159.

4 Linder 1987, 42. According to Honoré (1986, 161–62), the essential content of the original text, the core of the laws, is not paraphrased but is preserved intact: "the editorial policy was that of fidelity to the texts" (161). Corcoran 1996, 19: "In conclusion, the transmitted texts are seldom identical with what the imperial chancery originally issued, yet the extent of alteration, although sometimes drastic, is not usually so. Abbreviation is the most common fate of constitutions in the legal sources".

5 Cf. Coyle 2004, 223.

6 Linder 1987, 55.

7 See Corcoran 1996, 10: "Thus, interpolations may simply repeat or clarify the original text, perhaps explaining or eliminating anachronistic terms. [...] the level of alteration in Cod. justin. material can be assessed by comparison with other versions of the same texts [...] since Cod. justin. incorporates so much of the independently surviving Cod. theod.". Linder (1987, 48) on the content of Cod. justin.: "The complete dependence of Justinian's editors on the *Theodosian Code* as a source for the laws of the fourth and early fifth centuries, through 438, enables us to determine the degree to which the text was edited by them and to what extent they used the considerable latitude granted them by Justinian". The same applies to *Basilica*, which repeats, Hellenized, the Justinian provisions. The deviations observed between the two texts are due to the adaptation to the new social conditions, cf. Troiannos 1997.

further issues: a) whether they were able to detect all the laws, and b) whether they made a selection, having deliberately omitted some laws.

In both codes there are long periods during which there are no laws against heretics, or against Manichaeans. Both codes lack laws by certain emperors. How could this be explained? Did these emperors not issue laws against heretics whereas all other emperors did? Or, were their laws not included in the codes? In any case, what does not seem to be a coincidence and raises many questions is that some of these emperors were themselves regarded by the ruling emperors and compilers of the codes, as 'heretics' (i.e. not maintaining the Catholic faith). In this section, I will attempt to answer these very crucial questions.

The codification of the Cod. theod. took place from 429 to 438, under the reign of Theodosius II. We do not know if all of the older laws, namely those issued from Constantine up to Arcadius, were included. Although chapter 16.5 starts with the laws of Constantine (as the whole code does), it does not include laws against heretics, or against Manichaeans, issued by the emperors Constantius II (337–361), Julian (361–363) and Jovian (363–364). Thus, the laws included in chapter 16.5 (*De Haereticis*) of the Cod. theod. are not representative of the state's religious policy throughout the fourth and first half of fifth centuries. To be specific, in chapter 16.5 there are in total 66 laws against heretics, 64 of which were issued in the 63 years between 372 and 435. The chapter starts with two laws issued by Constantine in 326,[8] and after these, the next law recorded is the one issued by Valentinian and Valens in 372 (against Manichaeans). Linder points out a relevant omission of the laws concerning the privileges granted to the Jews, issued by Constantius II and Julian the Apostate.[9] For Julian it is self-evident that even in case he had issued edicts concerning religion, these would not have been included in the code. Thus, I will focus on Constantius II, supporter of the Arian party, since his reign was the longest-lasting (25 years). Two alternative suppositions could be made: (1) during the reign of the first Christian emperors there was no criminalization of heresy and therefore they did not decree laws against heretics, (2) Constantius II issued laws against heretics and Manichaeans, but Theodosius II did not include these laws (as well as those from other emperors) in the code.[10] Presumably, the material selected by the editorial committee reflects the image

---

8   The first is about the privileges of the adherents of the Catholic faith and the second about the right of Novatians to possess their own church buildings.

9   Linder (1987, 34) remarks: "Thus, whether deliberately or not, the Theodosian Code reflected a choice among existing laws, rather than a comprehensive collection".

10   For the chaotic religious policy of Constantius II, see Beck 1978, 135.

that Theodosius II wanted to project, that of a Catholic-Christian empire, inaugurated by Constantine; for this reason he chose to begin his code with Constantine's laws.[11] Given such a background, it would be very likely that he did not include laws that spoiled this picture, especially laws issued by 'heretical' (not Catholic) or pagan emperors (Julian), as well as laws that followed a more moderate and tolerant policy toward some heretics, giving them privileges. One such example could be a law issued by Gratian, which is recorded in the Ecclesiastical histories of Socrates and Sozomenus, and which granted to all heretics – except Manichaeans, Photinians, Eunomians – the right to congregate and practice their religion.[12] Thus, since Constantius II supported the Arian party and to him the Catholics were the heretics, it would be understandable that his laws (on religion) were not included in the code.

Consequently, since there are not any laws against Manichaeans included in the code before 372 (deliberately or not), the picture of the state's policy and of the effect it had upon Manichaeans cannot be reconstructed before that period.[13] Although restricted in time (372–445), the rest of the source material of the Cod. theod. has the advantage that this period witnessed a great number of laws concerning Manichaeans. These enable us to investigate the questions at stake in this study. In the words of Linder, who studied the same material of *Roman Imperial Legislation on the Jews*, "This corpus is of prime importance for [my] research. The large concentration of material from a period measured in decades makes it particularly useful for the study of developments within a short or medium period of time".[14]

The next law gap appears from 445 up to 527 (82 years). The Cod. justin. records only four laws against heretics during this period. The first was decreed by Marcian (450–457) against Eutychians and Apollinarians in 455. Another two laws against heretics in general were issued by Leo I (457–474) in 457 and 466–472. Finally, for the period from 474 up to 527, there is just one law, and this is against Manichaeans, issued either in 487 or in 510, and thus attributed either to Zeno (474–491), or to Anastasius I (491–518). In any case, the

---

11   Turpin 1985, 339–53, 344, 353.

12   Socrates *HE*: 5.2.1–8; Sozomenus *HE*: 7.1.3.

13   As Turpin (1985, 351, 347, 350–53) highlights, "Finally, it is important to remember that although Theodosius' interest in general legislation resulted in an impressive collection of edicts and epistles, even this collection is not complete", "the *Theodosian Code* was, in one important way, organized according to religious rather than legal criteria". The fact that Theodosius II, firstly, chose to begin his code with Constantine, and secondly, made a choice among existing laws means that he was motivated by religious rather than legal considerations. Thus, as Corcoran (1996, 12) concludes, what is included in the codes is "neither full nor necessarily representative". Cf. Tolan 2016, 229–31.

14   Linder 1987, 55.

anti-heretical legislation of the Leonid dynasty was poor. Alternatively, the absence of laws was the result of a conscious decision of the editorial team of the code. In any case, as Corcoran points out, when the "amount of missing legislation" is considerable, it is "extremely difficult to be certain that any text (of whatever nature) is introducing a change in the law".[15]

It is clear that the reconstruction of the state's policy towards heretics, and in particular towards Manichaeans, is influenced by the image that the compilers of the two codes intended to present. The selection of the specific laws that were included in the codes by the compilers reflects the priorities of the editing committees and aimed to serve the religious policies of the ruling emperors. So, the picture cannot be complete; some pieces of the puzzle are still missing.

1.4   *Reiteration of Laws: Mindless Procedure?*

Another 'problem' pointed out by many researchers is whether the reiteration of edicts was just a mindless process of recirculation, a mere repetition of what the previous laws had decreed. Thus, they question whether the laws actually reflect social reality.[16]

However, recirculation of a law could also mean that its subject was of paramount importance, or that it was repeated because it was not being upheld. Both apply in our case. As Corcoran points out commenting on the former possibility, "many legal points need constant reiteration, no matter how often they have been stated before [...] It is likely therefore that rescripts continued to be more important than is often assumed".[17] Regarding the latter, the laws themselves firmly reiterate that they were repeated because the previous laws were not implemented. As we will see in the course of this chapter (especially in section 3.4), each law against Manichaeans re-enforced the validity of the previous ones and supplemented them with additional measures. Thus, it remains to study the sources themselves to reveal whether the above reservation applies to the laws under investigation.

---

15   Corcoran 1996, 12.
16   On the question whether Roman law reflects aspects of the 'real world', see, e.g., Johnston 1999; Aubert and Sirks 2002. Cf. Gaudement 1972, on legislative reiteration. Regarding "The Reflection of Reality in Conciliar Legislation" see Halfond 2010, 99–130. Generally, on Roman Public Law, see the standard works of Kaser 1971; Mitteis 1891; Mommsen 1899.
17   Corcoran 1996, 294.

2 Time-Space Mapping of the Manichaean 'Sect' in Roman Territory

Studying the laws of the Theodosian and Justinian code, one quickly realizes that the Manichaeans were the most persecuted heresy, more than any other religious group. The presence of Manichaeans in both codes is constant, in contrast to the presence of other heretics/religious groups for which there is a periodicity, indicative of temporal or regional tensions and a de-escalation of their persecutions.

2.1 *Quantitative Dimensions of the 'Problem'*

In the Cod. theod., there are eighteen laws against the Manichaeans. The Eunomians, who are the next most persecuted religious group in the code, follow with seventeen[18] laws against them, while eleven laws are against the Donatists, who are the next in the list. Against the Arians and Montanists (or Phrygians or Tascodrogitae) there are nine laws, against the Macedonians six laws, and five each against Priscillianists, Apollinarians and Hydroparastates. The references for all the other religious groups/heresies in the laws, such as the ascetics (Apotactites, Encratites, Saccophori, Messalians, Euchites), the adoptionists (Photinians, Paulianists, Marcellians), the Nestorians, the Marcionites and the Gnostics (Valentinians), vary from one to three. In the above classification, I have included the religious groups that the code itself classified as heretics in chapter 16.5 of the code. The pagans and the Jews are treated as distinct religious groups, and the laws relating to them – some in their favour and some against them – constitute separate chapters, specifically ch. 16.8 and 16.9 for the Jews and ch. 16.10 for the pagans.

In the Cod. justin., and in particular in chapter five (first book), entitled *Concerning Heretics, and Manichaeans and Samaritans*, of a total number of twenty-two laws, seven are repetitions of the Cod. theod.'s laws. In the remaining fifteen laws, dating from 455 (Marcian) to 531 (Justinian), there are: seven laws against the Manichaeans, four laws against the Montanists (and three against the Tascodrogitae), four against the Samaritans, three against the pagans and the Ophites, respectively, and one each against the Jews, the Monophysites (adherents of Eutyches), and the Apollinarians. Finally, there are five laws which are not addressed against particular heretics, but against heretics in general.

---

18 Mainly sixteen since one of them is twice mentioned (it is addressed to the same prefect at the same date). There are another three laws in 'favour' of Eunomians, cancelling previous laws and penalties against them.

As one can notice, the Manichaeans in both codes head the list, followed by (or together with) the religious group that constituted a major problem for the state at the time each code was composed.

2.2   Time-Mapping

Studying the temporal distribution of persecutions per sect, the Manichaeans seems to be a constant target, unlike other sects, for which a periodicity is observed.

Starting from the Cod. theod. which covers the period 372–445, the so called *noble*[19] heresies (Arians, Macedonians or Pneumatomachi, Apollinarians) are the target of the laws during the first decades (380s–390s) and reappear later during the 420s. The Donatists, Montanists and Priscillianists appeared as a problem at the turn of the fourth to fifth century (Montanists and Priscillianists remaining as a target, up to the 430s). As far as the Manichaeans are concerned, they are steadily and continuously the focus of the laws from the 370s up to the 440s. The only heresy that seems to rival them are the Eunomians, who appear constantly in the laws from the 380s up to the 430s. I consider that this is due to the fact that at the time the Cod. theod. was composed, the Eunomians (neo-Arians) were the heresy of the day. Relevant remarks for the next period (445–531) which is covered by the Cod. justin., cannot be made because, as mentioned in the introduction, there is a law-gap of 82 years, while the majority of laws (eleven out of fifteen) are Justinian's laws issued between 527–531.[20]

2.3   Space-Mapping

Theodosian laws are general laws in the form of edicts that had *empire-wide* or *province-wide* applicability. The most common type of law was the "imperial epistle, addressed usually to a government official".[21] The latter, who is called upon to implement the law, was usually the highest in the hierarchy of the administrative structure, namely one of the four Praetorian Prefects (*Praefectus Praetorio*), or one of the two Prefects of the City (*Praefectus Urbi*), i.e. Rome and Constantinople. In the case of the laws against heretics, it is reasonable to assume that the geographical area administered by the particular Prefect (and recipient of the law), is in principle, the one confronted with the

---

19   See Introduction, 5.3.2.2.

20   However, in the Cod. justin., which covers the next period (455–531), the Eunomians disappeared; while the Manichaeans are not merely persecuted constantly, but seem to be the main target of the laws, followed by the Montanists who reappeared in the code.

21   Turpin 1985, 342–43.

problem of the specific heretics. This does not exclude the possibility that a similar problem was faced in other geographical areas.[22]

The *province-wide* applicability, which is the norm for the majority of laws against Manichaeans (and not only them), is a valuable tool for developing a chrono-geography of the sect, and a credible indicator that enables us to compare the mobility of the 'Manichaean problem' between East and West.[23] Thus, while initially (372–383), the Manichaeans equally troubled both the eastern (two laws) and western (three laws) part of the Empire, it seems that later (384–422), the 'problem' lay only in the western part (five laws).[24] Lastly, for the period (423–445), the Manichaeans again 'annoyed' similarly the eastern (four Laws) and western (three laws) parts.

How to explain the absence of persecutions of Manichaeans in the eastern part of the empire for 40 years? How could one interpret this silence, from the edict of Theodosius in 383 until the two edicts addressed to Asclepiodotus, the Praetorian Prefect of the East, in 423? Were there no Manichaeans in the East, or were they there but did they not create any problems? Were the officers of the East more operative and effective in their job in restraining them? Or were the bishops efficiently filling the legislative gap or supplementing the officials' work? Or further, was there cooperation in the East between bishops and government officials in the fight against the crime of the Manichaean heresy?

I consider it most likely that the authorities had their attention focused on other heretics during this period of time. The conflicts with the *noble* heresies (Arian, Eunomians Macedonians, Apollinarians) and especially with the Eunomians, almost fully occupied the state and Church of the Eastern Empire at the time. Eighteen out of a total of twenty laws relating to the Eunomians

---

22 Salzman 1993. Corcoran (1996, 201, 203) remarks: "we can see clearly how this system of promulgation developed. [...] one single act of legislation generated both edicts and letters to officials, with versions edited to include only appropriate matters for particular recipients or areas. [...] Thus, a single act of the emperor might [...] generate multiple copies of documents with different formats and/or content"; 201–02: "Letters to praetorian prefects are very common in Cod. theod. after 324, while instructions ordering them to disseminate the imperial will by letter or edict to governors and the population at large are preserved in many of the fuller versions of laws among the Sirmondian constitutions and the Novels".

23 For a 'geography' of heresy traced in Epiphanius' *Panarion*, see Young 2006, 235–51, 242: "Beginning at Constantinople, one can draw an arc that swept easterly, passing through Asia, then south down through Antioch and Palestine, and finally ending at Alexandria. This arc was a "heresy-belt" [...]. Once one entered beyond the arc of these cities, one entered into the wilderness of heresy".

24 There is also one additional law (Cod. theod. 16.5.38) issued in Ravenna in 405 by Arcadius, Theodosius and Onorio, with empire-wide applicability.

were issued during this period (381–423). The problem had a local dimension: seventeen out of these laws were addressed to Praetorian Prefects of the East. In addition, the fact that the question of Manichaeans returned more aggressively in the East after 423, suggests that the Manichaean 'threat' never ceased to exist.

Therefore, it seems more reasonable to assume that the Manichaeans of the East at the time were not the state's priority, than to assume that they did not bother the state with their activities, or that they had migrated westwards. Regarding the western part, it is evident that the works and polemics of Augustine played a significant role in the intensification of the persecutions of western Manichaeans between 389 and 408.[25] Finally, for the Cod. justin. laws, one cannot make similar observations, since the western part of the empire did not exist anymore, and all laws concerned the eastern part.

3 The Profile (Crime) of Manichaeans in the Eyes of the Law

The aim of the present section is to determine the gravity that the Manichaean question occupies in the laws. What did Manichaeism and Manichaeans mean to the emperor, the authorities, and the state? Why were Manichaeans persecuted more than other heretics? What was their 'crime'? What was the nature of the threat that the state and the authorities considered it so important to confront?

In order to answer these questions, I will examine: (1) How the laws themselves classify the Manichaeans; with which other religious groups are they categorized, (2) the rationale behind the persecution of the Manichaean heresy, as developed by the laws; what exactly was persecuted (dogma, cult, gatherings), (3) the human subjects of the persecution, i.e. were all Manichaeans persecuted or only the Elect? (4) the mechanisms employed (inquisitors) to detect and suppress the heresy, and (5) the nature of the threat as it is revealed through the procedure of the prosecution and the penalties imposed.

In this analysis, I will also take into account the way the other religious groups were treated by the law. The comparison between the attitude of the law towards Manichaeans and its attitude towards other religious groups will highlight the differences to better understand the rationale of the law in persecuting Manichaeans.

---

25   Augustine wrote his main anti-Manichaean works between 388 and 404.

3.1 Grouping Heretics[26]

Were all heretics the same in the eyes of the law? Did they receive the same treatment? Can we discern in the laws the difference in meaning that the terms 'heretic' and 'infidel' (follower of another religion) has today? And how were Manichaeans considered? Were they thought of as heretics or as infidels?

In book sixteen of the Cod. theod., which concerns religion, all heretics, among them the Manichaeans, appear in the same chapter entitled *De Haereticis* (16.5). Pagans and Jews, as said before, are dealt with in a separate chapter.[27] One could say that the Roman state did not distinguish the Manichaeans from other heretics, as it did with pagans and Jews, who existed prior to the Christians as religious groups. But it did regard them as heretics in the same way it considered the Arians, or other *noble* heretics. Was that so?

In order to answer this question, I will examine whether there are patterns in the way heretics are grouped together in the individual laws of the chapter, which would reflect a different position and treatment of the Manichaeans in relation to other heretics. This is because each separate law reflects the specific rationale of the persecution at a theoretical, procedural, and penal level. In chapter 16.5 of the Cod. theod. there are six laws that exclusively concern the Manichaeans and another twelve where Manichaeans are classified along with other heretics. In that latter group, the Manichaeans were persecuted together with: Priscillianists (6), Montanists (5), Donatists (4), ascetic movements (4), Gnostic sects (1), pagans (2), and Jews (1). The only instance where they are mentioned together with the *noble* heretics is a single umbrella-law, which indiscriminately covers *noble* heresies, ascetic groups, and Manichaeans.[28]

Thus, there definitely is a distinction in the way the Manichaeans were classified. They are mainly categorized with Priscillianists, Montanists, and Donatists. Concerning the Priscillianists, this seems reasonable, since they were accused of Manichaeism. As for the other two, Donatism and Montanism, both were anti-clerically oriented, threatening the authority of the bishop in two distinct ways. Montanism in addition shared many similarities with Manichaeism, such as extreme asceticism, participation of women in the class of clergy. I shall return to this issue in chapter four. Lastly, all three of these groups constituted a major problem for the Church during the first quarter of the fifth century, when the Cod. theod. was edited.

---

26 Regarding the use of the terms 'heresy' and 'heretics' in both *emic* and *etic* discourse, see Introduction, section 5.3.2, as well as ch.[4], Introduction.

27 Pagans: Cod. theod. 16.10 and Jews: Cod. theod. 16.8 and 16.9. Yet they also appear in Cod. theod. 16.5.43, 46 and *NVal*. 18 (438).

28 Cod. theod. 16.5.11 (383). Cod. theod. 16.5.59 (423) which also mentions together Manichaean and noble heretics just renews the validity of previous laws and penalties.

The fact that there was discrimination and a different treatment of the several sects is reflected most clearly in a law (16.5.65, 428) addressed against all heretics (twenty-three in number). Although this law is very reminiscent of the umbrella-law of Theodosius I in 383, there is a noteworthy difference: it does not put all heretics in the same basket. Instead, it ranks them according to the threat they pose. Thus, we have a ranking within the same law, which as stated by the law itself, serves to distinguish the severity of the crime, as well as to differentiate the treatment of each heresy with regard to the penalties. The Manichaeans are not simply placed in the third and more 'threatening' group, but are the last in this list as the worst of the worst: those "who have attained to the lowest villainy of crimes", in the words of the law. For this reason, the Manichaeans received extra penalties over and above those decreed for the rest of the heretics in the third group. The Manichaeans constituted themselves a separate (fourth) category of heretics.[29]

The *sui generis* status of Manichaeans is also apparent in the chapter *De Apostatis* (16.7), where only pagans, Jews and Manichaeans are considered as apostates.[30] Neither *noble* heretics nor schismatics are anywhere characterized as apostates. This is an indication that, at least for the law, Manichaeans were rather closer to the meaning that the word 'infidel' (ἀλλόθρησκος) has today, than the word 'heretic'.[31]

The Cod. justin. clarifies this section's focus on identifying whether Manichaeans were considered as 'heretics or infidels' from the outset. Manichaeans comprise a separate group alongside pagans and Samaritans which is distinguished from the rest of heretics. The title of the chapter is *De haereticis et Manichaeis et Samaritis*. Out of the seven laws of the Cod. justin. against Manichaeans, three exclusively concern the Manichaeans. In the other four, they

---

29   Cod. theod.16.5.65.2 (428) (Coleman-Norton, 642–45, 643): "since not all must be punished with the same severity [...] and Manichaeans, who have attained to the lowest villainy of crimes, nowhere on Roman soil should have the right of assembly and of prayer – the Manichaeans also being deserving of expulsion from municipalities". On classification and cataloguing of heresies in Cod. theod., in particular 16.5.65, see R. Flower (2013), "'The Insanity of Heretics must be restrained': heresiology in the *Theodosian Code*". As Flower remarks, "all the heretical groups named in the first sixty-four laws in this chapter of the Code also appear in the sixty-fifth".

30   Cod. theod. 16.7.3 (383). Cf. Linder 1987, 168.

31   See also Lieu 1992, 146: "The Roman state, in meting out the same penalties to those who became Manichaeans as to those who apostasised to Judaism and paganism, placed Manichaeism in a different category from heresies within the main body of the church like Donatism and Arianism".

are persecuted together with pagans (4), Jews/Samaritans (3), Montanists/
Tascodrogitae (3), and Ophites (3).[32]

3.2   The 'Topos' of the Crime: Doctrine or Gatherings?

Why were Manichaeans seen as the worst of worst? What was their crime? For
what were they persecuted? Was it for their doctrines or for their gatherings?
What was the nature of the threat they posed?

According to Barnard, "the criminalization of heresy was a novel development in post-classical Roman law".[33] In earlier times, religious behaviour was
prosecuted in case it promoted teachings or practices that were framed as
being socially dangerous and undermining social stability. Thus, the rationale
of the prosecution was the disturbance of social order. Yet, also those whose
religious practices could be associated with other crimes, like magic, "were
criminally prosecuted on that account".[34] In any case, there was not a law persecuting "religious beliefs or practices *per se* on a principal basis and through
judicial proceedings".[35] Being an adherent of a sect, or professing heterodox
doctrines did not constitute a crime, and this "position did not change under
the earlier Christian emperors".[36]

The laws of Constantius against the Jews and the pagans, for example,
could be placed in such a context. The same applies to the two laws against
heretics of the Cod. theod. 16.5 issued by Valentinian and Valens. The former
was against Manichaeans (372) and the latter against heretics in general (376).
Both of them were targeting the gatherings of the heretics.[37] Thus, what was
condemned as a crime in the legislation until then were the gatherings of a
sect rather than adherence to the sect or its beliefs. This situation changed
radically with the famous *Cunctos Populos* of Theodosius in 380 (Cod. theod.
16.1.2). What *Cunctos Populos* made clear was that all those who deviate from
the correct doctrine as precisely established at the Council of Nicaea were to
be seen by the state as 'heretics'. Criminalization of the 'false' doctrine began;
henceforth, religious beliefs and practices would be prosecuted *per se*.[38]

---

32   We note that in Cod. justin. the Manichaeans are categorized with religious groups which
      are either outside Christianity (pagans, Jews) or in the fringes of Christianity (Gnostic
      sects) or in any case with pre-Nicene groups.
33   Barnard 1995, 125.
34   Barnard 1995, 125.
35   Barnard 1995, 125.
36   Barnard 1995, 125.
37   Cod. theod. 16.5.3 (372), 16.5.4 (376).
38   On the "imposition of doctrinal uniformity" by Theodosius I, see Hunt 2007, 57–68.

3.2.1   The Manichaeans

Did this ruling apply to the Manichaeans? Was the problem with Manichaeans, according to the decrees against them after *Cunctos Populos* (380), the correct doctrine, their teachings and beliefs?

An examination of the Cod. theod. and Cod. justin. laws against the Manichaeans suggest instead that the concerns they raised were of a socio-political and moral nature, and that the sense of threat that they instilled was associated with their congregations. To be specific, the laws against the Manichaeans targeted: (1) their congregations and buildings of assemblies,[39] (2) activities that were associated with these congregational activities,[40] such as occult rituals, social unrest and proselytizing, and (3) the Manichaeans themselves, all of them: their presence in the cities,[41] their misleading activities,[42] their name,[43] their life.[44] What is not explicitly targeted in these laws is their doctrines.

Thus, the declared aim of the law was to suppress the Manichaean gatherings which were associated not only with religious purposes but also with sedition. This exclusive emphasis on their gatherings is observed *only* for the Manichaeans, while, as I will examine below, the problem with the *noble* heresies was due mainly to their doctrine.[45] By contrast, the problem with the Manichaeans was not deviation from the correct doctrine. The most likely explanation for this is that their doctrines were not considered comparable to those of the Catholic Church. There was no common ground for the comparison; thus, a relevant discourse was apparently considered meaningless. This may also explain why Manichaean doctrines never were addressed in ecclesiastical synods.[46] The declared problem with them was not theological or ecclesiastical. It was their gatherings, because these were associated with occult rituals, magic, and socially and politically subversive activities. That is to say, they were associated with different crimes; they posed a qualitatively different threat.

---

39   Cod. theod. 16.5.3 (372), 16.5.7 (381), 16.5.9 (382), 16.5.11 (383), 16.5.35 (399), 16.5.38 (405), 16.5.43 (407), 16.5.65 (428).
40   Cod. theod. 16.5.18 (389), 16.5.38 (405), *NVal.* 18 (445).
41   Cod. theod. 16.5.7 (381), 16.5.62 (425), 16.5.64 (425).
42   Cod. theod. 16.5.7 (381) (crypto-Manichaeism), Cod. justin. 1.5.16 (527) (pseudo-conversions).
43   Cod. theod. 16.5.38 (405), Cod. justin. 1.5.12 (527).
44   Cod. justin. 1.5.11 (487 or 510), 1.5.12 (527), 1.5.16 (527).
45   Cod. theod. 16.5.12, 16.5.13.
46   Cf. Lieu 1992, 127.

3.2.2   The *Noble* Heretics

In contrast, as the relevant argumentation of the Cod. theod. shows, the problem with the *noble* heretics was their false doctrine. The gist of the relevant laws was the following: all those who do not agree with the Nicene Creed (Arians, Macedonians, Eunomians, Apollinarians), believe in wrong doctrines. For this reason, they are prohibited from teaching their doctrines, ordaining, worshipping and assembling.[47] The same rationale is repeated in the Cod. justin., this time for Eutychians (Monophysites) and Apollinarians. For those whose doctrines disagree with the teachings of the (by then) four Ecumenical Councils of the Church, it was forbidden to assemble, to teach, to write, to publish texts against Chalcedon, to possess books containing these arguments, and to ordain clerics.[48] The only difference in the argumentation from the Cod. theod. are the additional Ecumenical Councils as guarantors that the law represents the correct faith.

Presumably, the problem in the case of *noble* heresies was their false doctrine (teaching and writings) and their 'invalid' ordinations. Their gatherings are prohibited, because the false doctrine is taught there, and the worship

---

47   I indicatively quote some excerpts of these laws. Cod. theod. 16.5.6, 16.5.12 (383) (Coleman-Norton, 389): "should not usurp and have any regulations for creating priests", 16.5.13 (384) (Coleman-Norton, 392–93): "The Eunomians, the Macedonians, the Arians, and the Apollinarians [...] who say that they teach what is proper either not to know or to unlearn, should be expelled [...]", 16.5.14 (388) (Coleman-Norton, 415): "They should not have the ability of ordaining clergymen", 16.5.31, 16.5.32 (396) (Coleman-Norton, 467): "Eunomians' authors and teachers; and particularly their clergymen, whose frenzy has prompted so great error, should be expelled", 16.5.33 (397) (Coleman-Norton, 469): "We order teachers of Apollinarians to depart with all promptitude from the dwellings of the city", 16.5.34, 16.5.36, 16.5.58, 16.5.60 (423) (Pharr, 462): "heretics whose name and false doctrine We execrate, namely, the Eunomians, the Arians, the Macedonians [...] if they persist in the aforesaid madness, they shall be subject to the penalty which has been threatened", 16.5.65 (428) (Coleman-Norton, 643): "Arians, indeed, Macedonians, and Apollinarians, whose villainy is this, that [...] they believe falsehoods", 16.5.66.

48   Cod. justin. 1.5.8 (455) (Coleman-Norton, 854–55): "Also it may not be lawful for them to create and to have bishops or priests and other clergymen [...] Moreover on no Eutychian or Apollinarian should be bestowed the ability of publicly or privately summoning gatherings and of assembling meetings and of arguing about heretical error and of asserting a villainous dogma's perversity. Also none it should be permitted either to declare or to write or to proclaim or to emit anything contrary to the venerable Chalcedonian Synod or to publish others' writings on the said subject; none should dare to have books of this character and to keep writers' sacrilegious documents. [...] Moreover we order those persons who through zeal of learning shall have heard disputes about unpropitious heresy to undergo the loss of ten pounds of gold, which must be paid into our fisc. Moreover all papers and books of this kind, which shall have contained the deadly dogma of Eutyches, that is, of Apollinaris should be burned by fire [...]".

is performed by irregularly/non-canonically (from a Catholic point of view) ordained clergy. Therefore, whenever, the target of the laws against *noble* heretics is their congregations, this is linked either with their wrong dogma and teaching, or with the illegitimate ordinations, baptisms, etc. The same is true for schismatics, whose illegal ordinations and anabaptisms/rebaptisms (i.e. questions of ecclesiastical organization) were the target of the law.[49]

In sum, while *noble* heretics were persecuted for erring in doctrine, on the basis of the rationale inaugurated by Theodosius, the Manichaeans were persecuted for reasons that existed in the pre-Theodosius era. A comparison with the underlying rationale for persecutions of pagans and Jews will allow us to add some flesh to the bones of this argument.

3.2.3   The Jews

Many of the laws concerning the Jews in the Cod. theod. are more beneficial than condemnatory. Their aim is: (1) the protection of the synagogues and of Jews from attacks,[50] and (2) ensuring privileges and rights (e.g. trade rights in determining the prices of their products).[51] Yet, there are also other laws that targeted the Jews for punishment.

Jews were persecuted mainly when their activities were framed as threatening Christians. One such case concerns conversion: when Jews who had converted to Christianity were attacked, abused or disinherited by their fellow Jews.[52] But above all, they were persecuted when they were believed to have compelled Christians to convert to Judaism using coercion and violence. This chiefly applied to slaves and to the context of mixed marriages. In such cases, the penalty for the Jew was death, while the penalty for the apostate was confiscation of property.[53]

---

49   Cod. theod. 16.5.54, 16.5.57, 16.6.4, 16.6.5, Cod. justin. 1.5.20.

50   Protection of synagogues seven out of 29 laws totally: Cod. theod. 16.8.9 (393), 16.8.12 (397), 16.8.17 (404), 16.8.20 (412), 16.8.21 (412), 16.8.25 (423). Protection of Jews and their patriarchs: 16.8.11 (396), 16.8.12 (397), 16.8.21 (412).

51   Privileges: Cod. theod. 16.8.2, 4 (330/31) 16.8.10 (396), 16.8.13 (397).

52   Cod. theod. 16.8.1 (315) (Coleman-Norton, 66): "We will that it should be made known to Jews and their elders and patriarchs that if after this law anyone shall have dared to assail with rocks or with another kind of madness-which we have learned is being done now-anyone who has fled their deadly sect and has turned his attention to God's cult, he must be delivered immediately to the flames and with all his accomplices must be burned", 16.8.5 (336), 16.8.28 (426).

53   Cod. theod. 16.8.6 (339); 16.9.2 (339); 16.8.7 (357); 16.8.19 (409); 16.8.26 (423). It is noteworthy that the strictest laws against Jews were issued by Constantius, who did not issue any laws against heretics.

In this very specific context, the legal problem with the Jews was, on the one hand, that they (were said to) attempt to convert Christians to Judaism (in this connection they were accused of circumcising slaves and other Christians), whereas on the other hand, they hampered Jewish conversions to Christianity.

3.2.4   The Pagans

Pagans were not persecuted for their doctrines and teachings either, but for their practices. This involved: (1) their sacrifices,[54] associated with divination, prediction of the future (using animal entrails),[55] and magic (incantations, conspiring against the life and future of other persons), and (2) the worship of idols and icons.[56] Otherwise, at least initially (that is, before 435),[57] neither their festal gatherings in the temples (without sacrifices), nor the temples as such were targeted by the laws.[58] Instead, as was true in the case of the Jews, there are laws that actively aimed to protect the buildings of the temples from Christians fanatic. The laws of Arcadius and Honorius of 399 may have had such a background.[59] Could these laws be a delayed reply to Libanius' plea for the protection of Greek temples which were vandalized by the Christian monks?[60] In addition, another law from 423 threatened Christians who assaulted and robbed pagan and Jews with huge fines.[61] Thus, pagans too, were not persecuted for their doctrine, but for practices characterized in the words of the law as "a pagan superstition".[62]

Recapitulating what has been discussed above: *noble* heresies were persecuted for the deviation from the correct dogma and irregular priesthood. The latter was also the problem with the schismatics. The Manichaeans were persecuted for socially dangerous practices performed in their gatherings, and certainly not for their doctrine. The assemblies of pagans were not just allowed,

---

54   Cod. theod. 16.10.1 (321), 16.10.2 (341), 16.10.4 (346), 16.10.5 (353), 16.10.6 (356), 16.10.7 (381), 16.10.8 (382), 16.10.9 (385), 16.10.10 (391), 16.10.11 (391), 16.10.12 (392), 16.10.13 (395), 16.10.15 (399), 16.10.16 (399), 16.10.17 (399), etc.

55   Cod. theod. 16.10.9 (385), 16.10.12 (392), etc.

56   Cod. theod. 16.10.6 (356), 16.10.10 (391), 16.10.12 (392), 16.10.19 (408), 16.10.23 (423).

57   Cod. theod. 16.10.25 (435) (with the exemption of 16.10.16 in 399, which however contradicts the laws 16.10.17 and 16.10.18 of the same year).

58   Cod. theod. 16.10.8 (382); 16.10.17 (399).

59   Cod. theod. 16.10.15, 16.10.18 (both in 399).

60   Libanius' famous open letter *Pro templis* (Oration 30), to the Emperor Theodosius I, is dated ca 388 CE (384–391).

61   Cod. theod. 16.10.24 (423).

62   Cod. theod. 16.10.12.2 (392), 16.10.16 (399), 16.10.17 (399) (Pharr, 465): "amusements shall be furnished to the people, but without any sacrifice or any accursed superstition", 16.10.20.pr. (415).

but were protected, at least until the first decades of the fifth century, provided they did not make sacrifices. Finally, the synagogues were protected, while Jews were persecuted only when they were considered to exercise subversive tactics against Christians or Christian communities.[63]

We note that the theoretical framework for the persecution of Manichaeans, pagans and Jews is the same (bad practices, not dogma), and continues in the same spirit of the law as it was in the pre-Theodosian era. However, there is an important difference: pagans and Jews were not persecuted, either themselves, or their congregations, unless they violated the law. For Manichaeans, this alternative did not exist, unless they ceased being Manichaeans. Manichaeans were thus framed as constituting a problem in every respect. For the moment, the above observation suffices. Only in the case of Manichaeans and similar sects was there criminalization of their gatherings *per se* in advance, because they were considered beforehand as socially dangerous and subversive. All of this is clearly reflected also in the persecuted persons, the prosecution processes, and the *poenae* imposed. It is to all of these that we turn now.

3.3   *Persecuted Persons*

Were all the Manichaeans persecuted, or only the Elect? In light of the general framing of Manichaeism as a problem, it should not be surprising that the answer to this question seems to be both. In the first decrees, the distinction between the two classes is noticeable. Elect and hearers are distinguished from each other, as they had to face different penalties. Diocletian's rescript (302) decreed: burning in the flames for "the authors and leaders" of the sect, and "capital punishment" for the "followers" (hearers/catechumens), "if they continued recalcitrant". Better was the treatment of those hearers/catechumens who were governmental officials or members of the upper social classes, who were sentenced to forced labour in the mines (metalla, μεταλλισθῆναι). The confiscation of property applied to all.[64] According to the edict of Valentinian

---

63   This is what the laws *tell us*. In all cases, there is, of course, an enormous amount of negotiating power that would allow many people to persecute others under a veneer of legality.

64   Rescript of Diocletian cited in Gardner and Lieu 2004, 116–18: "We order that the authors and leaders of these sects be subjected to severe punishment, and, together with their abominable writings, burnt in the flames. We direct that their followers, if they continue recalcitrant, shall suffer capital punishment, and their goods be forfeited to the imperial treasury. (7) And if those who have gone over to that hitherto unheard-of, scandalous and wholly infamous creed, or to that of the Persians, are persons who hold public office, or are of any rank or of superior social status, you will see to it that their estates are confiscated and the offenders sent to the (quarry) at Phaeno or the mines at Proconnesus". As Lieu (2015, 124) states: "the famous rescript of Diocletian and Galerius of 302 [...] consigned the Elect of the sect to the flames along with their books, and the followers (i.e. Hearers)

II and Valens (372), the teachers (Elect) of the sect were punished with severe penalties (not specified) and the followers ("those persons who assemble") were socially isolated, as "infamous and ignominious".[65] The last time the distinction between the two classes is discernible, though not clearly enough, is the law on apostates of Theodosius (and Valentinian II, 383), according to which heavier penalties were imposed upon the "artificers" (Elect?) of the sect, varying at "the discretion of the judges and the nature of the crime committed".[66]

Any possible distinction between the two classes is lost in the later laws. In all following decrees, the relevant references are addressed to Manichaeans as a whole. So, ten years after the law of Valentinian II and Valens (372), when a burst of laws against Manichaeans began, all were equally targeted: Elect, catechumens, *Manichaeos* and *Manichaeas*. The first law of Theodosius in 381 contains this innovation of making this clarification: Manichaean men and Manichaean women. The goal of the law was essentially to eliminate the *loci cultus* of the Manichaeans, depriving Manichaean men and women from the right "of leaving or of taking any inheritance".[67] At first sight, it seems that by mentioning the two sexes separately, the purpose of the law was to prevent the possibility that any property could be transferred in the community by the women of the sect, as they also had hereditary rights.[68] So, apart from the fact that there were women in the sect, one could say that the law does not reveal much about the activities of Manichaean women. However, the reference to both *Manichaeos* and *Manichaeas* is repeated again in a later law, and this, in combination with the fact that the Manichaeans were the only sect in both the Cod. theod. and Cod. justin. for which there is separate mention of the two sexes, is an indication that the Manichaean women were active members.[69]

---

to hard labour in mines and quarries". Nevertheless, it is possible that Diocletian's distinctions between "the authors and leaders" on the one hand, and the "followers" on the other, is a reference rooted in 'foreignness' and 'Romanness' rather than a reference to the 'Elect' and 'hearer' distinction.

65   Cod. theod. 16.5.3 (Coleman-Norton, 333). See also Lieu's comments (1992, 143f).
66   Cod. theod. 16.7.3 (383) (Coleman-Norton, 386); Linder, 1987 169–71, 172 fn. 3; Pharr 1952, 466.
67   Cod. theod. 16.5.7.pr. (381) (Coleman-Norton, 367).
68   From Adrianus onwards, hereditary rights were also extended to female Roman citizens who could bequeath or take any inheritance with the consent of their guardian/spouse, etc. Cf. Lieu 1992 145. From Kellis' documentary material it seems that the women of the village owned a big share of the village's property. See Franzmann's "The Manichaean Women in the Greek and Coptic Letters from Kellis" (2022a).
69   Cod. theod. 16.5.40 (407) in the version of Cod. justin. 1.5.4: Manichaeos seu manichaeas vel donatistas meritissima severitate persequimur. A third reference to Manichaean women is found in Justinian's *Nov.* 109 (541), which, however, is directed against all heretic women (among them Manichaeas) by depriving them of the right of dowry.

On the contrary, the decrees concerning *noble* heretics only persecute the clergy and their teachers, and not the ordinary believers. Priests and bishops were persecuted especially when they ordained and baptized.[70] Later, Justinian persecuted also the 'heretical' laymen who held imperial (public) positions.[71]

3.4 *Inquisitional Mechanisms for the Prosecution of Manichaeans*

What was the procedure for the prosecution of the Manichaeans when they were persecuted? How was the research aiming to detect and repress Manichaeans conducted? The laws against heretics of the Cod. theod. and Cod. justin. show that two basic models for prosecuting mechanisms existed. In the first model, a body of specialized investigators was formed for this particular purpose. In the second model, the already existing civil and military state structure (later also that of the church), was enlisted in order to enforce the laws. The degree to which officials (higher or low-ranking), other administrative staff, and ecclesiastical authorities were engaged in the second model, varies and depends on the case and on the time period. The first model is found only in the Cod. theod., while the second is found in both codes. In both cases, the instructions on how the investigation will be conducted were given by the emperor to the praetorian prefect of the respective prefecture.[72]

3.4.1 Codex Theodosianus

In the Cod. theod. there are three cases of laws that belong to the first model. The first concerns Manichaeans and some extreme ascetics, behind which, according to a previous law, Manichaeans were hiding.[73] The second concerns an investigation of heretics in general.[74] Targets of the third law were the Manichaeans, the Priscillianists, the Donatists, and the pagans.[75] In all the above three cases, the emperor decreed the praetorian prefect (and recipient of the law), who also had the criminal jurisdiction, to form a body of inquisitors for the detection and the repression of the aforementioned heretics.

In detail, in the first case, emperor Theodosius I ordered (on March 31, 382) Florus, the praetorian prefect of the East, to appoint *inquisitores* who would

---

70   Cod. theod. 16.5.12, 16.5.13, 16.5.14, 16.5.21, 16.5.31, 16.5.32, 16.5.33, 16.5.34, 16.5.36, 16.5.58, 16.5.65, Cod. justin. 1.5.8 (455).

71   Cod. justin. 1.5.8; 1.5.12; 1.5.18.

72   The same applies to Cod. justin.. Although the name of the recipient has not been preserved in the two laws that will be discussed, later laws from Cod. justin. confirm the above practice.

73   Cod. theod. 16.5.9 (382) and 16.5.7 (381).

74   Cod. theod. 16.5.15 (388).

75   *Sirm.* 12 (407/408).

conduct searches aimed at detecting and bringing to trial the Manichaeans and some extreme ascetics of his prefecture.[76] Moreover, he was prompted to encourage Roman citizens to denounce Manichaeans, "without the odium of delation".[77] It is true that Roman law, as well as society regarded informants (*delatores*) with suspicion. In legislation, informers are discouraged even with the threat of the death penalty if proven as slanderers. Constantine, in two decrees addressed to Roman citizens, prescribed a death sentence for malicious accusers who groundlessly accused someone, because they coveted his property or his life.[78] However, in a subsequent decree, Constantine made an exception to his own rule, encouraging the accusers of magicians, of astrologers and of other such criminals. In these cases, informers were not treated with any suspicion, but instead received a reward.[79] Theodosius followed the same tactic in the above decree, adding the Manichaeans to the list of those whom it was permitted to accuse, as they also had the stigma of magicians.[80] Citizens could fearlessly denounce Manichaeans within the confines of the law. We do not know whether a reward was also offered. The issue of informers returns in 445, in a law (the last of the Cod. theod. against Manichaeans), which is exclusively dedicated to the Manichaeans. This law highlights that everyone could accuse Manichaeans safely since the sect was a public crime: "This heresy shall be a public crime, and every person who wishes shall have the right to accuse such persons [Manichaeans] without the risk attendant upon an accusation".[81]

A similar procedure (appointment of investigators) was followed again by Theodosius I in June 14, 388, this time for the heretics of the West. The praetorian prefect of Italy, Trifolius, was asked to appoint "as observers certain very faithful persons, that they can both restrain them and bring them, when arrested, to the courts".[82] It is worth noting the instruction of Theodosius that

---

76   Cod. theod. 16.5.9 (382). The persecuted ascetics were: Encratites, Saccophori, and Hydroparastates. As Beskow (1988, 5) states: "This is probably the first time we encounter this term [inquisitors], later to be so ominous in Church history, and its use here ought not to be over-interpreted."

77   Cod. theod. 16.5.9.1 (382) (Pharr, 452). The law combines two methods: denunciation by investigators appointed by judge and denunciation by private informer. Cf. Barnard 1995, 128.

78   Cod. theod. 10.10.1 (313), 10.10.2 (319) (*De delatores*).

79   Cod. theod. 9.16.1 (319/20). Cf. Lieu 1992, 147.

80   Cod. theod. 16.5.9 (382). Cf. Lieu 1992, 142–50. On the question "Did the Manichaeans practice magic?", see BeDuhn 1995a, 419–34.

81   *NVal.* 18.2 (445). Manichaeism was defined as a public crime, i.e. "a crime that could be prosecuted by any person", see Pharr 1952, 531, fn. 4.

82   Cod. theod. 16.5.15 (Coleman-Norton, 418).

the body of investigators should consist of "very faithful persons". It is also interesting that the stages of the prosecution process are recorded in detail: (1) assemblies, discussions, secret meetings shall be restrained; (2) heretics shall be arrested, and (3) brought before the courts. Although the decree did not concern specific sects but was addressed against "all persons of diverse and perfidious sects", the whole context is reminiscent of the Manichaeans. Its target was the gatherings of the heretics, which are associated with something occult and conspiratorial: "should not be allowed to have anywhere an assembly, to enter into discussions, to conduct secret meetings, to build impudently by the offices of an impious hand altars of nefarious transgression and to apply the simulation of mysteries, to the true religion's injury".[83] Even the derogatory expressions 'miserable conspiracy' and 'madness' are some of those attributed to Manichaeans. The above assumption is supported by the following factors: (1) the fact that the decree concerned heretics of Italy, where the problem at that time were the Manichaeans, as shown by the laws that follow during the following years,[84] (2) the fact that the very same year the edict was issued (388), Augustine's first work against the Manichaeans, *De Moribus Manichaeorum*, was published. Probably Augustine's publication could have incited (to a certain extent) the persecution of the western Manichaeans.

The third case took place again in the Prefecture of Italy twenty years later. The decree, issued in the name of the emperors Honorius and Theodosius II, was directed to the praetorian prefect Curtius, and concerned the persecution of Manichaeans, Priscillianists, Donatists and pagans.[85] The specific copy of the law was the one posted in the *agora* (forum) of Carthage in June 5, 408. The novelty of the decree was the proposed collaboration between bishops and secret agents, officials of the state's secret services. The body of prosecution this time was comprised of the local bishops and three *agentes in rebus* (agents of the secret services), namely, Maximus, Julianus, and Eutychus. The bishops were entitled to use their ecclesiastical power and were granted the power of execution so that by collaborating with the secret agents they could track down the heretics, suppress their activities and report them to the governors who acted as judges of the provinces. However, the latter step did not always happen, and the report did not always reach the judges. And as it seems, the blame was put on the agents: "These men [*agentes in rebus*], however, shall

---

83   Cod. theod. 16.5.15 (Coleman-Norton, 418).

84   Cod. theod. 16.5.18 (389) 16.5.35 (399), 16.5.40 (407), 16.5.41 (407), 16.5.43 (408).

85   *Sirm.* 12 (408). It is the developed form of the law 16.5.43 (407), from which such useful information is missing.

know that the measure of the statutes must be observed in all respects", so that heretical deeds shall immediately be reported "to the judges to be punished according to the force of the laws".[86] Apparently, the emperors trusted the bishops more than their own civil servants. The reason for recruiting the Church in the prosecutorial procedure was the inefficiency and negligence of the state structure in implementing the law. The current edict inaugurated the creation of local networks of cooperation between the regional bishops and provincial governors.

The fourth case of the Cod. theod. belongs to the second model of prosecution, that of the mobilization of civil and military state officials. This concerns the law that the emperor Theodosius II addressed on May 30, 428, to Florentius, the praetorian prefect of the East.[87] As discussed above, this was the law that persecuted three categories of heretics, classified them according to the severity of their crime and by the corresponding penalties. The first group (*noble* heretics) was not allowed to have churches in the cities. The second group (Judaizers) were prohibited from building new churches. For the third group (among which we find the Manichaeans), their gatherings and prayers throughout the Roman territory were banned. Moreover, the Manichaeans had to be expelled from all municipalities.[88] Thus, the target of the inquisition was mainly the third group, and in particular the Manichaeans who had to be banished from all cities. For the enforcement of the law, "all civil and military power [...], the power of the municipal councils and defenders and the judges" was mobilized.[89] The accusations were reported to the governors of the provinces who also had jurisdiction over criminal matters at first instance. In case of negligence by the officials or by the administrative staff, a fine was prescribed. In case the governors/judges imposed lighter penalties than the law stated (or none at all) they were subjected to the penalties imposed on the heretics they had favoured. One can realize that the prosecutorial procedure could also be interrupted at the stage of litigation.

Judging, however, by the edict that was sent to the same prefect ten years later (in 438), the administrative dysfunction still continued. Theodosius II ordered the prefect Florentius that he had to follow the bureaucratic process step by step:

---

86   *Sirm.* 12 (408) (Pharr, 438; Coleman-Norton, 507).
87   Cod. theod. 16.5.65 (428).
88   Cod. theod. 16.5.65.2 (428).
89   Cod. theod. 16.5.65.3,5 (428) (Pharr, 463).

Therefore your [...] Authority, [...] by your Excellency's duly posted edicts should cause to come to all persons' notice and should order to be announced also to the provinces' governors what we have decreed [...] that also by their like care they may notify to all communities and provinces what we necessarily have ordained.[90]

3.4.2 Codex Justinianus

In the Cod. justin., as said, only the second model is found, in which the practice of cooperation between state and Church dominates, yet with an upgraded role of the Church. The responsibility for the enforcement of the law was the duty of all officials of the state, "as it pertains to each".[91] The clergy played the role of inspector, and had to check whether the provisions were observed and to report offenders to the emperor.[92] In other words, the bishops became the supreme inquisitorial body for the prosecution of heretics in the service of the emperor.

The main target of the two laws that I will examine were the Manichaeans. The first was issued by Justin and Justinian (in 527) and persecuted Manichaeans, heretics, pagans, Jews, and Samaritans.[93] The second was issued by Justinian (between 527 and 529) and persecuted only the Manichaeans.[94] Apart from the general objective, which was to identify Manichaeans "wherever on earth [Roman territory] appearing" and put them to death,[95] the two laws were focused on two specific target groups. The first group consisted of the Manichaeans who had infiltrated the imperial or other public or military services. Officials in the administration and in the army were asked to detect, after a diligent search, their Manichaean colleagues and deliver them to the authorities. Anyone who demonstrably knew any Manichaeans and did not

---

90 *NTh.* 3.1.10 (438) (Coleman-Norton, 713). The decree is addressed against the third group of the previous law. This time, the Manichaeans ("ever odious to God") head the list, followed by "Eunomians (authors of heretical fatuity) [...], Montanists, Phrygians, Photinians, Priscillians, Ascodrogitans, Hydroparastatans, Borborians, Ophitans". It is for this reason more probable that the inquisitional mechanisms of the previous law targeted the third group and primarily the Manichaeans.

91 Cod. justin. 1.5.12.21 (Coleman-Norton, 998). Specifically, in Constantinople, in charge were those who had glorious magistracies, and in the provinces, the governors (whether greater or lesser).

92 Cod. justin. 1.5.12.22. In Constantinople, in charge were the archbishop and the patriarch. In the other cities were the bishops and also those who occupied "patriarchal, metropolitan and minor positions".

93 Cod. justin. 1.5.12.

94 Cod. justin. 1.5.16.

95 Cod. justin. 1.5.12.3 (Coleman-Norton, 996).

turn them in would be punished as a Manichaean, even though he might not be one himself.[96]

The second target group comprised the apostates and the crypto-Manichaeans. Manichaeans' fake conversion and crypto-Manichaeism, it seems, were believed to have taken on large dimensions. For this reason, there was a great reservation about the sincerity of Manichaean conversions. According to the law, the ex-Manichaean, in order to prove to all that he converted "not in pretence, but in earnest", should immediately report and deliver, "to a lawful judge", his ex-comrades with whom he "appeared to have communed".[97] Thus, converted Manichaeans became part of the persecutory mechanism.

3.5 The Dilemma Between Tolerance and Repression

The main purpose of prosecuting and imposing penalties on heretics, as is reflected in Roman legislation, was both the prevention of the crime through the 'terror of the punishment' and the 'correction' of the heretics, namely by their conversion to the 'correct' faith.[98] That the same objective was also the aim in the case of Manichaeans is clearly illustrated in the *Sirm.* 12 (408). The constitution explains in a most enlightening manner that the aim of the law was their correction, and not their prosecution. This allows us to understand why the laws against Manichaeans, as well as against other heretics, were usually not enforced. At the same time, it explains why there was such room for tolerance by the authorities in implementing the laws, which in turn resulted in their continuous repetition.

> The heretics [Donatists, Manichaeans, Priscillianists] and the superstition of the pagans ought to have been corrected by the solicitude alone of those religious men, the priests of God [...] by their sedulous admonition and by their authoritative teaching. Nevertheless the regulations of Our laws have not become ineffective, which also by the terror of punishment that has been proposed shall lead back [...] those persons who go astray.[99]

---

96   Cod. justin. 1.5.16.5. Cf. Lieu 1994a, 117.

97   Cod. justin. 1.5.16 (Coleman-Norton, 1007). Cf. Lieu 1994a, 117.

98   As Troiannos (1997, 16–17) observes, Basil of Caesarea in his letter to Andronicus (epist. 122) sets out the purpose of Church's and state's penal system, rejecting a retributive character and emphasizing its value as a means of prevention. Later on, in the Isaurian *Eclogae* the purpose of punishment is clearly stated: prevention and correction. In all Byzantine legislation prevention stands out as the most basic purpose of a penalty.

99   *Sirm.* 12, 407/08 (Pharr, 482–83; Coleman-Norton, 506).

The rationale and the practice of three more laws testifies to the fact that the ideal for the state was for the Manichaeans to convert and no longer comprise a threat.[100] These laws annul the punishments (*abolitio*) and absolve all repenting Manichaeans from the prosecution of all previous laws. The three following edicts are the exception to the rule of the state's policy of 'terror' and marked the adoption of an alternative religious policy, that of *philanthropy*. Hereafter, I will refer to them as the *decrees of philanthropy*.

> Although it is customary for crimes to be expiated by punishment, it is Our will, nevertheless, to correct the depraved desires of men by an admonition to repentance. Therefore, if any heretics, whether they are Donatists or Manichaeans or of any other depraved belief and sect who have congregated for profane rites, should embrace, by a simple confession, the Catholic faith and rites, which We wish to be observed by all men, even though such heretics have nourished a deep-rooted evil by long and continued meditation, to such an extent that they also seem to be subject to the laws formerly issued [16.5.1–40], nevertheless, as soon as they have confessed God by a simple expression of belief, We decree that they shall be absolved from all guilt.[101]
>
> We command that the Manichaeans, heretics, schismatics, astrologers and every sect inimical to the Catholics [...]. By the issuance of this notification We grant to them a truce of twenty days. Unless they return within that time to the unity of communion, they shall be expelled from the City.[102]
>
> We command that Manichaeans, heretics, schismatics, and every sect inimical to the Catholics shall be banished from the very sight of the various cities, [...] unless a speedy reform should come to their aid.[103]

However, in practice, as is reflected in the rest of the legislation, this remained only wishful thinking. In the case of Manichaeans, this tactic of philanthropy did not work. On the contrary, as we shall see below, it opened the door to the phenomenon of false-conversions.[104] The authorities realized this fact, and returned to the policy of 'tolerance through terror', issuing a series of decrees

---

100   Cod. theod. 16.5.41, 16.5.62, 16.5.64. 16.5.40.
101   Cod. theod. 16.5.41 (407) (Pharr, 457; Coleman-Norton, 504).
102   Cod. theod. 16.5.62 (425) (Pharr, 462; Coleman-Norton, 635).
103   Cod. theod. 16.5.64 (425) (Pharr, 462; Coleman-Norton, 633–34).
104   See ch.[8], section 5.

expelling Manichaeans from the cities and the empire.[105] The only option left was the physical eradication of the Manichaeans.

In their debut on the political scene, the emperors Justin and Justinian made it clear that their patience with heretics was exhausted, thus confirming that the policy of tolerance until then was applied:

> We permitted the heretics to assemble and have their own name for this reason: that, ashamed by Our forbearance, they may come to their senses and turn to the better of their own accord. 1. But an unbearable audacity has possessed them, and, disregarding the sanction of the law [...] [...].[106]

The two emperors renewed and confirmed the validity of all previous laws against heretics and assured that in the future they would not let the law again become a dead letter, as had happened before.

3.6 Crime and Punishment: The Nature of the Crime/'Threat' As It Is Revealed Through the Prosecuting Process and the Penalties Imposed

3.6.1 Characterization of the Crime (Classification)

But which were the penalties that the Manichaeans would be discharged of if they did repent? And what do these penalties reveal about the nature of their crime? In criminal law, the penalties reflect the seriousness of each crime, and on this basis the characterization of the crime takes place.

Studying the laws against Manichaeans, one observes that they emphasize two determinants of the identity of the sect and its adherents, aiming to underline the severity of the crime. In terms of the law of the era, the sect was characterized as *publicum crimen*[107] and the Manichaeans themselves as *infames*, a brand inducing the forfeiture of their status of Roman citizens (*cives Romani*). Starting already from the first laws, it became gradually embedded that Roman civil law did not apply to the Manichaeans: Manichaeans were deprived of the right to live "under [the] Roman law" (*vivere/vivendi iure Romano*):[108] "they

---

105 As a result, a series of edicts expelling Manichaeans from cities and empire, were issued: Cod. theod. 16.5.7 (381), 16.5.11 (383), 16.5.18 (389), 16.10.24 (423), 16.5.62 (425), 16.5.64 (425), *Sirm.* 6 (425) (the latter three are probably experts of a longer law), 16.5.65 (428), NVal. 18 (445).

106 Cod. justin. 1.5.12.pr. (527) (Frier et al., 203).

107 Cod. theod. 16.5.40 (407) = Cod. justin. 1.5.4: Ac primum quidem volumus esse publicum crimen, quia quod in religionem divinam conmittitur, in omnium fertur iniuriam. NVal. 18 (445): Sitque publicum crimen et omni volenti sine accusationis periculo tales arguere sit facultas.

108 Cod. theod. 16.5.7.pr. (381) (Coleman-Norton, 367) (due to the crime of sacrilege).

should have nothing in common with all other persons",[109] "this class of men [...] have no customs and no laws in common with the rest of mankind".[110]

One of the consequences of the loss of Roman citizenship was the retroactive effect of the law in terms of prosecutions and penalties. The concept of retroactivity was twofold. In his first edict in 381, Theodosius I decreed the following, which was unprecedented in Roman jurisprudence: the Manichaeans will be prosecuted not only for acts that they will do in the future, but also for acts that were done in the past, before the issuance of the law. And he justified his decision by invoking the severity of the crime:

> The general rule of this law issued [...] shall be valid not only for the future but also for the past [...] For although the order of [...] imperial statutes indicates to those who must observe them the subsequent observance [...] and is not customarily prejudicial to previous acts, nevertheless, in this sanction only, since it is Our will that it shall be especially forceful, We recognize by Our sense of just inspiration what an inveterate obstinacy and a pertinacious nature deserve. [...] We sanction the severity of the present statute not so much as an example of a law that should be established but as one that should be avenged [...].[111]

In particular, the above law stated that since the sect and its gatherings were outlawed, i.e. after Valentinian's decree in 372, any testament, conveyance, donation, etc., that was made or accepted by a Manichaean, after that day, would be rendered invalid.

The other dimension of retroactivity was the *post mortem* accusability and prosecution. In the law of 407, the emperors Arcadius, Honorius, and Theodosius II made it clear from the outset that the Manichaean heresy had to be considered as a *public crime* and on this ground they legitimized *post mortem* prosecution.[112] Later, in 445, the same argument was used, as we have seen, to grant the right that "every person who wishes" could "accuse such persons without hazard of an accusation".[113]

---

109 Cod. theod. 16.5.18.1 (389) (Coleman-Norton, 421): Nihil ad summum his sit commune cum mundo (because they disturb the world).

110 Cod. theod. 16.5.40.pr. (407) (Pharr 457) = Cod. justin. 1.5.4. Huic itaque hominum generi nihil ex moribus, nihil ex legibus sit commune cum ceteris, because they committed a public crime, parallelized to that of high treason.

111 Cod. theod. 16.5.7.1 (381) (Pharr 451).

112 Cod. theod. 16.5.40 (407) = Cod. justin. 1.5.4.

113 NVal. 18.2 (445) (Pharr 531; Coleman-Norton, 730).

But what exactly was the content of the concept of public crime in the case of Manichaeans? In the next sections examining the rationale of the law and the penalties imposed, I will attempt to discern the dimensions of this 'threat' (national, political, social, religious and moral).

3.6.2   The National Dimension of the 'Threat'

The only decree explicitly stating the link between Manichaeans and Persia, which expressed fears of a national threat due to the activities of the Manichaeans, was Diocletian's rescript. In 445, Valentinian III, in his novella against the Manichaeans, refers implicitly to Diocletian's decree, in fact to indicate the seriousness of the threat: "A superstition condemned also in pagan times, inimical to public discipline [...] We speak of the Manichaeans [...]"; yet, without making any allusion to the Persian threat.[114]

So, in the wording of the law there is no explicit link between Manichaeans and Persians. Nevertheless, the fact that the prosecution procedure and the penalties imposed on Manichaeans were similar to those of traitors indicates that there was a latent national threat to the authorities.[115] As stated above, the characterization of the sect as public crime in 407 made the *post mortem* prosecution legal, something which otherwise applied only in the case of traitors. In the words of the law: "Also the legal inquisition extends beyond death. For, if in crimes of treason it is allowed to accuse a deceased person's memory, not undeservedly the said person also ought to undergo judgment in this case".[116] The term public crime here is identical to that of high treason. The above heretics (Manichaeans and Donatists), in addition to not being considered Roman citizens, also were treated as traitors. In practice, *post mortem* prosecution in this case meant that if someone was found out after death to have been a Manichaean, his will became void, as did a number of other legal titles.[117] Furthermore, the Manichaeans as traitors were never granted amnesty, as was an option for other crimes and other heretics.[118] At times and in various occasions – usually on account of the Easter celebration – prisoners were

---

114   *NVal.* 18.pr. (445) (Coleman-Norton, 730). Cf. Barnard 1995, 135.
115   Barnard (1995, 134–36) examining the similarities of the procedures of prosecution between heretics and traitors, argues that "there was [...] some indirect historical connexion between heresy and *maiestas* through Manichaeism"; however as she notes "it would be unwarranted to translate this historical link into a contemporary conceptual connexion".
116   Cod. theod. 16.5.40.5 (407) = Cod. justin. 1.5.4 (Coleman-Norton, 502). In mortem quoque inquisitio tendatur. nam si in criminibus maiestatis licet memoriam accusare defuncti, non immerito et hic debet subire iudicium.
117   Cod. theod. 16.5.40.5 (407).
118   Edict of Gratian (378/9) in Socrates *HE*: 5.2.1–8; Sozomenus *HE*: 7.1.3.

pardoned for a specified period. Amnesty was given to all who had not committed any of the capital crimes (*capitalia crimina*), namely: treason, murder, witchcraft (including poisoning/φαρμακεία), sacrilege, moral crimes (adultery, seduction, rape) kidnapping, and counterfeiting (imperial documents or currencies).[119]

As far as the penalties are concerned, apart from the socio-economic measures against the descendants of the deceased Manichaeans entailed by the *post mortem* prosecution, from some point onwards (485 or 510) the death penalty (re)appeared in Roman anti-Manichaean legislation, commonly used for traitors.[120] As highlighted by Barnard, the death penalty was "an inappropriate penalty for heresy" and was imposed only in some isolated cases of sects linked to other offenses (rebellion, witchcraft, violence), when other non-theological factors were involved.[121]

Of course, as mentioned above, there were the *decrees of philanthropy*, which annulled all guilt and prosecution if Manichaeans repented. Moreover, several edicts against Manichaeans stressed that in case of conversion the former Manichaean was exempted from accusations, penalties, and prosecution. Doing something similar in the case of traitors was inconceivable. High treason was punished irrevocably. It therefore seems that there was a considerable reservation: hence the ambiguous attitude of the law towards Manichaeans. Probably the tactic of philanthropy was a result of necessity, when and where the situation was out of control. In addition, even in this case, we do not know for how long these laws were applied, because they were followed by others that did not provide this opportunity, and seemed contradictory to the former. In any case, the above discourse applies to the pre-Justinian era. Under Justinian, tolerance and patience were exhausted. Repentance was not always a safe alternative option.

3.6.3   The Socio-Political Dimension of the Threat
The dimension of subversion of the public order is a permanent concern in legislation linked with the congregations of the Manichaeans.

---

119   Cod. theod. 9.38.1–12 and *Sirm.* 7 and 8. The Manichaeans were associated with the crimes of treason, of witchcraft, of sacrilege, and of sex-crimes.

120   Manichaeism is the first and perhaps the only 'heresy' for which the death penalty was prescribed.

121   Barnard 1995, 140, 146 fn. 95: "The death penalty was applicable to e.g. *maiestas*, counterfeiting, magic, arson, adultery, abduction of a woman for sexual purposes, sodomy, certain instances of violation of tombs and (for the lower orders) murder and grave forms of violence".

Right from the introductory part of his novel, Valentinian underlines that the Manichaean heresy "is inimical to the public discipline". The second article of the novel decrees: "let" Manichaeism "be a public crime".[122] The conviction that the Manichaeans upset urban communities and corrupted peaceful citizens runs throughout all anti-Manichaean laws. The Manichaeans are described as corrupters of the public discipline, who attract people and collect a multitude of followers;[123] they form secret groups in hidden gatherings in the towns, in the countryside, in private homes, and in public spaces;[124] they instigate seditious mobs[125] and disturb the world.[126] For these reasons, citizens are forbidden to talk to or about a Manichaean.[127] Here, the term public crime acquires the meaning of subversive socio-political action.

The first measure to face the above 'threat' was that the Manichaean community should not be allowed to own meeting places, in other words, real estate. Initially, the detected places were confiscated.[128] But then, in order to exclude any possibility of acquiring such premises in the future (by the members of the Manichaean community), a series of financial measures and penalties were introduced.[129] The forfeiture of Roman citizenship from Manichaeans also served this purpose.[130] Since the Manichaeans were deprived of the right *vivere iure Romano* (to live under the Roman law), they were forbidden to inherit, bequeath, transfer, or donate their property to other Manichaeans, but above all to their community for the purpose of the assemblies of the sect.[131] Consequently, the only solution left for them was to use places that belonged to non-Manichaeans; this was done, as evidenced in the law by the appearance of penalties for those in whose properties the Manichaean congregations took place.[132]

However, it was not only the Manichaean gatherings which caused disturbance in civic communities, but the very presence of Manichaeans themselves. The ultimate goal of the law was to deactivate the Manichaeans socially,

---

122　*NVal.* 18pr, 2 (Coleman-Norton, 730).
123　Cod. theod. 16.5.9, 16.5.11.
124　Cod. theod. 16.5.9.
125　Cod. theod. 16.5.38.
126　Cod. theod. 16.5.18.
127　Cod. theod. 16.5.38.
128　Cod. theod. 16.5.3 (372).
129　Cod. theod. 16.5.7 (381), 16.5.9 (382), 16.5.18 (389), 16.5.38 (405), 16.5.40 (407), 16.5.43 (407), 16.5.59 (423), 16.10.24 (423), 16.5.65 (428), *NVal.* 18 (445), Cod. justin. 1.5.15 (527).
130　Cod. theod. 16.5.7 (381).
131　Cod. theod. 16.5.9 (382) urged Manichaeans to return the estates that had been given to the community to their legal (non-Manichaeans) heirs.
132　Cod. theod. 16.5.40 (407).

and the best solution for that purpose seemed to be their physical isolation. Thus, from 389 onwards, a series of edicts decreeing the penalty of exile for Manichaeans began.[133] The Manichaeans were deprived of the right "of dwelling in cities".[134] They were forbidden to live, especially, in metropolises and populous cities, in order not to infect the citizens through social intercourse.[135] Step by step, the Manichaeans were expelled initially from the major cities, followed by exile from all cities, and at the end from all over the Roman world.[136] This escalation of the measures indicates, firstly, that the Manichaean 'danger' was gradually dispersed throughout the empire and, secondly, that even a single Manichaean, found anywhere in the empire, was considered a threat.[137] The fact that the 'corruption' of the citizens, according to the law, was spread is reflected in: (1) the determent and intimidation of citizens who harboured or abetted Manichaeans,[138] (2) the penalties imposed on administrative officials who did not enforce the law.[139]

3.6.4   The Religious Dimension of the Threat: Sacrilege
According to the rationale of the law issued in 407, the Manichaean "heresy shall be considered a public crime", "because what is committed against divine religion is effected to the injury of all persons".[140] One further capital crime of which Manichaeans were accused was that of sacrilege.[141] This was the offense

---

133   Cod. theod. 16.5.18 (389).
134   NVal. 18.3 (445) (Coleman-Norton, 730).
135   Cod. theod. 16.5.3 (372), 16.5.7 (381), 16.5.18 (389), 16.10.24 (423), 16.5.62 (425), 16.5.64 (425), Sirm. 6, 16.6.65 (428), NVal. 18 (445), Cod. justin. 1.5.12 (527).
136   Cod. theod. 16.5.18 (389), 16.5.62, 16.5.64, Sirm. 6, NVal. 18.pr. (445) (Coleman-Norton, 730): "We speak of the Manichaeans, whom the statutes of all previous emperors have judged execrable and worthy to be expelled from the whole world". Cod. justin. 1.5.12.3, p. 53. As Pharr (1952, 453) and Coleman-Norton (1966, 422) note, the Latin word mundus has a broader meaning than "orbis terrarum, the Roman world, the Roman Empire, the civilized world" and means "the 'universe', 'mankind'".
137   Cod. justin. 1.5.12.3.
138   Cod. theod. 16.5.35 (399), 16.5.40 (407), 16.5.65 (428), NVal. 18 (445).
139   Cod. theod. 16.5.40.8 (407), 16.5.43 (408), 16.5.65.5 (428), NTh. 3.9–10 (438), NVal. 18 (445), Cod. justin. 1.5.16.1, 1.5.18.11.
140   Cod. theod. 16.5.40.1 (407) (Coleman-Norton, 502; Pharr, 457). Here lies the cornerstone of the political theology of Christian Roman Empire: Undermining the 'correct'/official religion is equivalent to undermining the state and its citizens. As Pharr (1952, 457, fn. 85) notes, "This is the fundamental principle on which was based the persecution of Christianity by the pagan Emperors and the persecution of heresy and paganism by the orthodox Christian Emperors. The Emperors were also influenced by their desire to promote the unity of the Empire".
141   In Cod. theod. 9.38.7 (384) and 9.38.8 (385) sacrilege is classified among capital punishments.

that forced Theodosius I to deprive Manichaeans of the status of Roman citizenship in 381, and to innovate with the retroactivity of his law:

> We regard as guilty of sacrilege on the ground of violation of this described law [Valentinian's in 372] those persons who, even after the law originally had been issued, have not at all been able to be restrained at least by divine admonishment from illicit and profane assemblies.[142]

What was the content of the crime of sacrilege in the case of the Manichaeans? In the above law there are hints that something 'occult' was happening in their congregations. Expressions like, 'profane assemblies' (*profanis coitionibus*) for their gatherings, 'funereal mysteries' (*feralium mysteriorum*) for their cult and 'sepulchres' (*sepulcra*) for their meeting places, imply that something occult was occurring during the Manichaean mysteries.[143] In addition to the above law, such references or allusions to sacrilegious rituals exist in a series of laws,[144] with expressions such as 'profane rites', 'depraved desires',[145] 'obnoxious Manichaeans and their detestable assemblies',[146] 'sacrilegious rite in these rather deadly places',[147] 'crimes [...] obscene to tell and to hear [...] so detestable an outrage to the Divinity,'[148] and 'Manichaeans' loathsome blasphemies'.[149] Characteristic is also the concern of the law, to protect citizens from being contaminated from touching the sacrilegious Manichaeans!

> We call heretics other persons, just as the accursed Manichaeans and those about like these; indeed it is unnecessary that they even should be named or should appear anywhere at all or should defile what they have touched. But the Manichaeans – as we have said – thus ought to be expelled and none ought either to tolerate or to overlook their denomination, if indeed a person diseased with this atheism should dwell in the same place with others.[150]

---

142   Cod. theod. 16.5.7.1 (381) (Coleman-Norton, 368).
143   Cod. theod. 16.5.7.3 (381) (Coleman-Norton, 368).
144   Cod. theod. 16.5.9 (382), 16.5.11 (383), 16.5.38 (405), 16.5.43 (408), 16.5.65 (428), NVal. 18 (445).
145   Cod. theod. 16.5.41 (407).
146   Cod. theod. 16.5.35 (399) (Coleman-Norton, 480).
147   *Sirm.* 12 (407/08) (Coleman-Norton, 507): sacrilegi ritus funestioribus locis.
148   NVal. 18.pr. (445) (Coleman-Norton, 730).
149   Cod. justin. 1.5.16.2 (Coleman-Norton, 1006).
150   Cod. justin. 1.5.12.2–3 (527) (Coleman-Norton, 996).

Tangled up with occult rituals was also the dimension of moral corruption:[151]

> [It is] a crime by which not only the bodies but also the souls of deceived persons are polluted inexpiably. [...] For nothing seems too much to be able to be decreed against those persons whose unholy perversity in the name of religion commits deeds unknown or shameful even to brothels.[152]

Sacrilege in turn, was interconnected with another capital crime, magic; this formed an extra link between Manichaeans and Persians. The occult, profane, sacrilegious scenery referenced above, that the law reiterates took place during Manichaean rituals, was associated with magical practices. According to the edict directed to Florentius, the praetorian prefect of the East, in 428, it was imperative that Manichaeans should be expelled from "municipalities, since to all these must be left no place wherein even on the very elements may be made an injury".[153] In the version of the same law in the Cod. justin., apart from exile, they should be "delivered over to capital punishment, since there must be left to them no place in which an outrage may even be committed against the elements (by magic)".[154]

The treatment of Manichaeans and magicians by the law, as far as the prosecution and the sentences are concerned, had much in common. As mentioned above, while informers generally were deterred and were risking their lives in case their accusations proved slanderous, the informers for magicians and Manichaeans were encouraged without fear of punishment.[155] In addition, the magicians, as with the Manichaeans and traitors, were never granted pardon, since magic was one of the capital crimes. As far as the penalties are concerned, not only were magicians and Manichaeans both subjected to capital punishment, but they faced the same method of execution, which was to

---

151   Cod. theod. 16.7.3.pr. (Manichaeans' "nefarious retreats" and "wicked recesses/seclusion")
        (Coleman-Norton, 385), 16.5.41 (depraved desires).

152   *NVal.* 18.pr., 4 (Coleman-Norton, 730–31).

153   Cod. theod. 16.5.65.2 (428) (Coleman-Norton, 643): Manichaeis etiam de civitatibus expellendis, quoniam nihil his omnibus relinquendum loci est, in quo ipsis etiam elementis fiat iniuria.

154   Cod. justin. 1.5.5 (428): Manichaeis etiam de civitatibus expellendis et ultimo supplicio tradendis, quoniam nihil his relinquendum loci est, in quo ipsis etiam elementis fiat iniuria". For the disturbance of the elements by magic arts, see also Cod. theod. 9.16, especially 9.16.5 (Pharr, 237–38): "Many persons who dare to disturb the elements by magic arts do not hesitate to jeopardize [...]".

155   Cod. theod. 9.16; Cod. theod. 16.5.9 (382), *NVal.* (445).

be burned at the pyre, or decapitation. Thus, in these cases, the content of the term public crime meant insulting religion by sacrilege and magic.

To sum up, according to what was presented above, the crimes that constituted the content of the term *public crime* in the case of Manichaeans were: high treason, subversion of public order, sacrilege, magic and moral corruption. However, I consider that apart from the above 'threats' there was an underlying fear of another one that is not explicitly stated in the legislation of the Christian emperors, while it is highlighted in Diocletian's rescript: "there is danger that, in process of time, they will endeavour, as is their usual practice, to infect the innocent, orderly and tranquil Roman people, as well as the whole of our empire".[156]

Which usual practice is Diocletian talking about? The sense given through the anti-Manichaean law is for something driven underground, slowly, steadily, methodically; for something that was 'poisoning' citizens silently, through their daily social life and intercourse. As is highlighted in a line of the law, such heretics "have nourished by long and long-lasting meditation a deep-seated evil, to such an extent that they also appear subject to previously issued laws [16.5.1–40]".[157]

The Manichaeans 'contaminate' people even just by their sight or their touch, without doing something dramatic.[158] Through everyday social contact they somehow draw upon themselves the sympathy of people who protect them and hide them in their homes, even risking their safety.[159] I consider that the 'threat' was intensified by a series of interrelated characteristics of the idiosyncrasy of Manichaeism. First in this regard is the exclusivity required by Manichaeism, as in Christianity, which was an outcome of Manichaean eschatology. As underlined by Honoré, who comments on the desire of the law for the Manichaean 'expulsion from the world', "the author of the text understands the doctrine he is attacking. For the Manichees believe that the whole cosmos must be enlisted in order to release the sparks of light imprisoned".[160] I should note, here, that the idea of the conversion of the whole cosmos at the

---

156   Rescript of Diocletian.
157   Cod. theod. 16.5.41 (Coleman-Norton, 504).
158   Cod. theod. 16.5.7.3 (381), 16.5.62 (425), 16.5.64 (425), *Sirm.* 6 (425) (Coleman-Norton, 633): "Manichaeans [...] ought to be barred from the very sight of the various cities, in order that these may not be befouled by the contagion of even the presence of criminals", Cod. justin. 1.5.12 (527).
159   Cod. theod. 16.5.35; *NVal.* 18; Cod. justin. 1.5.4.7.
160   Honoré 1986, 214. Cf. Cod. theod. 16.5.18.

end of history is no stranger to Christianity (i.e. restoration of everything).[161]
The common denominator of exclusivity and of the specific eschatological
perspective was the necessity of mission. It can be noted that the three above
characteristics were common to Manichaeism and Christianity. Taking into
account that Manichaeism also was presented as an alternative Christianity
and the Manichaeans as the true Christians and exemplary ascetics, one realizes why for both the state and the Church, the Manichaeans were the 'worst of
the worst'.[162] Therein lies the difference with the Jews and the pagans. All three
were persecuted for practices that threatened public order, morality, yet not for
their doctrine. But while the Jews and pagans were religious groups with distinct
and entrenched boundaries around their collective identity, the corresponding
limits of the identity of Manichaeans were blurred.[163] Moreover, this ambiguity of the boundaries of the sect was magnified by crypto-Manichaeans and
false conversions, since perjury and renunciation of faith for the sake of safety
was believed to be acceptable in Manichaeism.[164] Unlike the Jews and pagans,
who were persecuted only when infringing the law, the Manichaeans, as the
Christians earlier, were persecuted for anything they did. This means they were
persecuted for their own existence, for their name: "But the Manichaeans – as
we have said – thus ought to be expelled and none ought either to tolerate or
to overlook their denomination".[165]

In conclusion, I would like to make the following remarks. According to
Roman imperial law the Manichaeans were traitors, magicians, and sacrilegious. This could obviously have been the biased opinion of those who persecuted them; hence it runs a high risk of being subjective. On the other hand, it

---

161   The concept of rehabilitation was developed by great theologians, such as Origen and
      Gregory of Nyssa.

162   Cod. theod. 16.5.65.2 (Manichaeans, who have attained to the lowest villainy of crimes).

163   Lim 2001, 198: "Judaism was regarded by the Romans as a *Volksreligion* that had its own
      recognized hierarchy, distinctive laws, rituals, and institutions. Thus for a nonconform-
      ing minority religion the secret to survival rested on being set apart and hedged by
      clear group boundaries. Whenever purveyors of religious ideas aggressively sought con-
      verts across established social and ethnic lines, their success met with stiffer opposi-
      tion. Though universalistic in aspiration, the so-called mystery religions did not seek to
      monopolize religious devotion but offered added options under the rubric of polytheism.
      But the missionary efforts of Christians and later of Manichaeans, neither of whom could
      boast unambiguous ethnic identities, posed a more threatening challenge to the existing
      order; their brand of transgressive proselytism alarmed local opponents and caused them
      to be intermittently persecuted by the state".

164   See for instance: Cod. theod. 16.5.7, Cod. theod. 16.5.9, Cod. justin. 1.5.16. I will return to
      this issue in ch.[8].

165   Cod. justin. 1.5.12.3 (Coleman-Norton, 996).

is an objective fact that the state considered them as traitors, magicians, and sacrilegious, and imposed upon them penalties of property measures, exile and capital punishment.

In the next section, I will investigate the effects of the implementation – or not – of such penalties on the everyday life of the Manichaeans.

4   Effects of the Implementation – or Not – of the Law on the Everyday Life of the Manichaeans

The relationship between law and social reality is dialectical. Law to some extent 'anticipates' social reality, attempting to transform it. At the same time, it follows social reality, responding to its demands.

On the one hand, the Roman anti-heretical laws, with the privileges provided and the punishments imposed, sought to transform the identities of the citizens subjected to it, affecting their social and economic status; they shaped the profile of law-abiding, loyal and faithful Roman citizens, as opposed to that of the heretic, who was a threat to public order and faith. On the other hand, the law reflects the social attitudes and practices that come either to correct or to reward.

The goal of this section is to explore this twofold question, namely, the relationship between the Roman anti-Manichaean laws and social reality of the Roman Manichaeans. What does the law reveal for the everyday life of the Manichaeans? And how did it affect and remodel this social reality? How in turn does this daily reality come to reshape the content of the law? The laws themselves with the prohibitions on the one hand reveal aspects of daily life of Manichaeans and on the other transform their daily routine. Each law is a witness of practices that were believed actually to take place, but also creates the need for the adoption of new practices that are reflected in subsequent laws, etc. Thus, my aim is to examine the effect that the persecution and the penalties imposed (exile, property penalties, capital punishment) had diachronically upon specific sectors of the everyday life of Manichaeans, namely, Manichaean communities, religious life, social relations, family life, and social profile.

The first general observation is that, compared to Diocletian, Christian emperors were much more lenient and tolerant with the Manichaeans. Although Diocletian's rescript (302) did offer the alternative that Manichaeans would be exempted from prosecution (capital punishment) if they did not "continue recalcitrant", this applied only for their followers (catechumens). For the leaders and the authors of the sect and their books, burning in the fire was inescapable.[166] Thus, provided that Diocletian's rescript was enforced, it seems that the daily life of Manichaeans became much easier under the Christian emperors. Initially, and for a long period of time, probably there were no laws that specifically targeted Manichaeans. The first anti-Manichaean law was issued by Valentinian I and Valens in 372. Before that, there is no known law recorded either in imperial legislation or in other sources. It is thus reasonable to assume that from the so-called edicts of toleration in 311 and 313 until 372, the Manichaeans enjoyed some kind of religious freedom, as other religious groups did, living either in urban communities or in rural areas and gathering freely, either publicly or privately.[167]

However, from 372 onwards the situation would change. Before proceeding to the investigation of the impact that the imposed penalties had on the daily life of the Manichaeans, I will examine the question of the non-implementation of laws.

4.1　The Question of the Non-Implementation of the Law

As pointed out above, the laws were not always enforced. Apart from those cases where this was the result of an intentional religious policy, as in the case of the *decrees of philanthropy*, the laws were not always implemented either for the unrepentant Manichaeans, or because there was significant room for silent tolerance. The laws themselves firmly reiterate that they are repeated because the previous laws were not applied. There are several examples of laws which renew earlier ones and make it clear that unlike the previous laws, they will be enforced vigorously and effectively.[168] Frequent also are the references to the penalties faced by officials responsible for the non-execution of the law.

166　See section 3.3 in this chapter.

167　Galerius' Edict (311) and the Edict of Milan (313), in Eusebius *HE* 8.17 and 10.5, respectively. Cf. Corcoran 2015, 77. According to Eusebius (*Vit. Const.* 3.63–66), later, Constantine, as monarch, changed his religious policy of tolerance and issued a decree against all heretics, naming five specific heresies (Novatians, Valentinians, Marcionites, Paulians and those called Cataphrygians). Even if it were meant, Constantine's edict did not explicitly mention the Manichaeans. Cf. Matsangou 2017a, 401.

168　Cod. theod. 16.5.40 (407), 16.5.43 (407), *Sirm.* 12 (408) (Pharr, 483): "All statutes [...] not only are to continue but are to be brought to fullest execution and effect"; 16.5.65.3.5 (428) (Pharr, 463): "All the laws formerly issued and promulgated at various times against such persons [...] shall remain in force forever, by vigorous observance", "the foregoing provisions shall be so enforced"; Cod. justin. 1.5.5; *NTh.* 3.1.9 (438) (Coleman-Norton, 713): "what rules have been enacted in countless constitutions against Manichaeans (ever odious to God), [...] with cessation of inactivity should be entrusted to speedy execution."; Cod. justin. 1.5.19. On the questions of repetition and non-implementation of the laws, cf. Athanassiadi 2018, 170, 189.

This description of inertia is highlighted and is constantly repeated.[169] Justin and Justinian's statement (in 527) confirms that the law was a "dead letter" and declares that a new stance on religious policy is going to be applied: "Unless that, too, seems to be a law of our enactment, which though (merely) confirmed by us, is not neglected as before, when it was a dead letter".[170]

So, why were the laws not applied? Did social networks play a protective role? Did Manichaeans have sound popular support? Or was it just tolerance? Was it negligence or inefficiency of the state apparatus? Or was corruption involved? Did Manichaeans have access to powerful persons of authority and shared interests with them? It seems that all these options played a role to a certain extent.[171]

Firstly, the entire process for implementing the laws could face obstacles in both stages of the prosecution process, namely at the stage of accusation, and at the stage of judgment. The reasons for which the accusation did not reach the officer who had the criminal jurisdiction[172] over the case varied:

(1) Cover-up by citizens: Citizens who offered Manichaeans asylum rather than denouncing them; landlords who remained silent even when they were aware that Manichaean gatherings were taking place in their houses; caretakers of landed estates who hosted Manichaean gatherings in the houses of their employers, without the permission of the owners.

(2) Cover-up by officials who were responsible for detecting and identifying Manichaeans. This was possibly due to a benign tolerance, because of negligence, or even because of self-serving purposes. Typical of the latter is the case of the secret agents (*agentes in rebus*) who, as stated above,[173] were slow to report the identified heretics (Manichaeans, Donatists, Priscillianists, pagan) to the governors of the provinces. Probably the

---

169 Cod. theod. 16.5.40.8 (407), *Sirm.* 12 (408), 16.5.65.5 (428), *NVal.* 18.4, Cod. justin. 1.5.16.1, 1.5.18.11, 1.5.20.8.

170 Cod. justin. 1.5.12.12 (527) (Kruger 1967, 2:54): Πλὴν ἀλλ' ἡμέτερον ἂν εἶναι καὶ τοῦτο δοκοίη τῶν ἀνακτησαμένων αὐτὸ καὶ μὴ περιιδόντων, καθάπερ ἔμπροσθεν, ἀμελούμενόν τε παρ' ἐνίων καὶ μέχρι μόνων γραμμάτων κείμενον. Cf. Lieu 1998b, 207.

171 Besides, the same happened with the treatment of other heretics. For noble heresies: Cod. theod. 16.5.12 (383); 16.5.24 (394); 16.5.58 (415); 16.5.65 (428); Cod. justin. 1.5.8 (455). For Donatists: Cod. theod. 16.5.46 (409); 16.11.3 (412); 16.5.54 (414); 16.5.55 (414); 16.5.65 (428); Cod. justin. 1.5.20 (530). Already since 376 there are hints of negligence or complicity of governors (Cod. theod. 16.5.4). However, from 407 onwards there is a steady reference to officials of all levels who do not apply the law and whose penalties vary according to their position.

172 The governor of the province at first instance, or the praetorian prefect in the court of highest appeal.

173 See section 3.4.1 in this chapter.

delay was related to the negotiation for the amount of the bribe. "Avarice and corruption" of *agentes in rebus* "were notorious".[174] But also in the case of the decentralized inquisitorial model, which involved all the state officials in the uncovering of Manichaeans, several officials in charge did not report them to the judge, as revealed by the relevant penalties. For example, Valentinian in his Novel of 445, decreed that the punishment of "the chief men of every government service or of every office staff" who permitted Manichaeans "to be in governmental service" would be "a fine of ten pounds of gold".[175] Whereas, under Justinian's governance, officers who failed to denounce their Manichaean colleagues were equally guilty, even though not adherents of the sect.[176]

(3) Manichaeans' camouflage. The Manichaeans concealed their identity behind other movements (e.g. ascetic) in order not to be accused. As the law of 381 denounces:

Nor with malignant fraud they should defend themselves under pretence of those fallacious names, by which many, as we have discovered, desire to be called [...] Encratites, Apotactites, Hydroparastates, or Saccophori.[177]

As to the stage of judgment, the prosecuting procedure could be obstructed or cancelled for the following reasons: (1) The accusation was cancelled by means of the defence of prescription, common practice according to the testimony of the law.[178] (2) The accused person devised ways to circumvent the law by tricks.[179] Perhaps some defendants found ways to elicit specific decrees that excluded certain persons or groups of heretics from penalties. A known case is that of Priscillian who, although condemned as a Manichaean, bribed Macedonius, the master of the offices, and managed to have an imperial rescript issued, restoring him to his church.[180] (3) Deferral of the trial, or annulment of the punishment inflicted by the Governor of the province due to

---

174   Pharr 1952, 594.
175   *NVal.* 18.4 (445) (Coleman-Norton, 731). On *NVal.* 18, see Enßlin 1937, 373–78.
176   Cod. justin. 1.5.16.1 (527).
177   Cod. theod. 16.5.7.3 (381) (Coleman-Norton, 368, slightly altered).
178   Cod. theod. 16.5.9 (382). About the defence of prescription, see below, section 4.2.2 in this chapter.
179   Cod. theod. 16.5.65 (428). *NVal.* 18.3 (445): Manichaeans "by any fraud should not be sought what we openly prohibit"; Cod. justin. 1.5.16 (52[7;]) (Coleman-Norton, 1006): For the Manichaean apostate: "he shall be liable to extreme punishments, not retreating to any excuse nor being able to postpone by any subterfuges the punishments imposed on him".
180   Chadwick 1976, 40–41.

connivance or favouritism, although the crimes had been reported to him.[181] (4) Judges ordered minor punishments or no punishments at all.[182] (5) Sloth, negligence, or corruption of officers of all ranks, of the whole administrative structure, civil and military.[183] (6) Contemporary bureaucratic problems.[184] (7) Grace awarded by the Emperor.[185]

To sum up, the non-implementation of the laws could be attributed to both the interlocking relationships or interests between Manichaeans and officials, and to the fact that the Manichaeans had popular support. The latter probably constituted an important social force, a factor which the officials, governors, judges in charge on matters of criminal prosecution of Manichaeans, should take into consideration for any decisions they had to make.[186]

Something similar may have underlain the change of religious policy in the case of the *decrees of philanthropy*. In November 15, 407 the setting of persecutions in Africa unexpectedly changed. By a new law, the Manichaeans and the Donatists (and heretics more generally), were exempted from all charges, prosecutions and penalties of previous laws if they would convert, even at the last minute (in the midst of their trial). A simple condemnation of error and confession of the Name of the Almighty (*omnipotentis nomen*) could suffice for the absolution from all guilt and the annulment of the punishments, even in the midst of their afflictions.[187] What dictated this change in tactics? Just eight years before, the then vicarius of Africa "sought out" the Manichaeans of his diocese, brought them "before the public authorities", and punished them with the "most severe correction".[188]

---

181 Cod. theod. 16.5.40.8.
182 Cod. theod. 16.5.65.5.
183 *Sirm.* 12 (408): "the governors' mischievous sloth, their office staffs' connivance, the municipal senates' contempt". Cod. theod. 16.5.40.8 (407): "The governor of the province, if by dissimulation or by partiality he shall have deferred these crimes when reported or shall have neglected ...". 16.5.65.3 (428). *NTh.* 3.1.9 (438); *NVal.* 18 (445); Cod. justin. 1.5.12 (527); Cod. justin. 1.5.18 (527–29): "but persons who have not denounced these things whether they should be in office staffs or should serve in other magistracies, to which these matters refer-shall deposit a penalty of twenty pounds of gold for each person and similarly a fine of thirty pounds of gold pursues every magistracy (both military and civil) both here and in the several countries".
184 *NTh.* 3.9 (438); *NVal.* 18.1,4 (445).
185 Cod. theod. 16.5.65.3 (428).
186 Chadwick 1976, 40–41.
187 Cod. theod. 16.5.41.
188 Cod. theod. 16.5.35 (399) (Pharr, 456).

Perhaps the change in tactics was born from necessity, in light of the large number of Manichaeans in Africa at the turn of the fourth to the fifth century (known from other sources) and who may have been unmanageable by other means, including the usual policy of 'tolerance through terrorism'. It is not improbable that such a law could stimulate mass conversions or fake conversions, which in turn caused the need for set abjuration formulas, since the process of conversion and acceptance by the Catholic Church had to be carried out by less time-consuming procedures.[189] We can imagine a complete reversal of the previous scene of persecution. Instead of Manichaeans who were brought by force before the vicar, now a throng of former Manichaeans or pseudo-converts willingly turned up before Porphyrius, the new proconsul of Africa, making repentance statements in order to take advantage of the sudden change of the law.

If this is plausible, however, it is equally certain that this opportunity did not last for long. A few months later, on June 5, 408 a new law, this time persecuting the Manichaeans, was "posted at Carthage" in the agora.[190] As it seems, the practice of benevolence did not yield the expected results.[191] The persecuted Manichaeans now probably fled from Africa to Rome and to other cities of the West. This possibly explains why the tactic of *philanthropy* was adopted anew in August 425 for the Manichaeans, heretics, schismatics and astrologers of Rome[192] and then for those of the other cities of Italy and Gaul.[193]

Subsequently, I will examine in what way the punishments inflicted upon Manichaeans (i.e. exile and property penalties), affected the religious, social, and personal lives of Manichaeans.

4.2   Impacts of the Exile and Property Penalties on the Everyday Life of Manichaeans

4.2.1   Manichaean Communities (Exile Penalty)

What does the law reveal about the Manichaean communities? Did they exist at all, and if so, where?

The evidence presented above suggests that despite persecutions Manichaeans persisted throughout the period examined (fourth to sixth centuries) in both the Western and Eastern parts of the empire. And as it seems, they

---

189   Lieu 1994a, 208.

190   *Sirm.* 12 (408) (Coleman-Norton, 507).

191   Maybe there were side effects (false conversions) with the mass repentance statements which the new law was invited to correct, returning back again to the classic tactics of intimidation.

192   Cod. theod. 16.5.62 (425).

193   Cod. theod. 16.5.64 (425) = *Sirm.* 6.

were very active. It is more likely that they preferred to live in the cities, but this does not mean that there were no Manichaeans in the countryside. However, it is reasonable to assume that they preferred the cities, actually the large ones, since missionary activities were a key component of Manichaeism, and the cities would provide better opportunities for their missionary operations. This is also shown by the persistence of the law to take them out of the cities, although, to judge by the constant repetition of the measure until Justinian's laws, these attempts were not wholly effective.

Laws of exile appeared already from the first anti-Manichaean laws and (under the reign of Theodosius I and II) followed an escalated trajectory. Initially, according to the law of Valentinian I and Valens in 372, the Manichaeans had to be socially isolated: "segregated from the company of men as infamous and ignominious".[194] During the next decade, the measure was intensified by a series of Theodosius I's laws (381, 382, 383, and 389). With the first one in 381, Theodosius forbade Manichaeans to appear and be seen in municipalities.[195] In 383 he decreed that the transgressor of the previous laws (i.e. anyone who appeared in municipalities and participated in prohibited gatherings),[196] "should be expelled", "by all good persons' common agreement".[197] The culmination of his exile policy was his law of 389, by which the Manichaeans "should be expelled [...] indeed from the whole world, but especially from this city [Rome]".[198] The laws of Arcadius and Honorius (399–408) that followed made no reference to exile. The measure reappears with intensity in the laws of Theodosius II and Valentinian III, from 423 onwards. Following in the footsteps of Theodosius I, these emperors exiled Manichaeans firstly from the metropolises,[199] then from all the cities either big or small,[200] and finally "from the whole world".[201]

---

194 Cod. theod. 16.5.3 (372) (Coleman-Norton, 333).
195 Cod. theod. 16.5.7.3 (381) (Coleman-Norton, 368): "they should be restrained completely from sight in a crowded community".
196 Cod. theod. 16.5.7.3 (381); 16.5.7 (381); 16.5.9 (382).
197 Cod. theod. 16.5.11 (383) (Coleman-Norton, 388).
198 Cod. theod. 16.5.18 (389) (Coleman-Norton, 422). The Latin word for 'world' "is *mundus*, which means 'the universe', 'mankind' – a concept larger than [...] 'the earth' especially the world of men wherein the Roman Empire's laws could be enforced." cf. fn. 136.
199 Cod. theod. 16.10.24 (423), 16.5.62 (425).
200 Cod. theod. 16.5.64 (425); *Sirm.* 6 (425); 16.5.65.2 (428).
201 *NVal.* 18 (445) (Coleman-Norton, 730): "We speak of the Manichaeans, whom the statutes of all previous emperors have judged execrable and worthy to be expelled from the whole world".

The years that followed until Justinian, as noted in the introduction, witnessed another legislative gap of 82 years (445–527). An exception to this is the law attributed either to Leo or to Anastasius (in 487 or 510 respectively), the first to decree capital punishment for any Manichaean who would appear or be found anywhere. According to the law, the Manichaeans "have no freedom or permission to reside anywhere" in the Roman Empire.[202] However, as can be inferred by the Justinian laws to come, this law was not successful in its goal to eradicate Manichaeans from the Roman Empire, or alternatively it was never enforced. If indeed there was no other law during these 82 years, it is reasonable to assume that any possible outcome which had been brought about by the religious policy of the Theodosian dynasty (379–457) was annulled. As reflected in the laws issued by Justinian just after he assumed the governance of the empire, the Manichaeans not only had not disappeared, but one could find them even within the state structure itself, holding public offices (both civil and military), in the capital and the provinces.[203]

Making a final assessment of the measure, one could say that it did not yield much. Furthermore, it is not impossible, that it caused the opposite results, and led to the dispersal of the Manichaeans throughout the empire.

4.2.2   Manichaean Assembly Places and Their Ownership Status (Property Penalties)[204]

That there were Manichaean communities in both large and small cities, even when Manichaeans were persecuted, is evidenced by the ongoing penalties of exile from these cities. That these communities had places of gathering (churches), either in 'small towns' or in 'famous cities'[205] is supported by the property penalties. As emphasized above, the main target of the law was the congregations of the Manichaeans and the most effective measure for their suppression was the deprivation of such places. They should not be allowed to own buildings for their gatherings. The property measures were taken for this purpose. Once these measures were legislated, they became part not only of all subsequent laws but, as we will see, a quasi-part of precedent legislation, since they had retroactive applicability.[206]

---

202   Cod. justin. 1.5.11 (Frier et al., 201; Coleman-Norton, 940): Θεσπίζομεν τοὺς τὴν ὀλεθρίαν τῶν Μανιχαίων αἱρουμένους πλάνην μηδεμίαν ἔχειν παρρησίαν ἢ ἄδειαν καθ' οἱονδήποτε τῆς καθ' ἡμᾶς πολιτείας διάγειν τόπον· εἰ δέ ποτε φανεῖεν ἤτοι εὑρεθεῖεν, ὑπάγεσθαι κεφαλικῇ τιμωρίᾳ (Kruger 1967, 2:53).

203   Cod. justin. 1.5.12.1 (527), 1.5.16.1 (527), 1.5.18.5–6 (527).

204   Parts of this section comprise the basis of Matsangou 2022.

205   Cod. theod. 16.5.7.3 (381).

206   Cod. theod. 16.5.7 (381), 16.5.9 (382), 16.5.18 (389), 16.5.38 (405), 16.5.40 (407), 16.5.43 (407), 16.5.59 (423), 16.10.24 (423), 16.5.65 (428), NVal. 18 (445), Cod. justin. 1.5.15 (527).

By the law of Valentinian I and Valens in 372, the Manichaean gather-ings were banned. The "houses and habitations" in which such assemblies of Manichaeans were found, were confiscated and appropriated "to the fisc's resources".[207] It is important to note that this was the first law of the Cod. theod. against heretics. Manichaeans were also the first target of Theodosius' religious policy. During his reign, although things became worse for all here-tics, judging from his first three decrees issued in 381, 382, and 383, his main tar-get initially seemed to be only the Manichaeans, especially their gatherings.[208] The last edict in 383, in addition to the Manichaeans, condemned also Arians, Semi-Arians and other ascetical groups. The decree prohibited such heretics: a) to congregate, b) to build private churches or use private homes as churches, c) to conduct any proselytizing activity, and d) to practice their religion pub-licly or privately.[209] Theodosius, with three laws issued in 381, 382 and 389, introduced and established the property restrictions for Manichaeans. From then onwards, the Manichaeans were deprived of the right that all Roman citi-zens had, to handle their property as they wished.

It is interesting to see in detail what is revealed about the Manichaean con-gregations according to the legislation. Firstly, from the testimony of the law issued in 381, it seems that some Manichaeans were still illegally assembling during the period 372–381, in clear violation of the law of 372.[210] Moreover, it seems that apart from the meeting places that had escaped the confiscation, new premises were transferred or donated to the community by Manichaean men and women;[211] perhaps by *Electi* and *Electae* who according to the Man-ichaean rules should not own property. In order to stop this practice and pun-ish those who did not restrain "from illicit and profane assemblies" after the law of 372, Theodosius' law of 381 forbade Manichaeans to inherit, bequeath, trans-fer or donate their property, except when it would pass into non-Manichaean hands. All prohibitions would apply, retroactively.[212] The latter meant that the community could not acquire any new assembly places in the future, but in addition would lose the edifices that were transferred to it between 372 and 381 illegally, since the law was retroactive. The confiscation would take place after

---

207 Cod. theod. 16.5.3 (Coleman-Norton, 333) addressed to the Prefect of Rome.
208 Cod. theod. 16.5.7 (381), 16.5.9 (382), 16.5.11 (383). Cf. Beskow 1988, esp. 2–5.
209 Cod. theod. 16.5.11 (383).
210 Cod. theod. 16.5.7.1 (Coleman-Norton, 368), addressed to the Prefect of Illyricum: "we regard as guilty [...] those persons who, even after the law originally had been issued, have not at all been able to be restrained [...] from illicit and profane assemblies".
211 Cod. theod. 16.5.7.pr. (Coleman-Norton, 367): "If any Manichaean – man or woman – from the day of the law enacted long ago and originally by our parents has transmitted his own property to any person whatsoever, by having made a will ...".
212 Cod. theod. 16.5.7.1 (Coleman-Norton, 368): "The rule of this law [...] should prevail not only for the future but also for the past".

"an immediate investigation".[213] If the property was given to a legal heir, such as
a husband, children, or any relative who was Manichaean, the aforesaid property "should be claimed [by the fisc] under the title of vacancy".[214] The reason
that brought Theodosius to this highly unusual step in Roman legal practice, as
he confessed, was that he did not want the time that had passed in the interim
to benefit the Manichaeans who had previously broken the law. In other words,
the Manichaeans who participated in illegal assemblies after 372 should not
be able to use the defence of prescription in order to claim ownership of the
aforementioned property.[215] According to the new law, paternal and maternal
property could only be inherited by children who were not Manichaeans.[216]

Despite these prohibitions, it seems that conveyances and donations to
Manichaean communities by Manichaean individuals continued. Presumably,
it was common practice for Manichaeans to leave their property to the community rather than to their children.[217] This practice was the target of the law
of 382 which decreed that the Manichaeans "should leave nothing" to "the
secret and hidden assemblies" of such "outlawed persons", and had to "restore
all his [their] property to persons who are his [their] own folk, not by character, but by nature".[218] However, two subsequent laws, of 383 and 389, indicate
that the community continued to acquire congregation premises in the following years.[219]

With the passage of time, however, the persistence of the law to some
extent seems to have achieved its purpose. Gradually, Manichaean real estate

---

213   Cod. theod. 16.5.7.pr. (Coleman-Norton, 367–68).

214   Cod. theod. 16.5.7.pr.-1 (Coleman-Norton, 368).

215   Cod. theod. 16.5.7.1 (Coleman-Norton, 368): "For, although the orderly arrangement of
       celestial statutes indicates observance of a sacred constitution in respect to matters about
       to follow afterward and has not been wont to be prejudicial to completed matters, nev-
       ertheless in this ordinance only, which we wish to be specially vigorous, by a sense of
       just instigation we recognize what a habit of obstinacy and a persistent nature deserve
       [...] We sanction the present statutes' severity not so much as an example of a law to be
       established but as of a law to be vindicated, so that a defence of time cannot also profit
       them". See also Cod. theod. 16.5.9.1 (Coleman-Norton, 379): "None should make void the
       establishment of this accusation by the usual prescription". Cf. Lieu 1992, 146.

216   Cod. theod. 16.5.7.2.

217   According to 1Keph. 80, 192.3–193.22 (Gardner 1995, 202) the Manichaean catechumens
       apart from fasting, prayer and almsgiving had to donate to their religious community
       some edifice for religious purposes. The above is also recorded in Augustine's Faust. 5.10.

218   Cod. theod. 16.5.9.pr.-1. (Coleman-Norton, 378–79), addressed to the Prefect of the East.

219   Cod. theod. 16.5.11 (383), addressed to the Prefect of the East; 16.5.18 (389), addressed to
       the Prefect of Rome. In his last edict of 389, Theodosius renewed the enforcement of con-
       fiscations and of intestability and emphasised, once more, that the Manichaeans being
       infamous "should have nothing in common with the world" (Coleman-Norton, 422).

had begun to leave Manichaean hands. The older generations were dying and according to the provisions of the new laws, their descendants could not obtain the paternal or maternal property unless they were Catholic. Thus, the buildings to which the sect had access were reduced in number. Hence, as depicted in the edict of Arcadius and Honorius in 407, the Manichaeans were forced to rent or to use places of non-Manichaeans for their gatherings.[220]

Arcadius and Honorius had already issued two decrees that targeted Manichaean gatherings, renewing the penalties of the previous laws.[221] However, their law of 407 attempted to deliver the final blow to Manichaean real estate. In addition to the hitherto forbidden acts (i.e. the act to inherit, to bequeath, to transfer or to donate property), the current law made it illegal for Manichaeans "to buy, to sell, or finally to make contracts". As decreed in the previous laws too, their property could be given to relatives only if they were Catholic: "We permit such kinsmen to have the right to take such property, unless polluted with an equal guilt". In addition, a system of monitoring of all heirs-relatives up to the second degree was established, in order to verify whether they could be entitled to the property. Despite the prohibition of the previous laws, this suggests that some properties had been bequeathed, transferred, or donated to Manichaeans. Moreover, by the same law, any property found in the hands of Manichaeans had to be confiscated. An extra measure in order to further safeguard that no property would remain in Manichaean hands was the *post mortem* persecution. Finally, a new category of prosecuted persons appeared in the laws, against whom 'the stings of authority' were also directed: the owners and the caretakers of the landed estates or houses on which Manichaean congregation assembled.[222]

---

220 Cod. theod. 16.5.40, addressed to the Prefect of Rome. The law prosecuted Manichaeans, Phrygians and Priscillians. The same law is reproduced in Cod. justin. 1.5.4.

221 Cod. theod. 16.5.35 (399); 16.5.38 (405).

222 Cod. theod. 16.5.40.3–4 (Coleman-Norton, 502; Pharr, 457): "We also wish the heretics themselves to be withdrawn from every gift and inheritance coming under any title whatsoever. Furthermore we do not leave to anyone so convicted the capacity of donating, of buying, of selling, finally of contracting". Cod. theod. 16.5.40.2. For that purpose, the aforesaid property should have been ceded "to all nearest kinfolk, in such a way that the order, just as in successions, of ascendants and of descendants and of collateral blood-relatives-even to the second degree-may be maintained. And so, finally, we allow these relatives to have the right to take the property, if they themselves are not polluted also by an equally guilty conscience". Cod. theod. 16.5.40.5: "Also the legal inquisition extends beyond death. For, if in crimes of treason it is allowed to accuse a deceased person's memory, not undeservedly the said person also ought to undergo judgment in this case". Cod. theod. 16.5.40.7: The owner who, "although not implicated by participation in the crime, nevertheless knows of it and does not forbid it", would lose his estate. In case

Indeed, the last law did not leave a lot of room which would allow any legal ploy and as is apparent, it had some effect. This is also demonstrated by the fact that the references of the laws to property measures noticeably declined in number in the coming years.

However, "devices for the circumvention" of the law were always found, or alternatively for not enforcing it.[223] This explains how in the law that the emperor Theodosius II sent in 428 to the praetorian prefect of the East, Florentius, several heretics, among them Manichaeans, are reported as assembling again in public places; they had once more their own places of assemblies which they "try boldly to call churches", indeed, of building themselves these so-called churches.[224] These churches were either (1) gifts or property left to the community, or (2) private houses which belonged to non-Manichaeans, since the law prosecuted the owners and the procurators of those estates.[225] In brief, it seems that everything forbidden by all the previous laws had in effect taken place. Was this law a mere repetition of what the previous laws had banned? Or were they the result of the forty years (383–423) that the attention in the eastern part of the empire was drawn to Eunomians? In any case, because this law covered the entire range of heretics, especially in the version of the Cod. theod., it is not clear whether the above practices, and particularly the "building of new churches" concerned the Manichaeans. As Linder points out, the usefulness of laws that deal with several heretics in common is somewhat problematical.[226] The fact that in the version of the same law in the Cod. justin. the same practices are repeated this time only for the Manichaeans cannot be proof that they concerned Manichaeans in the original law as well.[227] What can be argued is that this modification reflects the new circumstances (of the Justinian era) and is indicative of the situation that Justinian had found; that is the situation which dominated the previous years, before his accession to the throne. The latter is also echoed in the statement that Justin and Justinian made in their edict in 527: "We have permitted [they meant previous

---

he was not aware, it was prescribed that "the overseer or the manager of the estate" would be punished.

223   Cf. Cod. theod. 16.5.65.3,5 (428) (Coleman-Norton, 643): such heretics shall not "plan anything for circumvention of the laws". See also: Cod. theod. 16.5.9.1 (382); 16.5.40.8 (407); 16.5.43 (407); *Sirm.* 12 (408); *NVal.* 18.3–4 (445); Cod. justin. 1.5.16.1,5 (527–29); 1.5.18.10–13 (527–29); 1.5.19 (529). Reported reasons for the non-implementation of the laws are administrative inefficiency, tolerance, sloth, negligence and corruption (on the part of the state); Manichaean social networks, popular support (on the part of the Manichaeans).

224   Cod. theod. 16.5.65 (Coleman-Norton, 645). The law is reproduced in Cod. justin. 1.5.5.

225   Cod. theod. 16.5.65.3 and Cod. justin. 1.5.5.1–2. Cf. Lieu 1992, 202.

226   Linder 1987, 60.

227   Cod. justin. 1.5.5.1–2.

emperors] heretics to assemble and to have their own denomination" and they subsequently clarified: "we call heretics other persons, just as the accursed Manichaeans and those about like these".[228] It is also important to note that the exile penalty inflicted solely on Manichaeans (according to the version of the law in the Cod. theod.), in the version of the Cod. justin. is altered to capital punishment.[229]

In light of all this, we cannot exclude the probability that tightening reforms of the original versions of other older laws (predating Justinian) included in the Cod. justin. took place as well. An example of this would be the law attributed to Anastasius or Zeno (510 or 487 respectively), which is considered to be the first law that imposed the death penalty on Manichaeans.[230] In any case, for Justin and Justinian, as is stated in their edict of 527, both the latter and former laws were a 'dead letter' (μέχρι μόνον γραμμάτων κείμενον).[231]

For the laws of Justinian that follow in the Cod. justin., the death penalty for the Manichaean "wherever on earth appearing" (τὸν ὁπουδὴ γῆς φαινόμενον Μανιχαῖον) was an undisputable option.[232] The Manichaeans were now prosecuted because they were Manichaeans: not for their congregations, but for their 'name'.[233] The Manichaean gatherings and estates did not concern laws promulgated by Justinian. Since the Manichaeans themselves did not have the option to live in Roman territory, it was obvious that they ought not dare to assemble. Consequently, because Manichaeans should not exist at all, the relevant property penalties concerned the investigation of the religious beliefs of the persons who held the property of the deceased Manichaeans.[234]

---

228   Cod. justin. 1.5.12 (Coleman-Norton, 995–96): Τοὺς αἱρετικοὺς ἡμεῖς μὲν διὰ τοῦτο καὶ συνιέ-
        ναι καὶ προσηγορίαν ἔχειν ἰδίαν συνεχωρήσαμεν [...] Αἱρετικοὺς δὲ καλοῦμεν τοὺς ἄλλους, ὡς
        τούς γε καταράτους Μανιχαίους καὶ τοὺς τούτοις παραπλησίους.
229   Cod. theod. 16.5.65; Cod. justin. 1.5.5.1, Cf. Coleman-Norton 1966, 2:644, fn. 10.
230   Cod. justin. 1.5.11.
231   Cod. justin. 1.5.12.12.
232   Cod. justin. 1.5.12.3 (Coleman-Norton, 996): καὶ ταῖς εἰς ἔσχατον τιμωρίαις ὑπάγεσθαι τὸν
        ὁπουδὴ γῆς φαινόμενον Μανιχαῖον; Cod. justin. 1.5.15; 1.5.16; 1.5.18; 1.5.19.
233   Cod. justin. 1.5.12.2–3 (Coleman-Norton, 996): "Manichaeans [...] indeed it is unnecessary
        that they even should be named [...] and none ought either to tolerate or to overlook their
        denomination". As Perczel (2004, 224, fn. 59) remarks "It is also the innovation of Justin's
        and Justinian's decree that it differentiates between "heretics" who have the right to be
        named in their own name and thus, to exist, and the "Manichees" who even cannot be
        named and thus, have no right to exist within the boundaries of the Roman Empire".
234   Cod. justin. 1.5.15 (527–29).

4.2.3   Social Relationships

As is natural, and as always happens in societies where some groups of citizens are persecuted by authorities, there are some fellow citizens who either because of personal relationships, or because of ideological kinship, or simply for humanitarian reasons, stand by or conceal the persecuted, defying the risks and the penalties of the law that they would probably face. In our case, the corresponding class of citizens against which the law is directed, because of protecting Manichaeans, consists of: (1) the owners of the private houses in which the Manichaeans assembled, (2) the caretakers of such estates, and (3) the citizens that hid Manichaeans in their homes. When did the above persons appear in the laws and what did they risk by breaking the law?

As mentioned above, the reason that made the appearance of owners and caretakers necessary in the life of Manichaeans was that the community did not possess enough real estate for conducting its congregations. The penalties the above persons had to face, according to law of 407, were: The owner who, "although not implicated by participation in the crime, nevertheless knows of it and does not forbid it", would lose his estate. In case he was not aware, it was specified as "the overseer or the manager of the estate" who would be subject to a particularly harsh sentence: "after he has been chastised with a lead-tipped scourge, should be consigned to the perpetual labour of the mines". If the inquisition proved that the leaseholder was also involved, the punishment would be deportation (*deportatio*).[235] In the next relevant law (in 428), the treatment of the procurators depended on their civil status. Those of servile condition were subjected to the same penalty as indicated previously, whereas the free-born were subjected to "a fine of ten pounds of gold or exile".[236]

On the contrary, for the citizens who hid Manichaeans in their homes, the laws did not mention any specific penalties, apart from warnings stressing that it was an illicit and risky practice.[237] The phenomenon normally would take on larger dimensions during the persecutions. So, the first time the 'protectors' appeared in the law was during the persecution of 399, when the vicarius of Africa was ordered to conduct an inquisition in order to identify the Manichaeans of his diocese. The wanted Manichaeans had to be "sought, they should be brought to a magistrate and should be checked by appropriate and very severe correction". "The stings of authority" would also be directed "against those persons" who would protect the aforesaid heretics "in their own houses".[238] The fact that the issue reappeared in subsequent laws (in 407, 445,

---

235   Cod. theod. 16.5.40.7 = Cod. justin. 1.5.4 (Coleman-Norton, 502).
236   Cod. theod. 16.5.65.3 (428) = Cod. justin. 1.5.5.1.
237   Cod. theod. 16.5.35 (399), Cod. justin. 1.5.4.7 (407), *NVal.* 18.3 (445).
238   Cod. theod. 16.5.35 (399) (Coleman-Norton, 480).

and 527) may be an indication that this practice was continuing.[239] When those Manichaeans who had infiltrated the imperial service later were targeted by the law, they enjoyed similar protection from some of their colleagues.[240]

On the other end of the spectrum of citizens, we find the informers (*delatores*), who for their own reasons (e.g. personal antipathy, hostility, loathing, ideological or selfish reasons), denounced the Manichaeans to the authorities. As we mentioned above, although the informers were in great disrepute and subjected to severe penalties if proven malicious, those who were informers of Manichaeans, like the informers of magicians and traitors, were encouraged to denounce such persons without risking being accused of slanderous defamation.[241] However, it seems that some side effects arose from this encouragement of informers from the very beginning. As is reflected in the law for apostates of 383,[242] some, combining the above exhortation of the law for accusations (382)[243] with the provisions of the law that enabled the retroactive accusation (381),[244] falsely denounced their dead fellow-citizens as apostates to Manichaeism (probably for selfish reasons) disqualifying them from "making a testament".[245] The law of 383, against apostates, addressed these side effects by setting the following prerequisites: firstly, a time limitation of five years was prescribed for a future opening of the trial, starting from the date of death of the accused, and secondly, the informer ought to be able to demonstrate that he had denounced the accused person of apostasy during his lifetime. Otherwise, he would be considered as complicit.[246]

Both the protectors and *delatores* testify to the intensification of inquisitional procedures and persecutions of Manichaeans.

4.2.4   Family Relationships and Social Profile

Apart from the *decrees of philanthropy*, the option of repentance with the resulting exemption from prosecution always seemed to be an alternative option and was highlighted in several laws. One can imagine that this option would have given rise to important intra-family dilemmas.

---

239 Cod. justin. 1.5.4 (407), *NVal.* 18 (445): Nec cuiquam licitum tutumque sit aut celare tales aut talibus conivere, cum omnia de his a nobis confirmata sint retro principum constituta. Cod. justin. 1.5.12.
240 Cod. justin. 1.5.16 (527), 1.5.18.
241 Cod. theod. 16.5.9 (382), *NVal.* 18 (445).
242 Cod. theod. 16.7.3 (383).
243 Cod. theod. 16.5.9 (382).
244 Cod. theod. 16.5.7 (381).
245 Cod. theod. 16.7.3.1. See also, about this law, Linder (1987, 168–74).
246 Cod. theod. 16.7.3.1.

All had started with the law of Theodosius I in 381, which under the perpetual stigma of *infamia*, deprived Manichaeans of the right to live under the Roman law. This produced many legal disabilities, among which was the withdrawal of the right to make a testament and to inherit. "The inheritance of paternal or maternal property should be conferred only on those children who, though born from Manichaeans", never were Manichaeans, or in case they had once been Manichaean, "have departed from the paternal depravity".[247] The only option which the children of Manichaeans had in order to inherit the property of their parents, apart from finding a way to circumvent the law, was to renounce the Manichaean religion and to profess the Catholic faith. It is probable that this was most often the case. But how many of these confessions of faith were sincere, and to what extent was that just a solution to save the family assets? Since a simple confession would suffice for the annulment of the penalties, why could they not make a statement of repentance, and become crypto-Manichaeans? Perhaps Theodosius' law of 383 for the apostates, for "those who have preferred at any time to attend the Manichaeans' nefarious retreats",[248] pertained to such cases. That is, some of those accused as apostates could have been children of Manichaean parents, who, for the aforementioned reasons, professed their Catholic faith, but had found it difficult to withdrawn themselves from the association of their family and previous life.[249]

A similar dilemma could have been encountered by all the other relatives who were the legal heirs or beneficiaries. As indicated above, in order to ensure that the Manichaean property was transferred to Catholic hands, the authorities investigated the religious beliefs of all relatives up to the second degree of kinship. For that purpose, the property should have accrued "to their next of kin, in such a way that the order of ascendants and descendants and collateral cognates, even to the second degree, [...] be observed, as in hereditary successions".[250] Apparently, all these questions of inheritance strained family relationships and created intra-family conflicts among the legal heirs and beneficiaries, as is also reflected in the law for the apostates.[251] Such claims may have been common in the everyday life of Manichaeans. This is also revealed by the *sanctio pragmatica* issued by Justinian in response to a question concerning matters relevant to Manichaean property.[252]

---

247   Cod. theod. 16.5.7.2 (381), 16.5.40.5 (407) (Coleman-Norton, 502).
248   Cod. theod. 16.7.3 (383) (Coleman-Norton, 385).
249   Cod. theod. 16.5.7 (381).
250   Cod. theod. 16.5.40.2 (407) (Pharr, 457).
251   Cod. theod. 16.7.3 (383).
252   Cod. justin. 1.5.15 (527–29).

4.2.5   Professions

What is interesting is the transformation of the social profile of the Manichaeans, as reflected in the legislation which seems to have taken place between the fourth and sixth century (372–531 CE). At the beginning, as we can read through the first laws of Theodosius I, the social profile that the Manichaeans themselves wished to project was that of solitaries, ascetics, monks, who were following a solitary life. They were self-proclaimed as ascetics "of approved faith and chaste character", and desired to be called Encratites, Apotactites, Hydroparastates, or Saccophori.[253] Thus, the Manichaeans initially are presented (in the legislation) as figures on the fringes of society, as non-conformists. In the laws that follow, those of Arcadius and Honorius, this picture is lost. In the laws of these emperors there are no references that could help us form a picture about the Manichaean social profile and status, apart from a brief notice regarding the slaves of the persecuted Manichaeans. However, this only serves to show that there were Manichaeans, and indeed persecuted Manichaeans, in the upper classes of society. According to the law, their slaves shall "be without guilt, if abandoning their masters' sacrilege, they shall have crossed with more faithful service to the Catholic Church".[254] It is worth noting that according to the law, those accused of a public crime lost the right to protect their slaves, who could be tortured in order to turn in their masters.

In contrast, in the Cod. justin., after the legislative gap of 82 years, the image of the social profile of Manichaeans is totally changed. The Manichaeans now seem to be fully integrated in society, holding public offices in the state's civil and military structure. This should not be surprising, since the last law of the Cod. theod. hints at this forthcoming evolution.[255] This suggests that there were Manichaeans who performed imperial service at least since 445. However, the penalties inflicted upon the responsible officers did not stop them from permitting Manichaeans to perform imperial service. Justinian's laws create the impression that there were many of them in such offices in the early sixth century in both Constantinople and the provinces.[256] From the very first words of their edict in 527, Justin and Justinian denounced that the Manichaeans and those like them with "intolerable audacity" had "infiltrated themselves, having disregarded the laws' command [Valentinian's Novel?], into governmental

---

253   Cod. theod. 16.5.7.3 (381) (Coleman-Norton, 368), 16.5.9 (382).

254   Cod. theod. 16.6.40.6 (407) (Coleman-Norton, 502).

255   NVal. 18 (445) (Coleman-Norton, 731): Imperial officers shall be punished with a fine "if they allow anyone polluted by this [the Manichaean] superstition to be in governmental service".

256   NVal. 18 (445), Cod. justin. 1.5.12 (527), 1.5.16 (527), 1.5.18 (527–29).

services".[257] And this was happening, although "in the certificates of appointment [of] many officials concerning their office, it is added that the person who obtains it must be orthodox".[258] The question is whether this intrusion was accidental and due to the dynamics of the spread of Manichaeism, or if it was the result of a tactical method and strategy.

4.3   The Death Penalty

What has been exposed above concerns the effect that the property penalties and the penalty of exile could have on the ordinary life of Manichaeans. Here, I will examine what the threat of the death penalty meant for their daily life. The first thing to note is that nowhere in the Cod. theod. is the death penalty recorded as a punishment inflicted on Manichaeans. The first time that the death penalty appears is in the Cod. justin. where, as it seems, it is the only option. The terms that are used are *ultimate sentence* and *capital punishment*. In the Cod. theod., the punishment to which the Manichaeans were subjected, as said, were exile and property penalties. It is further remarkable that in the Roman legislation (of the period) the combination of exile, property penalties, and the parallel deprivation of Roman citizenship all coexist in the severe form of exile which is called *deportatio*. Usually, mere exile was not accompanied by property penalties and the loss of Roman citizenship.[259] *Deportatio* was considered equivalent in severity to the ultimate sentence or capital punishment. Indeed, the last two terms, in early Byzantine legislation, did not always signify the death penalty, but also meant other penalties which by their severity resembled death.[260] Thus, the terms *ultimate sentence* and *capital punishment*, apart from the death penalty (hanging, decapitation and burning at the stake), could also mean forced labour in the mines, or deportation, or loss of Roman citizenship. Yet a contradictory definition is recorded elsewhere.[261]

---

257   Cod. justin. 1.5.12.1–2 (527) (Kruger, 2:53; Coleman-Norton, 996; Frier et al. 203): 1. Τοὺς δὲ εἰσῆλθέ τις οὐκ ἀνεκτῇ τόλμα, καὶ τῆς τῶν νόμων ἀμελήσαντας παραγγελίας στρατείαις, ὧν οὐκ ἐᾷ μετεῖναι τοῖς τοιούτοις αὐτὰ τὰ τῶν βασιλικῶν συμβόλων δηλοῖ γράμματα, παρενέβαλον αὐτούς. 2. Αἱρετικοὺς δὲ καλοῦμεν τοὺς ἄλλους, ὡς τούς γε καταράτους Μανιχαίους καὶ τοὺς τούτοις παραπλησίους.

258   Cod. justin. 1.5.12.11 (527) (Kruger, 2:54; Coleman-Norton, 997): 11. Ὅπερ ἐστὶν οὐ καθάπαξ καινόν· τὰ γοῦν ταῖς πλείσταις τῶν στρατειῶν θεῖα διδόμενα τῆς ζώνης σύμβολα προσκείμενον ἔχει τὸ δεῖν ὀρθόδοξον εἶναι τὸν ταύτης μεταλαμβάνοντα.

259   B 60.54.6 = D 48.22.7.

260   B 60.51.26= D 48.19.28 pr. §§ 1–15; (title 51) Ἐσχάτη τιμωρία ἐστὶ τὸ φουρκισθῆναι καὶ καυθῆναι καὶ ἀποκεφαλισθῆναι καὶ μεταλλισθῆναι καὶ περιορισθῆναι· ταῦτα γὰρ πλησιάζει καὶ μιμεῖται θάνατον. Τὸ δὲ προσκαίρως ἢ διηνεκῶς ἐξορισθῆναι ἢ εἰς δημόσιον ἔργον δοθῆναι ἢ ῥοπαλισθῆναι ἢ ἄλλως ὑποστῆναι ποινὴν οὐκ ἔστι κεφαλικόν. B 60.51.2 = D 48.19.2: Κεφαλικὴ καταδίκη ἐστὶν ἢ θάνατον ἢ ὑπεύθυνον ποινῆς ἢ πολιτείας ἔκπτωσιν ἐπάγουσα.

261   B 60.51.20 = D 48.19.21: Μόνος ὁ θάνατός ἐστιν ἐσχάτη τιμωρία.

After what was presented above, one naturally wonders whether the terms *ultimate sentence* and *capital punishment*, used by the Cod. justin. as penalties for the Manichaeans, signified exclusively the death penalty, or whether it was left to the discretion of the judges to decide on a case-by-case basis.

The first law in which the term capital punishment is recorded is the one attributed to Zeno or Anastasius (487 or 510):

> We ordain that those who prefer the Manichaeans' deadly error should have no freedom or leave to dwell in any place whatever of our State; and if they ever shall appear or be found, they should be subject to capital punishment.[262]

The version of the same law in *Basilica*, determines also the way of execution, which was decapitation: "the Manichaean who lives in Roman territory once appeared/perceived should be decapitated".[263]

Justinian, as mentioned, did not leave the opportunity to Manichaeans to exist anywhere in Roman territory. The ultimate sentence for the Manichaean "wherever on earth appearing" was the only option.[264] As mentioned above in section 3.4, apart from the general objective, which was to identify and put to death the Manichaeans who were found in Roman territory, Justinian's laws focused in particular on the following groups: (1) the Manichaeans that had intruded into the imperial service, (2) the apostates, and (3) the crypto-Manichaeans. The Manichaeans were now prosecuted because they were Manichaeans: Not for their congregations, but for their 'name'.[265] What seems now to have troubled the authorities were the issues of apostasy and false conversion.

By his law (Cod. justin. 1.5.16) Justinian targeted the converted Manichaeans because they were suspected of both apostasy and crypto-Manichaeism.[266] This does not mean that there were no more Manichaeans, but certainly it was a transitional era, a turning point, during which massive conversions must have occurred due to the intensification of the persecutions. For the

---

262   Cod. justin. 1.5.11 (Coleman-Norton, 940, altered): Θεσπίζομεν τοὺς τὴν ὀλεθρίαν τῶν Μανιχαίων αἱρουμένους πλάνην μηδεμίαν ἔχειν παρρησίαν ἢ ἄδειαν καθ' οἱονδήποτε τῆς καθ' ἡμᾶς πολιτείας διάγειν τόπον· εἰ δέ ποτε φανεῖεν ἤτοι εὑρεθεῖεν, ὑπάγεσθαι κεφαλικῇ τιμωρίᾳ.

263   B 1.1.25 (= Cod. justin. 1.5.11): Ὁ Μανιχαῖος ἐν Ῥωμαϊκῷ τόπῳ διάγων ὀφθεὶς ἀποτεμνέσθω. Basilica, which means the royal/imperial [laws], is an extensive collection of laws compiled during the Macedonian dynasty (begun under Basil I and was completed during the reign of Leo VI), and constitutes a revised and updated version of Justinian's legislation.

264   Cod. justin. 1.5.12.3, 1.5.15, 1.5.16, 1.5.18, 1.5.19.

265   Cod. justin. 1.5.12.

266   Cod. justin. 1.5.16.

law, the apostate (a person who returned to Manichaeism after having been converted) "shall be subject to the ultimate punishment" (ταῖς ἐσχάταις ἔσται τιμωρίαις ὑπεύθυνος).[267] The apostates "will receive no clemency" (οὐδεμιᾶς τεύξονται φιλανθρωπίας). The problem was that the converted Manichaeans could be blamed for apostasy very easily. For example, if they happened to speak to an old friend on the road instead of denouncing him to the authorities. To the 'proper penalty' was also subjected all those who had Manichaean books and did not deliver them to the authorities in order to be burnt.[268]

But those whom the law deemed as "most worthy of the ultimate penalty" (ἐσχάτων τιμωριῶν ἀξίους) were those who pretended to have been converted (i.e. the crypto-Manichaeans), who:

> having pretended to abandon this impious error [...] later are seen to delight in rascally men's association and to cherish those persons' interests and in every way to conceal with them their impieties.[269]

Thus, apart from being accused of apostasy, the converted Manichaean was at risk of being accused as a crypto-Manichaean. According to this law, in order to demonstrate the sincerity of their reform and persuade the authorities that they had converted in earnest (not in pretence), the ex-Manichaeans had to denounce their former comrades.[270] This was the only way to "be secure" after their conversion. Under Justinian, the alternative options for Manichaeans became dramatically limited. They either had to die as Manichaeans, or they had to live as *delatores*.

In the middle of the sixth century, during the reign of Justinian, 230 years after the persecutions of the Manichaeans by Diocletian, it seems that a circle of tolerance was shrinking, and the daily life of Manichaeans had to confront once again the pre-Christian reality. But for the state and the authorities now, it was much more difficult and complicated to identify them. This is because in the years that had passed a transformation of the Manichaean identity had taken place. Justinian's inquisitors did not search out Manichaean churches

---

267 Cod. justin. 1.5.16.pr. (Coleman-Norton, 1006; Frier et al. 209): "after our so great benevolence" (τὴν τοσαύτην ἡμῶν φιλανθρωπίαν), "and many admonitions" (τὰς πολλὰς προαγορεύσεις) and "time given for repentance" (τοὺς ἐνδεδομένους ἐπὶ τῇ μεταμελείᾳ καιρούς).

268 Cod. justin. 1.5.16.pr., 2,3.

269 Cod. justin. 1.5.16.4 (Coleman-Norton, 1006): ὅσοι προσποιησάμενοι τὸ ἀπολιμπάνειν τὴν ἀσεβῆ ταύτην πλάνην [...] μετὰ ταῦτα χαίροντες φαίνονται τῇ τῶν ὀλεθρίων ἀνθρώπων συνδιαγωγῇ καὶ τὰ ἐκείνων θάλποντες καὶ πάντα τρόπον αὐτοῖς τὰ ἀσεβήματα συγκρύπτοντες.

270 Cod. justin. 1.5.16.5.

and congregations but Manichaeans who had infiltrated state structures or in other social structures (e.g. guilds).[271] The limits of the sect had become even more blurred.

5 Conclusions

Despite the reservations raised by scholars regarding the use of legal codes as historical sources, this chapter argued that under certain preconditions, the Roman legal sources are valuable to shed light on many aspects of the history of Manichaeism in the late Roman Empire. Although the gaps in the law that exist do not allow us to fully reconstruct the entire period under investigation (fourth to sixth centuries), our source material, especially the Cod. theod., is extremely important because it contains a large number of anti-Manichaean laws issued in a short period of time. This brief window enables us to capture historical changes, both at the level of the formation of imperial religious policy and at the level of the everyday life of the persecuted. As the analysis showed, the laws are not necessarily mindless reiterations of previous ones. In our case, every subsequent law, apart from reinforcing the validity of the previous ones, is a clarification, supplement, or correction of past laws, in order to make them more effective. Our source material gives the impression that legal institutions and social reality are in a continuous dialogue.

By examining the available data, it becomes immediately apparent that Manichaeism was the most persecuted heresy. Both codes have more numerous laws against Manichaeans than against other heretics. From the time that laws against heresies appeared in the codes, Manichaeans, in contrast to other religious groups, are steadily their target. Furthermore, in contrast to the *noble* heretics, of whom only the clergy and their teachers were persecuted, the Manichaeans were persecuted as an entire community (both Elect and catechumen). In addition, the Manichaeans were the only sect some laws (both codes) separately mention female and male members. However, employing the tool of *province-wide applicability* of the laws, which enables a diachronic geography of the sect to emerge, there is a notable absence of laws against the Manichaeans of the eastern part of the empire for a period of 40 years. The most likely explanation for this is that the Eunomians monopolized the interest of both religious and state authorities in the East during this period (383–423).

---

271   Cod. justin. 1.5.16.1.

A core question of this chapter was the Manichaeans' religious profile from a legal perspective. In the eyes of the law were the Manichaeans Christian heretics or not Christian at all? Although the Cod. theod. classified Manichaeans in the chapter of heretics, after examining: (1) with which groups they were co-classified, (2) the rationale of the persecution, (3) the prosecution procedure and, (4) the imposed penalties, it becomes clear that the Manichaeans were considered as a *sui-generis* class of heretics.[272] This is also reflected in the rationale of the law regarding the nature of the crime of Manichaeans. Unlike *noble* heretics, who were persecuted for their doctrine, Manichaeans were persecuted for socially dangerous and subversive practices. Unlike Jews and pagans, whose religious identity was distinct, the boundaries of the Manichaean identity were blurred: a factor that made them more threatening. For this reason, Manichaeans, as Christians earlier, were persecuted just for being Manichaeans and not when they broke the law, as was the case with Jews and pagans.

The policy of repression that Christian emperors initially opted for was that of 'tolerance through terror'. In this context, the tools employed were *infamia* and the characterization of the sect as a *public crime*. The crimes that constituted the content of the term *public crime* in the case of the Manichaeans were: high treason, sedition, sacrilege, magic, and moral corruption. Concerning the former, in contrast to the representation of Manichaeism by the sources examined in ch.[2], Roman imperial legislation defines no explicit link between Manichaeans and Persians; yet, the penalties of Manichaeans and traitors have much in common. The above policy legitimized: (1) the deprivation of the right of the Manichaeans to own property (depriving them likewise of their assembly places), and (2) the exile penalty. *Infamia* was proven to have been effective over a specific period of time. However, during Justinian's time, the measure had lost its focus and was no longer an effective tool.[273] As for the exile penalty, it probably led to the dispersal of the Manichaeans throughout the empire. The change in policy with the *decrees of philanthropy* could be seen as an attempt to manage the large number of Manichaeans in North Africa. It is notable that the promulgation of the *decrees of philanthropy* in the early fifth century coincides with the dating of the earlier set abjuration formulas. This reinforces the view that the latter were established in times of massive conversions. The fact that soon the policy of 'tolerance through terror' was adopted anew, probably implies the large dimension of false conversions.

---

272   In Cod. justin. the Manichaeans are clearly distinguished from heretics.
273   On the application of *infamia* and its various uses over time (Diocletian-Justinian), see Bond 2014.

Likely connected to the latter is a transformation of the Manichaean social profile that took place between the fourth and sixth century. While the laws of Theodosius I present the Manichaeans as ascetics following a solitary life, in the laws of Justinian they appear to be fully integrated into society and the state's apparatus. With Justinian the 'end of tolerance' policy was inaugurated. Thenceforth, the real persecution began; the only option left was the physical eradication of the Manichaeans.

Regarding the question of the impact of laws on the everyday life of Manichaeans, as we have seen, the stigma of *infamia* (and the consequent deprivation of property rights) brought about a series of unbearable effects such as: social marginalisation, many legal disabilities, family disputes, real estate loss, and the removal of community assembly places. Yet, certain legal loopholes and imperial policies of tolerance, at least until Justinian's time, left space for some action.

Finally, in contrast to ecclesiastical literature, which quite commonly uses the term 'Manichaean' to refer to other heretics, an issue discussed in the next chapter, the legal usage of the term Manichaean is literal and refers to the actual Manichaean community. This is because the laws contain references to the whole range of heretics and there is a clear distinction in the way that the Manichaeans were classified and treated in relation to other heretics. In practice, however, it is quite possible that, apart from Manichaeans, other 'heretics' were labelled as Manichaeans and were persecuted.[274]

---

274   Cf. Minale 2011.

CHAPTER 4

Classifying Manichaeism

> Mani is not of Christian origin, for God's sake!
> Nor was he like Simon cast out of the Church.
>
> CYRIL OF JERUSALEM[1]

⁘

1 Introduction

The previous chapter highlighted the fact that although the Cod. theod. classified Manichaeans among Christian heretics, it treated them as a distinctive
religious category, differentiating them from intra-Christian heresies. The
question of this chapter is how the rest of the sources, both Christian and
pagan, classify the Manichaeans in their heresiological accounts (treatises,
catalogues, lists, etc.).

Recently, an increasing number of researchers, such as Berzon, have
adopted Cameron's critique on modern scholars who consider "heresiology as
sterile or boring, as mere scholastic exercises".[2] In his *Classifying Christians:
Ethnography, Discovery, and the Limits of Knowledge in Late Antiquity*, Berzon
interprets "heresiology as a Christianized mode of ethnography".[3] "The heresiologists," he argues, "devised and ordered a Christian epistemological system
that thrust two competing realities into contention: knowledge of the heretical world and the rejection of that knowledge".[4] Through the taxonomy of a
great variety of different groups, beliefs, practices and concepts, the heresiologists provide "information through an organized system or principles, by
which readers locate and retrieve data readily (the reference function) or grasp
meaning through the fact of arrangement (a specific impression)".[5] The her-

---

1 Cyril of Jerusalem, *Catech.* 6.20–1. For the original text in Greek see section 2.1.1 in this chapter.
2 Cameron 2003, 484; cf. Berzon 2016, 14–16; Flower 2013, 172–74.
3 Berzon 2016, 42, 27–57.
4 Berzon 2016, 18.
5 Berzon 2016, 224. Cf. Foucault (2005/1966) esp. his discussion on "Mathesis and 'Taxinomia'"
   (79–85). As Berzon (2013, 37 & 145–46) states: "The heresiologists' codification of differences
   of praxis and theology, from cosmology to Christology to dietary practices and clothing

esiologists' goal with their "*quasi*-scientific" classification and cataloguing of heresies is to make sense of their world and of the world's history. In order to answer the question 'how and why were Manichaeans classified in the way they are classified', we must first ask what kind of options were available to the authors in order to make sense of the Manichaeans? In other words, we have to take into account the categories that existed on their mental map by which they could classify and make sense of Manichaeans. These, it can be argued, were Hellenism (paganism), Judaism and Christianity (all in the broad sense, including Gnosticism).

The aim of this chapter is to examine not only the Catholic perspective on the classification of Manichaeans, but also the corresponding perspective of all other Christian denominations as well as that of the pagans. In other words, how did the followers of other religious groups regard Manichaeans? To pagans, were Manichaeans just one Christian heresy alongside others? For the adherents of the several Christian parties was Manichaeism a rival Christian version? Or was it regarded as not Christian at all, what we today would call a different religion?

1.1   *Methodological Ruminations*

The investigation of the above query touches upon some hermeneutical and methodological questions which are quite problematic. For this reason, a further illumination of some vital concepts and terms, already discussed in the introduction, is necessary at this point.

First of all, it has to be clarified that, although the query itself is interconnected with the debated issue of the origin of Manichaeism (the same question in the *etic* discourse), our analysis here concerns only the *emic* level of the discourse. In this context, it is worth mentioning Gardner's theory of stratigraphy, which is based on the textual Manichaean tradition. By comparing texts attributed to Mani himself (*Epistles*) with the (later) texts ascribed to the community of the faithful (*Kephalaia*), Gardner argues that Mani's 'Manichaeism' was radically different from the 'Manichaeism' of his followers. While Mani's point of departure was a Christian tradition, later (for Gardner possibly quite fast, even during Mani's lifetime),

---

preferences, became metrics of heresy as a name and thus a charge – and the tools by which Christians could try to excise and limit the profusion of diversity [...] The ethnography of heresy at once narrows the order of the world to its Christian aegis and yet defines the world by its Christian (theological) governance. [...] The ethnographic impulse of heresiology emerges out of a desire to impose a fixed order on its world. Christianity can, above all else, explain the conditions, both past and present, of the world".

The development of [...] [the] scholastic tradition in the [Manichaean] community altered [fundamentally] [Mani's] presentation.

It was his followers, and a peculiar trajectory of development, (which would in many ways have astonished its originator), that led to the carving out of a discrete identity called 'Manichaeism' (similarly) 'Christianity', and so on.[6]

Regardless of whether we agree with Gardner's view concerning Mani's religious point of departure, for the question of the current chapter, this separation of Manichaeism at an earlier and a later stage of development is important. The issue here is not Mani's religious identity, but that of the (much) later Manichaeans.

The second issue pertains to the 'insider–outsider' problem.[7] The sources of information for the religious profile of East-Roman Manichaeans are *ab extra* and, indeed, distinctly polemical. For an explanation of the religious profile of the Manichaeans (which is the ultimate goal of this chapter), the *ab intra* self-understanding of the Manichaeans is of vital importance. Unfortunately, real evidence, such as Augustine provides for the West (his anti-Manichaean works preserve theses and attitudes of his Manichaean opponents) do not exist in the relevant repertoire of East-Roman authors.[8] Besides, as pointed out in the introduction, even the Manichaean testimonies themselves are contradictory regarding the use of autonyms by the Manichaeans.[9] Whereas for the Latin Manichaeans the use of the autonym 'Christian' is central, "we

---

6   Gardner 2010, 147.

7   According to Jensen (2011, 46, 30) "the insider–outsider distinction is really a 'pseudo problem' in epistemic and interpretive terms [which ...] obscures more than it discloses."

8   Similar Manichaean texts might have been preserved in AA but they do not provide evidence for this particular question.

9   Cf. Introduction, 5.3.4 (Defining Terms: Manichaeism in relation to Christianity). Manichaeans distinguishing themselves from Christians: *1Keph.* 105. According to Brand (2019, 185) this text is an exception of the Manichaeans of Egypt; *1Keph.* 151: 370.16–375.15 (On the ten advantages of the Manichaean religion), Cf. Gardner and Lieu (2004, 265–68 [no 91]). Manichaean self-identification as Christians: *2PsB* 7.11–9.1 (A bema psalm no 222 in the Medinet Madi Psalm-Book codex, cf. Allberry 1938), Cf. Gardner and Lieu (2004, 238 [no 78]): "It is worth reiterating that the Manichaeans regarded themselves as the true church of the saints". Augustine, *Faust.* 5.1: The famous pronouncement of Faustus claims for the Manichaean Elect the status of true Christians. For more on the self-designation of Manichaeans, see: Lieu 1998b, 205–27; Pedersen 2013a and 2013b; Gardner 2010; Brand 2019; Lim 2008; Baker-Brian 2011, 15–24. According to Brand (2019, 185), the textual evidence from Kellis "stands against the otherwise stimulating argument by Richard Lim that "the people whom we have grown accustomed to calling Manichaeans mainly represented themselves as Christians". See also Brand 2017, 105–119.

have no clear evidence for any use of the name 'Christian' as an autonym" by the Egyptian Manichaeans.[10] It is also worth noting that the Egyptian texts (Coptic) were written for internal use, while the Latin was "with a view to outsiders" (Christians).[11] Nevertheless, in order to reconstruct the religious profile of Byzantine Manichaeans, I consider equally important the opinion of the non-Manichaeans of the time, for whom Manichaeans were a lived and daily reality. Despite the fact that they were their religious opponents, these individuals were their interlocutors in the religious discourse of the era. Furthermore, it is important that these opinions come from followers of different religious groups who were rivals to each other. The fact that there was a variety of Christian parties within Christianity serves as a valuable tool which helps us to construct a more comprehensive picture. This is because it enables us to compare how different Christian 'sects' saw the Manichaeans, as those different sects did not perceive the Christian doctrine and faith in the same way. Of particular importance is the view of the pagans (clearly outsiders) on the issue, as it sheds light on Manichaeism from a third more neutral angle. While this does help to complement the general picture, unfortunately the relevant evidence is scant.

The last thorny issue is the clarification of the content of the terms *heresy* and *religion* (briefly discussed in the introduction). The ancient Greek word αἵρεσις (heresy) means 'choice' and thus also in antiquity it was used to mean 'school of thought' or a 'philosophical tendency'. Gradually, the term acquired a pejorative connotation (i.e. the wrong choice); since the mid-second century it could (additionally) indicate the 'deviant doctrine and the team that supported it'.[12] However, during the period under examination, the term still

---

10   Pedersen 2013b, 192. Cf. Brand 2019, 185.

11   Pedersen 2013a, 1. Researchers also remark that the use of the name and adjective 'Manichaean' in both Latin and Coptic texts is very rare. In particular, Egyptian Manichaeans used to express their religious self-understanding through many different autonyms (e.g. 'the Holy Church', 'Sons of the Living Race', etc). As Brand (2019, 186) concludes, these "Self-designators used by Kellites cannot indisputably support the hypothesis of a Manichaean self-identification as Christians".

12   For the meaning of the term heresy in antiquity and the evolution of its content, see: Chadwick 1998, 561; Kazhdan 1991, 918; Mango 1980, 94–104; *Lampe Patristic lexicon*, 51; Young 1982, 199; Boulluec 1985, 2 vols; Athanassiadi 2018, 179. Cf. *LSJ*, s.v. Αἵρεσις as inclination, choice: Polybius, *Historiae* 2.61.9 (διὰ τὴν πρὸς τοὺς Ἀχαιοὺς αἵρεσιν); Plutarchus, *Quaestiones convivales* 2.708b. Αἵρεσις as system of philosophic principles, or those who profess such principles, sect, school: Polybius, *Historiae* 5.93.8 (ἦν δὲ τῶν ἐπιφανῶν ἀνδρῶν ἐκ τοῦ Περιπάτου καὶ ταύτης τῆς αἱρέσεως); Polystratus, *Περὶ ἀλόγου καταφρονήσεως* (P.Herc. 336/1150) (p. 20 W.) (καὶ ἡ τῶν ἀπαθεῖς καὶ κυνικοὺς αὐτοὺς προσαγορευσάντ[ω]ν αἵρεσις); Dionysius of Halicarnassus, *De compositione verborum* 2 (καὶ μάλιστα οἱ τῆς Στωικῆς αἱρέσεως ἡγεμόνες); Diogenes Laertius, *Vitae philosophorum* 7.191 (Αἵρεσις πρὸς

had a broader connotation. Thus, apart from meaning 'choice', the relevant literature used the word αἵρεσις as a technical term to denote different religious choices, especially the rival ones (i.e. those of the opponents). The concept and criminalization of heresy as an intra-Christian religious choice which deviates from the 'correct' Christian dogma first appeared and was gradually established after the *Cunctos Populos* (*CP*) of 380.[13] Thus, especially before the *CP*, the term 'heretic' was attributed by Church Fathers to every opposing religious group, not only within Christianity but also to pagans and Jews. Athanasius of Alexandria, for example, in his *Historia Arianorum*, tells us that the Arians surpass (in deviance) all the other heresies, and as examples of these he lists pagans, Jews, Manichaeans, and Valentinians.[14] The leading ancient authority in the field of heresiology, Epiphanius, presented his genealogy of heresy by enumerating Hellenism and Judaism among the first heresies.[15] On the other hand, pagans themselves considered the Christians as heretics. The Emperor Julian, for example, asserted that heresies were the doctrines of the 'Galilean' and not those of the Greeks or the Jews.[16] Apart from the term heresy, however, the term θρησκεία (religion) was also used by the authors.[17] Didymus the Blind, for example, exhorts believers to stay away from the Manichaean θρησκεία and walk away from places that Manichaeans frequented.[18] The

---

Γοργιππίδην, title of work by Chrysippus). Αἵρεσις as faction, party: Appianus, *Bellum civile* 5.1.2 (ἐς Σικελίαν καὶ τὴν ἰσχὺν Πομπηίῳ Σέξστῳ συνῆψαν, οἱ δὲ κατέμειναν παρὰ Ἀηνοβάρβῳ καί τιν' αἵρεσιν ἐφ' ἑαυτῶν καθίσταντο).

13   Cod. theod. 16.1.2 (February 28, 380).

14   Athanasius, *H. Ar.* 66.4 (Opitz, 219): ὑπερβάλλουσι [Ἀρειανοὶ] τὰς ἄλλας αἱρέσεις. [...] καὶ "Ελληνες μέν, [...] Ἰουδαῖοι δὲ [...] Μανιχαῖοι γὰρ καὶ Οὐαλεντῖνοι [...] οἱ δὲ Ἀρειανοὶ τῶν μὲν ἄλλων αἱρέσεών εἰσι τολμηρότεροι καὶ μικροτέρας ἑαυτῶν ἀδελφὰς ἀπέδειξαν ἐκείνας.

15   Epiphanius, *Pan.* pr.3.1–2: ἐν δὲ ἑκάστῳ τόμῳ ἀριθμός τις αἱρέσεων καὶ σχισμάτων ἔγκειται, ὁμοῦ δὲ πᾶσαί εἰσιν ὀγδοήκοντα, ὧν αἱ ὀνομασίαι καὶ αἱ προφάσεις αὐταί· πρώτη Βαρβαρισμός, δευτέρα Σκυθισμός, τρίτη Ἑλληνισμός, τετάρτη Ἰουδαϊσμός, πέμπτη Σαμαρειτισμός. As Young (1982, 199–200) comments: "for Epiphanius the word is by no means confined to Christian deviations; such things as Greek philosophical schools and the various Jewish parties like the Pharisees and Sadducees are described as αἱρέσεις. Of course, the word αἵρεσις simply means 'division'. Long before it acquired the technical sense of 'heresy', the word was the classical designation for different philosophical schools [...] In very general terms, then, we may say that what Epiphanius meant by heresy was everything outside the one, holy, catholic and orthodox Church". Cf. Cameron 2003, 471: "Judaism was regarded as a heresy by Epiphanius, Islam by no less a person than John of Damascus".

16   Julian quoted by Cyril of Alexandria, *c. Jul.* (lib. 1–10), 2.9.5: οὔτε "Ελληνας οὔτε Ἰουδαίους, ἀλλὰ τῆς Γαλιλαίων ὄντας αἱρέσεως, ἀνθ' ὅτου πρὸ τῶν ἡμετέρων εἵλοντο τὰ παρ' ἐκείνοις.

17   And I dare to say in its current meaning. Cf. Tolan 2014, 58; See Introduction, 5.3.3.1 (Defining Terms: Religion).

18   [Pseudo-Didymus], *Trin.*, 42.33–36: ἐκ τῶν λεχθησομένων στοχάζεσθαι τὰ σιωπώμενα, καὶ μακρὰν φεύγειν τήνδε τῆς θρησκείας ἀπώλειαν, καὶ τὸ ποτὲ συναυλίζεσθαι τοιούτοις ταύτην ἐπιτηδεύουσιν.

church historian Socrates, in his *Historia Ecclesiastica*, uses alternatively both terms (θρησκεία and αἵρεσις) to refer to Manichaeism.[19] Further, another term which was used by the writers as an alternative expression for the terms θρησκεία and αἵρεσις, was the multivalent word δόγμα/dogma (belief, doctrine, tenet etc.). As we read in the *sc*, Aristocritus in his *Theosophy* "tries to demonstrate that Judaism, Paganism, Christianity, and Manichaeism are one and the same doctrine δόγμα/dogma".[20] Mani proclaims in his epistle to Edessa (quoted in the *cmc*), that he will offer "the truth and the secrets" that his Father disclosed to him to those "who were prepared to be chosen by him from the dogmas (religions)".[21]

Recapitulating, it could be argued that the use of the term 'heresy' in the relevant literature is inclusive (and broader in content) of both the modern meanings attributed to the terms *heresy* and *religion*. For this reason, it should always be interpreted contextually. Further, as noted, all three terms, αἵρεσις, θρησκεία and δόγμα are interchangeably attributed to what we would today define as religion.

Thus, after the above clarifications, the question to be asked here is whether the Manichaeans constituted a distinctive religious category to their contemporary Christians and pagans, one that was distinguished from other Christian parties: in other words, a different θρησκεία.

In order to answer this question, I will examine the opinion of the Manichaean specialists of the era. These are authors who have either written long treatises against the Manichaeans (Catholics and one pagan), or writers who, as reflected in their texts, were highly preoccupied with Manichaeans.

---

19   Socrates, *HE* 1.22.15 (sc 477: 206): ἡ Μανιχαίων παρεφύη θρησκεία; 6.9.4 (sc 505: 298): γυναῖκά τινα Μανιχαίαν τὴν θρησκείαν (a woman, Manichaean in religion) εἰς τὰ ἱερὰ μυστήρια προσδεξάμενος, μὴ πρότερον τῆς Μανιχαϊκῆς αἱρέσεως ἀποστήσας αὐτήν; 5.2.1 (sc 505: 152): νόμῳ τε ἐθέσπισεν μετὰ ἀδείας ἑκάστην τῶν θρησκειῶν ἀδιορίστως ἐν τοῖς εὐκτηρίοις συνάγεσθαι, μόνους δὲ τῶν ἐκκλησιῶν εἴργεσθαι Εὐνομιανούς, Φωτεινιανοὺς καὶ Μανιχαίους.

20   *sc*, ch. 7.223–26 (Lieu 1994a, 252; 2010, 124–25): πειρᾶται δεικνύναι τὸν Ἰουδαϊσμὸν καὶ τὸν Ἑλληνισμὸν καὶ τὸν Χριστιανισμὸν καὶ τὸν Μανιχαϊσμὸν ἓν εἶναι καὶ τὸ αὐτὸ δόγμα.

21   *cmc* 64.1–65.22 (Koenen and Römer, 44, 46): το(ῖ)ς ἑτοίμοις ἐκλεγῆναι αὐτῶι ἐκ τῶν δογμάτων Cf. 68.8–9: ἔκ τε τῶν δογμάτων καὶ τῶν ἐθνῶν, [...]. On the content of the terms religion, sect and supertitio see also Linder 1987, 58: "'Secta' is another term applied to the Jews in the legal texts, but, unlike the pair 'religio-superstitio', it did not evolve in the religious sphere. Originally it signified a philosophical school, a group distinct from others by a specific set of customs, mores, and opinions. Nevertheless, when the chancellery applied it to the Jews, it carried unmistakeably religious connotations which emerged whenever the Jewish ...".

2   Manichaean Religious Profile According to the Christian Authors

2.1   *Manichaeans as 'Heretics' (Real Manichaeans)*[22]

2.1.1   The Opinion of the Manichaean Specialists

Were Manichaeans regarded by Church Fathers as Christian heretics, that
had lapsed from the correct Christian dogma, or were they not regarded as
Christian at all?[23] The majority of the texts characterize Manichaeans as heretics. However, as we saw, everyone except the Catholics were considered heretics; yet, although the same term is used, the distinction between heretics and
people of a different religion/faith (ἀλλόθρησκος) still exists.

Serapion, bishop of Thmuis and author of the oldest Christian treatise
against the Manichaeans (326), makes clear from his introduction that the
main aim of his work is to stress the danger of the most recently appeared
heretics, the Manichaeans. According to him they surpass previous heretics
(Valentinians, Marcionites) in deceiving the faithful, invoking the name of
Christ, and presenting themselves as Christians while they were not.[24]

In the middle of the fourth century (348–350), Cyril, bishop of Jerusalem,
introducing the Manichaean heresy in his sixth lecture to the catechumens,
gives the religious stigma of Mani: "Mani is not of Christian origin, for God's
sake! Nor was he like Simon cast out of the Church".[25] It could be said, that
in this statement, Cyril distinguishes the meaning of Christian heretic from
that of the 'infidel' (outsider of the Christian faith). Cyril emphasizes that Mani
was never a Christian heretic, as was Simon who was excommunicated from
the Church.[26] Mani is a heretic, but not a Christian heretic. At the end of
the presentation of Manichaean doctrines and practices, Cyril, aiming to point
out that there is nothing in common with Christianity, asks his students to

---

22   This section is an extended version of Matsangou 2017b, 161–63.

23   On this question see also Coyle 2004, 224–26. According to Aubineau (1983, 64), Greek
      theologians and writers had no personal experience and contact with Manichaeans, as
      happened in the case of Augustine.

24   Serapion, *c. Manichaeos* 3.5–27. Serapion also in his treatise sometimes uses the term
      αἵρεσις with the meaning of choice (9.8, 10.2) and at others with the meaning of heretics
      (αἱρεσιῶται: 37.23, 49.4; αἱρεσιωτῶν: 40.5, 46.42).

25   Cyril, *Catech.* 6.21 (Reischl and Rupp 1848, 184): Οὐκ ἔστιν ἀπὸ χριστιανῶν ὁ Μάνης, μὴ
      γένοιτο· οὐδὲ κατὰ τὸν Σίμωνα ἐξεβλήθη τῆς Ἐκκλησίας.

26   Contra Cyril, the author of *De Trinitate* (PG 39:989.39–41, previously attributed to
      Didymus, ca. 380) regarded Manichaean doctrines as stemming from Simon and the
      Gnostics (Τοῦτο τοίνυν τὸ δόγμα ἔκροιά τίς ἐστι τοῦ ἐξελθόντος βορβόρου ἀπὸ Σίμωνος, τοῦ ἐκ
      Σαμαρείας Μάγου).

consider what agreement there can be between ours (doctrines and practices) and theirs.[27]

Titus, the bishop of Bostra and author of a more extensive treatise against Manichaeans (362–364), seems to answer the above question with clarity:

> Mani's teachings differ on nearly every point from what Jesus' apostles taught [...] The teaching of the two opposite principles, for instance, comes from the Persians, and the concept of 'matter' is from Aristotle, [...] The doctrine of the transmigration of souls is from Plato, and it is common for both barbarians and pagan Greeks to call the sun 'God' and to believe in fate and horoscopes. [...] Like the pagans Mani worships many gods, the only difference being that he gives them barbarian names.[28]

Thus, according to Titus, Manichaeism is a synthesis of Persian and Greek elements. Moreover, Titus makes the comparison between Manichaeans and Arians, which is particularly illuminating for our question.

> The division [Arian controversy] is not about the existence of the hypostases or their properties as such, but only about in what manner these properties exist. [...] For all are agreed in their belief in the one principle that has no beginning, and the important thing is that all honour the Son, just as they honour the Father [...] Against this, the heretics who are completely outside the Church, including the Manichaeans, have introduced non-existing principles and new properties; they are not Christians at all [...].[29]

Titus is very clear when he distinguishes between Arians whom he considers as Christians and Manichaeans whom he did not consider to be Christians at all.

As can be noticed, while these authors call the Manichaeans heretics, at the same time they are clear that Manichaeans are not Christians. We also note that these Catholic authors avoid characterizing the Arians as heretics, or they do not regard them as such. They attribute the term 'heretic' mainly to Marcionites, Manichaeans and Gnostics. Among them, the Manichaeans were their contemporary heresy.[30]

---

27 Cyril, *Catech.* 6.35 (Reischl and Rupp 1848, 204): τίς συμφωνία τῶν σῶν πρὸς τὰ ἐκείνων; τί τὸ φῶς πρὸς τὸ σκότος, τί τὸ τῆς Ἐκκλησίας σεμνὸν, πρὸς τὸ [τῶν] Μανιχαίων μυσαρόν.

28 Titus of Bostra, *c. Manichaeos* 4.16–21, in Pedersen 2004, 52–53.

29 Titus of Bostra, *c. Manichaeos* 3.73–74, in Pedersen 2004, 47.

30 An exception to this was Athanasius of Alexandria who called Arians heretics, but this was due to his personal adventure with them.

Apparently, before the CP defined the content of the term heresy by the law, there would have been intense discussions about who is or is not a heretic, a query linked to several other questions related to practical and canonical issues. In this context, Basil, the bishop of Caesarea, in a letter he wrote in 374 answering questions of Amphilochius, the young bishop of Iconium, defines the meaning of the term 'heretic', distinguishing it from that of a 'schismatic' and 'parasynagoge'. This letter later became church canon. According to Basil, who Augustine notes had also written a treatise against Manichaeans,[31] a heretic is one who is completely estranged and alienated in terms of faith, because his perception of God is completely different. I would say that this meaning is closer to the concept of the follower of a different faith. It is also noticeable, that Basil, like the previous authors, makes no reference to Arians or even to Eunomians who were his main adversaries, but he does consider as heretics Manichaeans, Valentinians, Marcionites and Montanists.[32]

As stated in the previous chapter, when Manichaeans were classified with other heretics, the laws addressed to the Prefects of the East mainly categorized them with the Montanists.[33] Basil provides the religious interpretation for this classification. He considers that Mani's claim that he is the Paraclete, and Montanus' belief that he is the mouthpiece of the Paraclete are both blasphemies against the Holy Spirit; according to the Church Fathers, this was the only unforgivable sin. In addition, as Basil explains, the Montanists had inaugurated a different type of baptism, which he considers invalid and for this reason they had to be re-baptized. However, as is reflected in the letter, Church Fathers were not unanimous in considering Montanists as heretics, which shows that – compared to Manichaeans – they were regarded as a less divergent type of heresy.[34]

In practice, however, the theoretical clarity of Basil's definitions was blurred and this was intensified by the fact that Manichaeans identified themselves as Christians.[35] As Epiphanius complains, even in his own age the Manichaeans – although heretics – are called by the people and call themselves Christians.

---

31   According to Augustine's c. Julianum, Basil wrote a work Adversus Manichaeos which is now lost.

32   Basil of Caesarea, Ep. 188.1 (Courtonne, 121–22): Αἱρέσεις μὲν τοὺς παντελῶς ἀπερρηγμένους καὶ κατ' αὐτὴν τὴν πίστιν ἀπηλλοτριωμένους [...] Αἱρέσεις δὲ οἷον ἡ τῶν Μανιχαίων, καὶ Οὐαλεντίνων, καὶ Μαρκιωνιστῶν, καὶ αὐτῶν τούτων τῶν Πεπουζηνῶν· εὐθὺς γὰρ περὶ αὐτῆς τῆς εἰς Θεὸν πίστεως ἡ διαφορά.

33   See ch.[3], 3.1.

34   Dionysius, for example, argued that Montanists did not need baptism, which reveals that he considered them a Christian heresy.

35   An example is Didymus the Blind who in his Comm. Zach. (4.124.1–3) ranks Manichaeans among Christian heretics: Οὐ μόνοι δὲ οἱ πειραστικῶς τῷ Σωτῆρι προσιόντες Ἰουδαῖοι ἀδόκιμον ἔχουσιν λόγον, ἀλλὰ καὶ οἱ ἐν τῷ χριστιανισμῷ ψευδοδοξοῦντες αἱρετικοί.

Even today in fact, people call all the heretics, I mean Manichaeans, Marcionites, Gnostics and others, by the common name of "Christians," though they are not Christians. However, although each sect has another name, it still allows this one with pleasure, since the name is an ornament to it.[36]

Two remarks are necessary at this point. Firstly, for Epiphanius, 'all the heretics' were [mainly] the Manichaeans, the Marcionites and the Gnostics.[37] Secondly, Epiphanius' testimony clearly illustrates that simple people considered Manichaeans as Christians; the latter explains why Church Fathers insisted so much on pointing out that the Manichaeans were not Christians but merely pretended to be.[38]

For the Church Fathers (as opposed to simple people), it is neither sufficient that Manichaeans are self-proclaimed Christians, nor that Christ is a central figure in Manichaeism.[39] As Gregory of Nyssa (381) critically comments:

I know that Manichaeans refer to Christ's name. So what? Because the name of Christ is respected by Manichaeans, is that a reason for counting them among Christians?[40]

---

36 Epiphanius, *Pan.* 29.6.6 (Williams, 128): καὶ γὰρ καὶ νῦν ὁμωνύμως οἱ ἄνθρωποι πάσας τὰς αἱρέσεις, Μανιχαίους τέ φημι καὶ Μαρκιωνιστὰς Γνωστικούς τε καὶ ἄλλους, Χριστιανοὺς τοὺς μὴ ὄντας Χριστιανοὺς καλοῦσι καὶ ὅμως ἑκάστη αἵρεσις, καίπερ ἄλλως λεγομένη, καταδέχεται τοῦτο χαίρουσα ὅτι διὰ τοῦ ὀνόματος κοσμεῖται.

37 In the same manner Chrysostom states (*Hom. Gal.* 2:11, PG 51.379.26–33) that at the time of the apostles all over the world there were no heresies, but only two dogmas (religions): Greeks and Jews; neither Manichaeus, nor Marcion, nor Valentinus existed. And he wonders: Why should I enumerate all the heresies? The same taxonomy appears in his *De sacerdotio* (*Sac.* 4.4.28–32) where Greeks, Jews, and Manichaeans besieged the Church. However, in a later work (c. 404, *Hom. Heb.* 63.73.53–54) he adds the Arians to his list of heretics; yet as constituting a new category of heresy, distinct from the old ones of which Manichaeism is the newest: πρώτη μὲν πάντων αἵρεσις ἡ Μαρκίωνος [...] Εἶτα ἡ Μανιχαίων· αὕτη γὰρ πασῶν νεωτέρα. Μετ' ἐκείνας, ἡ Ἀρείου.

38 On this see also Gardner and Lieu 2004, 9: "For the lay faithful in the Roman Empire it was a kind of superior Christianity, and the metaphysical details that attract the attention of scholars (and the higher echelons of the elect) had little profile".

39 Accoring to Pedersen (2004, 9) it is "proven misunderstanding that the Jesus-figure was seen as a secondary element in Manichaeism for tactical missionary purposes. [...] Jesus was not merely one among many Manichaean saviours. Jesus was at the centre of Manichaeaism, the saviour par excellence".

40 Gregory of Nyssa, *Adv. Macedonianos* 3.1 (Mueller, 101.22–25): Οἶδα καὶ Μανιχαίους τὸ ὄνομα τοῦ Χριστοῦ περιφέροντας. τί οὖν; ἐπειδὴ σεβάσμιον παρὰ τούτοις τὸ παρ' ἡμῶν προσκυνούμενον ὄνομα, διὰ τοῦτο καὶ αὐτοὺς ἐν Χριστιανοῖς ἀριθμήσομεν.

Along the same lines is Augustine's criticism of Manichaeans, stating in his Confessions:

> [...] your name [God], and that of the Lord Jesus Christ, and that of the Paraclete, [...] were never absent from their lips; but it was no more than sound and noise with their tongue. Otherwise their heart was empty of truth.[41]

In 383, Gregory of Nyssa wrote a letter to Letoius, the bishop of Melitene, which later became a canon of the Church, like the abovementioned letter of Basil. In it, he ranks Manichaeans among the atheists, along with Jews and pagans.[42] Since, according to the *CP* a heretic was now anyone who deviated in the slightest detail from the Nicene faith, Arians, Macedonians, Eunomians were counted as heretics too. Thus, Gregory distinguishes Manichaeans from the *noble* heretics by moving them into the category of atheists.

It is relevant to recall at this point that the edict against apostates to Judaism, paganism and Manichaeism was also issued (21 of May 383) exactly at the same period during which Gregory composed his letter (Easter of 383).[43] According to this law, anyone who at anytime preferred to frequent Manichaean congregations was an apostate. We note that just as in the law, Gregory ranks only the Manichaeans in the same category with Jews and pagans. This is an indication that, for both the State's laws and the Church's canons, Manichaeans were closer to being regarded as 'people of a different religion', rather than 'heretics'.[44]

Authors of the following centuries share the same opinion, that the Manichaeans were not Christians but were self-proclaimed Christians.[45] Severianus of Gabala, wondering in what way Manichaeans could claim to be called Christians, since their teachings have nothing in common with Christianity, echoes Cyril of Jerusalem:

---

41   Augustine, *Conf.* 3.6 (10), 44. Cf. Gardner and Lieu 2004, 131.

42   Gregory of Nyssa, *Ep. Letoium* (PG 45:221–236 [225]): εἴ τις ἠρνήσατο τὴν εἰς Χριστὸν πίστιν, ἢ πρὸς Ἰουδαϊσμόν, ἢ πρὸς εἰδωλολατρείαν, ἢ πρὸς Μανιχαϊσμόν, ἢ πρὸς ἄλλο τι τοιοῦτον ἀθείας εἶδος αὐτομολήσας ἐφάνη.... As Silvas (2010, 463) notes: "Scarcely any other of Gregory's writings survives in so many manuscripts, some 150 in all".

43   Klaus Fitschen dates the letter later, to around (390), cf. Silvas 2007, 213.

44   Cod. theod. 16.7.3. On this issue, see also Lieu, 1992, 146: "The Roman state, in meting out the same penalties to those who became Manichaeans with those who apostasised to Judaism and paganism, placed Manichaeism in a different category from heresies within the main body of the church like Donatism and Arianism".

45   See for example Cyril of Alexandria's *De incarnatione Domini* 9 (PG 75:1428); Macarius of Magnesia, *Apocriticus* 3.151.25–28 (§25).

Where did you hear in the Gospel of Jesus Christ, that the Sun and the Moon are creators? Where did Christ say that they draw up the souls, and lead them upwards? Where did you read this?[46]

In his biography of the life of Porphyrius (437–449), Mark the Deacon considers the Manichaean 'mythologies' worthy of ridicule and laughter. He focuses his criticism on the Manichaean Christ, and declares in a clever play of words of his argumentation:

And they also confess Christ, but say that he only incarnated in appearance; thus, they can only be said to be Christians in appearance as well.[47]

It is worth noting here that the introductory paragraph of the *sc* emphasized the distinction between the 'others' (the Manichaeans and their heresy) and the 'we' (the Christians):

Below are seven chapters [...] against [...] Manichaeans and their [...] heresy, [...] showing how they [...] must anathematize their former heresy and inform us Christians.[48]

Of particular importance for our question is the opinion of two authors, who – unlike the previous – were not ecclesiastical authorities, namely: the Nestorian geographer Cosmas Indicopleustes and the historian Agathias. Both of them lived in the time of Justinian I.

The Egyptian geographer and later monk Cosmas Indicopleustes, in his *Topographia Christiana* (536–547) uses the terms *religion* and *heresy* in the same way that one would use them today:

---

46 Severianus of Gabala, *De Spriritu Sancto* (PG 52:825.30–33): Ποῦ ἤκουσας ἐν τῷ Εὐαγγελίῳ Ἰησοῦ Χριστοῦ, ὅτι ὁ ἥλιος καὶ ἡ σελήνη δημιουργοί εἰσι; ποῦ εἶπεν ὁ Χριστός, ὅτι ταῦτα ἀντλοῦσι τὰς ψυχάς, καὶ ἀνάγουσιν αὐτάς; ποῦ ἀνέγνωκας τοῦτο; See also a parallel argument in *Homiliae Cathedrales cxxiii* of Severus of Antioch: "From where did the Manichaeans, who are more wicked than any other, get the idea of introducing two principles, both uncreated and without beginning, that is good and evil, light and darkness, which they also call matter?"

47 Mark the Deacon, *Vit. Porph.* 86 (Lieu 2010, 96–97): Ὁμολογοῦσιν δὲ καὶ Χριστόν, δοκήσει γὰρ αὐτὸν λέγουσιν ἐνανθρωπῆσαι· καὶ αὐτοὶ γὰρ δοκήσει λέγονται Χριστιανοί. For an English translation see Lieu 2010, 96–101.

48 *sc* pr. (Lieu 2010, 116–17, altered): Κεφάλαια ἑπτὰ [...] κατὰ τῶν [...] Μανιχαίων καὶ τῆς [...] αὐτῶν [...] αἱρέσεως, [...] παριστῶντα πῶς δεῖ τούτους [...] ἀναθεματίζειν τὴν γενομένην αὐτῶν αἵρεσιν καὶ ἡμᾶς τοὺς Χριστιανοὺς πληροφορεῖν.

No religion therefore, neither the Judaic, nor the Samaritan, nor the Pagan, nor the Manichaean, believes or hopes that there is a resurrection [and] an ascension into heaven for men; but such of these religions as think that heaven is a sphere, namely the Pagan and the Manichaean, are consistent with themselves in holding their unbelief. For, where are they able to find a place in the sphere for the kingdom of heaven? [...]

And, in like manner, every heresy among the Christians can be refuted;[49]

Regardless of Cosmas' knowledge concerning cosmo-geography and his views on the spherical heaven, it is clear that for him Manichaeism is another religion; it is in a class with the religions of pagans, Jews and Samaritans, which he distinguishes from the heresies within Christianity.

Agathias, as it seems, shared Cosmas' classification of Manichaeism as a distinct religion. Presenting in his *Historiae* the Persian Zoroastrians of his era, Agathias finds that they have much in common with the Byzantine Manichaeans. As he says: (1) they believe in two principles, the one is good (and the cause of all good things in the world), and the other is against it. Both the Zoroastrians and the Manichaeans attribute barbarian names to the two principles; (2) the faithful bring offerings to their priests; (3) they honour the water to the point that they may not wash, and are allowed only to drink and water plants.[50] Regardless of the degree to which the information provided about Zoroastrians is accurate,[51] Agathias' testimony is important for our

---

49   Cosmas Indicopleustes, *Top.* 6.30.1–7 & 6.33.1 (SC 197:47, 51; McCrindle 259–60, slightly
      altered): Οὐδεμία τοίνυν θρησκεία, οὐκ Ἰουδαῖος, οὐ Σαμαρείτης, οὐχ Ἕλλην, οὐ μανιχαῖος,
      πιστεύει ἢ ἐλπίζει ἀνάστασιν ἀνθρώπων καὶ ἄνοδον αὐτῶν γίνεσθαι ἐν τῷ οὐρανῷ. Ἀλλ' αἱ μὲν
      αὐτῶν ὅσαι τὸν οὐρανὸν δοξάζουσι σφαῖραν, τουτέστιν "Ἕλληνες καὶ μανιχαῖοι, ἁρμοδίως ἑαυ-
      τοῖς καὶ τὴν ἀπιστίαν κέκτηνται. Ποῦ γὰρ ἔχουσι δοῦναι ἐν τῇ σφαίρᾳ τόπον τῆς βασιλείας τῶν
      οὐρανῶν; [...] Ὁμοίως δὲ καὶ πᾶσα αἵρεσις ἐν χριστιανοῖς.
50   Agathias, *Hist.* 2.24.9–11 (CFHBSB 2:72–73; CFHBSB 2.1:58–59): νῦν δὲ ὡς τὰ πολλὰ τοῖς
      καλουμένοις Μανιχαίοις ξυμφέρονται, ἐς ὅσον δύο τὰς πρώτας ἡγεῖσθαι ἀρχὰς καὶ τὴν μὲν ἀγα-
      θήν τε ἅμα καὶ τὰ κάλλιστα τῶν ὄντων ἀποκυήσασαν, ἐναντίως δὲ κατ' ἄμφω ἔχουσαν τὴν ἑτέ-
      ραν· ὀνόματά τε αὐταῖς ἐπάγουσι βαρβαρικὰ καὶ τῇ σφετέρᾳ γλώττῃ πεποιημένα. τὸν μὲν γὰρ
      ἀγαθὸν εἴτε θεὸν εἴτε δημιουργὸν Ὁρμισδάτην ἀποκαλοῦσιν, Ἀριμάνης δὲ ὄνομα τῷ κακίστῳ
      καὶ ὀλεθρίῳ [...] ἑορτήν τε πασῶν μείζονα τὴν τῶν κακῶν λεγομένην ἀναίρεσιν ἐκτελοῦσιν, ἐν ᾗ
      τῶν τε ἑρπετῶν πλεῖστα καὶ τῶν ἄλλων ζώων ὅπόσα ἄγρια καὶ ἐρημονόμα κατακτείνοντες τοῖς
      μάγοις προσάγουσιν ὥσπερ ἐς ἐπίδειξιν εὐσεβείας. ταύτῃ γὰρ οἴονται τῷ μὲν ἀγαθῷ κεχαρισμένα
      διαπονεῖσθαι, ἀνιᾶν δὲ καὶ λυμαίνεσθαι τὸν Ἀριμάνην. γεραίρουσι δὲ ἐς τὰ μάλιστα τὸ ὕδωρ, ὡς
      μηδὲ τὰ πρόσωπα αὐτῷ ἐναπονίζεσθαι μήτε ἄλλως ἐπιθιγγάνειν, ὅ τι μὴ ποτοῦ τε ἕκατι καὶ τῆς
      τῶν φυτῶν ἐπιμελείας.
51   On this see de Jong 1997, 229–50; cf. Cameron 1969/1970.

inquiry because it reveals the image that a secular historian of the era had of Manichaeans.

As can be deduced, for all authors we examined, the Manichaean heresy was not one of the many 'factions' within Christianity. On every occasion it is emphasized that Manichaeans pretended to be Christians for tactical reasons. It is repeatedly stressed that this was not a matter of ignorance, but instead was a tactic which served their missionary strategy.[52] As Chrysostom warns his contemporaries:

> And if you hear that somebody is not a Greek or a Jew, do not rush to conclude that he is a Christian, [...] because this is the disguise the Manichaeans and all heresies use, in order to inveigle the naïve.[53]

According to Serapion, when Manichaeans claim that they honour the Gospels and Christ they are merely pretending; they feign in order to convert those who honour them sincerely.[54] According to Mark the Deacon, when the Manichaean missionaries aimed to proselytize among the pagans, they foregrounded common elements with Hellenism.[55] Titus, who addressed the first two books of his treatise to the pagans and the other two to the Christians of his city (Bostra), explains this attitude thoroughly: "Next to the Christians they behave as participating to the Christian tradition".[56] "However, towards

---

52 Chrysostom, *Hom. 1 Tim.* (PG 62:558.27–36): Οὐ περὶ Ἰουδαίων λέγει ταῦτα· [...] ἀλλὰ περὶ Μανιχαίων, καὶ τῶν ἀρχηγετῶν τούτων. Πνεύματα δὲ πλάνης ἐκάλεσεν αὐτούς, εἰκότως· [...] Τί ἐστιν, Ἐν ὑποκρίσει ψευδολόγων; Αὐτὰ ἃ ψεύδονται, οὐ κατὰ ἄγνοιαν οὐδὲ οὐκ εἰδότες, ἀλλ' ὑποκρινόμενοι ψεύδονται. John of Caesarea, *Adv. Manichaeos hom. 1*, 17.274–75 (Richard, 92): "invoking Christ's name they deceive the simple-minded (τῇ τοῦ Χριστοῦ προσηγορίᾳ τοὺς ἀπλουστέρους ἐξαπατῶσι)".

53 Chrysostom, *Hom. Heb.* 8.4 (PG 63:9–236, p. 73): Καὶ μὴ, ἐὰν ἀκούσῃς, ὅτι οὐκ ἔστιν "Ἕλλην, οὐδὲ Ἰουδαῖος, εὐθέως Χριστιανὸν εἶναι νομίσῃς, [...] ἐπεὶ καὶ Μανιχαῖοι καὶ πᾶσαι αἱρέσεις τοῦτο ὑπέδυσαν τὸ προσωπεῖον, πρὸς τὸ οὕτως ἀπατᾷν τοὺς ἀφελεστέρους.

54 Serapion, *c. Manichaeos* 36 (HTS 15:52–53): ἀποδέχεσθαι γὰρ νενομίκασι τὸ εὐαγγέλιον, μέμφεσθαι δὲ ἐσπουδάκασι τῷ νόμῳ καὶ τοῖς προφήταις [...] τιμῆσαι δὲ ὑπονενοήκασι τὰ εὐαγγέλια, σχηματιζόμενοι μᾶλλον τὴν τῶν εὐαγγελίων τιμήν, ἵνα τὸν σχηματισμὸν δέλεαρ τῶν ἀπατωμένων λάβωσιν. οὐδὲ γὰρ ἐπειδὴ συντέθεινται τοῖς εὐαγγελίοις, τιμᾶν ὁμολογοῦσι τὰ εὐαγγέλια, ἀλλ' ἐπειδὴ τετίμηται τὸ ὄνομα τοῦ Ἰησοῦ, προσποιοῦνται τὴν τιμήν, ἵνα τοὺς τιμῶντας μεταποιήσωνται, ὡς βούλονται.

55 Mark the Deacon, *Vit. Porph.* 85 (Lieu 2010, 97): "In fact the Manichaeans say that there are many gods, wishing in this way to please the Hellenes (i.e. pagans); besides which, they believe in horoscopes, fate, and astrology ...".

56 Titus of Bostra, *c. Manichaeos* 3.1.18–19 (CCSG 82:243): Παρὰ δὲ χριστιανοῖς, τὰ χριστιανῶν δῆθεν μετιών.

the pagan Greeks, [they] abandon the Christian material and instead set out to prove that his [Mani's] message accords with their traditions".[57] The latter Manichaean attitude is also criticized by Alexander, which will be discussed in the subsequent section.

2.1.2   Lists of Heretics by Ecclesiastical Authors

That the Manichaeans constituted a distinct kind of heretics (outside Christianity) for the Church Fathers and ecclesiastical writers is also illustrated by the classification of Manichaeans in the lists of heretics that abound in Byzantine literature. These lists also present the rationale which lies behind the classification, namely the common type of 'failure' of the heretics who were co-classified.

A similar investigation referring to the laws was carried out in the previous chapter. There, it was observed that the Cod. theod. usually categorized the Manichaeans along with Priscillianists, Montanists, Donatists and ascetic groups. Although pagans and Jews were allocated special chapters in the laws, there were some laws (e.g. *De Apostatis*) in which Manichaeans were categorized together with these groups. The Cod. justin. categorized Manichaeans with pagans, Jews, Samaritans and Montanists.

In the corresponding lists of the Church Fathers, the Manichaeans are usually categorized either together with docetic, dualistic, Gnostic sects, specifically with Marcionites and Valentinians, with Greeks and Jews, with ascetical groups, and in some rare cases with the Montanists.

By comparing the two kinds of classification, certain remarks can be made. What is missing from the lists of the Church Fathers are the Priscillianists and the Donatists, which is understandable since these two religious groups were active in the western part of the Empire. In the lists of the laws, the Marcionites and the Valentinians are missing; this is also explicable since these sects were active at an earlier stage, thus they did not constitute a threat to the state at the time the Cod. theod. was composed (fifth century).

2.1.2.1   *Together with Docetic, Dualistic, Gnostic Sects*

In general, the lists of the Church Fathers categorized the Manichaeans together with the docetic, dualistic, and Gnostic sects, when the focus of the classification is the genealogy of the Manichaean heresy.[58] In specific, the

---

57   Titus of Bostra, *c. Manichaeos* 4.2, in Pedersen 2004, 50. Cf. French translation CCT 21, 385.

58   [Pseudo-Didymus], *Trin.* 6.19.2: ἀπὸ δὲ τῆς προαιρέσεως τοῦ ἐξοβλήτου καὶ ἀπερριμμένου Οὐαλεντίνου τοῦ μανιχαΐσαντος. Theodoret (*Haer.* PG 83:337.39–41) divides heretics into four groups, each one occupying one of the books of *haer*. The first book begins with Simon and ends with Mani: Τούτων δὲ τῶν δογμάτων πρῶτος μὲν εὑρετὴς Σίμων ὁ μάγος ὁ Σαμαρείτης, ἔσχατος δὲ Μάνης ὁ γόης ὁ Πέρσης.

common *topoi* of their 'crime' are: the complex theology and cosmogony (parallel conflicting powers); the belief that emanations of the divine forces are entrapped inside the cosmos;[59] the docetic Christology (a consequence of dualism), according to which Jesus was never incarnated, had never assumed the flesh, but instead appeared as if he had a phantasmal body;[60] and the belief in reincarnation and metempsychosis (μεταγγισμὸν τῶν ψυχῶν).[61] Finally, like the Marcionites, the Manichaeans were accused of rejecting the OT and of making only fragmentary use of the NT, and misrepresenting it (e.g. Paul's letters and similes like the parable of two trees).[62]

59　Basil of Caesarea, *Hom. Hexaem.* 2.4.17–22 (370): Ἔμψυχος ἄρα ἡ γῆ; καὶ χώραν ἔχουσιν οἱ ματαιόφρονες Μανιχαῖοι, ψυχὴν ἐντιθέντες τῇ γῇ; Chrysostom, *Hom. Gen. A' Logos* (PG 54:584.55–57). Epiphanius, *Pan.* 42.11.17 (Sch.24.d): τοῖς οὕτω φρονοῦσιν ὅτι ἡ αὐτὴ ψυχὴ ἐν τοῖς ἀνθρώποις καὶ ζῴοις ὑπάρχει. τοῦτο γὰρ παρὰ πολλαῖς τῶν πεπλανημένων αἱρέσεων μάτην ὑπολαμβάνεται. καὶ γὰρ καὶ Οὐαλεντῖνος καὶ Κολόρβασος, Γνωστικοί τε πάντες καὶ Μανιχαῖοι [...].

60　Severianus of Gabala, *c. Manichaeos* 16–23; Chrysostom, *Hom. Matt.* 49 (PG 58:498.33–37): Ἐμφράττων τὸ Μαρκίωνος καὶ Μανιχαίου στόμα, τῶν τὴν κτίσιν ἀλλοτριούντων αὐτοῦ; *Hom.* 82 (PG 58:739.35–39): Ὁρᾷς ὅση γέγονε σπουδή, ὥστε ἀεὶ ἀναμιμνήσκεσθαι, ὅτι ἀπέθανεν ὑπὲρ ἡμῶν; Ἐπειδὴ γὰρ ἔμελλον οἱ περὶ Μαρκίωνα καὶ Οὐαλεντῖνον καὶ Μανιχαῖον φύεσθαι, ταύτην ἀρνούμενοι τὴν οἰκονομίαν, διηνεκῶς ἀναμιμνήσκει τοῦ πάθους καὶ διὰ τῶν μυστηρίων. Chrysostom, *Hom. 2 Tim.* (PG 62:607.9–13): Ὅρα γοῦν Μαρκίωνα καὶ Μάνην καὶ Οὐαλεντῖνον [...] τὰ τοῦ Θεοῦ μετρήσαντες ᾐσχύνθησαν ἐπὶ τῇ οἰκονομίᾳ. Cyril of Alexandria, *Inc.* 9–10 (PG 75:1428–1433); *Comm. Isaiam* (PG 70:253): Παιδίον δὲ λέγων γεγεννῆσθαι, διελέγχει σαφῶς τῆς τῶν Μανιχαίων δόξης τὸ ἀδρανές, οἳ παραιτοῦνται λέγειν, ὅτι γέγονε σὰρξ ὁ Λόγος'; *Comm. Jo.* 2.318: μετὰ δὲ τὴν ἐνανθρώπησιν, εἰ οὕτως εἰρῆσθαι φήσομεν, εἰκὼν ἦν ἄρα, καὶ δόκησις, καὶ σκιά, καὶ οὐ κατὰ ἀλήθειαν ἄνθρωπος, κατὰ τὸν ἄθεον Μάνην. *In illud: Pater, si possibile est, transeat* (against Marcionites and Manichaeans), attributed to Chrysostom but according to Severus of Antioch is a work of Severianus of Gabala (PG 51:37.61–38.5): στόμα διὰ Μαρκίωνος τοῦ Ποντικοῦ καὶ Οὐαλεντίνου, καὶ Μανιχαίου τοῦ Πέρσου, καὶ ἑτέρων πλειόνων αἱρέσεων ἐπεχείρησεν ἀνατρέψαι τὸν περὶ τῆς οἰκονομίας λόγον, λέγων, ὅτι οὐδὲ ἐσαρκώθη, οὐδὲ σάρκα περιεβάλετο, ἀλλὰ δόκησις τοῦτο ἦν καὶ φαντασία, καὶ σκηνὴ καὶ ὑπόκρισις, καίτοι τῶν παθῶν βοώντων, τοῦ θανάτου, τοῦ τάφου, τῆς πείνης. Theodoret, *Eranistes* 66: Βαλεντινιανῶν αὕτη καὶ Μαρκιωνιστῶν καὶ Μανιχαίων ἡ δόξα. Ἡμεῖς δὲ ὁμολογουμένως ἐδιδάχθημεν σαρκωθῆναι τὸν θεὸν λόγον, 117: Ἐγὼ τοῦτο ἐρῶ. Σίμων καὶ Μένανδρος καὶ Κέρδων καὶ Μαρκίων καὶ Βαλεντῖνος καὶ Βασιλείδης καὶ Βαρδισάνης καὶ Μάνης ἠρνήθησαν ἄντικρυς τὴν ἀνθρωπότητα τοῦ Χριστοῦ, 128: Τοὺς οὖν ἀρνουμένους τοῦ κυρίου τὴν ἀνθρωπότητα, Μαρκιωνιστάς φημι, καὶ Μανιχαίους, καὶ τοὺς ἄλλους, ὅσοι ταύτην νοσοῦσι τὴν νόσον, πῶς ἂν πείσαις. SC, ch. 4 (Lieu 2010, 120–21): Χριστὸν Ἰησοῦν καὶ φέγγος προσονομάζουσιν ἐν σχήματι ἀνθρώπου φανέντα.

61　Epiphanius, *Pan.* 29.6.6, 42.11.17 (Sch.24.d): πάσας τὰς αἱρέσεις, Μανιχαίους τέ φημι καὶ Μαρκιωνιστὰς Γνωστικούς τε καὶ ἄλλους [...] Οὐαλεντῖνος καὶ Κολόρβασος, Γνωστικοί τε πάντες καὶ Μανιχαῖοι καὶ μεταγγισμὸν εἶναι ψυχῶν φάσκουσι καὶ μετενσωματώσεις τῆς ψυχῆς.

62　Serapion, *c. Manichaeos* 39 (HTS 15:56): καὶ Οὐαλεντινιανοὶ μὲν ὧδε, Μανιχαῖοι ὧδε, ἑτέρωθι δὲ Μαρκίων πτύσματα καὶ οὐ ῥήματα κατὰ τοῦ νόμου μαρτυροῦσι. Athanasius, *Ep. Aeg. Lib.* 4.(1) (Metzler, 42): Ἐπεὶ πόθεν Μαρκίωνι καὶ Μανιχαίῳ τὸ εὐαγγέλιον ἀρνουμένοις τὸν νόμον; Chrysostom, *Hom. 2 Cor.* 21 (PG 61:545.33–36): Καίτοι γε πολλοὶ κατατέμνειν αὐτὸν [Παῦλο] ἐπεχείρησαν αἱρετικοί· ἀλλ' ὅμως κατὰ μέλος ὢν πολλὴν ἐπιδείκνυται τὴν ἰσχύν. Κέχρηται μὲν

2.1.2.2   Together with Greeks (Pagans) and Jews

The Manichaeans are classified together with the pagans and the Jews when it is necessary to emphasise their atheism.[63] They were seen to be of the same type of religious deviancy and severity. Further, the common *topoi* with the Greeks (pagans) were many. According to the church historian Socrates, Manichaeism is a camouflage of the religion of the Hellenes, a Hellenized Christianity (a pseudo-religion).[64] In specific, the Manichaeans are paralleled to the Greeks for: their mythologies and sophisms;[65] because they believe in many gods (polytheism);[66] for worshiping the sun and the moon;[67] because they support the view that matter is eternal (ἀΐδιος: without beginning, not generated by God) and that the souls are pre-existent;[68] because they deny

γὰρ αὐτῷ καὶ Μαρκίων καὶ Μανιχαῖος, ἀλλὰ κατατέμνοντες·; Pseudo-Chrysostomus, *In sancta lumina sive In baptismum et in tentationem* 3.7: Μαρκιωνιστῶν καὶ Μανιχαίων […] οἱ αἱρετικοὶ οὗτοι περιτρώγοντες τὰς γραφάς, τὰ μὲν περικόπτοντες, τὰ δὲ ἐῶντες, νομίζουσι φυγεῖν τὸν ἔλεγχον.

63   Gregory of Nyssa, *Ep. Letoium* (PG 45:221–236, 225): εἴ τις ἠρνήσατο τὴν εἰς Χριστὸν πίστιν, ἢ πρὸς Ἰουδαϊσμόν, ἢ πρὸς εἰδωλολατρείαν, ἢ πρὸς Μανιχαϊσμόν, ἢ πρὸς ἄλλο τι τοιοῦτον ἀθεΐας εἶδος. Chrysostom, *Sac.* 4.28–30.

64   Socrates, *HE* 1.22 (SC 477: 202, 204): […] Παρεφύη γὰρ μικρὸν ἔμπροσθεν τῶν Κωνσταντίνου χρόνων τῷ ἀληθεῖ χριστιανισμῷ ἑλληνίζων χριστιανισμός, δόγμα διὰ τοῦ Μανιχαίου χριστιανισμὸν ὑπεκρίνατο […] 3. ὁ Μανιχαῖος […] τὴν Ἐμπεδοκλέους καὶ Πυθαγόρου δόξαν εἰς τὸν χριστιανισμὸν παρεισήγαγεν […] 8. Τῶν βιβλίων τοίνυν τούτων αἱ ὑποθέσεις χριστιανίζουσι μὲν τῇ φωνῇ, τοῖς δὲ δόγμασιν ἑλληνίζουσιν.

65   Nilus of Ankara, *Ep. 321* (to presbyter Philon): τοὺς ματαίους συλλογισμούς τε, καὶ σοφισμοὺς τῆς τῶν Ἑλλήνων σοφίας, οὕσπερ εἰσφρῆσαι τετόλμηκας τῇ σεπτῇ Ἐκκλησίᾳ […] Πέπαυσο τοίνυν ἐν προσποιήσει δῆθεν (10) διδασκαλίας πνευματικῆς τὰ Μανιχαίων μυθεύματα.

66   Mark the Deacon, *Vit. Porph.* 85 (Lieu 2010, 96–97): Θεοὺς γὰρ πολλοὺς λέγουσιν, ἵνα Ἕλλησιν ἀρέσωσιν; Socrates, *HE* 1.22 (SC 477: 204): καὶ γὰρ θεοὺς πολλοὺς σέβειν ὁ Μανιχαῖος προτρέπεται ⟨αὐτὸς⟩ ἄθεος ὤν.

67   Alexander of Lycopolis, *Tract. Man.* 5.1–8 (Brinkmann, 7): "Such are their chief tenets, Sun and moon they honour most of all …" (τὰ μὲν κεφαλαιωδέστερα ὧν λέγουσίν ἐστιν ταῦτα. τιμῶσι δὲ μάλιστα ἥλιον καὶ σελήνην). Cyril, *Catech.* 15.3 (Reischl and Rupp 1967, 158): παιδευέσθωσαν οἱ ἐκ Μανιχαίων ἐπιστρέψαντες, καὶ τοὺς φωστῆρας μηκέτι θεοποιείτωσαν, μηδὲ τὸν σκοτισθησόμενον τοῦτον ἥλιον τὸν Χριστὸν εἶναι δυσσεβῶς νομιζέτωσαν. Chrysostom, *Hom. Gen.* 1 (PG 54:58148–59). Theodoret, *Haer.* (PG 83:380.12–14): συντόμως ἐρῶ τῆς δυσσεβοῦς αἱρέσεως τὰ κεφάλαια. Οὗτοι τὸν ἥλιον καὶ τὴν σελήνην θεοὺς ὀνομάζουσι; Socrates, *HE* 1.22.8 (SC 477: 204): καὶ τὸν ἥλιον προσκυνεῖν διδάσκει. SC, ch. 5 (Lieu 2010, 120–21): τοὺς τὸν ἥλιον λέγοντας εἶναι αὐτὸν καὶ τῷ ἡλίῳ εὐχομένους ἢ τῇ σελήνῃ ἢ τοῖς ἄστροις καὶ θεοὺς φανοτάτους αὐτοὺς ἀποκαλοῦντας ἢ πολλοὺς ὅλως εἰσάγοντας θεοὺς καὶ τούτοις εὐχομένους. [John of Caesarea or of Damascus?], *Disputatio cum Manichaeo* 45–46 (Richard, 124): Ἀπόκριναι δέ μοι, διὰ τί τὸν ἥλιον προσκυνεῖτε; 46. MAN. Ὅτι φωστήρ ἐστι τοῦ κόσμου, τοῦ ἀγαθοῦ θεοῦ γέννημα. From this excerpt of the dialogue Bennett (2009, 33–34) concludes that the text is addressed to the Manichaeans rather than to Paulicians or other dualists.

68   Gregory of Nazianzus, *De filio* (*orat. 29*), 11.4: ὁ δὲ μόνου θεοῦ καὶ ἴδιον, τοῦτο οὐσία. οὐκ ἂν μὲν συγχωρήσαιεν εἶναι μόνου θεοῦ τὸ ἀγέννητον οἱ καὶ τὴν ὕλην καὶ τὴν ἰδέαν συνεισάγοντες

the resurrection[69] (like Gnostics and Jews), whereas they accept the reincarnation of Empedocles and Pythagoras;[70] because they hold pantheist views and argue that the one universal soul of the cosmos is divided and exists in every part of the natural world;[71] because they believe in fate (invoke the εἱμαρμένη); because they highly esteem astrology;[72] and because they apply magical practices.[73]

The Manichaeans are also classified along with Greeks and Jews because they both (each one for their own reason) challenge the incarnation of Christ.[74] At some times, the problematic Christology of Manichaeism is paralleled with the docetic views of Gnosticism, and at some others with the denial of the divinity of Christ by the pagans and Jews.[75]

ὡς ἀγέννητα. τὸ γὰρ Μανιχαίων πορρωτέρω ῥίψωμεν σκότος. Chrysostom, *Hom. Gen.*[1-9] (hom. 1) (PG 54:581. 48–51): Εἰ περὶ κτίσεως ᾔδεισαν φιλοσοφεῖν Μανιχαῖοι καλῶς, οὐκ ἂν τὴν ἐξ οὐκ ὄντων, τὴν φθειρομένην, τὴν ῥέουσαν, τὴν ἀλλοιουμένην τοῖς τῆς ἀγεννησίας πρεσβείοις ἐτίμησαν. Εἰ περὶ κτίσεως ᾔδεισαν Ἕλληνες φιλοσοφεῖν [...]; *Hom. Gen.*[1-67] 2 (PG 53:29.55–57): Κἂν γὰρ Μανιχαῖος προσέλθῃ λέγων τὴν ὕλην προϋπάρχειν, κἂν Μαρκίων, κἂν Οὐαλεντῖνος, κἂν Ἑλλήνων παῖδες.

69   Epiphanius, *Pan.* 78.3.2 (3: 453). Cosmas Indicopleustes, *Top.* 6.30.1–7 (SC 197:47): Οὐδεμία τοίνυν θρησκεία, οὐκ Ἰουδαῖος, οὐ Σαμαρείτης, οὐχ Ἕλλην, οὐ μανιχαῖος, πιστεύει ἢ ἐλπίζει ἀνάστασιν ἀνθρώπων. Chrysostom, *Hom. Gen.*[1-9] 7 (PG 54:613.38–614); *Hom. 1 Cor.* (homiliae 1–44), 38: τί λέγουσιν ἐνταῦθα οἱ τὰ Μανιχαίων νοσοῦντες [...] Θάνατον ἐνταῦθα, φησίν, οὐδὲν ἄλλο λέγει ὁ Παῦλος, ἢ τὸ ἐν ἁμαρτίᾳ γενέσθαι, καὶ ἀνάστασιν τὸ τῶν ἁμαρτιῶν ἀπαλλαγῆναι.

70   Theodoret, *Haer* (PG 83:380.39–41): Ψυχῶν δὲ μετενσωματώσεις λέγουσι γίνεσθαι, καὶ τὰς μὲν εἰς πτηνῶν, τὰς δὲ εἰς κτηνῶν, καὶ θηρίων, καὶ ἑρπετῶν σώματα καταπέμπεσθαι. SC, ch. 6 (Lieu 2010, 122–23): καὶ τοὺς μετεμψύχωσιν, ἣν αὐτοὶ καλοῦσι μεταγγισμόν, εἰσηγουμένους, καὶ τοὺς τὰς βοτάνας καὶ τὰ φυτὰ καὶ τὸ ὕδωρ καὶ τὰ ἄλλα ἄψυχα πάντα ἔμψυχα εἶναι ὑπολαμβάνοντας.

71   Basil of Caesarea, *Hom. Hexaem.* 8.1: Ἐξαγαγέτω ἡ γῆ ψυχὴν ζῶσαν. Ἔμψυχος ἄρα ἡ γῆ; καὶ χώραν ἔχουσιν οἱ ματαιόφρονες Μανιχαῖοι, ψυχὴν ἐντιθέντες τῇ γῇ; Chrysostom, *Natal.* 1 (PG 49:358.55–359.50). Chrysostom, *Hom. Gen.*[1-9] (hom. 1) (PG 54:581.48–582): κτίσεως [...] ἀγεννησίας πρεσβείοις ἐτίμησαν. Theodoret, *Haer* (PG 83:380.42–43): Πάντα δὲ νομίζουσιν ἔμψυχα, καὶ τὸ πῦρ, καὶ τὸ ὕδωρ, καὶ τὸν ἀέρα, καὶ τὰ φυτά, καὶ τὰ σπέρματα. SC, ch. 6 (Lieu 2010, 122–23): καὶ τοὺς τὰς βοτάνας καὶ τὰ φυτὰ καὶ τὸ ὕδωρ καὶ τὰ ἄλλα ἄψυχα πάντα ἔμψυχα εἶναι ὑπολαμβάνοντας.

72   Mark the Deacon, *Vit. Porph.* 85.13–19 (Lieu 2010, 96–97): Ἐκ διαφόρων γὰρ αἱρέσεων καὶ δογμάτων Ἑλληνικῶν συνέστησαν ταύτην αὐτῶν τὴν κακοδοξίαν, [...] καὶ εἱμαρμένην καὶ ἀστρολογίαν φάσκουσιν, ἵν᾽ ἀδεῶς ἁμαρτάνωσιν, ὡς μὴ ὄντος ἐν ἡμῖν τοῦ ἁμαρτάνειν, ἀλλ᾽ ἐξ ἀνάγκης τῆς εἱμαρμένης. John of Caesarea, *Adv. Manichaeos hom.* 2, 10.149–50 (Richard, 96): ἀστρονομίαν γὰρ δῆθεν ἀσπάζονται καὶ κίνησιν τοῦ παντὸς ὑποτίθενται.

73   Mark the Deacon, *Vit. Porph.* 85.2–6, 88.22–23 (Lieu 2010, 96–97 & 98–99): Ἰουλία, ἥτις ὑπῆρχεν τῆς μυσαρᾶς αἱρέσεως τῶν λεγομένων Μανιχαίων, [...] ὑπέφθειρεν αὐτοὺς διὰ τῆς γοητικῆς αὐτῆς διδασκαλίας, πολλὰ δὲ πλέον διὰ δόσεως χρημάτων [...] φαρμακὸς Ἰουλία.

74   SC, ch. 4 (Lieu 2010, 120–21): σὺν Ἕλλησι καὶ Ἰουδαίοις ἀπιστοῦντες τῷ μυστηρίῳ τῆς θείας ἐνανθρωπήσεως.

75   Severianus of Gabala, *On the Nativity of Our Lord.* Theodoret, *Eranistes* 143.20–23: Ἐγὼ τὴν θεότητα λέγω μεμενηκέναι, καταποθῆναι δὲ ὑπὸ ταύτης τὴν ἀνθρωπότητα. {ΟΡΘ.} Ἑλλήνων

The Manichaeans are often grouped or even identified with several ascetical sects, like the Encratites, Apotactites, Hydroparastates, or Saccophori for their extreme asceticism, which is considered a social threat.[76] The same classification is reflected also in the laws.[77] In some laws Manichaeans were identified with these extreme ascetics, and in some other laws they coexisted as separate groups. The rationale behind their persecution was the fear of a disturbance to civil communities. Manichaean asceticism was criticized heavily by many Christian authors (Catholics, Arians, etc.), who pointed out its side-effects on anthropology, ethics, and social life (these will be further examined in ch.[5]).

Finally, as in the laws, Church authors sometimes rank Montanists and Manichaeans in the same category.[78]

2.1.2.3   The Worst of the Worst

The Manichaeans usually either lie at the top of such lists or are the last ones in them, in order to emphasise that they are the worst of the religious groups with which they are classified. As the Church authors explain, the Manichaeans are worse than Gnostics, docetics, dualists, pagans and Jews not because they are the last heresy to appear, but because their system is a synthesis of all the deluded dogmas and practices of all previous heresies. The newfangledness (καινοτομία), which they are accused of by the authors, is their unoriginality, their 'copy-paste' assemblage of the worst doctrines and practices of the other religions.[79]

ταῦτα μῦθοι καὶ Μανιχαίων λῆροι. Chrysostom, *Anom.* 7 (PG 48:759.48–53): Οὐκ ἀκούεις ἔτι καὶ νῦν Μαρκίωνος ἀρνουμένου τὴν οἰκονομίαν, καὶ Μανιχαίου, καὶ Οὐαλεντίνου, καὶ πολλῶν ἑτέρων.

76   Chrysostom, *Hom. 1 Tim.* 12 (PG 62:557.47–49): Περὶ Μανιχαίων, καὶ Ἐγκρατιτῶν, καὶ Μαρκιωνιστῶν, καὶ παντὸς αὐτῶν τοῦ ἐργαστηρίου τὰ τοιαῦτά φησιν. Macarius of Magnesia, Apocriticus 25: Τοιοῦτοι δὲ Μανιχαίων παῖδες ἐξεφοίτησαν· [...] Ἐγκρατηταὶ γὰρ καὶ Ἀποτακτῖται καὶ Ἐρημῖται καλοῦνται, οὐ Χριστιανοί τινες. Theodoret, *Haer.* 1.20 (PG 83:369.35–372): Κʹ. Περὶ Τατιανοῦ καὶ Ὑδροπαραστατῶν, ἤτοι Ἐγκρατιτῶν.

77   Cod. theod. 16.5.7 (381); 16.5.9 (382).

78   As Basil explains in his letter to Amphilochius (ep. 188), the Montanists, as the Manichaeans, blaspheme against the Holy Spirit, a crime identical to infidelity to God. See above in 2.1.1 and ch.[3], section 3.1 (Grouping Heretics). Didymus the Blind, *Trin.* 18.

79   Eusebius, *HE* 7.31.2 (LCL 265:226–27): δόγματά γε μὴν ψευδῆ καὶ ἄθεα ἐκ μυρίων τῶν πρόπαλαι ἀπεσβηκότων ἀθέων αἱρέσεων συμπεφορημένα καττύσας. Pseudo-Athanasius, *Sermo contra omnes haereses* (PG 28:513.1–2): Εἴπωμεν καὶ πρὸς τοὺς ἀσεβεστάτους Μανιχαίους, τοὺς τρυγιοὺς τῶν κακῶν. Cyril, *Catech.* 6.20–21 (Reischl and Rupp 1848:182, 184): Καὶ μίσει μὲν πάντας αἱρετικοὺς, ἐξαιρέτως δὲ τὸν τῆς μανίας ἐπώνυμον [...] Ἀλλ' οὐχ ὅτι πρὸ ὀλίγου χρόνου ἦν, διὰ τοῦτο μίσει· ἀλλὰ διὰ τὰ δυσσεβῆ δόγματα μίσει τὸν τῆς κακίας ἐργάτην, τὸ δοχεῖον παντὸς ῥύπου, τὸν πάσης αἱρέσεως βόρβορον ὑποδεξάμενον. Φιλοτιμούμενος γὰρ ἐν κακοῖς ἐξαίρετος γενέσθαι, τὰ πάντων λαβὼν, καὶ μίαν αἵρεσιν πεπληρωμένην βλασφημιῶν καὶ

Compared to the Gnostics, docetics, and dualists, they are the worst in deceiving the faithful, pretending that they are Christians,[80] as well as for their blasphemy against the Holy Spirit. During his debate with Mani, bishop Archelaus argues before the pagan judges that Marcion, Valentinian and Basilides are saints in comparison to Mani, who claims that he is the Paraclete.[81]

Compared to the pagans (Greeks), the Manichaeans are considered to be worse: not only did they not reject the Greek myths, but they also fabricated myths that were far worse.[82]

Manichaeans surpassed even the pagans in idolatry. With their theory that the divine substance is entrapped in every plant and in every animal, they came to honour everything; deifying all creatures, "they became more Greek

---

80 πάσης παρανομίας συστησάμενος, λυμαίνεται τὴν ἐκκλησίαν [...] κλέπτης γάρ ἐστιν ἀλλοτρίων κακῶν, ἐξιδιοποιούμενος τὰ κακά.; 16.9: Μάνης ὁ τὰ τῶν αἱρέσεων πασῶν κακὰ συνειληφώς. καὶ οὗτος τελευταῖος βόθρος ἀπωλείας τυγχάνων, τὰ πάντων συλλέξας; Epiphanius, Pan. 67.1.1 (GCS 37:132–33; Williams, 316): "After the savage onset of this rotten, poisonous teaching of Mani, the worst of all heresies and like that of a snake [...]" (Μετὰ τὴν μοχθηρὰν ταύτην καὶ ἰοβόλον ὑπὲρ πᾶσαν αἵρεσιν καὶ ἑρπετώδη τοῦ Μάνη βαρβαρικὴν θηριοβολίαν τῆς διδασκαλίας). Basil of Caesarea, Hom. Hexaem. 2.4: ἡ βδελυκτὴ τῶν Μανιχαίων αἵρεσις, ἣν σηπεδόνα τις τῶν Ἐκκλησιῶν προσειπὼν οὐχ ἁμαρτήσεται τοῦ προσήκοντος; Amphilochius of Iconium, c. Haer. 715: ἀλλὰ καὶ τῆς βδελυρᾶς καὶ ἀκαθάρτου αἱρέσεως τῶν Μανιχαίων. Cyril of Alexandria, Inc. Cyril of Scythopolis, Vit. Euth. 39 (TU 49.2:39.25–26): ἀπεστρέφετο, ἐξαιρέτως δὲ τὰς ἐξ ταύτας αἱρέσεις τέλειον μῖσος ἐμίσει. τήν τε γὰρ Μανιχαικὴν βδελυρίαν ἐμυσάττετο. Severus of Antioch, Homiliae Cathedrales cxxiii: "the Manichaeans, who are more wicked than any other". Oecumenius, Commentarius in Apocalypsin 60: τὸ κατάρατον καὶ βδελυρὸν τῶν Μανιχαίων φῦλον. Peter of Sicily, Hist. ref. Man. (ἱστορία χρειώδης ἔλεγχός τε καὶ ἀνατροπὴ τῆς κενῆς καὶ ματαίας αἱρέσεως τῶν Μανιχαίων, τῶν καὶ Παυλικιάνων λεγομένων) ch. 33: Ἡ δὲ ἐσκοτισμένη καὶ βορβορώδης καὶ στασιώδης καὶ παμμίαρος καὶ αἰσχρουργὸς τῶν Μανιχαίων αἵρεσις, ὑπὸ πάντων ἐθνῶν διωκομένη διὰ τὸ ἀνίατον αὐτὴν ὑπάρχειν καὶ πάσης βδελυρίας ἀνάμεστον [...]. The same opinion about the Manichaeans expressed in the laws: Cod. theod. 16.5.65 (428): "and the Manichaeans, who have attained to the lowest villainy of crimes [...]".

81 Serapion, c. Manichaeos 3 (HTS 15:30): τελευταῖον δὲ ἔκτρωμα τῆς πονηρίας πάσας τὰς τῶν ἄλλων πονηρίας ἐλαττώσασα καὶ μείζονι πονηρίᾳ τὰς τῶν ἄλλων πονηρίας δευτέρας ἀποδείξασα ἡ τοῦ Μανιχαίου προῆλθε μανία.

81 AA 42.1–3 (Vermes, 108): "Indeed I would beatify Marcion, Valentinian and Basilides and other heretics, in comparison with this fellow". See Gardner and Lieu 2004, 10: "It seems certain that Mani himself came to understand his Twin to be the Paraclete, foretold by Jesus, the 'comforter' and 'Spirit of Truth' who would be sent afterwards according to the divine will. Since Mani asserts that with the Paraclete, 'I have become a single body, with a single Spirit! (Keph. 15: 23–24)', he himself came to be proclaimed as the Paraclete. This then became one of the most characteristic assertions of the Manichaeans, and one of the most offensive to their catholic opponents; however, it was not intended to mean that Mani was the Holy Spirit, as that equation is part of catholic not Manichaean tradition". About Mani as the Paraclete in the Manichaean sources, see ch.[2], 2.2.1, fn. 51.

82 Titus of Bostra, c. Manichaeos 3.1.13–15 (CCSG 82:243): Παρ' "Ελλησι μὲν οὐ τὰ ἐκείνων ἀνατρέπων, [...] κακοηθέστερον ἑλληνισμὸν ὑφηγεῖται.

than the Greeks ("Ἕλληνες Ἑλλήνων γεγονότες)".[83] They are worse than pagans, who do not accept, hence they are not occupied with the Christian Scriptures; unlike them, the Manichaeans use the texts of the Gospels selectively while distorting their meaning; they also say that some Gospel passages belong to matter (i.e. Evil).[84] A typical example, and the repeated target of harsh criticism by Christian authors, was what Augustine claimed to be the favourite passage of Manichaeans: "For our knowledge is imperfect and our prophecy is imperfect; but when the perfect comes, the imperfect will pass away" (1 Cor 13:9–10). According to the ecclesiastical writers, Mani claimed that he himself and his apocalypse were the 'perfection' that Paul was referring to. In other words, as the authors criticize with irony, Paul left room for Mani to complete the knowledge that Paul did not possess.[85]

For the Church Fathers, Manichaeans were worse than Jews because while Jews considered some foods as unclean, the Manichaeans abhorred the whole creation.[86] The Manichaeans were considered worse than pagans, Samaritans, Jews and fornicators (!) for their occult rituals, which were considered as an insult to the divine and a sacrilege.[87]

The extent to which Manichaeans were demonized is well illustrated in the following narrative of Athanasius. The Arian bishops Leontius, George, and Narcissus, realizing that the majority of clergymen took Athanasius' side, visited the Emperor Constantius, to persuade him to persecute (by issuing an edict?) the Catholic faith (and of course Athanasius); otherwise, as they emphasized, there was a fear that both the Arians and the Emperor would be accused as heretics, and "if this come to pass", in their words, "you must take care lest we be classed with the Manichaeans".[88]

---

83   Serapion, c. Manichaeos 42.17.

84   Serapion, c. Manichaeos 36 (HTS 15:53): ἔδει γὰρ αὐτούς, εἴγε τὰ εὐαγγέλια ἐτίμων, μὴ περιτέμνειν τὰ εὐαγγέλια, μὴ μέρη τῶν εὐαγγελίων ἐξυφελεῖν. Titus of Bostra, c. Manichaeos 4.33–38 (That John participated in Matter!). Cf. Augustine, Conf. 5.11.21 (the same aspect supported by Faustus).

85   Titus of Bostra, c. Manichaeos 3.10–11 & 4.86–89. Epiphanius, Pan. 66.61.2 (Williams, 285): "And he claims that what St. Paul said leaves room for him". Cf. AA 15.3 & 41.

86   Chrysostom, Hom. 1 Tim. (PG 62:558).

87   Cyril, Catech. 6.33 (Reischl and Rupp 1848, 202): Ὁ δὲ Μανιχαῖος θυσιαστηρίου μέσον, οὗ νομίζει, τίθησι ταῦτα, καὶ μιαίνει καὶ τὸ στόμα καὶ τὴν γλῶσσαν.

88   Athanasius, H. Ar. 30.2 (Opitz, 199): ἡμεῖς δὲ ἐμείναμεν μόνοι. καὶ φόβος μὴ καὶ ἡ αἵρεσις γνωσθῇ καὶ λοιπὸν ἡμεῖς καὶ σὺ χρηματίσωμεν αἱρετικοί. κἂν τοῦτο γένηται, σκόπει μὴ μετὰ Μανιχαίων λογισθῶμεν (trans.: http://www.newadvent.org/fathers/28154.htm, altered). Did Constantius finally issue an edict? Could that be one of the edicts issued by 'heretic' emperors, which were not included in the Cod. theod.? About whether Constantius was finally associated with Manichaeism by his Catholic opponents, see Rohrbacher 2005, 326.

2.1.3   Taxonomical Lists in the Canons for the Converted Heretics

The taxonomical lists of the converted heretics organized according to the procedure for their reception into the Church are also illuminating for our inquiry into the status of Manichaeism as a Christian heresy or not.

The church canons entitled "How to receive those who return from heresies" determine the procedures to be followed for the reception of the converted heretics into the Church. Depending on the type of heresy to which the former heretics belonged and the degree of its deviation from the official religion, the converted heretics were classified into separate categories. The procedure to be followed was different for each of these categories. The closer a heresy was to the official faith, the simpler the procedure was. Respectively, the more a heresy deviated from the official faith, the more complex and time consuming the procedure was.[89]

The oldest known source which makes reference to the corresponding procedure for converted Manichaeans is the letter of Basil of Caesarea to Amphilochius of Iconium in 374.[90] Basil's letter was very soon recognized as canonical, and as such, it was incorporated into the body of Eastern Church canons. In this letter, Basil, as an authoritative senior bishop, responds to the questions of the new and inexperienced bishop Amphilochius; he treats issues concerning the administration of penance, including the procedure for the reception of repentant heretics into the Church. In this context, Basil defines the content of the term heresy, differentiating it from the corresponding meaning of the terms schism and παρασυναγωγή (*conventicle*). In the category of heretics Basil incorporates Manichaeans, Valentinians, Marcionites, and Montanists (*old* heretics). According to the canon, the converted heretics had

---

89   The Greek title: Περὶ τοῦ πῶς δεῖ δέχεσθαι τοὺς ἐξ αἱρέσεως ἐπιστρέφοντας. The latin title: "Quomodo recipiendi sint qui ex haeresibus accedunt".

90   Basil of Caesarea, *Ep. 188*, cf. Joannou 1963, 2: 92–99. Although according to Gelasius of Cyzicus and Evagrius the Scholastic, Manichaeism was condemned at the first Ecumenical Council, the only relevant canons that have survived concern Cathars and Paulicians (followers of Paul of Samosata). Cf. Gelasius' *HE* 2.27.8 (Hansen, 84): Αὕτη ἐστὶν ἡ πίστις, [...] ἐν Νικαίᾳ ... κατὰ Ἀρείου ... καὶ κατὰ Σαβελλίου τε καὶ Φωτεινοῦ καὶ Παύλου τοῦ Σαμοσατέως καὶ Μανιχαίου καὶ Οὐαλεντίνου καὶ Μαρκίωνος καὶ κατὰ πάσης δὲ αἱρέσεως. According to Evagrius' *HE* (2.18.324; Bidez and Parmentier, 88) Manichaeism was condemned in both the first and fourth Ecumenical Councils. As the bishops of Egypt in the fourth declare: "Φρονοῦμεν καθὼς καὶ οἱ ἐν Νικαίᾳ τριακόσιοι δέκα ὀκτὼ ἐξέθεντο καὶ ὁ μακάριος Ἀθανάσιος καὶ ὁ ἐν ἁγίοις Κύριλλος, ἀναθεματίζοντες πᾶσαν αἵρεσιν, τήν τε Ἀρείου, καὶ Εὐνομίου, καὶ Μάνου, καὶ Νεστορίου, καὶ τῶν λεγόντων ἐξ οὐρανοῦ τὴν σάρκα τοῦ Κυρίου ἡμῶν ὑπάρχειν, καὶ μὴ ἐκ τῆς ἁγίας καὶ θεοτόκου καὶ ἀειπαρθένου Μαρίας, καθ' ὁμοιότητα πάντων ἡμῶν, χωρὶς ἁμαρτίας." The seventh canon of the second Ecumenical Council (381), entitled "How to receive those who return from heresies", does not refer by name to the Manichaeans neither to Marcionites nor to Gnostics.

to be baptized, unlike schismatics and participants in *conventicles*, for whom it was sufficient to repent.

After the *CP* (380), according to which heretics were considered to be all those whose faith differed from the faith of Nicaea, the situation changed dramatically with regard to heretics. Thereafter, the state used its *carrot-and-stick* policy (i.e. privileges to Catholics and penalties to heretics) to press the heretics to convert, and the Church systematized the canons and the procedures for the reception of the converted. These church canons were also sanctioned by the decisions of the Ecumenical Councils.

Thus, the *new* (*noble*) heretics were added to the *old* heretics, and separate procedures gradually formed for the converted from the various kinds of heresies. So, in the seventh canon of the second Ecumenical Council in Constantinople (381), apart from the procedure for the *old* heretics, a second one for the heretics of the Trinitarian debate was added; later, after the Ecumenical Council of Chalcedon a third category for the heretics on the Christological dogma was further added. As depicted in the 95th canon of the Quinisext Council (692), which recapitulates the previous canons, the converted heretics were categorized into three groups, which corresponded to three different procedures:[91]

(1)   the first procedure, the simplest, was applied to the heretics (according to the Synod of Chalcedon) who had appeared after the Christological debate (e.g. Nestorians, Eutychians, Severians, and the like). For them it would suffice to anathematize their previous heresy and its heresiarch.

(2)   the second procedure was applied to the heretics of the Trinitarian debate (e.g. Arians, Macedonians, Apollinarians), Sabbatianoi and Cathars, who apart from the anathema had to be anointed with holy oil on their forehead, eyes, nose, lips and ears.[92]

(3)   the third procedure, the strictest, was applied to two categories of heretics. The first comprised the Eunomians,[93] Montanists, Sabellians and many other unnamed heretics which sprung from Galatia. The second comprised the Manichaeans, Valentinians and Marcionites. The procedure – identical for both – was strenuous and long-lasting. As the canon postulates, these heretics should be received into the Church as if they were

---

91   *ACO* (*Constantinopolitanum quinisextum* 691/2). Cf. Joannou 1963, 1.1: 230–33.

92   Saying: 'Signaculum doni spiritus sancti' (σφραγίς δωρεάς πνεύματος ἁγίου).

93   As one can observe, the heresy of the Eunomians – though new – was the only one classified among the old. The same harsh treatment was also given to Eunomians by the law. This is because, first, they had a different type of baptism (one immersion instead of three) and, secondly, because it was considered as the most threatening of the new heresies (in the eastern part of the Empire).

Greeks/pagans. In brief, the stages of the procedure were as follows: first they had to anathematize their heresy and its heresiarch, then they had to be exorcized, and then to be anointed with holy oil. Thereupon, after a long period of attending Christian catecheses to be instructed in the Christian doctrine, they had to be baptized (or re-baptized).

The same procedures (and classification) are also attested at the turn of the seventh century by Timothy the Presbyter (of Constantinople). Timothy categorizes converted heretics into three groups: (1) those who had to be baptized (he ranks Manichaeans here), (2) those who had to be anointed with holy oil, and (3) those for whom it would suffice to anathematize their previous fallacy and any other heresy. Presumably, those in the first category had to pass through the other two steps before being baptized.[94]

That the procedure for the repentant Manichaeans was long-lasting is illustrated by Mark the Deacon in his *Life of Porphyry of Gaza*. The converted *Electi* and *Electae* who accompanied the Manichaean missionary Julia (after her bitter defeat during the debate with Porphyrius, the bishop of Gaza), first confessed their repentance and anathematized Mani and, after being catechized for many days by the bishop Porphyrius, were baptized.[95]

However, as early as the time of the Second Ecumenical Council, Gregory of Nyssa, in his letter to the bishop of Melitene Letoius (383/390), seems to add a new procedure for the reception of the converted apostates to Judaism, paganism and Manichaeism. Gregory's letter was a response to Letoius' letter which raised a series of issues (similar to those asked by Amphilochius to Basil) concerning the administration of penance in the Church. In his letter, Gregory is indeed especially severe in arguing that for the apostate to Manichaeism (or to Judaism, or to paganism) who converts to Christianity, the duration of penance should be the whole of his life, and that he would be permitted to receive the Holy Communion only at the moment of his death.[96]

---

94   Timothy the Presbyter, *Recept. Haer.* (PG 86A.11–74 [13, 69]).
95   Mark the Deacon, *Vit. Porph.* 91 (Lieu 2010, 101): "Now all those who heard about what happened were seized with great astonishment, not only those of our faith, but also the foreigners, and the two men and two women who accompanied Julia and all those who had been beguiled by her, rushed to throw themselves at the feet of the most blessed bishop, crying: 'We have been led astray!' And they asked for pardon. The blessed one made all of them anathematize Mani, the founder of their heresy, the one after whom they were called Manichaeans. And, having duly instructed them for very many days, he admitted them to the holy catholic church".
96   Gregory of Nyssa, *Ep. Letoium* 225. The letter, written a few years after the Council of Constantinople, seems like a commentary on and completion of the seventh canon of the Council. For this letter see also Silvas 2007, 211–25.

In conclusion, as is reflected in the canons of the Church, the converted Manichaeans are always placed in the group for which the most austere and time-consuming measures are postulated. The rationale of the whole procedure for their reception into the Church can be reduced to two words: converted Manichaeans had to be received 'as Greeks' (ὡς Ἕλληνες).

To recapitulate, as has been demonstrated by the examination of (1) the opinion of the specialists, (2) the ecclesiastical lists of heretics, and (3) the taxonomical lists of the converted heretics, although Manichaeans are often named by the authors as heretics, it seems they constituted for them a distinctive *heretical* category entirely outside of Christianity. Furthermore, the fact that the Manichaean issue and doctrines had never been addressed in any of the ecumenical synods (beyond its mere inclusion in the lists of anathematized heretics) shows that the Church's authorities in no way regarded Manichaeism as a form of Christianity. Neither relevant synodic tomes, nor epistles, canons, or definitions clarifying the failure of the Manichaean doctrine were ever issued. Wherever there is a reference to Manichaeism in the proceedings of the Synods, it is to emphasize that the adversaries of the conflicting parties think as μανιχαΐζοντες or μανιχαιόφρονες, something that would advocate for the condemnation of their views.

It is also important to note, that in all the above cases, the word *Manichaean* concerns real Manichaeans because it exists in parallel with and is distinguished from other heresies, either *new/noble* or *old.*

2.2   *Heretics as 'Manichaeans' (Imagined Manichaeans)*[97]

How did *noble* heretics see Manichaeans? What was the relationship between them? Many patristic texts give the impression that there was a close relationship between Manichaeism and the *noble* heresies of the era. To be specific, Manichaeism is often presented as the root of all Triadological and Christological heresies.

For example, Athanasius of Alexandria links Arianism to Manichaeism due to the notion of *subordinatio*. According to him, the Arians introduce two *Logoi* as the Manichaeans introduce two Gods. This is because, as for the Manichaeans the creator of this world is not the one God but another whom their imagination invented, similarly for the Arians the Logos of God (Word, Wisdom) is different from the incarnated Logos (Son).[98]

For Basil of Caesarea and his brother Gregory of Nyssa, the doctrine of the Anomians (extreme Arians) is verging on Manichaeism because they could

---

97   This section is an extended version of Matsangou 2017b, 163–65.

98   Athanasius, *c. Ar.* (*Oratio I* 53. 3–4 and *Oratio II* 39–41; *Oratio III contra Arianos* (35. 2–3) [347]; *Ep. Aeg. Lib.* (16. 1–2) [55–56]; *Ep. Adelph.* col. 1073.

not distinguish between γενητός ('created') and γεννητός ('begotten'), introducing likewise two first principles: the κτιστόν ('created') and the ἄκτιστον ('uncreated'). As Gregory argues, Eunomius (Anomoean) premising that the terms ἀγενησία (ingenerateness) and γέννηση (generation) signify two different substances, and identifying the essence of God as ἀγενησία (ingenerateness) and the essence of the Son as γέννηση (generation), deduced that the Father and the Son are of two different substances. In this way, he argues, the Manichaean doctrine of the two principles intruded into the Church.[99]

Arius on the other hand, defending his faith in the one God, considers that, by attributing the term ὁμοούσιος ('homoousios') to the Logos, the Catholics introduced the Manichaean emanations.[100] Arians considered that the content of the term ὁμοούσιος and the principle of consubstantiality were analogous to the Manichaean tenet that Jesus was an "emanation of the Father of Greatness".[101] As some Arian clerics argued in a letter addressed to Alexander (the bishop of Alexandria), the term ὁμοούσιος (Father's emanation according to them), which is used by both Catholics and Manichaeans, renders the essence of God composite, dividable, and mutable, which in turn leads to polytheism.[102] According to the church historian Philostorgius (who was himself an Anomoean), the Arian orator Aetios, whom he considered a teacher *par excellence*, regarded Manichaeism as an overt polytheism, while seeing Catholicism as a covert one.[103]

---

99 Basil of Caesarea, *Adv. Eunomium*, II. 34 (PG 29:652): Εἰ μὲν οὖν, δύο ἀρχὰς ἀντιπαρεξάγων ἀλλήλαις, ταῦτά φησι, μετὰ Μανιχαίου καὶ Μαρκίωνος συντριβήσεται. Gregory of Nyssa, *c. Eunomium* Cap.1.35 (Book I, 1, §§503–523, 503–04; Jaeger, 172): πρὸς τὸν μανιχαϊσμὸν ῥέπειν τὸ δόγμα τῶν Ἀνομοίων [...] μὴ δύο ἑτερογενῆ πράγματα ἐν τῷ τῆς ἀρχῆς λόγῳ ὑπολαμβά-νοιτο καὶ διὰ τούτου πάροδον λάβοι τῶν Μανιχαίων τὸ δόγμα. τὸ γὰρ κτιστὸν καὶ τὸ ἄκτιστον ἐκ διαμέτρου πρὸς ἄλληλα τὴν κατὰ τὸ σημαινόμενον ἐναντίωσιν ἔχει. εἰ οὖν τὰ δύο (ἐν) ταῖς ἀρχαῖς ταχθείη, κατὰ τὸ λεληθὸς ἡμῖν ὁ μανιχαϊσμὸς εἰς τὴν ἐκκλησίαν τοῦ θεοῦ εἰσφθαρήσε-ται. On this see also Lieu 1994a, 107. Chrysostom, *Anom.* (*homilia 7*) (PG 48:758–59): Οὐκ ἀκούεις ἔτι καὶ νῦν Μαρκίωνος ἀρνουμένου τὴν οἰκονομίαν, καὶ Μανιχαίου, καὶ Οὐαλεντίνου, καὶ πολλῶν ἑτέρων.

100 Arius, 'Epistle ad Alexandrus', in Epiphanius, *Pan.* 69.7–8 (pp. 157.20–159.13), esp. 69.7.6 (158.11–14). See also Lieu 1994a, 102 and Edwards 2015, 141.

101 Lieu 1992, 126.

102 Athanasius, *De synodis Arimini in Italia et Seleuciae in Isauria* 16.3–5 (Opitz, 243–44): ὡς Οὐαλεντῖνος προβολὴν τὸ γέννημα τοῦ πατρὸς ἐδογμάτισεν, [...] Μανιχαῖος μέρος ὁμοούσιον τοῦ πατρὸς τὸ γέννημα εἰσηγήσατο [...] εἰ δὲ τὸ 'ἐξ αὐτοῦ' καὶ τὸ 'ἐκ γαστρὸς' καὶ τὸ 'ἐκ τοῦ πατρὸς ἐξῆλθον καὶ ἥκω' ὡς μέρος αὐτοῦ ὁμοουσίου καὶ ὡς προβολὴ ὑπό τινων νοεῖται, σύνθετος ἔσται ὁ πατὴρ καὶ διαιρετὸς καὶ τρεπτὸς [...].

103 Philostorgius, *HE* 3.15. Cf. Amidon 2007, xvii, 54 fn. 57. Philostorgius (who was Eunomius' encomiast) in his *Ecclesiastical History* (425–433), records a debate that took place in Alexandria ca. 356, between two mighty orators, the Manichaean Aphthonius and the Arian Aetius. I will discuss this in ch.[7], 3.3.

In the next step of the development of Christian theological debates, the Christological, Manichaeans still remained the negative paradigm for all. According to Socrates the Scholastic, representatives of the Antiochene School (dyophysites) dogmatized as did the Manichaeans.[104] In contrast, Theodoret of Cyrrhus (accused of being a dyophysite and Nestorian by his Catholic and Monophysite opponents) systematically correlates Monophysite Christology to Manichaean Docetism.[105] As is reflected in his letter to Eusebius of Ankara, he considered that the Monophysite theses strengthened and renewed the Manichaean heresy.[106] In general, testimonies linking Monophysitism and Manichaeism are many and from all sides.[107] Theodorus of Raithou considered Eutyches as successor and defender of Mani's and Apollinarius' dogma.[108] Nestorius, in an epistle he addressed to Cyril, bishop of Alexandria, blames Cyril and his clerics as Manichaean-minded (μανιχαιόφρονες), apparently due to their Monophysite wording on Christology.[109]

The case of Severus of Antioch, a moderate Monophysite himself, who "stigmatized his extreme Monophysite opponents as 'Manichaeans' on Christological issues" is characteristic.[110] For Severus, the Manichaeans were "more wicked [heretics] than any other".[111] Severus in turn, "himself was accused by Antiochene monks of being a Manichaean in the Synod of 536 for not believing

---

104   Socrates, *HE* 7.32.20.

105   Theodoret, *Ep. Sirm.* 82. 3–10.

106   Theodoret, *Ep. Sirm.* 82, in 449 (SC 98: 198–200). According to his letter his religious opponents, who renew the Manichaean heresy, calumniated him to the emperor as heretic because he combats them. Presumably by 'those who renew the Manichaean heresy' he meant the Monophysites: Οἱ γὰρ τὴν Μαρκίωνος καὶ Βαλεντίνου καὶ Μάνητος καὶ τῶν ἄλλων δοκητῶν αἵρεσιν ἐπὶ τοῦ παρόντος ἀνανεούμενοι, δυσχεραίνοντες ὅτι τὴν αἵρεσιν αὐτῶν ἄντικρυς στηλιτεύομεν, ἐξαπατῆσαι τὰς βασιλικὰς ἐπειράθησαν ἀκοάς, αἱρετικοὺς ἡμᾶς ἀποκαλοῦντες.

107   Justinian, *c. monophysitas* 93: οἱ Ἀκέφαλοι [...] δικαίως κληρωσάμενοι προσηγορίαν τὰ τῶν εἰρημένων ἀθέων φρονοῦντες ἀνδρῶν [Ἀπολιναρίου τοίνυν καὶ Μανιχαίου], εἰ καὶ τὰς προσηγορίας αὐτῶν δολερῶς ἀπωθοῦνται. According to Gardner and Lieu (2004, 174) since the above "fragments are all cited in polemics against Monophysites by Orthodox writers [...] are very likely to be fabrications".

108   Theodorus of Raithou, *Praeparatio* 2–7 (pp. 187–91). Ephraim of Antioch, *Capita xii*, 262: Κατὰ πάσης μὲν αἱρέσεως τῇ ἀληθείᾳ μαχομένων, ἐξαιρέτως δὲ κατὰ τῆς Νεστοριανῆς ἤτοι Ἰουδαϊκῆς αἱρέσεως καὶ Μανιχαϊκῆς τρυγίας τοῦ πεπλανημένου Εὐτύχεως.

109   Nestorius, *Ad Cyrillum Alexandrinum II* 180; ep. 5: γίνωσκε δὲ πεπλανημένον σαυτὸν ὑπὸ τῶν τῆς σῆς ἴσως διαθέσεως κληρικῶν, ὑπὸ τῶν ἐνταῦθα ἀπὸ τῆς ἁγίας συνόδου καθῃρημένων, ὡς τὰ Μανιχαίων φρονούντων. Cf. *ACO* (*Ephesenum anno 431*), 1.1.1, 32[9–11].

110   Lieu 1994a, 110.

111   Lieu 1994a, 110. Severus of Antioch, *Homiliae Cathedrales cxxiii*, in Gardner and Lieu 2004, 161.

that Mary was the Mother of God".[112] For the seventh-century author whose works have been passed on under the name of the (later) authority Oecumenius of Tricca, the followers of Eutyches (extreme Monophysites) argue like the Manichaeans since they support the docetic view of incarnation.[113]

Origenists of the meta-Chalcedonian controversy are also considered as Manichaean-minded due to their protology (pre-existence of the souls) and eschatology (apocatastasis, final restoration).[114]

As can be deduced from the above, not only the Catholics but also the *noble* heretics compared their religious opponents to Manichaeans and considered that a fundamental part of their theology connected them directly and substantially to Manichaeism.

Furthermore, the different Christian parties are (in most cases) not identified with, or accused of being Manichaeans. Instead, it is their theology, Triadology, and Christology that is compared to Manichaeism, and is underlined that they think as the Manichaeans do (μανιχαιόφρονες). I have the impression that the tone in many texts is more admonitory and exhortative, rather than denunciatory. Their aim is pastoral (i.e. caring for believers), because the correct wording of the dogma had soteriological dimensions. In such a context, Nilus the bishop of Ankara addressed a letter to the presbyter Philon, in which he rebukes Philon because he dissimulated the Manichaean teachings as Christian when preaching to his flock.[115]

---

112 *Acta Synodus (Constantinopolitana et Hierosolymitana anno 536)*, 3.72.9–10 & 16–17. Cf. Lieu 1994a, 110 fn. 361.

113 Oecumenius, *Commentarius in Apocalypsin* 13.2 (p. 60) (Suggit, 46): "He has become a human being, without discarding his divinity, and he is truly a human being [...] This has nothing to do with analogy, as Nestorians say, nor with semblance or appearance, as Eutychians say and the accursed and disgusting tribe of the Manichaeans". About the identity of the author see Suggit 2006, 3–16.

114 Cyril of Scythopolis, *Vit. Sab.* 124. Justinian, *Epistula ad synodum de Origene* 122–124. Evagrius, *HE* 4.38.420 (Bidez and Parmentier, 188–89): Ἰουστινιανὸς [...] συζεύξας καὶ τοῦ λιβέλλου τὸ ἴσον ἀτὰρ καὶ τὰ πρὸς Βιγίλιον περὶ τούτων ἐπεσταλμένα. Ἐξ ὧν ἁπάντων ἔστιν ἑλεῖν ὅπως ἐσπουδάσθη τῷ Ὠριγένει Ἑλληνικῶν καὶ Μανιχαϊκῶν ζιζανίων ἐμπλῆσαι τῶν ἀποστολικῶν δογμάτων τὸ λιτόν. As Perczel (2004, 205–36) argues, the reason that the Origenists were associated with the Manichaeans by anti-Origenist authors is that they used a common vocabulary, mythical schemes and motifs. Originists of the sixth century, appealing to the same audience as Manichaeans, combat Manichaean dualism using its own means. To his question of whether finally "this similarity of language testifies to any direct influence of Manichaean thought on the Origenists", Perczel answers "I think it does".

115 Nilus of Ankara, *Ep. 321* (book 2) (PG 79:356–57). Cf. Kyrtatas (2005, 67) on the Christian "belief that salvation depended on orthodox dogma".

Even in some cases where the word *Manichaean* is used, it seems from the context that it is not used literally. Through their letters, many Catholic bishops, among them Pamphilus of Abydus and Quintianus of Ausculanum, call the Monophysite bishop of Antioch Petrus Cnapheus, to the correct Christology:

> Pamphylos: [...] arguing likewise in your writings [...] wouldn't I call you a Manichaean?
> Quintianus: When you claim that Christ has only one nature, how do you mean this? Created as Arius says, or phantasmal as Manichaeus does?[116]

Athanasius' rhetorical question to Adelphius can be interpreted from the same point of view:

> Why then, [Arians] who adopt their [Valentinian, Marcionite, Manichaean] beliefs, do not also inherit their names? For it is reasonable, since they hold their misbeliefs, to also have their names, so as to be called Valentinians, Marcionites and Manichaeans.[117]

Athanasius' question is revealing for the use of the term 'Manichaean' as a label, and as a religious abuse in the Triadological debate during the fourth century.

A further illustration of how insulting it was considered for one to be called a Manichaean is his next sentence:

> Perhaps then they will become ashamed because of the bad odour of these names and so they will be enabled to perceive into what depth of impiety they have fallen.[118]

A corresponding question in the Christological debate during the fifth century is that of Eutherius of Tyana, the leader of the Nestorian party at the

---

116   *Acta Synodus* (*Constantinopolitana et Hierosolymitana anno 536*), 3.9.31–33 (Pamphylos: ἀλλ' ἐν τοῖς συγγράμμασιν ἔφης [...] οὐ Μανιχαῖόν σε λέξω;) & 3.15.23–24 (Quintianus: εἰ δὲ φύσεως μιᾶς ἐστιν ὁ Χριστὸς καὶ οὐ δύο, τί οὐ λέγεις τὸν Χριστὸν κτιστὸν ὡς ὁ Ἄρειος ἢ ἄκτιστον ὡς ὁ Μανιχαῖος;).

117   Athanasius, *Ep. Adelph.* col. 1073: Διὰ τί οὖν, τὰ τούτων φρονοῦντες, οὐχὶ καὶ τῶν ὀνομάτων αὐτῶν γίνονται κληρονόμοι; Εὔλογον γὰρ ὧν τὴν κακοδοξίαν ἔχουσι, τούτων ἔχειν καὶ τὰ ὀνόματα, ἵνα λοιπὸν Οὐαλεντινιανοὶ καὶ Μαρκιωνισταὶ καὶ Μανιχαῖοι καλῶνται.

118   Athanasius, *Ep. Adelph.*, col. 1073.20–30 (*NPNF*² 4:1381, altered): Τάχα κἂν οὕτως διὰ τὴν τῶν ὀνομάτων δυσωδίαν αἰσχυνόμενοι κατανοῆσαι δυνηθῶσιν, εἰς ὅσον βάθος ἀσεβείας πεπτώκασι. See also the episode with Constantius and the Arian bishops (section 4.2.1), Athanasius, *H. Ar.* 30.4–7 (358).

third Ecumenical Council of Ephesus in 431. Eutherius blames Monophysites as apostates to Manichaeism and wonders "how not to call you Manichaeans since you have the same misbeliefs?"[119]

To sum up: in the above cases, even when the word *Manichaean* is used, it acquires the meaning of μανιχαΐζων or μανιχαιόφρων. Furthermore, for both Catholics and *noble* heretics, Manichaeism constituted the worst heresy *par excellence*, which became the benchmark for calculating the degree of heresy.[120] The latter indicates that Manichaeism was active as a missionary religion and reflects the trouble that it caused. In the words of Serapion of Thmuis, Manichaeism makes the rest of the heresies appear harmless.[121]

Because the Manichaeans were considered the worst of the worst heretics by all the Christian parties, the term 'Manichaean' with the meaning of μανιχαΐζων became a label of abuse very early (i.e. during the Arian controversy) and continued to exist long after the period covered in this study. Therefore, in the literature under examination, alongside the real Manichaeans, there appeared the imaginary ones.

3 Manichaean Religious Profile According to the Pagan Authors

The most important testimony for the Manichaean religious profile which comes from the pagan world is the work of the philosopher Alexander of Lycopolis, *Contra Manichaei opiniones disputatio*. Alexander's work is the oldest treatise against the Manichaeans. Around 300, at the time Alexander wrote it, the Manichaean missionary activity in Egypt must have caused a general disturbance and alarm, as illustrated by the decree of Diocletian (302) and the circular letter attributed to Theonas, the bishop of Alexandria (282–300).[122]

The Manichaean religious identity, as depicted by Alexander, has been much discussed by scholars. As the translators of the text (Van der Horst and Mansfeld) commented in their introduction, "very interesting for the students of Manichaeism is the fact that so early a witness as Alexander presents Mani

---

119 Eutherius of Tyana, *Confutationes quarundam propositionum* 14.45–50: πρὸς Μανιχαίους ηὐτομολήσατε, καὶ πῶς φεύγετε τὴν ἐκείνων προσηγορίαν, ὧν φαίνεσθε κληρονόμοι τῆς ἀφορήτου κακοδοξίας.

120 It has been argued that both Arius and the Antiochian School developed their Triadology and Christology, respectively, in response to the Manichaean Docetism. See Lyman 1989, 493–503 (esp. 501–03); Perczel 2004, 205–36.

121 Serapion, *c. Manichaeos* 3.21–23, p. 30.

122 All the three sources were firstly discussed in ch.[2], 2.1. An introductory section on Alexander and his work is also provided in ch.[1], section 5.

as a Christian heretic".[123] This remark, which is also important for the question of the origin of Manichaeism, has attracted a lot of attention and has been repeatedly quoted in later works.[124]

The opinion of the translators was based mainly on the two opening chapters of Alexander's text. Alexander starts his work on Manichaeism by presenting Christian philosophy. He says that, although 'simple', it was effective in stimulating moral progress by instigating people to desire what is good. According to him, this 'simple' Christian philosophy was rendered decadent within the systems of thought of later heretics, worst of all Mani (εἰς ἀνήνυτον πρᾶγμα τὴν ἁπλῆν ταύτην ἐμβεβλήκασιν φιλοσοφίαν). Reading the two first chapters this way, it could indeed be inferred that Alexander presents Manichaeism as a Christian heresy. This thesis conforms also to Gardner's theory. Alexander met Manichaeism at an earlier stage of the religion's development, earlier than the Church Fathers; hence it is probable that the Manichaeism he faced was more Christian than the Manichaeism described by later Church Fathers.

However, I believe that the importance attributed to this first image of Manichaeism in Alexander's introduction has been overstated. Furthermore, the thesis that Alexander regarded Manichaeism as one of the Christian heresies is reinforced by the translation of the text; it presupposes such an interpretation, and is in turn derived from the conviction of the translators of the Christian origin of Manichaeism. They worked on the translation in the period immediately after the discovery of the CMC, when the hypothesis of the Christian origin of Manichaeism was convincing to most researchers. In the words of the translators "the Christian origin [of Manichaeism] has now been definitely proved by the new codex of Cologne".[125] The new translation and the emphasis on the importance of this specific part of Alexander's discussion of Manichaeism led later scholars to regard it as highly significant for the discourse concerning the origins of Manichaeism; this stimulated interpretations of the text from this perspective. Thus, Alexander's criticism

---

123 Van der Horst and Mansfeld 1974, 6.

124 Gersh 1976, 211: "but the writer [Van der Horst] draws attention to the important point that the pagan philosopher presents Mani as a Christian heretic (p. 6 and n. 11)". Lieu, 1994a 158: "Alexander [...] regarded [Manichaeism] as an eccentric form of Christianity". Lieu (2010, 162), slightly modifying his previous opinion, states: Alexander "saw Manichaeism as a 'complex' off-shoot of the Christian school". Van Oort 2013, 277: "In modern research, Alexander's *Against the Doctrines of Manichaios* is important for two main reasons. Firstly, because it is a highly significant source for our knowledge of early Manichaeism. A major characteristic of Alexander's description is that he considers it to be a form of Christianity. In the past decades, this assessment of Mani's religion has been confirmed by several discoveries of Manichaean texts".

125 Van der Horst and Mansfeld 1974, 6 fn. 11.

(in another chapter of his text) that Manichaean teachings relied on the voice of the prophets instead of being based on the reason of the apodictic principles of the Greek philosophers, was interpreted as a criticism of Christianity.[126] As Lieu argues, for "a pagan philosopher like Alexander [...] the Manichaeans were no different from the Christians", in that both relied on the prophets.[127] This interpretation, however, is incompatible with his position on Christianity, as will be shown below.

My thesis does not intend to challenge the translators' opinion regarding the origin of Manichaeism. As was made clear from the outset, the origin of Manichaeism does not fall within the scope of my research. What I doubt is the suggestion that Alexander presents Mani as a Christian heretic, or that Alexander's whole treatise represents Manichaeism as a Christian heresy. It is interesting to note here that the older translation by James Hawkins did not stimulate relevant discussion concerning the origin.[128] I quote below the two translations of the same passage:[129]

The philosophy of the Christians is termed simple. [...] But this being divided into many questions by the number of those who come after, there arise many, just as is the case with those who are devoted to dialectics [...] so that now they come forward as parents and originators of sects and heresies [...] wish to become the heads of the sects [...] 2. So in these matters also, while in novelty of opinion each endeavours to show himself first and superior, they brought this philosophy, which is simple, almost to a nullity. Such was he whom they call Manichaeus, Persian by race [rest is missing from translation].[130]

The philosophy of the Christians is a simple philosophy [...] Since this simple philosophy has been slit up into numerous factions by its later

---

126 Alexander, *Tract. Man.* 5.30–33 (Van der Horst and Mansfeld, 59): "The role attributed by the philosophers of the Greeks to the postulates, namely the underived propositions upon which proofs are based is represented among these people by the voice of the prophets".

127 Lieu 1994a, 170.

128 See *ANF* 6:411–35.

129 Alexander, *Tract. Man.* 1–2 (Brinkmann, 3–4): Ἡ Χριστιανῶν φιλοσοφία ἁπλῆ καλεῖται [...] Εἰς πλεῖστα δὲ ταύτης ὑπὸ τῶν ἐπιγενομένων μερισθείσης ζητήσεις συνέστησαν πλείονες καθάπερ ἐν τοῖς ἐριστικοῖς [...] καί τινες ἤδη καὶ αἱρέσεων προὔστησαν· [...] τῶν αἱρέσεως ἡγεῖσθαι ἠξίουν [...] οὕτω δὲ καὶ ἐπὶ τούτων τῇ καινότητι τῶν δοξῶν ἑκάτερος τὸν πρὸ αὐτοῦ ὑπερβάλλεσθαι σπουδάζων εἰς ἀνήνυτον πρᾶγμα τὴν ἁπλῆν ταύτην ἐμβεβλήκασιν φιλοσοφίαν· ὥσπερ ὁ λεγόμενος Μανιχαῖος, ὃς Πέρσης μέν τίς ἐστιν τὸ γένος, κατά γε τὴν ἐμὴν δόξαν πάντας ὑπερβαλὼν τῷ θαυμάσια λέγειν.

130 *ANF* 6:413–14.

adherents, the number of issues has increased just as in sophistry [...]
some of these men [...] wanted to be leaders of the sects [...] 2. as each
of them strove to surpass his predecessor by the novelty of his doctrines,
they converted the simple philosophy into a hopelessly complicated
and ineffectual thing. An example of this tendency is the man named
Manichaeus, a Persian by birth, whose astonishing doctrines, in my opinion, far surpass those of all the others.[131]

What makes the difference is that according to the translation of Hawkins,
Christian philosophy was "divided into many questions by the number of
those who come after [in life] (ἐπιγενομένων)",[132] while, according to the translation of Van der Horst and Mansfeld, Christian philosophy was "split up into
numerous factions by its later adherents". The literal translation is the first. The
second requires an interpretative proposal.[133] Thus, according to a more literal and neutral translation, Alexander says that Manichaeism is a heresy, but
he does not say that it is a Christian heresy. The content of the term heresy
during the period under investigation, as has been indicated above, was broad
and polysemous.[134] Especially at the time Alexander wrote his treatise and
in the context of pagan philosophy, the term still had the meaning of 'school
of thought', a 'system of philosophical principles, etc. Indeed, in a subsequent
chapter of his treatise Alexander himself uses the term αἵρεσις in the sense of
philosophical school.[135]

---

131   Van der Horst and Mansfeld 1974, 48–52.
132   Translation of 'ἐπιγενομένων', ἐπιγενόμενος = to be born after, come into being after, οἱ ἐπι-
      γινόμενοι ἄνθρωποι posterity, Id.9.85; οἱ ἐπιγενόμενοι τούτῳ σοφισταί who came after him,
      the following, the next, become or come into being afterwards.
133   Similar is the critique concerning the translation by Gersh (1976, 212): "in some ways the
      authors may be felt to be prone to excessive diligence in this respect [trans.] [...] per-
      haps the interpretation of the sentence [...] might well have been left to the reader's own
      ingenuity".
134   See section 1.1 in this chapter (*Methodological Ruminations*).
135   Alexander, *Tract. Man.* 24.20 (Brinkmann, 35): εἰ δὲ κατ' αὐτῶν τὴν καλλίστην αἵρεσιν ὁ
      νοῦς κατ' αὐτούς ἐστιν τὰ ὄντα πάντα. The expression 'καλλίστην αἵρεσιν' is translated by
      Van der Horst and Mansfeld (1974, 93) as 'best school'. Moreover, the Catholic writers
      themselves, from the beginning to the end of the period under investigation, repeatedly
      stressed that Manichaeism is a heresy that claims to be Christian. According to the tes-
      timony of Epiphanius, even in the 370s there were people (Christians) who considered
      Manichaeans as Christians. It is thus expected that when Manichaeism first appeared
      in Roman territories to be considered by the pagans as a form of Christianity. John of
      Damascus (*Haer.*) also classifies Islam (the Ismailite religion, θρησκεία τῶν Ἰσμαηλιτῶν) as
      a Christian heresy, the last of his time. Was it?

Consequently, I will argue that in the rest of Alexander's treatise, comprising his whole argumentation refuting the Manichaean doctrines, nothing suggests that he believes that he is confronting a Christian heresy. I would rather say that he seems to consider it as a 'pagan/Hellenic' heresy.

The Manichaean missionaries that Alexander met, among them Papos and Thomas, instead of using quotations from the Christian Scriptures (NT) in their propaganda, are said to have used fables from Greek mythology as supporting arguments. For example, they invoke the battle of the Giants to prove that the Greek poets were aware of the rebellion of matter (= evil principle) against God. They present the dismemberment of Dionysus by the Titans as supporting evidence for their doctrine of the dispersal of divine light particles in matter.[136] Alexander is especially critical. Manichaeans, he writes, have surpassed the poets. Their stories are of the same kind as those of the Greek poets; however, while for the poets they were allegories aiming to teach moral lessons, Manichaeans meant them literally. Alexander confesses that he himself knows such persons who mix together and quote material from poetry in order to support their arguments and doctrines.[137] As he testifies, the Manichaean missionaries, applying such methods, succeeded to convert even some of his fellow-philosophers.

> I, for one, do not wish to deny that these doctrines are capable of influencing the minds of those who uncritically accept this theory, especially since deceitful expositions of this kind were successful in making converts out of certain fellow-philosophers of mine.[138]

In addition to Greek myths, according to Alexander, Manichaeans took ideas from Greek philosophers (e.g. Plato, Aristotle, Pythagoras) which, however, they distorted. They talked about matter, but they did not mean it as Plato and Aristotle, but as "the random motion within each individual thing",

---

136   Alexander, *Tract. Man.* 5 (Van der Horst and Mansfeld, 57): "The more cultivated among them, who are not unfamiliar with Greek mythology, call to our memory parts of our own tradition. They quote the mysteries, comparing the dismemberment of Dionysus by the Titans to the dividing up, in their own teachings, of the divine power over matter. They also refer to the battle of the giants as told in our poetry, which to their mind proves that the poets were not ignorant of the insurrection of matter against God".

137   Alexander, *Tract. Man.* 10 (Van der Horst and Mansfeld, 70–71): "They surpass by far the mythographers [...] Their stories are undoubtedly of the same sort, since they describe a regular war of matter against God, but they do not even mean this allegorically, as e.g. Homer did [...]". For the presentation of the Manichaean mythology in Alexander, see Widengren 1985, 830.

138   Alexander, *Tract. Man.* 5.15–19 (Van der Horst and Mansfeld, 58).

which is something completely different.[139] Elsewhere, Alexander criticizes Manichaean pantheistic views[140] and the Manichaean misconception of Pythagoras' theory.[141] Thus, Alexander's work is a confirmation of the Church Fathers' claim that the Manichaeans in their propaganda to pagans/Greeks "set out to prove that [...] [their] message accords with their traditions".[142]

The Manichaean prophets, as described by Alexander, look like decayed Greek poets and philosophers, rather than Christian prophets. Their teachings are presented as a parody and a caricature of Greek mythology and philosophy. As Mansfeld comments, Alexander "argues against the Manichaeans from a Platonist point of view, often treating his opponents as if they were some sort of crypto-Stoics".[143] The latter is also illustrated in his presentation of the Manichaean doctrines, which are recorded in "their old and new scriptures (γραφὰς παλαιάς τε καὶ νέας)".[144] These are doctrines that had nothing in common with Christianity, and were later combated by the Church writers. Both Alexander and Christian authors like Titus of Bostra and Serapion of Thmuis developed the same rationale in their treatises against Manichaeans. Apart from the main target of their criticism, which was dualism and its consequences for anthropology and ethics, there are many other parallels in their rhetoric.[145] For example, a recurrent target of both the Church Fathers' and Alexander's criticism is the Manichaean theory of the construction of the salvific machinery for the pumping of the souls from matter, through the sun and the moon:

> The sun and the moon [...] continually separate the divine power from matter and send it on its way toward God.[146]

---

139   Alexander, *Tract. Man.* 2.18–26 (Van der Horst and Mansfeld, 52–53).

140   Alexander, *Tract. Man.* 22.15–19.

141   Alexander, *Tract. Man.* 6.

142   Titus of Bostra, *c. Manichaeos* 4.2.

143   Van der Horst and Mansfeld 1974, 47. Cf. Stroumsa and Stroumsa 1988 & Stroumsa 1992.

144   Alexander, *Tract. Man.* 5. Cf. ch.[2], 3.3.

145   See for example chs 13 and 14. As Alexander states (13.14–18), according to the Manichaean theory, natural disasters should "belong to the domain of the good", because they "would render possible the return to God of a great part of the power which has been confined within matter". Similarly, Titus of Bostra (*c. Manichaeos* 2.24–29), ca. 70 years later, points out that Manichaeans contradict themselves arguing, on the one hand, that matter's increase is harmful and that the birth of children increases matter, while, on the other hand, they consider matter's destruction through natural disasters as evil, and massive deaths through calamities as human woes. On the analogies between the work of Alexander and Titus of Bostra, see ch.[1], sections 5 & 6.

146   Alexander, *Tract. Man.* 3.30–33 (Brinkmann, 6; Van der Horst and Mansfeld, 55): ἥλιον καὶ σελήνην ταῖς [...] τὴν δύναμιν τὴν θείαν τῆς ὕλης ἀποχωρίζοντας καὶ πρὸς τὸν θεὸν παραπέμποντας. For the whole procedure of the pumping of light particles from matter, through

They say that both sun and moon separate the divine power from matter bit by bit and transmit it to God, the moon receiving it within itself from the time when it is new until when it is full, and then giving it to the sun, which sends it on towards God.[147]

This notion is denounced as absurd, and a "scientific" explanation is provided:

They would not have been in this plight, had they, at least occasionally, attended the lectures of astronomers; then they would not have been unfamiliar with the fact that the moon (which according to some does not possess a light of its own) is illuminated by the sun.[148]

For Alexander, the Manichaean idea that Man was created by matter according to the image of an icon of Man that appears in the sun, is beyond any imagination.

Is it not more fantastic than any myth when they say that man is a product of matter copied from the image which is visible in the sun?[149]

In general, Alexander's whole argumentation does not give the impression that he refutes a Christian heresy. On the contrary, in his argumentation, he commends and adopts Christian theses to refute the Manichaean theories and doctrines, which is a surprising choice from a pagan philosopher.[150] He juxtaposes the correctness of Christian teaching to the problematic theses of Manichaeism, especially in the topics of anthropology and ethics (free will).

---

the sun and the moon, see Ch. 4.4–12: "For at each increase the moon receives the power which is separated from matter and during this time it is filled with it; and when it has become full, it transmits it to the sun as it wanes. The sun, again, passes it on to God; and when it has done this, again receives that part of Soul which has migrated towards it since the last full moon".

147   Alexander, *Tract. Man.* 22.1–6 (Brinkmann, 29–30; Van der Horst and Mansfeld, 86): Λέγουσι δὲ ὅτι καὶ ἥλιος καὶ σελήνη τὴν θείαν δύναμιν κατὰ μικρὸν διακρίναντες ἀπὸ τῆς ὕλης πρὸς τὸν θεὸν ἀποπέμπουσιν, τῆς σελήνης ἐν ταῖς νουμηνίαις μέχρι τῆς πανσελήνου εἰς ἑαυτὴν δεχομένης ταύτην εἶτα τῷ ἡλίῳ ⟨δι⟩δούσης, τοῦ δὲ πρὸς τὸν θεὸν παραπέμποντος.

148   Alexander, *Tract. Man.* 22.6–14 (Brinkmann, 30; Van der Horst and Mansfeld, 86–87): εἰ δ' ἦσαν καὶ κατὰ μικρὸν εἰς ἀστρονόμων θύρας φοιτήσαντες, οὐκ ἂν ταῦτα πεπόνθεσαν οὔτε ἠγνόησαν ἂν ὅτι ἡ σελήνη – κατά τινας ἄμοιρος οὖσα ἰδίου φωτός – ὑπὸ τοῦ ἡλίου καταλάμπεται.

149   Alexander, *Tract. Man.* 23.10–12 (Brinkmann, 32; Van der Horst and Mansfeld, 88): Τίνας δὲ μύθους οὐχ ὑπερβέβηκεν τῷ ἀπιθάνῳ καὶ ταῦτα, ὅτε κατὰ τὴν ὀφθεῖσαν ἐν ἡλίῳ εἰκόνα τῆς ὕλης τὸν ἄνθρωπον δημιούργημα εἶναι λέγωσιν. See in 23.10–67 the whole section about the ⟨The Origin of Man⟩ (Van der Horst and Mansfeld, 88–91).

150   This is one of the reasons why Edwards (1989 and 2015) challenged the pagan identity of Alexander. See below in this section.

Our first question should be: what then, is the use of all the effort which
is spent on education? For we could become good even when asleep.
Or what reason do these people hold out to their own catechumens the
highest hope for reaching the good? For these would be in possession of
their proper good even when spending their time in whoring.[151]

He criticizes the elitist division of the members of the sect into two classes
and compares it with the corresponding Christian teaching on the equality
between all men.

This was, I believe, correctly understood by Jesus, and this is why, in order
that farmers and carpenters and masons and other skilled workers should
not be excluded from the good, he instituted a common circle of all these
people together, and why, by means of simple and easy conversations, he
[...] helped them to achieve a desire for the good.[152]

He is shocked, as Stroumsa comments, by the elitist approach of salvation
in Manichaeism only for the few Elect, and criticizes the closed Manichaean
communities from a social perspective.[153]

Finally, Alexander accuses Manichaeans of talking about Christ, while in
fact, they do not know him; they change even his name, instead of Χριστός (the
anointed, from chrism), he says, they call him Χρηστός (good).

Christ (Christos) however, whom they do not even know, but whom they
call chrestos (good), introducing a new meaning instead of the generally
received one by changing the 'i' into 'e', they hold to be the Intellect.[154]

151   Alexander, *Tract. Man.* 16.12–17 (Brinkmann, 23; Van der Horst and Mansfeld, 79): πρῶτον
μὲν τίς χρεία τοῦ περὶ τὴν παίδευσιν πόνου; γενοίμεθα γὰρ ἂν καθεύδοντες σπουδαῖοι. ἢ διὰ τί
μάλιστα τοὺς ἀκροωμένους αὐτῶν οἱ τοιοῦτοι ἄνδρες εἰς ἐλπίδα ἄγουσι τοῦ καλοῦ; καὶ γὰρ καλινδούμενοι σὺν ταῖς ἑταίραις τὸ οἰκεῖον ἔχοιεν ἂν ἀγαθόν.

152   Alexander, *Tract. Man.* 16.29–35 (Brinkmann, 24; Van der Horst and Mansfeld, 80): ὃ δοκεῖ
μοι κατανενοηκέναι ὁ Ἰησοῦς καὶ ἵνα μὴ ἀπεληλαμένοι ὦσι τοῦ ἀγαθοῦ γεωργοί τε καὶ τέκτονες
καὶ οἰκοδόμοι καὶ οἱ ἄλλοι ἀπὸ τῶν τεχνῶν, κοινὸν συνέδριον καθίσαι πάντων ὁμοῦ καὶ διὰ ἁπλῶν
καὶ εὐκόλων διαλέξεων καὶ εἰς θεοῦ ἔννοιαν αὐτοὺς ἀπενηνοχέναι καὶ τοῦ καλοῦ εἰς ἐπιθυμίαν
ἐλθεῖν ποιῆσαι.

153   Stroumsa and Stroumsa 1988, 50.

154   Alexander, *Tract. Man.* 24.1–4 (Jesus as Νοῦς) (Brinkmann, 34; Van der Horst and Mansfeld,
91–92): Τὸν δὲ χριστὸν οὐδὲ γιγνώσκοντες, ἀλλὰ χρηστὸν αὐτὸν προσαγορεύοντες τῇ πρὸς τὸ η
στοιχεῖον μεταλήψει ἕτερον σημαινόμενον ἀντὶ τοῦ κυρίως περὶ αὐτοῦ ὑπειλημμένου εἰσάγοντες
νοῦν εἶναί φασιν. Alexander, by saying that the Manichaeans do not know Christ (Τὸν δὲ
χριστὸν οὐδὲ γιγνώσκοντες), does not speak literally, but wants to emphasize the difference
between the Christ of the Manichaeans and the Christ of the Christian churches. See
below, fn. 157.

Alexander's testimony that Manichaeans use to call Jesus Chrestos instead of Christos is attested by an original Manichaean letter found in Kellis (probably Mani's canonical epistle?). In the greetings in the introductory paragraph of the epistle we read: "Manichaios, apostle of Jesus Chrestos, and all the brothers who are with me ... Peace through God the Father, and our lord Jesus Chrestos".[155] Moreover, Alexander's testimony shows that he had access to original Manichaean texts, since the difference in the pronunciation between the vowels 'ι' (ióta) and 'η' (eta) did not exist in his time.[156]

In any case, Alexander's statement is impressive for a pagan, who seems to defend the Christ of the Christians. For Alexander, even the Christ of the Manichaeans, a figure who is supposed to be the crucial point for ranking Manichaeans among Christians, is completely different from the Christ of the Christian Churches.[157] Alexander's assertion is reminiscent of remarks made by Gregory of Nyssa and Augustine, that the name of Christ on the lips of the Manichaeans was just a sound, empty of meaning.[158]

Continuing his critique, Alexander wonders why then, if they mean the same Christ as the Churches do, they do not accept the Old Testament.[159] Here, unlike his previous criticism that Manichaean missionaries rely on their prophets' voice, he seems to reproach them because they reject the OT. It is really astonishing that Alexander's arguments seem to become an advocate of Christianity against Manichaeism. As Edwards points out, it is strange that a pagan philosopher adopts and supports so many Christian theses. Edwards considers it unexpected that Alexander uses the Greek term ἐκκλησία, which has a political meaning, with the religious content that the Christians ascribed to it. "We should not, however, expect a pagan author to designate the concourse of the faithful by the name which they [Christians] had stolen from the vocabulary of political affairs".[160] According to Edwards, what Alexander is trying to prove is that the doctrine of Manichaeans is self-contradictory, in that they contradicted themselves in claiming that they were Christians. Edwards,

---

155 Gardner and Lieu 2004, 167. According to Pedersen (2013b, 190) "it is highly probable that" this spelling "is a Manichaean self-designation".

156 Suetonius also calls Jesus Chrestos.

157 Alexander, *Tract. Man.* 24.4–8 (Brinkmann, 34–35): εἰ μὲν τὸ γνωστὸν καὶ τὸ γιγνῶσκον καὶ τὴν σοφίαν αὐτὸν λέγοντες, ὁμόφωνα οὕτως τοῖς ἀπὸ τῶν ἐκκλησιῶν περὶ αὐτοῦ λέγουσι διαταττόμενοι οὕτω γε ἀλώσονται. See fn. 39 in this chapter, for Pedersen's opinion about the Manichaean Jesus.

158 See also Gardner and Lieu 2004, 131. Cf. ch.[4], 2.1.1.

159 Alexander, *Tract. Man.* 24.4–9.

160 Edwards 1989, 484. As Edwards also states (1989, 484): "only political senses of ἐκκλησία and ἐκκλησιαστικός are attributed by Liddell and Scott to any pagan source".

however, does not exclude the possibility that such parts of the text could be a later addition, by the hand of a Christian author.[161]

Summarizing the basics of the Manichaean religious profile as presented by Alexander, it is clear that apart from the initial link he makes between Manichaeism and Christianity, in the remaining twenty-four chapters of his treatise, the Manichaeism he presents is a heresy that one cannot seriously argue was considered as Christian. It is a heresy which in its missionary propaganda used Greek fables instead of the New Testament, and whose doctrines are grounded on an erroneous understanding of Greek philosophy. It was a heresy, moreover, which had no moral rules unlike Christianity, and was a heresy which did not speak about the Christ that Christian Churches proclaim.

Some other brief pagan testimonies concerning the religious profile of Manichaeans must be discussed here. Around the middle of the fourth century (364), the famous orator Libanius, in a letter addressed to Priscianus (governor of Palaestina Prima under Constantius), pleaded for the Manichaeans, requesting their protection from [Christian] abusers. It is notable, that this is the only testimony we have that speaks in favour of Manichaeans. In his brief description, nothing suggests that he saw Manichaeism as a Christian heresy.

> Those who venerate the sun without (performing) blood (sacrifices) and honour it as a god of the second grade and chastise their appetites and look upon their last day as their gain are found in many places of the world but everywhere they are only few in number. They harm no one but they are harassed by some people. 2. I wish that those of them who live in Palestine may have your authority for refuge and be free from anxiety and that those who wish to harm them may not be allowed to do so.[162]

---

161   Edwards 1989, 486: "The difficulties of the passage are more readily discernible than their causes, but we have ample reasons for doubting its integrity in its present form unless we believe that the author was a pagan who adopted Christian assumptions and vocabulary at points where the argument moved him to more than ordinary passion". In a later publication Edwards challenges more decisively the prevailing view that Alexander was a pagan (justifying likewise the tradition of the Church and Photius). After examining the arguments that Alexander draws from the Platonic tradition, Edwards (2015, 140) characteristically states: "In short we cannot maintain, without a battery of ancillary hypotheses, that our author was a pagan. More probably he was a Christian who had been to school with the Platonists, and was resolved to defeat the Manichees by a priori reasoning without appeal to any contested word of revelation". Cf. ch.[2], 2.1, fn. 32. However, as argued in ch.[1], section 5, the thesis that supports Alexander's Christian origin is weak since Alexander in the whole of his work speaks as an exponent of the Greek culture (see ch.[4] fn. 136, 'our own tradition', 'our poetry') and his argumentation is exclusively based on Greek philosophy.

162   Libanius, *Epist. 1253* (Lieu 2010, 42–43): Πρισκιανῷ.1. Οἱ τὸν ἥλιον οὗτοι θεραπεύοντες ἄνευ αἵματος καὶ τιμῶντες θεὸν προσηγορίᾳ δευτέρᾳ καὶ τὴν γαστέρα κολάζοντες καὶ ἐν κέρδει

In his *Commentary on the Manual of Epictetus*, the pagan philosopher Simplicius (sixth century, ca. 530) echoes Alexander's criticism of the Manichaean myths. In a much more derogatory tone than Alexander, he states that these kinds of myths do not even deserve to be called mythology.

> Why do I quote their views at length? For they fabricate certain marvels which are not worthy to be called myths. However, they do not use them as myths nor do they think that they have any other meaning, but believe that all the things which they say are true.[163]

As Simplicius confesses, a Manichaean teacher had informed him that the Manichaeans interpret these myths literally, something which coincides with Alexander's testimony.[164] In refuting the Manichaean doctrines, Simplicius uses neo-platonic argumentation, just as Alexander does.[165] Pedersen argues for an influence from Alexander on Titus and from Titus on Simplicius. As he notes, this would be interesting because it shows that "it was not only Christian writers of Late Antiquity who were influenced by the Platonists, but that the opposite was also now and again the case".[166] Along the same lines of criticism, full of irony, moves another philosopher of the sixth century, Asclepius of Tralles.[167]

ποιούμενοι τὴν τῆς τελευτῆς ἡμέραν πολλαχοῦ μέν εἰσι τῆς γῆς, πανταχοῦ δὲ ὀλίγοι. καὶ ἀδικοῦσι μὲν οὐδένα, λυποῦνται δὲ ὑπ᾽ ἐνίων. 2. βούλομαι δὲ τοὺς ἐν Παλαιστίνῃ τούτων διατρίβοντας τὴν σὴν ἀρετὴν ἔχειν καταφυγὴν καὶ εἶναί σφισιν ἄδειαν καὶ μὴ ἐξεῖναι τοῖς βουλομένοις εἰς αὐτοὺς ὑβρίζειν.

163 Simplicius, *Comm. Man. Epict.* 35 (Hadot, 326.105–07) (Lieu 2010, 105–07): Καὶ τί ταῦτα μηκύνω; τέρατα γὰρ πλάττοντές τινα, ἅπερ μηδὲ μύθους καλεῖν ἄξιον, οὐχ ὡς μύθοις χρῶνται, οὐδὲ ἐνδείκνυσθαί τι ἄλλο νομίζουσιν.

164 Simplicius, *Comm. Man. Epict.* 35 (Hadot, 325.90–92): – οὐ γὰρ ἀξιοῦσι μυθικῶς τινος τῶν λεγομένων ἀκούειν –, ἀλλ᾽ ὡς ἐμοί τις τῶν παρ᾽ αὐτοῖς σοφῶν ἐξέφηνε, καὶ κραταιοῦ λίθου καὶ ἄνω ⟨ἀνα⟩γλύφους αὐτὰς νομίζουσι [...] ("they do not think it right to listen to any of the things they say allegorically, but they are thinking of those things which are made or solid stone and carved, as one of their wise men informed me", in Lieu 2010, 104–05).

165 Cf. Lieu 1994a, 193 and 2010, 162.

166 Pedersen 2004, 68.

167 Asclepius of Tralles, *In Aristotelis metaphysicorum* 292: οἱ ἀτυχεῖς Μανιχαῖοι, ἐπειδὴ ἠπόρουν πόθεν τὰ κακά, μὴ ἰσχύσαντες ἐπιλύσασθαι ταύτην τὴν ἀπορίαν εἰρήκασιν ὅτι ἔστιν ἀρχὴ τῶν κακῶν, ὥσπερ καὶ τῶν ἀγαθῶν [...] τί ἐστι τὸ λεγόμενον ὑπ᾽ αὐτῶν ὡς ὅτι τοιαύτη ἐστὶν ἡ φύσις τῶν ὄντων, ὥστε συντρέχειν τὴν κατάφασιν τῇ ἀποφάσει, καθάπερ φασὶν οἱ θεοχόλωτοι Μανιχαῖοι; τούτῳ γὰρ τῷ ὀνόματι προσηγόρευσεν αὐτοὺς ὁ ἡμέτερος φιλόσοφος Ἀμμώνιος.

4   Conclusions

The examination of a variety of sources (treatises, lists, canons, Synod's minutes, etc.) has shown that although Manichaeans are often called heretics by
the authors, both Christian (of all denominations) and pagan sources regarded
Manichaeism as a religious category distinct from Christianity. This is also
illustrated in some of the Manichaean texts, especially in the *Kephalaia*. Apart
from the term heresy, the authors describing and classifying Manichaeism
used the terms 'religion' and 'dogma'. Furthermore, the term 'heresy' itself had
a broad meaning during the investigated period and also signified religion.
However, in the process of time, it becomes gradually more and more apparent that our sources treated Manichaeism as another religion, this being also
reflected in the increased use of the term religion. A corresponding evolution
is also noted in the legal codes (from the Cod. theod. to Cod. justin.).

Thus, it seems that for the specialists (Christian writers of different confessions and pagans) the 'Manichaean Church' was not one of the many Christian
Churches. However, simple people considered Manichaeism as a Christian
heresy, and it was therefore an option for those who searched for an alternative choice within Christianity. As Edwards remarks, Manichaeism probably
survived for centuries in the Roman Empire in contrast to Persia where it was
extinguished, "because it had the status of a heresy and not a new religion, so
that those who wished to escape the hegemony of the Catholic Church could
adopt it without divorcing themselves entirely from the faith in which they
were reared".[168] The latter explains why Church Fathers insisted so much on
pointing out that the Manichaeans were not Christians but merely pretended
to be. Indeed, the high appeal of Manichaeism to ordinary people, in combination with the fact that the autonym Christian was mainly used by the
Manichaeans for their communication with the surrounding Christianized
world, partly explains the claim of Christian authors that their self-designation
as Christians served tactical and missionary reasons.

Because the Manichaeans were considered the worst of the worst heretics
by all the Christian parties, the term 'Manichaean' with the meaning of μανιχαΐζων became a label of abuse very early (during the Arian controversy), and continued to exist long after the period covered in this study. So, in the literature
under examination, imaginary Manichaeans appeared alongside the real ones.

In his treatise, Alexander challenges the Christianness of the Manichaeans to
the same degree as ecclesiastical (Christian) authors. It is true that the first two
introductory paragraphs of Alexander's treatise initially give the impression

---

168   Edwards 2015, 142.

that he regards Manichaeism as a form of decadent Christianity. However, when one reads the whole text, it becomes clear that Alexander mainly juxtaposes Christianity with Manichaeism, treating Manichaeism and Christianity as two different religious categories which he compares. The emphasis of Alexander's critique is that whereas Manichaeans are self-identified as Christians, they differ radically from Christians on a number of substantial issues. At this point, his aspect coincides fully with that of the Christian specialists.

Manichaean Beliefs and Practices

> If anyone is able to demolish the unbegotten dualism [...] he would
> at the same time cut down the entire forest of his words.
>
> ACTA ARCHELAI[1]

∵

1 Introduction

As the previous chapters underlined, both the anti-heretical legislation and
Byzantine literature (Christian and Pagan) regarded the Manichaeans as the
'worst of the worst' heretics. Manichaeism itself constituted the worst heresy
par excellence. But what, exactly was the *nature* of their crime according to
Christian and pagan authors?

Unlike the laws, which targeted the Manichaean gatherings, the main object
of both Christian and pagan anti-Manichaean literature were Manichaean
doctrines. This is to be expected, since that was the work of the teachers, i.e.
the "priests of God"[2] and the philosophers. References to the Manichaean
assemblies, testimonies concerning the Manichaean rituals, or allusions to
what was happening during them, are quite rare in reality. The three main doctrinal issues that predominate in the discourse are: (1) Manichaean (ontological) dualism, namely the idea of two first principles, one good (the light/spirit)
and one evil (darkness/matter); (2) docetic Christology, which is seen as a consequence of that same dualism. Since matter is identified with the principle

---

1   *AA* 68.2 (Vermes, 150–51).
2   As is emphasized in *Sirm.* 12 (Pharr, 482): "The heretics [Donatists, Manichaeans, Priscillian-
ists] and the superstition of the pagans ought to have been corrected by the solicitude alone
of those religious men, the priests of God [...] by their sedulous admonition and by their
authoritative teaching".

of evil, Christ could not have acquired a material (physical) body; and (3) the Manichaean attitude towards the Bible and the use of the Christian Scriptures, a theme connected with missionary practices.

The biggest part of the discussion in literature concerns the Manichaean tenet of the two principles; the authors found this unacceptable and absurd and saw it as the source of a series of contradictions in Manichaean dogma, ethos, and praxis. They placed great emphasis on the theoretical discourse because, as Hegemonius argues, if the unbegotten ontological dualism would be demolished, then at the same time the whole Manichaean edifice would be deconstructed.[3] However, the discourse regarding dualism, for both Christian and pagan authors, was not just a theoretical discussion at a theological level, but also focused on the implications that dualism had on cosmology and anthropology. In turn, this formed an ethos that for the authors entailed problematic behaviour. It is exactly the latter which is the focus of this chapter: this behaviour had an obligatory character for the Manichaeans and also had serious religious and social consequences for the Christian and pagan anti-Manichaean authors. Thus, the target of this chapter is not the contradictions of dualism and its 'fatal' consequence on dogma (e.g. docetic Christology, etc.), but the effect dualism had on the Manichaean ethos, and on the observable behaviour on everyday Manichaean life.

In order to reconstruct a more comprehensive and reliable picture, I consider it necessary to conduct a comparative examination per subject of all the sources at our disposal (Greek, Semitic, Latin). So, the information and argumentation culled from the East-Roman anti-Manichaean sources will be complemented and compared to the influential anti-Manichaean writings of Augustine, without whose detailed observations little would be known about Manichaeism in the West. Finally, both the Greek sources and Augustine will be assessed in light of the authentic Manichaean sources. In this way, three different perspectives on the same issues will be presented and compared.[4]

---

3   *AA* 68.2 (Vermes, 150–51).

4   This chapter relies on the excellent work of Jason BeDuhn with regard to the collection of original Manichaean sources (Syriac, Arabic, Coptic, Iranian, Turkic, Chinese, etc.) that he provides in his *The Manichaean Body in Discipline and Ritual*, a reworking of his doctoral dissertation. Without these sources this work would have been much more difficult. Of course, the interpretation and argumentation are entirely my responsibility.

2   Manichaean Beliefs and their Implications in Religious
     Everyday Life

2.1   *The Manichaean Cosmogonic Myth*
2.1.1   The Two First Principles
There are numerous versions of the Manichaean cosmogonic narrative, which
vary according to time and place.[5] Yet, the core of the myth remains common
in all versions and in all narrative means through which it is expressed (e.g.
writings, sermons, hymns). Before proceeding to examine the implication of
dualism, I consider it appropriate to present very briefly the core of the myth.

All start from the Manichaean premise that there are two distinct co-eternal
principles: the good (identified with the light) and the evil (identified with
darkness and matter). In 'pre-cosmic' time they combated each other and this
led these two separate principles to be mingled; in specific, a part of the light
was swallowed by/trapped in matter, or according to some, the light 'sacrificed'
itself for this very purpose. At an ontological level, a consequence of this mixture was the cosmological and anthropological mixture. Since the primordial
mixture took place, the two principles conducted a series of stratagems on a
macrocosmic and microcosmic scale, in order to gain control of the situation
and of the universe; the good trying to free itself from the mixture, and the evil
trying to maintain its sovereignty through the mixture.[6]

At the macrocosmic level, the stratagem of the powers of light was to create
the cosmos (from the mixed material, i.e. matter containing divine particles)
which operates "as a huge machine" that liberates the captured light from
the mixture with evil.[7] On the other hand, the stratagem of evil was for the

---

5   According to BeDuhn (2000b, 72–73), this testifies on the one hand that "the details of
    Manichaean cosmogony were negotiable in the Manichaean proselytization process" and,
    on the other hand, the "inability or disinterest" of the "centers of Manichaean authority" to
    control the modifications of the myth.

6   Sources for the narrative of primordial combat between good and evil and primordial mix-
    ture: (1) Greek Sources: (a) *CMC* 132.11–13, (b) Epiphanius, *Pan.* 66.25 (Turbo's narrative)
    (c) Abjuration formulas, *SC* 1.9–25, 3, 4; (2) Latin Sources: (a) *AA* 7.1–2, (b) Augustine:
    (b1) *Faust.*, (b2) *Ep. 236* to Deuterius (§ 2), (b3) *Nat. bon.*, (b4) *Duab.*, (b5) *Haer.* 46.114–132,
    (b6) *Mor. Manich.*, (b7) *Fund.*; (3) Semitic sources: (a) Theodore bar Konai (*Scholia*),
    (b) Al-Nadim (*Fihrist*), (c) Ephrem (*Prose Refutations* cxii), (d) Severus of Antioch (*123
    Cathedral Homily*, esp. pp. 164.10–166.15); (4) Coptic Sources: *1Keph.* 7 (concerning the
    Five Fathers 34.13–36.26), *1Keph.* 63 (156.29–30), *1Keph.* 72 (177.6–178.23), *1Keph.* 85, *1Keph.*
    109. (262.25–27), *1Keph.* 59, *2PsB* 155.20–39, *2PsB* 86.27–30, *2PsB* 54.8ff. (Psalm 246), *2PsB*
    9.3–11.32 (Psalm 223); (5) Iranian Sources: M801, Turfan treatises, M442 + M555 + M5361, M33
    (6) Turkic Sources: TIIK2a.I.R, (7) Chinese Sources: *Compendium*. See BeDuhn 1995b. Cf.
    Boyce 1975, 3–10.

7   Indicatively see: *2PsB* 9.3–11.32 (Psalm 223); Al-Nadim, *Fihrist* ch. 9 (Dodge, 782); Augustine,
    Haer. 46. See also BeDuhn 2000b, 76.

powers/archons of Darkness, to 'engineer' the creation of man. Man, as cosmos, is also a product of a mixture of matter with the encapsulated divine element. Thus, both the cosmos and humans consist of a mixture of matter (evil/darkness) and divine particles (good/light). Until the end of time, which is the third moment according to the eschatology of Manichaean myth, two parallel and opposite processes are in progress. On the one hand is the liberation of light and thus the destruction of matter through the draining of the light imprisoned in it, and on the other hand is the counter-attack by matter, which aims to keep light contained within it.

Despite the variety of versions of the narrative of primordial combat (between good and evil) and the resulting primordial mixture, these differ only in their details; what exists in all versions, and must be kept in mind given its direct relevance to the question of the present chapter, is the presence of the divine element (sometimes referred to as the *Soul* or *Living Self*) in both man and the material world, as a consequence of the primordial mixture. Further, there are two additional key features of the narrative attested in the sources and underlined by several researchers, which are also important for my question:

(1) *The literal instead of the allegorical interpretation of the mythic narrative.*
According to BeDuhn, the preference of some researchers for a metaphorical rather than a literal interpretation merely helps the interpreter not to feel that he offends the "culturally other" as being inferior. As BeDuhn points out, "in the Manichaean case, the tradition insists upon a literal interpretation".[8] Manichaean "literary devices contribute to the characterization of a universe which, however, is not itself a metaphor or poetic representation. [...] Such a universe must really exist; it must be there literally".[9] The literalness of the Manichaean myth was, as we have seen, one of the recurrent targets of attack by their opponents, like Alexander, Serapion, Epiphanius, Augustine, Simplicius, etc.[10]

---

8   BeDuhn 2000b, 261–62.
9   BeDuhn 2000b, 70.
10   Alexander, *Tract. Man.* 10. Serapion, *c. Manichaeos* 33 (HTS 15:49): ἐνταῦθα λοιπὸν πολὺς ὁ γέλως καὶ μεγάλη ἡ χλεύη, [...] μῦθος Ἑλληνικός [...] λέγονται γὰρ μῦθοι οἱ μῦθοι, ἀλλ' ὡς μῦθοι πιστεύονται· [...] νῦν δὲ [...] πιστεύεται δὲ παρὰ τοῖς ἄφροσιν ὡς ἀλήθεια. *Epiphanius Pan.* 66.46.11–12 (Williams, 273): "(11) Raise your mask, Menander, you comedian! That is what you are, but you conceal yourself while you recite the deeds of adulterers and drink. For you say nothing original – you mislead your dupes by introducing the Greeks' works of fiction in place of the truth. (12) Hesiod, with his stories of the theogony, probably had more sense than you, and Orpheus, and Euripides. Even though they told ridiculous stories, it is plain that they are poets and made things up that were not real. But to compound the error, you tell them as though they were". Augustine characterized the "Manichaeans as materialists who treat spiritual realities in terms of physical properties", cf. BeDuhn 2000b, 115. Simplicius, *Comm. Man. Epict.* 71.44–49 & 72.12. Cf. ch.[4].

(2) *The correspondence between macrocosm and microcosm*: It is a common
     feature of religions that divine beings serve as exemplars which the
     faithful are called to imitate. However, in Manichaeism this macrocosm-
     microcosm relationship is more direct and substantial. In Manichaeism,
     "the universal macrocosm and the human microcosm both derive from
     a primordial mixture of antithetical substances, and both exist as battle-
     grounds of opposing forces".[11] Thus, the structure of the human body is
     analogous to the body of the Universe[12] and human attitudes and actions
     should be an imitation of divine beings to ensure a positive ending.[13] At
     the level of the microcosm, the acceptance of this narrative entailed cer-
     tain behaviours which could be classified in the following groups accord-
     ing to their purpose:

     (1) Protective purpose: Behaviours aiming at the non-injury of the
          entrapped divine element in matter (practiced by fasting and
          almsgiving).
     (2) Preventive purpose (the barring): Behaviours that aim to prevent
          further entrapment of the divine element in matter (e.g. through
          procreation).
     (3) Liberative purpose: Behaviours (practiced during rituals) aimed at
          releasing the divine element entrapped in matter.

2.1.2   The Creation of the Cosmos by the Demiurge (Stratagem of Light)
"All sources agree the world is crafted by the forces of light [usually by the
Living Spirit], although various deities play the role of demiurge according to
the different versions" of the myth.[14] Yet, the world's status is mixed,[15] and
is simultaneously material (evil) and divine. Part of the divine substance is
dispersed and bound in all kinds of plant and animal life. All plants, animals,
and men have divine elements trapped within them. By the creation of the
cosmos the forces of light had as their aim the cosmic separation of light
from darkness:

---

11   BeDuhn 2000b, 117.
12   Cf. Turbo's Narrative in *AA* 9.4 (Vermes, 52); Epiphanius, *Pan.* 27.4 (Williams, 256): "For
      this body of ours may be called a ⟨miniature⟩ world which answers to ⟨this⟩ great world,
      and all people have roots below which are fastened to the realms on high".
13   I will analyse this further in section 2.3 (Manichaean rituals).
14   BeDuhn 2000b, 76. Cf. Ephrem, *Prose Refutations*, xxxiv–xxxv. In some sources the
      machinery for the pumping of the light particles consists of three wheels. In the narrative
      of Turbo it consists of one wheel with twelve jars, see *AA* 8.5.
15   Colditz 2015, 55.

The King of the World of Light commanded one of his angels to create this world and to build it from those mixed particles, so as to rescue the particles of Light from those of Darkness.[16]

Patristic sources are not always clear as to who (in the Manichaean myth) is the creator of cosmos. Some of them correctly attribute the creation of the cosmos to the forces of light, while others apparently attribute it to Satan, Devil, etc., who is identified with matter or the archon of matter.[17]

According to the narration of Turbo, the world was created by the Living Spirit, one of the forces of light:

Then the Living Spirit created the world, and equipped with three other powers it went down and led out the princes and fixed them to a cross in the firmament, the sphere which is his body. And again that Living Spirit created the heavenly bodies, which are remnants of the soul, and made them circle the firmament, and again he created the earth; there are eight of them.[18]

Yet, "The world itself is not of God, but formed from the material [archons'] element, and for that reason everything in it is destroyed".[19] In the SC too, it is clear that the Manichaean creator of the world belongs to the forces of light and creates the sky, the earth and the sea with raw material from the evil powers:

(I anathematize) the (god) who flayed the evil gods, as he postulates in his myths, and from their skins and sinews made the heavens and from their knees, the earth, and from their sweat, the sea, (namely), the (god) who is called the Demiurge by Mani himself.[20]

---

16   Al-Nadim, *Fihrist* 9.1 (Dodge, 781).

17   Theodoret, *Haer.* (PG 83.380.28–30): Τὸν δὲ διάβολον ποτὲ μὲν Ὕλην καλεῖ, ποτὲ δὲ τῆς Ὕλης ἄρχοντα.

18   AA 8.1 (Vermes, 48–49); Epiphanius, *Pan.* 66.25.8–26.3 (Williams, 254).

19   AA 11.1 (Vermes, 55); Epiphanius, *Pan.* 66.29.1. See also AA 12.3 (Vermes, 56): "He says that God has no part in the world and does not rejoice over it, because in the beginning he suffered theft by the princes and trouble was caused to him"; Epiphanius, *Pan.* 66.31.1.

20   SC, ch. 3 (Lieu 2010, 118–19, altered): τὸν ἀποδείραντα τοὺς πονηροὺς θεούς, καθὼς αὐτὸς μυθολογεῖ, καὶ ἐκ τῶν βυρσῶν αὐτῶν καὶ τῶν νεύρων ποιήσαντα τοὺς οὐρανοὺς καὶ ἐκ τῶν γονάτων αὐτῶν τὴν γῆν καὶ ἐκ τῶν ἰδρώτων τὴν θάλασσαν, τὸν λεγόμενον παρ' αὐτοῦ τοῦ Μάνεντος Δημιουργόν. See also fourth anathema.

In the sc we also find the Manichaean conviction that the creation of the world by the forces of light was a necessity (the stratagem of light), in order that the light captured by the matter would be freed:

> I anathematize those who say that the human souls are consubstantial with God and, being part of (the) good (principle) were swallowed up by the Hylē and out of this necessity the world was created.[21]

Some sources, like Theodoret, identify the forces of light with God (and the forces of darkness or matter with the Devil), while they clearly state that: (1) "the parts of the world do not come from him but are the works of Hylē", as well as that (2) "God was forced to create the world". In other words, the world's creation was his stratagem in order to liberate "the light which was mingled with the Hylē".[22]

However, some other sources are ambiguous as to whether God (the Christian equivalent to the forces of light) was the demiurge. Here, the aspect that the cosmos (or part of it) is created 'by' and not 'from' Satan/the Devil seems to prevail.

> they call the sun, Christ. If then the world, according to them, was made by the evil God, and the sun is in the world, how is the Son of the good God an unwilling minister in the works of the evil God?[23]
>
> Manichaeans [...] declare that not the whole world is God's creation, but [only] part of it.[24]
>
> As for the Manichaeans and other heretics, some of them claim that it [the world] is not the work of a good God, while others cut off a part of

---

21   sc, ch. 6 (Lieu 2010, 122–23): Ἀναθεματίζω τοὺς τὰς ἀνθρωπίνας ψυχὰς λέγοντας ὁμοουσίους εἶναι τῷ θεῷ καὶ μοῖραν οὔσας τοῦ ἀγαθοῦ ὑπὸ τῆς ὕλης καταποθῆναι καὶ ἐκ τῆς ἀνάγκης ταύτης τὸν κόσμον γεγενῆσθαι.

22   Theodoret, Haer. (PG 83.377D, Lieu 2010, 95): Ἐντεῦθεν ἀναγκασθῆναί φασι τὸν Θεὸν δημιουργῆσαι τὸν κόσμον. Τὰ δὲ τοῦ κόσμου μέρη οὐκ αὐτοῦ λέγουσιν, ἀλλὰ τῆς Ὕλης εἶναι ποιήματα. Ἐδημιούργησε δὲ, διαλῦσαι αὐτῆς τὴν σύστασιν βουληθείς, καὶ εἰς εἰρήνην ἀγαγεῖν τὰ μαχόμενα, ὥστε κατὰ βραχὺ καὶ τὸ ἀνακραθὲν τῇ Ὕλῃ Φῶς ἐλευθερῶσαι. See also Titus of Bostra and Severus of Antioch.

23   Cyril, Catech. 6.13.20–23 (Reischl and Rupp 1848, 174; LFHCC, 67): τὸν δὲ Χριστὸν τὸν ἥλιον τοῦτον καλοῦσιν. Εἰ τοίνυν ὁ κόσμος κατ᾽ αὐτοὺς ὑπὸ τοῦ Πονηροῦ ἐγένετο, ὁ δὲ ἥλιος ἐν κόσμῳ, πῶς ὁ υἱὸς τοῦ Ἀγαθοῦ ἐν τοῖς τοῦ Πονηροῦ ἄκων δουλεύει.

24   Epiphanius, Anacephalaiosis 66.2 (Williams, 215): Μανιχαῖοι, [...] κόσμον δὲ οὐ τὸν πάντα, ἀλλὰ μέρος ἐκ θεοῦ γεγενῆσθαι ὁριζόμενοι; John of Damascus, Haer. 66.

it and ascribe it to some kind of self-acting matter, judging that it is not worthy to be included in God's creation.[25]

As Chrysostom explicitly states, the Manichaeans use Paul's saying "the God of this world" to argue that "the devil is here intended, desiring from this passage, very foolishly, to introduce another creator of the world besides the true one".[26] This confusion of the sources is justified because, as BeDuhn aptly remarks, "although this mixture is depicted as a stratagem for the victory of good, it definitely entails negative consequences".[27]

2.1.3 The Living Self/Soul

The sum total of the light-elements enslaved in matter and in the cosmos comprised the *Living Self*, which is something like the universal soul. The concept of the *Living Self* is crucial to interpret Manichaean behaviours and attitudes (religious and social) and to comprehend the relevant criticism by anti-Manichaean sources. According to the Manichaean sources, the *Living Self* is spread, divided, and bound in the whole cosmos (i.e. in all living plants and animals). Sometimes, it is identified with the Soul of the cosmos, sometimes with Jesus, and it is consubstantial with God. Other synonymous terms for the *Living Self* found in the Manichaean literature are the *Cross of Light* and *Jesus Patibilis* (Suffering).[28] The psalms that the Manichaean believers chant in their congregations often speak in the voice of the *Living Self*:

Since I went forth into the darkness I [...] am in the midst of my enemies [...] The strangers with whom I mixed [...] I am the life of the world; I am the milk that is in all trees; I am the sweet water.[29]

---

25   John Chrysostom, *Scand.* 4.12: Μανιχαῖοι δὲ καὶ ἕτεροι πάλιν αἱρετικοί, οἱ μὲν οὐκ ἀγαθοῦ θεοῦ ἔργον ἔφησαν αὐτὴν [creation] εἶναι, οἱ δὲ ἐν αὐτῆς ἀποτεμόντες μέρος, αὐτομάτῳ τινὶ προσέρριψαν ὕλῃ καὶ ἀναξίαν ἔκριναν τῆς τοῦ Θεοῦ δημιουργίας εἶναι.

26   John Chrysostom, *Hom. 2 Cor. (Hom.* 8) (PG 61:455): Μανιχαῖοι δέ φασι τὸν διάβολον ἐνταῦθα λέγεσθαι, ἐκ τούτου δημιουργὸν τῆς κτίσεως ἕτερον ἐπεισαγαγεῖν παρὰ τὸν ὄντα βουλόμενοι, σφόδρα ἀνόητως. Cf. John of Damascus, *c. Manichaeos*, 67.17–20 (PTS 22:385): Ἀκούσατε δὴ πρὸς θεοῦ, ὦ ἄνδρες, ἀκούσατε, τί φησιν ὁ θεώλεστος Μάνης. Οὐκ ἔστι, φησίν, ὁ κόσμος τοῦ θεοῦ, ἀλλὰ τοῦ διαβόλου. Ἀπαλλοτριῶσαι ἡμᾶς βούλονται τοῦ θεοῦ ἡμῶν.

27   BeDuhn 2000b, 75.

28   The Living Self identified with the Soul of cosmos: *1Keph.* 72, 177.6–178.23. The Living Self identified with Jesus: *1Keph.* 55, 135.17–21; *2PsB* 121.32–33; *2PsB* 155.20–39. The Living Self as the Cross of Light: *1Keph.* 63.156.29–30; *1Keph.* 72.177.6–178.23. The Living Self as *Jesus Patibilis*: Augustine, *Faust.* 2.4. For more sources on the Living Self, cf. BeDuhn 2000b, esp. 72–88; BeDuhn 1995b, 170–196.

29   *2PsB* 54.11ff.

Finally, another guise of the *Living Self* is the five elements of nature (air, light, good fire, good water, good wind) which are also its constituents.[30]

The mixture of the cosmos and the concept of the *Living Self* in combination with (1) the literalness of the Manichaean myth and (2) the correspondence between macrocosm-microcosm, constitute the basis of Manichaean religious behaviour in ascesis and rituals. The belief of the presence of the *Living Self* throughout the natural world entailed the adoption of behaviours that had protective, preventive, and liberative purpose, and led to the creation of very specific and strict codes of behaviour and rules for everyday life. The most discussed commands in both Manichaean and anti-Manichaean literature are the so called "three seals" (particularly applicable to the Elect), which are: "the seal of the mouth", which means fasting; "the seal of the breast", which bans marriage and procreation; "the seal of the hands", the command to avoid injury to the *Living Self*.[31]

However, not surprisingly, the above commands could not be followed by all Manichaeans and for this reason the Manichaean community and Church were divided from the beginning into two classes of believers: the Elect and the catechumens (also called hearers or auditors). The catechumens had to observe two other sets of commandments. The first set comprised fasting (only on lord's day), prayer (to the sun and the moon) and alms-giving to the Elect; the second set obliged them (1) to 'offer' someone to the service of the church (e.g. a child, a relative) and (2) to construct or donate church edifices.[32]

Manichaean asceticism, as well as the dualistic structure of the Manichaean Church, was criticized by both Christian and pagan authors. It is true that ascetic practices existed in Christianity from the beginning and also existed in the pagan world before Christianity. However, what bothered the anti-Manichaean critics in terms of Manichaean asceticism was the perversion of

---

30   *2PsB* 201.13ff; *1Keph.* 85; *2PsB* 54.8ff; Augustine, *Haer.* 46.7.

31   One can find explicit references to the "three seals" in the *2PsB* 115.28–116.16–18: "The seal (σφραγίς) of the mouth for the sign of the Father, the rest of the hands for the sign of the Son, the purity of virginity (παρθενία) [for the] sign of the holy Spirit [...] Let us seal our mouth that we may find the Father, and seal (σφραγίζειν) our (?) hands that we may find the Son, and guard our purity that we may find the Holy Spirit". For Manichaean sources on fasting cf. *1Keph.* 79: Concerning the Fasting of the Saints (Gardner 1995, 200); *1Keph.* 80: The Commandments of Righteousness (Gardner 1995, 201–02); *1Keph. 81*: The chapter of fasting, for it engenders a Host of Angels (Gardner 1995, 202–05). See also Augustine, *Mor. Manich.* 39.

32   *1Keph.* 80, 192.3–193.22 (Gardner 1995, 201–02). As Gardner and Lieu (2004, 74) comment: "The practice of lay families giving a child to the church was well established in Manichaeism, and indeed counted as one of the essential religious acts of the catechumenate". Cf. Sims-Williams 1985, 573–82. Cf. ch.[3], fn. 217 & ch.[6], fn. 38.

the meaning of ascesis; according to the anti-Manichaean authors, this was the result of Manichaean cosmological and anthropological dualism.

2.2 Manichaean Ascesis: "The Seal of the Mouth" (Fasting)

The major point of criticism concerning the Manichaean ascesis is devoted to the Manichaean fasting, otherwise known as "the seal of the mouth". Manichaean fasting was attacked and criticized by both Christian and pagan authors.

There are two different lines of attack, based on two contradictory interpretations: contempt for creation versus deification of creation. These, in turn, are based on two contradictory Manichaean assumptions: the materiality of food versus foods containing divinity (light particles). Thus, on the one hand the Manichaean fasting is considered as an insult to God while, on the other, it is seen as pantheism (i.e., a form of idolatry).

2.2.1 First Interpretation of Manichaean Fasting: The Materiality of Food

According to the first interpretation (i.e., contempt for creation), which is perceived as an insult against creation and therefore against God, Manichaeans abstain from food because they consider it full of matter (evil). Titus of Bostra says that Mani "blames the fruits that come from the earth altogether as nourishment of matter".[33] Amphilochius of Iconium connects Manichaean with Encratite attitudes in his work *Concerning False Asceticism*, declaring:

> The leaders of the Manichaeans have ordained, once and for all, to abstain from eating living beings, because of the impiety that dwells in them, and have said at the same time that things that grow from the earth are living beings.[34]

According to Macarius of Magnesia, who also links Manichaeans with other extreme ascetics (Encratites, Apotactites, etc.), the followers of the Manichaeans do not eat meat, and do not drink wine, because they consider these loathsome and abominable.[35]

---

33 Titus of Bostra, *c. Manichaeos* 2.55.2–4 (CCSG 82:219): τοὺς καρποὺς τοὺς ἀπὸ γῆς ἅμα διαβάλλει ὡς θρεπτικοὺς τῆς ὕλης.

34 Amphilochius of Iconium, *c. Haer.* 1067–71: Ἐκείν⟨ων [τῶν Μανιχαίων] γ⟩ὰρ ⟨οἱ⟩ ἔξαρχοι ἅπαξ νομοθετήσαντες ἐμψύχων ἀπέχεσθαι διὰ τὴν ἐνοικοῦσαν ἐν αὐτοῖς ἀσέβειαν, καὶ τὰ φυόμενα ἐκ τῆς γῆς ἔμψυχα εἶπον.

35 Macarius of Magnesia, *Apocriticus* 3.25, 27: Τοιοῦτοι δὲ Μανιχαίων παῖδες [...] Οἴνου δὲ γεῦσιν καὶ κρεῶν μετάληψιν μυσαρὸν εἶναι λέγει.

As Augustine explains, the Manichaean Elect: "do not eat meat on the grounds that the divine substance has fled from the dead or slain bodies, and what little remains there is of such quality and quantity that it does not merit being purified in the stomachs of the Elect"; they "do not drink wine either, claiming that it is the gall of the princes of darkness, when they eat grapes".[36] Augustine also attacks the theory of his former coreligionists about the impurity of the foods: "You neither eat meat nor drink wine. You say that some foods are unclean," and that "flesh is composed of nothing but filth".[37]

Especially for the Elect the "contact with any profaning substance must be strictly avoided, hence the prohibition on the consumption of 'dead' meat or 'polluting' wine".[38] Hearers on the other hand, as Augustine informs us, could eat meat but should not kill the animals:

> You, as a concession, allow your followers, as distinct from the priests, to eat animal food.[39]
>
> They warn these same Auditors ... if they eat meat, not to kill the animals. From them [the princes of Darkness], they claim, all flesh has its origin.[40]

Yet, they considered that eating the wrong food – especially consuming meat – wakes the carnal impulse to concupiscence and causes the desire for procreation. As Mani, in presenting his doctrine during the debate in Carchar, said before the judges:

> Thus you men have intercourse with your wives arising from an occasion such as follows: when one of you has been satiated with meats and other foods, then the impulse of concupiscence is aroused within him and so is increased his enjoyment in procreating a son; so that it is not from some virtue, or philosophy or from any other rational process, but only from satiety with food, and lust and fornication.[41]

We note that there was a correlation between fasting and sexual abstinence, nutrition and procreation, gluttony and concupiscence.[42] The consumption of food with a high 'matter' content, such as meat, should be avoided, because

---

36   Augustine, *Haer.* 46.11 (Lieu 2010, 89).
37   Augustine, *Mor. Manich.* 27, 35 & 37 (BeDuhn 2000b, 35).
38   Durkheim (1915/1954, 342–552) in Beduhn 2000b, 124.
39   Augustine, *Faust.* 30.5–6 (*NPNF*[1] 4:566).
40   Augustine, *Haer.* 46.
41   *AA* 16.7 (Vermes, 63–64).
42   Cf. Van Oort, 1987.

its materiality, when consumed, is like reinforcing the dark (the material) side of the self; it is like adding to the congenital evil forces within man. "Specifically, meat and wine were regarded as dominated by the dark elements that would re-infect the believer striving for personal purification and lead directly to sensuality and ignorance".[43] Indeed, as BeDuhn notes, there are various Manichaean texts that show the relationship between the 'evil' substance in food and the 'evil' congenitally present in the human body and their mutual reinforcement when they come into contact.[44] According to *Kephalaia*:

> [a] difficult part comes into him by the nourishment that he has eaten [...] or in the water that they have drunk. Again, trouble and confusion and anger (will) increase in him, a[nd / l]ust multiplies upon him together with depression and grief; becau|se of the nourishment of the bread he has eaten and the water he has drunk, | which are full of bothersome parts, a vengeful counsel. They shall | enter his body, [mixed in] with these foods, and they even become joined in with the wicked parts of the body and | the sin that is in him; transferring the anger and the lust and | the depression and the grief, these wicked thoughts of the body.[45]

2.2.1.1   Critique of the 'Seal of the Mouth' Based on the Interpretation of Fasting as 'Abstinence from the Materiality of Foods'

According to the Church Fathers, the above interpretation was a distortion of the real meaning of fasting, which constituted a divine hubris and for this reason was heavily criticized.

"Don't think", John Chrysostom warns his disciples, the fact that "the Manichaeans abhor wheat is the result of a high philosophy, or that they have defeated gluttony. They fast because they have taken a loathing for God's creation".[46] As Macarius notes, "All creation is accursed for them and suspect and harmful for everyone. So, by cursing and calumniating the beauty of the creatures, they blaspheme God".[47] For the Church Fathers, however, what is in fact blameworthy and harmful is not the material world, the "foods which God

---

43   Gardner and Lieu 2004, 22.

44   BeDuhn 2000b, 222. Cf. M801; *1Keph.* 104, 114.269.17–270.24, 86.215.1–216.13.

45   *1Keph.* 86, 215.12–215.23.

46   John Chrysostom, *Hom. Matt.* (hom. 55), (PG 58:547.55–548): "Ἵνα γὰρ μή, διὰ τὴν ἄκραν φιλοσοφίαν καὶ τὴν ὑπεροψίαν τῆς γαστρός, ὑποπτεύσῃς περὶ αὐτῶν ὡς τὰ σῖτα βδελυττομένων, οἷον περὶ ἐκείνων τῶν ἀπαγχονιζόντων ἑαυτούς, διὰ τῆς εὐχῆς σε παιδεύουσιν, ὅτι οὐ βδελυττόμενοι τὰ κτίσματα τοῦ Θεοῦ, τῶν πλειόνων ἀπέχονται, ἀλλ' ἢ φιλοσοφίαν ἀσκοῦντες.

47   Macarius of Magnesia, *Apocriticus* 27: Τοιούτῳ γὰρ λόγῳ πᾶσα μὲν ἡ κτίσις κατ' αὐτὸν ἐπάρατος, πᾶσα δ' ὕποπτος ἡ ζωὴ καὶ πᾶσιν ἐπιβλαβής· ὅθεν οἱ τοιοῦτοι τῷ θείῳ προσέκρουσαν τῶν δημιουργημάτων τὸ κάλλος ὑβρίσαντες.

created to be received", but the false ascesis of the Manichaeans who ignore that "everything created by God is good, and nothing is to be rejected if it is received with thanksgiving" (1 Tim. 4:1–5). This verse was one of the statements that the converted Manichaean had to confess and recite during the anathema of his previous fallacy.[48]

Criticism comes from all Christian parties. As the neo-Arian ecclesiastical author Julian, in his *Commentary in Job* remarks, the saying of Job that:

> "a branch shall come forth out of his dung-heap" (Job 8:16LXX) does not mean that he disparages the seed as Manichaeans and Pseudo-Encratites do (because neither the human body is evil, nor foods are bad, nor their excretion is shameful. Because nothing that springs out of the good is bad).[49]

Furthermore, Church Fathers often blame the Manichaeans that they fast in pretence. For this reason, Cyril, trying to protect his catechumens, admonishes them

> not to offer food to Manichaeans because they pretend that they are fasting, taking sad faces; [not to offer food to Manichaeans] who calumniate the creator of food, while in fact they devour greedily the most delicious foods.[50]

Could these catechumens of Cyril be former Manichaeans offering food (alms service) to the Manichaean Elect? If this was the case, it would seem as if only the Elect were Manichaeans to Cyril.

As Augustine points out, the "great difference" between the meaning of Catholic and Manichaean fasting, is that while the character of the former is "symbolic" and aims at "the mortification of the body", the Manichaeans do not eat because they consider food "naturally, evil and impure".[51] In addition,

---

48   *sc*, ch. 7 (Lieu 2010, 123).

49   Julian Arianus, *comm. Job* 67.7–9.

50   Cyril, *Catech.* 6.31 (Reischl and Rupp 1848, 198, 200): Μηδεὶς προσφερέσθω τοῖς ψυχοφθόροις Μανιχαίοις, τοῖς ἀχύρων ὕδασι τὸ στυγνὸν τῆς νηστείας προσποιουμένοις· τοῖς διαβάλλουσι μὲν τὸν τῶν βρωμάτων ποιητὴν, τὰ κάλλιστα δὲ τῶν βρωμάτων λαιμαργοῦσι.

51   Augustine, *Faust.* 30.5–6 (*NPNF*[1] 4:565–67). In the same manner Cyril (*Catech.* 4.27) pointing out the meaning of true fasting as opposed to the false, explains: we abstain "from wine and meat" not "as from things abominated" but "as good things" which we transcend in the quest of a spiritual banquet. Augustine (*Mor. Manich.*16.51, *NPNF*[1] 4:106/144), also

Augustine testifies that the command which prohibited the consumption of meat applied only to the Elect.

2.2.2 Second Interpretation of Manichaean Fasting: Divinity Within Foods

According to the second line of interpretation, which is the very antithesis of the first, Manichaeans abstain from food because they believe that divine particles are trapped in the food. In the words of Turbo "every soul and every animal that moves, has its share of the substance of the good Father".[52]

As Titus of Bostra characteristically comments, the Manichaeans accuse all those who kill animals in order to eat them, because they believe that the animals contain part of the divine soul. They say that the power of good is trapped within them.

> Therefore, they strongly accuse those who kill quadrupeds and birds, who are useful to humans as sustenance, because (they think that) these too are animated by that same power of good, and contain (it) within themselves.[53]

They abstain from eating animated foods, and they consider as such even the plants, Amphilochius adds.[54] And not only this, but as Theodoret of Cyrrhus complements: "They consider everything as animate: fire, and water, and air, and plants, and seeds".[55] The Christian philosopher Nemesius, bishop of Emesa, in examining the belief that the Manichaeans have about the soul, clarifies

> They [the Manichaeans] say that it [the soul] is immortal and incorporeal, but that there is only one, the soul of the universe, which is chopped

---

criticizes Manichaeans' rigidity and irrationality when someone does not observe their fasting: "is it not most unreasonable, to expel from the number of the elect a man who, perhaps for his health's sake, takes some animal food without sensual appetite; while, if a man eagerly devours peppered truffles, you can only reprove him for excess, but cannot condemn him as abusing your symbol?".

52 *AA* 8.7 (Vermes, 51).
53 Titus of Bostra, *c. Manichaeos* 2.61.1–4 (CCSG 82:229): Ἐντεῦθεν δὴ καὶ τὰ τετράποδα καὶ τὰ πετεινά, ὅσα χρήσεις ἀνθρώποις ἔχει τροφῆς, βαρέως αἰτιᾶται τοὺς θύοντας, ὡς ἐκείνης τῆς δυνάμεως τοῦ ἀγαθοῦ καὶ ταῦτα ψυχούσης καὶ ἐν αὐτοῖς κατεχομένης.
54 Amphilochius of Iconium, *c. Haer.* 1067–71.
55 Theodoretus, *Haer.* (PG 83:380.42–43): Πάντα δὲ νομίζουσιν ἔμψυχα, καὶ τὸ πῦρ, καὶ τὸ ὕδωρ, καὶ τὸν ἀέρα, καὶ τὰ φυτά, καὶ τὰ σπέρματα.

up and divided into particular bodies, both inanimate and animate [...]
So the souls of particular things are parts of the universal soul.[56]

Augustine's reports on the same subject are similar: the Manichaeans "think
that the souls of men as well as of beasts are of the substance of God and are,
in fact, pieces of God. [...] God [...] left a part of himself mingled with the
Prince of Darkness".[57] "They say that this part of the divine nature permeates
all things in heaven and earth and under the earth; that it is found in all bodies, dry and moist, in all kinds of flesh, and in all seeds of trees, herbs, men and
animals".[58] Manichaeans "say that earth, and wood, and stones have sense
[sensum]".[59]

As is indicated by the abjuration formulas, the converted Manichaean had,
among others, to anathematize "those who suppose that grass and plants and
water and other things without souls in fact all have them [souls]".[60] At the
turn of the seventh century, Timothy the Presbyter, in his instructions concerning the reception of the converted Manichaeans, attributes to his contemporary Manichaeans the same beliefs and attitudes: "and they say that fire, air,
earth, water, plants, trees and seeds have souls".[61]

2.2.2.1 Critique of the 'Seal of the Mouth' Based on the Interpretation of Fasting as 'Protection of the Divinity Within Foods'

The above Manichaean belief, which is grounded in the concept of the *Living
Self*, is interpreted by the anti-Manichaean authors as pantheism (deification
of nature) and idolatry.

According to the anonymous author of Alexandria, "the Manichaeans
manifestly worship the creation (and that which they say) in their psalms is
an abomination to the Lord".[62] In combating Manichaean pantheism, Basil of
Caesarea in his eighth homily in *Hexaemeron* (ca. 370), entitled "On birds and

---

56   Nemesius of Emesa, *De natura hominis* 2.32.20–23 (Morani, 32; Sharples and Van der
     Eijk 2008, 71): Ἑξῆς ἐπισκεψώμεθα καὶ τὴν δόξαν τῶν Μανιχαίων, ἣν ἔχουσι περὶ τῆς ψυχῆς.
     φασὶ μὲν γὰρ αὐτὴν ἀθάνατον καὶ ἀσώματον, μίαν δὲ μόνην εἶναι τὴν τῶν πάντων ψυχὴν κατα-
     κερματιζομένην καὶ κατατεμνομένην εἰς τὰ καθ' ἕκαστα σώματα ἄψυχά τε καὶ ἔμψυχα [...].
     Cf. Nemesius of Emesa, *De natura hominis* 2.17.10–15 (Sharples and Van der Eijk 2008, 53)
     "some have thought that the soul of all things was one and the same, divided up among
     individuals and again returning to itself, as do the Manichaeans".
57   Augustine, *Ep. 236* (§ 2) in Gardner and Lieu 2004, 244.
58   Augustine, *Nat. bon.* 44.1 in BeDuhn 2000b, 77.
59   Augustine, *Faust.* 15.4 in BeDuhn 2000b, 77.
60   *SC*, ch. 6 (Lieu 2010, 122–23): τοὺς εἰσηγουμένους, καὶ τοὺς τὰς βοτάνας καὶ τὰ φυτὰ καὶ τὸ
     ὕδωρ καὶ τὰ ἄλλα ἄψυχα πάντα ἔμψυχα εἶναι ὑπολαμβάνοντας.
61   Timothy the Presbyter, *Recept. Haer.* (PG 86A:11–74 [13, 69]).
62   P.Rylands 3, Gr. 469 (Roberts 1938, 38–46, 42; Lieu 2010, 37).

those (living) in water" argues that the biblical verse (Gen 1.24) "Let the earth bring forth living creatures", does not mean that the earth is animated and that therefore the Manichaeans are right in putting the soul within earth. It is not that the earth brought forth something that was stored within it, but the creative logos of God did.[63]

Cyril of Jerusalem, in his sixth catechetical lecture, becomes particularly caustic comparing and criticizing pantheistic views with pagan idolatry:

> Wickedness flourished upon idolatry and cat and wolf and dog instead of God were venerated; and lion [...] (and) snake and dragon were worshiped. I am ashamed to say, but I will do so, that even the onions were worshiped by some [people].[64]

Similar are also the comments of John Chrysostom: "Many heretics dare to bring down God's substance to even more despised beings". Manichaeans are doing the same by "introducing the substance of God in dogs and apes and in beasts of all sorts (because as they argue the soul of all these beings originates from the same substance)".[65]

Indeed, according to Titus of Bostra the Manichaeans go so far as to say that even the stones and the woods have a soul.

> Mani [...] is not ashamed to say that even the stones have a soul and suggests that everything is animate even those which are clearly inanimate, because as he argues, [...] the nature of the good is even bound to lifeless stones. [...] And he brings as proof of the soul of stones and trees the sound in the air of stone and tree as if it were their articulate voice that he once heard.[66]

---

63 Basil of Caesarea, *Hom. Hexaem.*, 8.1–15.

64 Cyril, *Catech.* 6.10.4–18 (Reischl and Rupp 1848, 168): Ἐπεδαψιλεύσατο δὲ ἡ πονηρία τῆς εἰδωλολατρίας· καὶ αἴλουρος καὶ λύκος καὶ κύων ἀντὶ Θεοῦ προσεκυνήθησαν, καὶ λέων [...] Ὄφις καὶ δράκων, [...] προσεκυνήθησαν· [...] Αἰσχύνομαι λέγειν, πλὴν λέγω· καὶ κρόμμυα γὰρ ἤδη παρά τισι προσεκυνήθη. Cyril's sixth *Catechesis* was mainly devoted to Manichaeans.

65 John Chrysostom, *Natal.* (PG 49:359): πολλοὶ δὲ τῶν αἱρετικῶν καὶ εἰς ἔτι τούτων ἀτιμότερα τοῦ Θεοῦ κατάγειν τολμῶσι τὴν οὐσίαν [...] καὶ οἱ τὰ αὐτὰ ἀσεβοῦντες αὐτοῖς Μανιχαῖοι, εἰς κύνας καὶ πιθήκους καὶ θηρία παντοδαπὰ τὴν οὐσίαν εἰσάγοντες τοῦ Θεοῦ (τὴν γὰρ ψυχὴν τούτοις ἅπασιν ἐκ τῆς οὐσίας ἐκείνης εἶναί φασιν).

66 Titus of Bostra *c. Manichaeos* 2.60.1–28 (CCSG 82:227, 229): [Μάνης] [...] Οὐκ αἰσχύνεται καὶ τοὺς λίθους ἐψυχῶσθαι λέγων, καὶ τὰ πάντα ἔμψυχα καὶ τὰ σαφῶς ἄψυχα εἰσηγούμενος, ὡς, ἀπ' ἐκείνης δὴ τῆς τοῦ ἀγαθοῦ δυνάμεως ἔτι καὶ ἐν λίθοις κατεχομένης, [...] ὥστε τὴν φύσιν τοῦ ἀγαθοῦ καὶ ἐν λίθοις ἀψύχοις φάσκειν πεπεδῆσθαι. [...] Καὶ ποιεῖται τεκμήριον τῆς τῶν λίθων καὶ τῶν ξύλων ψυχῆς τὸν ἐν ἀέρι κτύπον λίθου τε καὶ ῥάβδου, ὥσπερ ἐνάρθρου φωνῆς αὐτῶν πώποτε διακούσας. [...] Ὅπερ τοίνυν ἐχρῆν τεκμήριον ποιήσασθαι τῶν παντελῶς ἀψύχων ὡς

The above text of Titus reminds us of Mani's testimony in the *CMC*, according to which Mani did not pick vegetables and did not cut wood, because he believed that they were alive. All plants and trees possess speech and talked to Mani. A date-palm tree began to speak and asked protection from him; vegetables lamented "like human beings, and as it were, like children" when they were cut.[67]

As Nemesius of Emesa further informs us, not all individual bodies participate equally in the Living Soul. Animate beings participate more in it and inanimate bodies less. The animate "have a greater", the inanimate "a lesser share".[68]

Augustine was well aware of this Manichaean belief. In criticizing it, he becomes self-deprecating, since he had believed in the same things when he was a Manichaean hearer for nine years: "Gradually and unconsciously I was led to the absurd trivialities of believing that a fig weeps when it is picked, and that the fig tree, its mother, sheds milky tears".[69] Furthermore, Augustine in examining the pantheistic view which is based on the assumption that the divine substance resides within foods, highlights a distinction that the Manichaeans made between animal and plant food. As Augustine remarks, the Manichaeans believe that what is bright in colour, agreeable in smell and pleasant in taste encapsulates huge amounts of divine substance; all the above are qualities of plants, fruits, vegetables and flowers, but not of animals and of foods of animal origin. In this way, Augustine provides us with lists of approved and disapproved foods.[70]

κτυπούντων ἐξ ἀνάγκης εἰς ἀέρα – τοῦτο γὰρ μόνου σώματος οὐχὶ δὲ ψυχῆς – τοῦτο ψυχώσεως σημεῖον ἔλαβεν.

67 *CMC* 8.1–10.12 (Koenen and Römer, 4, 6; Cameron and Dewey, 13): ὅ[τε δὲ ὁ φοῖνιξ εἶπεν] [...] μεθ᾽ οὗ πάντα τὰ φ[υτ]ὰ λαλεῖ, [... κ]αὶ ἐτάκ[η ὀλοφυρό]μενον παραπλησ[ίως ἀν]θρωπείοις προσώ[ποις] καὶ ὡσεὶ παιδίοις. οὐαὶ ο[ὐ]αὶ δὲ τὸ αἷμα κατεκέχυτο τοῦ τόπου τοῦ κοπέντος διὰ τῆς δρεπάνης ἧς μετὰ χεῖρας εἶχεν. ἔκραζον δὲ καὶ ἀνθρωπείαι φωνῇ διὰ τὰς πλήξεις αὐτῶν.

68 Nemesius of Emesa, *De natura hominis* 2.32.22–33.2 (Morani, 32–33; Sharples and Van der Eijk 2008, 71): τὴν τῶν πάντων ψυχὴν κατακερματιζομένην καὶ κατατεμνομένην εἰς τὰ καθ᾽ ἕκαστα σώματα ἄψυχά τε καὶ ἔμψυχα, καὶ τὰ μὲν πλείονος αὐτῆς μετέχειν, τὰ δὲ ἐλάττονος· πλείονος μὲν τὰ ἔμψυχα, ἐλάττονος δὲ τὰ ἄψυχα, πολλῷ δὲ πλείονος τὰ οὐράνια, ὡς τῆς καθ᾽ ὅλου ψυχῆς μέρη τὰς καθ᾽ ἕκαστον εἶναι ψυχάς.

69 Augustine, *Conf.* 10.18 (Chadwick 1991, 48–49).

70 Augustine, *Mor. Manich.* 16.39–41, 39 (*NPNF*[1] 4: 139): "Tell me then, first, where you get the doctrine that part of God, as you call it, exists in corn, beans, cabbage, and flowers and fruits. From the beauty of the color, say they, and the sweetness of the taste; this is evident; [...] Why do you look upon a yellow melon as part of the treasures of God, and not rancid bacon fat or the yolk of an egg? Why do you think that whiteness in a lettuce proclaims God, and not in milk?"; *Duab.* 8. Cf. BeDuhn, 2000b, 37. Lieu 1981a, 153–173, 167: "A daily provision for 30 melons to be given to the main monastery and an equal number for its chapter house from the lands of the three Ordos (lines 79–81 AG) shows that the

As BeDuhn underlines, "the strict code of vegetarianism entails a qualitative distinction between the condition of light in plants vs. animals".[71] Indeed, the descriptions by the Manichaean sources of the presence of the *Living Self* in the material world and especially in plant life are very vivid and poetic, so it is logical that they did not escape Augustine's attention and his relevant comments. The *Living Self* is described as "treasure hidden in the field",[72] "milk that is in all trees",[73] the "sweetness of the fruits".[74] As Mani is presented to teach his disciples in the *Kephalaia*, the sun is the one that "gives a strength to the elements; and also it gives scent and a taste to the entire Cross of the Light".[75]

Seizing upon the latter, one should remember that in Manichaean sources the *Living Self* is identified with the *Cross of Light*, which is one dimension of the Manichaean Jesus.[76] According to a Manichaean psalm, the *Cross of Light* is a "sheep bound to the tree, [...] Jesus that hangs to the tree".[77] The concept of the *Living Self* represented as Jesus (*patibilis*) spread and imprisoned in the cosmos, is also illustrated in a Manichaean text cited by Theodore bar Konai. According to it, Jesus reveals to Adam and through him to all the Manichaeans that he was consumed, eaten, devoured by everything that exists in the natural world (e.g., panthers, dogs, elephants, men).[78]

Unlike Greek patristic sources Augustine's works clearly illustrate the above identification of the *Living Self* with Jesus (*patibilis*): "And Christ himself, they say, was crucified in the whole world".[79] In the words of Faustus "we believe [that] ... the suffering Jesus ... hung from the tree for everyone".[80] Interesting also is the information, provided by Augustine and attested in Manichaean sources, that humans were considered by Manichaeans as the biggest depositories of divine substance.[81]

Manichaean preference for melons, because of the exceptionally large number of light particles which they were alleged to hold, was not only theological but culinary".

71   BeDuhn 1995b, 191.
72   *2PsB* 155.23.
73   *2PsB* 54.28–29 (Psalm 246).
74   *2PsB* 155.27.
75   *1Keph.* 65.162.12–13 (Gardner 1995, 171).
76   *1Keph.* 63.156.29–30.
77   *2PsB* 155.22; *2PsB* 155.24.
78   Theodore bar Konai, *Scholia* in BeDuhn 2000b, 73.
79   Augustine, *Commentary on Psalm* 140.12 in Gardner and Lieu 2004, 245.
80   Augustine, *Faust.* 20.2.536.9–24 and 20.11, 550.14–19 (in Gardner and Lieu 2004, 219; Lieu 2010, 13–16).
81   Augustine, *Haer.* 46.6 in BeDuhn 2000b, 94: the Manichaeans "believe that this portion of the good and divine substance which is held mixed and imprisoned in food and drink is more strongly and foully bound in the rest of men, even their own Auditors, but particularly in those who propagate offspring". Cf. BeDuhn 2000b, 88.

Furthermore, East-Roman sources do not provide us with any information concerning the fasting periods of the Manichaeans. Augustine, once more, is illuminating; according to him, the Elect abstain from meat and wine and eat only in the evening, while hearers fast only on Sundays (or Bema?).[82] The latter is testified by Manichaean sources. According to *Kephalaia*, the catechumens, "who have not strength to fast daily should make their fast [only] on the lord's day".[83]

The pagan philosopher Alexander of Lycopolis is the only one of the East-Roman authors who simultaneously points out and examines the two contradictory interpretations of Manichaean fasting. Alexander considers both of them equally incomprehensible and ridiculous. As he notes, "since" according to Manichaeans "it is God's decree that matter shall perish", according to their doctrine, they "abstain from eating any animals, and should rather eat vegetables and all the other things that are without feeling".[84] As Alexander critically comments on the above Manichaean attitude:

> They abstain from eating ensouled things. If they do so for some other reason, we need not bother. If, however, they do so because the divine power is either more absent from these or more plentifully present within them, this choice of theirs is ridiculous. For plants are either of a more material nature, and it is not reasonable to use that which is inferior as food and substance; or, on the other hand, the divine power is more plentiful within them, – why should such things be used in that case as food, since the nurturing and growth-fostering part of soul is of a more bodily nature?[85]

---

82   Augustine, *Ep. 236* (§ 2).

83   *1Keph.* 79: 191.32–192.1 (Gardner 1995, 200). About the Manichaean fasts see also Henning 1945, 146–64.

84   Alexander of Lycopolis, *Tract. Man.* 4.25–27 (Van der Horst and Mansfeld, 56–57): ἐπεὶ οὖν ἀπόλλυσθαι τὴν ὕλην ἐστὶ θεοῦ δόγμα, ἀπέχεσθαι μὲν ἐμψύχων πάντων, σιτίζεσθαι δὲ λάχανα καὶ πᾶν ὅ τι ἀναίσθητον.

85   Alexander of Lycopolis, *Tract. Man.* 25.1–9 (Brinkmann, 36; Van der Horst and Mansfeld, 94): Ἀπέχονται δὲ ἐμψύχων. εἰ μὲν γὰρ ἑτέρου τινὸς χάριν, οὐ περιεργαστέον· εἰ δὲ διότι ἡ δύναμις ἡ θεία τούτων ἄπεστι μᾶλλον ἢ ἐνυπάρχει πλείων, γελοῖον αὐτὴ αὐτῶν ἡ προαίρεσις αὕτη. εἴτε γὰρ τὰ φυτὰ ἔνυλα μᾶλλον, εἰς τροφὴν καὶ δίαιταν χρῆσθαι τῷ χείρονι πῶς εὔλογον; εἴτε πλείων ἐν τούτοις ἡ δύναμις ἡ θεία, τί πρὸς τὴν τροφὴν τὰ τοιαῦτα χρήσιμα, τοῦ θρεπτικοῦ καὶ αὐξητικοῦ μέρους τῆς ψυχῆς ὄντος σωματικωτέρου.

2.2.3   Some Concluding Remarks Concerning the Representation
of the Manichaean "Seal of the Mouth" by the East-Roman
Anti-Manichaean Sources

After comparing the testimonies provided by East-Roman sources with those provided by Augustine in the light of the authentic Manichaean findings, some remarks can now be made to illuminate two issues arising from the above analysis.

Firstly, I would like to further highlight an issue which concerns the problem of the incompatibility between the two interpretations of Manichaean fasting (contempt for creation versus deification of creation). Where does the problem lie? Is it due to the misinterpretation of Church Fathers or due to the Manichaean practice? In other words: could the two contradictory interpretations be explained by the Manichaean narrative and precepts? Secondly, I would like to highlight the additional information that Augustine gives that is absent from East-Roman sources.

Concerning the first issue, this incompatibility is due to Manichaean premises. Both contradictory attitudes were meaningful according to the rationale of Manichaean discipline and are supported by the Manichaean narrative. The fundamental basis of the second interpretation (deification of creation) is the concept of the *Living Self* imprisoned in the natural world (divinity within foods). Whereas, the basis of the first interpretation (contempt for creation) is that the world is a mixture of divine and evil elements (materiality of food). Thus, the Manichaeans fasted because (some) foods are poisonous 'abominations', foul of 'deadly' matter. As BeDuhn points out:

> Manichaeans erect walls between themselves and the world not just to flee its poison, but also to restrain themselves from harmful action upon its goodness.[86]
>
> The Manichaean sources reflect apparently contradictory evaluations of the world. On the one hand, the world is identified as a locale of evil [...] from which Manichaeans strive to escape. On the other hand, the world is filled with a divine presence [...] which Manichaeans endeavor not to afflict by their actions. The abhorrence and reverence attested in the sources can be characterized as opposite reactions, attitudes or moods.[87]

---

86   BeDuhn 2000b, 230.
87   BeDuhn 1995b, 437: "In the Manichaean case, therefore, abhorrence is only one part of a larger set of rationales supporting ascetic practices". As BeDuhn (2000b, 208) concludes, "The Elect compressed their contact with the world, which is problematic for both its

Therefore, it could be said that the purpose of the Manichaean fasting ("seal of the mouth") was both protective, so as not to injure the entrapped divine substance within foods, and preventive, to limit the materiality rates inside humans. The latter was manifested by an abstinence from animal products, which was particularly important for the class of the Elect and their preparation for the ritual meal.

The second question concerns the comparisons with Augustine, namely (1) where Augustine differs from the authors of the eastern Empire, and (2) which further information he provides:

2.2.3.1   *Concerning the First Interpretation (Materiality of Foods)*

According to East-Roman authors, the Manichaeans seem to argue that materiality pertains without exception to all foods, including plants. However, Augustine's testimony seems to be that impurity concerned mainly foods from animals and animal products. Animal food is poisonous, and this is because animals have been slain.

2.2.3.2   *Concerning the Second Interpretation (Divinity Within Foods)*

Most Eastern patristic sources do not refer to the qualitative distinction that the Manichaeans made between animal and plant foods because of their high content either of matter or light. This is underlined and emphasized by Augustine. Exceptions are Nemesius of Emesa who differentiates between the share that animate and inanimate bodies have in the Light (Universal Soul), and Alexander who, although not distinguishing between plants and animals, notes that the content of matter or light was a criterion for the suitability of food for the Manichaeans.

Thus, for East-Roman sources, all kinds of food, according to the first interpretation, whether plant or animal, are considered as abominations, whereas according to the second interpretation they are considered as containers of divine particles. On the contrary, Augustine, notes this distinction, presents the Manichaeans' argumentation for this distinction (brightness, colour, odour, etc.), and ridicules their rationale. Thus, according to Augustine, the reason why meat and foods from animal products are considered as abominations is that they contain high percentages of matter and correspondingly low percentages of divine substance. Nevertheless, at this point it should be highlighted that the Manichaean position on the issue is ambiguous.[88]

---

profanity and its sacrality, to the single point of ingestion. Their resolution of the problematized world, therefore, was metabolic", Cf. Brand 2019, 201.

88 See for example *Kephalaia* (*1Keph.* 86, 215.12–215.23), where water consumption may have the same effect.

Moreover, particularly important is that Augustine's works clearly distinguish between the Elect and auditors. The "seal of the mouth" applies only to the Elect. Whereas hearers could eat meat (although deterred from doing so), the Elect who violated the "seal of the mouth" was expelled from the class of the Elect. Unlike Augustine, reports from East-Roman sources do not make this distinction, and they refer to Manichaeans in general. Further, Augustine is well aware of the Manichaean beliefs that inanimate things have articulated voices and of the identification of *Living Self* with the crucified Jesus. Lastly, Augustine provides us with some details concerning the everyday religious life of Manichaeans (e.g. days and time of fasting).

2.3   *Manichaean Rituals*

As underlined in the introduction, the acceptance of the Manichaean narrative entailed certain behaviours, which according to their purpose can be classified as protective, preventive, and liberative behaviours.

The purpose of the Manichaean fasting ("seal of the mouth") was both protective, and preventive. The purpose of the Manichaean rituals was liberative, and as such, they aimed to release the already entrapped divine element in the material world. On the macrocosmic level, the luminaries (sun and moon) were created by the powers of light to release the light from the material world. On the microcosmic level, this project was undertaken by the Elect Manichaeans, who released the divine particles entrapped within foods during the ritual meal.[89]

Furthermore, in order to analyse and correctly comprehend the discourse concerning Manichaean behaviours in rituals, it is important to stress once more the peculiarity of the macro-microcosmic relationship in Manichaeism. As underlined in the introduction, although it is common in many religions that divine beings serve as exemplars which the faithful are called to imitate, and that rituals could be interpreted as re-enactments of divine archetypes, in Manichaeism this macro-microcosmic relationship is more direct and substantial. This is because the Manichaean believer was not just asked to imitate the behaviour and deeds of the divine figures of his religion, but he himself, or rather his soul (as a part of the divine substance), was called to remember his own deeds which took place in a remote past (during the primordial struggle) and to act respectively, in the same way as then.[90]

---

89   As Augustine wrote to his epistle to Deuterius (*Ep. 236*, § 2), the Manichaeans say that the part of God which was "mingled with the prince of darkness" and which is "spread over the world, defiled and bound, is purified by the food of the elect and by the sun and moon", see BeDuhn 2000b, 77; Gardner and Lieu 2004, 244–45.

90   On this see BeDuhn 2000b, 82–83.

2.3.1   Sun and Moon Worship

A constant target of attack and criticism by anti-Manichaean authors was the important role that the sun and moon had in the Manichaean narrative, as well as the attitude of Manichaean followers towards them. In brief, the main points of the anti-Manichaean criticism on this subject are: (1) the central position the luminaries have in Manichaean narrative as a part of the divine substance, and their role in distilling the particles of light from cosmos; (2) the identification of Christ either with the sun or the moon; (3) the deification of the two luminaries by Manichaean sources; (4) the prayers and rituals devoted to their worship.

The two former issues, which concern Manichaean beliefs, will be discussed briefly. The two latter issues, which concern Manichaean attitudes, are the main questions to be examined in this section, by investigating whether according to the sources the Manichaeans worship the sun and the moon as gods, and what kind of information is recorded concerning the relevant rituals.

All kinds of sources, such as Christian (Greek, Semitic, Augustine), pagan, Muslim and Manichaean ones are unanimous about the important position and role which the two great luminaries had in the Manichaean cosmogonic myth. In specific, the key points of the narrative which were criticized are the following:

A.   *The powers of light created the two luminaries of pure divine essence*: The demiurge (i.e. the *Living Spirit*) clears from the mixture that part of the light that had not been affected by matter and creates the sun and moon,[91] which as Turbo comments, are the remnants of the universal *Soul*.[92] The sun is made of good fire and the moon is made of good water.[93]

B.   *The luminaries were created in order to capture the light from the world each day*: "The demiurge and his agents construct the world as a huge machine, distilling light from its unfortunate mixture with evil; each part functions towards this liberative purpose, from the rotation of the sun

---

91   Alexander, *Tract. Man.* 3.18–22 (Van der Horst and Mansfeld, 55): "Then God [...] sent another power which we call Demiurge. When this power had arrived and had put its hand to creating the universe, then that part of the other power which had suffered nothing untoward as a result of the mixture was separated from matter, and this first part of the other power became sun and moon".

92   *AA* 8.1 (Vermes, 49): "And again that Living Spirit created the heavenly bodies, which are remnants of the soul". Epiphanius, *Pan.* 66.49.1 (GCS 37:86): Εἶτα πάλιν φάσκει ὁ αὐτὸς ὅτι μετὰ τὸ ἐσταυρωκέναι τοὺς ἄρχοντας ἐν τῇ σφαίρᾳ ἔκτισε τοὺς φωστῆρας, ἅ ἐστι τῆς ψυχῆς λείψανα.

93   Augustine, *Haer.* 46.7; *1Keph.* 136 (337.10–338.18) & *1Keph.* 145 (348.12–27), cf. Gardner and Lieu 2004, 227 (no 72). Al-Nadim, *Fihrist* ch. 9 (Dodge, 789). Ephrem, *Prose Refutations* 41 (Mitchell): "The moon is a vessel into whose midst the light is poured".

and moon to the exhalations of trees and plants".[94] The demiurge "created the sun and the moon for sifting out whatever there was of light in the world".[95] He "founded sun and moon, [and] he set them on high, to purify the soul".[96] This extraction, or pumping takes place on a daily basis. Thus, "every day through these luminaries, the sun and the moon [...] the whole cosmos and all creation is taken away".[97]

C. *The description of the construction of mechanical devices for the light-pumping, as well as of the way the light is transported from the earth to the moon and the sun and finally to the kingdom of Glory:* Then, the pumped souls are daily sent via the luminaries "to the aeons of the Father",[98] in other words to the Kingdom of Light (God):[99] "The sun and moon [...] daily take up the refined part to the heights".[100] The "Light in the world ... [thus] rises up on a Column of Praise".[101] "The great luminaries, both the sun and the moon [...] [send over] (διαπεμπούσας) the victorious among the souls into the great aeon of light".[102]

---

94 BeDuhn 2000b, 76, cf. Ephrem, *Prose Refutations* (second discourse to Hypatius) 34–35.

95 Al-Nadim, *Fihrist* ch. 9 (Dodge, 782).

96 *2PsB* 9.3–11.32 (Psalm 223).

97 Epiphanius, *Pan.* 66.31.1 (GCS 37:69; Williams, 260): τούτου χάριν πέμπει καὶ συλᾷ ἀπ' αὐτῶν τὴν ψυχὴν αὐτοῦ καθ' ἡμέραν διὰ τῶν φωστήρων τούτων, ἡλίου καὶ σελήνης, ὑφ' ὧν ὅλος ὁ κόσμος καὶ πᾶσα ἡ κτίσις ἁρπάζεται. AA 12.3 (Vermes, 56): "For this reason he sends and steals from them every day the soul that is his by means of these heavenly bodies, namely the sun and the moon, by which the whole world and every creature is seized". Severianus of Gabala, *De Spriritu Sancto* 825.31–34: Ποῦ ἤκουσας ἐν τῷ Εὐαγγελίῳ Ἰησοῦ Χριστοῦ, ὅτι ὁ ἥλιος καὶ ἡ σελήνη δημιουργοί εἰσι; ποῦ εἶπεν ὁ Χριστός, ὅτι ταῦτα ἀντλοῦσι τὰς ψυχὰς, καὶ ἀνάγουσιν αὐτάς; ποῦ ἀνέγνωκας τοῦτο.

98 AA 8.7 (Vermes, 51): "So when the moon has handed the load of souls it carries to the aeons of the father, they remain in that Column of Glory, which is called the perfect man. This man is a column of light, for it is filled with pure souls, and this is the cause of the salvation of souls"; Epiphanius, *Pan.* 66.26.8 (GCS 37:60): τῆς οὖν σελήνης μεταδιδούσης τὸν γόμον τῶν ψυχῶν τοῖς αἰῶσι τοῦ πατρός, παραμένουσιν ἐν τῷ στύλῳ τῆς δόξης, ὃς καλεῖται ἀὴρ ὁ τέλειος. ὁ δὲ ἀὴρ οὗτος στῦλός ἐστι φωτός, ἐπειδὴ γέμει ψυχῶν τῶν καθαριζομένων. αὕτη ἐστὶν ἡ αἰτία δι' ἧς αἱ ψυχαὶ σῴζονται.

99 Alexander, *Tract. Man.* 3.29–31 (Van der Horst and Mansfeld, 55): "sun and the moon, [...] continually separate the divine power from matter and send it on its way toward God".

100 *2PsB*, 10.30–11.2 (Allberry). See also Gardner and Lieu 2004, 178, Psalm 223 (9.3–11.32), no 56, entitled: *The community sings 'the knowledge of Mani'*.

101 Al-Nadim, *Fihrist* ch. 9, 782.

102 P.Kellis GR. 98, 60–70 in Gardner 2007a, 121–22 (*Prayer of the Emanations/Εὐχὴ τῶν Προβολῶν*): Προσκυνῶ καὶ δοξάζω τοὺς μεγάλους φωστῆρες ἥλιον καὶ σελήνην [...] διαπεμπούσας τὰς νικώσας τῶν ψυχῶν εἰς τὸν μέγιστον αἰῶνα τοῦ φωτός. Cf. Nemesius of Emesa, *De natura hominis* 2.33.8–10 (Morani, 33; Sharples and Van der Eijk 2008, 71–72): "They say that pure souls turn towards light, being themselves light, but those tainted by matter go into the elements and again from the elements into plants and animals." (καὶ τὰς μὲν

For the pumping of light, a machine is usually postulated, described as an "instrument with twelve jars", a wheel through the rotation of which ("revolve by the sphere") the enlightened Manichaean souls (Elect) are sent to the moon. The luminaries are described as 'ships' or 'passage-boats' or 'palaces' carrying the souls of Elect: from the moon the souls travel to the sun and from the sun to the "pillar of glory, which is called the perfect air", or "the aeons of the Father". Thereby, the Manichaeans explained the monthly phases of the moon (full moon = full of souls, new moon = empty of souls) and the daily path of the sun from the east to the west (or rather the reverse).[103] What is drained and

---

καθαρὰς ψυχὰς χωρεῖν εἰς τὸ φῶς, φῶς οὔσας, τὰς δὲ μεμολυσμένας ὑπὸ τῆς ὕλης χωρεῖν εἰς τὰ στοιχεῖα καὶ πάλιν ἀπὸ τῶν στοιχείων εἰς τὰ φυτὰ καὶ τὰ ζῷα·).

103   The way of distilling the light (construction of an instrument): AA 8.5 (Vermes, 50): "When he [the son of the living Father/Jesus] had arrived, he set up a machine devised for the salvation of souls, that is a wheel, holding twelve jars. It rotates in this sphere, draining the souls of the dying which the greater heavenly body, the sun, takes away with its rays, purifies and hands on to the moon, which is how the disc of the moon, as we call it, is filled up. 6. He says those two heavenly bodies are ships or merchant boats, and when the moon is full, it carries souls to the eastern region, and so effects its waning or decline, by being relieved of its load. Then again the boats are refilled and once more loaded, as the souls are drained by means of the jars, until it releases its correct portion of souls. 7. [...] So when the moon has handed the load of souls it carries to the aeons of the father, they remain in that Column of Glory, which is called the perfect man. This man is a column of light, for it is filled with pure souls, and this is the cause of the salvation of souls". The same text by Epiphanius, Pan. 66.59.5–60.26. Alexander of Lycopolis, Tract. Man. 4. 2PsB 54.8ff: "as the sphere turns ... as [the sun receives] the refined part of life". Cf. fn. 14 of this chapter. Sun and moon as ships: AA 8.6, 13.2 (Vermes 50, 57): "He says those two heavenly bodies are ships or merchant boats". Epiphanius, Pan. 66.26.6 (GCS 37:60): πλοῖα γὰρ ἤτοι πορθμεῖα εἶναι λέγει τοὺς δύο φωστῆρας; 66.31.6 (GCS 37:70–71): αἱ δὲ προβολαὶ πᾶσαι, ὁ Ἰησοῦς ὁ ἐν τῷ μικρῷ πλοίῳ καὶ ἡ μήτηρ τῆς ζωῆς καὶ οἱ δώδεκα κυβερνῆται καὶ ἡ παρθένος τοῦ φωτὸς καὶ ὁ πρεσβύτης ὁ τρίτος ὁ ἐν τῷ μεγάλῳ πλοίῳ καὶ τὸ ζῶν πνεῦμα καὶ τὸ τεῖχος τοῦ μεγάλου πυρὸς καὶ τὸ τεῖχος τοῦ ἀνέμου καὶ τοῦ ἀέρος καὶ τοῦ ὕδατος καὶ τοῦ ἔσωθεν πυρὸς τοῦ ζῶντος πρὸς τὸν μικρὸν φωστῆρα οἰκοῦσιν. Theodoret of Cyrrhus, Haer. PG 380.17–19: "And sometimes they said that are boats [the sun and the moon] carrying the souls of the dead from the Matter to the Light" (ποτὲ δὲ πλοῖα λέγοντες εἶναι τὰς τῶν τελευτώντων ψυχὰς ἀπὸ τῆς Ὕλης μετάγοντα πρὸς τὸ Φῶς). SC, ch. 6 (Lieu 2010, 122–23): "out by means of the Sun and the Moon, which they also say are boats" (τὸν θεὸν καὶ ταύτας διὰ τοῦ ἡλίου καὶ τῆς σελήνης ἐξαντλεῖν, ἃ καὶ πλοῖα εἶναί φασιν). Ephrem, Prose Refutations in BeDuhn 2000b, 293–94: "they greatly magnify and call it 'the ship of light which ... bears away the burden of their refinings to the house of life' (cxvi); and they say, 'the moon receives the light which is refined, and during fifteen days draws it up and goes on emptying it out for another fifteen days' (xxxvi). Moreover, 'they say that the sun receives the light from the moon' (xxxviii); 'and it is the sun that goes and comes every day on account of its purity to the house of life, as they say' (xli). And elsewhere, 'they say concerning the sun that it purifies from evil, because it goes and comes every day to the domain of the good one, which is a purification' (lxxxiv)". Augustine, Faust. 20.6 (Lieu 2010: 79): "Your statements about the sun himself are so false and absurd [...] First of all, you call the sun a ship

fills the moon and the sun, is the divine substance that has been stolen during the primordial battle by the princes of Darkness from the powers of Light.[104]

D. *The identification of Christ sometimes with the sun*[105] *and sometimes with the moon:*[106] The reason the Manichaeans identify Christ with the sun, as Theodoret of Cyrrhus explains, is because the sun departed from the sky at the time of the crucifixion.[107] Criticism from all sides concerning the above Manichaean beliefs abounds.[108] Simplicius wonders:

> Then consider the enormous absurdity [...] They don't believe that the light of the moon is from the sun, either, but think it to be souls which the moon draws up in the period from the new to the full moon, and then channels towards the sun in the period from the full to the new moon.[109]

[...] Next, [...] you maintain that he is triangular [...] Light shines ... through a triangular window in heaven". Manichaean sources: *CMC* 34 (see esp.: 33–35 & 79–93) (Koenen and Römer, 20): Τιμόθεος [...] τοῦ φωτὸς πατέρων καὶ πάντα τὰ γιγνόμενα ἐν τοῖς πλοίοις ἀπεκάλυπτέ μοι. ἀνέπτυξε δ᾿ αὖ πάλιν τὸν κόλπον τοῦ κίονος καὶ τοὺς πατέρας καὶ τὰ σθένη τὰ ἀλκιμώτατα. *1Keph.* 65.162.24–26 (Gardner 1995, 171). *2PsB* 134.24 (Allberry): "The ships are the sun and the moon", and 147.34–37: "Lo, the ships are moored for thee, the barks are in the harbor. Take thy merchandise aboard and sail to thy habitations".

104 *AA* 11.2 (Vermes, 55): "However that which the princes stole from the first man is the very thing that fills the moon, which is purified every day from the world". Epiphanius, *Pan.* 66.29.2 (GCS 37:66): ὃ δὲ ἐσύλησαν οἱ ἄρχοντες ἀπὸ τοῦ πρώτου ἀνθρώπου, αὐτό ἐστι τὸ γεμίζον τὴν σελήνην, τὸ καθαριζόμενον καθημερινὸν ἀπὸ τοῦ κόσμου.

105 *AA* 60.1 (Vermes, 137): "you say that God transformed himself into a man or into the sun. You wish to prove by this that our Jesus was made man only in outward appearance". Cyril, *Catech.* 6.13 (Reischl and Rupp 1848, 174): τὸν δὲ Χριστὸν τὸν ἥλιον τοῦτον καλοῦσιν; *Catech.* 15.3.29–32 (Reischl and Rupp 1967, 158): παιδευέσθωσαν οἱ ἐκ Μανιχαίων ἐπιστρέψαντες, [...] μηδὲ τὸν σκοτισθησόμενον τοῦτον ἥλιον τὸν Χριστὸν εἶναι δυσσεβῶς νομιζέτωσαν; *Catech.* 11.21: Φιμούσθωσαν οἱ λέγοντες τὸν ἥλιον εἶναι τὸν Χριστόν· ἡλίου γάρ ἐστι δημιουργός, οὐχ ὁ ἥλιος ὁ φαινόμενος. Theodoret, *Haer.* (PG 83:380B): Οὗτοι τὸν ἥλιον ..., ποτὲ μὲν αὐτὸν ἀποκαλοῦντες Χριστόν. *SC*, ch. 5 (Lieu 2010, 120–21): Ἀναθεματίζω τοὺς [...] τὸν κύριον ἡμῶν Ἰησοῦν Χριστὸν [...] ἥλιον λέγοντας εἶναι αὐτόν; *SC*, ch. 6 (Lieu 2010, 122–23): Ἀναθεματίζω οὖν καὶ καταθεματίζω τοὺς εἰρημένους Μανιχαίους καὶ τοὺς τὸν Ζαραδὴν καὶ τὸν ⟨Βούδδαν καὶ τὸν⟩ Χριστὸν καὶ τὸν Μανιχαῖον καὶ τὸν ἥλιον τὸν αὐτὸν εἶναι λέγοντας; *SC*, ch. 7 (Lieu 2010, 124–25): Καὶ αὐτὸς γὰρ [Ἀριστοκρίτος] ἐν αὐτῇ κατὰ τὸν Μανιχαῖον τὸν Ζαραδὴ θεοποιεῖ, φανέντα, ὡς καὶ αὐτός φησι, παρὰ Πέρσαις, καὶ τοῦτον εἶναι λέγει τὸν ἥλιον καὶ τὸν κύριον ἡμῶν Ἰησοῦν Χριστόν.

106 *SC*, ch. 4 (Lieu 2010, 120–21): Ἀναθεματίζω οὖν τοὺς [...] ἀγέννητον ἀποκαλοῦσι Χριστὸν Ἰησοῦν καὶ φέγγος προσονομάζουσιν ἐν σχήματι ἀνθρώπου φανέντα, τὸν μὲν τῆς κακῆς ἀρχῆς, τὸν δὲ τῆς ἀγαθῆς μυθολογοῦντες.

107 Theodoretus, *Haer.* (PG 83:380B.13–16): Οὗτοι τὸν ἥλιον [...] ποτὲ μὲν αὐτὸν ἀποκαλοῦντες Χριστόν, καὶ τούτου τεκμήριον ἱκανὸν παρέχουσι, τὸ τὸν ἥλιον ἐκλείπειν· ἐν τῷ τοῦ σταυροῦ καιρῷ·.

108 Epiphanius, *Pan.* 66.23.1–7; Severianus of Gabala, *c. Manichaeos*; Augustine, *Conf.* (Gardner and Lieu 2004, 132).

109 Simplicius, *Comm. Man. Epict.* 35 (Hadot, 326.99, 101–04; Brennan & Brittain, 39): Πόση δὲ καὶ ἡ περὶ τοῦτο ἀλλοκοτία [...] Καὶ τὸ φῶς τῆς σελήνης οὐκ ἀπὸ τοῦ ἡλίου νομίζουσιν, ἀλλὰ

2.3.1.1   *Divinization or Just Honour?*

The Greek patristic sources are not entirely clear as to whether the Manichaeans considered and worshiped the two luminaries as gods or not. According to Cyril, the Manichaeans had made the sun and moon into gods.[110] According to Titus, Mani claims that the sun is consubstantial with God.[111] Theodoret of Cyrrhus states that they call the sun and the moon gods, while in the sc the converted Manichaeans anathematized those who "pray to the sun or to the moon or to the stars and call them the brightest gods or, in short, introduce many gods to whom they pray".[112] Thus, for a number of sources, the Manichaeans deify the two luminaries or call them gods, whereas, in some cases the Manichaeans just honour the two luminaries as if they were gods. For example, Chrysostom in his first homily in *Genesis* argues that the Manichaeans (as the Greeks) honour created things as if they were Gods, attributing the privilege of ingenerateness to something that comes from non-existence, which will be destroyed and will be lost. Chrysostom uses the sun as an example. It is not the sun to be worshiped, but its creator. The sun is bright but was created to worship the one who created it, and not the sun itself.[113] As he stresses addressing his flock:

> Don't you see that this sun is a material body, subjected to decay and perishable? And let the Greeks and the Manichaeans get overwhelmed with grief listening to this. Not only sun, but earth, and sea and the whole creation [are perishable] are subjected to futility.[114]

ψυχὰς εἶναι, ἃς ὑπὸ νουμηνίας ἕως πανσελήνου ἀπὸ τῆς γῆς ἀνασπῶσα, ἀπὸ πανσελήνου πάλιν ἕως νουμηνίας εἰς τὸν ἥλιον μεταγγίζει.

110   Cyril, *Catech.* 4.6: Ἐπεὶ οὖν ἐπλανήθησαν ἀπὸ τοῦ ἑνὸς Θεοῦ διαφόρως πολλοί· καὶ οἱ μὲν ἥλιον ἐθεοποίησαν; 15.3.29 (Reischl and Rupp 1967, 158): παιδευέσθωσαν οἱ ἐκ Μανιχαίων ἐπιστρέψαντες, καὶ τοὺς φωστῆρας μηκέτι θεοποιείτωσαν […].

111   Titus of Bostra, *c. Manichaeos* 2.54.28–29 & 40–44 (CCSG 82:217, 219): Ὁ τοίνυν Μάνης ἐκθειάζων, ὡς τῆς φύσεως ὄντα τοῦ ἀγαθοῦ, τὸν ἥλιον […] Ὥστε καὶ οἱ πέμπτον στοιχεῖον ὁριζόμενοι εἶναι τὸν ἥλιον πρός γε τὰ σαφῆ μὴ φιλονεικούντων, καὶ οὕτως αὐτὸς ὁ χαλεπώτατα μανείς, τὸν τῶν ὅλων δημιουργὸν βλασφημῶν, ἥκιστα πιστευέσθω, ἥλιον συγκρίνων θεῷ καὶ ἐκ τῆς οὐσίας αὐτοῦ λέγων εἶναι τοῦτον.

112   Theodoret, *Haer.* (PG 83:380B.13.14): συντόμως ἐρῶ τῆς δυσσεβοῦς αἱρέσεως τὰ κεφάλαια. Οὗτοι τὸν ἥλιον καὶ τὴν σελήνην θεοὺς ὀνομάζουσι. sc, ch. 5 (Lieu 2010, 120–21): Ἀναθεματίζω […] τοὺς … τῷ ἡλίῳ εὐχομένους ἢ τῇ σελήνῃ ἢ τοῖς ἄστροις καὶ θεοὺς φανοτάτους αὐτοὺς ἀποκαλοῦντας ἢ πολλοὺς ὅλως εἰσάγοντας θεοὺς καὶ τούτοις εὐχομένους. On this issue see also: Serapion, *c. Manichaeos* 42; Socrates, *HE* 1.22.8 (sc 477:204): καὶ γὰρ θεοὺς πολλοὺς σέβειν ὁ Μανιχαῖος προτρέπεται ⟨αὐτὸς⟩ ἄθεος ὢν καὶ τὸν ἥλιον προσκυνεῖν διδάσκει, καὶ εἱμαρμένην εἰσάγων.

113   Chrysostom, *Hom. Gen.* (PG 54:581.48–58).

114   Chrysostom, *Natal.* (PG 49:360.7–12): τὸν ἥλιον, οὗ τὸ σῶμά ἐστιν αἰσθητὸν καὶ φθαρτὸν καὶ ἐπίκηρον, κἂν μυριάκις ἀποπνίγωνται Ἕλληνες καὶ Μανιχαῖοι ταῦτα ἀκούοντες; Οὐχ οὗτος δὲ μόνον, ἀλλὰ καὶ γῆ, καὶ θάλασσα, καὶ πᾶσα ἁπλῶς ἡ ὁρωμένη κτίσις τῇ ματαιότητι ὑποτέτακται.

Alexander too, seems to be ambivalent on the issue. Initially he is clear in explaining that for the Manichaeans, "Sun and moon they honour most of all, not as gods, but as the means by which it is possible to attain to God".[115] Commenting on this, Lieu argues that "Alexander of Lycopolis [...] probably comes closest to the Manichaean position when he says that the Manichaeans do not regard the sun and the moon as gods but as a way to reach God".[116] Indeed, as one reads in the Manichaean *Prayer of the Emanations*, "the great light-givers, both sun and moon" are praised, for through them the souls succeed to have access "into the great aeon of light".[117] However, further in his text, Alexander contradicts himself saying that "the sun and the moon, heavenly bodies which alone among the gods they profess to revere".[118] Van der Horst, in his footnotes, also refers to the above contradiction, without however commenting on it further.[119]

At this point, it is interesting to examine the opinion of the other pagan authors on the subject. According to Libanius (fourth cent.), the Manichaeans "venerate the sun [...] and honour it as a god of the second grade".[120] Thus for Manichaeans, the sun is a god, yet a second class one. Contrary to Libanius, Simplicius, the pagan philosopher of the sixth century, speaks only about honour. The Manichaeans

> Out of all the heavenly bodies they honour only the two light-bearers, claiming that these alone belong the Realm of Good and despising the others as belonging to the Realm of Evil.[121]

The Manichaean sources are not entirely clear on this matter. The Manichaean Faustus (around 400), according to Augustine, "repels the charge of sun-worship and maintains that while the Manichaeans believe that God's power dwells in the sun and his wisdom in the moon, they yet worship one deity,

---

115 Alexander of Lycopolis, *Tract. Man.* 5.1–8 (Brinkmann, 7–8; Van der Horst and Mansfeld, 57): τιμῶσι δὲ μάλιστα ἥλιον καὶ σελήνην οὐχ ὡς θεούς, ἀλλ' ὡς ὁδὸν δι' ἧς ἔστιν πρὸς θεὸν ἀφικέσθαι.

116 Lieu 1994a, 288.

117 P.Kellis GR. 98, 60–69 (Gardner 2007a, 111–128, esp. 121–22, *Prayer of the Emanations/Εὐχὴ τῶν Προβολῶν*).

118 Alexander of Lycopolis, *Tract. Man.* 7.8–9 (Brinkmann, 11; Van der Horst and Mansfeld, 64): ὁ ἥλιος καὶ ἡ σελήνη, οὓς μόνους θεῶν αἰδεῖσθαί φασιν.

119 Van der Horst and Mansfeld 1974, 57, fn. 207 and 64 fn. 241.

120 Libanius, *Epist.* 1253 (Lieu 2010, 42–43): Πρισκιανῷ. 1. Οἱ τὸν ἥλιον οὗτοι θεραπεύοντες ἄνευ αἵματος καὶ τιμῶντες θεὸν προσηγορίᾳ δευτέρᾳ.

121 Simplicius, *Comm. Man. Epict.* 35 (Hadot, 326.99–101; Lieu 2010, 104–05): Πόση δὲ καὶ ἡ περὶ τοῦτο ἀλλοκοτία, τὸ ἐκ πάντων τῶν ἐν τῷ οὐρανῷ μόνους τοὺς δύο φωστῆρας τιμᾶν, τῆς τοῦ ἀγαθοῦ μοίρας λέγοντας αὐτούς, τῶν δὲ ἄλλων καταφρονεῖν, ὡς τῆς τοῦ κακοῦ μοίρας ὄντων.

Father, Son, and Holy Spirit. They are not a schism of the Gentiles, nor a sect".[122] However, according to the *Kephalaia*, in recounting the benefits of the sun to his disciples, Mani stresses that "people [...] have not perceived its greatness and its divinity".[123]

From what has been advanced so far, an answer to the first question could be that the two luminaries were considered by the Manichaeans as divine beings, consisting of pure divine substance. Yet, as they were made from the first light (first principle), in the Manichaean pantheon they were classified at a lower level: in the words of Libanius, they were gods of the second grade. Although it is not clearly reflected in all sources, one could also say that according to earlier sources (e.g. Cyril, Libanius, etc.) the Manichaeans deified the sun and moon, while according to later sources (Simplicius) they simply honoured them. If this was the case, it seems that over time, and given their persecution from the late fourth century onwards, the Manichaeans would avoid confessing such a faith publicly. An example of this reticence can be seen in the reaction of Faustus and Secundinus.[124] On the contrary, in other more tolerant environments, they would not have a problem to confess this, as the following Manichaean prayer illustrates: "if somehow we have done things that displease the gods of the Sun and the Moon [...] (then), Majesty, now we beg to be freed from these ten kinds of sins. Release my sins!"[125]

2.3.1.2   *Sun and Moon Worshipping Ceremonies*

The anti-Manichaean corpus contains several references to the Manichaean worshipping and veneration of the two luminaries. Some of them linked Manichaean sun-worship with Hellenic idolatry and polytheism, the magoi (i.e. the priests of Zoroastrianism), the astrologers (mathematicians), and the cult of Mithras. For example, in the second debate between Archelaus and Mani, which was in Diodoris, Archelaus called Mani a "barbarian priest and conspirator with Mithras".[126] According to Epiphanius,

---

122 *NPNF*[1] 4: 435–453, 435, cf. Augustine, *Faust.* 20.2,536.9–24 and 20.11,550.14–19.

123 *1Keph.* 65.159, p. 168.

124 As Gardner and Lieu (2004, 194) point out commenting on the *Prayer of Emanations*: "The fact that the hymn did not try to disguise or modify its polytheism gives the impression that it was composed in the first half of the fourth century, viz. before the dominance of Christianity compelled the Manichaeans to veil their cult in a semblance of monotheism". Gardner in a later publication (2007a, 112 fn. 34) is sceptical of the above aspect: "I would probably not express this point in the same way".

125 Excerpt from a manuscript in Turkic language dated from 8th–11th centuries and entitled *Xuastuanift* in BeDuhn 2000b, 54–55.

126 *AA* 40.7 (Vermes, 105). The Manichaean Secundinus claimed that "Augustine's description of Manichaeism [...] must be referring to Mithraism instead of Manichaeism" (Lieu in Vermes 2001, 105, fn. 213).

Mani [is a pagan with the pagans and] worships the sun and moon, the stars and daemons, the man ⟨is heathen⟩, and his sect teaches heathen religion. ⟨And besides this⟩ he knows the lore of the magi and is involved with them, and he praises astrologers and practices their mumbo jumbo.[127]

In the fifth anathema, the converted Manichaean had to anathematise his former companions who prayed to the sun and the moon: "(I anathematize) those who [...] pray to the sun or to the moon or to the stars and [...] in short introduce many gods to whom they pray".[128]

What seems to impress our sources regarding this Manichaean ceremony was the obeisance of Manichaeans to the luminaries. "Tell me this: why do you prostrate yourselves before the sun?" John the Orthodox asked this question to a Manichaean and the Manichaean replied: "because the sun is a luminary begotten by the good God".[129] As Socrates the Scholastic comments, Mani teaches his disciples to kneel before the sun.[130]

As reflected in the seventh anathema of the sc, the Manichaeans prayed twice a day to the sun: in the dawn towards the rising and in the evening towards the setting sun. During these prayers they made specific gestures and movements.

7. (I anathematize) those who do not pray towards the east only but also towards the setting sun and follow its movement foolishly and maniacally in their abominable and magical prayers.[131]

127　Epiphanius, *Pan.* 66.88.3 (GCS 37:131; Williams, 315–16): ὦ Μάνη, [...] ἥλιον προσκυνῶν καὶ σελήνην καὶ τὰ ἄστρα καὶ δαίμονας, ὁ ἀνήρ, ἀγαπητοί, τυγχάνει καὶ ἡ αὐτοῦ αἵρεσις τὰ τῶν Ἑλλήνων ὑφηγεῖται, τὰ μάγων ἐπίσταται καὶ ἐν αὐτοῖς ἐγκυλινδεῖται, ἀστρονόμους ἐπαινεῖ, τὰ αὐτῶν περιεργαζόμενος.

128　sc, ch. 5 (Lieu 2010, 120–21): Ἀναθεματίζω [...] καὶ τοὺς τὸν ἥλιον λέγοντας εἶναι αὐτὸν ['Ιησοῦν Χριστὸν] καὶ τῷ ἡλίῳ εὐχομένους ἢ τῇ σελήνῃ.

129　[John of Caesarea], *Disputatio cum Manichaeo* (Διάλεξις 'Ιωάννου 'Ορθοδόξου πρὸς Μανιχαῖον), 45–46.219–220 (Richard, 124): Ἀπόκριναι δέ μοι, διὰ τί τὸν ἥλιον προσκυνεῖτε; 46. ΜΑΝ. Ὅτι φωστήρ ἐστι τοῦ κόσμου, τοῦ ἀγαθοῦ θεοῦ γέννημα. Based on this reference, Bennett (2009, 33–34) supports the view that the text combats Manichaeans and not Paulicians or Bogomils. About the authorship of the work which earlier was attributed to John of Caesarea, see Bennet (2009).

130　Socrates, *HE* 1.22.8 (SC 477: 204): καὶ τὸν ἥλιον προσκυνεῖν διδάσκει.

131　sc, ch. 7 (lines 213–16) (Lieu 2010, 122, 124–25 & 1994, 7): Ἀναθεματίζω οὖν καὶ καταθεματίζω...τοὺς μὴ πρὸς ἀνατολὰς μόνας εὐχομένους, ἀλλὰ καὶ πρὸς δυόμενον ἥλιον, καὶ τῇ τούτου κινήσει συμπεριφερομένους ἐμπλήκτως καὶ μανικῶς ἐν ταῖς μιαραῖς αὐτῶν καὶ γοητευτικαῖς προσευχαῖς.

That the Manichaeans assembled in order to pray to the luminaries is also attested by Augustine: all together (hearers and Elect) "they adore and pray to the sun and the moon".[132] Augustine provides us with some complementary information for the reconstruction of the sun and moon worship rituals.

> 6. [...] Hence it is that you bend your backs and bow your necks to the sun, while you worship not this visible sun, but some imaginary ship which you suppose to be shining through a triangular opening.[133]
>
> 18. In the daytime they offer their prayers towards the sun, wherever it goes in its orbit; at night, they offer them towards the moon, if it appears; if it does not, they direct them towards the north, by which the sun, when it has set, returns to the east. They stand while praying.[134]

The cult of the two luminaries is also testified by the Manichaean sources. As the CMC records, Mani himself taught a hairy ascetic – whom he found on a lofty mountain – the way to prostrate before the two luminaries (among other commandments).[135] A typical Manichaean wonder story, in which many of the above discussed practices and beliefs are illustrated, is the account of the Manichaean missionary Gabryab.

> Thereupon, on the fourteenth day ⟨of the month⟩ Gabryab with his [assistants] [stood] in supplication and praise, and towards evening, when Jesus (= moon) rose, Gabryab stood in prayer before Jesus and spoke thus:
>
> 'You are a great god [and] bringer of life and a true resurrector of souls, help me this time, beneficent lord! Make this girl better and help her through my hand, so that your divinity is visible before the whole people, and the fact that we really (are) your true servants'. [...]
>
> And all night long Gabryab and his helpers stayed with the girl. They sang hymns and performed the [...] praise, until mor[ning] ⟨came⟩ and the sun rose. And he stood before the magnificent, huge [Mithra (i.e. sun) god] in praise. And with a loud voice he said:
>
> 'You are the bright eye of [the] whole world and you are the great ford and gate for all departed souls. Unworthy and unhappy (are) the dark beings who do not believe in you and who have averted their eyes

---

132 Augustine, *Ep. 236* (§ 2) to Deuterius, in Lieu 2010, 91. See also Gardner and Lieu 2004, 244–45 (no 81, *Augustine on Manichaean ethics*).

133 Augustine, *Faust.* 20.6 (*NPNF*[1] 4: 437).

134 Augustine, *Haer.* 46.18, in Gardner and Lieu 2004, 191. See also Lieu 1994a, 294.

135 *CMC* 128.5–12 (Koenen and Römer, 92): [ἐκήρυ]ξα δὲ αὐτῷ τὴν | [ἀνάπα]υσιν καὶ τὰς ἐντο[λὰς κα]ὶ τὴν εἰς τοὺς φω[στῆρα]ς προσκύνησιν. Cf. Colditz 2015, 55.

and their gaze from you. Help me, great light god, and by our hand give help and improvement to this girl, so that she may receive grace, and that there will be a new gate and a land of liberation for the patient souls, for whom redemption is at hand."[136]

Apart from the Manichaean Elect and missionaries, the Manichaean catechumens had among their primary duties to pray to the sun and the moon. As we read in the *Kephalaia*:

> The first work of the catechumenate that he does is fasting, prayer, and almsgiving. Now, [...] the pra[yer is this]: he can pray to the sun and the moon, the great li[ght-givers.[137]

According to the famous *Prayer of Emanations* the Manichaean believer prostrated and glorified all the divine beings of the Manichaean pantheon that were classified into ten groups. The classification followed "a kind of descent in the divine hierarchy from the eternal realm to the present and immediate".[138] The sixth prostration and prayer was devoted to the two luminaries.

> I worship and glorify the great light-givers, both sun and moon and the virtuous powers in them: Which by wisdom conquer the antagonists and illuminate the entire order, and of all oversee and judge the world, and conduct the victorious souls into the great aeon of light.[139]

It has been pointed out already by Jenkins (the first editor of the text), that the *Prayer of Emanations* had to be recited in a liturgical context. As Jenkins notes (1995), "to judge from the material and the contents, the text was in all likelihood prepared for liturgical purposes [...] This argument for the liturgical use of the board is strengthened by its content".[140] Recently, Iain Gardner supported the view that the *Prayer of Emanations* was the daily prayers of the Manichaean catechumens, which they accompanied by physical prostrations. Indeed, as Gardner remarks, "the text must have been composed in Aramaic, and most probably by Mani himself".[141]

---

136   Lieu 1994a, 31; cf. Lieu 1992, 105–06, fn. 134.
137   *1Keph.* 80 (Gardner, 202).
138   Gardner 2011, 247.
139   Gardner 2007a, 121–22.
140   Jenkins 1995, 248.
141   Gardner 2011, 259.

By combining the testimonies of our sources with modern research becomes apparent that what our authors describe was the daily prayers of the Manichaean catechumens. It is worth keeping in mind for the following discussion (because it touches on the question of Manichaean secrecy) that sun and moon worshiping is nearly the only ritual that our sources appear to know something about.

2.3.2   The *Sacred Meal* of the Elect

As has been shown above, the great luminaries (sun and moon) undertook the task of liberating the entrapped divine element in the material world at a macrocosmic scale. At the microcosmic scale, this project was executed by the Elect Manichaeans who, during their sacred meal, released (by eating) the divine substance entrapped within food.[142]

Yet, according to Mani's teaching in the *Kephalaia*, the sun's "releasing action, by which it releases the living soul, is a full day ahead of all releasing actions!"[143]

2.3.2.1   *The Manichaean Ritual Meal According to East-Roman Sources*

Before proceeding to examine the sources, I would like to make it clear from the outset that the records concerning the ritual meal of the Elect, provided by the East-Roman anti-Manichaean sources, are actually very scant. In addition, it has to be noted that the testimonies of sources do not concern what took place during the ritual meal itself, but rather are a criticism of the relationship between Manichaean Elect and catechumens, prompted by what was happening during the ritual meal.

In Turbo's account a prayer is cited,[144] the so called 'Apology to the Bread' (ἡ πρὸς τὸν ἄρτον ... ἀπολογία) as this prayer is called by the source in which it is first recorded.[145] According to the text, the Manichaean catechumens

> if [...] have anything good to eat they offer it to those Elect; and when they [the Elect] want to chew bread, they first pray, saying this to the bread: "I did not harvest you nor grind you nor knead you nor put you in the oven; someone else made you and brought you to me; I am innocent

---

142   See for example: (1) Manichaean sources: *1Keph.* 79 (Concerning the Fasting of the Saints); *1Keph.* 81 (The Chapter of Fasting, for 2 it engenders a Host of Angels); *1Keph.* 93. (2) Augustine, *Ep. 236* (§ 2), cf. BeDuhn 2000b, 77 & Gardner and Lieu 2004, 244–45. See also Puech 1979, 235–294; BeDuhn 2011, 301–19, esp. 313–15.

143   *1Keph.* 65 (Gardner 1995, 171): "The strength that it gives to its limbs is a great strength, being mightier than all strengths!".

144   *AA* 10.5–7; Epiphanius, Pan. 66.28.7.

145   P.Rylands 3, Gr. 469 (Roberts 1938, 38–46; Gardner and Lieu 2004, 114–5; Lieu 2010, 36–37).

as I eat you". When he has said this to himself, he replies to the person who brought it: "I have prayed for you", and then the person goes.[146]

Cyril, in his sixth Catechetical lecture, cites the same prayer slightly differently:

> Then having received the bread into his hand (as some of them who have repented have confessed), the Manichaean says to the bread, "I did not make you;" and he utters curses against the Highest, and curses him that made (the bread), and thus eats what was made [...] And again he says, "I did not sow you; may he who sowed you be scattered! I did not reap you with a sickle; may the one who reaped you be reaped to death! I did not bake you with fire; may he who baked you be baked!" What a lovely return of kindness this is![147]

The earliest primary source which records a preliminary form of this prayer is the circular epistle against the sect of Manichaeans, attributed to Theonas, the bishop of Alexandria (282–300 CE):

> And the Manichaeans manifestly worship the creation (? and that which they say) in their psalms is an abomination to the lord ... (saying) "Neither have I cast it (sc. the bread) into the oven: another has brought me this and I have eaten it without guilt". Whence, we can easily conclude that the Manichaeans are filled with much madness; especially since this "Apology to the Bread" is the work of a man filled with much madness.[148]

---

146   *AA* 10.5–7 (Vermes, 54); Epiphanius, *Pan.*, 66.28.7 (GCS 37:65): καὶ ὅταν μέλλωσιν ἐσθίειν ἄρτον, προσεύχονται πρῶτον, οὕτω λέγοντες πρὸς τὸν ἄρτον· "οὔτε σε ἐγὼ ἐθέρισα οὔτε ἤλεσα οὔτε ἔθλιψά σε οὔτε εἰς κλίβανον ἔβαλον, ἀλλὰ ἄλλος ἐποίησε ταῦτα, καὶ ἤνεγκέ μοι· ἐγὼ ἀναιτίως ἔφαγον". καὶ ὅταν καθ᾽ ἑαυτὸν εἴπῃ ταῦτα, λέγει τῷ κατηχουμένῳ "ηὐξάμην ὑπὲρ σοῦ", καὶ οὕτως ἀφίσταται ἐκεῖνος.

147   Cyril, Catech. 6.32 (Reischl and Rupp 1848, 200, 202; Lieu 2010, 55): Εἶτα δεξάμενος εἰς χεῖρας τὸν ἄρτον, (ὡς οἱ ἐξ αὐτῶν μετανοήσαντες ἐξωμολογήσαντο), Ἐγώ σε οὐκ ἐποίησά, φησιν ὁ Μανιχαῖος τῷ ἄρτῳ· καὶ κατάρας πέμπει εἰς τὸν ὕψιστον, καὶ καταρᾶται τὸν πεποιηκότα, καὶ οὕτως ἐσθίει τὸ πεποιημένον. [...] Καὶ πάλιν, Ἐγώ σε οὐκ ἔσπειρά, φησι· σπαρείη ὁ σπείρας σε. Ἐγώ σε οὐκ ἐθέρισα δρεπάνοις· ἐκθερισθείη ὁ θερίσας σε. Ἐγώ σε πυρὶ οὐκ ὤπτησα· ὀπτηθείη ὁ ὀπτήσας σε ὀπτηθείη ὁ ὀπτήσας σε. Καλὰ τὰ ἀμοιβαῖα τῆς χάριτος.

148   P.Rylands 3, Gr. 469 (Roberts 1938, 38–46, 42–43; Lieu 2010, 36–37): [ταῦτα βδέλυγμά ἐστιν κ(υρί)]ῳ τῷ θεῷ· καὶ οἱ Μανιχ(εῖ)c δηλονότι προσκυ[νοῦσι τὴν κτίσιν] ἐν ταῖς ἐπαοιδαῖς βδέλυγμά ἐστιν κ(υρί)ῳ [... οὐδὲ εἰς κλείβα[νον ἔβαλον ἄλλος μοι ἤνε[γκε ταῦτα ἐγὼ] ἀν[α]ι[τίω]c ἔφαγον· ὅθεν εἰκότως ἐστιν γνῶναι ὅτι πολλῆς μανίας πεπλή[ρ]ωνται οἱ Μανιχῖc· καὶ μάλιστα, ἐπὶ καὶ ἡ πρὸc τὸν ἄρτον αὐτῶν, ἀπολογία ἔργον ἐστιν ἀν(θρώπ)ου πολλῆς μανίας πεπληρωμένου· Cf. Lieu 2010, 36–37; Gardner and Lieu 2004, 114–15.

Modern researchers unanimously agree that the offerings of the foods to the Elect by the catechumens and the prayer of the former (the Apology to the Bread) can be interpreted as a part of the sacred meal of the Elect. However, a prayer with the same words has not been found in genuine Manichaean sources. The only parallel we possess is Mani's praying over bread and salt in his *Homilies* (58.18–19), but the exact text is missing.[149] According to BeDuhn, the Manichaean ritual meal of the Elect consisted of two parts: (1) the offering of the food by the auditors to the Elect (alms-service), and (2) the central ritual of the holy meal, during which the auditors had to withdraw[150] and only the Elect could participate. It is probable that both the offerings and the prayer took place during the first phase of the ceremony (act of alms service).

It is difficult to discern when the delivery of alms ended, and the ritual of the meal started. What is certain is that they were both phases of the same ceremony. The ritual of the meal had to commence after the official offerings ended and the catechumens departed. As BeDuhn notes, the majority of the sources state that the catechumens brought their alms a little while before the beginning of the holy meal and not during the whole day.[151] They stayed there until a petitionary prayer over them took place, and after that they left. Both Iranian and Latin sources say that the Elect blessed the catechumens when the latter offered the food.[152] An Iranian fragment (M 580) also mentions that the catechumens were advised to ask the Elect to absolve their sins. However, in our texts, it is not clear whether the apology-prayer occurred during the offering of the alms by the catechumens, or just after the latter had departed. That there was a holy meal to the community is certain. Nevertheless, it is very difficult to reconstruct the whole ritual, due to lack of information for the main part of it, the liturgical meal.

I will further discuss the structure of the ritual in chapter [7]. What interests us here are the religious implications, which the anti-Manichaean authors stress, caused by Manichaean dualism and practiced through the Manichaean religious behaviour in the ritualized context of the holy meal.

---

149   BeDuhn 1996, 6. Cf. Lieu in Vermes 2001, 54, fn. 69.

150   From the few references we have at our disposal (177 M & Augustine) we assume that auditors probably were not present at the second phase of the ceremony itself. However, there is an exception, a monastic manuscript testimony which speaks of "specially appointed Auditors in serving the Elect and making sure that all was in order, before, during, and after the meal" (BeDuhn 2000b, 159).

151   BeDuhn 2000b, 143–147.

152   In *1Keph.* 115, there is a petitioner prayer and memorial over the catechumens that bring the offerings. Cf. BeDuhn 1996, 1–15, esp. 5–6.

2.3.2.1   *Criticism of East-Roman Anti-Manichaean Sources on*
           the Ritual Meal

As already indicated, our sources do not comment on the ritual meal as such. Their criticism mainly targets the dual structure of the Manichaean Church (the two classes), which the anti-Manichaean authors interpret as a relationship of exploitation of the catechumens by the Elect.

In commenting on the Apology to the Bread, Cyril notes that it is a curse rather than a prayer (blessing), pointing out the hypocrisy of those Manichaeans who exploit their feeders:

> The Manichaeans are children of laziness; they do not do any work and gobble up the possessions of those who do work; they welcome with smiling faces those who bring them food, but repay them with curses instead of blessings for when some simple person brings them [anything], he [the Manichaean] says, "Stand outside for a little while, and I will bless you." Then having received the bread into his hand, [...] he says to the bread, "I did not make you" [...] and curses him that made (the bread), and thus eats what is made.[153]

The same opinion is also shared by Epiphanius in his commentary on Turbo's Manichaean narrative:

> Their so-called Elect [Manicheans] [...] instruct their catechumens to feed these people generously. They offer their Elect all the necessities of life, so that ⟨whoever⟩ gives sustenance to Elect souls may appear supposedly pious. (5) But silly as it is to say, after receiving their food the Elect all but put a curse on the givers under the pretence of praying for them, by testifying to their wickedness rather than to their goodness. For they say: "I did not sow you. I did not reap you. I did not knead you. I did not put you into the oven. Someone else brought you to me and I eat. I am guiltless." (6) And if anything, they have stigmatized as evildoers the persons who feed them – which, indeed, is true.[154]

---

153   Cyril, *Catech.* 6.32,1–4/9 (Reischl and Rupp 1848, 200; Lieu 2010, 55, slightly altered): Ἀργίας ἔκγονοι Μανιχαῖοι, οἱ μὴ ἐργαζόμενοι καὶ τὰ τῶν ἐργαζομένων κατεσθίοντες· οἱ τοὺς προσφέροντας αὐτοῖς τὰ βρώματα μειδιῶσι προσώποις δεχόμενοι, καὶ ἀντὶ εὐλογιῶν κατάρας ἀποδίδοντες. Ὅταν γάρ τις αὐτοῖς [τι] προσενέγκῃ ἀνόητος, Μικρὸν ἔξω, φησί, στῆθι, καὶ εὐλογήσω σε. Εἶτα δεξάμενος εἰς χεῖρας τὸν ἄρτον, [...] Ἐγώ σε οὐκ ἐποίησά, φησιν ὁ Μανιχαῖος τῷ ἄρτῳ· [...] καὶ καταρᾶται τὸν πεποιηκότα, καὶ οὕτως ἐσθίει τὸ πεποιημένον. See also Cyril *Catech* 6.31.

154   Epiphanius, *Pan.* 66.53.4–6 (GCS 37:89–90; Williams, 278): οἱ ἐκλεκτοὶ αὐτῶν καλούμενοι [...] παρακελεύονται οὖν τοῖς αὐτῶν κατηχουμένοις τρέφειν αὐτοὺς δαψιλῶς. οἱ δὲ πᾶν ὁτιοῦν ἀναγκαῖον προσφέρουσι τοῖς ἐκλεκτοῖς ἑαυτῶν, ἵνα δῆθεν εὐσεβὴς ὀφθείη ⟨ὁ⟩ τρέφων τὰς ψυχὰς

In a similar fashion, Theodoret of Cyrrhus remarks:

> They consider all things animated beings, [including] fire, water, air, plants and seeds. On this account, those called "Perfect" among them did not break bread, or cut vegetables, but they stir up against those who do these things openly, as being bloodthirsty; yet, they eat the things cut and the things broken.
>
> Instead, you persist in your ingratitude, and launch insults, and you are afflicted with the disease of Manichaeus, who on the one hand is satisfied up with all kinds of food and drinks, and on the other hand reproaches those who supply them, the reapers, as well as the bakers, and curses those who cut the bread in two pieces, since he refuses to cut it; but he eats the slice.[155]

It is noteworthy that, in contrast to Epiphanius, Cyril and Theodoret (in his second text) do not clearly juxtapose the Elect with the catechumens. Instead the difference is made between those who do not work (whom they call Manichaeans) with those who work (farmers, bakers, etc.) in order to produce food which the Manichaeans consume.

That the Manichaean Elect simply exploited the hearers as a means of their support is also the target of Augustine's criticism.

> As for your not plucking fruits or pulling up vegetables yourselves, while you get your followers to pluck and pull and bring them to you, that you may confer benefits not only on those who bring the food but on the food which is brought, what thoughtful person can bear to hear this? For, first, it matters not whether you commit a crime yourself, or wish another to commit it for you. You deny that you wish this![156]

τὰς ἐκλελεγμένας. οἱ δὲ λαβόντες, ὡς γέλοιόν ἐστιν εἰπεῖν, προφάσει τοῦ εὔξασθαι ὑπὲρ τῶν ἐνη-νοχότων, μᾶλλον δὲ σχεδὸν κατάραν αὐτοῖς ἐπιτιθέασιν, ἐπιμαρτυρήσαντες αὐτοῖς κακίαν μᾶλλον ἢ ἀγαθωσύνην. φάσκουσι γὰρ οὕτως· ὅτι ἐγὼ οὐκ ἔσπειρά σε, οὐκ ἐθέρισά σε, οὐκ ἤλεσα, εἰς κλί-βανον οὐκ ἔβαλον. ἄλλος ἤνεγκε, καὶ ἔφαγον. ἀναίτιός εἰμι. καὶ μᾶλλον πονηροποιοὺς ὑπέδειξαν τοὺς ἑαυτῶν τροφεῖς. καὶ γὰρ ἀληθές.

155   Theodoret, *Haer.* (PG 83:380(C–D).42–47) (Cope, 130): Πάντα δὲ νομίζουσιν ἔμψυχα, καὶ τὸ πῦρ, καὶ τὸ ὕδωρ, καὶ τὸν ἀέρα, καὶ τὰ φυτά, καὶ τὰ σπέρματα. Οὗ δὴ χάριν οἱ καλούμενοι τέλειοι παρ᾽ αὐτοῖς, οὔτε ἄρτον κλῶσιν, οὔτε λάχανον τέμνουσιν, ἀλλὰ καὶ τοῖς ταῦτα δρῶσιν, ὡς μιαιφό-νοις προφανῶς ἐπαίρονται· ἐσθίουσι δὲ ὅμως τὰ τεμνόμενα καὶ τὰ κλώμενα. Cf. Theodoret, *De providentia orationes decem* (PG 83:581.28): ἀλλὰ μένεις ἀχάριστος, καὶ λοιδορούμενος, καὶ τὰ Μανιχαίου νοσῶν, ὃς σιτίων καὶ ποτῶν ἀπολαύων, λοιδορεῖται τοῖς χορηγοῦσι, καὶ θερισταῖς ὁμοῦ καὶ ἀρτοποιοῖς, καὶ τοῖς τὸν ἄρτον διχῇ τέμνουσιν ἐπαρᾶται, αὐτὸς τέμνειν μὲν οὐκ ἀνεχόμενος, ἐσθίων δὲ τὸ τεμνόμενον.

156   Augustine, *Mor. Manich.* 17.

From the Manichaean point of view however, this behaviour is related with another command, the "seal of the hands". According to it, the Manichaean Elect had "to avoid injury to water, fire, trees and living things [...] hence [the seal] bans the procurement of food" by the Elect.[157] Indeed, the Manichaean normative code of behaviour protected the Elect from injuring the *Living Self*, since it was a command forbidding the Elect from being preoccupied with the gathering, procurement, and preparation of food. One of the three principal commandments (seals) the Elect had to observe, was to "acquire 'the rest [of the] hands', so that he will keep his hand still before the Cross of Light".[158] The sin of injuring the *Living Self* and violating the "seal of the hands" was a task laid upon the hearers who were obliged by the religion's commandments to feed the Elect. One of the three primary duties of the catechumens was daily almsgiving to the Elect.[159]

Revealing in this respect is a Manichaean text which reflects the extent of anxiety catechumen Manichaeans had due to their task of providing alms-offerings for the Elect. A Manichaean catechumen confesses his fears, before the Manichaean congregation and Mani, that the pain inflicted upon the *Living Self* by him (through his offering to the Elect) be proved fatal for himself.

> I know that each time I would provide an alms/-offering for the Elect, I know and sense that [...] I awake pain for it in various / form [s ...] [...] Indeed, due to this my heart trembles. / I become very afraid. I will venture to this place to speak / befo[re] you. Perhaps the good I perform will not repay the sin I am doing to the living soul?[160]

Ecclesiological dualism also affected the soteriological perspective and expectations. Turbo's account defines three classes of people: the Elect, the hearers, and the unbelievers (outsiders).

The latter class consists of those who do not accept the two principles, clearly the outsiders, the non-Manichaeans. As Turbo states, the fate of the 'infidel', among them being those who follow the words of the Jewish prophets

---

157   Lieu 2010, xviii–xix. Augustine, *Mor. Manich.* in Lieu 2010, 75.
158   *1Keph.* 80, 192.3–193.22 (Gardner 1995, 201).
159   *1Keph.* 80 (Gardner 1995, 202): "The first work of the catechumenate that he does is fasting, prayer, and almsgiving. Now, [...] The alms]/giving also is this: he can place it [...] / in the holy one, and give it to them in righteous[ness ...] /.". The whole text: The Chapter of the Commandments of Righteousness (192,3–193,22, pp. 201–202).
160   *1Keph.* 93 (Gardner 1995, 242–45). A Catechumen asked the Apo/stle: When I would give an Offering to the Saints, shall I inflict a Wound on the Alms? Cf. Gardner's introductory comments on the moral of the chapter: "The catechumen must not be afraid of causing sin in the task of preparing and offering alms [...] The offering of alms is also a means for the salvation of the catechumen" (243).

(i.e. Jews and Christians), is to "die for all age, bound up within a heap of earth, since he has not learnt the knowledge of the paraclete".[161]

Anyone who does not possess the knowledge of the two principles or is not aware of the primordial mixture and the presence of the *Living Self* in the material world will suffer in the *Gehenna* in order to be educated. If necessary, they will suffer endless metempsychoses (μεταγγισμός) until the end of time and the final consummation:

> If a soul has gone forth which has not understood the truth, it is handed over to demons to tame it in hell-fire, and after it has been educated, it is transferred into other bodies to be tamed, and then it is thrown into that great fire until the final reckoning.[162]

In theory, the catechumens were atoned for any injury they had caused to the *Living Self* if they offered a steady living for the Elect. For this reason if they have anything good to eat they offer it to those Elect.[163] As Augustine explains, "the Elect get others to bring their food to them, that they may not be guilty of murder".[164] In turn, auditors are forgiven by serving the Elect, who liberate the divine substance from the foods.[165] However, in case they neglected their duties, they would be punished by successive reincarnations in catechumens' bodies. As the eschatological aim of each individual was the liberation from the "birth-and-death" cycle and the return to the primitive light, reincarnations (μεταγγισμός) counted as a punishment.

---

161 *AA* 11.3 (Vermes, 55–56). Epiphanius, *Pan.* 66.30.2 (GCS 37:67): καὶ εἴ τις ἀκολουθεῖ τοῖς λόγοις αὐτῶν [παρ' ὑμῖν προφητῶν] ἀποθνήσκει εἰς τοὺς αἰῶνας, δεδεμένος εἰς τὴν βῶλον, ὅτι οὐκ ἔμαθε τὴν γνῶσιν τοῦ παρακλήτου.

162 *AA* 11.2 (Vermes, 55). Epiphanius, *Pan.* 66.29.3 (GCS 37:66–67): καὶ ἐὰν ἐξέλθῃ ἡ ψυχὴ μὴ γνοῦσα τὴν ἀλήθειαν, παραδίδοται τοῖς δαίμοσιν ὅπως δαμάσωσιν αὐτὴν ἐν ταῖς γεένναις τοῦ πυρός, καὶ μετὰ τὴν παίδευσιν μεταγγίζεται εἰς ⟨ἕτερα⟩ σώματα, ἵνα δαμασθῇ, καὶ οὕτω βάλλεται εἰς τὸ μέγα πῦρ ἄχρι τῆς συντελείας. The Greek text here uses the term 'μεταγγισμός' instead of 'μετενσωμάτωσις' or 'μετεμψύχωσις'.

163 *AA* 10.5 (Vermes, 54). Epiphanius, *Pan.* 66.28.6 (GCS 37:65): καὶ διὰ τοῦτο εἴ τι κάλλιστον ἐν βρώμασι τοῖς ἐκλεκτοῖς προσφέρουσι. The same belief is also testified by Manichaean sources, see *1Keph.* 91 and 127 and *2PsB.* 111.25. Cf. Brand 2019, 202.

164 Augustine, *Faust.* b4, 6.8.

165 Augustine, *Haer.* 46. Augustine, *Mor. Manich.* 61.

Anyone who has not given his food to the Elect will be subjected to the punishments of hell and is to be transformed into the bodies of catechumens, until he has suffered many miseries.[166]

Nevertheless, in the texts of the Church Fathers it is not always clear whether the catechumens had the option of atonement through their offerings, or whether they had to undergo further painful reincarnation in what they had killed. As Turbo emphasizes, anyone who would harm any kind of life would suffer the same fate in retribution of his misconduct.

I shall also tell you how souls are transmitted to other bodies. First of all a small part of it is purified; then it is transmitted into a dog or a camel or the body of another animal. But if it has committed murder, a soul is transferred into the bodies of lepers; if it has cut the harvest, into those of the dumb. [...] Harvesters who gather the harvest are compared with the princes [of darkness] [...] For that reason it is necessary for them to be transformed into hay or beans or grain or corn or vegetables, so that they too are cut down and harvested. Anyone who chews bread must also be chewed by becoming bread. He who kills a chicken must also become a chicken himself, or if a mouse he too will be a mouse.[167]

Cyril ridicules the Manichaean teachings concerning reincarnation, and considers them irrational and absurd, as worthy of laughter, and of censure and of dishonour.

Let no one join himself to the soul-wasting Manichees [...] who teach, that he who plucks up a herb, is changed into it. For if he who crops a herb, or any vegetable, is changed into it, into how many will husbandmen [farmers] and the tribe [children] of gardeners be changed? Into how many doth the gardener put his sickle, as we see; – into which then

---

166 AA 10.5; Epiphanius, *Pan.* 66.28.6 (GCS 37:64–65): καὶ εἴ τις οὐ δίδωσι τοῖς ἐκλεκτοῖς αὐτοῦ εὐσέβειαν, κολασθήσεται εἰς τὰς γεέννας καὶ μετενσωματοῦται εἰς κατηχουμένων σώματα, ἕως οὗ δῷ εὐσεβείας πολλάς.

167 AA 10.1–3 (Vermes, 52–53). Epiphanius, *Pan.* 66.28.1–5: (GCS 37:62–64): Ἐρῶ δὲ ὑμῖν καὶ τοῦτο, πῶς μεταγγίζεται ἡ ψυχὴ εἰς ἕτερα σώματα. πρῶτον καθαρίζεται μικρόν τι ἀπ᾽ αὐτῆς, εἶτα μεταγγίζεται εἰς κυνὸς ἢ εἰς καμήλου ἢ εἰς ἑτέρου ζῴου σῶμα. ἐὰν δὲ ᾖ πεφονευκυῖα ψυχή, εἰς κελεφῶν σώματα μεταφέρεται· ἐὰν δὲ θερίσασα εὑρεθῇ, εἰς μογγιλάλους. [...] οἱ δὲ θερισταί, ὅσοι θερίζουσιν, ἐοίκασι τοῖς ἄρχουσι [...] διὸ ἀνάγκη αὐτοὺς μεταγγισθῆναι εἰς χόρτον ἢ εἰς φασήλια ἢ εἰς κριθὴν ἢ εἰς στάχυν ἢ εἰς λάχανα, ἵνα ⟨καὶ αὐτοὶ⟩ θερισθῶσι καὶ κοπῶσι. καὶ εἴ τις πάλιν ἐσθίει ἄρτον, ἀνάγκη καὶ αὐτὸν βρωθῆναι ἄρτον γενόμενον. εἴ τις φονεύσει ὀρνίθιον, ⟨καὶ αὐτός⟩ ὀρνίθιον ἔσται· εἴ τις φονεύσει μῦν, καὶ αὐτὸς μῦς ἔσται.

of these is he transformed? Ridiculous doctrines truly, and fraught with their own condemnation and shame! A shepherd both sacrifices a sheep and slays a wolf; into which is he changed? Many men have both netted fishes and limed birds; into which are they changed?[168]

Augustine becomes extremely caustic when commenting upon the 'racist' Manichaean soteriology. The best scenario for the reincarnation of the auditors, he says, was to reincarnate in melons and cucumbers (!) if they were diligent in their duties as hearers.[169]

This (ecclesiological) eclecticism is also attested in the Manichaean texts.[170] The Elect are ascertained to rise to heaven upon their death. The lifestyle suggested by Mani for the Elect is a remedy for the "inherent pathology" of their body and its materiality.[171] Thus, after their death, the Elect are rewarded with their ascent to paradise, while the catechumens will undergo further reincarnations. However, the hearers, because they supported the Manichaean religion, were in a more favourable position than the outsiders and in that sense, they were in a way Elect too.[172] Instead, those souls who were subjugated to evil (the outsiders) "have become alienated from the life and freedom of the sacred light. Therefore, they cannot be taken back into those peaceful kingdoms, but will be confined in the terrible 'mass'".[173]

According to the *sc*, the converted Manichaean had to anathematize all those who supported transmigration as a punishment for not observing the *anapausis* of the hands.

---

168   Cyril, *Catech.* 6.31 (Reischl and Rupp 1848, 200; LFHCC, 75–76): τοῖς διδάσκουσιν, ὅτι ὁ τήνδε τὴν βοτάνην ἐκτίλλων, εἰς αὐτὴν μεταβάλλεται. Εἰ γὰρ ὁ ἐκτέμνων βοτάνας ἤ τι τῶν λαχάνων, εἰς τοῦτο μεταβάλλεται, γεωργοὶ καὶ κηπουρῶν παῖδες εἰς πόσα μεταβληθήσονται; Κατὰ τοσούτων ὁ κηπουρὸς ἤνεγκε τὴν δρεπάνην, ὡς ὁρῶμεν· εἰς ποῖα ἄρα μεταβάλλεται; Γέλωτος ἀληθῶς τὰ διδάγματα καὶ καταγνώσεως πλήρη καὶ αἰσχύνης. Ὁ αὐτὸς ἀνὴρ ποιμὴν ὢν προβάτων, καὶ πρόβατον ἔθυσε καὶ λύκον ἀπέκτεινεν· εἰς ποῖον ἄρα μεταβάλλεται; Πολλοὶ τῶν ἀνθρώπων ἰχθύας ἐσαγήνευσαν, καὶ ὄρνεα ἴξευσαν· εἰς ποῖον ἄρα μεταβάλλονται οἱ τῆς ἁρπαγῆς; cf. Nemesius of Emesa, *De natura hominis* 2.33.10–19 (Morani, 32): καὶ οὕτω τὴν οὐσίαν αὐτῆς κατατέμνοντες καὶ σωματικὴν ἀποφαίνοντες καὶ πάθεσιν ὑποβάλλοντες ἀθάνατον εἶναί φασι. περιπίπτουσι δὲ καὶ τοῖς ἐναντίοις. φάσκοντες γὰρ ἀνατρέχειν τὰς μεμολυσμένας ψυχὰς ἐπὶ τὰ στοιχεῖα καὶ συγκαταμίγνυσθαι ἀλλήλαις, πάλιν αὐτὰς ἐν ταῖς μετενσωματώσεσί φασι τιμωρεῖσθαι κατὰ τὸ μέγεθος τῶν ἁμαρτημάτων ἑνοῦντες αὐτὰς καὶ πάλιν χωρίζοντες καθ' ὑπόστασιν.

169   Augustine, *Faust.* 5.10.

170   Lieu 1994a, 289.

171   BeDuhn 2000b, 258.

172   BeDuhn 2000b, 103 (216–17).

173   Augustine, *Fund.*, in Gardner and Lieu 2004 (no 53), 171–72.

And (I anathematize) those who introduce metempsychosis which they call transmigration (μεταγγισμός) and those who suppose that grass and plants and water and other things without souls in fact all have them and think that those who pluck corn or barley or grass or vegetables are transformed into them in order that they may suffer the same and that harvesters and bread-makers are accursed, and who call us Christians who do not accept these stinking myths simpletons.[174]

As is illustrated by the anathema, Manichaeans considered those who do not accept these beliefs as naive. Moreover, the contradistinction between the Christian and Manichaean identity is also emphasized here.

What is striking, is that both Christian and pagan authors in their criticism of the Manichaean sacred meal (and fasting), do not comment at all on the redemptive theology which lies behind it.[175] References and criticism of the East-Roman sources to the Manichaean ritual meal are restricted to the first phase of the ritual (the phase of almsgiving), and target the relationship of exploitation between the two classes. Our sources do not comment at all on the objective, the very purpose of the sacred meal itself (second phase), that the ultimate goal of the ritual was the liberation of the trapped divine elements within food, by the Elect. Indeed, Augustine is merciless in his frequent criticism of the Manichaean belief that the Elect, by their teeth and their stomachs, liberate the divine substance, becoming likewise the saviours of God: "And, if some [Manichaean] 'saint' ate this fig [...] he would blend it in his bowels and breathe forth angels from it, even groaning in prayer and belching up little pieces of God".[176]

The beliefs and practices that Augustine attributes to the Manichaeans are also attested in Manichaean sources. According to the *Kephalaia*, the ultimate aim of the fasting of the Elect Manichaeans was the preparation of their bodies, so that during the sacred meal they could function as 'machines' which

---

174 *SC*, ch. 6 (Lieu, 1994a, 248): καὶ τοὺς μετεμψύχωσιν, ἣν αὐτοὶ καλοῦσι μεταγγισμόν, εἰσηγουμένους, καὶ τοὺς τὰς βοτάνας καὶ τὰ φυτὰ καὶ τὸ ὕδωρ καὶ τὰ ἄλλα ἄψυχα πάντα ἔμψυχα εἶναι
ὑπολαμβάνοντας, καὶ τοὺς τὸν σῖτον ἢ κριθὴν ἢ βοτάνας ἢ λάχανα τίλλοντας εἰς ἐκεῖνα μεταβάλλεσθαι οἰομένους, ἵνα τὰ ὅμοια πάθωσι, καὶ τοὺς θεριστὰς καὶ τοὺς ἀρτοποιοὺς καταρωμένους
καὶ ἡμᾶς τοὺς Χριστιανοὺς τοὺς μὴ παραδεχομένους τοὺς ὀδωδότας μύθους τούτους ἀπλαρίους
ἀποκαλοῦντας.

175 The question of this silence is worth investigating. One naturally wonders how the above beliefs escaped the criticism of the East-Roman authors. Cf. Lieu 2010.

176 Augustine, *Conf.* 3.10(18) in Lieu 2010, 83–85. Cf. Augustine, *De Nat. bon.* 44.20, 45; Augustine, *Ep. 236* (§ 2); Augustine, *Mor. Manich.* 15, 17 (Description of the Symbol of the Hands Among the Manichaeans); Augustine, *Haer.* 46; Augustine, *Commentary on Psalm* 140.12; Augustine, *Faust.* 31.4. See also Gardner and Lieu 2004, 245.

would liberate the divine substance. Thus, the effectiveness of the sacred meal depended on whether the Elect strictly observed the seals of mouth and hands.[177] As Mani explains, what the other sects of the world are doing wrong in their fasting and rituals is that they do not keep the seals of mouth and of hands, which will finally open the gates for the liberation of the divine substance trapped within the alms-offerings.[178] In contrast to other Churches, in the Manichaean Church, it is due to the observation of the commandments that the divine light "is healed by the Elect, by the psalms [and] prayers and ble[ssings]".[179]

As Gardner underlines, "for the Manichaeans the human body and its digestive processes worked in a very literal way so as to purify the divine light, and thus to discard the evil waste matter".[180]

2.3.3   Holy-Oil (?)
Apart from the Apology to the Bread, Turbo's narration refers to what he calls the end of the Elect's meal. He quotes Mani's words:

> Mani has commanded only his Elect, of whom there are no more than seven, "When you finish eating, pray and put on your heads oil which has been exorcized with many names, as a support for this faith." The names have not been revealed to me for only the seven employ them.[181]

Could this mystery that Turbo refers to be equivalent to the Christian mystery of the Holy Oil? In the early Christian Church, this mystery – as all other mysteries – was connected to the Holy Liturgy and took place during the

---

177   *1Keph.* 79: 'Concerning the Fasting of the Saints' (191.9–192.3). Cf. Gardner and Lieu 2004, no 79 (The profits of fasting). *1Keph.* 94, 240.1–12.

178   *1Keph.* 87, 217.1–11.

179   *1Keph.* 93, 238.2–4, p. 244.

180   Gardner 1995, 202, cf. *1Keph.* 81, 193,23–194. 13 (The Chapter of Fasting, for it engenders a Host of Angels) (Gardner 1995, 203).

181   Epiphanius, *Pan.* 66.30.3 (GCS 37:67–68; Williams, 259): ἐνετείλατο δὲ τοῖς ἐκλεκτοῖς αὐτοῦ μόνοις, οὐ πλέον ἑπτὰ οὖσι τὸν ἀριθμόν· ἐὰν παύσησθε ἐσθίοντες, εὔχεσθε καὶ βάλλετε ἐπὶ τῆς κεφαλῆς ἔλαιον ἐξωρκισμένον ὀνόμασι πολλοῖς, πρὸς στηριγμὸν τῆς πίστεως ταύτης. τὰ δὲ ὀνόματά μοι οὐκ ἐφανερώθη· μόνοι γὰρ οἱ ἑπτὰ τούτοις χρῶνται. AA 11.4 (Vermes, 56): He also instructed only his elect, who are not more than seven in number, that when they have stopped eating they should pray and put on their head olive oil over which they have sworn an oath, invoking many names to confirm this pledge. But he did not reveal the names to me, for only those seven use these names. Cf. AA 63.5 (Vermes, 143): "Finally early one morning he climbed a high roof top, where he began to invoke certain names which Turbo told us only seven of the elect have been taught".

meeting for the *agapai* (ἀγάπαι) as part of it. The aim of the Holy Oil mystery was the strengthening of faith (στηριγμὸν τῆς πίστεως), the awareness of the sinful, and the therapy of the bodily and the psychic illnesses. As is indicated in the above passage, the use of oil by the Manichaean Elect had the same purpose of faith strengthening (πρὸς στηριγμὸν τῆς πίστεως), as in Christianity.

2.3.4 The Ceremony of the 'Dried Fig'

2.3.4.1 *Text and Translation*

Cyril in his sixth Catechetical lecture, apart from the Apology to the Bread and the olive-oil rite (?), records an occult ritual, the identity of which remains a true mystery: the ceremony of the dried fig (τῆς ἰσχάδος).[182] As mentioned in ch.[1], a part, or even the whole chapter that describes the ritual was heavily abridged in a series of English translations.[183] This protracted concealment partly explains the absence of references or of any commentary of the text in modern scholarship until Van Oort's publication in 2016.

Cyril is the only author in Greek anti-Manichaica who mentions this particular ceremony; the testimony of Peter of Sicily repeats Cyril's account.[184] Just after his reference to the Manichaean holy meal and his critique about the feeding of the Elect by the hearers (6.32), Cyril states:

> These are also great evils, but yet small in comparison with the others. *I do not dare give an account about their λουτρὸν of men and women. I do not dare say in what they baptise the dried fig they give to their wretched. But I will only reveal it speaking symbolically (through symbols/signs). Let men think about those (things/products) of the wet dreams (= nocturnal emissions), and women of the menstruation/menses.* We truly pollute our mouth speaking about these things. For the fornicator, in a moment/an hour, because of lust, performs the deed. However, he [soon] condemns his deed, realizing that, as a defiled, he is in need of λουτρῶν and he acknowledges that his deed is abominable/loathsome. But the Manichaean places these things in the middle of the altar, as/where he thinks [right], and defiles both his mouth and his tongue.[185]

---

182 Cyril, *Catech.* 6.33.

183 See ch.[1], section 2.3 (Cyril of Jerusalem).

184 Peter of Sicily, *Hist. ref. Man.* 33, ch. 72.

185 Cyril, *Catech.* 6.33 (Reischl and Rupp 1848, 202): Μεγάλα μὲν κακὰ καὶ ταῦτα, ἀλλ᾽ ἔτι μικρὰ πρὸς τὰ ἄλλα. Οὐ τολμῶ ἐπὶ ἀνδρῶν καὶ γυναικῶν τὸ λουτρὸν αὐτῶν διηγήσασθαι. Οὐ τολμῶ εἰπεῖν, τίνι ἐμβάπτοντες τὴν ἰσχάδα, διδόασι τοῖς ἀθλίοις. Διὰ συσσήμων δὲ μόνον δηλούσθω. Ἄνδρες γὰρ τὰ ἐν τοῖς ἐνυπνιασμοῖς ἐνθυμείσθωσαν, καὶ γυναῖκες τὰ ἐν ἀφέδροις. Μιαίνομεν ἀληθῶς καὶ τὸ στόμα, ταῦτα λέγοντες. [...] Ὁ μὲν γὰρ πορνεύσας, πρὸς μίαν ὥραν δι᾽ ἐπιθυμίαν

In the above translation I purposely kept the Greek form λουτρὸν/ῶν, because this is the key word for the interpretation of the text and, therefore, for the understanding of the context in which Cyril places the ritual. Apart from its literal interpretation (i.e. washing or bath), 'λουτρόν' in the religious language of the era meant baptism, 'baptism of tears' (confession) and 'baptism of blood' (martyrdom).[186] In all English translations the word λουτρὸν is translated as baptism. The latter is problematic, for as is known the Manichaeans did not practice any baptism in water.[187] Before proceeding to the interpretation of the text, I will present other parallel testimonies that exist in anti-Manichaean literature.

2.3.4.2   Parallel Testimonies in Greek Anti-Manichaean Literature
Cyril himself refers once again to the ceremony of the dried fig at another point of the sixth catechesis where he talks about the roof-top ritual performed by Terebinthus, which cost him his life.

> Terebinthus [...] having gone up to the roof-top of the house, and invoked the daemons of the air, whom the Manichaeans to this day invoke upon their detestable ceremony of the fig.[188]

By this testimony, Cyril provides additional information on the puzzle of the rite: attaching to it a flavour of magic, Cyril reveals that during the ceremony the aerial demons were invoked,[189] and that the ritual was performed until his days.

Other references to a ceremony under the name *dried fig*, in Greek (or Latin) literature, do not exist. However, Cyril is neither the first nor the only one to accuse the Manichaeans of performing licentious practices during their rituals. The anonymous Alexandrian author of the encyclical epistle is the first

---

τελεῖ τὴν πρᾶξιν· καταγινώσκων δὲ τῆς πράξεως, ὡς μιανθεὶς οἶδε λουτρῶν ἐπιδεόμενος, καὶ γινώσκει τῆς πράξεως τὸ μυσαρόν. Ὁ δὲ Μανιχαῖος θυσιαστηρίου μέσον, οὗ νομίζει, τίθησι ταῦτα, καὶ μιαίνει καὶ τὸ στόμα καὶ τὴν γλῶσσαν. The omitted sentences in previous translations are in italic. See also the translations by Fox and Sheldon (Lieu 2010, 55) and Van Oort 2016b, 432.

186   The second time that the word λουτρῶν is mentioned could mean both washing and confession (baptism of tears).

187   Stroumsa 1999, 405–20.

188   Cyril, *Catech.* 6.23 (Reischl and Rupp 1848, 186; LFHCC, 71): Τερέβινθος [...] ἐπὶ δώματος ἀνελθών, καὶ προσκαλεσάμενος τοὺς ἀερίους δαίμονας, οὓς οἱ Μανιχαῖοι μέχρι σήμερον ἐπὶ τῆς μυσαρᾶς αὐτῶν ἰσχάδος ἐπικαλοῦνται.

189   Sacrilege and magic were often interwoven. Cf. the anti-Manichaean law Cod. theod. 16.5.65.

who accuses Manichaeans of using the *Electae*'s menstrual blood during their rites. As the author warns his readers:

> We may be on our guard [...] particularly against those women whom they call "Elect" and whom they hold in honour, manifestly because they require their menstrual blood for the abominations of their madness.[190]

In the rest of Greek literature, there are another two references to Manichaean practices that combine magic and orgies. As Theodoret points out,

> They especially use magic in practicing their impious mysteries. In this way, I tell you, their teaching is hard to eradicate, and it is extremely difficult to remove anyone who has partaken of their loathsome orgies from the activity of the soul-destroying demons, who bind their souls by the spells of those initiating them.[191]

It is not improbable that Theodoret, here, is denoting the dried fig ritual.

The Manichaean mysteries were also anathematized and condemned as abominable, unclean, and magic-filled by the ex-Manichaeans during the ritual of their conversion: "I anathematize and condemn [...] and their abominable and unclean and magic-filled mysteries".[192] Another practice attributed to Manichaeans in the *sc*, which had to be anathematized, was that of washing themselves in their own urine instead of water.

> So I anathematize these and I curse (them) as being unclean in their souls and bodies, with all the rest of their evils, and as not suffering their

---

190 P.Rylands 3, Gr. 469 (Roberts, 1938; Lieu, 2010, 36–37): ἐπιτηρῶμεν [...] μάλιστα τὰς λεγομέ- νας παρ' αὐτοῖς ἐκλεκτάς, ἃς ἐν τιμῇ ἔχουσιν διὰ τὸ δηλονότι χρῄζειν αὐτοὺς τοῦ ἀπὸ τῆς ἀφέδρου αἵματος αὐτῶν εἰς τὰ τῆς μανίας αὐτῶν μυσάγματα.

191 Theodoret, *Haer.* (PG 83:380.48–53) (Lieu 2010, 95–97): Κέχρηνται δὲ καὶ γοητείαις διαφερόν-τως, τὰ δυσαγῆ αὐτῶν ἐκτελοῦντες μυστήρια· ταύτῃτοι καὶ δυσέκνιπτος αὐτῶν ἡ διδασκαλία, καὶ τὸν τῶν μυσαρῶν ὀργίων μετειληχότα λίαν ἐστὶ δυσχερὲς μετατιθέναι τῆς τῶν ψυχοφθόρων ἐνεργείας δαιμόνων, ταῖς τῶν τελούντων ἐπῳδαῖς τὰς ἐκείνων καταδεσμούντων ψυχάς. In antiq-uity the word orgies meant the 'secret rites' of Demeter, Orpheus, Cabeiri, Cybele and most commonly, the rites/mysteries of Dionysus-Bacchus.

192 *sc*, ch. 7 (Lieu 2010, 124–25): ἀναθεματίζω καὶ καταθεματίζω [...] καὶ τὰ μυσαρὰ τού-των καὶ ἀκάθαρτα καὶ γοητείας πλήρη μυστήρια. The same is reproduced by the *LAF* (PG 1:1465A–1465D). Both Cyril and *sc* use the word μυσαρὰ in order to characterize the Manichaean mysteries.

filth to be washed away by water lest, they say, the water be defiled, but even polluting themselves with their own urine.[193]

According to Kessler, by urine one could mean 'semen'. However, his suggestion is not supported by the specific context of the text, where the discussion clearly concerns the act of washing.[194]

2.3.4.3   *The Charge of Sacrilege in Anti-Manichaean Laws*

As examined in ch.[3], sacrilege[195] was one of the capital crimes due to which Manichaeism was characterized as a public crime[196] and by which Manichaeans were deprived of the status of Roman citizenship.[197] Expressions that define the content of the crime of sacrilege exist in a series of laws.[198] The overall impression is that during these 'sacrilegious rites'[199] the 'elements' were 'injured' by magic. According to the law of 428, the Manichaeans had to be expelled "from municipalities, since to all these must be left no place wherein even on the very elements may be made an injury".[200]

---

193   *sc*, ch. 7. (Lieu 2010, 122–23 and Lieu 1994a, 250): Τούτους οὖν ἀναθεματίζω καὶ καταθεματίζω ἀκαθάρτους ὄντας, σὺν τοῖς ἄλλοις αὐτῶν κακοῖς, τὰς ψυχὰς καὶ τὰ σώματα καὶ μὴ ἀνεχομένους τὰς ῥυπαρίας αὐτῶν ὕδατι ἀποπλύνειν, ἵνα μή, φασίν, τὸ ὕδωρ μολυνθῆναι, ἀλλὰ καὶ τοῖς οἰκείοις οὔροις ἑαυτοὺς μιαίνοντας. See also the same in *LAF* (PG 1:1461/1472A, 1465), cf. Lieu 2010, 138.

194   Kessler in Lieu 1994a: 293–94. In the *LAF* the converted Manichaeans had also to condemn the immoral practices that took place at the Feast of the Bema. However, according to Lieu (1994a, 225), this "must now be seen as Byzantine polemics against Paulicians". Anastasius of Sinai (*Hexaemeron* 7b. 530–32) also speaks about Manichaean mysteries where men and women congregate nude in imitation of Adam and Eve (6th/8th?): Μανιχαῖοι δὲ ὁμοῦ τε καὶ ἄνδρες καὶ γυναῖκες γυμνοὶ ἐν ταῖς αὐτῶν ἐκκλησίαις συνάγονται κατὰ μίμησιν τοῦ Ἀδὰμ καὶ τῆς Εὔας.

195   In the laws of Cod. theod. 9.38.7 (384) and Cod. theod. 9.38.8 (385), Theodosius I classifies sacrilege among the capital crimes. Sacrilege was also the offense that forced Theodosius I to innovate with the retroactivity of his law (16.5.7, 381).

196   Cod. theod. 16.5.40 (407).

197   Cod. theod. 16.5.7 (381).

198   Cod. theod. 16.5.9 (382); 16.5.11 (383); 16.5.38 (405); 16.5.43 (408); 16.5.65 (428); *NVal.* 18 (445); 16.5.35; 16.5.38; Cod. justin. 1.5.16.

199   Cod. theod. 16.5.41. See also *NVal.* 18 (Pharr, 531): "obscene to tell and to hear" and "so detestable an outrage to the Divinity of God".

200   Cod. theod. 16.5.65 (428) (Coleman-Norton 1966, 2, 643). Cf. the same law in Cod. justin. (Cod. justin. 1.5.5).

2.3.4.4   *Parallel Testimonies by Augustine*

Augustine too charges Manichaeans with the crime of sacrilege and of the consumption of human semen during their ritual meal.[201] As he states in *De haeresibus*, the Manichaean "Elect are forced to consume a sort of eucharist sprinkled with human seed in order that the divine substance may be freed".[202] Manichaeans themselves, Augustine comments, rejected these accusations, clarifying that these practices were performed by some other groups (e.g. Catharists); yet they conceded, that "the Manichaean books" were "common to all of them".[203] These books, especially the myth of the *Seduction of the Archons*, Augustine believed, were "the source of the [aforementioned] obscene practices".[204] The *Seduction of the Archons* was a scene from the Manichaean cosmogonic myth cited in the *Thesaurus*.[205] According to it, the divine powers "exploiting the 'deadly unclean lust'" of the archons of evil appeared before them as attractive beautiful males and females, "so that the divine substance which is imprisoned in them may be set free and escape".[206] So, as Augustine explains, the Manichaeans

> imagine that they are imitating divine powers to the highest degree and so they attempt to purge a part of their god, which they really believe is held [...] in human seed as it is in all celestial and terrestrial bodies, and in the seeds of all things.[207]

Augustine adds that "some of them [who] were brought to trial [...] admitted that this is no sacrament, but a sacrilege".[208] As Augustine argues in *De moribus Manichaeorum*, even if Manichaeans did not perform these things of which they were accused, and instead only claimed that their Elect set free the *Living Soul* from all seeds by eating and drinking (their food), this would inevitably raise suspicion; one would reasonably think that this purification concerned not only plant but also animal and human seeds. Continuing his argumentation, Augustine considers it likely that this purification took place during the secret assemblies of the Elect.

---

201   Augustine, *Haer.* 46.9–10; *Mor. Manich.* 18.66 and 19.70 (pp. 150.17–151.5); *Nat. bon.* 45–47.
202   Augustine, *Haer.* 46.9–10, in Gardner and Lieu 2004, 144–45, 144.
203   Augustine, *Haer.* 46.9–10, in Gardner and Lieu 2004, 145.
204   Augustine, *Haer.* 46.9–10, in Gardner and Lieu 2004, 145.
205   Tardieu 2008, 37; Lieu 2010, 149; Reeves 2011, 108–109.
206   Augustine, *Haer.* 46.10. Cf. Tardieu 2008, 37.
207   Augustine, *Haer.* 46.10. Cf. Tardieu 2008, 37.
208   Augustine, *Haer.* 46.10. Cf. Tardieu 2008, 37.

And as your followers cannot bring these seeds to you for purification, who will not suspect that you make this purification secretly among yourselves, and hide it from your followers, in case they should leave you?[209]

Augustine's accusations of immorality were not concealed such as Cyril's; however, no scientific work has taken them seriously into account, with the exception of Van Oort's recent publications.[210] As the determining factor in this direction, Van Oort considers Alfaric's contribution, who, commenting on the "historical reliability of the described" events in *Haer.* 46. 9–10 concludes: "Leur Eucharistie aspergée de semence humaine semble aussi légendaire que le meurtre rituel si souvent imputé aux Chrétiens pendant les premiers siècles".[211] Therefore, Van Oort points out, "One gets the impression that, since Alfaric, most researchers have subscribed to this opinion and hence considered the subject to be legendary".[212]

2.3.4.5   *Parallel Accusations for Other Religious Groups*
It is true, that to blame religious opponents for immorality was "a fairly standard" accusation at that time.[213] Epiphanius, for instance, makes similar accusations against the Nicolaitans[214] and a group of 'Gnostics', known as Borborites (or Barbelognostics, or Stratiotics, etc.).[215] However, although the chapter of *Panarion against the Manichaeans* is by far the longest of the chapters devoted to the above 'heretics',[216] Epiphanius nowhere implies that the Manichaeans exercised similar practices during their rituals. This, firstly, challenges Cyril's credibility, and secondly indicates that Epiphanius was not aware of the content of Cyril's *Catecheses* (something that has been highlighted in ch.[2]). The latter applies also to the rest of the authors who wrote against Manichaeans until the ninth century, when Photius and Peter of Sicily clearly name Cyril as their source. So, it seems that Cyril's passage was neglected not only by contemporary researchers but also by Byzantine anti-Manichaean authors.[217]

---

209   Augustine, *Mor. Manich.* 18.66. See also *Nat. bon.* 45–47.
210   For a detailed overview of the fate of the passage in modern literature see Van Oort, 2016a 200–02.
211   Van Oort 2016a, 201.
212   Van Oort 2016a, 201.
213   Lieu 1992, 143 fn. 131.
214   Epiphanius, *Pan.* 25.2.2–3.2 (v. 1, pp. 268–274, esp. 269.23–270.2).
215   Epiphanius, *Pan.* 26 (v. 1, pp. 275–300, esp. 280.10 [ch. 4]–282.13).
216   Five times longer than the chapter devoted to Borborites etc., and twelve times longer than the respective to Nicolaitans. See also Coyle 2009a, 164–165.
217   An exception to this, likely, was Theodoret of Cyrrhus, see ch.[5], fn. 191.

Was, then, Cyril's account just a slander? Even if this were the case, the stereotypes of modern society and the taboos of contemporary researchers should not misinterpret or, even worse, silence any testimonies. The 'embellishment' of the past in order to be in line with modern ethical codes is not compatible with scientific ethos.

2.3.4.6   *Interpretation of the Text*

Without of course intending to confirm Cyril's testimony, I will investigate the framework in which Cyril places these practices, assuming that there is an element of truth in his words. Besides, although we do not know exactly what the Manichaean Elect did during their rituals, following Augustine's rationale, one can legitimately assume, on the basis of the Manichaean beliefs and the existing excerpt from *Thesaurus*, that Cyril's testimony sounds plausible. So, was the above ritual, a description of the mystery of baptism (as all English translations maintain) or of the holy meal, as Van Oort argues? Or does it concern another ritual altogether?

The only study on Cyril's text, as said, is that of Van Oort. Commenting on this 'gap', Van Oort points out that "in previous research the passage is regarded either as mere slander or simply as not worth mentioning".[218] Van Oort too, interprets the crucial word λουτρόν as baptism. However, since the Manichaeans did not practice baptism, he suggests a baptism of the fig, rather than of the bodies of the Manichaeans, placing the whole scene during the Manichaean sacred meal. In favour of his interpretation, Van Oort points to Cyril's statement that "the Manichaean sets these things [...] in the middle of *the altar* (θυσιαστήριον) and defiles both his lips and his tongue".[219] Thus, according to him,

> Cyril claims that the Manichaeans 'dipped' or 'baptized' (ἐμβάπτω) a fig (ἰσχάς) in some substance, which he indicates 'only indirectly' (διὰ συσσήμων) as a product of men's 'delusive dreams of the night' and women's 'menses'. In other words, some (dried) fig (ἰσχάς) is dipped in male sperma and female menstruation fluid.[220]

Van Oort considers it less plausible to interpret the word λουτρόν as either spiritual baptism, or another type of baptism which Cyril considered horrible.[221]

---

218   Van Oort 2016b, 432, fn. 6.
219   Van Oort 2016b, 435.
220   Van Oort 2016b, 435.
221   Van Oort 2016b, 434.

Arguing in favour of Cyril's reliability, he firstly points out that Cyril drew his information from inside sources: the converted Manichaeans and the Manichaean books,[222] in particular the *Thesaurus*, for in the next paragraph (34) which follows the puzzling text he refers to the *Seduction of the Archons*.

Furthermore, in support of his interpretation, Van Oort points out the importance that the fig and the human semen should have had in the Manichaean Eucharist. The main axes of his argumentation are the following: (1) the sexual symbolism of the fig in Antiquity (and not only),[223] (2) that Augustine emphasizes (in several of his works) the great importance that figs must have had in Manichaeism, in particular in their ritual meal as fruits containing much divine light,[224] (3) that Augustine also records similar practices which reveal the importance that Manichaeans might have attributed to human semen for the same reason as in the case of the figs,[225] (4) that, according to Augustine, the source of inspiration of those practices was the *Seduction*-myth from the *Thesaurus*[226] to which Cyril also refers, and (5) that Cyril's and Augustine's testimonies are two independent testimonies from each other. Van Oort concludes his article, presenting two pieces of Manichaean art (miniature-paintings) found in Kotcho (Central Asia) which, as he argues, reveal "the special place of the fig in Manichaean eucharistic meals".[227]

Agreeing with Van Oort, I also consider it plausible that Cyril's sources may have been of Manichaean provenance, i.e. former Manichaeans and the *Thesaurus*. As said in ch.[2], Cyril in all probability had access to the *Thesaurus*, since this was the book which was circulated during his time by the Manichaean missionaries in his area. This also may have been the book which Cyril says that he read himself and from which (as he says) originates the scene he quotes in ch. 34 that echoes the *Seduction of the Archons*.[228] Furthermore,

---

222   Van Oort 2016b, 437.

223   Van Oort 2016b, 435.

224   Van Oort 2016b, 435–36. The respective Augustine's works are: *Mor. Manich.* 2.40–41, 2.57 and *Conf.* 3.18. As Van Oort (2016b, 435) comments on *Mor. Manich.* 2.57: "when seeing a raven on the point of eating a fig, the true Manichaean will pluck the fig and eat it in order to release the light elements".

225   Van Oort 2016b, 436. See also Van Oort's (2016a) previous paper on Augustine concerning "Human Semen Eucharist Among the Manichaeans".

226   Van Oort 2016b, 436–37.

227   Van Oort 2016b, 437, 437–440.

228   Cyril, *Catech.* 6.34: "These persons say that the rain is produced by erotic mania. And they dare to say that there is a beautiful virgin in the heaven, together with a beautiful young man. [...] and that the latter during the winter, runs after the virgin like a madman [...] then as he runs he sweats; [and they say that] the rain comes from his sweat. These things are written in the Manichaean books. These things we have read disbelieving those who

taking into account the two basic assumptions of the Manichaean cosmogony, it makes sense for one to argue (agreeing with Augustine) that, indeed, the *Seduction-myth* could have inspired such practices.[229] As said, one basic assumption of the Manichaean cosmogonical narrative was that the *Living Spirit*, which the Manichaean Elect had to liberate during their meal, was dispersed and bound in all kinds of plant and animal life and in all kinds of seeds.[230] The other basic assumption was that in Manichaeism the link between macrocosm and microcosm was direct and substantial. The structures of the human and of the body of the Universe are interconnected. Thus, although it is common to all religions that believers imitate their divine archetypes, the Manichaean believer was not just called to imitate his divinities, but also to remember his own deeds during the primordial episode and to act accordingly. The example of the *Seduction of the Archons* indicated the way of action for Manichaeans.

However, concerning the great importance that figs must have had in Manichaeism, I would rather say that what becomes apparent in Augustine's writings is that all fruits and vegetables, especially those containing large amount of water and not only figs, had a special place in Manichaeism, particularly in the ritual meal. Melons and cabbages are equally cited in Augustine's texts. The only reference, as far as I know, of Augustine that correlates figs with the holy meal is *Conf.* 3, 18:

> Yet if some saint (i.e., a Manichaean Elect) ate the fig [...] then he would digest it in his stomach and breathe out angels, yes indeed particles of God when he groaned in prayer and even belched. These particles of the most high and true God would have remained bound in that fruit, if they had not been liberated by the tooth and belly of that Elect saint.[231]

---

affirmed them. For your safety, we have closely inquired into their deadly doctrines". See also ch.[2], 3.4.1. However, a similar scene exists also in Turbo's narration, so, possibly his source could have been *AA*.

229 According to the version of the *Seduction of Archons* provided by Bar Kōnay, "the Third Messenger appeared in the Sun in his radiant nakedness in a female form as the Virgin of Light ... before the male archons, and in a male form before the female. He thus awakens their sensual desires and makes them scatter with their seed the Light" (Lieu 2010, xvii).

230 Theodoret, *Haer.* (PG 83:380). Timothy the Presbyter, *Recept. Haer.* Augustine, *Nat. bon.* 44 in BeDuhn 2000b, 77. Ephrem the Syrian appears surprised about the "Manichaean project of metabolizing the whole world, and Augustine invoked the Manichaean slogan "purify all seeds", see BeDuhn 2000b, 249.

231 Augustine, *Conf.* 3.18. As Van Oort (2016b, 436) comments, "No doubt, here we have a surprising description of the Manichaeans' sacred meal, in which – equally surprising – the fig is considered to be the central element". In contrast, what Augustine says in

In addition, since the holy meal (at least theoretically) was the only daily meal of the Manichaean Elect, apart from figs, they would obviously eat other vegetables and fruits too.[232] Furthermore, it sounds odd that Cyril names the Manichaean holy meal as a baptism. So, if the ritual in question was neither the Manichaean holy meal, nor their baptism, what else could it have been?

In any case, the sentence "But the Manichaean places these things in the middle of the altar, as/where he thinks [right], and defiles both his mouth and his tongue" denotes that the framework was sacramental, not secular (e.g. baths). The latter is also supported by Cyril's first reference in 6.23, where he speaks about a ritual which Manichaeans exercise until his days (μέχρι σήμερον).

The interpretation of baptism in water should be excluded, for it is known, from the genuine Manichaean sources, that the Manichaeans were not baptised in water. However, it could have been another kind of "baptism", as Van Oort also suggests, although he considers this interpretation less likely.[233] So, what other kind of baptism might Cyril have meant? Put differently, what other meanings, apart from baptism in water, could the word λουτρὸν have?[234] I will briefly suggest two more alternative (to van Oort's) interpretations. As said, in the literature of the era, λουτρὸν also meant a 'baptism of tears', referring to the mystery of repentance, confession and absolution of sins (λουτρὸν παλιγγενεσίας).[235] As far as is known, the Manichaeans held rituals of confession daily, weekly and annually, in three different circumstances. The first concerned

---

Mor. Manich. 2.40–41 about figs does not testify Manichaean beliefs and practices, but it is Augustine's hypothetical deductive reasoning in his polemical argumentation, e.g. "I grant that He dwells more in a fig than in a liver" (2.40). Augustine trying to prove the absurdity of the Manichaean beliefs, says that if one took them seriously he would have to conclude that "In color alone the excrement of an infant surpasses lentils; in smell alone a roast morsel surpasses a soft green fig".

232   BeDuhn 2000b, 158: "the meal was conducted daily; testimony on this point is overwhelming".

233   Van Oort 2016b, 434.

234   Similarly, the word 'ἐπὶ' apart from 'before' (as is translated by both Lieu and Van Oort) could acquire other meanings too, such as: in, on, upon, at, over, during, in the time of, to, about, concerning, etc. So, the puzzling phrase "Οὐ τολμῶ ἐπὶ ἀνδρῶν καὶ γυναικῶν τὸ λουτρὸν αὐτῶν διηγήσασθαι" can also be translated: "I do not dare give an account about their baptism of/upon men and women" instead of "I dare not deal with their baptism before [in the presence of] men and women", cf. Van Oort 2016b, 432 and Lieu 2010 (translation by Fox and Sheldon).

235   Cyril (*Catech.* 6.33.9–12) also in the same paragraph states: "For the fornicator, in a moment/an hour, because of lust, performs the deed. However, [soon] he condemns his deed, realizing that, as a defiled, he is in need of λουτρῶν (washing or 'baptism of tears'), and he acknowledges that his deed is abominable".

the daily absolution of the sins of the catechumens. When they offered the food to the Elect, they were advised to "seek assembly and absolution from the Elect".[236] The third concerned the great confession that took place during the grand annual festival of the Manichaeans, the Bema.[237] Lastly, between the daily and the annual confession, "every week, all Manichaeans – Electi and Auditors alike – subjected themselves to a ceremony of contrition and reconciliation", or in other words, to the *rite of Confession* (ritualized confession).[238]

The other alternative interpretation could be that Cyril, by saying "baptism of men and women", meant it in the sense of baptism in the secrets of the Manichaean religion. In other words, the riddling ritual could have been an initiation ceremony. Thus, according to this interpretation, the baptised dried fig was consumed by the neophyte Manichaean communicants as their first communion or holy meal during their 'baptism/initiation' into the class of the Elect. This interpretation also fits well with the expression "the Manichaean places these things [the offerings] in the middle of the altar". Furthermore, apart from the sexual symbolism that the fig had in Antiquity, the fig-tree was considered as the tree of religious initiation. In many religious traditions (familiar to Mani) the fig-tree featured as the symbol of 'gnosis' and of the initiation in 'gnosis'.[239] Finally, in favour of this interpretation is the fact that it incorporates the 'baptism of tears', since a part of the initiation procedure was also the 'baptism of tears'. The candidates entering the Manichaean community had to go "through an initial confession and absolution as part of his or her initiation into the community".[240]

---

236 BeDuhn 2000b, see especially pp. 108, 143, 147, 202 & 208.

237 About the Bema festival and the great confession see BeDuhn 2010, 332. See also BeDuhn 2013, 271–72.

238 BeDuhn 2013, 271–299, 297. See in particular p. 271: "Between the daily prayers and sacred meal, and the annual high holiday of the Bema festival, Manichaeans punctuated their life with a weekly assembly that featured among its activities a rite of confession" and pp. 282–288: *The Rite of Confession*. Yet, according to BeDuhn 2013, 277: "Evidence for a Monday [weekly] rite of confession among western Manichaeans is far scarcer".

239 Nathanael was sitting under a fig-tree before becoming a disciple of Jesus. According to Vallas (1993, 40–44), the wild fig-tree (ἐρινεώς) was the tree of religious initiation and one of the prosonimia of Dionysus/Bacchus was Sykites, i.e. the fig-tree god. The enlightenment of Buddha took place under a *ficus religiosa* (a kind of a fig-tree). For the religious meaning of *ficus religiosa*, see Eliade 1982, 76.

240 BeDuhn 2013, 271–299, 291. In p. 284: "It may even be questioned whether, besides the initial confession at the time of conversion, the recurring weekly and annual confessions were anything but recitations of either brief general statements of repentance for sinfulness."

2.3.5   Bema

Bema was the most important annual feast in the Manichaean calendar during which Manichaeans commemorated Mani's martyrdom. The only explicit reference to Bema throughout the Greek anti-Manichaean literature is found in the *SC*:

> And (I anathematize) their abominable and unclean and magic-filled mysteries and that which they called the (Feast of the) Bema.[241]

According to Augustine's testimony, "at the feast a seat or tribunal [or a platform (bema) of five steps covered with precious cloth] was raised in the middle of the worshipping congregation. Upon this was placed a portrait of Mani (or a seated Elect representing Mani) to celebrate his continuing presence in the community of the Elect".[242] Surprisingly, there is a unique reference to Mani's icon in Greek anti-Manichaica. Eusebius of Caesarea, in an epistle addressed to Augusta Constantia (the stepsister of Constantine), reported that he saw with his own eyes Mani's icon to be surrounded by the Manichaeans ("Ἐθεωρήσαμεν δὲ καὶ αὐτοὶ τὸν τῆς μανίας ἐπώνυμον ὑπὸ τῶν Μανιχαίων εἰκόνι δορυφορούμενον").[243]

    In his letter, Eusebius explains to Constantia (who wished to have an icon of Christ) that worshiping icons was idolatry; as an example he recounts the scene with the Manichaeans he had recently happened to have witnessed. Could this have been a reference to Bema?[244]

3   Manichaean Beliefs and Their Implication in Everyday Social Life

As underlined in the previous section, the religious behaviours that were the target of our sources were interpreted by the anti-Manichaean authors as the result of the Manichaean cosmological dualism: the mixed status of cosmos. Accordingly, in the social sphere, the problematic behaviour and ethos that anti-Manichaean authors attributed to Manichaeans were interpreted as deriving from the Manichaean anthropological dualism: the mixed status of

---

241   *SC*, ch. 7 (Lieu 2010, 124–25): καὶ [ἀναθεματίζω] τὰ μυσαρὰ τούτων καὶ ἀκάθαρτα καὶ γοητείας πλήρη μυστήρια καὶ τὸ καλούμενον αὐτῶν Βῆμα.

242   Augustine on the bema festival (*Fund.* 8) in Gardner and Lieu 2004, no 77. See also Lieu 1985, 126; Lieu 2010, pp. xx–xxi & 79.

243   Eusebius, *Ep. Constantiam* (PG 20:1548): Ἐθεωρήσαμεν δὲ καὶ αὐτοὶ τὸν τῆς μανίας ἐπώνυμον ὑπὸ τῶν Μανιχαίων εἰκόνι δορυφορούμενον.

244   Cf. Gulácsi 2015, 48–50.

humans. The Manichaean anthropological model seems to rest on these three premises:

(1) The creation of man is the stratagem of Hylē (Matter).
(2) The ontological and cosmological division also characterizes human beings: both matter (evil) and light (divine) are mixed in humans.
(3) Evil acts independently of man's free will.

3.1 *The Manichaean Anthropology*

3.1.1 The Creation of Man as the Stratagem of Hylē (Matter)

According to the Manichaean cosmogonic myth, the archons of Darkness undertook the creation of man as "a countercreation" to the creation of the cosmos, in order to perpetually entrap the light in matter. The son of the *King of Darkness*, Ashaqlun, with his companion Nebroel (Namrael), ate the abortions of the daughters of Darkness, in which the form of the Messenger was imprinted, and then "came together". "Nebroel conceived of him and gave birth to a son, whom she called Adam. Then she conceived and gave birth to a daughter, whom she called Eve".[245] "The human species therefore is born out a series of cannibalistic and sexual acts".[246]

In Turbo's account, Adam and Eve were created by the princes of Darkness after their form and according to the image of the Primal Man. Thus, the rulers instilled in man their own evil desire (= sin):

> Concerning Adam and how he was created, he says this, that the one who says: "Come let us make a man in our image and likeness" and following the form that we have seen, is a prince who says this to his fellow princes, namely: "Come give me some of the light which we have received, and let us create following the form of ourselves, who are princes, and following that form we have seen, which is the First Man"; and so they created man. They made Eve too in a similar way, and gave her some of their lust in order to deceive Adam, and through this method was produced the formation of the world by means of the creation of the prince.[247]

---

245 A summary provided by Tardieu 2008, 80.
246 Lieu 2010, xvii.
247 *AA* 12.1–2 (Vermes, 56). Turbo's account from Epiphanius' *Pan.* 66.25–31, 66.30.5–6 (GCS 37:68; Williams, 259–260): Περὶ δὲ τοῦ Ἀδὰμ πῶς ἐκτίσθη λέγει οὕτως· ὅτι ὁ εἰπών "δεῦτε, καὶ ποιήσωμεν ἄνθρωπον κατ᾽ εἰκόνα ἡμετέραν καὶ καθ᾽ ὁμοίωσιν", ἢ καθ᾽ ἣν εἴδομεν μορφήν, ἄρχων ἐστὶν ὁ εἰπὼν τοῖς ἑτέροις ἄρχουσιν ὅτι δεῦτε, δότε μοι ἐκ τοῦ φωτὸς οὗ ἐλάβομεν, καὶ ποιήσωμεν ἄνθρωπον κατὰ τὴν ἡμῶν τῶν ἀρχόντων μορφὴν ⟨καὶ⟩ καθ᾽ ἣν εἴδομεν, ὅ ἐστι ⟨ὁ⟩ πρῶτος ἄνθρωπος. καὶ οὕτως ἔκτισαν τὸν ἄνθρωπον. τὴν δὲ Εὔαν ὁμοίως ἔκτισαν, δόντες αὐτῇ ἐκ τῆς ἐπιθυμίας αὐτῶν πρὸς τὸ ἐξαπατῆσαι τὸν Ἀδάμ. καὶ διὰ τούτων γέγονεν ἡ πλάσις τοῦ κόσμου ἐκ τῆς τοῦ ἄρχοντος δημιουργίας.

Next, then, Matter also created from itself plants or seeds, and when they had been stolen by some of the princes, he summoned all the leading princes, and took from them all their powers, and made this man following the image of that first man and bound the soul in him.[248]

Among the East-Roman anti-Manichaean sources in Greek that present the cosmogonic Manichaean myth, there are only two that mention two names quite similar to those of Ashaqlun and Nebroel: Theodoret of Cyrrhus and the *sc*.

They say that man was not created by God but by the ruler of matter. They called him Saclas. They say that Eve was created by Saclas and Nebrod in the following manner. Adam was created in the form of an animal, but Eve was soulless and motionless.[249]

In addition, the Abjuration formula presents the first human couple as the fruit of demons' intercourse.

I anathematize all these myths and condemn them together with Manichaeus himself and all the gods proclaimed by him and those who say that out of the sexual union which was glimpsed Adam and Eve were generated, issuing forth from Sakla and Nebrod, and to put it simply, (I anathematize) whatever is contained in the Manichaean books, especially their magical works.[250]

That the Manichaeans considered the creation of man as a stratagem of the matter, is emphasized also by Titus of Bostra. As said in ch.[2], Titus seems

---

248 *AA* 8.3 (Vermes 49–50). Epiphanius' *Pan.* 66.26.3–4 (GCS 37:58–59): τότε τοίνυν καὶ ἡ ὕλη
     ἀφ᾽ ἑαυτῆς ἔκτισε τὰ φυτὰ καὶ συλωμένων αὐτῶν ἀπό τινων ἀρχόντων ἐκάλεσε πάντας τοὺς τῶν
     ἀρχόντων πρωτίστους καὶ ἔλαβεν ἀπ᾽ αὐτῶν ἀνὰ μίαν δύναμιν καὶ κατεσκεύασε τὸν ἄνθρωπον
     ⟨τοῦ⟩τον κατὰ τὴν ἰδέαν τοῦ πρώτου ἀνθρώπου ἐκείνου, καὶ ἔδησε τὴν ψυχὴν ἐν αὐτῷ. αὕτη ἐστὶ
     τῆς συγκράσεως ἡ ὑπόθεσις.

249 Theodoret, *Haer.* (PG 83:377.55) (Lieu 2010, 95, slightly altered): Καὶ τὸν ἄνθρωπον δὲ οὐχ
     ὑπὸ τοῦ Θεοῦ πλασθῆναι λέγουσιν, ἀλλ᾽ ὑπὸ τοῦ τῆς Ὕλης ἄρχοντος· Σακλᾶν δὲ τοῦτον προσα-
     γορεύουσιν· καὶ τὴν Εὔαν ὡσαύτως ὑπὸ τοῦ Σακλᾶ καὶ τοῦ Νεβρὼδ γενέσθαι· καὶ τὸν μὲν Ἀδὰμ
     θηριόμορφον κτισθῆναι, τὴν δὲ Εὔαν ἄψυχον καὶ ἀκίνητον.

250 *sc*, ch. 3 (Lieu, 1994a, 240; 2010, 118–19, slightly altered): Τοὺς μύθους τούτους ἅπαντας ἀνα-
     θεματίζω καὶ καταθεματίζω σὺν αὐτῷ Μανιχαίῳ καὶ τοῖς εἰρημένοις ἅπασι παρ᾽ αὐτοῦ θεοῖς καὶ
     τοὺς λέγοντας ἐκ τῆς συνουσίας τῆς ὑποδειχθείσης παρὰ τοῦ Σακλᾶ καὶ τῆς Νεβρὼδ γεγενῆσθαι
     τὸν Ἀδὰμ καὶ τὴν Εὔαν, καὶ ἁπλῶς εἰπεῖν ὅσα ταῖς μανιχαϊκαῖς, μᾶλλον δὲ ταῖς γοητευτικαῖς
     αὐτῶν περιέχεται βίβλοις.

to have at his disposal a particular Manichaean text, which he examines and which contains a chapter entitled 'Concerning the first human moulding' (Περὶ τῆς ἀνθρωπίνης πρωτοπλαστίας), that criticized the biblical Genesis and Exodus. According to it, as Titus says, when the princes of Darkness realized that by the creation of cosmos, the luminaries would gradually drain all the light from matter, and that this would lead to their death, they contrived the creation of human flesh (= Adam) as a prison in which the soul (Living Self) will remain in the world bound to the body.

> They say in these words, he, or one of his followers who wrote the chapter Concerning the first moulding. When the archons [of Darkness] realized that through the withdrawal of the portion of light that had fallen into them, soon they will die, they contrived the descent of the soul in the bodies [...]. And their first creature moulded is Adam, a means/tool of desire and bait for the souls from above and a device which trap them in the bodies.[251]

3.1.2 Both Evil and Divine are Congenital in Man

Further argumentation in support of the view that man was created by the princes of Darkness was presented by Mani in the debate with Archelaus. As Mani said, the good God could not create creatures that are full of evil, death, and corruption such as men.

> Moreover, how could he form creatures, if there were no pre-existent matter? For if it was from things that did not exist, it would follow that these visible creatures are better, and full of all virtues. But if they are full of evil, and death is in them and corruption and everything that is contrary to the good, then how can we say that they are not made from another nature?[252]

As Mani states in his Fundamental Letter, even today one can observe that the bodies are created by the archons of Darkness.

---

251 Titus of Bostra, c. Manichaeos 3.4–5.5 & 3.5.16–19 (CCSG 82:247, 249): Φησὶ δὲ πρὸς λέξιν αὐτὴν ἐκεῖνος, ἢ ἕτερός τις τῶν ἀπ' ἐκείνου, ἐπιγράψας τὸ κεφάλαιον Περὶ τῆς ἀνθρωπίνης πρωτοπλαστίας. Ἐπειδὴ γὰρ ἔγνωσαν οἱ ἄρχοντες ὡς ἐκ τοῦ παραιρεῖσθαι τὸ ἁπαξαπλῶς ἐμπῖπτον εἰς αὐτοὺς μέρος τοῦ φωτός, ταχὺς ἐπ' αὐτοὺς ὁ θάνατος ἥξει, τὴν εἰς τὰ σώματα τῆς ψυχῆς κάθοδον ἐμηχανήσαντο [...] Καὶ πλάσμα αὐτῶν ἐστι πρῶτον ὁ Ἀδάμ, ὄργανον ἐπιθυμίας καὶ δέλεαρ τῶν ἄνωθεν ψυχῶν καὶ μηχάνημα τοῦ αὐτὰς εἰς σώματα ἐμπίπτειν.

252 AA 16.5 (Vermes, 63).

And yet as we (even) today can observe that the principle of evil, which forms bodies, takes and creates out of them (the bodies) forces, in order to form (new bodies).[253]

In the same fashion, Turbo declares before the judges during the first debate with the bishop Archelaus in Carchar:

If indeed you consider how men produce offspring, you will discover that it is not God who is the creator of man, but another, who is himself also of an unbegotten nature, who has no founder, nor creator nor maker, but only his own evil has produced him as he is.[254]

However, although man is a creation of the archons, since his creation he has imprisoned in his body the light that was caught by the principle of evil in the primordial time. Because, as said, the princes created man "after that form" which they "have seen, which is, the First Man"; thus, by creating man they tied within him the image of Primal Man.

Next, then, Matter [...] summoned all the leading Princes, and took from them all their powers, and made this man following the image of that first man and bound the soul in him.[255]

Thus, from his very creation, man inherently carries both divine and evil 'parts'. Furthermore, divine or evil particles are rooted within him through the consumption of food. Indeed, according to Manichaean sources, the human body contains "the richest concentrations of both two substances", each of which is trying to prevail "over the other".[256]

3.1.3   The Dichotomy of Man
The consequence of the above assumptions is the dichotomy of man, with two conflicting identities. God is the originator of souls, whereas matter is the

253 Augustine, *Fund.*, Frg. 9: (6.4) in Lieu 2010, 11. *Letter to Menoch*, in Lieu 2010, 13 (Bodies the other power, Adam was made by the archons of Darkness).

254 *AA* 16.6 (Vermes, 63).

255 *AA* 8.3 (Vermes, 49–50). Epiphanius, *Pan.* 66.25–31, 66.26.3–4 (GCS 37:58–59): τότε τοίνυν καὶ ἡ ὕλη [...] ἐκάλεσε πάντας τοὺς τῶν ἀρχόντων πρωτίστους καὶ ἔλαβεν ἀπ' αὐτῶν ἀνὰ μίαν δύναμιν καὶ κατεσκεύασε τὸν ἄνθρωπον ⟨τοῦ⟩τον κατὰ τὴν ἰδέαν τοῦ πρώτου ἀνθρώπου ἐκείνου, καὶ ἔδησε τὴν ψυχὴν ἐν αὐτῷ. αὕτη ἐστὶ τῆς συγκράσεως ἡ ὑπόθεσις. As Didymus the Blind states, the Manichaeans argue that human souls are "of the same substance as God" and "had been joined to the bodies", see Bennett 1997, 76.

256 BeDuhn 2000b, 88. About human beings as depositories and storehouses of matter and light, see BeDuhn 2000b, 88, 231, 155.

originator of bodies. Souls are of divine nature and provenance, while the origin of bodies is evil. This, according to anti-Manichaean authors, entailed a polarity between body and soul and a disdain of the former.

> So since this is the body of princes and matter [...] air is the soul of men and animals, birds, fish and reptiles and everything there is in this world; because as I told you this body is not that of a deity, but of the matter of shadows, and for that reason it must be kept in obscurity.[257]
> 7. I therefore anathematize and condemn those who teach these myths and say that bodies are of the evil (principle). 6. [...] I anathematize those who say that the human souls are consubstantial with God and, being part of (the) good (principle) were swallowed up by [matter] the Hylē and out of this necessity the world was created.[258]

As Serapion of Thmuis critically comments, the Manichaeans held the absurd and outrageous view that man's essence is a mixture of good and evil essences. The substance of the body is of the evil one, while the essence of the soul is a spoil from God that the evil one inserted in the body. The flesh, its essence, its form, and all its works are from the imposter. Thus, they argue that man consists of two opposite essences.

> For which reason then did Manichaeans bring accusations against the body?[259]
> The Manichaeans say (this): we carry our body from Satan, but the soul is of God. And so, it is that the body is naturally evil, as it proceeds from evil, while the soul is naturally good, having its origin from what is good.[260]

---

257 *AA* 10.4, 8 (Vermes 54–55). Epiphanius, *Pan.* 66.28.5, 9 (GCS 37:64 & 66): τοῦ δὲ σώματος τούτου ὄντος τῶν ἀρχόντων καὶ τῆς ὕλης [...] ὁ ἀὴρ ψυχή ἐστι τῶν ἀνθρώπων καὶ τῶν ζῴων καὶ τῶν πετεινῶν καὶ τῶν ἰχθύων καὶ τῶν ἑρπετῶν καὶ εἴ τι ἐν κόσμῳ ἐστίν· εἶπον ⟨γὰρ⟩ ὑμῖν ὅτι τὸ σῶμα τοῦτο οὐκ ἔστι τοῦ θεοῦ, ἀλλὰ τῆς ὕλης ἐστὶ καὶ σκότος ἐστὶ καὶ αὐτὸ σκοτωθῆναι δεῖ.

258 *SC*, chs. 6, 7 (Lieu 1994a, 248, 246; Lieu 2010, 122–23): 7. Ἀναθεματίζω οὖν καὶ καταθεματίζω τοὺς ταῦτα μυθολογοῦντας καὶ τὰ σώματα λέγοντας εἶναι τοῦ πονηροῦ 6. ... Ἀναθεματίζω τοὺς τὰς ἀνθρωπίνας ψυχὰς λέγοντας ὁμοουσίους εἶναι τῷ θεῷ καὶ μοῖραν οὔσας τοῦ ἀγαθοῦ ὑπὸ τῆς ὕλης καταποθῆναι καὶ ἐκ τῆς ἀνάγκης ταύτης τὸν κόσμον γεγενῆσθαι.

259 Serapion, *c. Manichaeos* 10.1–3 (HTS 15:33): Πόθεν οὖν κεκινημένοι Μανιχαῖοι διαβολὰς κατὰ τῶν σωμάτων ἐπηνέγκαντο [...].

260 Serapion, *c. Manichaeos* 12.3–8 (HTS 15:49; Lieu 2010, 51): φασὶ γὰρ Μανιχαῖοι· "τὸ σῶμα ἐφορέσαμεν τοῦ Σατανᾶ, ἡ δὲ ψυχὴ τοῦ θεοῦ. Καὶ τὸ μὲν σῶμα οὕτω πέφυκε κακόν, ἐκ κακοῦ προελθόν, ἡ δὲ ψυχὴ πέφυκε καλή, ἐκ καλοῦ ἔχουσα τὴν ἀρχήν· οὐκοῦν δύο ἀρχαὶ καὶ δύο οὐσίαι [...]".

He (the teacher, i.e. Mani) wants to say that this visible creation is the creation of the deceiver, and man is a creature of the evil one and, while soul is of God, it is however bonded to the evil one. And so, man has been formed, after taking the essence of the body from the essence of the evil one, while the essence of the soul has been taken from God as spoil or plunder, plundered by the evil one. In this way, from the plundered essence and from that of the evil one, man has been formed from soul and body. And the evil one is not the cause of the soul [...] but is the agent only of its introduction into the body [...] whereas the flesh itself and its formation and its features and its general shape and its entire essence are the work and making of the deceiver. Therefore, man is formed out of opposites, they state.[261]

Augustine criticizes the conflicted human identity of the Manichaean anthropological model along similar lines.

You say that all your members and your whole body were formed by the evil mind (maligna mente) which you call Hylē, and that part of this formative mind (fabricatricis') dwells in the body along with part of your God.[262]

So, "every living being has two souls, one of the race of light, and the other of the race of darkness".[263]

The above wording of Augustine (and Serapion's) reveals another dimension of the division of man, which is caused by the two rival souls that reside within him. As BeDuhn argues in interpreting the Manichaean anthropogony, the two roots do not simply correspond to the dipole of matter and spirit, as many

---

261   Serapion, c. Manichaeos 51.12–25 (HTS 15:72–73; Lieu 2010, 53): καὶ τοῦτο τὸ φαινόμενον ποίημα τοῦ ἀπατεῶνος ποίημα εἶναι βούλεται καὶ εἶναι μὲν τὸν ἄνθρωπον πλάσμα [μὲν] τοῦ πονηροῦ καὶ εἶναι μὲν τὴν ψυχὴν ἀπὸ θεοῦ, εἶναι δὲ παρὰ τῷ πονηρῷ ἡρμοσμένην, καὶ γεγονέναι τὸν ἄνθρωπον τὴν μὲν οὐσίαν τοῦ σώματος ἀπὸ τῆς οὐσίας εἰληφότα τοῦ πονηροῦ, τὴν δὲ οὐσίαν τῆς ψυχῆς ὡς σκῦλον ἢ λάφυρον ἀπὸ θεοῦ ληφθεῖσαν, ὑπὸ δὲ τοῦ πονηροῦ λαφυραγωγηθεῖσαν. οὕτως ἔκ τε τῆς λαφυραγωγηθείσης καὶ τῆς οὐσίας τοῦ πονηροῦ γεγονέναι τὸν ἄνθρωπον ἐκ ψυχῆς καὶ σώματος, καὶ τῆς μὲν ψυχῆς μὴ αἴτιον εἶναι τὸν πονηρὸν μήτε πεποιηκέναι οὐσίαν ψυχῆς, τῆς δὲ εἰσκρίσεως μόνης τῆς ἐν σώματι ἐνεργὸν εἶναι. σκυλεύσας γάρ, ὥς φασιν, εἰσέκρινε τῇ σαρκί, τὴν δὲ σάρκα αὐτὴν καὶ τὴν πλάσιν αὐτὴν καὶ τὸν χαρακτῆρα καὶ τὴν τοιάνδε μορφὴν καὶ τὴν οὐσίαν ὅλην ἔργον εἶναι καὶ πλάσιν τοῦ ἀπατεῶνος. ἐξ ἐναντίων οὖν γεγονέναι τὸν ἄνθρωπον ὁμολογοῦντες.

262   Augustine, Faust. 20.15.

263   Augustine, Faust. 6.8 in BeDuhn 2000b, 95. Cf. Duab. 1.16.

modern scholars understand it, but to two roots within the body, a good and an evil one.[264]

The above dimension of polarity emphasized by BeDuhn is not discernible in the following letter attributed to Mani and addressed to Menoch, one of his catechumens.

> For just as souls are begotten from souls, so the creation of the body derives from the nature of the body. Therefore, what is born of the flesh is flesh; and what of the spirit, is spirit; [...] So just as God is the originator of souls, so the devil is the originator of bodies through lust that is in the Devil's snare by means of the lust for a woman, by which the Devil traps, he hunts not souls but bodies [...]. Wherefore see how foolish are they who say that his creative act was established by the good God [...] In short, abolish the root of this evil stock and gaze at once on your own spiritual self [...] the root of all evils is lust.[265]

The text above identifies evil with nature, through the passions and the desires of the flesh (carnal lust). Lust, which is identified with flesh and matter, is the cause of evil, but because of this, man himself is not responsible, but his nature.

Athanasius of Alexandria is familiar with the Manichaean terminology (ἄρχοντα τῆς κακίας) and aware of the above 'problematic' rationale. As he says, Manichaeans claim that since human flesh is created and dominated by the archons of evil, the sin is the nature of human flesh rather than the result of human deeds.[266] According to Severianus of Gabala the Manichaeans misinterpret Paul by saying that flesh comes from the evil one. They scorn the body and appreciate only the soul, whereas in the Scripture one can find examples where the flesh is esteemed by the Spirit, while the soul is not worthy to receive the gifts of the Spirit.[267]

---

264 BeDuhn 2000b, 95.

265 *Letter to Menoch* 2–4, in Gardner and Lieu 2004, 172–74 (no 54). According to Gardner and Lieu (2004, 172) "The authenticity of this text (Latin) remains open to dispute".

266 Athanasius, [*Apoll.*] [Sp.] 1116.5–8 & 1144.30–34: ... Μανιχαῖος εἰσηγήσατο τὴν γνώμην, τοῦ ἀνθρώπου τὴν σάρκα καὶ αὐτὴν τὴν γέννησιν ὑπὸ τὸν ἄρχοντα τῆς κακίας τάσσων ...

267 Severianus of Gabala, *c. Manichaeos*, 17 & 22 (Aubineau, 122, 128): Ἀλλὰ προφέρουσιν τὸ ἀποστολικὸν οἱ Μανιχαῖοι καὶ συκοφαντοῦσι τὴν ἀποστολικὴν φωνὴν λέγουσαν ὅτι ἡ σὰρξ πονηρά ἐστιν. [...] Λέγουσιν τὴν ψυχὴν εἶναι τοῦ θεοῦ, τὴν δὲ σάρκα τοῦ διαβόλου. Εὑρίσκομεν ἀπὸ τῆς γραφῆς τὴν μὲν σάρκα καταξιουμένην Πνεύματος ἁγίου, τὴν δὲ ψυχὴν μὴ δεχομένην τὰ τοῦ πνεύματος· κατὰ τὴν λέξιν λέγω, οὐχ ὅτι οὐ καταξιοῦται, ἀλλὰ πρὸς τὸν αἱρετικῶν λόγον ἐνίσταμαι. Cf. Aubineau 1983, 63–67. Apart from the specialists, there exist many relevant references in the whole byzantine literature. For example, see Cosmas Indicopleustes, *Top.* 5.178. Criticism is made by all Christian parties: Theodorus Heracleensis vel Theodorus Mopsuestenus, *Frg. Matt*: οὐ μὴν θατέρου κατὰ τοὺς τῶν Μανιχαίων λήρους, οἳ

The coexistence of evil and good in man had negative results for the psyche. Manichaean texts describe the body as a corpse, a prison for the soul.[268] The powers of light in man work in order to liberate the elements of good.

3.1.4   Evil Acts Independently of Man's Free Will

Thus, the human person was divided in two opposite parts. As Augustine criticizes commenting on Manichaean anthropology: "Two souls, or two minds, the one good, the other evil, are in conflict with one another in one man, when the flesh lusts against the spirit, and the spirit against the flesh".[269] Consequently, according to the Manichaean thesis, man does not sin consciously (i.e. by free choice of the will) but it is another opposing nature within man makes him sin. "They ascribe the origin of sins not to a free choice of the will, but to the nature of the opposing element, which they hold is intermingled in man".[270] One of the passages that Manichaeans invoked in order to support the above position, as is indicated in the Epistle to Menoch, was Paul's letter to the Romans: "The good which I wish, I do not do; but I perform the evil which I abhor (Rom. 7.15)".[271] In this very same letter, Mani explains to Menoch, his 'daughter' (i.e. female catechumen), that the evil exists outside men's actions, as an autonomous entity.

> In short, every sin is outside the body, because it is active; [...] For every sin, before it is committed, does not exist; [...] but the evil of lust, because it is natural, exists before it is committed;... If sin is not natural, why are infants baptised, who are agreed to have done no evil of themselves?... (Let those answer), whom I have to question with these words, – if every evil is committed by an act, then before anyone does evil, why does he receive the purification of water when he has done no evil of his own accord?[272]

διαφόρους εἰσάγουσιν δημιουργούς, ἄλλον τὸν τῆς ψυχῆς καὶ ἄλλον τὸν τοῦ σώματος. Julianus Arianus: "⟨ἐκ⟩ σαπρίας δ᾽ ὁ ῥάδαμνος" λέγει οὐχ ἵνα φαυλίσῃ τὸ σπέρμα κατὰ Μανιχαίους καὶ Ψευδεγκρατίτας (οὔτε γὰρ τὸ σῶμα κακὸν οὔτε αἱ τροφαὶ φαῦλαι [...].

268   BeDuhn 2000b, 89, 95: "Even the good soul can be corrupted by its contact with evil, and lose its divine identity".

269   Augustine, *haer.* (Lieu 2010, 91).

270   Augustine, *haer.* (Lieu 2010, 91).

271   *Letter to Menoch* in Lieu 2010, 13.

272   *Letter to Menoch*, 6–8. Gardner and Lieu (2004, 172 fn. 67) challenge the authenticity of the letter and one of the reasons is its "preoccupation with theological issues (such as infant baptism) which could not possibly have been of interest to Mani".

The idea that man is created by the archons of Darkness, that evil exists innately in man, and that man 'sins' due to his nature and not due to his conduct entailed two major consequences according to the anti-Manichaean authors: (1) the abolition of free will, and (2) the lack of effort (resignation) for moral improvement. In turn, both of them had implications on the ethics and attitudes in everyday social life.

3.2   Implications of Manichaean Dualism in Ethics of Social Life

3.2.1   Abolition of Free Will (Determinism vs. Personhood)

For the authors, a first major side-effect of the Manichaean anthropology was the adoption of a deterministic stance, which entailed the abolition of man's free will. For both Christian and pagan authors the Manichaean anthropological proposal was problematic, because attributing the 'evil' human deeds to another entity that man could not control eliminated free will and was against the concept of the human person and free agency. The latter entailed the annihilation of the human guilt for the 'evil' deeds that man committed. Man was not responsible for his misconduct: an evil nature within him acts against his virtuous one.[273] In the words that the converted Manichaean had to recite during the anathema: "I therefore anathematize and condemn those [...] who deny free will and say it is not in our power to be good or evil".[274] As Augustine confesses,

> For, still I thought that it is not we who sin but some kind of alien nature in us which sins. It gratified my pride to think that I am beyond blame, and when I had done something evil, not to confess I had done it ... but

---

273   Many Manichaeologists challenge anti-Manichaean authors' claim regarding Manichaean determinism. As BeDuhn (1995b, 393–94 and 2000b, 225) states, "Manichaean treatment of the self has defied the most well-intentioned and ingenious efforts to classify it as a form of determinism. There is no unanimity even in the Christian sources; Ephrem, for example, states that the Manichaeans believe in free will." "In brief, Manichaeism ascribes no fault to the soul prior to its 'awakening' [...] Only when the soul is collected, and establishes dominion over the body, does it assume responsibility for action", [determinism under preconditions]. As Pedersen (2004, 173) remarks, the original Manichaean literature "often lays claim to man's freedom and sense of responsibility; the importance in Manichaean texts of themes such as ethical commandments, penance and eternal perdition would seem to render it impossible for Manichaeism to have been a deterministic doctrine".

274   *sc*, ch. 7 (Lieu, 1994a, 248, 250): τὰ σώματα λέγοντας εἶναι τοῦ πονηροῦ, [...] τὸ αὐτεξούσιον ἀναιροῦντας καὶ μὴ ἐν ἡμῖν εἶναι λέγοντας τὸ εἶναι καλοῖς ἢ κακοῖς. See also Zacharias of Mytilene, *Adv. Manichaeos* 4.7–9 (Demetrakopoulos, 4): Τὸ κακὸν τοίνυν οὐκ οὐσία, ἀλλὰ τοῦ θείου νόμου παράβασις ἐκ μόνου τοῦ αὐτεξουσίου κινήματος.

instead I liked to excuse myself and accuse something else which existed within me and yet was not really I.[275]

Soon enough, it was pointed out by the anti-Manichaean authors that this rationale (anthropology) had ethical implications which in turn would lead to the adoption of behaviours with social consequences. The necessity to answer the Manichaean challenge was an important reason for the development of the theology of αὐτεξούσιον (free will) and the freedom of choice, especially by the Greek Church Fathers.[276] The core of their rationale is this: Evil is not self-existent at an ontological level, it is not an entity but the absence of being, the not-being. It is not a substance but an event that has happened (συμβεβηκός). It exists only through the deeds of man, who in front of a range of good and bad choices chooses the evil ones.

As Serapion emphasizes, the Manichaean theory that human nature is a mixture of good and evil essences promotes a weak moral responsibility. Serapion refutes the Manichaean belief that "the body is naturally evil, as it proceeds from evil, while the soul is naturally good, having its origin from what is good"[277] arguing that: The choice of doing the good is up to each person (10). In any case, people can change (16), not in terms of their essence, but their skills and their quality (17). The body and its limbs are mere tools; they do not determine the quality of man's operations which depend on man's disposition and freedom of choice (18). The vices and virtues could be acquired; yet, they also could be lost (19). Both our life and our achievements depend on our free choice (23).[278] For Serapion, even the demons are not evil by nature as spring-

---

275   Augustine, *Conf.* 10.18 (Lieu 1992, 184).
276   For example, by Serapion of Thmuis, Titus of Bostra, Zacharias of Mytilene, John of Caesarea, etc.
277   Serapion, *c. Manichaeos*, 12.3–8 (HTS 15:34; Lieu 2010, 51): καὶ τὸ μὲν σῶμα οὕτω πέφυκε κακόν, ἐκ κακοῦ προελθόν, ἡ δὲ ψυχὴ πέφυκε καλή, ἐκ καλοῦ ἔχουσα τὴν ἀρχήν.
278   Serapion, *c. Manichaeos*, 16–23 (HTS 15:36–37, 40) (in the text above is provided a summary of the content): 16. διὰ τοῦτο οὐδὲ εἰκόνα τὴν παλαιὰν λαμβάνουσι, καίτοι ἄνθρωποι καὶ αὐτοί εἰσιν. οὐ τοῦ εἶναι ἄνθρωποι ἐπαύσαντο· μενούσης τῆς οὐσίας, οὐ μένουσιν οἱ τρόποι. αἱ οὐσίαι οὐ λέλυνται, οἱ δὲ τρόποι καταλέλυνται· ἕστηκεν ἡ ἑκάστου οὐσία, ἡ τοῦ ἀνθρώπου οὐσία· [...] οὐ τὸν χαρακτῆρα τοῦ προσώπου λέλυκε, μένει ὁ τῆς ὄψεως χαρακτήρ· οὐ τὴν ὄψιν τῆς φύσεως ἀνήρηκεν. [...] 17. καὶ αἱ μὲν οὐσίαι οὐκ ἠλλάγησαν· μένει γὰρ τὸ σῶμα σῶμα, οὐχ ἕτερον γεγονός· οὔτε γὰρ τὸ σῶμα εἰς τὸ ἀσώματον μετετέθη· οὔτε ἡ ψυχὴ ἑτέρα τῇ οὐσίᾳ ὑπῆρξεν· ἀλλὰ μενουσῶν τῶν οὐσιῶν τὰ ἐπιτηδεύματα οὐκ ἔμεινε. [...] 18. ὀφθαλμοῦ ἦν τὸ βλέπειν, οὐ τὸ πῶς βλέπειν· καὶ γλώττης ἦν λαλεῖν, οὐ πῶς λαλεῖν· ἡ γὰρ ποιότης τῶν κινημάτων ἐν τῇ προαιρέσει κεῖται [...] 19. μεταβέβληνται οὖν αἱ κακίαι καὶ αἱ ἀρεταί· καὶ κτηταὶ καὶ ἀπόκτηται. ἔχεις, οὐκ ἔχεις· εὗρες καὶ ἀπολώλεκας· ἔχεις ὃ εὗρες· οὐκ ἔχεις ὃ ἀπολώλεκας. 23. [...] προαιρέσει γὰρ ζῶμεν, προαιρέσει τὸ κατόρθωμα ἀποταμιευόμεθα.

ing from an evil root, or because their substance is darkness. Instead, they are evil because of their deliberate choices.[279]

Titus of Bostra, answering the classical Manichaean question: "whence evil?" (Πόθεν οὖν τὰ κακά;), argues that evil is not an autonomous entity, does not exist as an individual being, and that there is no other first principle opposing God; God is the only authority. Evil exists only through human deeds (2). Furthermore, good and evil are qualities that could be acquired through man's choices. God wanted to give man the freedom of choice. Therefore, he did not create him either as good or evil, in order to give him the opportunity to attain goodness via virtue and through pain (7). Thus, since he is God's creation, man is by nature innately beautiful (καλὸς); whether he will become good (ἀγαθὸς) or bad (κακὸς) depends upon his intentions and his choices. So, goodness and badness are qualities that are acquired through human praxis (8).[280]

As Didymus the Blind remarks, the Manichaeans argue that the body is evil by nature (8) and "flesh belongs to sin" (12). However, sin is the result of man's disposition and not of his nature. Men are characterised (either good or evil) by their deeds. No one is inherently bad, "not even the Devil himself is evil by nature: instead, he became so, as a result of a change effected by his own free will" (6). Soul and body are not inherently bad or good, but are receptive of

---

279 Serapion, c. Manichaeos, 29.9–14 (HTS 15:44): εἰ δὲ βούλεσθε μαθεῖν ὅτι καὶ οἱ δαίμονες αὐτοὶ οὐκ ἀπὸ ῥίζης εἰσὶ κακοὶ οὐδὲ ῥίζαν ἀτοπίας ἔχουσιν, ἀλλὰ κἀκεῖνοι ἀπὸ προαιρέσεως ἐπὶ τοῦτο ἐληλύθασιν, οὐ πονηροὶ τὴν φύσιν ὄντες, οὐκ ἀγνοίᾳ ἀναγεγραμμένοι, οὐ νὺξ καὶ σκότος τὴν οὐσίαν τυγχάνοντες, ἀλλ᾽ ἕξει καὶ ἐπιτηδεύμασι τῇ ἐπιχειρήσει τῶν τοιούτων γεγονότες.

280 Titus of Bostra, c. Manichaeos, 2.1–8.12 (CCSG 82:97, 99, 109, 111, 113): [...] Καὶ γὰρ δὴ οἱ ἐξ ἐκείνου, ἐπειδὰν περὶ τῶν ἀσυστάτων ἀρχῶν ἐν λόγῳ διελεγχθῶσιν, ἐπὶ ταύτην κατάγονται τὴν ἐπαπόρησιν, ὡς δυσαπόδεικτον καὶ πολλὰς παρέχουσαν λαβὰς κατὰ τοῦ προσδιαλεγομέ-νου, φάσκοντες· Πόθεν οὖν τὰ κακά; Φαμὲν δὴ θαρσαλέως ἡμεῖς ὡς, ἑνὸς ὄντος θεοῦ τοῦ πάντα δημιουργήσαντος, οὐδὲν μὲν κατ᾽ οὐσίαν ἐν τοῖς οὖσι κακόν [...] Μόνη δὲ εὐλόγως καὶ δικαίως πρὸς κακίαν ἡ τῶν ἁμαρτανόντων ἀνθρώπων ἀδικία, καὶ ἀληθῶς γε κακία τυγχάνει, οὐ μὴν ἐξ ἀνάρχου κακίας ἥντινα μὴ οὖσαν ὡς ἀπὸ ταύτης γε οὔσης ἐπενόησεν ὁ Μάνης [...] κατ᾽ οὐσίαν οὐδὲν τῶν ὄντων κακόν [...] Οὕτω δὴ κατεσκεύακε τὸν ἄνθρωπον φύσει μὲν οὔτ᾽ ἀγαθὸν οὔτε κακόν, ἐπιτρέψας δὲ τῷ λογισμῷ τοῦ κρείττονος τὴν αἵρεσιν. [...] Ἡ μὲν γὰρ οὐσία τούτου καλή, τὸ δὲ κατ᾽ ἀρετὴν ἀγαθὸν οὔπω προσείληφεν. [...] Κατὰ δὴ τοῦτον τὸν λόγον καὶ ἄνθρωπος, καλὸς μὲν καὶ λίαν καλὸς οὐσίᾳ τε καὶ αὐτῷ τῷ εἶναι, τὸ δὲ ἀγαθόν, τὸ διὰ μόνης ἀρετῆς προσγι-γνόμενον, πόνῳ κτᾶται· [...] Οὐσίᾳ μὲν καὶ φύσει ἄνθρωπος καλὸς ὡς χρυσός, ὡς λίθος τίμιος, ὡς ἔργον θεοῦ, ἀγαθὸς δὲ ἢ τοὐναντίον κακὸς προθέσει. Ταῦτα γὰρ αὐτῷ παράκειται μὲν ὡς πρα-χθῆναι δυνάμενα· ποιότητες δέ εἰσιν ἐπισυμβαίνουσαι κατὰ τὴν ἐγγιγνομένην ἀγωγὴν καὶ τῆς προθέσεως αἵρεσιν, ὡς τὴν κακίαν ἐν πράξει μόνον συνισταμένην πρὶν πραχθῆναι μὴ ὑφεστάναι. Ἐξουσίαν μέντοι ἔχει κακίας ὁ ἄνθρωπος τῆς πραχθῆναι δυναμένης, οὐχ ἵνα πράξῃ ταύτην, ἀλλ᾽ ἵνα μὴ πράξας, ἄριστος ἀναδειχθῇ. Εἰ γὰρ τοῦ πράττειν τὴν ἐξουσίαν οὐκ εἶχε, φθόνον ἂν ἔδοξεν ὑπέχειν τοῦ δημιουργοῦ πρὸς ἐμπόδιον εὐδοκιμήσεως καὶ πρὸς στέρησιν ἐλευθεριότητος, ὡς οὐκ ἔχων ἐφ᾽ ἑαυτῷ τὸ γενέσθαι ἀγαθός [...] Ἀρετὴ γὰρ ἐν ἀνθρώποις σχεδὸν οὐδὲν ἕτερον ἢ κακίας παραίτησις.

both qualities by "the exercise of free will" (11). When talking about a rational species like man that are either good or evil, we do not mean that their substance is good or evil (19).[281]

As Epiphanius explains in his commentary on the Manichaean cosmogony:

> We must first consider the sort of thing that evil is [...] whether it is an object or, as it were, has a body or substance, or whether it can even have a root. And when [...] we shall find that evil is without substance and has no root, but is limited to the deeds of human activity at work. While we are doing it, evil exists; while we are not doing it, it does not. [...] For though God in his supreme goodness willed that all persons and creatures be ⟨good⟩ [...] he still, by allowing the freedom to choose, permits all creatures to undertake whichever action each chooses by its own will. Thus God cannot be responsible for the evils [...] But though this madman Mani (Μάνης) means to exempt God from evil, he has instead set evil over against God on equal terms. And at the same time, while he is abusing all creation, he is not ashamed to use our human errors as his excuse for interweaving ⟨a mixture of the two⟩ evenly matched ⟨principles⟩ with all created being.[282]

That the discourse on theodicy was one of the hotly debated issues is illustrated not only in the theological treatises but also in the live speeches and sermons of Church Fathers. Cyril of Jerusalem, teaching his disciples, emphasizes and admonished them "Learn also this: The soul comes into the world without sin (faultlessness). Thus, while we were born faultless, we now sin due to our freedom of choice. So, do not listen to those who support the opposite view".[283]

John of Caesarea, in his homily *Adversus Manichaeos*, answering the repeated Manichaean question: "whence evil?" (Πόθεν οὖν τὰ κακά;), develops

---

281   Didymus the Blind (Pseudo-Didymus), *c. Manichaeos* 6–20, 32 (PG 39:1092B–1105A; Bennett 1997, 309–315, 321 altered): 8. [...] οὐ κακὸν τὸ σῶμα τῇ φύσει [...] 12 [...] ἁμαρτίας εἶναι τὴν σάρκα, τοῦτο νομίζουσιν· [...] 6. [...] Ἀλλ᾽ οὐδ᾽ αὐτὸς ὁ διάβολος κατὰ φύσιν κακός, ἀλλ᾽ ἐκ τροπῆς τοῦ ἰδίου αὐτεξουσίου. [...] 37 οὐδὲ φύσει κακὴ ἡ κόλασις [...] 11. Εἰ οὖν διὰ πλειόνων ἡ σὰρξ καὶ τὸ πνεῦμα, ὁτὲ μὲν ἁμαρτίας, ὁτὲ δὲ ἁγιασμοῦ, καὶ πρὸς τὸ δοξάζειν τὸν Θεὸν ἔχοντα λέγεται οὐδὲν τούτων φύσει κακόν, ἢ ἀγαθόν ἐστιν· ἀλλ᾽ αὐτεξουσίως ἑκατέρων δεκτικόν· [...] 19 Μηδεὶς δὲ ὑπολάβῃ, ὅτι εἴδη λογικῶν πονηρῶν εἰρηκότες, οὐσίαν πονηρὰν λέγομεν [...] 20 Ἀμέλει γοῦν τὰ ὀνόματα τὰ προειρημένα πονηρά, οὐκ οὐσιῶν, ἀλλὰ προαιρετικῶν ἐστιν ἐμφανιστικά.

282   Epiphanius, *Pan.* 66.15.4–16.4.

283   Cyril, *Catech.* 4.18: Μάνθανε δὲ καὶ τοῦτο, ὅτι πρὶν παραγένηται εἰς τόνδε τὸν κόσμον ἡ ψυχή, οὐδὲν ἥμαρτεν· ἀλλ᾽ ἐλθόντες ἀναμάρτητοι, νῦν ἐκ προαιρέσεως ἁμαρτάνομεν. Μή μοι κακῶς τινος ἀκούσῃς.

the twofold meaning of it, distinguishing: the natural evil (e.g. illnesses, physical disasters), which according to him should not be called evil, and which frequently becomes the agent of salvation, from the human evil (sin) which is the real evil. Concluding his homily, he stresses that the gift of free will is necessary for the promotion of virtue, and that the cause of real evil is only our freedom of choice and disposition.[284]

This optimistic anthropological proposal, developed by Greek Church Fathers, emphasizes the free agency of man,[285] and reveals the extent of the problem that clerics faced educating their flock because of the moral fatalism and resignation promoted by Manichaeism. In turn, this can be seen as a sign of the success of Manichaean missionary propaganda in the East.[286]

As Stroumsa emphasizes, "Christian theologians focused precisely on those major implications of Manichaean doctrine that threatened the monotheistic conception of God and of the human person. Theodicy and ethics seem never more cogently developed in Patristic and early Byzantine works than in the context of anti-Manichaean polemics".[287]

---

284 John of Caesarea, *Adv. Manichaeos hom.* 2 14–15, 21 (Richard, 98, 102): 14. Ἐντεῦθεν οὖν λοιπὸν ἀνακύπτει τὸ παρὰ τοῖς ἀθέοις θρυλλούμενον· [...] Πόθεν οὖν τὰ κακά; [...] 15. Τὸ κακὸν διττὴν ἔχει τὴν σημασίαν· δηλοῖ γάρ ποτε μὲν τὴν κάκωσιν, ποτὲ δὲ τὴν ἁμαρτίαν, καὶ κυρίως μὲν κακὸν ἡ ἁμαρτία, καταχρηστικῶς δὲ ἡ κάκωσις κακὸν ὀνομάζεται. Ἡ γὰρ κάκωσις οὐ πάντως κακή· πολλάκις δὲ καὶ σωτηρίας πρόξενος γίνεται [...] 21. Ἰδοὺ καὶ τὸ θρυλλούμενον ἀποδέδεικται ὅτι τε ἀναγκαῖον πρὸς ἀρετὴν τὸ τῆς αὐτεξουσιότητος δώρημα τοῖς ἀνθρώποις καὶ ὅτι ἐκ μόνης προαιρέσεως καὶ αὐτεξουσιότητος ὑπάρχει τὰ κυρίως κακά· τὰ δὲ ἕτερα, ὅσα κακὰ ὑπάρχει, παρὰ θεοῦ γινόμενα, παιδευτικὰ τῶν ἀνθρώπων εἰσί, παιδαγωγοῦντα μᾶλλον πρὸς ἀρετήν. Διὸ οὔτε κυρίως κακὰ ταῦτα λεκτέον.

285 Contra Augustine's pessimistic perspective of the *man of fall* due to the consequences of the primeval sin. Cf. Gross (1960) in Pedersen (2004, 96).

286 Presumably, questions such as 'whence evil' would also have had arisen without the Manichaeans. However, this optimistic anthropology, which rejects any kind of predetermination and insists on free will, has been developed in contradiction to the Manichaean challenge. As Pedersen (2015b, 572–73) notes regarding Titus' anthropology, "His treatise is, firstly, original within Patristic literature, in the sense of intensifying or making a number of ideas unambiguous which otherwise only exist as unclear tendencies among other Greek Church Fathers, where they are combined with different, even conflicting, tendencies. This is, for example, the case with Titus' vehement insistence on man's ethical freedom, which leads to a denial of the traditional teaching in Greek Patristics on Adam's original immortality and the catastrophic "fall of man". Titus' theology corresponds to a large degree to later "Pelagian" viewpoints in the Latin language area".

287 Stroumsa and Stroumsa, 1988, 56. It is worth examining the influence of these early Byzantine works on later Syriac-speaking anti-Manichaean authors under Islam. John of Dara, for instance, as Ruani (2017, 203–22, esp. 221) has shown addressing the Manichaean question 'whence evil' and the issues of theodicy and free will, draws from Titus of Bostra to whom he refers and whom he quotes.

The anthropological implications of Manichaean dualism are pointed out not only by Christian theologians and clerics, but also by pagans. The neo-Platonist philosopher Simplicius, Proclus' pupil, gives a summary of the "Manichaean cosmogony as a classic example of the wrong solution to the problem of evil".[288]

> Since they didn't want to say that God was the cause of the bad, they posited the existence of a specific origin of the bad, taking it to be equal in honour and strength to the good (or rather, even stronger, since up to the present the bad has obviously been superior in all its undertakings). [...] The result is that in their flight from saying that the good is the cause of the bad they portray it as utterly bad – and so, as the proverb has it, by running from the smoke they fell into the fire.[289]

3.2.2 The Lack of Effort for Self-Improvement

The second important implication of Manichaean anthropology, highlighted by both pagan and Christian writers, was that it did not leave room for man's moral progress.

According to Alexander of Lycopolis, Manichaean anthropology and doctrine resulted into the lack of rules for the moral education of the people; it thus hindered and obscured morals.[290] Moral progress could be acquired in any place, even in the midst of debauchery.

> Our first question should be: what then, is the use of all the effort which is spent on education? For we could become good even when asleep. Or for what reason do these people hold out to their own catechumens the highest hope for reaching the good? For these would be in possession of their proper good even when spending their time in whoring.[291]

---

288 Lieu 1994a, 125, 171.

289 Simplicius, *Comm. Man. Epict.* 35 (Hadot, 326.112–327.121; Brennan and Britain, 40): Μὴ βουλόμενοι γὰρ αἴτιον τοῦ κακοῦ τὸν θεὸν εἰπεῖν, ἀρχὴν ὑπεστήσαντο ἰδίαν τοῦ κακοῦ, ἰσότιμον αὐτὴν καὶ ἰσοσθενῆ τιθέντες τῷ ἀγαθῷ, μᾶλλον δὲ καὶ ἰσχυροτέραν· [...] ὥστε φεύγοντες, αἴτιον αὐτὸν τοῦ κακοῦ εἰπεῖν, πάγκακον ὑπογράφουσι· καὶ, κατὰ τὴν παροιμίαν, φεύγοντες τὸν καπνὸν εἰς πῦρ ἐμπεπτώκασιν. See also Johannes Philoponus, *De opificio mundi*: 69 ς'. Ὅτι τὸ σκότος οὔτε οὐσία ἐστὶν οὔτε ποιότης, στέρησις δὲ μόνη τοῦ ἀντικειμένου φωτός. αἱ μὲν οὖν περὶ τοῦ σκότους τῆς Μανιχαϊκῆς καὶ ἀσεβοῦς μυθολογίας ζητήσεις παρείσθωσαν εὐθύνας ἤδη πρότερον παρασχοῦσαι πολλοῖς.

290 Alexander of Lycopolis, *Tract. Man.* 1.

291 Alexander of Lycopolis, *Tract. Man.* 16.12–17 (Brinkmann, 23; Van der Horst and Mansfeld, 79): πρῶτον μὲν τίς χρεία τοῦ περὶ τὴν παίδευσιν πόνου; γενοίμεθα γὰρ ἂν καθεύδοντες σπουδαῖοι.

For Titus of Bostra, Manichaean anthropology introduces coercion in human actions and abolishes the hope of change for the better. "Mani does not acknowledge the difference between things and an ethical being like man; he introduces coercion and banishes the hope of conversion",[292] and creates an impression that man cannot determine his own life. "To say that evil is external and therefore uncontrollable, can leave people feeling powerless to influence their own fate or luck".[293] Thus, "the Manichaeans require no anointing for battles, since they regard virtue and vice as necessities of nature".[294]

However, as Zacharias of Mytilene underlines, a change for the better (moral progress) is possible and is the result of education, whereby the choice of the good becomes an acquired habit/disposition (ἕξις). Talking about man, good is precisely this acquired state of mind (ἕξις), which is a quality, not a substance as it is in the case of God, while evil is the absence of this habit.[295]

In practice, for Church Fathers like John Chrysostom, the Manichaean belief that "evil is steadfast" (τὴν κακίαν ἀκίνητον εἶναί φασι) and that man's change for the better is impossible (ἀδύνατον [...] ἐπὶ τὸ βέλτιον μεταβολή), was a constant threat and had a bad influence on the moral behaviour and attitudes of the faithful. People who were eager to make progress were paralysed by this rationale; nobody would fight for virtue anymore (Πότε γὰρ ἐπιμελήσεταί τις ἀρετῆς [...];).[296] Chrysostom wonders:

> for if even now, that there are laws, the threat of hell, the desire for glory, [...] the condemnation of evil, and the praise of good, there are but a few who choose to strive for virtue; [imagine] if all the above did not exist, what would prevent everyone from being perished and corrupt?[297]

ἢ διὰ τί μάλιστα τοὺς ἀκροωμένους αὐτῶν οἱ τοιοῦτοι ἄνδρες εἰς ἐλπίδα ἄγουσι τοῦ καλοῦ; καὶ γὰρ καλινδούμενοι σὺν ταῖς ἑταίραις τὸ οἰκεῖον ἔχοιεν ἂν ἀγαθόν.

292 Titus of Bostra, c. Manichaeos 4.4.39–43 in Pedersen 2004, 55.

293 Lieu 1985, 141.

294 Titus of Bostra, c. Manichaeos 4.10, in Pedersen 2004, 51.

295 Zacharias of Mytilene, Adv. Manichaeos 3–4 (Demetrakopoulos, 3–4): ἀλλ᾽ ὡς ποιότητες· ὅθεν οὐ ψυχαὶ λέγονται, ἀλλὰ περὶ ψυχὴν θεωροῦνται, ἡ μὲν ὡς ἕξις τις οὖσα ψυχῆς, ἡ δὲ ὡς στέρησις ἕξεως (3.1–3). [...] Ἡ γὰρ ἀντιδιαστολὴ τοῦ καλοῦ εἰς τὸ κακὸν ἐπὶ Θεοῦ χώραν οὐκ ἔχει, ἀλλ᾽ ἐπὶ τοῦ ἐν ἀνθρωπίναις πράξεσι καλοῦ τε καὶ κακοῦ, τοῦ μὲν καθ᾽ ἕξιν τῇ τοῦ Θεοῦ δημιουργίᾳ συνεισερχομένου, τοῦ δὲ κατὰ στέρησιν ἕξεως ἐκ τοῦ αὐτεξουσίου κινήματος ἐπιγινομένου πολλάκις καὶ ἀπογινομένου (3.6–10). Τὸ γὰρ καλὸν τὸ ἐν τῇ ψυχῇ καὶ τὸ κατ᾽ ἀρετὴν ζῆν, τῇ γενέσει, καθὼς εἴρηται, οἷά τις ἕξις ἀρίστη συνεισέρχεται· τῇ δὲ τούτου ῥαστώνῃ τῇ ἐκ προαιρέσεως καὶ κακῆς ἀναστροφῆς καὶ συνηθείας φαύλης συμβαινούσῃ, τὸ κακὸν οἷά τις ἕξεως στέρησις πολλάκις ἐπιγίνεται (3.11–15) [...] Τὸ κακὸν τοίνυν οὐκ οὐσία, ἀλλὰ τοῦ θείου νόμου παράβασις ἐκ μόνου τοῦ αὐτεξουσίου κινήματος (4.7–8).

296 John Chrysostom, Hom. Matt. (hom. 1–90), hom. 26, PG 57:340.15–24.

297 John Chrysostom, Hom. Matt. (hom. 1–90), hom. 26, PG 57:340.24–30.

This statement of Chrysostom could be interpreted as a reference to the laws against heretics, which punished and deprived heretics of the privileges of the Catholics. In a similar fashion, Nilus in several of his letters emphasizes that "evil is not invincible, as the Manichaeans claim" (οὐ γάρ ἐστιν ἀκίνητον τὸ κακόν, ὡς οἱ Μανιχαῖοί φασιν). Indeed, pointing out the strength of free will, he argues that self-improvement is possible even for those who have reached "the depths of malice" (τῆς κακίας τὰ βάραθρα).[298] Relevant in this context are the worries of John of Caesarea in the sixth century and the instructions he gave when addressing his flock: "So, you must avoid them [Manichaeans] and do not even greet them; because 'evil companionships corrupt good morals'".[299]

Serapion of Thmuis, in order to prove that people can change, gives the example of the apostles. Unlike the example of Manichaeism, in which 'the apostle of Christ' Mani is identified with the Paraclete, Serapion underlines the human weakness of the apostles, stressing that the acquisition of virtue is the result of human effort and not an arbitrary victory of the powers of good over the powers of evil (= nature) within us.[300]

As Basil of Caesarea notes in his second *Homily on the Hexaemeron*, for some people, namely, the Marcionites, the Valentinians and the Manichaeans (the worst of all for Basil and the putrefaction of the Churches), darkness does not mean a place deprived of light; it is an evil power, or rather the evil itself, which is self-begotten and is hostile to the goodness of God. According to them, as Basil criticises, this darkness is fighting the human soul, bringing death and is opposed to virtue. Basil considers all these theories as an invention to serve as pretexts for committing sins freely, which finally would cause man's perdition.[301] Basil's homilies on the *Hexaemeron* were live speeches that

---

298 Nilus of Ankara, *Ep. 317 to Martinus the Chancellor*. As also Nilus argues in his epistle to the monk Thaumasius, "it's on our hand to make a progress, because evil is not unmovable, as the Manichaeans claim". See Cameron (1976b) about the authenticity of St. Nilus letters.

299 John of Caesarea, *Adv. Manichaeos hom. 1* 17.277–79 (Richard, 92): Φεύγετε τοίνυν καὶ τοῖς τοιούτοις χαίρειν μὴ λέγετε· Φθείρουσιν ἤδη χρηστὰ ὁμιλίαι κακαί.

300 Serapion, *c. Manichaeos* 24.9–25.4 (HTS 15:40–41): [...] διὰ τοῦτο καὶ τὰ τῶν ἁγίων ἁμαρτήματα λελάληται· τί γὰρ ἐλύπει σιωπῇ σιωπηθῆναι τὸ πταῖσμα; [...] ἵνα διαβληθῶσι, λελάληται· ἐκβεβλήκασι γὰρ τὴν διαβολήν, ἀλλ' ἵνα μὴ τῶν ἁμαρτημάτων σιωπηθέντων ἀναμάρτητοι τὴν φύσιν ὑπονοηθῶσιν. ὑπὲρ ἀληθείας τοίνυν ὁ λόγος. [...] Ὦ τοῦ καινοῦ θαύματος! ἐγράφησαν αἱ ἁμαρτίαι τῶν ἁγίων, ἵνα ἡ ἀλήθεια γνωσθῇ, ὅτι ἐκ τῶν ὁμοίων φύντες καὶ ὁμοίως φύντες ἀρετὴ τὸ μεῖζον εἰλήφασιν, οὐ φύσει νικήσαντες, ἀλλ' ἀρετῇ διαπρέψαντες.

301 Basil of Caesarea, *Hom. Hexaem.* (hom. 2, sec. 4.1–24, 22–24)/(2.4.22–24): Τί μακρὰν ἀποτρέχεις τῆς ἀληθείας, ἄνθρωπε, ἀφορμάς σε αὐτῷ τῆς ἀπωλείας ἐπινοῶν; Decret (1982, 1060–1064) commenting on this homily, points out that Basil's problem with Manichaeans was not abominations, the favorite accusation of Augustine, but the "inconsistency and absurdity" of "the dualistic doctrine of Mani", which with its view that "the human body" "derives its origin from the 'race of Darkness', is fundamentally impure and evil" has severe consequences in the life of young ascetics.

Basil gave in Caesarea around 370 during the holy week. Thus, it is reasonable to assume that among his audience there may have been some Manichaeans, something which is at any rate expected, since the first law against the Manichaeans was issued, as we have seen, only in 372. What is certain, however, is that these Manichaean views were raised as a topic of discussion and circulated in the society of Caesarea.

For John Chrysostom, all the trouble started from the Manichaean question 'whence evil', which, according to him, is the culmination of all evils.[302] As Simplicius points out, the quest for the source of evil is not only "a cause of impiety towards the divinity", but "has [also] undermined the foundations of good morals".[303]

Summarizing, both pagan and Christian writers related theodicy to ethical theory and both, in the words of Stroumsa, "insist on the misleading consequences entailed by such a false epistemology, in particular in the field of ethics".[304] For the anti-Manichaean authors (both Christian and pagan), the Manichaean anthropology had, in specific, the following consequences: matter and body were treated with complete disdain, the annihilation of human guilt and man's responsibility, and the abolition of free will and of the concept of personhood. In terms of social life, such consequences, led to behaviours that undermined the (established) social life-model (status quo) and challenged social institutions and organizations that were vital for social cohesion and economic prosperity, such as marriage, childbearing, labour (a number of professions were rejected), and charity.

3.3   The "Seal of the Breast" and Its Implications in Everyday Social Life

One of the three major commandments that the Elect had to observe was "the seal of the breast". This stemmed from the Manichaean belief that the creation of man was the stratagem of matter and man's body was created by the archons of Darkness. As Mani himself explains in his *Fundamental Letter*, even today one can observe that the bodies are not created by God, but by nature, which is identified with matter and evil.[305] The aim of the principle of evil was to entrap perpetually the divine substance in matter through the continual creation of new bodies through births. This could only succeed through the weakness and the passions of the body of man, which was co-substantial with lust since it had originated from the evil. Thus, man's carnal lust was the

---

302   John Chrysostom, *Oppugn.* (PG 47:365.22–28): οὐδ' ἂν ὁ τῶν κακῶν τούτων ἐπεισῆλθε κολοφῶν τὸ ζητεῖν, πόθεν τὰ κακά. [...] Καὶ γὰρ Μαρκίων, καὶ Μάνης, καὶ Οὐαλεντῖνος, καὶ τῶν Ἑλλήνων οἱ πλείους ἐντεῦθεν ἔλαβον τὴν ἀρχήν.

303   Simplicius, *Comm. Man. Epict.* 35 (Hadot, 322.3) (Lieu 2010, 101).

304   Stroumsa 1992, 340.

305   Augustine, *Fund.*, Frg. 9: (6.4). For the whole text see Gardner and Lieu 2004, 168–172.

trap of nature. As Mani teaches the catechumen Menoch, "the Devil is the originator of bodies through lust that is in the Devil's snare by means of the lust for a woman".[306] Thus, the desire for a woman is rendered as nature's (i.e. matter/evil) snare, a trap invented by the archons of Darkness. Consequently, for the Manichaeans, the institution of marriage, which is 'inextricably tied' to family and childbearing, ensured the success of the stratagem of Matter to entrap the divine substance in bodies through births.

Therefore, in order to prevent Matter's stratagem, Mani sanctioned the "seal of the breast" as a counter measure. According to the *Kephalaia*, the righteous (Elect) Manichaean had to "embra/[ce] continence and purity".[307] In other words, "the Seal of the Breast prevents fornication and marriage and therefore physical procreation, which prolongs the captivity of Light".[308]

3.3.1 Critique of the "Seal of the Breast"

The Manichaean prohibition of marriage and of procreation was too serious a matter to pass unnoticed. It was an issue that threatened the nucleus of social life, the family institution. Thus, it became one of the most hotly debated issues in anti-Manichaean polemics.

The first relevant testimonies come from the Egyptian authors. At the same time as Diocletian worried about the corruption of the innocent, orderly, and tranquil Roman citizens by the Manichaean evil deeds and practices, a Christian bishop and a pagan philosopher were equally troubled by these Manichaean practices. In his circular letter, the bishop of Alexandria warned the faithful and informed the Roman authorities that "Again the Manich[aea]ns" misinterpreting Paul's passage (1 Cor. 7:1ff.), "speak [falsely against marriage saying that] he [who does not] marry does well".[309] Alexander of Lycopolis provided the interpretation of such practice: The Manichaeans abstain "from marriage and love-making for fear that because of the continuing of the race, the divine power will dwell within the matter for a longer time".[310]

---

306   *Letter to Menoch* 2.3 in Gardner and Lieu 2004, 172–174 (no 54); Lieu 2010, 13.

307   *1Keph.* 80, 192.3–193.22 (Gardner 1995, 201): "[Once more] the enlightener speaks to his disciples: Know [and] / understand that the first righteousness a per[son] / will do to make truly righteous is this: he can embra/[ce] continence and purity".

308   Lieu 2010, xviii. Regarding the Manichaean rejection of marriage and procreation cf. Gardner and Lieu (2004, 22); Franzmann (2022b, 168): "the distinction between virginal, continent and married ones – with 'married' as a fully negative category – is amply illustrated in *PsB* 179.7–181.18". Arabic sources also testify that Manichaeans rejected marriage and procreation, cf. Al-Nadim, *Fihrist* 9 (Dodge, 788).

309   PRynalds 3, Gr. 469 (Roberts 1938, 38–46) (Lieu 2010, 36–37, 37; Gardner and Lieu 2004, 114–5).

310   Alexander of Lycopolis, *Tract. Man.* 4.25–30 (Brinkmann, 7; Van der Horst and Mansfeld, 57, altered): ἐπεὶ οὖν ἀπόλλυσθαι τὴν ὕλην ἐστὶ θεοῦ δόγμα, ἀπέχεσθαι μὲν ἐμψύχων πάντων,

On the opposite side, Manichaean polemics against the Catholic Church commented on Paul's passage, arguing: "Yet, these are men who have dared to say that this lust is a good thing in opposition to the evangelical and apostolic books, which they keep reading in vain; you may see how their holy men at one time have slept with their daughters, at other times have had intercourse with several concubines and wives as well ... when they perform this act, they think it has been permitted by God".[311]

Around half a century after Alexander's and Theonas' testimonies, *circa* 350, Didymus the Blind recorded (in his *Ecclesiastes*) a dialogue he had with a Manichaean, who maintained celibacy and abstinence from sex.[312] As one reads in the *Vita Sancti Epiphanii*, a similar discussion echoing Manichaean ideas concerning celibacy and marriage took place in the Nile Delta between Epiphanius and Hierax, an outstanding ascetic of the era.[313] Logically, such disputes and controversies on the issues of marriage and sexual life should have been part of the daily agenda.

As Theodoret of Cyrrhus remarks, the Manichaeans "maintain that marriage is the Devil's legislation".[314] According to Macarius of Magnesia, a certain Dositheus, a chief among the "children of the Manichaeans" (Μανιχαίων παῖδες), said freely (ἀποθρυλλῶν) that marriage is an unseemly action and very contrary to the law. This Dositheus claimed that as this world (humanity) began through mingling and communion, so, through abstinence and restraint of impulses and desires it has to be terminated.[315] So, according to Dositheus, marriage is illegal because it is contrary to the goal of the Manichaeans, which is the gradual dissolution of the cosmos into its constituent elements in order to release the divine substance. And, since the cause of man's creation was the sexual intercourse of the princes of Darkness, the only way to bring it to an end is to abstain from sex. Thus, Mani's plan counteracted the plan of Matter, aiming for the gradual release of the divine principle (through rituals), and to put an end to its further entrapment (with "the seal of the breast").

σιτίζεσθαι δὲ λάχανα καὶ πᾶν ὅ τι ἀναίσθητον, ἀπέχεσθαι δὲ γάμων καὶ ἀφροδισίων καὶ τεκνοποιίας, ἵνα μὴ ἐπὶ πλεῖον ἡ δύναμις ἐνοικήσῃ τῇ ὕλῃ κατὰ τὴν τοῦ γένους διαδοχήν.

311   *Letter to Menoch* 4, in Gardner and Lieu 2004, 173.

312   Didymus the Blind, *Comm. Eccl.* 274.17–275.2.

313   *Vita Sancti Epiphanii* 27 (PG 41:57–60). For more about Hierax, see ch.[7], section 3.2.

314   Theodoret, *Haer.* 83:380.28–31: Τὸν δὲ διάβολον ποτὲ μὲν Ὕλην καλεῖ, ποτὲ δὲ τῆς Ὕλης ἄρχοντα. Τὸν δὲ γάμον τοῦ διαβόλου νομοθεσίαν φησί. Timothy the Presbyter, *Recept. Haer.* (PG 86ᴬ: 20): καὶ τὸν γάμον, νομοθεσίαν τοῦ δαίμονος. Didymus, *De trinitate.*

315   Macarius of Magnesia, *Apocriticus*, 3.26: Διὰ μὲν κοινωνίας ὁ κόσμος τὴν ἀρχὴν ἔσχε· διὰ δὲ τῆς ἐγκρατείας τὸ τέλος θέλει λαβεῖν. I shall return to Dositheus, who may not have been a Manichaean at all, and about whom there is substantial literature in ch.[6], section 3.1.2.

However, as Titus of Bostra notes, although the Manichaeans condemn marriage as illegal and lawless because of the fear that it will lead to procreation, sex with precaution was considered desirable. As Titus points out, with astonishment:

> [The Manichaeans] curse the begetting of children, while on the contrary, they desire sexual intercourse if it does not lead to procreation. This is so, because they consider as bondage/slavery procreation (which is legislated by God), instead of considering as slavery the sensual pleasure/delight (ἡδονή).[316]

In contrast, for the Church Fathers, legitimate sexual intercourse was only that which aims at giving birth to children. Thus, one can imagine that their corresponding instructions and advice were diametrically opposed. As Didymus the Blind argues in his discussion with the Manichaean, the relationship of a couple is not a sin if they come together (have intercourse) at the right time (ἐν καλῷ καιρῷ), namely during woman's fertile days, for procreation.[317] This view is apparently in contrast to the advice that the Manichaean Elect gave to their catechumens, such as to abstain from sex during the fertile days of a woman and other suggestions for methods of contraception.[318]

In addition, in case the above contraception was ineffective, as Titus claims, the Manichaeans urged their partners to dispose of their foetuses through abortions.

> But those who often enjoy pleasure necessarily hate the fruit that derives from it and order women to break up and to reject conceptions by magical practices and not to wait for childbirth (at proper time).[319]

---

316 Titus of Bostra, *c. Manichaeos* 2.56.29–32 (CCSG 82:221): Τήν τε παιδογονίαν ὑβρίζοντες τὰς μίξεις αὐτοῖς ἄνευ γε ταύτης ⟨βούλονται⟩ συμβαίνειν, δοῦλοί γε ὄντες τῆς ἀναγκαίας διαδοχῆς πρὸς θεοῦ νενομοθετημένης, ἀλλ᾽ οὐ τῆς ἡδονῆς.

317 Didymus the Blind, *Comm. Eccl.* 274.17–275.2: τοῦτό ποτε καὶ π[ρὸς] τοὺς Μανιχαίους εἶπον ⟨ ⟩, ὅτι ʽσκόπησον, οἷον μέγεθός ἐστιν τα[ύ]της τῆς σωφροσύνης· μὴ γὰρ κολάσει ὑποβάλλεται, ἐὰν συνέλθῃ τῇ γυναικὶ ἑαυτοῦ ἐν [κα]λῷ καιρῷ· μὴ γὰρ ψόγον αὐτῷ φέρει, μὴ γὰρ παρανομία αὐτῷ λογίζεται.

318 Augustine, *Mor. Manich.* 18.65 (PL 32: 1178), cf. Lieu 1994a, 294; Lieu 2010, 75. See also Chadwick 2001 170: "Hearers who cooked selected food for the Elect and were allowed sexual relations at safe periods of the monthly cycle. They were discouraged from having children since this incarcerated sparks of divine light in soggy matter".

319 Titus of Bostra, *c. Manichaeos*, 2.56.48–52 (CCSG 82:223): Οἱ δὲ τὴν ἡδονὴν πολλάκις καρπούμενοι τὸ ἀπ᾽ αὐτῆς ἔργον ἀναγκαίως μισοῦσι, καὶ παρεγγυῶσι ταῖς παραγγελίαν ἐφαλλομέναις μαγγανείαις τὰς συλλήψεις ἐκλύειν τε καὶ ῥίπτειν καὶ τοὺς ἐν ὥρᾳ τόκους μὴ ἀναμένειν (CCT 273). Cf. Pedersen 2004, 32: "The Manichaeans encourage women to dispose of their

It is for this reason, Titus comments, that Mani befriends the young people, because the license to sin is given to them.[320] A well known case of a person who was labelled as a Manichaean and was sentenced to death in 386 was Priscillian the bishop of Avila. Among the charges against him, it is said, was that a "young [woman] Procula had become pregnant by Priscillian and had disposed of the unwanted child by abortion".[321]

The above stance of Manichaeans toward marriage and procreation, described by Eastern Church Fathers, is confirmed by Augustine's critique.[322] As Augustine's criticism has a confessional character it gives more detailed and intimate information since he knew things from within, having himself been an auditor for nine years. Thus, Augustine blamed his former companions:

> For (you do not forbid) sexual intercourse; but, as has been said long before by the apostle, you really forbid marriage, which is the only honourable justification for such a deed (1 Tim 4:3) ... Are you not the ones who are accustomed to advise us to observe as far as possible the period when a woman was fit for conception after the purification of her womb (menstruation), and at that time to refrain from sexual intercourse, lest the soul be entangled in the flesh?'[323]
>
> And, though you allow many of your followers to retain their connection with you in spite of their refusal, or their inability, to obey you, you cannot deny that you make the prohibition.[324]
>
> This proves that you approve of having a wife, not for the procreation of children, but for the gratification of passion.[325]

As I have argued above with regard to "the seal of the mouth", it is also in the case of "the seal of the breast" that Augustine's writings, unlike those of Eastern Church Fathers, make a clear distinction between the Elect and the auditors. The prohibition of marriage applied only to the Elect.[326] Auditors were allowed to marry, even though they, too, were encouraged "to avert

---

foetuses, and they are enemies of nature and the Creator". Cf. Pedersen (2004, 171–77), for Titus' portrayal of Manichaeism as determinism and immorality.

320   Titus of Bostra, c. Manichaeos 4.39–43. Pedersen 2004, 55: "he introduces coercion and banishes the hope of conversion, and that is why he becomes the friend of young people who want permission to sin".

321   See Chadwick 1976, 37.

322   Augustine, Haer. 46 (cf. Gardner and Lieu 2004, 187–191); Faust. 30.6 (NPNF¹ 4: 566–67).

323   Augustine, Mor. Manich. 18.65 (Lieu 2010, 75).

324   Augustine, Faust. 30.6 (NPNF¹ 4: 567).

325   Augustine, Mor. Manich. 18.65 (NPNF¹ 4).

326   As BeDuhn (2000b, 36) remarks: "Throughout his exposition, Augustine implicitly associates the seals exclusively with the Elect class. He clearly envisions a distinct set of values

procreation".[327] However, for Augustine, "there is no marriage where action is taken to prevent motherhood".[328] As BeDuhn comments, in Augustine's "Catholic point of view, the Manichaean encouragement of birth control is incompatible with marriage in the true sense".[329] "This avoidance of child-bearing led to Augustine's accusation that the Manichaeans had turned the bed-chamber into a brothel".[330]

Augustine also associates this problematic Manichaean stance toward marriage and reproduction with the dualistic background of the Manichaean doctrine. He further points out that the different treatment of auditors is a contradiction of the Manichaean doctrine for the sake of the Manichaean community and its missionary policies.

> They abstain from sexual intercourse, that he may not be bound more closely in the bondage of the flesh.
>
> The prohibition is part of your false doctrine, while the toleration is only for the interests of the society. [...] You see, then, that there is a great difference between exhorting to virginity as the better of two good things, and forbidding to marry by denouncing the true purpose of marriage.[331]

Recapitulating, according to both Eastern Church Fathers and Augustine, the Manichaeans considered childbearing as a more serious sin than sexual intercourse. As one can easily realize, such attitudes and behaviours threatened the Church Fathers who feared the negative influence of the Manichaean advice to young couples. As Chadwick aptly comments, "the Manichees were known to hold that procreation should be avoided, and horrified orthodox catholics by openly advising married couples to confine sexual intercourse to the 'safe period' of the menstrual cycle. They were naturally accused of justifying abortion".[332]

For Church Fathers, the heretics of the later times, referred to in the pseudo-Pauline letter to Timothy (1 Tim. 4.1–5), were unquestionably the Manichaeans. As Chrysostom stresses, apart from Paul's prophesy that they would abstain

---

for Auditors, and does not indicate that they were organized according to a Three Seals scheme".

327   Augustine, *Faust.* 6.3–5. Cf. Chadwick 1998, 582: "Hearers, who were allowed wives or concubines but were expected to avert procreation"; BeDuhn 2000b, 96. Augustine, *Mor. Manich.* 65 (BeDuhn 2000b, 36): "but do not prohibid marriage since your Auditors, who are in the second rank (*secundus gradus*) among you, are not forbidden to have wives".

328   Augustine, *Mor. Manich.* 18.65 (BeDuhn 2000b, 284).

329   BeDuhn 2000b, 36.

330   Lieu 1994a, 294. Augustine, *Faust.* 15.7, p. 480,6–8 (& Augustine, *Mor. Manich.* 18.65).

331   Augustine, *Faust.* 6.3 & 30.6 (*NPNF*[1] 4:288 & 567).

332   Chadwick 1976, 37.

from food and marriage ('forbid marriage and demand abstinence from foods'), they will give, for all related issues, the most destructive advice.[333] Macarius of Magnesia, commenting on the Manichaean concepts of chastity, purity, and virginity, states that these would not benefit the world at all, because they are based on wrong grounds.[334]

Also, Alexander's critique on the Manichaean beliefs concerning sexual abstinence is harsh, caustic, and relentless:

> As for their abstaining from marriage and love-making for fear that, because of the continuing of the race, the divine power will dwell within matter for a longer time, I wonder how they are able to convince themselves. For if God's providence is not strong enough to separate the divine power from matter both by means of births and through those things which are always the same and in the same way, what, then, is Manichaeus' inventiveness able to contrive for his sake? For surely, he does not say that he really has come to assist God in this task with a giant's mettle in order to quicken and speed up the departure of the divine power from matter through the abolishing of births.[335]

Along the same lines is Titus' of Bostra criticism. The Manichaeans became lawmakers in the place of God. They want to determine nature's processes and to eliminate the perpetuity of the human race. Thus, they become enemies of nature, or rather of God, nature's creator.[336] The notion that the divine

---

333 John Chrysostom, *Hom. 1 Tim.* (*homiliae 1–18*), 557.55–558.30: ἔσται καιρὸς ὅτε χαλεπώτε-ρον αὐτοὶ οἱ τῆς πίστεως μετεσχηκότες τοῦτο ἐργάσονται, οὐ μέχρι βρωμάτων, ἀλλὰ καὶ μέχρι γάμων, καὶ πάντων τῶν τοιούτων τὴν ὀλέθριον συμβουλὴν εἰσάγοντες. Οὐ περὶ Ἰουδαίων λέγει ταῦτα· [...] ἀλλὰ περὶ Μανιχαίων, καὶ τῶν ἀρχηγετῶν τούτων.

334 Macarious of Magnesia, *Apocriticus* 3.52.27: καὶ οὐδὲν οὐδαμοῦ τὸ κοινὸν ὠφέλησαν, κἂν παρ-θενεύειν, κἂν τὴν ἄκραν σωφροσύνην ἐν βίῳ διδάσκωσι.

335 Alexander of Lycopolis, *Tract. Man.* 25.10–21 (Brinkmann, 37; Van der Horst and Mansfeld, 94–95): Τὸ δὲ ἀπέχεσθαι γάμου καὶ ἀφροδισίων δεδιότας, μὴ κατὰ τὴν τοῦ γένους διαδοχὴν ἐπὶ πλέον ἐνοικήσῃ τῇ ὕλῃ ἡ δύναμις ἡ θεία, θαυμάζω πῶς καὶ αὐτοὶ ἑαυτοὺς ἀποδέχονται. εἰ γὰρ μὴ ἐξαρκεῖ ἡ τοῦ θεοῦ πρόνοια, ὥστε καὶ διὰ γενέσεων καὶ διὰ τῶν ἀεὶ ⟨κατὰ τὰ αὐτὰ⟩ καὶ ὡσαύτως ἐχόντων ἀποικονομήσασθαι τῆς ὕλης τὴν θείαν δύναμιν, τί ἡ τοῦ Μανιχαίου ἐπίνοια ὑπὲρ τούτου διαμηχανήσασθαι δύναται; οὐ γὰρ δήπου γιγαντείῳ λήματι ὡς ἀληθῶς φησιν τῷ θεῷ βοηθὸς πρὸς τοῦτο γεγονέναι, ἵνα τὰς γενέσεις ἀναιρῶν σύντομον ποιήσῃ τὴν τῆς θείας δυνάμεως ἀπὸ τῆς ὕλης ἀναχώρησιν.

336 Titus of Bostra, *c. Manichaeos* 2.56.33–38 & 53–55 (CCSG 82:223): ἐχθροί γε τὰ πάντα τῆς ἀληθοῦς καὶ γνησίας ἀρετῆς καὶ τῆς εὐσεβείας ὄντες, ὥσπερ αἰτιώμενοι τὸ ἀείζωον τοῦ τῶν ἀνθρώπων γένους καὶ βουλόμενοι αὐτοῦ που στῆναι τὸν δρόμον τῆς φύσεως, νομοθετοῦντες τῷ θεῷ καὶ ἀγανακτοῦντες πρὸς τὴν ἀγαθότητα, δι' ἣν ἀνεξικάκως ἔχει πρὸς τὴν αὐτῶν βλασφη-μίαν. [...] ἐχθροὶ τῆς φύσεως ἐγηγερμένοι, μᾶλλον δὲ τοῦ ταύτην δημιουργήσαντος, καὶ μανίαν κατὰ τοῦδε τοῦ παντὸς ἐκμαθόντες.

substance was entrapped into the flesh through the births and the subsequent practices (abstinence from lawful intercourse) were some of the things that converted Manichaeans had to abjure in a particular chapter of the abjuration formula.

> I therefore anathematize and condemn those who [...] say that bodies are of the evil (principle) [...] those who forbid marriage [...] and withholding [...] themselves from the lawful intercourse with woman [...] that is [the one which] is clearly referring to the procreation of children (childbearing), which the Manichaeans detest, so as not to drag, as they say, souls down into the mire of human flesh.[337]

These Manichaean positions on marriage, celibacy, sexual behaviour and procreation were further associated (as is expected) with moral deviations, and fuelled accusations of 'crimes' against nature (e.g. anal intercourse, homosexuality). There is no doubt that the rumours about such behaviours were reinforced by the anthropological perspective that the Manichaeans held (as interpreted by anti-Manichaean authors), according to which evil is congenital in man's nature, acting independently (*in absentia*) of man's own volition and intension, hence free will was absent.

The correlation that the opponents of Manichaeans made between celibacy and 'orgies', is clearly illustrated in the sc. The converted Manichaean anathematized abnormal sexual behaviour and acts which his former comrades, men and women, 'were forced' in a way to commit among them, since they abstained from 'normal'/lawful intercourse.

> [...] and because of this [withholding themselves from the lawful intercourse] "they commit shameless acts" (Rom 1:26–27) against nature with men and women even as do the women among them.[338]

---

337 sc, ch. 7 (Lieu 1994a, 248–250 & Lieu 2010, 122–125): Ἀναθεματίζω οὖν καὶ καταθεματίζω τοὺς [...] τὰ σώματα λέγοντας εἶναι τοῦ πονηροῦ [...] καὶ γαμεῖν κωλύοντας [...] καὶ τῆς νενομισμένης πρὸς τὰς γυναῖκας συνουσίας ἀπεχομένους [...] δηλαδὴ πρὸς παιδοποιΐαν, ἣν οἱ Μανιχαῖοι βδελύττονται, ἵνα μὴ ψυχάς, ὡς αὐτοί φασιν, εἰς τὸν βόρβορον τῶν ἀνθρωπίνων σαρκῶν κατάγωσι.

338 sc, ch. 7 (Lieu 2010, 124–25): [...] καὶ διὰ τοῦτο [τῆς νενομισμένης πρὸς τὰς γυναῖκας συνουσίας ἀπεχομένους] ἐν ἄρρεσι καὶ γυναιξὶ παρὰ φύσιν, ὥσπερ οὖν καὶ αἱ παρ' αὐτῶν γυναῖκες, "τὴν ἀσχημοσύνην κατεργαζόμενοι". See also Basil of Caesarea, *Asceticon* (PG 31:1256); Basil of Caesarea, *Quod deus non est auctor malorum* (PG 31:329–353): καὶ αἱ μὲν θήλειαι παρ' αὐτοῖς μετήλλαξαν τὴν φυσικὴν χρῆσιν εἰς τὴν παρὰ φύσιν, ἄρρενες δὲ ἐν ἄρσεσι τὴν ἀσχημοσύνην κατεργάζονται.

3.4 The "Seal of the Hand" and its Implications in Everyday Social and Economic Life

3.4.1 The Concept of the Living Self as the Basis for the "Seal of the Hand"

The concept of the *Living Self* is also the theoretical basis of the third Manichaean seal, which is related to both religious and social behaviour: "the seal of the hand".

According to the *Kephalaia*, the "the seal of the hand" or alternatively "the rest of the hands" is "to take great care not to harm the light soul trapped everywhere in matter and especially vegetation (*the Cross of Light*), for instance by plucking fruit".[339] As al-Nadim records, quoting Mani, "He who would enter the cult", apart from refraining "from eating meats, drinking wine, as well as from marriage", has also "to avoid [causing] injury to water, fire, trees, and living things".[340]

According to Turbo's presentation of the Manichaean doctrines and precepts:

> They also say that if anyone walks on the ground he harms the ground, and if he moves his hand he harms the air, because air is the soul of men and animals, birds, fish and reptiles and everything there is in the world.[341]

The concept and the importance of the *Living Self* for the Manichaeans has been presented in detail in the section above that examined the implications of Manichaean fasting, the "seal of the mouth". Further, "the seal of the hand", with its prohibition against injuring the divine substance in animals and plants, but also in the elements of nature (e.g. water, fire, air, earth), entailed implications in a number of daily activities in social and economic life.

3.4.2 Murderous Professions

At the economic level, "the seal of the hand" affected many productive sectors. A series of occupations, mainly in the primary sector (e.g. reapers, farmers, growers, breeders), but even in processing (e.g. food preparation, cooks, bakers, carpenters) and in the construction sector were scorned and should be avoided by the catechumens, because they were considered of a criminal nature.

---

339 *1Keph.* 80 (Gardner 1995, 201).
340 Al-Nadim, *Fihrist* 9 (Dodge, 788). Lieu 2010, xviii–xix.
341 *AA* 10.8 (Vermes, 55); Epiphanius *Pan.* 66.28.9 (Williams, 258).

Harvesters who gather the harvest are compared with the princes who originating from matter are in darkness, from when they chewed from the armour of the first man. For that reason it is necessary for them to be transformed into hay or beans or grain or corn or vegetables, so that they too are cut down and harvested. [...] He who kills a chicken must also become a chicken himself, [...] [...] He who has built himself a house, will be scattered through all bodies.[342]

And (I anathematize) those who [...] think that those who pluck corn or barley or grass or vegetables are transformed into them, in order that they may suffer the same experiences, and that harvesters and bread-makers are accursed [...].[343]

Alexander of Lycopolis criticizes the Manichaean elitist discrimination of professions which states that farmers, architects, builders, and other professionals are sentenced to be deprived of the good (ἀγαθόν). He compares it with the attitude of Jesus:

correctly understood by Jesus, and this is why, in order that farmers and carpenters and masons and other skilled workers should not be excluded from the good, he instituted a common circle of all these people together, and why, by means of simple and easy conversations, he led them towards an understanding of God and helped them to achieve a desire for the good.[344]

As Augustine critically remarks, agriculture is a crime for the Manichaeans.

They believe that [...] souls pass into [...] everything that is rooted [...] For they are convinced that plants and trees possess sentient life and can

---

342   *AA* 10.2–5 (Vermes, 53–54); Epiphanius, *Pan.* 66.28.2–5 (GCS 37:63–64; Williams, 257): οἱ δὲ θερισταί, ὅσοι θερίζουσιν, ἐοίκασι τοῖς ἄρχουσι τοῖς ἀπ᾽ ἀρχῆς οὖσιν εἰς τὸ σκότος, ὅτε ἔφαγον ἐκ τῆς τοῦ πρώτου ἀνθρώπου πανοπλίας. διὸ ἀνάγκη αὐτοὺς μεταγγισθῆναι εἰς χόρτον ἢ εἰς φασή-λια ἢ εἰς κριθὴν ἢ εἰς στάχυν ἢ εἰς λάχανα, ἵνα ⟨καὶ αὐτοὶ⟩ θερισθῶσι καὶ κοπῶσι.[...] εἴ τις φονεύ-σει ὀρνίθιον, ⟨καὶ αὐτὸς⟩ ὀρνίθιον ἔσται· [...] εἰ δέ τις οἰκοδομεῖ ἑαυτῷ οἰκίαν, διασπαραχθήσεται εἰς τὰ ὅλα σώματα.

343   *SC*, ch. 6 (Lieu 2010, 123): [...] τοὺς τὸν σῖτον ἢ κριθὴν ἢ βοτάνας ἢ λάχανα τίλλοντας εἰς ἐκεῖνα μεταβάλλεσθαι οἰομένους, ἵνα τὰ ὅμοια πάθωσι, καὶ τοὺς θεριστὰς καὶ τοὺς ἀρτοποιοὺς καταρωμένους.

344   Alexander of Lycopolis, *Tract. Man.* 16 (Brinkmann, 24; Van der Horst and Mansfeld, 80): ὁ Ἰησοῦς καὶ ἵνα μὴ ἀπελημαλένοι ὦσι τοῦ ἀγαθοῦ γεωργοί τε καὶ τέκτονες καὶ οἰκοδόμοι καὶ οἱ ἄλλοι ἀπὸ τῶν τεχνῶν, κοινὸν συνέδριον καθίσαι πάντων ὁμοῦ καὶ διὰ ἁπλῶν καὶ εὐκόλων διαλέ-ξεων καὶ εἰς θεοῦ ἔννοιαν αὐτοὺς ἀπενηνοχέναι καὶ τοῦ καλοῦ εἰς ἐπιθυμίαν ἐλθεῖν ποιῆσαι.

feel pain when injured, and therefore that no one can pull or pluck them without torturing them. Therefore, they consider it wrong to clear a field even of thorns. Hence, [...] they make agriculture, the mostly innocent of occupations, guilty of multiple murder.[345]

Indeed, as Augustine comments, they go as far as to say that "It is better for a man to be a usurer than a farmer ... For, they say, the person who gives money on usury does not injure the Cross of Light", while, "the person who is a farmer very much harms the cross of light [...] Those parts, they say, of God which were captured in that battle, were mixed altogether with the world and are in the trees, plants, fruit trees and fruit. He who furrows the ground troubles God's parts. He who plucks fruit from tree troubles God's parts".[346] On the contrary, for the Church Fathers it was usury that was a sin and not agriculture. Usurers were heavily criticized by many Christian authors.[347]

This discrimination and rejection of professions – especially of agriculture – is also evidenced by the Manichaean sources. An Iranian text, for example, records "regulations against engaging in agriculture",[348] and a Parthian text "reminds Auditors that they torture the living things".[349]

3.4.3 Dualism in the Economy

Another implication of the "seal of the hand" was the division of society into workers and non-workers. As mentioned above, the Elect did not work; or rather, their work was the ritual meal and their prayers. Catechumens were those who offered the Elect all the necessities of life. The Church Fathers are very critical about the dualistic structure of the Manichaean communities; they considered that the dual structure mainly served the Elect who exploited the catechumens as means of their support.

Epiphanius, in his commentary, ridicules the shockingly 'scandalous' and parasitical behaviour of the Elect towards their catechumens.

---

345 Augustine, *Haer.* 46.12 (Gardner and Lieu 2004, 189).

346 Augustine, *Commentary on Psalm* 140.12, cf. Gardner and Lieu 2004, 245: "Augustine on the Manichaean preference for money-lending over farming".

347 See for example Gregory of Nyssa, *Contra usurarios* v.9 p. 201, 203 & 206; Basil of Caesarea, *Homilia in divites*; Athanasius of Alexandria, *Syntagma ad monachos*; Theodoret of Cyrrhus, *Haer.* (PG 83:429). Cf. Brown 2012.

348 BeDuhn 2000b, 44 (M801.475–532).

349 BeDuhn 2000b, 107–08 (M580).

> But their other complete absurdities, such as their so-called "elect." [...]
> For they are drones who sit around and "work not, but are busybodies" [...]
> The holy apostle [...] says, "If any does not work, neither let him eat!"[350]

Augustine, as a former auditor himself, states clearly several times in his work that the Elect did not work but were nourished by their auditors.

> The Elect themselves perform no labors in the field, pluck no fruit, pick not even a leaf, but expect all these things to be brought for their use by their Auditors.[351]
> You yourselves do not pluck fruits or pull up vegetables, yet command your Auditors to pick them and bring them to you.[352]

It is important to note at this point, that unlike the ancient Greco-Roman world, which devalued manual labour for its connections with slavery, for Church Fathers, the issue of labour was very important for both individuals and society. According to the *Constitutiones Asceticae* (ascribed to Basil of Caesarea), labour is a factor of joy, as well as important to the mental and psychological health of the individual. Further (as the author argues developing a theory of ethics in economic life), social prosperity and peace depend on the balanced distribution of labour among the members of society.[353]

Attitudes against labour that resembled those ascribed to the Manichaeans were adopted by various religious groups of the era (e.g. Messalians), and by some monks and hermits. The representatives, however, of the official Church, seemingly rejected such practices. In one of his letters, Cyril of Alexandria argues that the real motive of the wandering ascetics, who were not working and depended on alms-giving of other people, was their laziness:

---

350 Epiphanius, *Pan.* 66.53.1–3 (1 Tim 1:7 & 2 Thess 3:11) (GCS 37:89; Williams, 277–78): Τὰ δὲ ἄλλα χλεύης ἔμπλεα, ὡς οἱ ἐκλεκτοὶ αὐτῶν καλούμενοι. [...] ἐκεῖνοι γὰρ καθεζόμενοι κηφῆνες καὶ "μηδὲν ἐργαζόμενοι, ἀλλὰ περιεργαζόμενοι" καὶ μηδὲ γινώσκοντες οἷς ἐπικηρυκεύεται ὁ ἅγιος ἀπόστολος, [λέγων] ὡς κατὰ προφητείαν γινώσκων ὅτι οὐκ ἐκ τῆς τοῦ θεοῦ διδασκαλίας ἐπιφοιτῶσιν, ἀλλὰ ἐκ τοῦ διαβόλου ἐμ(βε)βροντημένοι τινὲς ἀργοὶ καὶ αὐθάδεις κακῶν· φάσκει ⟨γὰρ⟩ λέγων "ὁ μὴ ἐργαζόμενος μηδὲ ἐσθιέτω", ἵνα παραχαράξῃ τὴν τῶν παρέργων τούτων ὑπόθεσιν. Williams 278, fn. 249: "Manichean sources indicate that the behavior of the elect sometimes gave scandal; Cf. *1Keph.* 88 219,1–221,17 ("Concerning the Catechumen who found fault with the Elect: why he is angry", Gardner 1995, 226).

351 Augustine, *Haer.* 46.114ff, in BeDuhn 2000b, 47.

352 Augustine, *Mor. Manich.* 57 in BeDuhn 2000b, 130.

353 Pseudo-Basil of Caesarea, *Asceticon* fus. 37: 39: 42; *Asceticon* brev.121: 143: 144–46.

There are some other men going about, as they say, who pretend to devote all their time to prayer, without working at all, and have turned piety into a pretext for laziness and a means of gaining a living, holding on to views that are not right. [...] The Church, therefore, does not accept those who act in this way [...]. If they still think that it is good not to work at all, in case everyone will imitate their behaviour, who will feed them? Some, then, use the idea that all time should be devoted to prayer and not even thinking about work as a cover for laziness and gluttony.[354]

In any case, catechumens had to nourish the Elect; thus, they necessarily had to work. By gardening or preparing food, they inevitably injured the divine substance within it. As a punishment, according to anti-Manichaean sources, they had to suffer what they had caused, that is to be reincarnated in what they had killed and to suffer the same fate.

Just as I said to you a moment ago, if anyone has harvested, he will be mown down, likewise if anyone has put corn to the grindstone, he too will be put to the grindstone, or if anyone has scattered seed, he will be scattered, or if he has cooked bread he will be cooked.[355]

Thus, reincarnation (μεταγγισμός) was a punishment for those who did not observe "the rest of the hands", while the Elect, "for this [same] reason" were "not permitted" "to do any work".[356] However, the Elect managed to convince their auditors that they had a way to be forgiven for violating "the seal of the hands": to feed them (the Elect) generously. "For this reason if they have anything good to eat they offer it to those Elect".[357]

---

354 Cyril of Alexandria, *Ep. 83 (to Calosyrius)* 7, 603–607: Περιέρχονται δὲ καὶ ἕτεροί τινες, ὡς φασί, προσποιούμενοι μόνῃ σχολάζειν τῇ προσευχῇ, καὶ οὐδὲν ἐργαζόμενοι, καὶ ὄκνου πρόφασιν καὶ πορισμοῦ ποιοῦνται τὴν εὐσέβειαν, οὐκ ὀρθὰ φρονοῦντες. [...] οὐκ ἀποδέχεται τοίνυν τοὺς τοῦτο δρῶντας ἡ Ἐκκλησία. [...] εἰ δὲ νομίζουσιν εἶναι καλόν, τὸ ἔργου μὴ ἅπτεσθαι, ὅταν πάντες τὰ αὐτῶν ζηλώσωσι, τίς ὁ τρέφων αὐτούς; ἀργίας τοίνυν καὶ γαστριμαργίας πρόφασιν ποιοῦνταί τινες, τὸ δεῖν οἴεσθαι μόνῃ σχολάζειν τῇ προσευχῇ, ἔργου δὲ ὅλως μὴ ἅπτεσθαι.

355 *AA* 10.7 (Vermes, 54–55). Epiphanius, *Pan.* 66.28.8 (GCS 37:65; Williams, 258): ὡς γὰρ εἶπον ὑμῖν πρὸ ὀλίγου, εἴ τις θερίζει, θερισθήσεται, οὕτως ἐὰν εἰς μηχανὴν σῖτον βάλῃ, βληθήσεται καὶ αὐτός, ἢ φυράσας φυραθήσεται ἢ ὀπτήσας ἄρτον ὀπτηθήσεται.

356 *AA* 10.7 (Vermes, 55). Epiphanius, *Pan.* 66.28.8 (GCS 37:65; Williams, 258): καὶ διὰ τοῦτο ἀπείρηται αὐτοῖς ἔργον ποιῆσαι.

357 Epiphanius, *Pan.* 66.28.6 (GCS 37:65; Williams, 257): καὶ διὰ τοῦτο εἴ τι κάλλιστον ἐν βρώμασι τοῖς ἐκλεκτοῖς προσφέρουσι.

Manichaeans instruct their catechumens to feed these people generously. They offer their Elect all the necessities of life, so that ⟨whoever⟩
gives sustenance to Elect souls may appear supposedly pious.[358]

For all these reasons, it is reasonable to guess that the Manichaean auditors
preferred other professions than agriculture, such as trade, as is indicated in
Epiphanius.[359] As Gardner and Lieu comment, "It is perhaps no accident that
the Manichaean community in fourth-century Kellis, the only such group from
the Roman Empire that we can study in their full socio-economic context,
appears to have centred on families of traders".[360]

    That the auditors daily supported the Elect with foods is also confirmed by
the Manichaean sources. The work of the Elect was to maintain their purity, in
order that the ritual meal and their prayers be effective. Terms such as, 'good
works', 'apostolate', 'soldiery', 'ministry', 'career', that characterise the work of
the Elect and the Elect himself as 'soldiers', 'collaborators in business', 'participants in the 'toil' of this mission', are revealing of the importance that their
'work' (or profession) had in the Manichaean community.[361] On the other
hand, one of the first works of the 'catechumenate', according to the commandments of the teacher (Mani), was almsgiving to the righteousness (Elect).[362]

    "The seal of the hands" for the Elect was established by Mani himself. As
is recorded in the *CMC*, when Mani was young and still in the community of
the Baptists in Mesopotamia, he took into consideration the warnings that
plants and water gave him, and himself first practiced the *anapausis* (rest) of
the hands.

> Rest, one of the leaders of their Law spoke to me, having observed did not
> take vegetables from the garden [...] He said to me: "Why did you not take
> vegetables from the garden [...]" After that Baptist had spoken to [me]
> [...] [it] wasted away, [wailing] like human beings, and, as it were, like
> children. Alas! Alas! The blood was streaming down from the place cut by
> the pruning hook which he held in his hands. And they were crying out in

---

358   Epiphanius, *Pan.* 66.53.4 (GCS 37:89; Williams, 278): παρακελεύονται οὖν τοῖς αὐτῶν κατη-
      χουμένοις τρέφειν αὐτοὺς δαψιλῶς. οἱ δὲ πᾶν ὁτιοῦν ἀναγκαῖον προσφέρουσι τοῖς ἐκλεκτοῖς ἑαυ-
      τῶν, ἵνα δῆθεν εὐσεβὴς ὀφθείη ⟨ὁ⟩ τρέφων τὰς ψυχὰς τὰς ἐκλελεγμένας.

359   Epiphanius, *Pan.* 66.1.8–12.

360   Gardner and Lieu 2004, 22. More about commercial activities of Kellites (textile trade and
      trade of agricultural goods) see Brand 2019 (90, 131, 134, 143–44, 153, 211 and 244–45). As
      Brand (2019, 90) states, "textile trade belonged to the professional and domestic world of
      Kellites". Manichaeans from Kellis "traveled into the Nile valley to conduct trade and sell
      agricultural goods from the oasis" (Brand 2019, 211). Cf. Ruffini 2016, 334–347.

361   *Tebessa codex*, in Gardner and Lieu 2004, 270–271.

362   *1Keph.* 80 (Gardner 1995, 202).

a human voice on account of their blows. [...] [from] the waters [a face] of a man appeared to me, showing with his hand the Rest, so that I might not sin and bring trouble to him.[363]

Thus, Mani "provides a prototype of the perfect Manichaean, exemplifying in his life the correct behaviour, and explaining through his spiritual experiences the rationale for that behavior".[364]

In addition, in the same text (CMC), the dual socio-economic structure of the Manichaean community is justified on Biblical grounds. Firstly, Mani in order to support his view that the Elect should not work, uses the example of the students of Jesus.

Consider, moreover, how even the disciples of the Savior ate bread from women and idolaters and did not separate bread from bread, nor vegetable from vegetable; nor did they eat, while laboring in the toil and tilling of the land, as you do today. Likewise, when the Savior sent his disciples out to preach in [each] place, [neither] mill nor [oven] did [they] carry [with] them, but [made haste], taking one [garment] from [...].[365]

Further, he displays and promotes the model of Martha and Maria from Luke (10:38–42). This became one of the favourite passages of the Manichaeans, an exemplar in order to justify the distinction between the two classes.[366]

---

363 CMC 9.2–10.17 & 12.1–6 (Koenen and Römer, 6, 8; Cameron and Dewey, 12–15): ἔλεγεν πρὸς ἐμὲ εἷς [τῶ]ν ἀρχηγῶν τοῦ νόμου αὐτῶν θεωρήσας με λάχανα ἀπὸ τοῦ κήπου μὴ λαμβάνοντα, ἀλλ᾽ ἀπαιτοῦντα αὐτοὺς ἐν λόγῳ εὐσεβείας· ἔλεγέν μοι· "σὺ τίνος χάριν οὐκ ἔλαβες λάχανα ἀπὸ τοῦ κήπου, ἀλλ᾽ ἐν μέρει εὐσεβείας αἰτεῖς παρ᾽ ἐμοῦ;" καὶ μετὰ τὸ εἰπεῖν δὲ ἐκ[εῖ]νον τὸν βαπ[τι-στὴν] πρὸς [ἐμὲ ...]. δὲ .[... κ]αὶ ἐτάκ[η ὀλοφυρό]μενον παραπλη[ίως ἀν]θρωπείοις προσώ[ποις] καὶ ὡσεὶ παιδίοις. οὐαὶ ο[ὐ]αὶ δὲ τὸ αἷμα κατεκέχυτο τοῦ τόπου τοῦ κοπέντος διὰ τῆς δρεπά-νης ἧς μετὰ χεῖρας εἶχεν. ἔκραζον δὲ καὶ ἀνθρωπείᾳ φωνῇ διὰ τὰς πλήξεις αὐτῶν. ὁ δὲ βαπτι-στὴς πάνυ ἐκινήθη ἐφ᾽ οἷς ἐθεώρησεν καὶ ἐλθὼν [π]ρ[ό]σθεν μου προσέπε[σεν. ὁπ]ηνίκα τοίνυν [...... ....] ἐμέ τις | [...... ....]ου| [...] [... ἐκ τῆς πηγῆς] τῶν ὑδάτων εἶδ[ος] ἀν(θρώπ)ου ὤφθη μοι ὑ[ποδει] κνύον διὰ τῆς χειρ[ὸς] τὴν ἀνάπαυσιν ὡς ἂν μὴ ἁμάρτω καὶ πόνον ἐπάγω εἰς αὐτόν.

364 BeDuhn 2000b, 78.

365 CMC 93.3–21 (Koenen and Römer, 64; Cameron and Dewey, 74–75): σκοπεῖτε τοίνυν ὡς καὶ οἱ μαθηταὶ τοῦ σ(ωτῆ)ρ(ο)ς [...] οὐδὲ ἐν τῇ ἐργασίαι καὶ γεωργίαι τῆς γῆς ἐργαζόμεν[οι] ἤσθιον ὃν τρόπον τήμερον διαπράττεσθ[ε]. ὁμοίως δὲ ὁπηνίκα ἀ[πέ]στειλεν αὐτοῦ τοὺ[ς μα]θητὰς ὁ σω(τὴ)ρ καθ᾽ ἕκ[αστον] τόπον κηρύξαι, [οὔτε] μύλον οὔτε κλί[βανον] συνεπεφέρον[το με] τ᾽ αὐτῶν, ἀ[λ]λ᾽ [......] γον τοπ.. [...... ....] μιαν ἐκ το [...... ....] λαμβαν [....."].

366 Appart from CMC and Tebessa codex (cited above) the model of the two biblical sisters Martha and Mary is known from the Manichaean Psalms (2PsB 192.21–24), whereby Mary behaves as a man, cf. Coyle 2009c, 176: "she hunts, she casts the net, and later, like her Gnostic counterpart, she becomes talkative" whereas "Martha, on the other hand, is a servant (though a joyful one)".

Likewise, he also reclined to eat in the house of Martha and Mary on the occasion when Martha said to him: "[Lord], do you not care (enough) for [me] so as to tell my [sister to] help [me]?", the Savior said [to] her: "Mary has chosen the [good] portion and it will not be taken away from her".367

Based on the same Biblical grounds, much later (fourth-fifth cent.), a Manichaean Elect in the Western part of the Roman Empire, elaborated and justified this position in his *Apologia for the Distinction between Elect and hearer*. According to him, "The rich, who [...] are themselves known as disciples of the second order" [have] to be "friends with the Elect, who are without these resources" and "are transitory visitors and strangers in the world". The text emphasizes the mutually supportive relationship of the two classes. As it explains, in order for the difference in nature of the two classes to be understood, one has to see "the example of the two sisters", Martha and Maria, "of whom one had chosen the most excellent lot, that is the higher rank of the Elect; whereas the other [...] carried out the housekeeping and domestic duty". The Elect are "poor in resources, and few in number, they walk by the narrow way". "Those possessing wealth are called hearers, or rather, as we have said, catechumens, who, since they have made their fortunes in this world, and are still below that rank of the perfect, because they possess wealth, are referred to by the term 'mammon' in the Gospel." [...] However, the catechumens who had difficulty in achieving the level of Election [how?] stayed in their homes; but they helped the Elect and, receiving them under their roofs and into their own homes, they provided them with the necessities of life".368

Apparently, the paradigm of Martha and Maria must have been used often for the defence of the dual structure of the community. In addition, the author of the *Apologia* answers Epiphanius' charge that Paul's saying "If any one will not work, let him not eat" (2 Thess 3:10)369 targeted the Elect Manichaeans, clarifying and giving reassurances that the above passage does not apply to the Elect: "However, I affirm that that [Apostle's saying] does not so much concern the order of these perfect ones".370

---

367   *CMC* 92.14–93.2 (Koenen and Römer, 64; Cameron and Dewey, 74–75): ὁμοίως δὲ καὶ [ἐ]ν τῆ οἰκίαι Μάρθας καὶ [Μα]ρίας ἐκλήθη. ὁπηνί[κα] εἶπεν αὐτῶι ἡ Μάρ[θα· ʼκ(ύρι)]ε, οὐ μέλει σοι περὶ [ἐμο]ῦ ἵνα εἴπης τῇ ἀ[δελφ]ῇ μου ἀντιλαβέ[σθαι μο]υ;ʼ ὁ σω(τὴ)ρ ἔφη [πρὸς αὐτ]ήν· ʼΜαρία τὴν [ἀγαθὴν με]ρίδα ἐπελέξατο καὶ οὐκ ἀφαιρεθήσεται ἀπʼ αὐτῆς.

368   *Tebessa codex* (*An apologia for the distinction between elect and hearer*) in Gardner and Lieu 2004, 268–272. According to the text apart from the Elect, "there are two other groups, namely the catechumens and the gentiles" (Gardner and Lieu 2004, 268). Cf. Lieu 2010, xxiii.

369   Epiphanius, *Pan.* 66.53.

370   *Tebessa codex, An apologia for the distinction between elect and hearer* Col. 21 (vi.1) in Gardner and Lieu 2004, 269–70.

Numerous Manichaean texts scattered across a wide temporal and spatial range attest to the fundamental division of the Manichaean community into Elect and catechumens, and that the latter supported the former. In ancient Kellis many letters were found confirming that the subsistence of the Elect depended on the alms of the catechumens.[371]

However, another aspect of the dualistic character of the socio-economic structure of the Manichaean community is also illustrated by the Manichaean sources: that of the model of barter economy. The catechumen nourishes the Elect with food, while "The Elect nourishes the Auditor through his wise knowledge".[372] As was established by Mani, "the second righteousness that [the Elect] should do is this":

> He can add to it [...] wisdom and faith so that / [...] from his wisdom he can give wisdom, to every person who will he/ar it from him. And also from his faith he can give faith, [to th]ese who belong to the faith. From hi[s grace] he can give freely / of love, shower it upon them, that he might join them to him. / For, when that one acquires a great riches [...] / in righteousness. By this second godliness / he may cause others to be sent, resembling him in [righteous]ness.[373]

The juxtaposition now is between those that preach and those that hear.[374] According to the Manichaean sources, both classes are necessary: "And who[ever] comes [...] no one is rejected [...] either in Auditorship [...] (or) in Righteousness [...] according to their order, zeal, and power".[375] "Each degree (*bathmos*) within the Manichaean community has a task 'in the yoke of Jesus'".[376] BeDuhn emphasizes repeatedly the importance that both classes had for the existence of the Manichaean community and Church.

> This study has shown the essential role played by the Auditors in the community, such that there was no "rest" for the Elect in the world without them, there was no metabolic salvation without their alms-service, there was no possibility of the Elect lifestyle without their support.[377]

---

371 For instance, see the letter 'An elect writes to ask for alms', P.Kell. v Copt. 31, in Gardner and Lieu 2004, 277–78 (no 96).

372 Turkic source R.i.2–8, 27–29/T II D 171, in BeDuhn 2000b, 113.

373 *1Keph.* 80, 192.3–193.22 (Gardner 1995, 201).

374 *2PsB* 241,47.13–14.

375 Sogdian parable-book (fragment M7420), in BeDuhn 2000b, 29.

376 BeDuhn 2000b, 27.

377 BeDuhn 2000b, 211.

However, it seems that such an argumentation regarding the role of the cat-echumens could not convince the opponents of the Manichaeans who still regarded the relationship of the two classes as exploitation. Thus, East-Roman anti-Manichaean sources, unlike their silence for the Manichaean idea that the stomachs of the Elect function like altars, are quite vocal in their criticism and ridicule of the Manichaean attitude that catechumens had to nourish the Elect.

> The Elect do not cut the cluster themselves but they eat the cluster, which shows them up as out-and-out drunkards rather than persons with a grasp of the truth. For which is the worse? The harvester cut the clus-ter once, but the eater tormented and cut it many times over, with his teeth and by the crushing of each seed, and there can be no comparison between the one who cut it once and the one who chewed and crushed it. ⟨But they do this⟩ only to give the appearance of ⟨abstaining from God's creatures⟩, ⟨while proving by their⟩ phony behavior how much evidence of the truth Mani has.[378]

Texts such as the *Apologia* (*Tebessa Codex*) reflect the need of the Manichaeans who lived in Roman territory to defend themselves against the above charges and ridicule. Additionally, it reveals that the topic of labour was highly dis-puted, and the criticism of opponents was effective.

4   Conclusions

As one may observe, the main target of anti-Manichaean critique concerns the Manichaean ascesis. References to rituals, apart from sun worship during the daily prayers of the catechumens, are really very scant. In specific, information concerning the ritual meal itself is non-existent.[379] The occasional charges for occultism (mainly the consumption of human semen and menstrual blood) and for crimes against nature are likely an arbitrary induction, made by the

---

378   Epiphanius, *Pan.* 66.53.7–9 (GCS 37:90; Williams 278): αὐτοὶ δὲ οὐ τέμνουσι τὸν βότρυν, ἀλλὰ ἐσθίουσι τὸν βότρυν, ἵνα ἐλεγχθῶσι παντάπασι μέθην μᾶλλον ἔχοντες ἤπερ ἀληθείας κατάληψιν. ποῖον γάρ ἐστι τὸ δεινότερον; ὁ μὲν γὰρ τρυγῶν ἅπαξ ἔτεμε τὸν βότρυν, ὁ δὲ ἐσθίων διὰ τῶν μασῃ-τήρων καὶ διὰ τοῦ καταδαμάζειν ἕκαστον κόκκον μᾶλλον πολυπλασίως ἐβασάνισε καὶ ἔτεμε, καὶ οὐχ ὅμοιος οὐκέτι ἔσται τῷ τέμνοντι ἅπαξ ὁ μασησάμενος καὶ καταδαπανήσας.

379   The rare testimonies about the sacred Manichaean meal indicate a small number of par-ticipants and possible secrecy of the ritual. On the contrary, the numerous references to the worship of the sun indicate a wider circle of participants.

opponents of Manichaeans, since this was a standard accusation that rival religious groups of the era made against each other. Thus, it could be argued, that the critique mainly focuses on the so-called three seals; namely, "the seal of the mouth" (fasting), "the seal of the breast" (avoidance of marriage and procreation), and "the seal of the hands" (not to injure the living soul trapped in the material world).

The implications of the seals of the mouth and breast concern the sphere of religious and social life respectively. The seal of the hands has both religious and social implications. On the religious level, it is related with the Manichaean holy meal. One pole of criticism is the ritualization of the feeding of the Elect by the catechumens. In the context of the sacred meal of the community, the catechumens were obliged to feed the Elect on a daily basis. The other pole of criticism (interrelated with the former) is the division of the Manichaean church into two separate categories, or classes of believers (Elect and catechumens). Further, the critique targets the hypocrisy of the Elect who encouraged the above practice (alms-giving) by cultivating soteriological expectations to the catechumens.

On the social level, anti-Manichaean criticism is related with the economic life of the Manichaean community. It attacks the social elitism which discriminates members of the Manichaean community, dividing them into workers and non-workers, the contempt that the Manichaean Elect had for labour, and the repudiation of a number of professions. What is emphasized on both levels (religious and social) is the relationship of exploitation of the catechumens by the Elect.

What East-Roman anti-Manichaean sources do not criticize at all, whereas Augustine criticizes it thoroughly and ridicules it, is the objective, the very purpose of the sacred meal. This was based on the Manichaean belief that the Elect by eating the food offered by the catechumens during the holy meal liberated the divine substance entrapped within it, 'breathing out angels' and 'bits of God'.[380] Their silence implies that they were not aware of it.

Generally, in the corpus of Greek anti-Manichaica, the distinction between Elect and catechumens is rare. Sources describing the Manichaean religious and social attitudes and behaviour do not differentiate between the two classes. Charges, accusations, and criticisms are addressed to Manichaeans in general. Specifically, sources do not clarify whether everyday fasting, fasting from meat and wine, abstinence from marriage and procreation, and praying to the sun was an obligation of the Elect or/and of the catechumens. An explanation for this is that either they were not well informed, or more likely that in

---

380   Augustine, *Conf.* x (18).

the framework of their polemics, their rhetoric equated the two classes. They generalized by attributing to all Manichaeans behaviours that applied only to the Elect.

The distinction of the two classes is clear only in the case of alms-giving by the catechumens to the Elect; yet this is not always the case. In some cases (e.g. in Cyril and Theodoret) it seems that the distinction is made rather between Manichaeans and non-Manichaeans, than between the Elect and hearers. Indeed, some texts give the impression that only the Elect were considered as Manichaeans, whereas catechumens were not considered as 'totally' Manichaeans. The charges concern mainly the Elect's attitudes and rules, while Church Fathers sometimes seem to defend the Manichaean catechumens, describing them as those 'simple persons' who bring Manichaeans their food. Characteristic is the example of Cyril of Jerusalem, who admonishes his (Christian) catechumens "Let no one bring offerings to the soul-destroying Manichaeans".[381] It could be argued that, in the above case, Cyril was addressing former Manichaean hearers among his catechumens, preventing them from offering alms service to the Manichaean Elect, as they used to do. If this was the case, it seems as if Manichaean catechumens could have been Christian and Manichaean catechumens simultaneously. Indeed, as BeDuhn comments, "it is possible [...] that some Auditors also participated in the rites of other religions. In practice, the boundaries of the Auditor class probably varied considerably in exclusivity of commitment from one region to the next".[382] In this context, it is likely that Christian authors, in their proselytizing policy, tried to appeal to Manichaean catechumens and take them over to their side, identifying the Manichaeans only with the Elect. In favour of the mobility hypothesis is the fact that, in the case of the Manichaean catechumens, there was not any prospect for them to be initiated into the class of the Elect. Catechumenate in the case of Manichaeism was not, necessarily, a transitional stage (at least during this life) as was the case of Christian catechumens who entered the class of believers after being baptized.

This obscurity in the boundaries of the class of catechumens was further intensified in the Roman East by the interconnection of Manichaeism with other extreme ascetic movements, which adopted common practices in the field of ascesis and had corresponding behavioural and social models. The latter issue is one of the key questions that will be examined in the next chapter.

---

[381] Cyril, *Catech.* 6.31.4–5 (Reischl and Rupp 1848, 198): Μηδεὶς προσφερέσθω τοῖς ψυχοφθόροις Μανιχαίοις.

[382] BeDuhn 2000b, 162. On the question of the status of the Manichaean catechumens, i.e. whether they were considered (by both insiders and outsiders) as members of the Manichaean community and Church, see BeDuhn 2000b, 211 ff., 29 ff. Puech 1979, 260–63.

CHAPTER 6

Manichaeism in Society

Children of Manichaeans have spread abroad; such heresies does
the country of the Pisidians contain, and of the Isaurians; Cilicia
also, and Lycaonia and all Galatia.

MACARIUS OF MAGNESIA[1]

∙∙∙

Some of these brethren ⟨refrain from all mundane labor⟩ – as
though they had learned this from the Persian immigrant, Mani.

EPIPHANIUS OF SALAMIS[2]

∙∙
∙

1 Introduction

This chapter will address the question of which groups were attracted to
Manichaeism in the East-Roman Empire, according to the available evidence.
It has been argued that the factors that made Manichaeism particularly
attractive in the Roman West were its critical, dualistic, aesthetic, ascetical,
and sectarian appeal, as well as its relationship with astrology.[3] Taking into
account these factors, I will attempt a sociological classification of the groups
to which Manichaeism was appealing in the Roman East. Examining the data
given by the Greek sources, several suggestions can be made about the following parameters: religious profile, age, gender and social status. The appeal
of Manichaeism to ascetics and monks (especially urban ones), as well as the
relationship between Manichaeans and other ascetics, due to their particular
importance, will be examined in a separate section of the present chapter.

---

1 Macarius of Magnesia, *Apocriticus*, 3.151.25–28, §25 (Grafer, modified). For the original text in
   Greek see section 3.1.2 in this chapter.
2 Epiphanius, *Pan.* 80.4.3 (Williams, 648). For the original text in Greek see section 3.2.3 in
   this chapter.
3 Lieu 1992, 151–191. On Manichaean attractiveness, see Chadwick 1990, 203–22.

© REA MATSANGOU, 2023 | DOI:10.1163/9789004544222_008

As explained in the introduction, we shall follow mainly what the Greek anti-Manichaean sources themselves say, and draw conclusions only after careful analysis of *all* of the evidence.

2 Manichaeism as an Appealing Model: To Whom and Why

2.1 *Religious Profile: Pagans and Christian Neophytes*

At a time when the empire's religious profile was changing and traditional Greek religion gradually gave way to Christianity, it seems that Manichaeism – which presented itself as a higher, more perfect, form of Christianity – was an attractive religious option for Christian neophytes (catechumens or believers), as well as for pagans. This is reported not only by Christian authors, but also by our main non-Christian witness, Alexander of Lycopolis. Alexander's work testifies that the Manichaean missions were successful among the pagans of Egypt. Especially Lycopolis (the birthplace of Plotinus and centre of Gnosticism), must have been a major centre of Manichaean propaganda since the middle of third century.[4] As mentioned in ch.[4], the Manichaean missionaries that Alexander met are described by him as people invoking the fables of the Greek poets and the ideas of the Greek philosophers. This attracted educated pagans to their movement and among them were some of Alexander's fellow philosophers.[5] Although Alexander claimed that the Manichaeans misinterpreted the Greek philosophers, their repertoire undoubtedly exerted a critical appeal and was an attractive factor for pagans with philosophical tendencies.[6]

Writing around 326, the Egyptian Serapion of Thmuis, in his work *Contra Manichaeos*, appears to be especially concerned about pagans who had only recently converted to Christianity.[7] He feared that their faith needed to be

---

4 Stroumsa 1992, 338. As Van Lindt (1992, 229) remarks, "all scholars agree that two main centers of Manichaeism were established in Egypt: one at Alexandria and a second in the neighbourhood of Lycopolis (Assiut)". According to Lieu (1994, 93): "It is very probable that the Manichaean community at Kellis was an offshoot of that at Lycopolis". Contra Lieu, Van Lindt argues that "on the basis of the new discoveries in Egypt, one may presume that the local center was situated in the Dakhleh Oasis, east of Assiut where the road to the oasis starts" (229, fn. 79). Cf. Brand (2019, 182, fn. 80), on Kellis – Lycopolis relationship.

5 Alexander, *Tract. Man.* 5.15–19.

6 Lieu 1992, 152–53, 165. For the success of Manichaean mission among pagan intellectuals see also Lieu 1994a, 94; Gardner and Lieu 2004, 38. As Pedersen (2004, 161) remarks, Alexander's presentation "appears to be adapted to people with a more philosophical taste in that the names of the Manichaean gods/hypostasisings of the deity are for the most part replaced by philosophical concepts".

7 Serapion was the cultural 'product' of two different types of education. On the one hand he was cultivated with Greek philosophical education and on the other he was a student of the narrow circle of Antonius' disciples. He knew and used Manichaean technical terms, such as:

fortified against Manichaean propaganda, for he considered these recent converts a precarious group particularly vulnerable to apostasy and to conversion to Manichaeism. It is possible that Serapion was also addressing those pagans who were (in principle) open to conversion to Christianity, but still had doubts about some issues, such as accepting the OT. When Serapion composed his treatise, pagans were still the majority in the empire, and were especially well represented among most officials in administrative functions. That Serapion's work addressed pagans is suggested by the fact that he criticizes the Manichaean cosmogony with the same arguments that Alexander used.[8] Yet unlike Alexander, Serapion states that he will not talk about the Manichaean's invented legends, such as the battles of the giants (γιγαντομαχίας), the emanations (τὰς προβολὰς) of the powers of light, the fighting (τὰς μάχας) etc.; according to him, these fables resemble the chatter of elderly women.[9] Serapion's statement gives the impression that he was aware of Alexander's treatise. Addressing an audience with the same concerns and preoccupations, Serapion seems to refer to Alexander's work and to declare that he will not tell them what Alexander had already said.

The main topic in Serapion's treatise is the age-old question concerning the origin of evil, and the Manichaean answers to it. Yet, although Serapion was a student and a friend of Anthony, the famous ascetic, his explanations for the existence of evil in the world largely avoided references to the forces of evil, which are so prominent in ascetic literature.[10] Serapion refers to the Devil only once, in order to refute the Manichaean idea that the human body originates from the Devil. His argumentation is philosophical, emphasizing human free will and free agency, a line of argumentation that Titus of Bostra further developed.[11] The philosophical language and rationale he employed strongly suggest that the audience he aimed to address was educated in Greek culture.

Apart from dualism and its impact on anthropology, the other major topic that Serapion elaborates upon is the defence of the OT against attacks by the

---

'roots/ρίζες', 'emanations/πρόοδοι/couriers', 'archons of evil/οἱ τῆς πονηρίας ἄρχοντες', that the OT is a creation of 'πονηροῦ τινος, ἀφεγγοῦς, ὅλου σκότους'.

8   See for example his criticism on Manichaean literalism; cf. Serapion, *c. Manichaeos* 33, 42.

9   Serapion, *c. Manichaeos* 35–36 (HTS 15:52): Ἀλλ' ἐπειδὴ γραῴδη καὶ μυθώδη φθέγγονται, οὔτε ἃ λέγουσιν εἰδότες [...] Καὶ τοιούτου μὲν τοιοῦτος ὁ ἔλεγχος, ἵνα πολλὴν συστείλωμεν ὁμιλίαν, τὰς προβολὰς αὐτῶν, τὰς μάχας, τὰς μυθοποιίας ἐκείνας καὶ γιγαντομαχίας σιωπῶντες.

10 The AA deals with the same issues. Probably, both were written during the same period (firstly Serapion). Nevertheless, in AA there is a detailed discussion about devil, as an autonomous entity which exists in man's life (not as an equal to Good power) using his free will.

11 See ch.[5], section 3.2. As Dix (1932, 236) comments, Serapion's "treatise shows the mind of a well-educated Greek theologian of a philosophic and dialectical piety rather than a mystic".

followers of Valentinus, Manichaios, and Marcion.[12] However, as Serapion states, he will not present the argumentation of those heretics in detail "lest their theses will be attracting".[13] This suggests two things: the first is that Manichaean arguments (combating OT) were convincing to some, and the second is that Serapion's audience were Christians of gentile origin, and not of Jewish origin. The OT was a "major obstacle" to the Christianization of the pagans and the Manichaean polemic against it was a great advantage in favour of the Manichaean mission among pagans.[14] In the AA, Mani's criticism of the OT appears to have persuaded "some simple folk" from the audience "as he spoke".[15] This forced Diodorus to seek the assistance of bishop Archelaus' authority and competence in order to convince them that the "Law of Moses does not belong [...] to the evil prince", as Mani had claimed.[16]

As Pedersen underlines, both Alexander's and Titus' works are a presentation of Manichaeism for philosophically educated circles.[17] The same is true, I argue, for Serapion's work. The use of philosophical terminology and concepts, especially in his interpretation of the origin of evil, as well as the rejection of the OT exerted a powerful pull on such circles.

In the middle of the fourth century, when Cyril delivered his lectures to the Christian catechumens in Jerusalem, the religious setting was different. Christianity had already been promoted by the emperors for two to three decades, being the favoured religion (but not yet the official religion of the Empire), and the number of Christian catechumens steadily increased. Cyril's sixth lecture, devoted to the Manichaeans, as well as the multitude of references to Manichaeans that appear in all his speeches show that the Christian catechumens were susceptible to what Cyril saw as Manichaean propaganda. The theme of his sixth lecture, entitled *About God's Monarchy*, was the interpretation of the first article of the Nicene Creed: "I believe in one God ...". Instead of arguing in favour of monotheism by attacking polytheism, as would be expected, Cyril instead targeted dualism: "Heretics dare to say that there are two gods, and two sources, those of good and evil, which were not born".[18] The most plausible background to this is that Cyril was aware of the appeal of Manichaean dualism to many. He seems afraid of the fact that the idea of evil

12   Serapion of Thmuis, *c. Manichaeos* 37–50.
13   Serapion of Thmuis, *c. Manichaeos* 40.5–6 (HTS 15:57): μὴ ταύτης τῆς ὑποθέσεως ἡμᾶς ἑλκούσης.
14   See Lieu 1992, 158, 155–58.
15   *AA* 45.6 (Vermes, 114).
16   *AA* 44.6 (Vermes, 112); *AA* 52.5 (Vermes 124). *AA* 44.3.
17   Pedersen 2004, 88.
18   Cyril, *Catech.* 6.13.1–2 (Reischl and Rupp 1848, 172): Ἐτόλμησαν αἱρετικοὶ λέγειν δύο θεούς, καὶ δύο πηγὰς ἀγαθοῦ τε καὶ κακοῦ, καὶ ταύτας ἀγεννήτους [εἶναι].

as the first principle responsible for the existence of all the evil in the world was more convincing (and comforting) to many than the Christian position that God is one and that he is good.[19]

Titus of Bostra continues along these lines; for him too, the two religious groups of pagans and of Christian neophytes were also more at risk of being charmed by Manichaean propaganda. In the first two books of his *Contra Manichaeos* (363–377/8), Titus addresses the pagans of Bostra who, it seems, were still numerous even in the last quarter of the fourth century. His argumentation is based on the 'common notions' (κοιναί ἔννοιαι) through which, as he says, he aims to empower the minds of the pagans against Manichaeans.[20] This suggests that Manichaean arguments were convincing and appealing to some pagans. Titus' evidence also confirms the view that Manichaean missionaries were particularly active in communities with a strong pagan element. Indeed, Bostra was the site of intense confrontation between pagans and Christians, and Titus had problems with the pagans induced by Julian.[21] Thus, Pedersen argues that there may have been an alliance between the pagans and the Manichaeans of the city which threatened the position of the Catholic Christians.[22] In his other two books, which are addressed to Christians, Titus' argumentation is based on the Christian Scriptures. He considers that the Christians who are more likely to apostatize to Manichaeism are those who either find it difficult to understand the Christian position in the discourse 'concerning the origin of Evil', or those who reject it. As Titus confesses in his fourth book, he hopes that his analysis of the concept of evil would be beneficial to the Christians who are uncertain about this issue.[23] This shows that in the discourse regarding evil there was fertile ground for Manichaean mission.

As shown in ch.[5], Titus refutes Manichaean dualism by claiming that the existence of evil in the world is neither due to an independent first evil principle nor due to man's evil nature, but is only realized through the actions of men. In the books addressed to the pagans, Titus uses arguments from Aristotelian ethics (possibly using the *Nicomachean Ethics*) in order to defend man's free will. One gets the impression that his readers were familiar with Platonic, Neoplatonic or Plotinian perceptions, which were characterized by a certain aversion to materiality and the human flesh, and thus had some ideological affinity with Manichaean dualism. For example, Titus argues strongly against

---

19 As Cyril points out (*Catech.* 6.20.8–11), those who are outside the Church (μᾶλλον δὲ τοὺς ἐκτὸς τῆς ἐκκλησίας) are in danger due to the Manichaean propaganda.

20 Titus of Bostra, *c. Manichaeos* 3.1.1–5.

21 Flavius Claudius Julianus, *Ep. 114*: "Ἰουλιανὸς Βοστρηνοῖς". See ch.[1], section 6.1.

22 Pedersen 2004, 4.

23 Pedersen 2004, 60.

the view that the body is a prison for the soul.[24] In the books he addressed to the Christians, the basis of Titus' argumentation is a reinterpretation of the Paradise narrative. Here again, it seems that Titus' readers were influenced by and familiar with Neoplatonism and Plotinus. Such theoretical positions within Christianity were expressed by theologians like Evagrius Ponticus, who had a great influence on ascetic environments and ascetic literature. Titus, in contrast to other more pessimistic Christian interpretations of the Paradise narrative, which disdain the human body, supported the integrity of human nature after the fall.[25]

Thus, it seems wholly plausible that the target audience of Titus was philosophically educated pagans and Christians, and more specifically, Neoplatonist pagans and Christian ascetics or mystics. The latter were Christians who in their anthropology emphasized the 'fallen' human nature as a result of the original sin. Both audiences represented trends in which there was an intense polarity between body and soul.

An additional factor attracting pagans and Christian neophytes to Manichaeism was its ascetical appeal.[26] Dress codes, for example, played an important role in promoting their ideas. As Titus observes, "in appearance the Manichaeans resemble ascetics or philosophers, but that is simply hypocrisy, a cover for magic and secret felonies (4.43)".[27] He declares that with his arguments he intends to persuade those pagans and Christians who were fascinated by the asceticism of the Manichaeans. However, as he confesses towards the end of his work, he had little hope of convincing "those who have been totally captured by Manichaeism". His hopes were on the strongest, those who had been immunized against it;[28] those who, like Augustine, were restless in nature and in their spiritual quest ended up being dissatisfied with Manichaeism.

The account of Mark the Deacon about the activities of the Manichaean missionary Julia from Antioch, who came to Gaza (ca. 400) in order to proselytize Christian neophytes, "confirms the view that Manichaeism had a special

---

24 Titus of Bostra, c. Manichaeos 1.17.25–26 (CCSG 82:39): σῶμα δὲ καὶ τὴν σάρκα τῆς ὕλης, πῇ μὲν κατέχουσαν ὡς ἐν εἱρκτῇ τὴν ψυχήν; 1.38.1–5 (CCSG 82:89): Ἐπειδὴ καὶ λόγος ἕτερος καταγέλαστός ἐστι τοῦ μανέντος, ὡς οἱ τῆς ὕλης, [...] ἀντεμηχανήσαντο τῆς σαρκὸς τὴν κατασκευήν, δεσμὸν μέγιστον ταῖς ψυχαῖς. Cf. 2.1–14 & 3.5. Cf. Pedersen 2004, 263.

25 Cf. Pedersen 2004, 320–65, esp. 349–65.

26 Cf. Lieu 1992, 180–187 (The ascetical appeal of Manichaeism).

27 Titus of Bostra, c. Manichaeos 4.43 in Pedersen (2004, 55); CCT 21, 417: "Or, leur apparence extérieure est celle des philosophes mais leur agir est celui des Chaldéens perdus et des magiciens en ce qui concerne les choses qu'ils cachent, mais c'est un ingrat pour celles qui sont connues".

28 Titus of Bostra, c. Manichaeos 4.112.

appeal to those recently converted".[29] As Mark the Deacon recounts, Julia entered into the Church undetected and secretly and gradually corrupted the neophytes through her bewitching teachings.

> About that time, a woman from Antioch named Julia arrived in the city [Gaza]. She belonged to the abominable sect of those known as Manichaeans. Now discovering that (among the Christians) there were some novices who were not yet confirmed in the holy faith, this woman infiltrated herself among them and surreptitiously corrupted them with her bewitching doctrine, and still further by giving them money.[30]

Apart from the unsteady Christian neophytes, Mark the Deacon attests that another target group of Manichaean missionaries were pagans, for whose proselytism the corresponding material was disseminated.

> In fact the Manichaeans say that there are many gods, wishing in this way to please the Hellenes (i.e. pagans); besides which, they believe in horoscopes, fate, and astrology.[31]

As time passed and the Christianization of the empire advanced, the number of authors who addressed the pagans decreased.

2.2 Age: Appealing to the Youth

Examining the parameter of age, there are some testimonies that support the argument that one more group to which Manichaeism seems to have had a special appeal (and for that reason was a very promising target), were young people. The anti-conformist style, the unconventional and antisocial behaviour, the vagabond lifestyle, and the profile of the ascetic-philosopher, were all feared by Christian writers as being attractive to the youth.

---

29 Lieu 1992, 158, cf. Mark the Deacon, *Vit. Porph.* 85–89.

30 Mark the Deacon, *Vit. Porph.* 85.1–7 (Lieu 2010, 96–97): Κατ' ἐκεῖνον δὲ τὸν καιρὸν ἐπεδήμησεν τῇ πόλει γυνή τις Ἀντιόχισσα καλουμένη Ἰουλία, ἥτις ὑπῆρχεν τῆς μυσαρᾶς αἱρέσεως τῶν λεγομένων Μανιχαίων, καὶ γνοῦσά τινας νεοφωτίστους εἶναι καὶ μήπω ἐστηριγμένους ἐν τῇ ἁγίᾳ πίστει, ὑπεισελθοῦσα ὑπέφθειρεν αὐτοὺς διὰ τῆς γοητικῆς αὐτῆς διδασκαλίας, πολλὰ δὲ πλέον διὰ δόσεως χρημάτων.

31 Mark the Deacon, *Vit. Porph.* 85.15–17 (Lieu 2010, 96–97): Θεοὺς γὰρ πολλοὺς λέγουσιν, ἵνα Ἕλλησιν ἀρέσωσιν, ἔτι δὲ καὶ γένεσιν καὶ εἱμαρμένην καὶ ἀστρολογίαν φάσκουσιν.

According to Titus, the Manichaeans with their views about childbearing and sexual life become friends with the young men and women because they felt allowed to sin freely.[32]

> Car il est ainsi en tout temps l'ami des adolescents et des jeunes parce qu'en plus des autres (choses) et aussi de ses histoires, ils se réjouissent de la licence de pécher et, sans bride qui les retienne, comme des poulains, ils courent impétueusement vers les plaisirs [...] il n'est aucune des actions qui sont prohibées qu'ils n'aient osée.[33]

The above excerpt highlights Titus' concern for the spread and perpetuation of Manichaean ideas to the next generations; the imaginative stories of Manichaeans, but mainly their attitude towards sex and childbearing would seem attractive at all times to teenagers and young people alike.

The general Sebastian, who persecuted Athanasius, the bishop of Alexandria, is depicted by the latter as a merciless Manichaean and an immoral young man.[34] Young and beautiful, but all pale, were the two men and two women who accompanied Julia.[35] Young were also the twenty-two Elect men and women who accompanied Mani in his debate in Carchar.[36] Further, let us not forget that Augustine too was attracted by Manichaeism at the tender age of nineteen as he writes in his *Confessions*.[37]

Moreover, as I have already mentioned, one of the duties of Manichaean catechumens was to give a child to the community of the Elect.[38] The latter is confirmed by the Kellis material; by the correspondence between travelling children alongside the Elect teacher and their families. In an epistle preserved at Ismant el-Kharab/Kellis (written probably in the 350s) a father (Makarios) instructs his young son (Matheos): "I may be grateful for you and God too may be grateful for you, and you will be Glorified by a multitude of people. [...]

---

32   Cf. Pedersen 2004, 55.

33   Titus of Bostra, *c. Manichaeos* 4.43 (CCT 21, 417).

34   Athanasius of Alexandria, *H. Ar.* 59.1 (Opitz, 216): ἔχοντες δὲ ὑπουργοὺς εἰς τὴν πονηρίαν τὸν δοῦκα Σεβαστιανόν, Μανιχαῖον ὄντα καὶ ἀσελγῆ νεώτερον καὶ τὸν ἔπαρχον καὶ τὸν κόμητα καὶ ὑποκριτὴν τὸν καθολικόν. Cf. *Oratio III c. Ar.* 3.50.2.

35   Mark the Deacon, *Vit. Porph.* 88 (Lieu 2010, 98–99): Τῇ δὲ ἐπαύριον παραγίνεται ἡ γυνή, ἔχουσα μεθ' ἑαυτῆς ἄνδρας δύο καὶ τοσαύτας γυναῖκας ἦσαν δὲ νεώτεροι καὶ εὐειδεῖς, ὠχροὶ δὲ πάντες, ἡ δὲ Ἰουλία ἦν προβεβηκυῖα.

36   *AA* 14.2.

37   Augustine, *Conf.* 4.1.1; cf. Lieu 1992, 151.

38   See ch.[5], 2.1, fn. 32. Cf. Gardner and Lieu 2004, 167: "Indeed, my loved one, I was obliged to write a mass of words to you this time; but God himself knows that these young people, whom you sent and who came, found me in how much pain".

Study (your) psalms, whether Greek or Coptic, ⟨every⟩ day (?) Do not abandon your vow"; "Write a daily example, for I need you to write books here".[39] From the instructions given by the father to his son, it is implied that the son was intended to become an Elect. However, a later correspondence informs us that his brother was finally the one that was given as Elect to the entourage of the Teacher.[40]

Aesthetics and dress code played an important role in the attraction of Manichaeism to young people. Apart from Titus' testimony, that Manichaeans looked like ascetics or philosophers, Epiphanius' text at some point suggests that Manichaean men had long hair, which they "called ... the Glory of God" (δόξαν θεοῦ).

> And once more, in another passage the same apostle [Paul] says, "A man ought not to have long hair, forasmuch as he is the glory and image of God." And you see how he [Mani] called hair the glory of God, though it is grown on the body and not in the soul.[41]

Paleness also, "seems to have been a hallmark of the Manichaeans, at least of the Elect, especially females".[42] In many writings the Manichaean Elect are described as pale and having sad faces.[43] The ascetic look was identified to such a degree with the Manichaeans, that, as Jerome says, any woman who looked like an ascetic was called a Manichaean. This implies that anyone who had ascetic tendencies could be labelled by his opponents as a Manichaean.[44]

---

39 P.Kell. v Copt. 19 (*A father instructs his young son*, no 93 in Gardner and Lieu 2004, 272–275, 273–274.

40 P.Kell. v Copt. 25 (*The son writes to his mother*, no 94 in Gardner and Lieu 2004, 275–276). Cf. Brand 2019, 140–45 & 293–99.

41 Epiphanius, *Pan.* 66.54.4 (GCS 37:90–91; Williams, 279): καὶ πάλιν ἐν ἄλλῳ τόπῳ ὁ αὐτὸς ἀπόστολος 'ἀνὴρ οὐκ ὀφείλει κομᾶν, δόξα καὶ εἰκὼν θεοῦ ὑπάρχων' (1 Cor 11:7). καὶ ὁρᾷς ὡς δόξαν θεοῦ ἔφη τὴν κόμην, ἐπὶ σώματος φερομένην καὶ οὐκ ἐν ψυχῇ; Corresponding testimony for long-haired men, and women who cut off their hair, is also provided by Jerome in his letter to Eustochium (*Ep.* 22, § 27f.): "Some women, it is true, disfigure their faces, that they may appear unto men to fast. [...] They cut off their hair and are not ashamed to look like eunuchs. [...] Avoid men also, when you see them loaded with chains and wearing their hair long like women, contrary to the apostles' precepts, not to speak of beards like those of goats, black cloaks, and bare feet braving the cold".

42 Coyle 2009d, 200.

43 Chrysostom, *Hom. Gen.* (PG 54:584–585): Πύξινον ἔχουσιν ἐκεῖνοι τὸ χρῶμα, καὶ κατεσταλμένην τὴν ὀφρὺν, καὶ ῥημάτων ἐπιείκειαν. John of Caesarea, *Adv. Manichaeos hom.* 1 17.273–74 (Richard, 92): οἳ πολλάκις ὠχρότητι σώματος τὸ δοκεῖν ἐγκρατεῖς εἶναι θηρώμενοι, τῷ σχήματι καὶ τῷ βλέμματι.

44 Jerome, *Ep.* 22 *ad Eustochium* (§ 13). Cf. Coyle 2009b, 154, fn. 53.

As we shall see in later section of this chapter, such practices (men with long and women with short hair, etc.), which were adopted by other ascetics too, were persistently condemned by the church canons.[45]

Lastly, in order to underline the importance that Manichaean missionaries gave to appearance, we should recall how Mani himself is described in the *Acta Archelai* and the impression he made on Marcellus and the audience of the debate.[46] The key-role that appearance played in the case of Mani's appeal is underlined also by the priest Diodorus in his letter to the bishop Archelaus: "For in actual fact the man is extremely forceful both in what he says and what he does, as is also clear in his appearance and his dress".[47]

The emphasis of Manichaean missionaries on the aesthetic appeal is also shown by the care and diligence that they devoted to the decoration of their books (picture book, hymns, etc.) with the use of calligraphy and illustrations by specialized scribes.[48] This may also explain why the Manichaeans, according to anti-Manichaean authors, had the tendency to create fanciful names and astonishing doctrines:

> His silly talk is chaotic; what he calls elements, and the twelve "water jars" as he futilely terms them, and the "device" by which he wants to astonish those who are led astray by him.[49]

2.3   *Gender: Manichaean Women*

The fact that there were women in the movement, and that they were able to climb to the rank of the Elect, is well known.[50] The question of this section is whether there are testimonies about the Manichaean women of the Eastern Roman Empire, and especially about the Manichaean Elect and their involvement in the religious life of the community. What were their duties? Did Manichaean women assume, for example, offices such as missionaries or teachers? Did they play a key role in proselytizing?

---

45   See below, section 4.1 in this chapter.

46   *AA* 14.3.

47   *AA* 44.4 (Vermes, 111).

48   Cf. Lieu 1992, 175–177 (*The aesthetic appeal of Manichaeism*); cf. Gulácsi 2015, 2005.

49   Epiphanius, *Pan.*, 66.50.6 (GCS 37:88; Williams 276, modified): ἀσύστατος αὐτοῦ ἡ φλυαρία· πρὶν γὰρ τοῦ εἶναι ἄνθρωπον ἐπὶ τῆς γῆς, ἐγένοντο τὰ κατ᾽ αὐτὸν καλούμενα στοιχεῖα καὶ οἱ δώδεκα μάτην καλούμενοι κάδοι καὶ ἡ μηχανή, ἣν βούλεται χαριστικοῖς ὀνόμασι φαντάζειν τοὺς ὑπ᾽ αὐτοῦ πεπλανημένους. Cf. Alexander of Lycopolis, *Tract. Man.* 2.

50   For a full treatment of women in Manichaeism, see Kristionat 2013. On Manichaean women see also Coyle 2009, Scopello 1997, 2001, 2005(a&b), Van Oort 2020, Franzmann (2022a & 2022b), and the volume on *Women in Western and Eastern Manichaeism*, edited by Scopello (2022).

Recent research has shown that "the prominence of women is a notable feature of the Manichaean documentary texts from Kellis".[51] The descriptions suggest independent women, who, in addition to household management and childbearing, were successful businesswomen supporting their community's economy and their husbands on their commercial trips. In religious life, too, they appear to have had an active involvement: they were "givers of the *agape*", "keepers of religious texts", they supported the itinerant Elect with supplies. It is not clear, however, whether apart from the catechumens there were also Elect among these women. In addition, there are no testimonies referring to missionary activities of any female Manichaean Elect. It remains an open question whether some of the titles attributed to some of these women, such as 'mother' and 'great mother' are familial or religious terms, or social markers of age and respect.[52]

Anti-Manichaean literature preserves several testimonies of female missionaries, but they are very few and scattered. Strangely, there are no relevant references to the activities of male Manichaean missionaries (except for the first generation of missionaries after Mani).

Apart from the brief reference in the *Acta*, where Mani is presented as arriving in Carchar "bringing with him twenty-two Elect young men and women,"[53] there are two other cases involving female missionaries, as well as an archaeological finding that may be relevant to our subject. All three have been examined thoroughly by Scopello,[54] Coyle,[55] and Kristionat.[56]

The oldest of these mentions is the one attributed to Theonas, the bishop of Alexandria. According to it, the Manichaean *Electae*, apart from being honoured, seem to have had missionary duties as well:

> we may be on our guard against those who with deceitful and lying words steal into our houses, and particularly against those women whom they call 'Elect', whom they honour.[57]

---

51 Gardner 1997, 161–175, 170. Brand 2019, 211: "This general trend is clearly visible in the Kellis papyri, where the women had a central role as key figures (or hub) in the family network when their husbands and sons traveled into the Nile valley to conduct trade and sell agricultural goods from the oasis". Cf. Franzmann (2022a).

52 Gardner et al. 1999, 19–20; Brand 2019, 128. Franzmann (2022a). Clackson 2000.

53 *AA* 14.2 (Vermes 2001, 58).

54 Scopello 2001, 35–44; Scopello 2005b, 44–7; Scopello 1997, 187–209; Scopello 2005a, 237–91 & 93–315.

55 Coyle 2009d, 194–198.

56 Kristionat 2013, 134–63.

57 P.Rylands 3, Gr. 469 (Roberts 1938, 42; Lieu 2010, 36–37): τῆς μανίας τῶν Μανιχέων ἵν' ἐπιτηρῶμεν τοὺς ἐν ἀπάταις καὶ λόγοις ψευδέσι εἰσδύνοντας εἰς τὰς οἰκίας· καὶ μάλιστα τὰς λεγομένας παρ' αὐτοῖς ἐκλεκτάς, ἃς ἐν τιμῇ ἔχουσιν. Cf. Lieu 2010, 36–37. Similar information to that

As Coyle points out, "the more interesting (and factual?) aspects of this text are that these women conducted door-to-door canvasses, and that they were indeed Elect, enhancing the impression that Manichaean missionary activity was confined to that class and that women were participants".[58]

The second and more extensive testimony concerns the missionary activities of the Manichaean Julia.[59] Coyle remarks that in the episode of Julia there is not a "clear reference" to her as an Elect, as is the case in Theonas' testimony.[60] However, if his suggestion is correct that "missionary activity was confined" only to the class of the Elect, then not only Julia, but also the other two ladies who accompanied her, should have belonged to the class of Elect. As is denoted in the text, all four companions of Julia participated in the discussions of the missionary endeavour.

> The next day the woman arrived with two men and the same number of women. All four of them were young and good-looking, but very pale; as for Julia she was well on in year. All of them, especially Julia, based their reasoning on the principles of worldly education. Their attitude was humble and their conduct gentle. [...] Then, having been asked to sit down, they began the enquiry.[61]

Besides, Mani's numerous companions belonged to the class of the Elect too. As is implied by a relevant reference in Augustine, missionary duties were mainly undertaken by those who belonged to the higher ranks of the Manichaean hierarchy, but also by any of the Elect who had the appropriate qualifications.[62]

---

of Theonas about Manichaean missionaries intruding the houses propagating their religion is provided by Ambrosiaster a century later. However, Ambrosiaster does not clarify whether the missionaries were male or female, but just that they deceive naive women. Like Theonas, Ambrosiaster uses 2 Tim's (3:6–7) comments on feminine weakness and persuasiveness to warn the faithful that the Manichaeans exploit this weakness. Cf. Lieu 1992, 180–187. Gardner and Lieu 2004, 119.

58   Coyle 2009d, 195–96.
59   Mark the Deacon, *Vit. Porph.* 85–91, 88.
60   Coyle 2009d, 198. Kristionat (2013, 158–63) is even more cautious/sceptical, challenging the historicity of Julia.
61   Mark the Deacon, *Vit. Porph.* 88 (translation by Gardner and Lieu 2004, 127 and Lieu 2010, 99 modified): Τῇ δὲ ἐπαύριον παραγίνεται ἡ γυνή, ἔχουσα μεθ᾽ ἑαυτῆς ἄνδρας δύο καὶ τοσαύτας γυναῖκας· ἦσαν δὲ νεώτεροι καὶ εὐειδεῖς, ὠχροὶ δὲ πάντες, ἡ δὲ Ἰουλία ἦν προβεβηκυῖα. Ὅλοι δὲ ὥρμουν ἀπὸ λόγων τῆς κοσμικῆς παιδείας, πολλῷ δὲ πλέον ἡ Ἰουλία. Τὸ δὲ πρόσχημα αὐτῶν ἦν ταπεινὸν καὶ τὸ ἦθος ἤπιον, [...] Εἶτα ἐπιτραπέντες καθίσαι, τὴν ζήτησιν ἐποιοῦντο.
62   Augustine, *Haer.* 46.16 (Gardner and Lieu 2004, 191): "[...] The rest are called merely the elect; but even any of their members who seem suitable are sent to strengthen and

Finally, we possess one tantalizing piece of archaeological evidence, which in all likelihood belonged to a tomb and was discovered near Salona in Dalmatia. It is a burial inscription that is dated to the early fourth century, and it belonged to a woman, the 'Elect' (παρθένος) Manichaean Bassa from Lydia (in Asia Minor), as indicated in the inscription: ΒΑϹϹΑ ΠΑΡΘΕΝΟϹ ΛΥΔΙΑ ΜΑΝΙΧΕΑ.[63] Scopello supports the view that Bassa was a Manichaean missionary who came to Dalmatia/Illyria in order to spread her religion.[64] Coyle has expressed some reservations about this interpretation and argues that the evidence of the monument is so scant that we can neither support nor exclude such an interpretation.[65]

Coyle concludes that the only testimony in which it is clearly stated that Elect women were involved in missionary activities is that of Theonas. Further, he considers that the account provided by Mark the Deacon does not indicate anything other than that in a male-dominated society, male authors preferred to attack active women like Julia.[66] As he notes, the "equality of the genders, at least among the Elect – surely [was] part of the motivation behind the attacks on Manichaean women".[67]

In the rest of our literature, there are a few brief references to Manichaean women that do not specify whether they concern *Electae* or catechumens, and in fact may not all be addressing real Manichaeans. The church historians Socrates and Sozomenus recount an episode about a woman in Alexandria, Manichaean in religion (γυναῖκά τινα Μανιχαῖαν τὴν θρησκείαν); the arch-presbyter Petrus admitted her to the holy sacraments of the Church without her having first withdrawing from the Manichaean heresy. However, according to the sources, this story was slander and part of a plot of Theophilus, the bishop of Alexandria, who disliked Petrus and wanted to expel him from the Church.[68] Another reference to Manichaean women in general is Titus'

---

support this error where it exists, or to plant it where it does not". See also ch.[2], section 7.3.4 (*The Participants*): "It seems that it was a common Manichaean practice for the leader of the debate to be accompanied by young Elect".

63 See Cumont 1912, 175–77.

64 Scopello 2001, 42; 2005a, 293–315.

65 Coyle 2009d, 197–98. Kristionat (2013 141–42), following Coyle argues that "due to the lack of comparison pieces, an identification of Bassa as a missionary cannot be clearly proven, 142. [...] The fact that she died far from her hometown does not automatically imply missionary activity".

66 Coyle 2009d, 198.

67 Coyle 2009d, 194.

68 Socrates the Scholastic, *HE* 6.9.3 Sozomenus, *HE* 8.12. Cf. ch.[7], section 3.4.

report that pregnant Manichaean women were forced to end their pregnancies through abortion, since Manichaeans eschewed childbirth.[69]

Apart from the references to unknown Manichaean women, testimonies that associate named Byzantine women with Manichaeism are the following: (1) the testimony of the sixth-century chronographer Malalas, who records that during the reign of Justinian many Manichaean women were punished and among them was the wife of the senator Erythrius;[70] (2) the information provided by Theodorus Anagnostes that the mother of the emperor Anastasius (491–518) was a zealous supporter of the Manichaeans.[71]

There are also testimonies about women who were attracted by Manichaeism, not because the idea of a promising career as missionaries-teachers appealed to them, but because of their weakness. According to the account provided by Mark the Deacon, the teachings of the apostle Julia, apart from the childish men, attracted also 'foolish weak women' (γυναικάρια).[72] As Ephrem the Syrian observes, folk women, because of their naivety, were especially vulnerable to the Manichaean propaganda as they were easily impressed.[73]

Of course, there would also have been women who consciously chose to become Manichaeans because they found something fascinating and intriguing in it. For this case, it makes sense to investigate what this could have been, because it shows the comparative advantage of Manichaeism over other religious options for this portion of the population. In other words, what was the more interesting and promising choice for a woman of that time who had spiritual queries and wanted to pursue an ascetic life? Would she become a Manichaean Elect, or a Christian nun?

In addition to the attraction exerted by asceticism on women due to a kind of autonomy that it offered them,[74] there were several other reasons that made

---

69   Titus of Bostra *c. Manichaeos* 2.56. See also in SC 7.211–213 another accusation of the same kind (homosexuality) against Manichaean women ("they commit shameless acts ... against nature with men and women even as do the women among them").

70   Malalas, *Chronographia* 17.21 (CFHBSB 35:352): Ἐν δὲ τῷ αὐτῷ καιρῷ κατὰ πόλιν πολλοὶ ἐτιμωρήθησαν Μανιχαῖοι, ἐν οἷς ἐτιμωρήθη καὶ ἡ γυνὴ Ἐρυθρίου τοῦ συγκλητικοῦ Ἐρυθρίου καὶ ἄλλαι ἅμα αὐτῇ.

71   Theodorus Anagnostes, HE 4.448. I shall return to both of them in the next chapter.

72   Mark the Deacon, *Vit. Porph.* 85 (Lieu 2010, 96–97): ἐφελκομένων γυναικάρια καὶ παιδιώδεις ἄνδρας κοῦφον ἔχοντας τόν τε λογισμὸν καὶ τὴν διάνοιαν.

73   Ephrem the Syrian, *Hymni*, in Lieu 1994a, 42–43: "and also today he [the demon] seduces the simple women through diverse pretenses: he catches one by fasting, the other by sackcloth and leguminous plants." Lieu 1992, 181: "It was the Devil, Ephrem warned, that had given Mani a pale complexion in order to deceive the unwary". This is more clearly a topos.

74   Burrus 1987. Cf. Coyle 2009b, 153. Regarding the attraction ascetic Christianity exerted on certain women, see Kraemer 1980, 298–307.

the option of 'Manichaean Elect' more appealing to women, and which are highlighted in the relevant academic discourse. First, the class of the Elect was open to them (i.e. they could be initiated into the class of the Elect) and as Elect they had equal status with their male counterparts. As Coyle points out, "finally, it appears certain that Manichaeans provided a more public and (to a certain extent, anyway) equal status to women, which could have been another factor in the attraction".[75] And what does equal status mean in our case? That they could wander, carry out missions and participate in debates. The Manichaean Elect women, as missionaries and teachers, could also (like men) compete against their religious opponents in the public debates conducted in various cities, "chose unique pour l' époque" as de Stoop comments.[76] Yet, it seems that Manichaean women, although they participated in the class of the Elect and assumed missionary and teaching tasks, could not assume "any office or ministry which belonged to the official hierarchy".[77]

More than thirty years ago, Peter Brown, based mainly on Julia's account and on a reference to Thecla in the Manichaean Psalm-book, recounted in his vivid narrative style:

> throughout the late third and fourth centuries, Paul and Thecla walked the roads of Syria together, in the form of the little groups of "Elect" men and women, moving from city to city. As members of the "Elect," Manichaean women traveled on long missionary journeys with their male peers. Christian bishops believed that Manichaean women were capable of acting as spokesmen in public debates.[78]

---

75 Coyle 2009d, 193.
76 De Stoop in Coyle 2009d, 205. Another important reason for the attraction of women to the Manichaean sect may have been the importance and roles of women in Manichaean narratives. In contrast to the culture of the era that was 'misogynistic', women in Manichaean literature are rather honoured; "specific women were even revered" (Coyle 2009b, 145). Coyle (2009a, 164 and 2009c, 176 ff.) highlights the important role of certain women in Manichaean texts, such as the 'Psalms of Heracleides' where they appear to have the important role of a guide and instructor. Indicative of women's position in Manichaeism is also the fact that the paradigmatic Manichaean exemplar was the female model/pattern of the evangelical sisters Martha and Maria. This model, where Mary acts like a man ("she hunts, she casts the net, and later like her Gnostic counterpart, she becomes talkative"), whereas "Martha, on the other hand, is a servant (though a joyful one)" exists also in *Cologne Mani Codex* (92.15–22), in the Latin fragment from Tebessa, and in the Manichaean *Psalms* (*2PsB* 192.21–24).
77 Van Oort 2020c, 499, 502; Kristionat 2013. See also Van Oort 2020b, 418–432 and Van Oort 2020a 433–442.
78 Brown 1988, 202. Cf. *2PsB* 143.4–16: "... Thecla, the lover of God ..."; 195.8–12: "... they went from village to village. They went into the roads hungry, with no bread in their hands".

Does recent research justify Brown's thesis? Is there sufficient evidence for this? Coyle, initially, in his paper "Prolegomena to a Study of Women in Manichaeism" questioned Brown's assertion and concluded that women do not "appear [in sources] to have shared the rootlessness that often characterized male Elect, at least in the West."[79] In a subsequent paper, however ("Women and Manichaeism's Mission to the Roman Empire"), he revisits his view, arguing that until the middle of the fifth century there is some (but not much) evidence that supports Brown's view for women being active in the mission. However, he points out that this evidence comes from polemical literature, while, on the contrary there is no relevant testimony in Manichaean sources.[80] Ten years after Coyle's second publication, the study of Kellis' findings so far does not seem to shed more light on our question.

In conclusion, I will further highlight three points worthy of note that could be indicative for the active role of Manichaean women in the East-Roman Empire: (1) it is true that the testimonies we have about Manichaean *Electae* in action are very few; yet, they all come from the eastern part of the empire;[81] (2) furthermore, it is striking that the only known evidence we have so far for the existence or/and the activity of Byzantine Manichaean missionaries concern female Elect (Alexandria, Julia and Bassa?). This probably shows the active involvement of women in the movement; (3) lastly, as shown above in chapter [3], Manichaeism was the only case in which the law turned against the women of a religious group (heresy).[82] The same applies to the LAF where both male and female Elect are anathematized.[83]

3   Appeal to and Relationship with Other (Extreme) Ascetic Groups[84]

In the sources examined in the previous chapters, the Manichaeans are often associated or even identified with several other ascetic groups, namely the Encratites, the Apotactites, the Hydroparastates, the Saccophori, and the Messalians. As these groups are classified together with the Manichaeans both

---

79   Coyle 2009b, 144. Coyle (2009b, 144–45) also concludes that there are not evidences "that women exercised 'special' ministries carried out by the Elect, such as preacher, lector, scribe, or cantor".

80   Coyle, 2009d, 204 ff.

81   Cf. Coyle 2009d, 198.

82   There are at least two laws in which the two genders, *Manichaeos* and *Manichaeas*, are mentioned separately: Cod. theod. 16.5.7 (381) and 16.5.40 (407) in the version of Cod. justin. 1.5.4. Cf. ch.[3], section 3.3. See also *Nov.* 109 (541).

83   LAF (PG 1:1468A, Lieu 2010, 140–41): ἀναθεματίζω καὶ καταθεματίζω [...] ἐκλεκτοὺς καὶ ἐκλεκτάς.

84   This section provides the basis for Matsangou 2021.

in legal and in ecclesiastical literature for their common practices, behaviours, and lifestyle, the investigation of what exactly these ascetics meant in the eyes of the state and Church, as well as their relationship with Manichaeans, must be explored here.

3.1 Encratites, Apotactites, Hydroparastates, Saccophori

3.1.1 Laws

In the legislation, the association of Manichaeans with the Encratites, Apotactites, Hydroparastates and Saccophori (Encratites et al., thereafter) first appears in the early 380s. This was in the context of the first three laws of Theodosius I against heretics which were issued in three successive years and were addressed to the Prefects of Illyria (in 381) and the East (in 382 and 383).[85]

Indeed, in the first law, it is not the Encratites et al. who are persecuted, but the Manichaeans, who hide "themselves under the pretense of those fallacious names".[86] In the next two laws, the Encratites et al. are persecuted alongside the Manichaeans as independent religious groups. The reason for their persecution (particularly in the first two laws) is their "secret and hidden assemblies"[87] in places which are portrayed as "wonted sepulchres of funereal mysteries";[88] or because, by their customs and behaviour they threaten to become "a profaner and a corrupter of Catholic discipline".[89]

As Beskow points out, "Theodosius was not the first Roman Emperor to take measures against the Manichaeans".[90] Diocletian, Valens and Valentinian I and Gratian had preceded him. But while the rescript of Diocletian targets Manichaeans because they injured "the civic communities" and infected "the innocent, orderly and tranquil Roman people [...]" with the damnable customs and perverse laws of the Persians", the laws of Theodosius, do not suppose that the values and the customs of the empire are threatened by Persians but by the practices of these ascetics.

In later laws, while the Manichaeans are persistently persecuted, these other ascetic groups do not reappear except for the Hydroparastates, who are found again in the laws of 428 and 438.[91]

---

85   Cod. theod. 16.5.7 (381) to Prefect of Illyria Eutropius; Cod. theod. 16.5.9 (382) to the Prefect of East Florus and Cod. theod. 16.5.11 (383) to the Prefect of East Postumianus.

86   Cod. theod. 16.5.7 (381) (Coleman-Norton 1966, 1: 368).

87   Cod. theod. 16.5.9.1 (Coleman-Norton 1966, 2: 379).

88   Cod. theod. 16.5.7.3 (Coleman-Norton 1966, 1: 368).

89   Cod. theod. 16.5.9.pr. (Coleman-Norton 1966, 2: 378).

90   Beskow 1988, 6–11, 6.

91   Cod. theod. 16.5.65 (428) = Cod. justin. 1.5.5; NTh. 3.1.9 (438).

3.1.2   Ecclesiastical Literature

In patristic literature, the association of Manichaeans with the aforementioned ascetic movements is common. Many years before the Theodosian laws, as early as the 350s–60s, the Arian writer Julian (357–365?), for example, attributed to Manichaeans and pseudo-Encratites convictions such as that the body is evil and food is poisonous (αἱ τροφαὶ φαῦλαι).[92] Amphilochius of Iconium, in his most extensive work, *On False Asceticism*, fights the Encratites, whom he characterizes as 'pseudo-ascetics'. He appears to consider the Manichaeans as mentors of their 'false' practices.[93] Indeed, as he explains, these Manichaean ascetic practices (adopted by the Encratites) were ordained by the Manichaean leaders. As he characteristically says:

> They abstain from eating animate beings (ἐμψύχων) according to the teaching of Manichaeans. Because their leaders have ordained, once and for all, to abstain from eating living beings [...].[94]

From Amphilochius' correspondence with Basil of Caesarea it seems that in the region of Lycaonia (Iconium was its Metropolitan Archbishopric) there were many ascetics such as Encratites et al. The young Amphilochius needed the pastoral guidance of Basil in order to deal with various challenging issues. Interestingly, there is a discussion between the two concerning the baptism of the Encratites, Hydroparastates and Catharoi. In his first letter to Amphilochius in 374, Basil expresses reservations towards the baptism of the ascetics mentioned above. Particularly, he cautions against the Encratites, because, as he says, in order to make themselves not acceptable (!) by the Church they established their own, peculiar baptism, counterfeiting even their own tradition. The only known source for the baptism of the Encratites is this brief and mysterious reference of Basil. Though Basil, initially, appears ambiguous, he finally suggests that their baptism could be accepted (for the sake of a pastoral economy and homogeneity, local ethos), provided that they would be anointed with Holy Oil before the faithful.[95] However, in his second letter, just a year later (375), Basil discusses the same issue with Amphilochius. This

---

92   Julianus Arianus, *comm. Job* 67.8.
93   Amphilochius, *c. Haer.* 1067–71. See ch.[5], 2.2.1.
94   Amphilochius, *c. Haer.* 1067–71.
95   Basil, *Ep.* 188.1.63–69 (to Amphilochius) (Courtonne, 123): Ἐπειδὴ δὲ ὅλως ἔδοξέ τισι τῶν κατὰ τὴν Ἀσίαν οἰκονομίας ἕνεκα τῶν πολλῶν δεχθῆναι αὐτῶν τὸ βάπτισμα, ἔστω δεκτόν. Τὸ δὲ τῶν Ἐγκρατιτῶν κακούργημα νοῆσαι ἡμᾶς δεῖ, ὅτι, ἵν᾽ αὐτοὺς ἀπροσδέκτους ποιήσωσι τῇ Ἐκκλησίᾳ, ἐπεχείρησαν λοιπὸν ἰδίῳ προκαταλαμβάνειν βαπτίσματι· ὅθεν καὶ τὴν συνήθειαν τὴν ἑαυτῶν παρεχάραξαν.

time, he appears more unbending in arguing that the Encratites, Saccophori and Apotactites have to be rebaptized, since their sect is an offspring of the Marcionites and other similar heretics, who abhor marriage, abstain from wine, and consider God's creations polluted. Presumably, the expression "similar heretics" included the Manichaeans, since in contemporary literature they were always grouped together with the Marcionites. Basil concludes his letter with the enigmatic phrase:

> Thus, they should not dare to claim that they were baptized to the Father, Son and Holy Spirit, those who perceive God as the source of evil, as their heresiarchs, Marcion and other heretics, did.[96]

In his *Panarion*, which was written in the same year (375), Epiphanius points out that even during his days the Encratites, though the heresy was ancient, were gaining new adherents, mainly in Pisidia and Phrygia Combusta but also in Asia, Isauria, Pamphylia, Cilicia, and Galatia. He seems astonished to observe that by his time Encratites have been 'planted' even in big cities such as Rome and Antioch.[97] According to Epiphanius' description, the Encratites had a dualistic standpoint. They speak about "different first principles" (ἀρχαὶ διάφοροι) and not "about one deity" (περὶ μιᾶς θεότητος).[98] They say, as Epiphanius states, that "there are certain first principles and that the ⟨power⟩ of the devil [...] is not subject to God; he has power of his own and acts as in his own right".[99] Further, Epiphanius points out the implications of their dualism in everyday life. They claim that marriage serves the Devil's plan. They detest meat, not "for the sake of continence or as a pious practice", but from fear lest they "be condemned for eating flesh". They "do not drink wine at all" claiming that it comes from the Devil and they "celebrate mysteries with water".[100] They use as their scriptures "principally the so-called Acts

---

96   Basil, *Ep.* 199.47.1–16 (to Amphilochius) (Courtonne, 163): Μὴ γὰρ λεγέτωσαν ὅτι "Εἰς Πατέρα καὶ Υἱὸν καὶ Ἅγιον Πνεῦμα ἐβαπτίσθημεν" οἵ γε κακῶν ποιητὴν ὑποτιθέμενοι τὸν Θεόν, ἐφαμίλλως τῷ Μαρκίωνι καὶ ταῖς λοιπαῖς αἱρέσεσιν. Both Basil's letters (188 and 199) later became canons of the Church.

97   Epiphanius, *Pan.* 47.1.2–3. Epiphanius dates them to the time of Tatian, considering them his successors.

98   Epiphanius, *Pan.* 47.1.4; 47.2.1. 4 (Williams 2013, 3 modified).

99   Epiphanius, *Pan.* 47.1.4 (Williams, 3): Φάσκουσι δὲ καὶ οὗτοι ἀρχάς τινας εἶναι τήν τε τοῦ διαβόλου ⟨δύναμιν⟩ [...] μὴ ὑποτασσομένου θεῷ, ἀλλὰ ἰσχύοντος καὶ πράττοντος ὡς κατὰ ἰδίαν ἐξουσίαν.

100   Epiphanius, *Pan.* 47.1.6 (Williams, 4): τὸν δὲ γάμον σαφῶς τοῦ διαβόλου ὁρίζονται· ἔμψυχα δὲ βδελύσσονται, ἀπαγορεύοντες οὐχ ἕνεκεν ἐγκρατείας οὔτε πολιτείας, ἀλλὰ κατὰ φόβον καὶ ἰνδαλμὸν τοῦ μὴ καταδικασθῆναι ἀπὸ τῆς τῶν ἐμψύχων μεταλήψεως. κέχρηνται δὲ καὶ αὐτοὶ

of Andrew, and of John, and of Thomas, and certain apocrypha". In order to support their views in their propaganda, they use selectively texts from OT (οἷς βούλονται λόγοις τῆς παλαιᾶς διαθήκης) where the patriarchs (Noah, Lot, etc.), whom they call drunkards, misbehaved under the influence of wine.[101] "They pride themselves on supposed continence, but all their conduct is risky. For they are surrounded by women, deceive women in every way, travel and eat with women and are served by them".[102]

The fact that in the area of Antioch, among the many other monastic communities, there also existed Encratite communities, is also testified by John Chrysostom. One of his lectures, which Chrysostom delivered when he was still a presbyter in Antioch (before 398), is dedicated to the monks of the Antioch monasteries. The targets of the homily are the Manichaeans and their leaders (ἀρχηγετῶν τούτων), the Encratites, the Marcionites, and the whole "factory" (ἐργαστηρίου) of those apostates from faith, who prevent marriage and abstain from food.[103] The following remarks are necessary at this point: First, it is interesting that Chrysostom refers to their leaders only in the case of the Manichaeans. Thus, for the second time, Manichaean leaders are mentioned in the discourse associating Encratites and Manichaeans.[104] Second, the term "factory" for Manichaeans and Encratites et al. also was used by the legislation.[105] This usage suggests an interplay between the rhetoric of church leaders and the language of the law. Third, the law against the apostates to Manichaeism was issued at the same time.[106] Possibly, this was not a coin-

μυστηρίοις δι᾽ ὕδατος· οἶνον δὲ ὅλως οὐ μεταλαμβάνουσι, φάσκοντες εἶναι διαβολικὸν καὶ τοὺς πίνοντας καὶ τοὺς χρωμένους ἀνόμους εἶναι καὶ ἁμαρτάδα.

101 Epiphanius, *Pan.* 47.1.5 (Williams, 3): κέχρηνται δὲ γραφαῖς πρωτοτύπως ταῖς λεγομέναις Ἀνδρέου καὶ Ἰωάννου Πράξεσι καὶ Θωμᾶ καὶ ἀποκρύφοις τισὶ καὶ οἷς βούλονται λόγοις τῆς παλαιᾶς διαθήκης; 47.2.3–4 (Williams, 4). Epiphanius (47.2.3) also accuses them of using the NT as it suits them. They even discredit Paul "calling him a drunkard" (τοῦτον μεθυστὴν καλοῦντες) when they disagree with his ideas.

102 Epiphanius, *Pan.* 47.3.1 (Williams, 5): Σεμνύνονται δὲ δῆθεν ἐγκράτειαν, σφαλερῶς τὰ πάντα ἐργαζόμενοι, μέσον γυναικῶν εὑρισκόμενοι καὶ γυναῖκας πανταχόθεν ἀπατῶντες, γυναιξὶ δὲ συνοδεύοντες καὶ συνδιαιτώμενοι καὶ ἐξυπηρετούμενοι ὑπὸ τῶν τοιούτων.

103 Chrysostom, *Hom. 1 Tim.* (PG 62:557.47–50): Περὶ Μανιχαίων, καὶ Ἐγκρατιτῶν, καὶ Μαρκιωνιστῶν, καὶ παντὸς αὐτῶν τοῦ ἐργαστηρίου τὰ τοιαῦτά φησιν, ὅτι ἐν ὑστέροις καιροῖς ἀποστήσονταί τινες τῆς πίστεως; 558.27–30: Οὐ περὶ Ἰουδαίων λέγει ταῦτα· πῶς γὰρ τό, Ἐν ὑστέροις καιροῖς, καὶ τό, Ἀποστήσονταί τινες τῆς πίστεως, ἔχει χώραν; ἀλλὰ περὶ Μανιχαίων, καὶ τῶν ἀρχηγετῶν τούτων.

104 The first time was by Amphilochius.

105 Cod. theod. 16.5.9.1 (382). In the law "all this workshop" comprise the Manichaeans, Encratites, Saccophori, and Hydroparastates.

106 Cod. theod. 16.7.3 (383).

cidence; Chrysostom's discussion about apostates, which reflects a fear of Manichaean influence on other groups of ascetics, could have been one of the factors that triggered the promulgation of the law.

In spite of the bishops' polemic and the laws and canons against them, these ascetic practices were still appealing, and the number of ascetics who adopted them seems to have continuously increased even in the fifth century. According to Macarius of Magnesia, "children of Manichaeans" (Μανιχαίων παῖδες) who were self-proclaimed with names difficult even to pronounce (Encratites, Apotactites and Hermits), mushroomed everywhere in Pisidia, Cilicia, Isauria, Lycaonia and Galatia,[107] in the same territories mentioned by Epiphanius (and Amphilochius). "Μανιχαίων παῖδες" literally means Manichaean children, but in our context, it could also be translated as the followers/disciples/servants of the Manichaeans, or ascetics who adopted Manichaean practices and attitudes. For Macarius, as for Chrysostom, these ascetics were not Christians but apostates from faith. They abstained from foods and held marriage to be illegal.[108] Macarius also speaks about a certain Dositheus of Cilicia, a leader among them, and about eight books by means of which he strengthened his doctrines.

At the head of their chorus doubtless stands Dositheus, a Cilician by race, who confirms their teaching in the course of eight whole books, and magnifies his case by the splendour of his language, saying again and again that marriage is an illegal act, and quite contrary to the law. Here are his words, "Through communion (koinōnia) the world had its beginning; through abstinence it has to be terminated."[109]

---

107 Macarius of Magnesia, *Apocriticus*, 3.151.25–28 (§25) (Grafer, modified): Τοιοῦτοι δὲ Μανιχαίων παῖδες ἐξεφοίτησαν· τοιαύτας αἱρέσεις ἡ τῶν ΠισσιδΓέ7ων ἔχει καὶ τῶν Ἰσαύρων χώρα, Κιλικία τε καὶ Λυκαονία καὶ πᾶσα Γαλατία, ὧν καὶ τὰς ἐπωνυμίας ἐργῶδες ἀπαγγεῖλαι· Ἐγκρατηταὶ γὰρ καὶ Ἀποτακτῖται καὶ Ἐρημίται καλοῦνται, οὐ Χριστιανοί τινες. Macarius was probably a bishop of Magnesia and a friend and supporter of John Chrysostom.

108 Macarius of Magnesia, *Apocriticus*, 3.151.36–40 (§27); 3.151.29–31 (§25): οὐ Χριστιανοί τινες, οὐδὲ πρόσφυγες τῆς οὐρανίου χάριτος, πίστεως μὲν εὐαγγελικῆς ἀποστάται καὶ Γἀπόδημοι7. "They are not Christians, nor [are they] refugees of celestial grace, [they are] apostates from evangelical faith and expatriates (ἀπόδημοι)". See also ch.[5], 3.3.1.

109 Macarius of Magnesia, *Apocriticus* 3.151.32–36 (§26) (Grafer, modified): Ἀμέλει Δοσίθεος ὁ κορυφαῖος παρ' αὐτοῖς, Κίλιξ τὸ γένος ὑπάρχων, δι' ὀκτὼ βιβλίων ὅλων κρατύνει τὸ δόγμα καὶ λαμπρότητι λέξεων μεγαλύνει τὸ πρᾶγμα, ἄθεσμον ἔργον καὶ λίαν παράνομον ἀποθρυλλῶν τὸν γάμον, λέγων· "Διὰ μὲν κοινωνίας ὁ κόσμος τὴν ἀρχὴν ἔσχε· διὰ δὲ τῆς ἐγκρατείας τὸ τέλος θέλει λαβεῖν". About Dositheus see also ch.[5], 3.3.1.

According to Goulet (the editor of the text), it is not easy to find out what
Macarius presupposes as historical or dogmatic relationship between Manichaeans, Encratites, and Dositheus. Most likely he suggests that Macarius
does not consider that the above ascetics (including Dositheus) were formally
members of the Manichaean movement, but describes them as "Manichaean
children" for their similarities with the latter.[110] Without disregarding Goulet's view, it is not unlikely that Macarius had in mind a closer relationship
between Manichaeans and the above ascetics, since in his next book he points
out that the Manichaean heresy is active and acquires followers "corrupting
the *oikoumene*" up to and during his time.[111] In addition, although we know
nothing about the eight books which Macarius claims that Dositheus had at
his disposal and through which he supported his doctrines,[112] the summary of
Dositheus' teachings based on these books (as recorded by Macarius) and their
number (eight), inevitably leads us to suspect a closer connection with Manichaeism. Especially the verbatim quotation of Dositheus' own words that:
"Since this world (humanity) had its beginning through communion, it has to
be terminated through abstinence" sounds very Manichaean.[113]

At this point, it is possible to make some concluding remarks concerning
Encratites et al. and their relationship with Manichaeans:

(1) References to and correlation of Manichaeans and Encratites et al.
     appear in ecclesiastical literature earlier than in legislation. A boom in
     the growth of the phenomenon of radical asceticism is recorded in eccle-
     siastical literature during the 370s–380s. Just after this boom (early 380s)
     the first laws against these ascetics appeared. The fast pace of this phe-
     nomenon seems to have continued at least during the first half of the
     fifth century, when the laws against Hydroparastates were promulgated.

(2) Both Amphilochius and Macarius present Encratites et al. as followers or
     disciples of the Manichaeans, who were regarded as the mentors of their
     ascetic practices. Moreover, it is emphasized that these practices were
     established by Manichaean leaders. This indicates an additional concern:
     the organized character of the Manichaean movement.

---

110 Goulet 2003, 59–60.
111 Macarius of Magnesia, *Apocriticus* 4.184.8–11(3): Αὐτίκα γοῦν ὁ ΜανΓῆ῀ς ἐν Περσίδι τὸ ὄνομα
     τοῦ Χριστοῦ ὑποκρινάμενος πολλὴν μὲν σατραπείαν, πολλὴν δὲ τῆς ἀνατολῆς χώραν τῇ πλάνῃ
     διέφθειρε καὶ μέχρι τήμερον φθείρει λυμαντικοῖς ὑφέρπων τὴν οἰκουμένην σπέρμασιν.
112 Goulet 2003, 60.
113 Interpreting Dositheus' statement in a Manichaean perspective, he seems to claim that
     marriage is illegal because it counteracts the plan of the forces of Light, which is the
     deconstruction of the cosmos. See ch.[5], 3.3.1.

(3) According to the first law of Theodosius (381), the Encratites et al. are names behind which the Manichaeans were hidden; the same is implied by the wording of Macarius for the Encratites et al. of his time (children of Manichaeans who are self-identified as Encratites, Apotactites, and Hermits).

(4) The areas where the presence of communities of such ascetics is recorded are the central provinces of Asia Minor, mainly Pisidia, Lycaonia, and Phrygia Combusta (τῇ κεκαυμένῃ),[114] but also major cities such as Rome and Antioch. Pisidia heads both lists given by Epiphanius and Macarius.

In addition, the intense presence of Encratites in Pisidia and Lycaonia is confirmed by archaeological monuments. Two burial inscriptions dating back to 375 prove that there were Encratite communities in Laodicea Combusta (κεκαυμένη) of Pisidia or Lycaonia,[115] a neighbouring city of Iconium.[116] From the burial inscriptions the following can be deduced: the members of this religious community self-identified as Encratites, meaning that the appellation 'Encratites' is not a label *ab extra*, but can also be an autonym; they called their movement a religion (τῆς Ἐνκρατῶν θρισκίας); they had active women in the class of deaconesses[117] (Ἐλαφία διακόνισσα τῆς Ἐνκρατῶν θρισκίας); they distinguished their own religion from that of the Catholics (independent self-understanding). One of the inscriptions records a provision for the protection of the tomb against those who drink wine (i.e. Catholic Christians): "And if any of the wine-bibbers intrudes (a corpse), he has to deal with God and Jesus Christ".[118] The above provision "in the context of this epitaph must be regarded as a piece of propaganda"[119] against the criticisms of Catholics (Epiphanius and

---

114 Epiphanius *Pan.* 47.1.2 (Williams, 3) says about Scorched Phrygia (Φρυγία τῇ κεκαυμένη): "Perhaps the country has come to be called this by divine dispensation, for this very reason – its inhabitants have been scorched by the perversity of such error, and so much of it. For there are many sects in the area".

115 Some ancient authors situate Laodicea Combusta in Lycaonia (not the Laodicea of Frygia) and others in Pisidia; cf. Socrates, *HE* 6.18.

116 Calder 1929, 645–46: (a) Αὐρ. Ἀντώνιος Μίρου ἅμα τῇ ἑαυτοῦ θίᾳ Ἐλα[φ]ίῃ διακονίσσῃ [τῶν Ἐν]κρατῶν [ἀνεστήσ]αμεν...(SEG 6 348) (b) Ἐλαφία διακόνισσα τῆς Ἐνκρατῶν θρισκίας ἀνέστησα τῷ πρ(εσ)β(υτέ)ρ(ῳ) Πέτρῳ ἅμα τῷ ἀδελφῷ αὐτῶ Πολυχρονίῳ μνήμης χάριν (SEG 6 349). Also, on the west side of Laodicea was found a burial "doorstone" with the inscription: [Με][ἱρος Ἀεντίνου τῶ[ν] Ἐνκ[ρ]α[τ]ῶν ζῶν κὲ φρονῶν ἀνέστ[η]σεν ἑαυτῷ τε κὲ τῇ ἀνεψιᾷ Τατῖ [κ]ὲ τῷ ἀδε[λ]φῷ Παύλῳ κὲ ἀδελφῇ Πρ[ί]βι μνήμης χάριν· εἰ δέ τις τῶν οἰν[ο]ποτῶν ἐπενβάλῃ, εἴσχι πρὸς τὸν Θ(εὸ)ν καὶ Ἰη(σο)ῦ(ν) Χ(ριστό)ν (SEG 6 345).

117 Cecire 1985, 175. Cf. Quispel 1985/2008, 356–60.

118 Calder 1929, 646: εἰ δέ τις τῶν οἰν[ο]ποτῶν ἐπενβάλῃ, εἴσχι πρὸς τὸν Θ(εὸ)ν καὶ Ἰη(σο)ῦ(ν) Χ(ριστό)ν.

119 Calder 1929, 646.

Basil wrote against Encratites during the same year), concerning the Encratite abstinence from alcohol (even for the Eucharist). It sounds like the last word of an Encratite in the debate with the Catholics, engraved in eternity.

(5) Despite the self-identification just mentioned, it is most likely, as suggested by many scholars, that Encratites et al. were not organized movements or "closed communities with distinct characteristics". Instead, they were "interchangeable names for irregular ascetic groups"[120] which adopted certain ascetic practices, as is revealed by their names. Encratites abstained from animal food and wine and they condemned marriage; Apotactites renounced marriage and private property; Hydroparastates substituted water for wine in the Eucharist (abstaining from all other drinks but water); and Saccophori wore the sackcloth. Such tendencies to self-negation had existed since the beginning of Christianity, from Paul's era, and earlier in the pagan world. Already from the mid-second century, well before the appearance of Manichaeism, there were Encratite groups in the eastern provinces, whose practices initially were broadly within the limits of 'acceptability' for the church leaders.[121] These same practices also were performed by the Manichaeans who, in addition, used the same apocrypha, especially the Acts of Thomas, and who also had women involved in the services and the ministries of their sect (as missionaries and Elect). Yet Manichaeans, in contrast to Encratites et al., were a distinct and well-organized religious group. Thus, while these ascetic groups initially were considered 'harmless' (although their practices were condemned), it seems that once they were associated with the Manichaeans, imperial and church leaders were alarmed.

3.2   Messalians

Another ascetic group associated with Manichaeism by anti-Manichaean authors are the Messalians (Euchites in Greek). Messalians appear chronologically later than Manichaeans. According to Theophanes the Confessor "the heresy of the Messalians, that is of the Euchites and Enthusiasts, sprouted up" during the reign of the emperor Valens (375/6).[122] Messalians, as well as Encratites et al., resided by and large in the provinces of central and southern

---

120   Beskow 1988, 8–11, esp. 9; Caner 2002, 85. Cf. Gregory 1991, 1350.

121   See for example the opinion of Dionysius of Alexandria in Basil's letter 188/199. Eusebius (*H.E.* 4.28–29) is the first one who mentions Encratites. Cf. Lössl 2021, 13 n. 53.

122   Theophanes, *Chron.* (de Boor, 63.14–20; Mango and Scott, 97–98): Τούτῳ τῷ ἔτει [under Valens] ἡ τῶν Μεσαλιανῶν αἵρεσις ἤγουν Εὐχητῶν καὶ Ἐνθουσιαστῶν ἀνεφύη.

Asia Minor (Lycaonia, Pamphylia, etc.),[123] as well as in the city of Antioch.[124] According to Photius, the Messalians reached their zenith during the fifth century. The last bishop who fought them was, according to Photius, Severus of Antioch.[125]

3.2.1 Laws

A single law issued in 428 exists in the codes (Cod. theod. & Cod. justin.) that persecuted, among many other heretics, the Messalians. This is the same law explored in ch.[3] which ranked heretics according to the severity of their crime and the corresponding inflicted penalty. The Messalians are co-classified along with the Hydroparastates and Manichaeans in the third and worst group. They have no right to gather and pray anywhere on Roman soil. The Manichaeans, as the worst of the worst, had in addition to be exiled/expelled from the municipalities.[126]

3.2.2 Ecclesiastical Synods

Messalianism was condemned as heretical by a series of local synods held at Antioch, Side, and Constantinople. The most important of these was the Synod convened at Side of Lycaonia in the 390s (or earlier in 383),[127] which was presided over by Amphilochius.[128] Next, Messalianism was condemned

---

123 ACO (Ephesenum anno 431), 1.1.7:117: περὶ τῶν λεγομένων ἐν τοῖς τῆς Παμφυλίας μέρεσι Μεσσαλιανιτῶν εἴτ' οὖν Εὐχιτῶν ἢ γοῦν Ἐνθουσιαστῶν εἴτε ὁπωσοῦν. About the many heretics who according to Epiphanius were found in Asia Minor and the 'heresy-belt' from Constantinople to Alexandria, see Young 2006, esp. 244. For differing views on Messalianism, in general, and on when and where they appeared, see Caner (2002 esp. 84–85). For Caner, the above testimonies provided by the church leaders are unreliable and serve their heresiological construction of the Messalian profile.

124 Epiphanius (Pan. 80.1.3–3.1, 3.6) seems to differentiate the origins of the Messalians of Asia Minor and those of Antioch. Whereas, according to him, the motherland of the latter was Mesopotamia, he considers the former as successors of an earlier movement dated at the reign of Constantius II and called by him pagan Messalians.

125 Photius, Bibl. 52.26–27. See Fitschen 1993, 354.

126 Cod. theod. 16.5.65 (428) = Cod. justin. 1.5.5.

127 As Anna Silvas (2007, 213) states, "Karl Holl [...] dated this synod of Side as early as 383, with Flavian's synod at Antioch following afterward. More recently however, Klaus Fitschen, [...] places Flavian's council first, and dates the Synod of Side well into the 390s. The maturity of doctrine and phraseology in this letter [...] points perhaps to a later rather than an earlier dating for this letter, so that the year 390 or thereabouts it might be reasonably nominated".

128 Photius, Bibl. cod., 12b.7–11: 52(12b): Ἀνεγνώσθη σύνοδος γενομένη ἐν Σίδῃ κατὰ τῆς αἱρέσεως τῶν Μεσσαλιανῶν ἤγουν Εὐχιτῶν ἤτοι Ἀδελφιανῶν. Ἐξῆρχε δὲ τῆς συνόδου Ἀμφιλόχιος ὁ τοῦ Ἰκονίου, συνεδρευόντων αὐτῷ καὶ ἑτέρων ἐπισκόπων τὸν ἀριθμὸν πέντε καὶ εἴκοσιν. Cf. Caner

by the Ecumenical Council of Ephesus in 431.[129] According to the decision of the synod, both priestly and lay Messalians (even those suspected to be such) should abjure their 'heresy' by a written statement. Otherwise, clerics were forfeiting their priesthood and were ex-communicated (ἐκπίπτειν καὶ κλήρου καὶ βαθμοῦ καὶ κοινωνίας), whereas laymen were anathematized. In addition, the suspects should not be confined in monasteries during their interrogation (a common penalty during the Byzantine era for criminals and heretics) in order to prevent the spread of Messalianism among the monks. The synod also condemned the book of the heresy, "the so called *Asceticon*".[130] Apart from Amphilochius, the bishops of Melitene (Letoius) and of Antioch (Flavianus) combated Messalianism actively.[131]

3.2.3 Ecclesiastical Literature

In the ecclesiastical literature, Messalians are reported first in the 370s by Ephrem the Syrian[132] and Epiphanius.[133] According to Epiphanius, Messalians came from Mesopotamia and could also be found in Antioch. Their basic features as depicted by Epiphanius are the following:

2002, 90: "Actions taken against certain Mesopotamian monks (Messalians) in the 380s and 390s at synods held in Antioch and Side".

129   *ACO (Ephesenum anno 431)*,1.1.7, 117–18.

130   *ACO (Ephesenum anno 431)*, 1.1.7: 117–18: Ὅρος τῆς αὐτῆς ἁγίας καὶ οἰκουμενικῆς συνόδου τῆς ἐν Ἐφέσῳ κατὰ τῶν δυσσεβῶν Μεσσαλιανιτῶν ἢ γοῦν Εὐχιτῶν· Συνελθόντες [...] ἐπίσκοποι Οὐαλεριανὸς καὶ Ἀμφιλόχιος [...] περὶ τῶν λεγομένων ἐν τοῖς τῆς Παμφυλίας μέρεσι Μεσσαλιανιτῶν εἴτ᾽ οὖν Εὐχιτῶν ἢ γοῦν Ἐνθουσιαστῶν εἴτε ὁπωσοῦν [...] χαρτίον συνοδικὸν περὶ τούτων [...] ὥστε τοὺς ὄντας κατὰ πᾶσαν ἐπαρχίαν τῆς Μεσσαλιανῶν ἢ γοῦν Ἐνθουσιαστῶν αἱρέσεως ἢ καὶ ἐν ὑποψίαις τῆς τοιαύτης νόσου γεγενημένους, εἴτε κληρικοὶ εἶεν εἴτε λαικοί, μεθοδεύεσθαι, καὶ ἀναθεματίζοντας κατὰ τὰ ἐν τῷ μνημονευθέντι συνοδικῷ διηγορευμένα ἐγγράφως, [...] τοὺς [...] καὶ μὴ ἀναθεματίζοντας, τοὺς μὲν πρεσβυτέρους καὶ διακόνους καὶ τοὺς ἕτερόν τινα βαθμὸν ἔχοντας ἐν ἐκκλησίαι ἐκπίπτειν καὶ κλήρου καὶ βαθμοῦ καὶ κοινωνίας, τοὺς δὲ λαικοὺς ἀναθεματίζεσθαι· μοναστήρια δὲ μὴ συγχωρεῖσθαι ἔχειν τοὺς ἐλεγχομένους ὑπὲρ τοῦ μὴ τὸ ζιζάνιον ἐκτείνεσθαι καὶ ἰσχύειν. See also Photius, *Bibl.* (*Codex 52* Bekker) 12b–13b: Ἐξήνεγκε δὲ καὶ ὅρον ἡ ἁγία καὶ οἰκουμενικὴ σύνοδος, ἡ ἐν Ἐφέσῳ τρίτη, ἀπογυμνώσασα αὐτῶν καὶ τὰ ἐν τῷ λεγομένῳ αὐτῶν βιβλίῳ ἀσκητικῷ βλάσφημα καὶ αἱρετικὰ κεφάλαια, καὶ καθυποβαλοῦσα τῷ ἀναθέματι. Ἔγραψε δὲ καὶ Ἀρχέλαος ὁ Καισαρείας τῆς Καππαδοκῶν ἐπίσκοπος ἀναθεματισμοὺς εἰκοσιτέσσαρας τῶν κεφαλαίων αὐτῶν.

131   Theodoret, *HE*, 4.10, p 230.2–5: Λητῶϊος μὲν οὖν ὁ τὴν Μελιτηνῶν ἐκκλησίαν ἰθύνας, ἀνὴρ ζήλῳ θείῳ κοσμούμενος, πολλὰ τῆς νόσου ταύτης σπάσαντα θεασάμενος μοναστήρια, μᾶλλον δὲ σπήλαια λῃστρικά, ἐνέπρησε ταῦτα καὶ τοὺς λύκους ἐκ τῆς ποίμνης ἐξήλασεν.

132   Ephrem the Syrian, *Beati Ephraem Testamentum* 421.

133   Epiphanius, *Pan.* 80.1.2: "For another sect has actually arisen after these, a foolish, entirely stupid one, wholly ridiculous, inconsistent in its doctrine, and composed of deluded men and women. They are called Messalians, which means 'people who pray'".

- They lack principles, authorities, rulers, (foundation of a name, or Legislation) constitution, rules; their prayer and fasting is also irregular.[134]
- They build certain places and call them prayers or houses of prayer. In some places, these houses resemble a church, purposing to counterfeit the truth and imitating the example of the Church.[135]
- Women played an important role in the sect. Men and women assemble together [in mixed companies]. They abandoned their homes and their families under the pretence of the world's renunciation, and they cohabit together, males and females.[136]
- Wandering in the open air and within cities, they spend their time in prayers and singing hymns.[137] Four centuries later, Theophanes completes the picture by adding that they danced using castanets while they chanted.[138]
- "In the summertime they sleep in the public squares, all together in a mixed crowd, men with women and women with men, because, as they say, they own no possession on earth. They show no restraint and hold their hands out to beg, as though they had no means of livelihood and no property".[139]
- In this way, as Epiphanius comments, they made their life a public show. Thus, even if they were chaste as they claimed, or had spouses, they provoked people "by their silly, extravagant activity".[140] Elsewhere, however, he denotes that "vice or sexual misconduct" among them is probable, but states that he is unable to know it.[141]

---

134 Epiphanius, *Pan.* 80.3.3 (Williams, 647): "But they have no beginning or end, no top or bottom, they are unstable in every way, without principles, and victims of delusion. They are entirely without the foundation of a name, a law, a position, or legislation".

135 Epiphanius begins his chapter with the (earlier) pagan Messalians, the predecessors of his contemporary – nominally Christian – Messalians, pointing out their habit to built assembly places that look like Christian churches. Cf. Epiphanius, *Pan.* 80.1.4; 80.2.1; 80.2.3; 80.3.3 (Williams, 647): "Today, however", Epiphanius explains, "these people who are now called Massalians ⟨have adopted⟩ their customs".

136 Epiphanius, *Pan.* 80.3.4 (Williams, 647): δοκοῦσι τοίνυν οὗτοι ἐπὶ τὸ αὐτὸ ἄνδρες τε καὶ γυναῖκες δῆθεν εἰς Χριστὸν πεπιστευκέναι λέγοντες, ὡς ἀποταξάμενοι τῷ κόσμῳ καὶ τῶν ἰδίων ἀνακεχωρηκότες, ὁμοῦ δὲ ἀναμὶξ ἄνδρες ἅμα γυναιξὶ καὶ γυναῖκες ἅμα ἀνδράσιν ἐπὶ τὸ αὐτὸ καθεύδοντες.

137 Epiphanius, *Pan.* 80.3.2: ἐπειδὴ γὰρ τὰ ἴσα ἐν ὑπαίθρῳ ἐξαγόμενοι, ἔξω βεβηκότες τῆς ἀληθείας, ἐπὶ τὸ εὔχεσθαι καὶ ὑμνεῖν ἐσχολάκασιν.

138 Theophanes, *Chron.* (de Boor, 63.14–20): οὗτοι ψάλλοντες βαλλίζουσι καὶ κροταλίζουσι.

139 Epiphanius, *Pan.* 80.3.4 (Williams, 647): ὁμοῦ δὲ ἀναμὶξ ἄνδρες ἅμα γυναιξὶ καὶ γυναῖκες ἅμα ἀνδράσιν ἐπὶ τὸ αὐτὸ καθεύδοντες, ἐν ῥύμαις μὲν πλατείαις, ὁπηνίκα θέρους ὥρα εἴη, διὰ τὸ μὴ ἔχειν, φησί, κτῆμα ἐπὶ τῆς γῆς. ἀκώλυτοι δέ εἰσι καὶ ἐκτείνουσι χεῖρας μεταιτεῖν ὡς ἀβίωτοι καὶ ἀκτήμονες.

140 Epiphanius, *Pan.* 80.8.4–6 (Williams, 652).

141 Epiphanius, *Pan.* 80.3.7 (Williams, 648): περὶ δὲ αἰσχρότητος ἢ λαγνείας οὐ πάνυ τι δύναμαι εἰδέναι. πλὴν οὐδὲ τούτου εἰσὶν ἀποδέοντες, μάλιστα ἐπὶ τὸ αὐτὸ κοινῇ τὸ κοιτάζειν ἐσχηκότες ἅμα γυναιξὶ καὶ ἀνδράσιν.

– Outlandish also was the appearance of Messalians, who, according to Epiphanius had long hair, were beardless and wore a sackcloth. As Epiphanius stresses, these practices were also adopted by some Catholic monks in the Mesopotamian monasteries. However, as he points out, both the female hairstyle and the sackcloth were practices alien to the Catholic Church.[142] Apart from the Saccophori and the Messalian monks, Manichaeans possibly wore the sackcloth too.[143]

Although all the aforementioned features also existed in Manichaeism (apart from the anarchist character), *argia* – the refusal to work – and its consequent begging is clearly the most important feature for Epiphanius, as well as the main reason for connecting Messalians with Manichaeans.[144] *Argia* seems to have been the hallmark of Manichaeans. Whoever was against manual labour was considered to have certainly learned it from the Manichaeans. Indeed, according to Epiphanius, the "horrid" Manichaean practice of idleness had found supporters among certain simple-minded Catholic monks in the Mesopotamian monasteries; misinterpreting the evangelical command (Mt. 19:21), they believed they should not work, and should "⟨be⟩ idle and without occupation and [...] ⟨be like⟩ drones".[145] As Epiphanius states:

> Some of these brethren ⟨refrain from all mundane labor⟩ – as though they had learned this from the Persian immigrant, Mani, if I may say so. They have no business to be that way. The word of God tells us to mark such people, who will not work.[146]

---

142 Epiphanius, *Pan.* 80.6.5–7 (Williams, 651): οἱ αὐτοὶ τίμιοι ἡμῶν ἀδελφοί, οἱ κατὰ Μεσοποταμίαν ἐν μοναστηρίοις ὑπάρχοντες [...] κόμαις γυναικικαῖς ⟨χρῆσθαι⟩ προβαλλόμενοι καὶ σάκκῳ προφανεῖ ἐπερειδόμενοι; Epiphanius (*Pan.* 80.6.6): ἀλλότριον γάρ ἐστι τῆς καθολικῆς ἐκκλησίας σάκκος προφανὴς καὶ κόμη ⟨μὴ⟩ ἐκτεμνομένη. His comment about beards: (80.6.7): Τὸ δὲ χεῖρον καὶ ἐναντίον οἱ μὲν τὸ γένειον, τὴν μορφὴν τοῦ ἀνδρός, ἀποτέμνουσι, τρίχας δὲ τῆς κεφαλῆς πολλάκις κομῶσι. καὶ περὶ μὲν οὖν τοῦ γενείου ἐν ταῖς διατάξεσι τῶν ἀποστόλων φάσκει ὁ θεῖος λόγος καὶ ἡ διδασκαλία μὴ φθείρειν τουτέστι μὴ τέμνειν τρίχας γενείου.

143 Cf. Lieu 1981a, 166.

144 Epiphanius, *Pan.* 80.7.5 (Williams, 652): "But I have been obliged to say this because of these Messalians, since they [...] have been made a sect with the horrid custom of idleness and the other evils". Ammonius of Alexandria (fifth-sixth cent.) connects Messalians with Manichaeans for the same reason (*argia*), *Fragmenta in Joannem, frag.* 193.

145 Epiphanius, *Pan.* 80.4.1–2 (Williams, 648): [...] ⟨εἶναι⟩ ἀργὸν [...] ἄεργον καὶ ἀκαιροφάγον, [...] ⟨ἐοικέναι⟩ τῷ κηφῆνι τῶν μελισσῶν.

146 Epiphanius, *Pan.* 80.4.3 (Williams, 648): τινὲς δὲ τῶν προειρημένων ἀδελφῶν, ὡς ἀπὸ τοῦ Μάνη μεμαθηκότες τάχα, ἵν' οὕτως εἴπω, τοῦ ἀπὸ Περσίδος ἀναβεβηκότος, ἅτινα οὐκ ἐχρῆν οὕτως εἶναι· σκοπεῖν δὲ μᾶλλον τοὺς τοιούτους παραγγέλλει ὁ θεῖος λόγος τοὺς μηδὲν ἐργαζομένους. As Caner (2002, 89) observes, Epiphanius associates "their [Messalians'] idleness with simple-minded Mesopotamian monks. Although he admits the latter to be orthodox

For Epiphanius, the right thing is to do both (work and pray), something which, as he states, many of the clerics did, though they were not obliged to. In addition, they shared the fruits of their work with the needy.[147] The way labour is combined with unceasing prayer is explained magisterially by Abbas Lucius in a conversation he had with a group of Messalian monks. To the claim of the Messalians that they do not work because they pray unceasingly, Abbas Lucius, first, forced them to admit that they do not pray when they sleep and eat. Then, he demonstrated how he achieves both simultaneously. As he explains, while he is working he prays unceasingly and gives a part from the money he earns to the poor who in turn pray for him when he eats or he sleeps.[148] The whole discussion reflects the confrontation between the two rival theories on the issue of labour that divided ascetic environments and troubled ecclesiastical and civil authorities.

The next portrait of the Messalians is outlined by Theodoret of Cyrrhus some decades later. Theodoret gives us an account of the Messalians of his time, in three of his works: *Haereticarum fabularum compendium* (after 453), *Historia ecclesiastica* (449–450) and *Historia Religiosa* (437–449). In the two former, he depicts their basic features in detail.

Like Epiphanius, Theodoret points out the anarchist, lawless, and irregular character of the movement: that they have neither teachings nor rules regulating their ascetic practices (fasting, etc.).[149] He also attests that they do not work, calling themselves *pneumatikoi*/πνευματικοί (spirituals), that they rest the whole day, doing nothing, because they supposedly spend their day in praying,[150] and because in addition, as Theodoret remarks, "they avert the manual labour as evil".[151] The Messalian *pneumatikoi* resembled the Manichaean Elect and the division of the Manichaean community into the two classes. Theodoret adds, interestingly, that when Messalians are interrogated it is easy for them to deny everything they believe and perform, by

---

Christians, he suggests that they 'had learned this [*argia*] from Mani'. Thus Epiphanius sought to discredit the Messalian trait he found most reprehensible by linking it with the great Mesopotamian heresiarch. His message was clear: 'the divine word tells us to mark such people who do not work'".

147 Epiphanius, *Pan.* 80.6.1–3 (Williams, 650).

148 *Apophthegmata patrum* (collectio alphabetica) PG: 65:253.17–43 (Ἀρχὴ τοῦ Λ στοιχείου. Περὶ τοῦ ἀββᾶ Λουκίου).

149 Theodoret, *HE* 231.10–11: μήτε νηστείας πιεζούσης τὸ σῶμα μήτε διδασκαλίας χαλινούσης καὶ βαίνειν εὔτακτα παιδευούσης.

150 Theodoret, *Haer.* (PG 83:429.41–43): ἔργον μὲν οὐδὲν μετίασι (πνευματικοὺς γὰρ ἑαυτοὺς ὀνομάζουσι), τῇ δὲ εὐχῇ δῆθεν ἐσχολακότες, τῆς ἡμέρας τὸ πλεῖστον καθεύδουσιν.

151 Theodoret, *HE* 229.9–10: ἀποστρέφονται μὲν τὴν τῶν χειρῶν ἐργασίαν ὡς πονηρίαν.

anathematizing those who accused them as slanderers.[152] In his words: "Trying
to hide their 'sickness', after being examined, they shamelessly repudiate and
renounce publicly those who have these beliefs".[153]

Further, apart from their behaviour and attitudes, Theodoret in explaining
their appellations informs us about some of their doctrinal positions. They are
called 'Euchites' (Εὐχῖται, translation of Messalians in Greek) because, as they
claim, only continual prayer (εὐχή) drives out from man his "indwelling demon"
(τὸν ἔνοικον δαίμονα), "who has been allocated/attached to him" from his birth
and who incites him to misconduct. They claim that this demon "cannot be
driven out of the soul either by baptism or by any other power".[154] Further, they
are called Enthusiasts (Ἐνθουσιασταὶ) because they claim that after the innate
demon is expelled they become possessed by the Holy Spirit, which enables
them to predict the future.[155] As Caner comments, "not only had" Messalians
"suggested the inefficacy of a basic church sacrament" (baptism), but they "had
also conjured the almost Manichaean specter of a congenitally indwelling
demon, an innate source of evil that could only be exorcised through constant
prayer".[156]

However, Theodoret does not make any comment on this point, but he does
link Messalians and Manichaeans in his *Historia Religiosa* (437–449). As he
remarks, the so-called 'Euchites' follow the example and adopt the customs
of the Manichaeans under the pretext of monastic life.[157] It seems that for
Theodoret, what was happening with the Encratites et al. also happened with

152 Theodoret, *Haer.* (PG 83:432.1–6): Πρόχειροι δέ εἰσιν εἰς ἄρνησιν, κἂν βιασθῶσιν, ἀναθεματί-
     ζουσιν εὐπετῶς τοὺς τούτων τι λέγοντας. [...] Αὐτίκα τοίνυν ἐπὶ τοῦ πανευφήμου Φλαβιανοῦ, τοῦ
     τῆς Ἀντιοχέων ἐπισκόπου, κρινόμενοι, συκοφαντίας ἐκάλουν τὰς γεγενημένας κατηγορίας.

153 Theodoret, *HE* 229.17–18–230.1–2: κρύπτειν δὲ τὴν νόσον πειρώμενοι, καὶ μετὰ ἐλέγχους ἀναι-
     δῶς ἐξαρνοῦνται, καὶ ἀποκηρύττουσι τοὺς ταῦτα φρονοῦντας ἅπερ ἐν ταῖς ψυχαῖς περιφέρουσι.

154 Theodoret, *Haer.* (PG 83:429.25–41): Μεσσαλιανοὶ δὲ (τοὔνομα δὲ τοῦτο μεταβαλλόμενον εἰς
     τὴν Ἑλλάδα φωνήν, τοὺς Εὐχίτας σημαίνει), τὸ μὲν βάπτισμά φασι μηδὲν ὀνεῖν τοὺς προσιό-
     ντας· ξυροῦ γὰρ δίκην ἀφαιρεῖται τῶν ἁμαρτημάτων τὰ πρότερα, τὴν δὲ ῥίζαν οὐκ ἐκκόπτει τῆς
     ἁμαρτίας· ἡ δὲ ἐνδελεχὴς προσευχή, καὶ τὴν ῥίζαν τῆς ἁμαρτίας πρόρριζον ἀνασπᾷ, καὶ τὸν ἐξ
     ἀρχῆς συγκληρωθέντα πονηρὸν δαίμονα τῆς ψυχῆς ἐξελαύνει. Ἑκάστῳ γάρ φασιν ἀνθρώπῳ
     τικτομένῳ παραυτίκα συνέπεσθαι δαίμονα, καὶ τοῦτον εἰς τὰς ἀτόπους πράξεις παρακινεῖν.
     Τοῦτον δὲ οὔτε τὸ βάπτισμα, οὔτε ἄλλο τι δύναται τῆς ψυχῆς ἐξελάσαι, ἀλλὰ μόνη τῆς προσευχῆς
     ἡ ἐνέργεια. Some parts between quotation marks in the text are from Cope's (1990, 195)
     translation.

155 Theodoret, *HE* 229.6–12: ἔχουσι δὲ καὶ ἑτέραν προσηγορίαν ἐκ τοῦ πράγματος γενομένην
     Ἐνθουσιασταὶ γὰρ καλοῦνται, δαίμονός τινος ἐνέργειαν εἰσδεχόμενοι καὶ πνεύματος ἁγίου
     παρουσίαν ταύτην ὑπολαμβάνοντες [...] ὕπνῳ δὲ σφᾶς αὐτοὺς ἐκδιδόντες τὰς τῶν ὀνείρων
     φαντασίας προφητείας ἀποκαλοῦσι; *Haer.* 83.429.45–46: ἀποκαλύψεις ἑωρακέναι φασί, καὶ τὰ
     ἐσόμενα προλέγειν ἐπιχειροῦσιν.

156 Caner 2002, 91.

157 Theodoret, *Phil. hist.* 3.16.7–8: ἀπεστρέφετο δὲ κομιδῇ καὶ τοὺς ὀνομαζομένους Εὐχίτας ἐν
     μοναχικῷ προσχήματι τὰ Μανιχαίων νοσοῦντας.

the Messalians. Manichaeans hid themselves behind the names of other ascetics; in the former case behind Encratites et al., in the latter behind Messalians.

Lastly, Theodoret, in contrast to Epiphanius, names some of their leaders, and mentions the bishops who fought the Messalians, such as, Amphilochius of Iconium, Letoius of Melitene, and Flavianus of Antioch.[158]

More than a century later, at the time of Timothy the Presbyter (sixth-seventh cent.), Messalianism does not seem to constitute a problem in the way that Manichaeism still did, to judge from Timothy's lists of converted heretics. In grouping the converted heretics, Timothy classifies Messalians in the third category (they had only to anathematize their previous heresy), as opposed to Manichaeans whom he places in the first, more deviant, group (they had to be baptized). Besides 'Euchites' and 'Enthusiasts', other names that Timothy uses for Messalians are: Markianists, Choreuts (dancers), Lampetians, Adelphians, and Eustathians.[159] Timothy, like Epiphanius and Theodoret, criticizes the stance of Messalians towards manual labour, which, as he remarks, they considered abominable. Moreover, Timothy emphasizes that they are against giving alms to the needy (neither to widows nor to the orphans), because, as they say, the truly poor (in spirit), are they themselves, hence everything must be provided to them.[160] Timothy, like Epiphanius, underlines the prominent role of the Messalian women, specifying further, that the women of the heresy assume important offices, such as those of a teacher or of a priest.[161] Timothy elaborates further on the interesting information provided by Theodoret, according to which:

> When Messalians are interrogated [by authorities] about their doctrines, they do not hesitate to renounce their faith and anathematize promptly

---

158 Theodoret, *Haer.* (PG 83:432.34): Ταύτης ἡγήσατο τῆς αἱρέσεως Σάββας, καὶ Ἀδέλφιος, καὶ Δαώδης, καὶ Συμεώνης, καὶ Ἑρμᾶς, καὶ ἄλλοι τινές. Ἔγραψε δὲ κατὰ τούτων ἐπιστολὰς ... Λητόϊος, ὁ τῆς Μελιτινῆς ἐπίσκοπος... Ἀμφιλόχιος, ὁ τοῦ Ἰκονίου; *HE* 229.12–14: ταύτης ἐγένοντο τῆς αἱρέσεως ἀρχηγοὶ Δαδώης τε καὶ Σάβας καὶ Ἀδέλφιος καὶ Ἑρμᾶς καὶ Συμεώνης καὶ ἄλλοι πρὸς τούτοις [...]; 230.3–231.4: Λητώϊος μὲν οὖν ὁ τὴν Μελιτηνῶν καὶ Ἀμφιλόχιος ... τὴν Λυκαόνων μητρόπολιν ... Φλαβιανὸς ... Ἀντιοχέων ἀρχιερεύς. Theophanes in his *Chronographia* (63.14–20) mentions the same bishops, but omits the heresiarchs Symeōnēs, and Ermas. Instead, he mentions that some considered also Eustathius of Sebasteia as Messalian heresiarch. Timothy the Presbyter mentions Cyril of Alexandria, Flavian and Theodot of Antioch, Letoius of Melitene and Amphilochius of Iconium, as bishops who combated Messalianism. However, he does not name the source of the Messalian *Kephalaia* he is referring to: Πρὸς δὲ εἴδησιν καὶ ἀσφάλειαν τῶν ἐντυγχανόντων, ἀναγκαῖον καὶ τὰ κεφάλαια τῶν δογμάτων αὐτῆς ὑποτάξαι· ἅπερ εἰσὶ ταῦτα."
159 Timothy the Presbyter, *Recept. Haer.* PG 86A:45–52. Cf. Fitschen, 1993.
160 Timothy the Presbyter, *Recept. Haer.* PG 86A:49.13, 52.15.
161 Timothy the Presbyter, *Recept. Haer.* PG 86A:52.18.

all those who still have or ever had the same beliefs, and to swear without fear that they hate and abhor such doctrines.[162]

Another new and interesting feature in Timothy's report is the Messalian concept of *apatheia*, which, when conquered, as they claim, provides a kind of immunity that makes them unaffected to the exposure of all kinds of sins.[163] The same information is provided by Jerome, according to whom the Manichaeans, Priscillians, and Messalians say that those who have overcome passions can freely and fearlessly sin.[164]

However, the most noticeable information concerning Messalians' *apatheia* is that neither perjury nor anathematization of their own faith could harm those who had conquered *apatheia*, since, as they say, they became *pneumatikoi* (spirituals).[165]

Thus, even betrayal of their own faith does not harm those who have conquered *apatheia*. *Apatheia* provides protection even in this case. Further, "the permission to perjure and anathematize" their own religion before danger was a tradition of the community "bestowed upon them by the tradition of their teachers".[166] This need for legitimization of apostasy (or pseudo-apostasy) is striking and may show that the situation for Messalians was difficult due to their persecution.

Fitschen, examining the existence of Messalians in Asia Minor after 431 CE, argues that whatever information Timothy offers derives from earlier sources; he himself seems to have no personal experience with Messalianism (current Messalians):

> There is an amazing fact in Timothy's report: he does not know one single current event about that heresy ... He merely reports on traditions from earlier sources [...] the anti-Messalian protagonists of the 4th and 5th century, namely Cyril of Alexandria, Flavian and Theodotus of Antioch, Letoius of Melitene and Amphilochius of Iconium. The records

---

162   Timothy the Presbyter, *Recept. Haer.* PG 86ᴬ:52.19.

163   Timothy the Presbyter, *Recept. Haer.* PG 86ᴬ:49.10: "they say that to surrender your self to delights/indulgency and licentiousness after having conquered apathy, is guiltless and not risky".

164   Jerome, *Dialogus adversus Pelagianos*, prol. 1, in Caner 2002, 92.

165   Timothy the Presbyter, *Recept. Haer.* (PG 86ᴬ:52.19): μήτε τῆς ἐπιορκίας μήτε τοῦ ἀναθεματισμοῦ βλάπτειν λοιπὸν δυναμένων τοὺς μετὰ τὴν ἀπάθειαν, ὡς αὐτοὶ λέγουσι, πνευματικοὺς γενομένους.

166   Timothy the Presbyter, *Recept. Haer.* (PG 86ᴬ:52.19): ἐπιορκεῖν τε καὶ ἀναθεματίζειν ἑαυτοὺς ἐπ᾽ἀδείας ἐχόντων αὐτῶν ἐκ τῆς τῶν διδασκάλων αὐτῶν παραδόσεως. The same attitude towards danger appears to be legitimized by Mani himself in the last anathema of *LAF* against Manichaeans. More details on this will be provided in ch.[8], 3.3.

of these bishops seem to be the basis for Timothy's survey on Messalian doctrine [...]. Therefore is doubtful whether Messalianism still had virulent power in the days of Timothy.[167]

Although I agree with Fitschen that it "is doubtful whether Messalianism still had virulent power in the days of Timothy", I disagree with the argumentation he employs to support it. Though Timothy, in his introduction, states that these earlier bishops had combated Messalianism through their writings and also kept minutes, we do not possess any texts of these that describe the behaviour or the doctrines of Messalians. What we do know about these bishops stems from the records of the third Ecumenical Synod, as well as the accounts of Theodoret and Theophanes, and concerns their active engagement in the fight against the spread of Messalianism.[168] So, the question whether Timothy based himself on their records or not must remain open. However, the fact that Timothy ranks the converted Messalians third in the procedure for their reception into the Church, while ex-Manichaeans had to follow the first most severe procedure, implies that Messalianism was not considered a real danger in Timothy's time.[169]

Evaluating the data of the sources, one observes a change in the profile of the Messalians over time. The image of mixed companies of men and women wandering through the cities, chanting, dancing with castanets and sleeping together in the public squares that Epiphanius had sketched gradually fades out. On the contrary, the Messalians of Theodoret's time are persecuted and interrogated. It seems that after the synods of Side and Ephesus, the show of eccentricity they performed (as described by Epiphanius) was scaled down since they were persecuted. Flavian of Antioch was one of the bishops who had been active in limiting the spread of the 'heresy'. He interrogated a certain Adelphius, "an old man on the edge of the grave", who was the leader of a group of Messalians who lived in Edessa.[170] From such interrogations new evidence

---

167 Fitschen 1993, 354.

168 *ACO* (*Ephesenum anno 431*), 1.1.7, 117.4–14; Theodoret, *HE* 230.1–14; Theodoretus, *Haer.* 432.1–6; Theophanes, *Chron.* 63.17–21.

169 Comparing Timothy's outline of the profile of the Messalians to that sketched by Epiphanius and Theodoret, I would argue, that Timothy is based on the latter's accounts enriching the Messalian portrait with additional details about their behaviour and doctrines.

170 Theodoret, *Haer.* (PG 83:432.6–22): Ἀλλ' ὁ πάνσοφος ἐκεῖνος ἀνὴρ τὴν λανθάνουσαν ἐφώρασεν αἵρεσιν. [...] Ἀδέλφιον· αὐτὸς γὰρ ἡγεῖτο τῶν ἐγκαλουμένων τὴν αἵρεσιν, ἀνὴρ πρεσβύτης καὶ τυμβογέρων, καὶ παρ' αὐτὰς λοιπὸν ὢν τοῦ θανάτου τὰς πύλας [...] Καὶ ἄλλα δὲ πολλὰ φρενίτιδος ἔργα τολμῶσι. Καὶ γὰρ ἐξαπίνης πηδῶσι, καὶ δαίμονας ὑπερπεπηδηκέναι νεανιεύονται ... Καὶ ἕτερα ἄττα δρῶσι παραπλησίως παραπληξίας μεστά, διὸ δὴ καὶ τῶν Ἐνθουσιαστῶν ἐσχήκασιν ὄνομα; *HE* 432.1–28.

emerged, which complemented the Messalian profile and which was related to both their doctrine (e.g. baptism, indwelling demon) and practices, especially to their attitude towards danger (whereby they were permitted to anathematize their own religion).[171] Stable elements of the Messalian profile over time remain: the non-institutional character and lack of rules, the participation of women in ministries, and above all idleness and the consequent demand to be nourished by others.

Fitschen points out that we must be careful when reading heresiological sources. In his article "Did 'Messalianism' exist in Asia Minor after AD 431?", he explains that he had put 'Messalianism' in inverted commas in order to highlight that it was an 'amorphous movement'. Based on the fact that in the condemnatory decision in the records of the third Ecumenical Council (431), various names are attributed to Messalians (Euchites, Enthusiasts), and no one is named as their heresiarch, Fitschen argues that Messalianism was not an organized heresy but a spiritual movement.[172] Disagreeing with the view that Messalianism was a movement, even a spiritual one, Caner argues that researchers reproduce stereotypes and labels of that era when they treat "such groups as separate historical phenomena", "distinct and isolated historical movements", and that they tend to "identify objections to manual labor with marginal or heretical ascetic groups such as Manichaeans, Messalians or circumcellions".[173] Further, Caner, questioning the credibility of the sources, argues that the later Messalian profile (e.g. from Theodoret or Timothy), with its doctrinal features, was a heresiological construction aimed at the marginalization of Christian ascetic practices that followed the apostolic paradigm of the wandering life and threatened church hierarchies. For this reason, Caner also suggests a shift in the focus of the methodology of Messalian scholarship "on behavioral rather than doctrinal features" of Messalianism.

> Through an alternative methodology that focuses on behavioral aspects of the Messalian profile [...] rather than doctrinal features [...] it will become apparent that what church leaders were confronting under the "Messalian" label was not in fact a novel movement, but rather a complex of ideals, practices, and assumptions deeply rooted in the apostolic model for Christian ascetic life.[174]

---

171   Contra this view, Caner (2002, 91–96, esp. 92) argues that the new doctrinal features were unfounded additions by later church authorities, in order for a dogmatically heretical Messalian profile to be generated.

172   Fitschen 1993, 352–355.

173   Caner 2002, 13, 85.

174   Caner 2002, 85. Indeed, as Caner (2002, 78) points out, "Manichaeans became the most notorious heirs to the apostolic paradigm for Christian life." The question of the

Taking into account the observations of these specialists, some clarifying remarks are necessary at this point:

The fact that Messalians, as well as Encratites et al., were not organized but amorphous movements, is first of all clearly stated by their opponents (e.g., Epiphanius, Theodoret). Besides, as is entailed by the legislation, the state also held the same view. There is only one law against Messalians (428) and three against Encratites et al., in one of which the latter are portrayed just as masks of Manichaeans (the target is Manichaeans, not the Encratites et al.), while the twenty-five laws against Manichaeism (eighteen in Cod. theod. and seven in Cod. justin.), which was an organized movement constituting a threat, are more numerous than those of any other heresy. Hence, it is not legitimate to put Manichaeans together in one conceptual basket with Messalians and Encratites by considering that these names were used just as alternative labels for various trends within Christian asceticism that Church and state authorities of the era wished to marginalize.[175]

The fact that the focus of church leaders' rhetoric is the behaviour and attitudes of the above ascetics rather than their doctrines is also evident in the examined primary sources. The same is true for Ephrem, who wrote at about the same time as Epiphanius.[176] As Caner points out, "Indeed, Epiphanius, Ephrem, and the Gangra synod demonstrate that by the fourth century ascetic practices, themselves, could be deemed heretical without reference to specific doctrinal deviations".[177] However, as we also saw, most of the authors we examined do not condemn these practices as such, but their interpretation which is grounded on doctrinal assumptions (e.g. meat is poisonous because it consists of matter, plants are alive, wine is of Devil, marriage is illegal and serves the Devil's plan). Therefore, focusing only "on behavioral rather than doctrinal features", as Caner suggests, is problematic because it completely leaves the doctrines out of the discussion, which are those that differentiate and finally make sense of the specific practices.

Messalian identity and its relationship with mainstream Christianity and spirituality has raised much discussion in scholarship. See for instance: Fitschen 1993, 352–55; Stewart 1991; Louth 2007, 110–121, esp. 112–13; Caner 2002, 97–103; Casiday 2003, 429; Hunt 2012. On the question of whether the 'problem' was just the practices in themselves or/and the doctrines behind them, see also Beskow (1988, 10) and Goodrich (2004, 209).

175   Contra Caner 2002, 15, 101.
176   Ephrem the Syrian, *Hymni contra Haereses* 22.4, p. 79. Caner 2002, 115, 90.
177   Caner 2002, 101.

3.3   Concluding Remarks Regarding Encratites et al., Messalians and Their Relationship with Manichaeans

Taking together the findings of the preceding analysis, I will attempt some concluding remarks regarding the relationship between Manichaeans and both the Encratites et al. and Messalians, with the ultimate aim of answering the question: what does this link (made by our sources) reveal about the Manichaeans?

The outbreak of the phenomenon of radical asceticism during the decades 370 and 380, which resulted in the increase of the number of anarchist ascetics (Encratites etc.), in combination with the simultaneous appearance of the Messalians, was connected by the official Church and state with Manichaean influence. Therefore, the laws against Manichaeans constituted the first priority of Theodosian religious policy.

Indeed, from the above presentation, it became apparent that both Encratites et al. and Messalians share a series of common features with the Manichaeans. In both cases, these features primarily concern the behaviour and attitudes of these ascetics, such as the wandering ascetic lifestyle even within the cities, women's active role in the sect, the renunciation of possessions, extravagant appearance, idleness and begging (Messalians), extreme forms of fasting, etc. Doctrinal issues which arose secondarily, mainly, underline the dualistic perspective of these movements. Indeed, both the 'indwelling daimon in every man' of the Messalians (Theodoret), and the 'distinct principles' (ἀρχαὶ διάφοροι) – among them the Devil as an autonomous entity – of the Encratites (Epiphanius) echo Manichaean positions.[178] Moreover, what is emphasized by our sources is that the Manichaeans were the mentors of the above ascetics. Manichaeans were presented as the teachers of the false ascetic practices of Encratites. Manichaeans were also deemed as the teachers of idleness, which was highlighted as the main feature of Messalians. The 'bad' influence of Manichaeans was considered to have transformed the above ascetical environments into 'factories' for producing apostates. Thus, it is logical to assume that for the authorities (civil and ecclesiastical) the independent and amorphous groups of ascetics, such as Encratites et al. and Messalians, were likely to be attracted, influenced, and even swallowed up by the highly organized sect of the Manichaeans. Their common practices and outlook were a serious reason for their appeal and possible recruitment by Manichaeans

---

178   Additional references to Messalian dogmatic theses by Timothy may refer to their successors, namely, the Lampetians and Markianists (end of 6th century). However, the conducted so far research does not allow us to say whether we can consider these groups as direct heirs of the Messalians. Cf. Fitschen 1993, 355.

into their movement. Moreover, according to some sources, the names of these ascetic groups were used as camouflage (or were considered as such) by disguised Manichaeans.

Therefore, the link between these ascetics and the Manichaeans, in the minds of Church and state leaders, seems to have been of crucial importance. Whether or not this link actually existed or was only in their minds, or whether the authorities sought to discredit Encratites et al. and Messalians by linking them with Manichaeans, are all probable alternative interpretations. To a certain extent, it is more likely that all had happened together at the same time. However, this may be, it is certain that the practices themselves were considered dangerous and alarmed both Church and state authorities. Their preoccupations were not only religious but clearly extended to the social domain as well.[179]

And while, initially, for both the Church and the state (in the law of 381) the terms Encratites et al. referred to practices (not illegal), the sudden shift of imperial religious policy which rendered illegal the Encratites et al. as groups in their own right (law of 382) indicates that it was soon realized that:

(1)   The boundaries between various ascetic groups were blurred. In practice, it was difficult to judge whether someone who adopted radical ascetic practices was a Manichaean or a Christian ascetic.

(2)   regardless of whether the Manichaeans were hidden behind other ascetic groups, or inspired, or even recruited the members of the other groups, the danger was that the adoption of such practices (and ideas) by a growing number of ascetics constituted a threat. Beyond the religious side effects, the lifestyle promoted through those ascetics, even in urban areas, was a threat to the social values and social institutions of the empire.

4   Socially Alarming Dimensions of Manichaean Attractiveness and Ways to Deal with Them

4.1   *Similar But Different*

4.1.1   Manichaean Ascesis (The Pseudo-Ascetics)

The fact that the spread of Manichaeism in the Roman Empire coincided with the growing prevalence of Christianity (one of whose essential elements was asceticism), gave the Manichaeans the opportunity to present themselves as exemplary ascetics. One of the main tricks that Manichaeans devised in order

---

179   Cf. Caner 2002, 14–15, 89.

to seduce the unwary, as Augustine states, was that of "making a show of chastity and of notable abstinence".[180] The image of the non-conformist, like a philosopher ascetic, in an era during which asceticism was fashionable, was attractive and influential. Manichaeans through their ascetic 'pale look' and their philosophic-scientific-religious speculations about the cosmos, charmed especially young people and women.[181] What annoyed the representatives of the Catholic Church about the Manichaeans' ascetic appeal, was that they promoted themselves not just as ideal ascetics, but as ideal *Christian* ascetics, while most Christian parties did not regard them as Christians at all. Thus, church leaders feared that ordinary Christians would be unable to distinguish the Manichaean 'pseudo-ascetics', and be led astray by them, because, while the forms of Manichaean and Christian *ascesis* were similar, the theological interpretation of ascesis was completely different.

As explained in ch.[5], for the Church Fathers, Manichaean fasting was based on totally false theological assumptions. Instead of fighting gluttony, their fasting was an insult to God and his creation. They had similar problems with the logic underlying Manichaean sexual abstinence. Marriage was rejected not for the sake of virginity (the early Christian writers saw virginity as a way of life to fortify spiritual progress), but because childbearing was construed as the Devil's plan. But while Christian and Manichaean asceticism were distinct on a doctrinal level, on a practical level there were few visible differences.[182]

A good example of this is the following hagiographical account about the early Manichaean missionary Mar Ammo. When he reached the border of the Kushan state, he explained to the guardian spirit of the East (Bagard) the commandments of Manichaean discipline: "'We do not consume meat or wine (and) we stay far from women', the spirit replies, 'Where I rule, there are many

---

180   Augustine, *Mor. Manich.* 1.2 (Stothert in *NPNF*[1] 4:46); cf. Lieu 1992, 180, 185 and 180–187 about the ascetical appeal of Manichaeism.

181   Cf. Caner 2002, 80.

182   Cf. Liebeschuetz 2011, 21, 32: "All these dualistic groupings clearly troubled many generations of leaders of main-line Christianity. For their ideas were obviously so closely related to those of Christianity that Christian leaders found it difficult to convince their followers that their doctrines were distinct from Christian doctrines, and even totally incompatible with them" [...] "the attitudes of the followers of some Gnostic sects and of Manichaeans to sexuality came close to Christian views. The way of life of Manichaean 'elect' was quite similar to that of Christian ascetics, particularly to that of the wandering encratite ascetics of Mesopotamia". See also Lieu 1992, 180–187. Stroumsa (1985, 276) states: "It is significant, moreover, that the Manichaeans, who had appeared in Eleutheropolis in the third century – close to the main monastic area and to the locus of the Archontics, are still found in the Judaean wilderness in the sixth century. It must remain the task of further research to evaluate whether dualist groups and Christian monks were more, throughout this period, than casual neighbors".

like you (already)'".[183] It is generally assumed that the Spirit here refers to the presence of Buddhists in the Kushan Empire, but that is precisely the point. Manichaean practices of fasting and of celibacy instead of marriage can be found in many religions and do not differ significantly from those promoted by Christian monks and ascetics. For this reason, Faustus refutes the Catholics' assertion that Paul's prophesy about those who abstain from meat and forbid marriage "applies to the Manichaeans more than to the Catholic ascetics, who are held in the highest esteem in the Church".[184]

Apart from the ascetic practices, there were also similarities in ascetic terminology, representations, and concepts. Expressions such as, 'good thoughts', 'good words', 'good deeds' were interreligious in ascetical environments and were present not only in Manichaean and Christian practices, but also in Zoroastrian and Buddhist. The terms, 'rest/*anapausis*',[185] 'quietness/*hesychia*', and 'discerning/*diakrisis*',[186] were widespread, as was the Pauline concept of the 'old' and the 'new man',[187] and especially the idea that the senses are gates which must be guarded.[188]

As Manichaean and Christian asceticism did not differ in form, there was a fear of Manichaean influence upon accepted forms of asceticism.[189] Further, through the ascetics, the Manichaean influence would spread into society, since ascetics at that time constituted spiritual exemplars and acted as mentors and instructors of believers. In order to enable the Christian faithful to distinguish true from false ascetics, instructions were given by Church Fathers. Ephrem warned the Christians in Mesopotamia not to admire Manichaeans as exemplary Christians, for, as he says, "their works are similar to our works, as their fasting is similar to our fasting, but their faith is not similar to our faith".[190] Also, it is interesting to note that the great ascetic exemplars in ascetic literature were represented as avoiding contacts with Manichaeans or with ascetics who held Manichaean views and practices. According to Athanasius, Antony, the great anchorite and father of monasticism,

---

183 BeDuhn 2000b, 33.

184 Augustine, *Faust.* 30.1–6 (trans. by Stothert in *NPNF*[1] 4:563–567).

185 About the Manichaean concept of *rest* in the documentary texts from Kellis, see Brand 2019, 177–78.

186 However with another meaning: the "gnosis of separation" = a practical knowledge.

187 *2PsB* 167.54–55; 153.20. *1Keph.* 86.215.1–3.

188 *2PsB* 150.23–31; *1Keph.* 38.100.1–6 & 86.215.1–216.13. Cf. Serapion, *c. Manichaeos* 53.43–47. Cf. Pedersen (2012, 133–43), about the Manichaean use of the term 'Μυστήριον'.

189 "The most intriguing question", as Van Oort (2009, 129) points out, is whether Manichaeism exerted any influence on "mainstream Christianity". The similarity between Manichaean and Christian ascetical ideals naturally raises the question of mutual influence. Cf. Drijvers 1981, 130.

190 Ephrem the Syrian, *Prose Refutations* cxix. Cf. Lieu 1992, 181; Lieu 1994a, 42.

[Did not have] friendly dealings with the Manichaeans or any other heretics; or, if he had, only as far as advice that they should convert to piety; for he thought and asserted that intercourse with these was harmful and destructive to the soul.[191]

As Lieu points out, "Athanasius might have felt it necessary to mention this so that Antony's ascetic endeavours would not be construed as a form of Manichaeism".[192] The hermit Marcianus from Cyrrhus, as Theodoret recounts, avoided Messalians, because under the pretext of monasticism they were Manichaean-minded.[193] Cyril of Scythopolis, in his *Life of Euthymius*, makes clear that the grand ascetic and abbot abhorred all the sects but especially he hated six heresies. Of these, he hated more than any other the Manichaean "disgust".[194]

Further, descriptions were provided that depicted the image of the pseudo-ascetic body and outfit, which could guide faithful readers to identify heretics. According to ecclesiastical authors, one could distinguish pseudo-ascetics by their conspicuous appearance: paleness, long hair among the men, short-cut hair among the women, and the wearing of dark sackcloth. Thus, the body could be used as a marker to identify heretics.[195] For Ephrem the Syrian, ascetic practices such as paleness and the wearing of sackcloth was just a show intended to deceive the naive. As Ephrem warned, "the faithful must learn to judge them not by the outward filth of their garments but by the inward filth of their doctrines".[196] The most representative example of this kind is Jerome's detailed description in his letter to Eustochium.[197]

---

191 Athanasius of Alexandria, *Vit. Ant.* 68.1.4–7 (Kennan, altered): Οὔτε Μανιχαίοις ἢ ἄλλοις τισὶν αἱρετικοῖς ὡμίλησε φιλικὰ ἢ μόνον ἄχρι νουθεσίας τῆς εἰς εὐσέβειαν μεταβολῆς, ἡγούμενος καὶ παραγγέλλων τὴν τούτων φιλίαν καὶ ὁμιλίαν βλάβην καὶ ἀπώλειαν εἶναι ψυχῆς.

192 Lieu 1992, 183: "Athanasius in his *Life of Antony* made the point that this great Christian ascetic studiously avoided contacts with the Manichaeans during his sojourn in the desert".

193 Theodoret of Cyrrhus, *Phil. hist.* 3.16.7–8: ἀπεστρέφετο δὲ κομιδῇ καὶ τοὺς ὀνομαζομένους Εὐχίτας ἐν μοναχικῷ προσχήματι τὰ Μανιχαίων νοσοῦντας.

194 Cyril of Scythopolis, *Vit. Euth.* (TU 49.2:39.20–30): καὶ ὁ μακάριος Σάβας καὶ ἄλλοι πλεῖστοι γέροντες ἐθαύμαζον τοῦ μεγάλου Εὐθυμίου [...] ὅτι πᾶσαν μὲν αἵρεσιν τῷ ὀρθῷ τῆς πίστεως λόγῳ ἐναντιουμένην ἀπεστρέφετο, ἐξαιρέτως δὲ τὰς ἓξ ταύτας αἱρέσεις τέλειον μῖσος ἐμίσει. τὴν τε γὰρ Μανιχαϊκὴν βδελυρίαν ἐμυσάττετο καὶ τοῖς τὰ Ὠριγένους φρονοῦσιν πολλοῖς τότε οὖσιν ἐν τοῖς μάλιστα περὶ Καισάρειαν τόποις καὶ σχήματι δῆθεν εὐλαβείας ἐρχομένοις πρὸς αὐτὸν διεμάχετο γενναίως τὴν παρ' αὐτοῖς μυθευομένην τῶν νοῶν προύπαρξιν καὶ τὴν ταύτῃ ἑπομένην τερατώδη ἀποκατάστασιν.

195 About the identification of heretics "by virtue of the senses"/observable attitudes, cf. Berzon 2013, 262–64.

196 Ephrem the Syrian, *Hymni contra Haereses* in Lieu 1992, 181.

197 Jerome, *Ep.* 22 (§ 27f).

Church canons also condemned these ascetic practices early on, in case their theoretical background was a theology directed against creation, or when the ascetic discipline was considered an end in itself. According to the canons of the Synod held at Gangra in Paphlagonia in 340, the following practices were condemned and those who adopted them were anathematized: those who abhor meat-eating,[198] those who condemn lawful marriage,[199] those who remain celibate not for the sake of chastity,[200] those boasting for practicing celibacy,[201] women wearing men's clothes under the pretence of asceticism,[202] women cutting off their hair pretending piety,[203] women who leave their husbands,[204] parents who abandoned their own children pretending asceticism,[205] children leaving their parents pretending piety,[206] those who fast on Sunday under the pretence of asceticism,[207] those who despise the assemblies of the Catholic Church and hold their private assemblies.[208]

Apart from the similarities in ascesis, there was a further remarkable resemblance between the grades of the Manichaean hierarchy and the corresponding ranks of the Christian priesthood.[209] It is striking therefore, that apart from the SC, no other Greek anti-Manichaean author documents this structure in detail, or comments on the similarity with the respective Christian hierarchy. So, they did not give any relevant instructions to Christian believers, as they did in the case of ascesis and other similarities.

Finally, as we shall see in ch.[7], similarities also existed between the form of Christian and Manichaean churches as well as between Christian and Manichaean sacred meals.[210]

4.2 Wandering Asceticism as a Challenge to Both Religious and Social Institutions

The anarchist, atypical, amorphous, un-institutional groups of wandering ascetics were a challenge to the institutional Church, official authorities,

---

198 Joannou 1962, 90 (no 2). (I, 2, Les canons des Synodes particuliers).
199 Joannou 1962, 89 (no 1).
200 Joannou 1962, 93 (no 9).
201 Joannou 1962, 93 (no 10).
202 Joannou 1962, 94–5, 482 (no 13).
203 Joannou 1962, 97 (no 17).
204 Joannou 1962, 95 (no 14).
205 Joannou 1962, 95 (no 15).
206 Joannou 1962, 96 (no 16).
207 Joannou 1962, 96 (no 18).
208 Joannou 1962, 91–92 (no 5 & 6).
209 See ch.[2], section 4.
210 See also chs. [3], 4.2.2 (Manichaean assembly places) and [5], 2.3.2 & 2.3.3 (Manichaean rituals).

hierarchies and worship. Both Messalians and Encratites (as denoted by Basil's letter) questioned the efficacy of Christian holy sacraments, in particular catholic baptism. It was an era characterized by competition between bishops and monks for which of these power-structures would gain power and control over the Christian landscape and would become the dominant authority in the conscience of faithful Christians. In this context, the Christian bishops also had to compete "with the Manichaean ascetic Elect [and other ascetics] who lived in their cities".[211]

The fact that the Manichaean ascetic model was that of the wandering asceticism is supported by both Manichaean and anti-Manichaean sources. Although it has been argued by some scholars that there were also Manichaean monasteries in Egypt that preceded and inspired the coenobitic type of Christian monasticism, this cannot be verified due to the lack of sufficient evidence at present.[212] Thus, from the sources we have at our disposal it is presumed that the Manichaean ascetic model in the Roman Empire should have been the wandering small *conventicula*: small groups of Elect surrounded by catechumens. The latter is also confirmed by the material from Kellis.[213] The case of the missionary Julia is one such example in action. In this respect, Libanius' testimony is also relevant. According to him, the Manichaeans "are found in many places in the world but everywhere they are only few in number".[214] Such small cells of Manichaean ascetics seem to have gathered in the countryside, outside the city walls, but especially within the cities.

Representatives of the official church rejected the individualism of wandering ascetics and supported the social character of coenobitic monasticism. The *Constitutiones Asceticae* (ascribed to Basil) was the result of an attempt to gain control over the enthusiastic waves of wandering ascetics who spread irregularly across the eastern provinces of the empire, without constitutions and with radical manifestations in discipline. It determined the terms and the

---

211   Caner 2002, 124. Cf. Maier 1995a, 52. On the "formation of the early Christian leadership", see Kyrtatas 1988, 365–383, 365.

212   On this issue, see Lieu 1985, 145. Lieu 1981a, 155–56, 155: "Modern scholars have not refrained from investigating the ascetical practices and organization of the sect and from assessing its influence on the development of Christian monasticism. Voobus, for instance, regards Manichaeism as a major stimulus to the growth of asceticism in the Syrian Orient but this has not gone unchallenged". Stroumsa 1986b, 307–319. Gardner 2000, 247–257. As Brand (2019, 246) concludes, "Stimulating as it may sound, there is no evidence from the Roman Empire for a Manichaean group style with elect living communally in monastic buildings".

213   The documentary material from Kellis portrays Elect as continually travelling in the Nile Valley, cf. Brand 2019, 140–145.

214   Libanius, *Ep. 1253* (Lieu 2010, 42–43): πολλαχοῦ μέν εἰσι τῆς γῆς, πανταχοῦ δὲ ὀλίγοι.

rules that should regulate the monastic life and became the basis upon which monasticism was organized thereafter.[215] In contrast to the Messalian and Manichaean view, according to which the Elect/*pneumatikoi* should not work, in order to offer their spiritual services through their prayers, the new model of economic life inspired by Basil stated that the monks not only had to work to feed themselves, but by their labour, they also had to support the needy. Basil implemented his vision in practice and founded a "new city" (καινὴν πόλιν) for the poor of Caesarea, on the outskirts of the city: the Basiliad (Basileias). This was a complex of buildings that included a hospital, hospices, and hostel.[216]

4.3 The Diffusion of Radical Ideas Into Wider Society

Another major side-effect of wandering asceticism was the diffusion of radical ideas into wider society. Although the Manichaean wandering ascetics used the "language of monasticism", they did not withdraw from society, but lived inside the world as the Messalians did because "their constant mission" was "to transform it", to 'cure' it by transferring their values to it.[217] Thus, in the words of Beskow, they "were regarded by the Roman authorities as socially harmful, not because they were ascetic, which might in itself be acceptable, but because they tended to upset law and order by questioning the laws of marriage, property, [labour] and social behaviour in general".[218] Throughout legislation, we find the fear that the Manichaeans would corrupt and infect society with their morals and customs. Therefore, the laws record the repeated insistence that Manichaeans should be exiled from the cities.

4.4 The Dilemma between Concealment and Disclosure: To Speak or Not to Speak?

Apart from the aforementioned patterns (i.e. the 'similar but different' argument, the example of great Christian ascetics, the human body as a marker of heresy) and measures (church canons, regulation of monastic life) an additional tactic of the Church Fathers' rhetorical strategy to combat Manichaean attractiveness (strange as it may sound) was the concealment of heretical information. As Berzon remarks:

---

215 Pseudo-Basil of Caesarea, *Constitutiones Asceticae* PG, 31:1381.46–49, 1385.25 (*Asceticon fus.*: 901–1052 and *Asceticon brev.*: 1052–1305). Basil's authorship of *Constitutiones Asceticae* is doubted, cf. Tzamalikos 2012, 196; Thomas, Constantinides-Hero & Constable, 2000, 30.

216 Basil in his epistles (94, 150, 176) calls it πτωχοτροφεῖον (*ptôchotropheion*), i.e., alms house. Gregory of Nazianzus, in his funeral oration (*Fun. oratio* 63.1.3) in honor of Basil, calls Basiliad καινὴν πόλιν. Cf. Rousseau 1994, 139–144; Crislip 2005, 103.

217 Gardner and Lieu 2004, 23.

218 Beskow 1988, 11. Cf. Drijvers 1984, 118.

In their position as pastoral caretakers, the heresiologists managed the information at their disposal with a dual mandate: reveal and restrict. [...] the fear of overexposing the heretics remained a looming concern [...] While heresiology served to protect its readers from the disease of heresy by means of identificatory and curative knowledge, the bishop of Salamis, like Hippolytus, Tertullian, and Theodoret, ensures his audience's protection by consciously restricting the flow of heretical information. [...] It was not lack of knowledge that defined down the scope of Theodoret's inquiry, but a defensive inclination to maximize potency and minimize peril.[219]

Thus, in some cases, our authors conceal information lest Manichaean beliefs and conduct would seem appealing. As Serapion declares at the end of his treatise:

> Let us stop here, indicating, by these few points, the meaning of all the rest, and systematically refute their views through what has already been said. It is necessary for those who are diligent to show caution, so that after overcoming any deceitful attraction, they may ensure that their ears have remained unharmed by their wickedness, as if they (their ears) were the key holders/keepers.[220]
>
> Those who happen to encounter a (heretical) doctrine must be in contact with it, as much as is enough for them to realize its harmful effect; that is, to understand from what has been said those things that have been silenced.[221]
>
> Now I leave aside that which is ridiculous and offensive in order to avoid filling my audience's ears with the sound of scandalous words and monstrous suggestions.[222]

---

219   Berzon 2013, 247–49.

220   Serapion, *c. Manichaeos* 40.5–6 & 53.43–47 (HTS 15:77): μέχρι τούτων στῶμεν, διὰ τῶν ὀλίγων καὶ τὰ ἄλλα ὑποδείξαντες καὶ διὰ τῶν προλεχθέντων τὸν ἔλεγχον κατασκευάσαντες. ἐπιμελείας δὲ τοῖς σπουδαίοις χρεία, ἵνα πᾶσαν γοητείαν ὑπερβεβηκότες ἀλήπτους τὰς ἀκοὰς ἀπὸ τῆς πονηρίας διαφυλάξωσιν, ὅπως κλειδοφύλακες.

221   Pseudo-Didymus, *Trin.* (PG 39:989.33–34): ἀνάγκη τοῦ δόγματος τοσοῦτον ἐφάψασθαι, ὅσον ἱκανόν ἐστι τὸ βλαβερὸν τοῦ δόγματος γνωρίσαι τοῖς ἐντυγχάνειν ὀφείλουσι δηλαδή, ἐκ τῶν λεχθησομένων στοχάζεσθαι τὰ σιωπώμενα.

222   Mark the Deacon, *Vit. Porph.* 86.3–5 (Lieu 2010, 96, 99): Τὰ γὰρ γέλωτος καὶ δυσφημίας ἄξια παραλιμπάνω, ἵνα μὴ πληρώσω τὰς ἀκοὰς τῶν ἐντυγχανόντων ἤχους βαρυτάτου καὶ τερατολογίας.

However, in other cases, they end up saying what they do not want to say (either explicitly or symbolically), although they stress that this is in the best interests of believers.

> We say things which we would prefer not to say, seeking not our own profit, but the profit of many that they may be saved.[223]
>
> I do not dare give an account [...] I do not dare say [...] But I will only reveal it speaking symbolically (through symbols/signs) [...] We truly pollute our mouth speaking about these things. The Church informs you about these things and teaches you, and touches the filth, so that you may be not besmirched: it speaks of wounds, that you may not be wounded. It is sufficient for you to know these facts; now do not attempt to learn about it by experience![224]

5 Political Reflections on the Anti-Manichaean Discourse

The question of the last sub-section is the investigation of a probable correlation between social stratification factors and Manichaean attractiveness. Was Manichaeism appealing to a particular social group? And if so, is there evidence of activities undermining governmental power and state authorities? To this end, I will firstly refer to the few relevant references I have traced in the anti-Manichaean literature. Secondly, I will focus on one episode, a dialogue in the Hippodrome in Constantinople held between Justinian and a group of protestors (the green dēmos); as far as I know, this has so far escaped the attention of Manichaean scholarship.

5.1 Dualism Means Anarchy?

Monotheism and monarchy were the ideal forms of religion and government respectively in the Late Roman Empire. One god and one ruler as his divine representative on earth were the cornerstones of Byzantine political theology. Therefore, Manichaean ontological dualism could lead to ἀναρχία (anarchy), ἀταξία (disorder), and στασιῶδες (sedition) at the political level. Revealing of

---

223　P.Rylands 3, Gr. 469 (Lieu 2010, 37).

224　Cyril, Catech. 6.33–34 (Reischl and Rupp 1848, 202, 204; trans. partly from Lieu 2010, 55): Οὐ τολμῶ εἰπεῖν [...] Διὰ συσσήμων δὲ μόνον δηλούσθω [...] Μιαίνομεν ἀληθῶς καὶ τὸ στόμα, ταῦτα λέγοντες [...] Παραγγέλλει ταῦτα ἡ Ἐκκλησία καὶ διδάσκει, καὶ ἅπτεται βορβόρων, ἵνα σὺ μὴ βορβορωθῇς. Λέγει τὰ τραύματα, ἵνα μὴ σὺ τραυματισθῇς. Ἀρκεῖ δέ σοι τὸ εἰδέναι μόνον· τὸ δὲ πείρᾳ παραλαβεῖν ἀπέχου.

the Byzantine political theology of the era is Gregory of Nazianzus' third theological oration, *De filio*.

> There are three main views about God: anarchy, polyarchy, and monarchy. The children of the Greeks [pagans] played with the first two – and will continue to play. Anarchy is synonymous with disorder, and polyarchy is characterized by constant conflicts, and therefore is also connected with anarchy and disorder. So, both (anarchy and polyarchy) lead to the same result, to disorder, and this subsequently leads to dissolution. This is because disorder is nothing but the study of dissolution. To us, only the monarchy is honoured; a monarchy that does not include a single person.[225]

For Gregory, theological πολυαρχία (polyarchy, includes polytheism, dualism) means by definition στασιῶδες (sedition), which then leads to ἀναρχία (anarchy) and this in turn to ἀταξία (disorder). The final stage of the above process is λύσις: the breaking down of laws and the dissolution of the government (πολιτείας). Conversely, the correct perception of God, which according to Gregory is μοναρχία (monarchy), ensures political peace and social order.[226]

Alexander's criticism of the ambiguity of Manichaean teachings could be a hint of such a kind, namely that dualism entailed sedition. For Alexander, the complexity of the Manichaean doctrine resulted in the lack of rules and laws, and this led the crowd to become seditious.

---

225   Gregory of Nazianzus, *De filio* 2.1–7: Τρεῖς αἱ ἀνωτάτω δόξαι περὶ θεοῦ, ἀναρχία, καὶ πολυαρχία, καὶ μοναρχία. αἱ μὲν οὖν δύο παισὶν Ἑλλήνων ἐπαίχθησαν, καὶ παιζέσθωσαν. τό τε γὰρ ἄναρχον ἄτακτον· τό τε πολύαρχον στασιῶδες, καὶ οὕτως ἄναρχον, καὶ οὕτως ἄτακτον. εἰς ταὐτὸν γὰρ ἀμφότερα φέρει, τὴν ἀταξίαν, ἡ δὲ εἰς λύσιν· ἀταξία γὰρ μελέτη λύσεως. ἡμῖν δὲ μοναρχία τὸ τιμώμενον· μοναρχία δέ, οὐχ ἣν ἓν περιγράφει πρόσωπον.

226   Orthodoxy as a political tool (*political orthodoxy*) aimed at religious unity and united worshiping that was directly linked (1) to social unity, prosperity and peace and (2) to the loyalty of citizens towards the state and the emperor. For more on Byzantine political theology and the formulation of the 'Kaiser-ideologie' by Eusebius, see Beck (1978, 87–108, *Politische Orthodoxie*; esp. 95–98: "Eusebios formuliert seine Kaiser-ideologie sehr personlich"); Mango (1980, 88): "One God, one Empire, one religion – these were the cornerstones of Byzantine political thinking [...] it was the emperor's duty – in fact, his highest duty – to enforce its [religion's] universal observance". See also Barnes 1981, 224–71. For the relationship/correlation between monotheism and monarchy (as the preferred forms of government and religion) in early Christian thought, see Peterson's (1935) *Monotheismus als politisches Problem*. Cf. Pettipiece 2007, 119: "On a more worldly level, however, this reflects a correlation that was being drawn between monarchy and monotheism as the preferred forms of government and religion as well as a trend towards the harmonization of Christian theology with a new political situation after the rise of Constantine".

[...] ethical instruction declined and grew dim, [...] and since the common people became more inclined to internal strife. For there was no norm or laws on the basis of which issues could be decided.[227]

As Stroumsa underlines, for "both Alexander and Titus, dualism meant anarchy", and was an attitude which could also have political implications.[228] When Manichaeans defended their belief in two first principles, this always resulted in the same question: Whence comes evil and disorder?

For Mani, as Titus of Bostra says, ἀταξία (disorder) originates from the principle of evil. Titus explains that, by ἀταξία Mani means the inequalities that exist in society. "Wealth and poverty, health and disease are not equally distributed among people. Instead of criminals, who manage to escape the punishment of the law, the innocent are punished. The corrupt people rule all the others".[229] Could such statements be interpreted as political ones? According to Pedersen "this is extremely unsure".[230] However, as Pedersen adds, "even though the Manichaeans have not fought for any alternative political or socio-economic system, it nonetheless makes sense to say the fact that in the eyes of the leading forces in society these accusations must have made Manichaeism unsuitable as ideological legitimation".[231]

However, are there testimonies according to which the fear that dualism means anarchy, disorder, and sedition would become real action, or does this remain just a fear? Is there any evidence that connects Manichaeans with political activities in the literature of the era, as is indicated by the law[232] (social unrest, upset of the urban communities, instigation of seditious mobs, etc.)? The whole picture does not reveal something like this. However, there are some occasional reports linking real or imagined Manichaeans to sedition and riots, but these cases concern mainly ecclesiastical disputes.

---

227 Alexander of Lycopolis, *Tract. Man.* 1.26–28 (Brinkmann, 4; Van der Horst and Mansfeld, 51): [...] τοῦ δὲ πολλοῦ πλήθους στασιαστικώτερον πρὸς αὐτὸ διατεθέντος, κανόνος δὲ οὐδενὸς ὑπόντος οὐδὲ νόμων [...].

228 Stroumsa 1992, 345; Pedersen 2004, 171.

229 Titus of Bostra, *c. Manichaeos* 2.15.3–9 (CCSG 82:123): Ἀταξίαν δὴ πολλὴν ψηφίζεται τῶν καθ' ἡμᾶς πραγμάτων, πλοῦτόν τε καὶ πενίαν, ὑγείαν τε καὶ νόσον ὡς ἄνισα διαβάλλων· ἔτι μὴν καὶ τὸ πολλάκις τὸν μὲν κακοῦργον διαφεύγειν τὴν τῶν νόμων τιμωρίαν, τὸν δ' ἀναίτιον τιμωρεῖσθαι, καὶ τοὺς φαύλους ἔστιν ὅτε τῆς κατὰ τῶν ἄλλων ἀρχῆς ἐπιβαίνειν.

230 Pedersen 2004, 172.

231 Pedersen, 2004, 172.

232 Cod. theod. 16.5.7; 16.5.9; 16.5.38. See ch.[3], 3.2.1 & 3.6.

One such case, as the Catholic church historian Theodorus Anagnostes recounts, is that of a Syro-Persian Manichaean painter, whose icons were so alien to the Catholic tradition that they caused a rebellion in Constantinople.[233] The sources (again Catholic church historians) report another case as a trouble-maker who they labelled as Manichaean. This was Philoxenos, the Monophysite bishop of Hierapolis, (nick)named by the authors as Xenaias. According to the authors, Xenaias disrupted the surrounding cities of Antioch and agitated the Syrian monks to rebel against the Catholic bishop of Antioch.[234] However, as the term 'Manichaean' was a label attributed to the Monophysite bishop Philoxenos, it could also be the case of the icon painter. In addition, both epi-sodes concern either conflicts among rival factions within the Church or theo-logical issues. However, political and religious events in Byzantine political theology are interconnected.

The latter is reflected in the uprising of 512 (after the Synod of Sidon, 511), during which both the Blue and the Green factions rose against the emperor Anastasius for a theological issue. Specifically, this concerned the Monophysite addition to the Trisagion hymn: "the One crucified for us" (ὁ σταυρωθεὶς δι' ἡμᾶς).[235] Jarry considers it likely that the Manichaeans participated in the revolt too, protesting the edict Anastasius decreed against them in 510, which, for the first time, inflicted on them capital punishment.[236]

The heroic gesture of a Manichaean who threw a pamphlet in front of the royal bookstore could also be interpreted as a political act. This occurred immediately after Justinian issued his edict against Manichaeans, which re-activated Anastasius' edict enforcing capital punishment for Manichaeans. The pamphlet, according to Zacharias of Mytilene (who undertook the task to refute it), was "challenging the truth of the one and only principle".[237] Was it a challenge to monotheism and/or the monarchy? In any case, even if it was a literary *topos*, the whole incident reflects practices which could have been real.

---

233   Theodorus Anagnostes, *HE* 4.467; Theophanes, *Chron.* 149.28–33. Cf. ch.[7], 3.9.2.

234   Theodorus Anagnostes, *HE* 3.444; Evagrius the Scholastic, *HE* 130 etc. (ch. 32).

235   The revolt of 512 (4/11) in Theodorus Anagnostes, *HE* 4.483(145.15–18); Theophanes, *Chron.* 159.14–18.

236   Jarry 1968, 302–305.

237   Zacharias of Mytilene, *Adv. Manichaeos* (*Antirresis*), (Cod. Mosquensis gr. 3942) (Demetrakopoulos, 1–2): Πρότασις Μανιχαίου παραλογιζομένη τὴν ἀλήθειαν τῆς μιᾶς καὶ μόνης παντοκρατορικῆς ἀρχῆς· Ἀντίρρησις Ζαχαρίου Μιτυλήνης ἐπισκόπου, εὑρόντος ταῦτα ἐπὶ τῆς ὁδοῦ, ῥίψαντος αὐτὰ Μανιχαίου τινὸς ἐπὶ βασιλέως Ἰουστινιανοῦ.

Apart from the above incidents, there is an episode cited by the Chronographer Theophanes in his *Chronicle*,[238] which has been neglected by previous Manichaean scholars. Theophanes places it in the beginning of the Nika Revolt, and according to some scholars echoes the protestors' dualistic views.

5.2 Excursus: The 'Circus Dialogue'

The famous dialogue which took place in the Hippodrome between the Greens and the Emperor Justinian has been characterized by scholars as noteworthy, curious, odd,[239] obscure in meaning, and "much misunderstood, both in details of interpretation and in its over-all purpose and significance".[240]

The dialogue is included among the sources under investigation, because Justinian through his *Mandator* (herald), addressing at some point the Greens, called them: "Jews, Samaritans and Manichaeans".[241] Thus, the question is whether the protesting Greens were just labelled as Manichaeans, or whether they were in fact Manichaeans or verging on Manichaeism (e.g. μανιχαΐζοντες, μανιχαιόφρονες). If the latter is true, what would this reveal for the social and political profile of the Manichaeans? In scholarship, this dialogue has been debated from many different angles. In specific, both the time frame of the event and its interpretation have been endlessly debated. Some historians have challenged Theophanes' historical context and argued that the dialogue did not take place during the Nika Revolt.[242] Some of them suggest this episode occurred more likely at the beginning and some others at the end of Justinian's reign.[243] What is not doubted is that the dialogue took place during Justinian's reign.

What is debated concerning the dialogue's interpretation is whether there are allusions revealing the religious identity of the protesting Greens. The different interpretations made by scholars in various points of the dialogue derive from their stance on this key issue. In brief, the theses of the researchers

---

238　Theophanes, *Chron.* 181.25–186. An abbreviated form of the dialogue is found in *Chronicon Paschale* 112–115.

239　Mango and Scott 1997, 280. See Bury 1889, 56; Bury 1897 92; Bury 1889/1958.

240　Cameron 1976a, 318.

241　Theophanes, *Chron.* 182.16. As Mango and Scott (1997, 282) note, in the Late Roman Empire it was a common practice "for an Emperor to address the crowd through a herald rather than by gesture or in writing".

242　Maas 1912, 49–51; Cameron 1976a, 322–329.

243　Cameron 1976a, 322–329, 323 (beginning); Maas 1912, 50 (end). See Cameron 1976a, 142; Bury suggested that the events took place between 11 and 19/1/532); Karlin-Hayter 1973 (11th or 10/1/532); Stein, Palanque, and Stein 1949 (few days before the executions); Mango and Scott (1997, 281): "it cannot be taken for granted that the dialogue had anything to do with the Nika revolt".

on the above question could be summarized as follows. According to Bury, there are hints in the dialogue revealing the Monophysitism of the Greens.[244] For Jarry, the protestors in the Green faction were Nestorians verging on Manichaeism.[245] Karlin-Hayter finds in the critical points of the dialogue "une profession incontestable de dualisme".[246] Cameron, exercising harsh criticism on the above scholars, claims that there is no hint in the dialogue revealing any kind of religious beliefs of the Greens.[247] Finally, the translators of Theophanes (Mango and Scott) hold a neutral stance on the issue.[248]

I believe that what complicates the discussion is that it concerns the well-known Greens, in combination with the theory (in research) which dissociates heresies from social-political motives and intentions; according to some researchers, heresies do not seem to have political goals and purposes. However, all agree that especially the dualistic heresies attracted discontented and dissatisfied persons and are a kind of heresy which by and large could be associated with socio-political causes and social consequences.[249]

Indeed, my first impression, realizing that the protestors were the Greens was to think that this is another example of the use of the term 'Manichaean' as a 'label'. Thus, I would propose to make a subtractive suggestion, namely, that to remove the word 'Green' from the dialogue, and to examine the crucial and controversial parts of the dialogue, as if we did not know this aspect of the protestors' identity.

The protestors come to the Hippodrome in order to complain and denounce their oppressors to the Emperor. The latter was something common and in fact the only opportunity they had to make requests, to express complaints, to exert criticism of the rulers, and to denounce the maladministration or the corruption of certain governmental officials. They start the dialogue saying that the injustice towards them (from a person with authority) is unbearable, but initially they are reluctant to name their oppressor, lest worse afflictions would find them. Eventually, they denounce a certain Calopodius (whom one can find in the τζαγγαρεῖα/shoemaker's quarter) and start cursing him. The

---

244   Bury 1889, 57, fn. 3.

245   Jarry 1968, 138–144.

246   Karlin-Hayter 1973, 95.

247   Cameron 1976a, 323, 141. According to Cameron (p. 323) the arguments of the above scholars who identify religious allusions and argue for "supposed religious arguments" of the Greens, are "too fragile to permit serious discussion". Cf. Cameron 1974, 92–120. Whitby (2009, 233–234) criticizes Cameron's view that the followers of the demes were merely hooligans with no political motivation and religious identity. Cf. Whitby 2006, 441–61.

248   Mango and Scott 1997, 280–285.

249   Jones 1959; Mango 1980, 103–04; Kazhdan 1991, 918–20. Cf. Garsoïan 1971, 85–113.

Mandator/Justinian gets angry, tells them that they did not come to watch but to insult their rulers, and invites them to settle down. The first critical part of the dialogue goes as follows:

- Herald: Silence, you Jews, Manichaeans, and Samaritans!
- [Protestors]: Do you call us Jews and Samaritans? May the Mother of God be with everyone. [or, the Mother of God be with all the Manichaeans].[250]

As Jarry points out, when Justinian called the protestors Jews, Samaritans and Manichaeans, they complained about the two first names, as if they were insulted, but they did not react to being called 'Manichaeans'. Jarry, supporting the view that the protestors were Nestorians verging on Manichaeism, interprets "Jews" as a label for the Nestorians, which was a usual way to label the Nestorians in the religious abuse of the era.[251] Cameron considers that all three names were 'labels' with no theological significance and underlines that the word 'Manichaean' was "an insult applied indifferently" to all religious opponents. Commenting on Jarry's observation, Cameron argues that the fact that the Greens did "only expressly repudiate the first two names [Jews, Samaritans] [...] does not mean they deserve the third [Manichaeans]". If this was the case, he says, "the Mandator would not have confused the issue by dragging in the other two names".[252]

These three religious groups are often associated with riots and uprising, either because they did rebel, or because they were suspected of doing so. During Justinian's reign there are several examples of rebellions by Jews and Samaritans.[253] The three religious groups are also co-classified as equally threatening religious groups in the law[254] and in the taxonomical lists of heretics by Church Fathers. As Cameron notes, "All three are in fact frequently linked in Byzantine religious abuse [...]. They are constantly evoked by John of Ephesus as the source of all trouble and temptation".[255]

Obviously, the fact that the protestors did not react to the name 'Manichaean' is not proof that they were Manichaeans. However, the fact that they were offended only by the first two names and not by the third, which, as we have seen, was the ultimate insult, may be an indication that they were somehow

---

250 Theophanes, *Chron.* (de Boor, 182.16–18; Mango and Scott, 277): – Μανδάτωρ· "ἡσυχάσατε, Ἰουδαῖοι, Μανιχαῖοι καὶ Σαμαρεῖται." – Οἱ Πράσινοι "Ἰουδαίους καὶ Σαμαρείτας ἀποκαλεῖς; ἡ θεοτόκος μετὰ ὅλων [τῶν μανιχαίων]". For the addition at the end see Jarry 1968, 139.
251 Jarry 1968, 138–144.
252 Cameron 1976a, 141, 323, fn. 2, 141.
253 Mango 1980, 112–13.
254 See for example Cod. justin., "Against heretics, Manichaeans and Samaritans" and Cod. theod. 16.7.3.
255 Cameron 1976a, 141 & 141 fn. 2.

related to, tolerant with, or were sympathetic to the Manichaeans. Moreover, if they were Manichaeans, their reaction to the 'labels' 'Jews' and 'Samaritans' would make sense.[256] A further argument in favour of the hypothesis that the protestors had a kind of relationship with the Manichaeans is a different version of the text, provided by Jarry, which strangely enough has not been commented upon by other scholars. According to this, at the end of the protestors' answer the word Manichaeans is added, thus becoming: "La mère de Dieu est avec tous les Manichéens".[257]

The next crucial verses of the text are the following:
- Herald: I am telling you: Get baptized in one [God].
- [Protestors]: shouted above each other and chanted, as Antlas demanded, 'I am baptized in one [God]'.[258]

These verses are among the most commented upon and obscure parts of the dialogue. Firstly, different opinions have been suggested concerning the grammatical clause (affirmative, interrogative, imperative) of the Mandator's words.[259] The discussed interpretive problems are twofold: the meaning of the word 'baptism' and the identity of Antlas. According *to* Bury, "the Greens apparently take up the words of the Mandator, 'εἰς ἕνα βαπτίζεσθε' (get baptized in one [God]), in a monophysitic sense".[260] However, as Jarry[261] observes (followed by Cameron),[262] the Monophysites did not administer baptism 'εἰς ἕνα' (in one, i.e. in the name of the one of the three persons of the Holy Trinity, which is something only Eunomians did), so there is not a hint of Monophysitism. Cameron argues that the 'εἰς ἕνα βαπτίζεσθε' is a question of abuse labelling the Greens as polytheists; as he wonders "Why doubt that the Greens are simply repudiating the imputation that they are pagans, as they had already repudiated the Mandator's other cheap smears" (i.e. as Jews and Samaritans).[263] Why however, suggest that the 'εἰς ἕνα' is an allusion to polytheism instead of dualism, since the Mandator had called them Manichaeans before and not pagans? It is far more plausible to assume that the above phrase is a hint that they did not administer baptism; alternatively, it may mean that they had another type of baptism, which was not considered by the Church as baptism.

256 Manichaean anti-Semitism/Judaism is well known. Cf. BeDuhn 2021, 302–23.
257 Jarry 1968, 139.
258 Theophanes, *Chron.* (de Boor, 182.20–22; Mango and Scott, 277): – Μανδάτωρ "ἐγὼ ὑμῖν λέγω, εἰς ἕνα βαπτίζεσθε." – Οἱ δὲ ἀνεβόησαν ἐπάνω ἀλλήλων καὶ ἔκραζον, ὡς ἐκέλευσεν Ἄντλας "εἰς ἕνα βαπτίζομαι."
259 Karlin-Hayter argues in favour of an affirmative type, Cameron of an interrogative and Bury and others of an imperative.
260 Bury 1889, 57.
261 Jarry 1968, 355–6.
262 Cameron 1976a, 320.
263 Cameron 1976a, 141.

The second hermeneutical problem is the identity of Antlas. Two suggestions have been made in terms of the punctuation of the phrase, which corresponds to different interpretations. The disagreement is whether there is a comma after the word 'ἔκραζον' (chanted), so the two versions are: (1) chanted, 'as Antlas demanded, I am baptized in one', and (2) chanted as Antlas demanded, 'I am baptized in one'. According to the first version, a certain Antlas had introduced a type of baptism, whereas according to the second, a certain Antlas in the Hippodrome commanded the protestors to shout 'I am baptized in one'.

Researchers that support the first version are Bury, Karlin-Hayter and Jarry. Bury, in supporting his view that the protestors were Monophysites, argues that Antlas is a nickname for Anastasius, a hypothesis grounded on the etymology of the word ἀντλῶ (pump), which Bury interprets "in the sense of 'fetch water', for the baptismal rite".[264] Thus, his interpretation should be: we are following the command of Anastasius and we apply the Monophysite baptism. The same etymological origin (ἀντλῶ) has been suggested by Karlin-Hayter yet resulting in a different interpretation. Karlin-Hayter interprets Antlas as "the one who sucks dry" and considers it as a nickname for the Emperor Justinian, which implies that the protestors' answer expressed a discontent over heavy taxation, which actually happened at the period of the Nika Revolt.[265] Jarry is the only scholar who takes Antlas as a real name, rather than an ironic nickname, and connects it with the known Omoforos ("Ατλας) of the Manichaean myth.[266]

The second version, 'chanted as Antlas demanded, I am baptized in one' (ἔκραζον ὡς ἐκέλευσεν "Αντλας· 'εἰς ἕνα βαπτίζομαι'), has been supported by Cameron. Consistent with his thesis that there are no religious allusions in the dialogue, Cameron argues that Antlas was the leader of the Greens, and criticizes Jarry's thesis: "It is building on sand [...] to take Antlas to be an otherwise unknown heresiarch who ordered a particular form of baptism".[267] Lastly, Mango and Scott consider Cameron's interpretation plausible, but do not exclude the possibility that there are hints targeting Justinian's economic policy, as highlighted by Karlin-Hayter.[268]

---

264 Bury 1889, 57, fn. 3: "we may assume it ["Αντλας] to be a nickname of Anastasius".
265 Karlin-Hayter (1981, 7–8) in Mango and Scott 1997, 282.
266 Jarry 1968, 139: "Atlas (ou Saclas) était un démon que les manichéens rêveraient fort; ils lui attribuaient même les tremblements de terre". Jarry here confuses two different Manichaean mythological figures.
267 Cameron 1976a, 319, 139.
268 Mango and Scott 1997, 282. The truth is that the name Antlas is quite strange to be a byzantine one, unless it was a nickname.

It is further important to highlight that the above answer of the protestors (chanted, as Antlas demanded, 'I am baptized in one') enraged the Mandator, who then threatened them: "Surely, if you do not keep quiet, I shall behead you".[269] This reaction is quite unexpected in the case of the second version (i.e. that their answer was just "I am baptized in one"). Capital punishment, as said in the previous chapters, had first been imposed on Manichaeans by the law of 487 or 510 (Zeno or Anastasius) and successively by Justinian's laws (527 onwards). What I am arguing here is not that the protestors were Manichaeans. During Justinian's age, the laws were very strict for the Manichaeans. They had to disappear from the Roman Empire, and in case they were found anywhere, the punishment was the ultimate (decapitation according to Basilica).[270] Thus, it is likely that they would not dare to appear so openly in broad daylight in front of the emperor and quarrel with him. However, I consider it a plausible hypothesis that the protestors had adopted Manichaean ideas or practices, in other words, that they were, in a way, μανιχαΐζοντες.

The next crucial point of the dialogue is the protestors' answer to the Mandator's threat to behead them:

– [Protestors]: Everyone tries to get office for security. So whatever we say in our distress, Your Majesty should not get angry, for deity endures everything.
– [Protestors]: We have a case, emperor, and we shall now name everything. We do not know even where the palace is, thrice-august, nor where is the state ceremonial. I come only once to the City, when I am seated on a mule (on the way to execution). And I would rather not then, thrice-august.[271]

The above answer of the protestors, one of the more obscure parts of the episode, has not been commented upon enough. Concerning the first part of the answer, Cameron considers that the phrase "Everyone tries to get office for security" is an abrupt transition and wonders whether a text is missing to explain it. However, I believe that there is coherence in the text; the current verses are linked with both the previous and the next verses. As far as the second part of the answer is concerned, the exclusion of the protestors from Constantinople, given the fact that they were the Greens, had troubled a lot the researchers.

---

269   Theophanes, *Chron.* (de Boor, 182.22–23; Mango and Scott, 277): ὄντως εἰ μὴ ἡσυχάσητε, ἀποκεφαλίζω ὑμᾶς.

270   Cod. justin. 1.5.16.

271   Theophanes, *Chron.* (de Boor, 182.23–29; Mango and Scott, 277–78): – Οἱ Πράσινοι ἕκα-στος σπεύδει ἀρχὴν κρατῆσαι, ἵνα σωθῇ· καὶ εἴ τι ἐὰν εἴπωμεν θλιβόμενοι, μὴ ἀγανακτήσῃ τὸ κράτος σου· τὸ γὰρ θεῖον πάντων ἀνέχεται." – Οἱ Πράσινοι· "ἡμεῖς λόγον ἔχοντες, αὐτοκράτωρ, ὀνομάζομεν ἄρτι πάντα· ποῦ ἐστιν, ἡμεῖς οὐκ οἴδαμεν, οὐδὲ τὸ παλάτιον, τρισαύγουστε, οὐδὲ πολιτείας κατάστασις. μίαν εἰς τὴν πόλιν προέρχομαι, ὅτ' ἂν εἰς βορδώνην καθέζομαι εἴθοις μηδὲ τότε, τρισαύγουστε.

According to Bury, "one might conclude from this that members of the Green faction were not allowed to reside in the city, and were confined to quarters in Pera and Galata, on the other side of the Golden Horn".[272] Cameron pointed out that the interpretation of the 'πολιτείας κατάστασις' (state ceremonial) as government is problematic, and considers it odd that the Greens did not know where the palace was.[273] According to some other interpretations, the Greens had been 'kept out of politics'.[274]

I consider that the dialogue from the point of the Mandator's threat onwards depicts an atmosphere of persecution. It seems that the protestors comprise a group that is persecuted, probably exiled from the cities, and certainly excluded from the capital which they visit only when driven to execution.[275] Within this climate of persecution, "everyone tries to get office for security" (ἕκαστος σπεύδει ἀρχὴν κρατῆσαι, ἵνα σωθῇ). As Cameron rightly interpreted, "seeking of office" means "presumably the office which is now protecting Calopodius".[276] Thus, the phrase should mean that everyone (in order to save his life) tries to hold an authoritative position, or to have access to persons of authority: in other words, to have the proper 'contacts'.

Could such a contact be Peter Barsymes, an outranked official and Theodora's favoured (PPO since 543, before he was a count and patrician), who, according to Procopius, amazed the Manichaeans, probably even joined the sect and did not hesitate to protect them openly?[277] Such a scenario could explain the infiltration of Manichaeans in the imperial administrative structure that Justinian faced from the very beginning of his reign.[278] The laws of the early sixth century present the Manichaeans as having intruded into the imperial service, holding public offices in the state's civil and military structure, in both Constantinople and in the provinces; a situation which forced Justinian to take drastic measures. Let us recall the law which invited officials in the administration, in the army and in the guilds, to denounce their fellow Manichaeans, or otherwise risk their lives (the punishment would be the same as if they were Manichaeans).[279] A victim of this policy would

---

272   Bury 1889, 57.
273   Cameron 1976a, 320.
274   Cameron 1976a, 320.
275   Bury 1889, 57, fn. 5: "Prisoners were drawn by mules to execution or punishment, and perhaps there is some such reference here".
276   Cameron 1976a, 320.
277   Procopius, *Hist. Arcana* 22.25 (Haury, 138): τοὺς καλουμένους Μανιχαίους ἐτεθήπει τε καὶ αὐτῶν προστατεῖν ἐκ τοῦ ἐμφανοῦς οὐδαμῇ ἀπηξίου. I will return to Barsymes in ch.[7], section 3.11.
278   See ch.[3], 3.4.2.
279   Cod. justin. 1.5.16.

have been the wife of the senator Erythrius, who according to Malalas was among the Manichaeans who were punished during Justinian's time. The latter further illustrates the influence that Manichaeans could have had over the ruling classes.

The conversation about persecutions is continued in the next verses of the Hippodrome episode:

– Herald: Every free man can go where he likes in public without danger.
– [Protestors]: To be sure, I am a free man, but I am not allowed to show it. For if a free man is suspected of being a Green, he is sure to be punished in public.
– Herald: Are you ready to die then, and will you not spare your own lives?
– [Protestors]: Let this colour be removed and justice disappears. Stop the murdering and let us face punishment. See here a gushing fountain, punish as many as you like.[280]

This dialogue, which I consider of particular importance, has not been substantially commented upon by the researchers. As it seems, the Greens, unlike the Blues, during Justinian's reign had problems of freedom. Initially they speak ironically about the supposed freedom they had according to the claim of the Mandator. However, what is really remarkable is their answer: "Let this colour be removed", to the new threat of the Mandator. It is impressive because the protestors make the same subtractive hypothesis as the one I made in order to interpret the text. So, what would happen if this "colour be removed"? It is likely that executions would take place, bypassing the legal prosecution process: "Let this colour be removed and justice disappears". What the protestors are requesting is to have equal treatment by the law. They call for the stopping of killings, of vigilantism, of executions without trial; they demand to be judged and penalized according to the legal procedure: "Stop the murdering and let us face punishment. See here a gushing fountain, punish as many as you like". They do not dispute the right that each one has to accuse them; on the contrary they offer themselves at the disposal of justice to be punished, if the legal prosecution will be observed.

So according to the dialogue, after the Mandator's statement that everyone is free to go "where he likes in public, without danger" the protestors become furious. Interpreting the text freely, they asked: what freedom are you talking

---

280   Theophanes, Chron. (de Boor, 183.1–7; Mango and Scott, 278): – Μανδάτωρ· "ἕκαστος ἐλεύθερος ὅπου θέλει ἀκινδύνως δημοσιεύει." – Οἱ Πράσινοι· "καὶ θαρρῶ ἐλευθερίας, καὶ ἐμφανίσαι
οὐ συγχωροῦμαι· καὶ ἐάν ἐστιν ἐλεύθερος, ἔχει δὲ Πρασίνων ὑπόληψιν, πάντως εἰς φανερὸν
κολάζεται." – Μανδάτωρ· "ἑτοιμοθάνατοι, οὐδὲ τῶν ψυχῶν ὑμῶν φείδεσθε;" – Οἱ Πράσινοι·
"ἐπαρθῇ τὸ χρῶμα τοῦτο, καὶ ἡ δίκη οὐ χρηματίζει· ἄνες τὸ φονεύεσθαι· καὶ ἄφες, κολαζόμεθα.
ἴδε πηγὴ βρύουσα, καὶ ὅσους θέλεις, κόλαζε ...".

about, since we are not allowed even to appear in public? We are punished even for the fact that we are Greens. If indeed, the green colour would be removed, we would not just be punished but killed without a trial. As it seems, they claim that if they were not Greens, things would be even worse for them, which reveals that apart from their identity as Greens, they had another distinct identity too. Thus, the text gives the impression that for the protestors the fact that they were Greens was a kind of protection for them; they were safeguarded behind the label of the Greens and being Greens, although they were punished, at least they were not killed. What is here described by the Greens (i.e. killing without observing the prosecuting process) is reminiscent of Justinian's law against Manichaeans: "Every Manichaean should be put to death, whenever found".[281] Relevant is the testimony from the *Erotapokriseis* (sixth cent.), according to which the laws of the time of Justinian condemned those who were undoubtedly killers, or Manichaeans, immediately, without trial, in order for the rest of the sect to be made into an example.[282]

Having clarified that the protestors also had another distinctive identity in addition to being Greens, the name of the Greens can be returned to the discussion. Passing in the next scene of the dialogue, the Blues enter the discussion. It seems that the above accusations from the side of the Greens about vigilantism and killings were addressed to the Blues. This can be deduced from a quarrel that follows between the Blues and the Greens in which the Emperor took the side of the Blues, resulting in the Greens' outburst:

– The Greens: Now, now, have pity O Lord. Truth is being suppressed. I want to quarrel with those who say events are controlled by God. For what is the source of this misery?
– Herald: God cannot be tempted with evil.
– The Greens: God cannot be tempted with evil? But who does me wrong? If there is a philosopher or hermit here, let him explain the difference.
– Herald: You God-hated blasphemers, will you never be silent?[283]

This is the last crucial part of the dialogue. Both Jarry and Karlin-Hayter argue that the idea of God as outlined by the Greens in the above dialogue is

---

281 Cod. justin. 1.5.12.
282 Pseudo-Caesarius, *Erotapokriseis*, 146.85: οὐδὲ γὰρ οἱ τήμερον νόμοι τὸν πρόδηλον φονέα ἢ Μανιχέα τῆς εἱρκτῆς ἐκφωνήσαντες μακρηγορίᾳ κρίνουσιν, ἀλλ᾽ αὖθις τοῦ κρίνεσθαι κατακρίνουσιν ἐν ὄψει τῆς φρικτῆς ὁμηγύρεως, ἐκείνην δι᾽ ἐκείνου σωφρονίζοντες.
283 Theophanes, *Chron.* (de Boor, 183.20–26; Mango and Scott, 278): – Οἱ Πράσινοι· "ἄρτι καὶ ἄρτι· κύριε ἐλέησον. τυραννεῖται ἡ ἀλήθεια. ἤθελον ἀντιβάλαι τοῖς λέγουσιν ἐκ θεοῦ διοικεῖσθαι τὰ πράγματα· πόθεν αὕτη ἡ δυστυχία;" – Μανδάτωρ· "ὁ θεὸς κακῶν ἀπείραστος." – Οἱ Πράσινοι· "θεὸς κακῶν ἀπείραστος; καὶ τίς ἐστιν ὁ ἀδικῶν με; εἰ φιλόσοφός ἐστιν ἢ ἐρημίτης, τὴν διαίρεσιν εἴπῃ τῶν ἑκατέρων." – Μανδάτωρ· "βλάσφημοι καὶ θεοχόλωτοι, ἕως πότε οὐχ ἡσυχάζετε;".

dualistic.[284] On the contrary, Cameron, once more rejecting the views which support religious allusions, interprets the doubts of the Greens about the divine governance as a "natural human reaction to the sight of evil".[285]

However, the identities of people are not monolithic. The fact that the protestors belonged to the Greens cannot exclude the possibility that they also had a religious identity. The latter would not mean that all the Greens necessarily had the same religious identity, though we cannot exclude the possibility that civilians' preferences for one or another faction (*dēmos*) was to a certain extent linked to their religious inclination. Thus, taking into account that the specific group of Greens had an additional identity, which apparently caused problems for them, why not hypothesize that this was a religious one, not least because religious issues were of particular importance in Byzantine society and culture? Further, if we assume that there are no religious allusions, certain parts of the dialogue do not make sense.

In my opinion, the above dialogue is an additional testimony that certain protestors, apart from being members of the Green faction, were in a way μανιχαΐζοντες, because they held some views that could sound as Manichaean. The doubts expressed by the Greens echo the classic Manichaean question, "whence evil"? The Greens question divine providence and governance of human affairs as well as "what is the source of this misery"; the Mandator responds (in defending God) that "God is not the source/cause of evil". Surely this is the eminent topic, the hallmark, that runs throughout Christian and pagan literature in its discourse with Manichaean dualism. The spirit of the dialogue in the Hippodrome recalls what was said by Titus: for Mani, ἀταξία (disorder) is due to the principle of evil, and by ἀταξία he means the inequalities in society [...] Instead of criminals, who manage to escape the punishment of the law, the innocent are punished. The corrupt people rule all the others".[286]

Thus, summing up, I consider that there are many indications in the dialogue to support the view that those who speak on behalf of the Greens were μανιχαΐζοντες and not just labelled as such. Although all individual evidence

---

284   Jarry 1960, 365–66: "Une telle alternative n'est ni nestorienne, ni monophysite. Cette idée d'un Dieu cruel, inflexible et méchant, Dieu de l'Ancien Testament, choisi pour gouverner un monde que le Christ vient lui racheter au prix de ses souffrances, est une idée marcionite. [...] En cette journée exceptionnelle, malgré la peine de mort prévue depuis 527 pour ce genre de délit, les Verts s'avouent manichéens"; Karlin-Hayter 1973, 95: "une profession incontestable de dualisme".

285   Cameron 1976a, 141: "natural human reaction to the sight of evil prospering and age-old theme in the schools of rhetoric, designed of course to shock the Mandator by its skepticism but in no way a 'manifestation d' opposition a l'orthodoxie".

286   Titus of Bostra, *c. Manichaeos* 2.15.3–9 (CCSG 82, 123). Pedersen 2004, 25.

is insufficient, I believe that the evidence in its totality permits us to support such a hypothesis. Μανιχαΐζοντες does not mean Manichaeans, although, as it seems, they were often treated in the same way as the Manichaeans were. So, what kind of Μανιχαΐζοντες were they? Jarry claims that they were Nestorians (extreme Chalcedonians) verging on Manichaeism. In ch.[8] I will make some assumptions based on church canons in order to further illuminate their religious identity.

6 Conclusions

From the above analysis it appears that our sources made a correlation between religious, age and gender factors and Manichaean attractiveness. Apart from the general appeal of Manichaeism, which is also reflected in the combat against it, what our sources steadily point out is the particular attraction Manichaeism had to Christian neophytes and pagans. For the former, the Manichaean response to the question of the origin of evil was of particular importance; for the latter, the critical dimension of the Manichaean discourse was particularly appealing.

Although the references are few, it seems (as is expected) that the anti-conformist attitudes, vagabond lifestyle, and extravagant appearance of Manichaeans were appealing to young people. This constituted a problem for both imperial and church authorities because it meant the dissemination of socially threatening ideas to a critical group prone to radicalization, and the perpetuation of these ideas to subsequent generations. That the young people were one of the target groups of the Manichaean missionary strategy is also testified by the Manichaean testimonies about the recruitment of young Elect.

It is noteworthy that the only testimonies we have regarding female Manichaean missionaries (two, perhaps three) concern the missionary activity of Manichaean women in the eastern Roman Empire. However, the scarcity of this evidence and the lack of corresponding material from Manichaean sources do not allow us to draw any secure conclusions. As current research evidences, the women of Kellis do not appear to have shared the wandering lives of their male Elect compatriots. There are no testimonies (at least to date) about female Kellites in the entourage of the Egyptian Manichaean teacher. Generally, references to all the above three groups (neophytes, the young, and women) must be interpreted with caution, since their 'vulnerability to heresy' is a common polemical *topos* in Christian literature.

The group to which Manichaeism was most appealing, and through them to the whole of society, since they acted as paradigms, were the ascetics. Both the Encratites et al. and Messalians are associated by our authors with

Manichaeans. Indeed, they had a lot of common features. Their main difference is that the former were amorphous movements, while Manichaeans were highly organized. Encratites et al. appeared chronologically before Manichaeans, and Messalians after them; both originated from the same motherland (Central Minor Asia, Antioch).

Anarchist and wandering forms of asceticism, to which both groups belonged, predated Manichaeism, though they were not widely accepted as is reflected in the canons of the Church and ecclesiastical literature. However, with the appearance of Manichaean ascetics in the Christian ascetical landscape, they were linked by Church and state authorities with the Manichaeans. Manichaeans were considered the mentors of both Encratites et al. and Messalians. All of them constituted a laboratory producing apostates from faith and cultivating social radicalism that threatened structural social institutions and values. The increase in the number of anarchist monks in the 370s and 80s, and mainly their presence in the cities, coupled with the appearance of Messalians in the foreground, necessitated repressive and persecutory measures. In the laws, the persecution of the Encratites et al. and Messalians by the state is sluggish and ends early, while it continues to preoccupy the Church (which is often contradictory in its stance) as is reflected in the canons and church synods. On the contrary, Manichaeism's persecution is intensified. The latter shows the gravity of the Manichaean issue, which went beyond the jurisdiction of ecclesiastical leaders and extended to the political sphere, whereas for the state the issue of Encratites et al. and Messalians was an intra-ecclesiastical affair.[287]

However, subversive action against the authorities or purely political radicalization (as the laws imply) in the ecclesiastical literature does not appear. Nor is there any evidence to correlate social stratification and Manichaean attractiveness. On the contrary, as we shall see in the next chapter, Byzantine Manichaeans come from all social classes. The only testimony involving the 'nomen Manichaeorum' in protest against the emperor is the Hippodrome episode. Whether this was just a label of abuse, or there was indeed a connection between Manichaeans and the party of Greens is beyond the scope of the current research as this incident requires a thorough investigation. In ch.[8] I will return to this subject with additional suggestions.

---

287   Because the boundaries between the several forms of asceticism were blurred, in the implementation of the law the Manichaean label could have been assigned to any kind of extreme ascetics. However, for our discussion, important is the normative and not any occasional framework.

Manichaean Communities, Churches, and Individuals

> Because the name of the church is applied to different things [...] I mean the meetings of the heretics, the Marcionites and Manichaeans and the rest [...] if you ever visit another city, do not merely inquire where the congregation for the *kyriakon* (κυριακόν) takes place [...] nor simply where the church is, but, instead, seek out (for) the Catholic church, because this is the specific name of the true Church.
>
> CYRIL OF JERUSALEM[1]

• • •

> Be careful! A Manichaean is coming ...
>
> JOHN CHRYSOSTOM[2]

∵

1 Introduction

This chapter will focus on specific cases of Manichaean communities and churches and on specific histories of Manichaean individuals – real or imagined. In particular, I will first examine the existence of a Manichaean community and a church in two cities in which a real Manichaean presence seems likely. These are Jerusalem and Antioch in the mid- and the late fourth century respectively. The primary sources on which the study of these two cases will be based belong to the literary genre of homilies. Homilies, when delivered at a specific time and place (i.e. oral speeches, as in our cases), unlike theological treatises, are the kind of sources from which much historical information can

---

1 Cyril, *Catech.* 18.26.1–16 (LFHCC 252, modified). For the original text in Greek see section 2.1.2 in this chapter.

2 Chrysostom, *Hom. Gen.*[1-9](hom. 1) (PG 54:583–584). For the original text in Greek see section 2.2.4 in this chapter.

be obtained. In both cases, the homilies delivered by two outstanding clergy-men of these two cities (Cyril and John Chrysostom) to their catechumens and flock abound in references to and warnings against Manichaeans, their beliefs, behaviours and practices. The works of these two pastors vividly records their concern and worries about a Manichaean influence upon their flock. Secondly, I will examine, case by case, a number of the references that I have been able to track down in Greek anti-Manichaean literature to specific individuals labelled as Manichaeans by the anti-Manichaean authors. This will be done to assess (where possible) whether they were real or imagined Manichaeans.

2   Manichaean Communities and Churches in Named Cities

2.1   *Jerusalem*[3]

2.1.1   Jerusalem's Religious Landscape

In a very fascinating study, J.W. Drijvers describes how Constantine's efforts transformed Jerusalem from an insignificant provincial town into the reli-gious centre of Christianity in a short period of time. Churches were erected to identify landmarks of the life of Jesus, Christian monasteries mushroomed, and hostels were built for pilgrims. However, as Drijvers notes, despite the Christianized image highlighted by Christian sources, the religious landscape of Jerusalem, Palestine, and the rest of the empire throughout the fourth cen-tury remained culturally rich and religiously diverse.[4] It was a transitional era, in which the passage from a dominant pagan culture to Christianity took place. Christianity had not yet been established as the official religion of the state and Christian dogma had not yet been fully formulated. In such an envi-ronment of religious diversity, freedom, and tolerance, various religious groups competed with each other for dominance. Amongst them were the Christians who, so it seems, were still a minority.

This religious pluralism of Jerusalem is amply recorded by Cyril, the bishop of the city (350–386), in his *Catecheses*. The *Catecheses* were the lectures that Cyril delivered daily during Lent for those Christian catechumens preparing to be baptized. According to a note in the manuscripts, *Catecheses* are the shorthand notes of Cyril's oral teachings.[5] This is also shown by Cyril's vivid language. As Cyril underlines, the ultimate goal of his teaching was to protect the catechumens from heretics.[6] To reach this goal, Cyril taught them what Christianity is, by explaining what it is not. For every Christian doctrine he

---

3   Elements from section 2.1 have been published in a different context in Matsangou 2017a.
4   Drijvers 2004, 1–30. See also Drijvers 2015, 211–20.
5   Drijvers 2004, 53.
6   Cyril, *Catech.* 4.2.14–19.

developed, he mentioned heretic 'fallacies' in juxtaposition. For example, in his lecture on the Holy Spirit he explains: "... I will not analyse the precise meaning of his [Holy Spirit] hypostasis; this is ineffable; I will expose the seducing teachings of heretics on this topic, so that no one could be misled by ignorance".[7] Thus, Cyril was 'forced' to expose the 'deluded' dogmas in order to educate his students on how to protect themselves from the other religious groups who lived and acted in the city: the pagans, the Jews, the Samaritans, and the heretics. In fact, Cyril's audience consisted of converts drawn from all these religious groups.

When it comes to heretics, it is clear that in Cyril's use of the word 'heretics' mainly refers to so-called 'Gnostic' and dualist groups such as Marcionites and Manichaeans. At that time, Arians were not always considered heretics since Christian doctrine had not yet been formulated; Arianism was supported by many bishops of the empire, as well as by some emperors of the Constantinian and Valentinian dynasties.[8] Indeed, at the time of the composition of the *Catecheses* (348–350), the emperor was the Arian Constantius II.

Among the heretics, the Manichaeans were apparently the greatest threat to Cyril's disciples. Cyril's references to contemporary Manichaeans are more frequent than to any other religious group. Indeed, Cyril devoted almost the entire sixth lecture, the one against heretics, to the refutation of Manichaeism.

Cyril's presentation of Manichaeism is not a theoretical theological refutation. He had to inform his disciples about the teachings of the Manichaeans so that they would be prepared to deal with them at any time.[9] The fact that he confronted a real problem is repeatedly stressed: "Even now, there are people who have seen Mani with their own eyes'";[10] "Even now, Manichaeans reject as a phantom Jesus' resurrection";[11] "Even now, Manichaeans invoke the daemons" during a mysterious ceremony.[12] From Cyril's records, the image of an active Manichaean community emerges. Firstly, intensive missionary activity is noted. Cyril gives the impression that there was systematic Manichaean propaganda in the area, supported by books that Manichaeans carried with them. During his time, Cyril notes, they were carrying the *Thesaurus of Life*.[13] Furthermore, as Cyril argues, Manichaeans performed some occult rituals

---

7   Cyril, *Catech.* 16.5.1–9.
8   Although condemned at the synod of Nicaea (325), Arianism prevailed throughout the period from Constantius II to Theodosius and was supported by emperors and the majority of the bishops of the eastern churches.
9   Cyril, *Catech.* 6.21.
10 Cyril, *Catech.* 6.20.3–5.
11 Cyril, *Catech.* 14.21.5–7.
12 Cyril, *Catech.* 6.23.9–11.
13 Cyril, *Catech.* 6.22.7–8.

(e.g. the ceremony of the dried fig), which threatened Christian mores.[14] An additional threat was social interaction. It seems that some of Cyril's disciples were associating with Manichaeans. Some of them may well have been former, converted, Manichaeans. This latter group was the most precarious among Cyril's catechumens.[15] Cyril admonished his disciples to stand apart from those who were suspected of belonging to the Manichaean heresy, at least until it was made sure that they had truly converted.[16] The latter can be interpreted as a hint of the existence of Crypto-Manichaeans.

It becomes apparent from Cyril's account of Manichaeism that the Manichaean community in Jerusalem was strong and active. Through their mission, rites, and social interaction, it seems that Manichaeans exerted influence upon Cyril's new Christian proselytes.[17]

2.1.2 Testimonies for the Existence of Manichaean Churches

Along with the many other things Cyril says about Manichaeans, he warns his audience that in the cities, apart from the Catholic Christian churches, there were other heretical churches too. He specifically mentions those of the Marcionites and Manichaeans, which could mislead the Christian catechumens and neophytes who were possibly not able to distinguish them from the Catholic churches. For this reason, he advised his disciples,

> Because the name of the church is applied to different things [...] I mean the meetings of the heretics, the Marcionites and Manichaeans and the rest [...] if you ever visit another city, do not merely inquire where the congregation for the *kyriakon* (κυριακόν) takes place (for other profane sects attempt to call their 'caves' κυριακά), nor simply where the church

---

14   Cyril, *Catech.* 6.33.1–17.

15   Cyril, *Catech.* 15.3.29–32.

16   Cyril, *Catech.* 6.36.3–4. Although Cyril does not mention it explicitly, I believe is referring to former Manichaeans since his admonition is just after an extensive presentation of the Manichaean heresy. Cf. Stroumsa 1985, 275; Lieu 1994a, 205.

17   Especially for the presence of Manichaeans in Palestine, there are many testimonies (apart from Cyril's): (1) the Manichaeans with the icon of Mani (Eusebius, *Ep. Constantiam*); (2) the Palestinian Manichaeans for whom Libanius sought protection (*Ep.* 1253); (3) the Manichaean missionaries (Akua, etc.) who arrived at Eleutheroupolis (Epiphanius, *Pan.* 66.1.1); (4) the proto-Manichaeans who went to Palestine (*AA* 62.7); (5) the missionary Julia in Gaza (Mark the Deacon, *Vita* 85–91); (6) the converted Manichaeans of Zif (Cyril of Scythopolis, *Vit. Euth.* 22); (7) the Samaritans who converted to Manichaeism(?) (Procopius, *Hist. Arcana* 11); (8) the μανιχαΐζοντες monks of the monastery of New Laura (Cyril of Scythopolis, *Vit. Sab.* 124). Cf. Stroumsa 1985, 273–278; Klein 1991, 49.

is, but, instead, seek out (for) the Catholic church, because this is the specific name of the true Church.[18]

Cyril is the only anti-Manichaean author who provides such concrete testimony for the existence of Manichaean churches – not only in Jerusalem, but in other cities too – and his testimony is of particular importance. The value of his *Catecheses* as a source is significant because, as mentioned, they were Cyril's lectures delivered to a live audience and reflected the historical reality in a specific time and place. Furthermore, Cyril's wording creates the impression that there was religious freedom in the mid-fourth century, that heretics such as the Manichaeans and the Marcionites could freely exercise their religion, and that they had places of worship which they called churches.

The above testimony of Cyril for the existence of Manichaean churches is confirmed by subsequent imperial legislation, which as discussed in ch.[3], finally prohibited the functioning of these churches.

2.1.3 The Form of the Manichaean Churches: House-Churches or Distinctive Church Buildings?

But what was the physical form of Manichaean churches? Were they recognizable and public or private and secret? Archaeological findings relating to Manichaean churches in the Roman Empire do not exist. Neither do any Manichaean sources known presently have specific information about this subject. However, what is once more illuminating, is the legislation against Manichaeans and, in addition, the Christian churches of the era. Judging by Cyril's warning to the catechumens against such a confusion, the Manichaean churches must have looked like Christian churches. It is more convenient to start from the latter.

The predominant view in New Testament and Early Christian studies is that the main type of early Christian churches was that of the house-church (κατ' οἶκον ἐκκλησία). Initially, these were the houses of wealthy Christians and later were houses that some Christian individuals offered to their community for religious purposes. Those places which did not differ in appearance from ordinary houses were called by Christians 'churches', or '*Kyriaka*' (Κυριακά), or 'praying houses' (εὐκτήριοι οἶκοι). As Gehring states, "On one point nearly all NT

---

18 Cyril, *Catech.* 18.26.1–16 (Reischl and Rupp 1967, 328; LFHCC 252, modified): Ἐπειδὴ δὲ τὸ τῆς ἐκκλησίας ὄνομα περὶ διαφόρων λέγεται πραγμάτων [...] κυρίως δὲ ἄν τις εἴποι καὶ ἀληθῶς ἐκκλησίαν εἶναι πονηρευομένων τὰ συστήματα τῶν αἱρετικῶν, μαρκιωνιστῶν λέγω καὶ μανιχαίων καὶ τῶν λοιπῶν [...] Κἄν ποτε ἐπιδημῇς ἐν πόλεσι, μὴ ἁπλῶς ἐξέταζε ποῦ τὸ κυριακὸν ἔστι (καὶ γὰρ αἱ λοιπαὶ τῶν ἀσεβῶν αἱρέσεις κυριακὰ τὰ ἑαυτῶν σπήλαια καλεῖν ἐπιχειροῦσι), μηδὲ ποῦ ἔστιν ἁπλῶς ἡ ἐκκλησία, ἀλλὰ ποῦ ἔστιν ἡ καθολικὴ ἐκκλησία.

scholars presently agree: early Christians met almost exclusively in the homes of individual members of the congregation. For nearly three hundred years – until the fourth century, when Constantine began building the first basilicas throughout the Roman Empire – Christians gathered in private houses built initially for domestic use, not in church buildings originally constructed for the sole purpose of public worship".[19] Building on Krautheimer's scheme for the evolution of the Christian meeting places, White suggests three phases for the pre-Constantinian churches: (1) the 'house church phase', (2) the *domus ecclesiae* (renovated houses),[20] and (3) the *aula ecclesiae* (larger halls, which externally "resembled domestic architecture").[21]

This process "is widely recognized".[22]

---

19   Gehring 2004, 1–2, cited in Adams 2016, 1. Adams (2016) challenges the aspect that dur-
      ing the first two/three centuries the "Christian meeting places were 'almost exclusively'
      houses" (198). Arguing that the evidence for house-churches was less substantial than
      scholars have usually argued, he suggests "a number of other kinds of space that could
      plausibly have served as Christian meeting venues", such as: shops, workshops, barns,
      warehouses, hotels, inns, rented dining rooms, bathhouses, gardens, watersides, urban
      open spaces and burial sites.

20   A characteristic example of a house renovated and transformed into *domus ecclesiae* is
      the Dura Europos building. Cf. White 1990, 120–22; Adams 2016, 89–95.

21   White 1990, 102–139 (esp. 129); White 1997; Krautheimer 1986. Cf. Adams, 2016, 3–4. Some
      literary evidence appears to indicate that there were large Christian churches (basilicas?)
      by the second half of the third century. Eusebius (*HE* 8.1.5, LCL 267:252–53) describing the
      growth of the Christian Church over the last thirty years before Diocletian's persecution
      states: "And how could one fully describe those assemblies thronged with countless men,
      and the multitudes that gathered together in every city, and the famed concourses in
      the places of prayer; by reason of which they were no longer satisfied with the buildings
      of older time, and would erect from the foundations churches of spacious dimensions
      throughout all the cities?" (πῶς δ᾽ ἄν τις διαγράψειεν τὰς μυριάνδρους ἐκείνας ἐπισυναγω-
      γὰς καὶ τὰ πλήθη τῶν κατὰ πᾶσαν πόλιν ἀθροισμάτων τάς τε ἐπισήμους ἐν τοῖς προσευκτηρίοις
      συνδρομάς; ὧν δὴ ἕνεκα μηδαμῶς ἔτι τοῖς πάλαι οἰκοδομήμασιν ἀρκούμενοι, εὐρείας εἰς πλάτος
      ἀνὰ πάσας τὰς πόλεις ἐκ θεμελίων ἀνίστων ἐκκλησίας.) According to the Neoplatonist phi-
      losopher Porphyrius (*Contra Christianos*, fr. 76, ca 268–270 CE), "the Christians, imitating
      the construction of temples, erect great buildings (μεγίστους οἴκους) in which they meet
      to pray, though there is nothing to prevent them from doing this in their own homes (ἐν
      ταῖς οἰκίαις) since, of course, their Lord hears them everywhere". (ἀλλὰ καὶ οἱ Χριστιανοὶ
      μιμούμενοι τὰς κατασκευὰς τῶν ναῶν μεγίστους οἴκους οἰκοδομοῦσιν, εἰς οὓς συνιόντες εὔχονται,
      καίτοι μηδενὸς κωλύοντος ἐν ταῖς οἰκίαις τοῦτο πράττειν, τοῦ κυρίου δηλονότι πανταχόθεν ἀκού-
      οντος). Cf. Adams 2016, 84 and White 1997, 104 for the translation in English. Grant (1977,
      150) interpreting Eusebius text argues "it is clear that there were at least some church
      buildings, probably basilicas, before Constantine's time." Contra Grand, White (1990,
      127–28) classifies the churches that Eusebius (*HE* 8.1.5) refers to in the category of *aula
      ecclesiae*, considering them as adapted and renovated *domus ecclesiae*, not with regard
      to their architectural style, but in terms of "numerical growth and social status". "In his
      view", *aula ecclesiae* "did not displace *domus ecclesiae* but overlapped with them" (Adams
      2016, 80).

22   Adams 2016, 3.

However, the earlier forms did not disappear at once, but continued to exist alongside "monumental basilicas" for a long time.[23] First of all, it is reasonable to suggest that a transitional period of time was needed until the number of new church buildings was large enough to replace all the house-churches. Yet, this is not the only reason.

During the period under investigation, there was a constant tension in ecclesiastical and religious affairs. The formation of doctrine, as well as the debates on the Triadological and Christological question took place precisely during this time. The different interpretations of the dogma, which had not yet crystallized, caused confrontations: in terms of ecclesiastical power, things were still fluid. Those who disagreed with the interpretation of one party (the 'others'), were labelled as heretics; thus, there were always some intra-Christian denominations (heresies for the group that prevailed each time) that were outlawed and therefore persecuted.

As a result of these intra-Christian conflicts, the buildings of the public churches changed hands according to the doctrine supported (each time) by the imperial and ecclesiastical authorities. The religious group that was displaced resorted to more private (mainly secret) home-based churches. The same practice was applied by all the persecuted parties, such as by the Arians when the Emperors were Catholics, and by the followers of Nicaea when the Emperors were Arians.[24]

An example of the latter case is what occurred in 380 Constantinople, where for the previous 40 years the bishops had been Arians and Gregory of Nazianzus undertook a campaign to restore the Nicene orthodoxy in the city. For this purpose, according to Sozomenus' depiction, Gregory had transformed much of his residence into a church, naming it Anastasia, because it was the place where the Nicene dogma was resurrected through the speeches of Gregory.[25]

---

23   As White (1990, 23) remarks: "One must also begin to question the notion, often implicitly presupposed in recent architectural histories, that the church's fortunes under Constantine brought about a universal transformation to basilical architecture virtually overnight. On the contrary, the archaeological evidence indicates that *domus ecclesiae* and *aula ecclesiae* forms continued well after that point when basilicas had supposedly become the norm. Thus we find that while monumental basilicas were springing up under the aegis of Constantine, other churches were still being founded following prebasilical patterns". Cf. Adams 2016, 4.

24   For "the different ways in which domestic space functioned" for several Christian groups during the fourth and fifth century (apart from official churches), see Maier 1995a. Cf. Gwynn 2010, 255.

25   Sozomenus, *HE*, 7.5.3: τὸ δόγμα τῆς ἐν Νικαίᾳ συνόδου, πεπτωκὸς ἤδη ἐν Κωνσταντινουπόλει καὶ τεθνηκός, ὡς εἰπεῖν, διὰ τὴν δύναμιν τῶν ἑτεροδόξων, ἐνθάδε ἀνέστη τε καὶ ἀνεβίω διὰ τῶν Γρηγορίου λόγων. Cf. Maier 1995a, 51. Anastasis (Ἀνάστασις) in Greek means resurrection.

Respectively, during Cyril's time, since the Emperor Constantius II (337–361) was an Arian, the Catholics assembled in house-churches. This was especially the case in cities where the bishop was also an exponent of the Arian party, such as Antioch, where the bishops were Arians or Homoian Arians. Therefore, when Cyril warns the catechumens of Jerusalem to be on guard because the Manichaean churches in other cities resemble those of the Christians, he did not mean the newly built basilicas, but rather the house-form churches.

Something similar happened later with the Novatians in Rome. According to the church historian Socrates the Scholastic, when Novatians were persecuted by Pope Celestine (422–32) and "their meeting places confiscated, their bishop Rusticulus conducted worship in households".[26] As Maier points out, alongside the splendour and the dignity of the basilicas, there was another *impressionistic* religious landscape composed by the dissidents, heretics, schismatics, etc.: in brief, by anyone who disagreed with the official Church. While a reconstructive project aiming to transform cities like Jerusalem and Rome into Christian metropolises was running, various movements were congregating on the fringes of the central religious scene.[27]

By observing what happened when an intra-Christian party was deposed from its position of power, one could argue that the Manichaeans who never became a recognized religion in the empire could always be found in this marginal landscape. The Manichaean churches that apparently existed throughout the fourth century and later, whether they were legal or not, never ceased to be considered as churches of heretics, by both the state and all Christian parties. Moreover, whereas in the case of the intra-Christian heresies, the same church-buildings changed hands depending on the faith of the Emperor (or of the local bishop), in the case of the Manichaeans, who had never officially held political or ecclesiastical positions of power, it is reasonable to assume that they never erected (or used) separate churches, such as the official Christian churches that began to be built under Constantine. Instead, it is likely that their churches always had the form of house-churches.

That the Manichaean churches in the Roman Empire may have always had the form of house-churches can also be inferred by the legal sources. As we saw in ch.[3], one of the main goals of anti-Manichaean laws was to deprive Manichaeans of their assembly places, in order to make it impossible for them to assemble. The most effective measures to this end were the confiscation

---

26   Socrates, *HE* 7.11.2 (SC 506: 45): Καὶ οὗτος ⟨ὁ⟩ Κελεστῖνος τὰς ἐν Ῥώμῃ Ναυατιανῶν ἐκκλησίας
      ἀφείλετο καὶ τὸν ἐπίσκοπον αὐτῶν Ῥουστικούλαν κατ᾽ οἰκίας ἐν παραβύστῳ συνάγειν ἠνάγκα-
      σεν. See also Maier 1995b, 234.

27   Maier 1995b, 235.

of such places and the property restrictions against Manichaean individuals. The impression created by the expressions used in these laws for the description of the Manichaean assembly places is that they had the form of private homes and not of "distinctive church buildings". Thus, according to the first anti-Manichaean edict (372) of the code (Cod. theod.), Manichaeans assembled in "houses and habitations".[28] As it appears from the following laws of Theodosius, such "houses and habitations"[29] that hosted Manichaean *conventicles* were found both in cities (small towns and in famous cities)[30] and in the country. The law continues to specify that they also looked like Christian churches: Manichaeans [and other heretics] "should not show walls of private houses after the likeness of churches".[31] The same impression is given by the wording of subsequent laws, where Manichaeans appear to assemble in "private buildings",[32] or "meet in private houses",[33] which, according to the law, they "try boldly to call churches".[34]

Apart from the wording of the law describing Manichaean assembly places, the fact that the target of the law itself was the real estate of Manichaean individuals confirms the hypothesis that these places were indeed houses.[35]

The domestic setting of Manichaean churches is also supported by Manichaean scholars. As BeDuhn argues, the "evidence unequivocally attests that Manichaeism within the Roman Empire operated as a cultic association largely confined to the domestic sphere, lacking any civic or public component".[36] Some additional reasons in favour of the house-church scenario could be drawn from the broader context of the marginal religious groups. First, apart from a place of worship, the domestic environment ensured secrecy when the sect was being persecuted. In addition, meetings in private places were a means of protest. As in the case of displaced persons, the choice of humble places was a form of resistance to the opulence of the imperial basilicas. Far from the official public gathering places, there was a network of houses, of deviant worship and teaching, where propaganda and resistance to the political and ecclesiastical authorities took place.[37] Furthermore, the domestic space was also suitable

---

28 Cod. theod. 16.5.3 (372).
29 Cod. theod. 16.5.11 (383): "to build private churches or use private homes as churches".
30 Cod. theod. 16.5.7 (381).
31 Cod. theod. 16.5.11 (383) (Coleman-Norton, 387).
32 Cod. theod. 16.5.65.
33 Cod. justin. 1.5.5.
34 Cod. justin. 1.5.5 (Coleman-Norton, 645).
35 See ch.[3], 4.2.2. Cod. theod. 16.5.7 (381); Cod. theod. 16.5.40 (407); Cod. theod. 16.5.65 (428). Cf. BeDuhn 2008b, 260.
36 BeDuhn 2008b, 259–60. Cf. Lieu 1992, 202.
37 Maier 1995b, 242; cf. Maier 1995a, 49–63.

for propaganda, promoting ideas, recruiting followers, and even for conducting debates. As we have seen in ch.[2], debates apart from public places or squares were also conducted in homes.[38] In this regard, a congregation based in the home of an individual from the upper social classes was of paramount importance. As highlighted in ch.[2], the interconnection with persons such as Marcellus could be very helpful for the successful dissemination of the ideas of a marginal or persecuted religious group.[39]

Especially in the case of Manichaeans, the network of many houses served the cellular and flexible structure of the movement (with small numbers of followers in each community), its survival during persecution since "individual units could easily go underground when threatened",[40] and the missionary spread of the sect, which was Manichaeism's predominant goal.

Lastly, for the record, and for the sense of completeness, it is worth mentioning that both legal and ecclesiastical anti-Manichaean sources (in our case Cyril) often call the Manichaean assembly places caves ('σπήλαια'/sepulchrum).[41] Presumably this should not be interpreted literally, since it is well documented that this was a technical term of religious abuse. In the polemic literature of the era, the word σπήλαιον/sepulchrum, which also means a tomb/grave, is often used for the place of worship of religious opponents. Its intended meaning is to name such 'heretical' structures as a place where anyone who enters dies, instead of being reborn/resurrected, having the exact opposite meaning of the church Anastasia, Gregory's church in Constantinople. The literary play with words relating to *life/life-bringing* versus *death/death-bringing* is not limited to *loci culti*, but also refers to the mysteries, the books of the opponents, and the opponents themselves (especially their mouths and souls).[42] We cannot, of

---

38   Cf. Maier 1995a, 52; Maier 1995b, 243.

39   Cf. Maier 1995a, 49–63; Maier 1995b, 237, 241, 244; cf. Lieu 2015, 125.

40   Lieu 1992, 202; BeDuhn 2008b, 260.

41   Cod. theod. 16.5.7 (*sepulcra constituent*); Cod. theod. 16.5.9 ('secret and hidden assemblies'); Cod. theod. 16.7.3 ('*sepulchrum/a*', 'nefarious retreats'). Cyril, *Catech.* 18.26.13 (Reischl and Rupp 1967, 328): κυριακὰ τὰ ἑαυτῶν σπήλαια καλεῖν ἐπιχειροῦσι.

42   For example, Ammianus Marcellinus (*Res Gestae*, 18.7.7) uses the term 'tombs' for "the famous martyrs' churches" of Edessa, cf. Barnes (1993) and Woods (2001, 258). At another point Ammianus (*Res Gestae*, 22.11.7) states that the use of the term 'tomb' by George the bishop of Alexandria for the temple of Genius was the cause of his murder by a pagan mob. Theodoret of Cyrrhus (*HE* 230) calls the Messalian monasteries *sepulchra*/dens of robbers (σπήλαια λῃστρικά). About the 'death-bringing' mysteries: Cod. theod. 16.5.5: "If any person by a renewed death should corrupt bodies that have been redeemed by the venerable baptismal font". Theodoret of Cyrrhus, *HE* 232: οὕτως ὁ θεῖος Φλαβιανὸς τὴν δυσώδη διορύξας πηγὴν καὶ γυμνῶσαι παρασκευάσας τὰ θανατικὰ νάματα (eucharistic wine). About persons: *AA* 48.3; Cyril, *Catech.* 6.27 (Reischl and Rupp 1848, 190): Λέγε, φησὶν, ὁ Ἀρχέλαος πρὸς τὸν Μάνην, ὃ κηρύσσεις. Ὁ δὲ [ὡς] τάφον ἀνεῳγμένον ἔχων τὸ στόμα [...]. Zacharias of Mytilene,

course, rule out the possibility that some of the Manichaean churches were actually caves (or cave-houses or cave-churches). This is especially the case in the areas examined, since the geography of the landscape makes the presence of churches, monasteries, and houses carved into the rocks very common.[43]

2.1.4 Manichaean House-Churches: Recognizable and Public or Secret and Private?

An additional question remains whether these Manichaean house-churches were known to local communities as Manichaean churches or places where Manichaeans used to gather, or whether Manichaeans instead met in secret. State religious policy towards the Manichaeans during the fourth century will be illuminating in order to answer this question. Based on the extant legal sources we can divide the investigated period into three phases that may correspond to different practices: (1) 302–313, (2) 313–372 (which includes the case of Jerusalem), and (3) 372/380s onwards (which includes the case of Antioch).

Regarding the first phase, after Diocletian's rescript (302), it is reasonable to assume that the Manichaean congregations continued secretly until the (so-called) edicts of 'religious toleration' (in 311 and 313). These granted all religious groups the right to meet freely and practice their religion and cults in public.[44] The same applies to the third phase[45] during which the main target of all the decrees were the Manichaean assemblies and churches. The secrecy surrounding the meetings of the Manichaeans is illustrated in the language of the law by expressions such as conventicles,[46] secret and hidden assemblies,[47] nefarious retreats,[48] and wicked seclusions.[49] Thus, the only period during which it is likely that the Manichaeans had recognizable (or even distinctive) church-buildings and met freely in public remains the second phase (within which Cyril's episcopacy falls), when they were not persecuted, specifically

---

The Syriac Chronicle 7: "the *Akoimetoi*, outwardly appeared to men honourable, and were adorned with the semblance of chastity, but were inwardly like whited sepulchres, full of all uncleanness"; Theodoret of Cyrrhus, *HE* 231.15–16 (about Messalians).

43   About the various and varying functions that the caves in the broader area of Palestine could have had, see Zangenberg 2014, 195–209.

44   Galerius' Edict (311) and the Edict of Milan (313), in Eusebius *HE* 8.17 and 10.5, respectively.

45   This phase was examined in detail in ch.[3].

46   Cod. theod. 16.5.7 (381): ne in conventiculis oppidorum.

47   Cod. theod. 16.5.9 (382).

48   Cod. theod. 16.7.3 (383): Eos vero, qui manichaeorum nefanda secreta et scelerosos aliquando sectari maluere secessus, ea iugiter atque perpetuo poena comitetur, quam vel divalis arbitrii genitor Valentinianus adscripsit vel nostra nihilo minus saepius decreta iusserunt.

49   Cod. theod. 16.10.24 (423).

from the edits of 'religious toleration' until the first anti-Manichaean laws in the 370s–380s.[50] Yet, the fact that there are no laws against Manichaeans included in the codes from that period does not necessarily mean that such laws were never issued or that there was a tolerance towards the Manichaeans. As said, it is probable that some laws were deliberately omitted by the compilers of the codes. Such an example could have been Gratian's law in 378/79 which advanced a tolerant policy towards some heretics. The law, in specific, forbade Manichaeans to congregate in houses of worship and practice their religion, while other religious groups were allowed to do so with special permission. Eusebius, in his *Life of Constantine*, records a law promulgated by Constantine against heretics which is not included in the Cod. theod.. In it, Constantine, as emperor, partly rescinded his policy of religious toleration and (probably sometime around 326–330) issued a decree against five specific heresies. These were: Novatians, Valentinians, Marcionites, Paulians, and those called Cataphrygians. The list of heretics concluded with the general wording "and against all heresies".[51] Manichaeans were not included among the five heresies. The decree forbade congregations and confiscated houses of worship of the above heretics. In any case, Constantine's edict did not explicitly mention the Manichaeans, so we cannot be sure whether the above decree had any effect on Manichaeans and their churches.

So, under the precondition that there was religious tolerance and no edict was issued between 313 and 372 against the Manichaeans, the latter, logically, should have benefited and, as Cyril claims, practiced their religion openly in their own churches.

As far as the ownership status of these house-churches is concerned, these buildings were either for collective use or private habitations.[52] In particular, they could have been houses that (1) either belonged to Manichaean individuals, (2) houses which Manichaean men and women had transferred as bequests to their community,[53] (3) or later (when Manichaean real estate had evaporated), houses of non-Manichaeans in which Manichaeans used to assemble.[54]

---

50   BeDunhn (2008b, 260) holds also the same view (i.e. that this is the only possible period during which Manichaean meeting places could have had a more public character). As an example of such a place BeDuhn brings the *topos Mani*, a private estate near Kellis, mentioned in the Manichaean *KAB*: 320, 513 (Bagnall 1997, 102, 112). Cf. Brand 2019, 243–46.

51   Eusebius, *Vit. Const.* 3.63–66. Modern scholarship dates the edict to between 324 and 330. Eusebius places it after Nicaea (325) and the synod of Antioch (326), see Cameron and Hall 1999, 306f. Cf. Matsangou 2017a, 401.

52   Cod. theod. 16.5.9 (382).

53   Cod. theod. 16.5.9 (382); Cod. theod. 16.5.65 (428).

54   Cod. theod. 16.5.40 (407); Cod. theod. 16.5.65 (428); Cod. justin. 1.5.5.

Another case of houses that possibly could have been turned into gathering places were the houses confiscated by the state that were derelict (hovels). As Lieu argues, "the large number of houses which had been declared 'derelict' (*caducus*) as a result of imperial confiscations at the end of the third century, might have offered ideal shelter for Manichaean conventicles".[55]

2.1.5   Manichaean Churches as Congregations

The Greek word ἐκκλησία ('church'/ecclesia), before it acquired the meaning of a specific building, signified an 'assembly' of people, which was its literal meaning. I have argued above that the target of all the decrees against Manichaeans was these congregations where the mysteries of the sect were celebrated. But why did Cyril worry about his catechumens, lest they be confused and be found watching the Manichaean mysteries? Was this possible? Could the Manichaean gatherings and mysteries exert any attraction over the converts to Christianity, forming likewise a disruptive factor for the Christianization of the empire?

As Drijvers points out, the biggest obstacle to the Christianization programme was the exclusivity required by the new religion. Even those who preferred Christianity, who at the time of Cyril were probably the minority, apparently had a problem with the strict Christian rule of monotheism. Conversion to Christianity meant a change of lifestyle; they had to get used to the one and unique worship, something difficult to achieve overnight. Therefore, for a long time, it is likely that Christians continued to visit other religious congregations too.[56] Something similar had happened with the early Jewish-Christians (Judeo-Christians), who continued to participate in traditional Jewish worship, such as continuing to go to the synagogue. At the same time, however, they participated in the new worship, meeting each other in the Christian house-churches for the Eucharistic meal.[57]

It is quite probable then that one could meet Cyril's catechumens or even Christian neophytes in Manichaean churches. Some of them might have been former Manichaeans. This could be inferred from Cyril's instructions to his disciples. At the end of a long list of forbidden things that his students were supposed to avoid, including astrologers, diviners, Samaritans, Jews and their Sabbaths, Cyril underlines that above all they had to avoid going to heretic

---

55   Lieu 1992, 202; Cod. theod. 16.5.3, 16.5.40.7.

56   Drijvers 2004, 115f. About Christians attending Hellenic cults, see Trombley 1993 and 1994, Fowden 1978 & 1998, Chuvin 1990, Bowersock 1990.

57   About Christians in Jewish synagogues, see Judith Lieu 2004. See also Judith Lieu 1998, 71–82 and 2016, esp. 52, 62, 95, 142, 243. Smith 1984, 8.

congregations.[58] Furthermore, in the lecture concerning the Manichaeans, and just after the description of the ceremony of the dried fig, Cyril wonders: "Are you receiving, oh man, the teaching of such a mouth? On meeting him, do you greet him with a kiss?".[59] "Let him who is in communion with them realize among whom he places himself".[60] The above could refer to social interaction. However, the combination of teachings, kissing, and communion suggests that it is a reference to a Manichaean congregation. What we learn about these congregations from researchers working on Manichaean sources is illuminating.

As said in ch.[5] the Manichaean ritual meal consisted of two parts: the alms-service, during which the catechumens brought the offerings to the Elect, and the central ritual, the holy meal, before which the catechumens had to depart. The same structure existed already from the second century in the Christian ritual meal (Holy Eucharist). For both ritual systems, the two parts were stages of the same ceremony. At the end of the first stage, before the withdrawal of catechumens, a prayer over them took place (δέησις ὑπὲρ τῶν κατηχουμένων).[61] Cyril 'reveals' some information about a petitionary prayer said by the Manichaean Elect over their catechumens, which, as he comments with sarcasm, is a curse rather than a blessing. As he claims, strengthening the reliability of his source, this was confessed to him by former Manichaeans.[62] Cyril is referring to the Apology to the Bread, which is a testimony known to us at present only by anti-Manichaean writers.[63] However, in order to draw some conclusions, it would suffice to say that Cyril's disciples could probably stay during the first part of the Manichaean ritual: the teachings and the offerings. What they saw would definitely be confusing because it was something very similar to what they knew from the Christian churches.

Therefore, it was not only the names which were common (Κυριακόν, Ἐκκλησία) and the buildings which were similar, but the structure of the rites was also identical, and this was the problem. Because while the content (i.e.

---

58   Cyril, *Catech.* 4.37.16–17.

59   Cyril, *Catech.* 6.33.14–15 (Reischl and Rupp 1848, 202): Παρὰ τοιούτου στόματος, ἄνθρωπε, δέχῃ διδασκαλίαν; Τοῦτον ὅλως ἀπαντήσας ἀσπάζῃ φιλήματι.

60   Cyril, *Catech.* 6.25.4–5 (Reischl and Rupp 1848, 190): Ὁ ἐκείνοις κοινωνῶν, βλεπέτω μετὰ τίνων ἑαυτὸν ἐντάσσει.

61   For the Manichaean holy meal, see BeDuhn 2000b, 144–148. For the stucture of the Christian Eucharist see Justinus Martyr, *Apol.* A: 65–67, and the text of the Divine Liturgy – attributed to Chrysostom – which is still in use in Eastern Christian worship. Cf. Dix 1949, 36–47, esp. 36–38, 41; Bradshaw 1996, 2002 and 2012. See also ch.[5], 2.3.2.

62   Cyril, *Catech.* 6.32.6–7.

63   P.Rylands 3, Gr. 469 (Roberts 1938, 12–42); *AA* 10.6; Epiphanius, *Pan.* 66.28.65; Cyril *Catech.* 6.32. See also Vermes 2001, 54, fn. 69.

the theology of worship of the Manichaean and the Christian holy meal) differed radically, the similarity in form, structure, and terminology made this difference indiscernible for catechumens and simple Christians. As BeDuhn points out in commenting on the different theology of the Manichaean and Christian sacred meal, in the Christian Eucharist, holiness enters the cosmos, consecrates matter (bread and wine) and saves the participant by his divinization. In Manichaeism, on the contrary, it is the participants (Elect) who liberate and save the divine elements already present in the material food.[64]

2.2 *Antioch*

2.2.1 Antioch's Religious Landscape

I have already highlighted in previous chapters that much of John Chrysostom's [hereafter Chrysostom] work consists of oral homilies, which he delivered, like Cyril, to his students and flock.[65] In Chrysostom's speeches too, the concerns, the worries and the warnings about Manichaeans abound.[66] Chrysostom delivered his lectures both at the congregations in Antioch, when he was a presbyter (386–398), and in Constantinople where he was a bishop (398–404). In the Antiochene homilies, the references to Manichaeans are much more numerous than those in Constantinople. This is to be expected because Chrysostom served the Antiochene church as a cleric for many more years (380–398: twelve as a presbyter and six as a deacon) than Constantinople.[67] Additionally, although Christianity was the official religion of the state (since 380), and anyone who deviated, even slightly, from the official doctrine was considered a heretic and was persecuted, Antioch still remained a strongly multireligious city in comparison to Constantinople.[68] Antioch was a Hellenistic city, and one of the largest and most important cities of the era; it was a city of merchants, administrators, yet, a city from which many known 'heresiarchs'

64　BeDuhn 2000a, 14–36, esp. 20–21. For the similarities between Manichaean and Christian ascesis and ranks of priesthood, see ch.[6], section 4.1 and ch.[2], section 4, respectively.

65　Liebeschuetz 2011, 133: "The writings of Chrysostom are of two kinds: sermons, and what might be called 'literary works', treatises". In his work he has a lot of references to the Manichaeans, however he had not written any treatise about them (cf. Chris L. de Wet, 2021, 225–52).

66　In Chrysostom's writings the fighting against Manichaeans is vital, cf. ch.[5], 2.2 & 3.3 about fasting, marriage and the idea of consubstantiality of creatures/creation with God; about the Manichaean belief that evil is steadfast and that man's change for the better is impossible, see ch.[5], 3.2. Chrysostom warned his fellow citizens that the Manichaeans, for all issues related to marriage, fasting, etc., gave the most destructive advices, see ch.[5], 3.3.1 & ch.[6], 3.1.2.

67　Maxwell 2006, 3; Liebeschuetz 2011, 119.

68　Maxwell 2006, 3; Liebeschuetz 2011, 115; Kelly 1995, 134.

arose.[69] Apart from heretics, the pagan and the Jewish communities of the city were still very large and active. The exponents of the official church had, therefore, to confront many opponents.[70] As Maxwell remarks,

> the diversity of the population in Antioch intensified the danger, from the preacher's point of view, of blurring the lines between Christian and non-Christian, or, perhaps worse, between orthodoxy and heresy. Every social interaction, every conversation in the marketplace could lead people astray. So Chrysostom made it his mission to explain carefully exactly what was and was not proper Christian belief and behavior.[71]

As one can notice, the religious landscape of Antioch at the end of the fourth century had many analogies to that of Jerusalem in the mid-fourth century, something that makes the comparison of the two cases stimulating. Manichaeans, as depicted in Chrysostom's writings, had an especially strong base in Antioch.[72] Apart from Chrysostom, other testimonies confirming this situation are those of Libanius and the account of the Manichaean missionary Julia. Libanius, at whose school of rhetoric Chrysostom studied before embarking on his Christian career,[73] composed his orations and letters at about the same time.[74] In one of his letters Libanius asked Priscianus, the governor of Palaestina Prima, to protect the Manichaeans of his region from the ill-treatment they suffered from Christians.[75]

2.2.2   The Sources

Sermons as historical sources are of great importance, especially if the particular context in which they were delivered (time, city, church) is known.[76] Chrysostom's sermons were delivered in the church, most likely during the

---

69   For instance: Nicolaus, Tatian, Paul of Samosata, Nestorius, Eutyches, etc. Cf. Young, 2006, 235–251, esp. 244–45.

70   Maxwell 2006, 4.

71   Maxwell 2006, 4.

72   Gardner and Lieu 2004, 110.

73   Liebeschuetz 2011, 117, 118: "Palladius tells us that the young Chrysostom studied rhetoric under a sophist whose name he does not give. [...] Socrates confirms that the sophist under whom Chrysostom studied rhetoric was Libanius". Socrates, *HE* 6.3.1 (SC 505: 265): Ἰωάννης Ἀντιοχεὺς μὲν ἦν τῆς Κοίλης Συρίας, υἱὸς δὲ Σεκούνδου καὶ μητρὸς Ἀνθούσης, ἐξ εὐπατριδῶν τῶν ἐκεῖ, μαθητὴς δὲ ἐγένετο Λιβανίου τοῦ σοφιστοῦ καὶ ἀκροατὴς Ἀνδραγαθίου τοῦ φιλοσόφου. See also Cameron 1998, 668–69.

74   Maxwell 2006, 3–4.

75   Libanius, *Ep.* 1253.

76   Sandwell 2008, 99.

service and usually commented on a passage from the Bible.[77] Some of them were delivered at the new cathedral of Antioch (Golden Church), while others at the Old Church (or elsewhere).[78] The whole style and spontaneity of their language reveals that they were intended for oral use, regardless of whether later on, in their published form, they would have been polished.[79]

In one of his homilies, for example, Chrysostom, after apologizing for his absence from the previous assembly, urges the faithful to attend the preaching of the day very carefully.

> [...] Please manifest for my sake willingness and seriousness during the teaching, [...] this is the favour I am asking you also today. [...] For this reason, I need to see around me insightful eyes, awakened minds, elevated way of thinking, tight and precise arguments, alert and fully awake souls.[80]

On another occasion, he points out that hearing requires training. This training will enable his listeners to distinguish the heretical teachings. So, Chrysostom prompts them to pay attention daily during the preaching for, as he stresses, "even if you should not comprehend today, you will comprehend tomorrow" (κἂν σήμερον μὴ καταλάβῃς, αὔριον καταλήψῃ).[81] Sometimes Chrysostom explains that he will go in-depth on a subject which in his previous preaching he had failed to develop sufficiently due to the lack of time.[82] Occasionally, he interrupts his speech in order to make sure that his audience understood him; if not, he repeats the point he was making. However, as it seems, sometimes his listeners turn out to be hopeless. Although Chrysostom repeats the same things over and over again, and his audience ought to have become teachers by then, they look like careless students who have not learned anything. So, Chrysostom explains that he cannot proceed to preaching, because then it would be as if he would be more interested in receiving applause rather than in caring for his students. This being the case, he considers it more important

77   Liebeschuetz 2011, 133.
78   Chrysostom, *Hom. Gal.* 2:11 (PG 51:371.25–26): Τῇ προτέρᾳ συνάξει ἐν τῇ ἐκκλησίᾳ τῇ καινῇ συναχθεὶς μετὰ τοῦ ἐπισκόπου, ταύτην ἐν τῇ παλαιᾷ εἶπεν εἰς τὴν περικοπὴν τοῦ Ἀποστόλου See also Mayer 1997, 72–73.
79   Maxwell 2006, 6–7.
80   Chrysostom, *Hom. Gal.* 2:11 (PG 51:371).
81   Chrysostom, *Hom. Heb.* 8. The homilies were issued by the presbyter of Antioch Constantine from the notes of the tachygraphers. The majority of researchers argue in favour of a Constantinopolitan provenance of all the homilies except for Opelt who supports an Antiochene derivation. Allen and Mayer (1995b) are in-between, see esp. 336–348.
82   Chrysostom, *Hom. 2 Cor.* 4:13 (homiliae 1–3), 2.

that his listeners learn the doctrines of their faith, rather than talking to them about pagans, Manichaeans and Marcionites about whom, as he argues, he could say a lot.[83]

Thus, there is broad scholarly agreement that Chrysostom's homilies were live lectures, delivered in a specific time and place. It is not easy, however, to settle the question of which lectures were preached in Antioch and which in Constantinople. Initially, scholars considered that homilies which belonged to a cohesive series according to the manuscript tradition were preached as a group in one of the two cities. This assumption has been challenged as problematic by Mayer and Allen, who support the view that the individual sermons in each series could have been delivered in different cities. So, as they argue, some series of speeches (Col., Phil. and Heb.) "contain material of both Antiochene and Constantinopolitan derivation".[84] According to Mayer, the only secure criterion of provenance is when the text itself certifies that Chrysostom was either presbyter or bishop; yet, such references are rare. Likewise, the dating and provenance of some sermons remain uncertain.[85]

2.2.3   Chrysostom's Main Target: Greeks, Jews, and Manichaeans

The main target of Chrysostom's polemic was the Jews and the Greeks. References to pagans amount to hundreds and to Jews up to thousands. However, as Chrysostom warns in one of his sermons:

> And if you hear that somebody is not a Greek or a Jew, do not rush to conclude that he is a Christian, [...] because this is the disguise the Manichaeans and all heresies use, in order to inveigle the naïve.[86]

In De sacerdotio (one of his treatises, ca. 388–390) Chrysostom likens the Church to a city in danger of being besieged by its enemies. He identifies those enemies as Greeks, Jews, and Manichaeans.[87] Regarding Chrysostom's references to heretics, there are many more against Manichaeans and Arians than against other 'heretics'. Yet, Arianism for Chrysostom, as well as for many

---

83   Chrysostom, *Hom. Heb.* 9 (PG 63).
84   Allen and Mayer 1995a, 271; Allen 2013, xii.
85   Mayer 2005; Allen 2013, xi–xv; Allen and Mayer 1995a, 270–289; About *In epistulam ad Hebraeos* (homiliae 1–34) see Allen and Mayer 1995b, 309–348. Allen and Mayer 1994, 21–39; Sandwell 2008, 99–100; Maxwell 2006, 6–7; Malingrey and Zincone in EAC 2014, 2:431.
86   Chrysostom, *Hom. Heb.* 8 (PG 63:73).
87   Chrysostom, *Sac.* 1–6.

Catholics at that time, was considered another kind of heresy, if one at all. Presenting briefly the heretics until his time Chrysostom says:

> [...] the first heresy of all was that of Marcion; [...] After this that of Sabellius [...] Next that of Marcellus and Photinus [...] Moreover that of Paul of Samosata [...] Afterwards that of the Manichaeans; for this is the most modern of all. After these the heresy of Arius. And there are others too.[88]

The Manichaeans are the last, as the most recent, in the list of the old heresies. After this group, another class of heretics follows, starting with Arius.

The Manichaeans in Chrysostom's sermons are classified and compared either with the Greeks and Jews or with the Marcionites and Valentinians. Indeed, as it seems, for Chrysostom (the same applies for Cyril) the above religious groups comprised mainly the heretics. "When Peter came to Antioch", Chrysostom points out, there were only Greeks and Jews, and not any Manichaeans, Marcionites or Valentinians; "but why should I number all the heresies?"[89] Something similar is repeated in *De sacerdotio*:

> For to what purpose does a man contend earnestly with the Greeks, if at the same time he becomes a prey to the Jews? or get the better of both these and then fall into the clutches of the Manichaeans? [...] But not to enumerate all the heresies of the devil [...].[90]

2.2.4 The Classic Exemplar of Heretic: Be Careful! A Manichaean is Coming!

The Manichaeans were the classic example that Chrysostom used in order to instruct his audience about how to deal with heretics, their false teachings, and practices. Many times, Chrysostom gives the impression that his listeners will encounter Manichaeans at every turn of Antioch's streets and will have to debate with them. Was Julia among them? Indeed, in some of his speeches,

---

88 Chrysostom, *Hom. Heb.* 8 (PG 63:73): Οἷον, πρώτη μὲν πάντων αἵρεσις ἡ Μαρκίωνος· [...] Μετ' ἐκείνην ἡ Σαβελλίου, [...] Εἶτα ἡ Μαρκέλλου καὶ Φωτεινοῦ, [...] Εἶτα ἡ Παύλου τοῦ Σαμοσατέως, [...] Εἶτα ἡ Μανιχαίων· αὕτη γὰρ πασῶν νεωτέρα. Μετ' ἐκείνας, ἡ Ἀρείου. Εἰσὶ δὲ καὶ ἕτεραι.

89 Chrysostom, *Hom. Gal.* 2:11 (PG 51:379): Τότε τοίνυν, [...] Ἢ γὰρ Ἕλληνες, ἢ Ἰουδαῖοι, οἱ τὴν γῆν οἰκοῦντες ἅπαντες ἦσαν· οὔτε δὲ Μανιχαῖος, οὔτε Μαρκίων, οὔτε δὲ Οὐαλεντῖνος, οὐκ ἄλλος οὐδεὶς ἁπλῶς· τί γὰρ δεῖ πάσας καταλέγειν τὰς αἱρέσεις.

90 Chrysostom, *Sac.* 4.4 (NPNF[1] 9): Τί γάρ, ὅταν πρὸς Ἕλληνας μὲν ἀγωνίζηται καλῶς, συλῶσι δὲ αὐτὸν Ἰουδαῖοι; ἢ τούτων μὲν ἀμφοτέρων κρατῇ, ἁρπάζωσι δὲ Μανιχαῖοι [...] καὶ τί δεῖ πάσας καταλέγειν τοῦ διαβόλου τὰς αἱρέσεις.

Chrysostom prepares the faithful on how to refute Manichaeans in these confrontations by 'setting up' potential dialogues. Such dialogues, for example, exist in his homilies on Genesis (386 and 388),[91] where Chrysostom defends the *ex-nihilo* (out of nothing) model of creation by combating the Manichaean claim that matter is a pre-existent first principle, eternal and antagonistic to God. In his first homily on *Genesis* which he delivered at the beginning of the Lent in Antioch in 386, Chrysostom cautions:

> Be careful! A Manichaean is coming saying, Matter is ingenerated; answer to him, *In the beginning God created the heavens, and the earth*, and you immediately debunked all his vain delusion. Yet, they say they do not believe the sayings of the Scriptures. So then, for this reason evade and avert him as a maniac. [...] And, they say, how could something possibly have come into being out of nothing?[92]

A little further on, Chrysostom sets up a new dialogue on the same subject:

> And say; *In the beginning God created the heavens, and the earth.* And if a Manichaean will come forward to speak, or a Marcionite, or those who are infected with the doctrines of Valentinus, or any other person, say to him this; and if you see him laughing, weep, as if he were a maniac.[93]

A similar dialogue (again on the pre-existence of matter) also appears in his second series of speeches on *Genesis* in 388:

> For if a Manichaean will come saying that matter was pre-existent, or a Marcionite, or a Valentinian, or a Greek, say to them; *In the beginning*

---

91   The first series of homilies, consisting of nine speeches on the first three chapters of *Genesis*, were delivered in Antioch in 386, at the beginning of Lent, in the metropolitan church. The second series of homilies, consisting of 67 speeches commenting on the entire book of *Genesis*, were "probably preached partially during Lent 388", cf. Malingrey and Zincone in *EAC* 2014, 2:431.

92   Chrysostom, *Hom. Gen.*[1-9] (hom. 1) (PG 54:583–584): Σκόπει δέ. Προσέρχεται Μανιχαῖος λέγων, Ἀγέννητός ἐστιν ἡ ὕλη· εἰπὲ πρὸς αὐτόν, Ἐν ἀρχῇ ἐποίησεν ὁ Θεὸς τὸν οὐρανὸν, καὶ τὴν γῆν, καὶ πάντα τὸν τῦφον αὐτοῦ κατέστρεψας εὐθέως. Ἀλλ' οὐ πιστεύει τῷ ῥήματι τῆς Γραφῆς, φησίν. Οὐκοῦν διὰ τοῦτο αὐτὸν ὡς μαινόμενον διάκρουσον καὶ ἀποστράφηθι [...] Καὶ πῶς ἐξ οὐκ ὄντων γένοιτ' ἄν τι, φησί.

93   Chrysostom, *Hom. Gen.*[1-9] (hom. 1) (PG 54:584–585): καὶ λέγε Ἐν ἀρχῇ ἐποίησεν ὁ Θεὸς τὸν οὐρανὸν καὶ τὴν γῆν. Κἂν Μανιχαῖος προσέλθῃ, κἂν Μαρκίων, κἂν οἱ τὰ Οὐαλεντίνου νοσοῦντες, κἂν ὁστισοῦν ἕτερος, τοῦτο προβάλλου τὸ ῥῆμα κἂν ἴδῃς γελῶντα, σὺ δάκρυσον αὐτὸν ὡς μαινόμενον.

God created the heavens, and the earth. But he does not believe in the Scriptures. So then, avert him as a maniac and confused.[94]

Elsewhere, discussing the same topic, Chrysostom stresses: "and you see again how the Manichaeans", explaining all things with their own reasoning and taking examples from earthly things, dare to say "It was impossible, [...] for God to create the world without matter".[95] As Chrysostom points out, the Manichaeans alienate creation from God (τὴν κτίσιν ἀλλοτριούντων)[96] and "very foolishly", "introduce another creator of the world besides the true one".[97]

However, despite Chrysostom's talent in instructing his flock, as it seems, some among them were convinced by the Manichaean argumentation. Interpreting Christ's saying to the robber "today you will be with me in paradise" (Luke 23:43), Chrysostom interrupts his speech in order to present in detail the Manichaean reasoning and argumentation and asks his audience repeatedly to ensure they had understood him: "Here be careful; because the Manichaeans, interpreting this passage, claim" that there will be no resurrection of the bodies because it is unnecessary. Chrysostom continues: "I wonder whether you understood what I said, or do I have to say it again? [...] They say, therefore, the robber entered Paradise without his body; how could this happen, since his body was not yet buried".[98] The Christian belief in the resurrection of bodies was indeed a thorny issue, provocative to common sense, and was a difficult issue that required delicate handling. The following interpretation of the words 'death' and 'resurrection' that Chrysostom identified as Manichaean in origin should have been more convincing:

But first it is worth while to hear what those who are infected with the Manichaean doctrines say here, who are both enemies to the truth and

---

94   Chrysostom, *Hom. Gen.*[1-67] (PG 53:29.54): Κἂν γὰρ Μανιχαῖος προσέλθῃ λέγων τὴν ὕλην προϋπάρχειν, κἂν Μαρκίων, κἂν Οὐαλεντῖνος, κἂν Ἑλλήνων παῖδες, λέγε πρὸς αὐτούς Ἐν ἀρχῇ ἐποίησεν ὁ Θεὸς τὸν οὐρανὸν καὶ τὴν γῆν. Ἀλλ᾽ οὐ πιστεύει τῇ Γραφῇ. Ἀποστράφηθι λοιπὸν αὐτὸν ὡς μαινόμενον καὶ ἐξεστηκότα.

95   Chrysostom, *Hom. Eph.* (hom. 1–24), *Hom.* 23 (PG 62:165): β'. Μανιχαίους δὲ ὁρᾷς πάλιν, πῶς πάντα ἀπὸ τῶν οἰκείων λογισμῶν τολμῶσι φθέγγεσθαι; Οὐκ ἠδύνατο, φησίν, ὁ Θεὸς ἄνευ ὕλης ποιῆσαι τὸν κόσμον. Πόθεν τοῦτο δῆλον; Χαμόθεν ταῦτα λέγουσι καὶ ἀπὸ τῆς γῆς καὶ ἀπὸ τῶν παρ᾽ ἡμῖν. Ὅτι ἄνθρωπος, φησίν, οὐ δύναται ἑτέρως ποιῆσαι. Kelly 1995, 58.

96   Chrysostom, *Hom. Matt.* (hom. 1–90), *Hom.* 49 (PG 58:498).

97   Chrysostom, *Hom. 2 Cor.* (hom. 1–30), *Hom.* 8. Cf. Kelly 1995, 96.

98   Chrysostom, *Hom. Gen.* (PG 54:613,39–44, 54.613.51–52): Ἆρα ἐνοήσατε τὸ λεχθέν, ἢ δεύτερον αὐτὸ πάλιν εἰπεῖν ἀνάγκη; [...] Εἰσῆλθεν οὖν, φησίν, εἰς τὸν παράδεισον ὁ λῃστὴς οὐ μετὰ τοῦ σώματος πῶς γὰρ, ὁπότε οὐκ ἐτάφη τὸ σῶμα αὐτοῦ.

war against their own salvation. What then do these allege? By death here, they say, Paul means nothing else than our being in sin; and by resurrection, our being delivered from our sins.[99]

2.2.5   Were Any Manichaeans Among Chrysostom's Listeners?

Examining Chrysostom's speeches, even the earlier ones (380s), one gets the impression that the Manichaeans during his preaching did not attend the congregation, at least overtly. Preaching usually took place after the readings and before the second part of the mass, when catechumens and non-believers had to depart. Nevertheless, Chrysostom seems sure that whatever he says will reach the ears of the Manichaeans. Therefore, sometimes he addressed them as if they were present and intended to provoke a confrontation with them through the faithful. In some of his later speeches (390s) it is clear that the Manichaeans were certainly absent, although Chrysostom would prefer them to have been present for a direct confrontation: "I would wish they were present, the Manichaeans who most deride all this, and those diseased in Marcion's way, so that I might fully stop their mouths".[100] Elsewhere he asks: "Where are those foul-mouthed Manichaeans who say that by the resurrection here [Paul] means the liberation from sin?"[101]

It would be reasonable to assume that, after a series of laws against Manichaeans during the 380s, their public appearances (especially inside churches) and their public debates were scarce. This would certainly be supported by the absence of representations of such debates in Chrysostom's works of the next decade (390s). Probably, some Manichaeans may even have abandoned Antioch because of Chrysostom's persistent and continuous polemic. One of them might have been the Manichaean missionary Julia, who departed for Gaza at about that time.[102] However, the Manichaean danger

---

99   Chrysostom, *Hom. 1 Cor.* (hom. 1–44), *hom.* 38 & 39 (PG 61:324) (*NPNF*[1], 12:228): Πρῶτον δὲ ἄξιον ἀκοῦσαι τί λέγουσιν ἐνταῦθα οἱ τὰ Μανιχαίων νοσοῦντες, καὶ τῆς ἀληθείας ἐχθροὶ, καὶ τῇ οἰκείᾳ πολεμοῦντες σωτηρίᾳ. Τί οὖν οὗτοι λέγουσι; Θάνατον ἐνταῦθα, φησὶν, οὐδὲν ἄλλο λέγει ὁ Παῦλος, ἢ τὸ ἐν ἁμαρτίᾳ γενέσθαι, καὶ ἀνάστασιν τὸ τῶν ἁμαρτιῶν ἀπαλλαγῆναι.

100   Chrysostom, *Hom. Matt.* (hom. 26) (PG 57:247): ἐβουλόμην παρεῖναι καὶ Μανιχαίους τοὺς μάλιστα ταῦτα κωμῳδοῦντας, καὶ τοὺς τὰ Μαρκίωνος νοσοῦντας, ἵνα ἐκ περιουσίας αὐτῶν ἐμφράξω τὰ στόματα.

101   Chrysostom, *Hom. 1 Cor.* 39 (PG 61:335) (*NPNF*[1], 12:409): Ποῦ νῦν εἰσι τὰ πονηρὰ τῶν Μανιχαίων στόματα, τῶν λεγόντων ἀνάστασιν αὐτὸν ἐνταῦθα λέγειν τῆς ἁμαρτίας τὴν ἀπαλλαγήν; And elsewhere (*Hom. 2 Cor.* 4:13 2 (PG 51:282.28) he wonders: Ποῦ νῦν εἰσιν οἱ τὴν Παλαιὰν διαβάλλοντες; *Hom. 2 Cor.* 4:13 (PG 51:281.16t): Εἰς τὴν ἀποστολικὴν ῥῆσιν τὴν λέγουσαν, "Ἔχοντες δὲ τὸ αὐτὸ Πνεῦμα τῆς πίστεως, κατὰ τὸ γεγραμμένον" καὶ πρὸς Μανιχαίους, καὶ πάντας τοὺς διαβάλλοντας τὴν Παλαιὰν καὶ διαιροῦντας αὐτὴν ἀπὸ τῆς Καινῆς, καὶ περὶ ἐλεημοσύνης.

102   Mark the Deacon, *Vit. Porph*, 85.1–7.

does not seem to have faded out. The homilies *in Matthaeum* have more references to the Manichaeans than any other work, giving the impression that the Manichaean danger in Antioch had increased during the last ten years of the fourth century. The latter is compatible with the hypothesis I made in chapter [3], that for a period of 40 years (383–423) in the Eastern part of the Empire, the Manichaean threat was underestimated. At this time, the authorities had their attention focused on the Eunomians, who were the main target of contemporary anti-heretical legislation. Chrysostom seems to fill the gap of the law in his own way.

Thus, the Manichaeans of Antioch may not have been present in the church, and would have been more discreet in public life. Yet, they still constituted a threat for the faithful who, in the context of social life, met them, discussed with them, or even befriended them. The Manichaean ideas, practices, and negative influence they had upon his audience (i.e. causing apostasies) must have been a real problem, engaging Chrysostom until the end of his career as a presbyter.[103]

For our preacher, Manichaean dualism created a chain of side effects at all levels, especially in terms of anthropology and ethics of social life. Chrysostom was particularly concerned about the appeal that the Manichaean view of free will had upon his flock. As he says, the Manichaeans, invoking the saying "No one can come to me, unless the Father who sent me draws him (John 6:44)", argue "that nothing lies in our own power" and will.[104] And they insisted that "evil is steadfast", although everyday life and scriptures are full of examples of

---

103 Apart from the aforementioned issues, Chrysostom often attacks: (1) the Manichaean tenet of consubstantiality (see indicatively: *Natal.*: PG 49:359–360, *Hom. 1 Cor.* 7, *Hom. Gen.*[1-9] (hom. 1)); (2) their claim that Christ did not assume human flesh (see indicatively: *Natal.*: PG 49:359; *Anom.* 7 PG 48:759 & 766; *Hom. Matt.* 82; *Hom. 2 Tim. 1–10:2*). Discussing on the nativity of Christ on Christmas Day of 386 (*Natal.* PG 49:359–360), Chrysostom observes that impiety is not the incarnation of God, but the Manichaean idea that the creatures share God's substance: τί λέγεις, εἰπέ μοι, ὦ ἄνθρωπε; [...] Οὐχ ὁρᾶτε τουτονὶ τὸν ἥλιον, οὗ τὸ σῶμά ἐστιν αἰσθητὸν καὶ φθαρτὸν καὶ ἐπίκηρον, κἂν μυριάκις ἀποπνίγωνται Ἕλληνες καὶ Μανιχαῖοι ταῦτα ἀκούοντες; Further, Chrysostom many times during his speeches defends OT against the Manichaean attacks and blames them for mangling the NT. The Manichaeans, as Chrysostom argues, curse the NT in two ways: (1) cutting it off from the Old, and (2) cutting off passages from it, which, as they claim, blame the OT. However, in order to outargue the Manichaeans, Chrysostom says that he would present a passage from NT that testifies the unity with the OT, and which, as he emphasizes, is still used today by the Manichaeans (τὴν καὶ παρὰ τοῖς Μανιχαίοις σωζομένην ἔτι καὶ νῦν). See indicatively: *Hom. Matt.* (1–90): 16 & 51; *Hom. Rom.* (1–32): 13; *Hom. 2 Cor. 4:13* (PG 51:281); *Hom. Gal.* 4.21–22 & 4.24; *Hom. Heb.* (1–34): 9; *Hom. 2 Cor.* (1–30): 21; *Hom. Eph.* 23; *Hom. 2 Cor. 4:13*, 1–3: 2.

104 Chrysostom, *Hom. Jo.* (*hom.* 1–88) *hom.* 46 (PG 59:257).

sinners who were sanctified. With such ideas, Chrysostom observes, no one cares about virtue (ἐπιμελήσεταί τις ἀρετῆς).[105] In fact, as Chrysostom points out, those who attribute sin to nature and to the members of the body find pretexts to sin fearlessly.[106] Chrysostom admonished the faithful not to search for the cause of their miseries, as the Manichaeans do, concluding that evil is a first principle.[107] Instead, they have to thank God even for their misfortunes and not just for the good things he gives them, in contrast to Manichaeans who blaspheme God although he "bestow[s] blessings on them every day".[108] Believers, by thanking God even for the lesser things, put the Manichaeans to shame for affirming that our present life is evil.[109] On the contrary, eunuchs and those who circumcise themselves, "cutting off their member as being hostile" "open the mouths of the Manichaeans", who "call the body a treacherous thing, and from the evil principle".[110]

Chrysostom condemns the Manichaean hyperbole in ascesis[111] and never ceases to warn his audience about the show of asceticism that Manichaeans perform, pointing out that they are pretending in order to appeal and deceive the faithful, and create apostates from faith, especially in the ascetic milieu.[112] For this reason, Chrysostom's attitude, especially towards extra-urban ascetics and hermits, is very cautious and sometimes ambivalent. On the one hand, he urges his flock to visit the monks, while on the other he points out the danger of the distorted Manichaean ascesis, and encourages urban asceticism which he considers more social and safer. "But inconsistency", as Liebeschuetz remarks, "is indeed found to some degree in all the ascetic writers, who are enthusiastic for the ascetic life, but must also emphasize that they do not adhere to the dualism of the Manichaeans".[113]

105 Chrysostom, *Hom. Matt.* (*hom. 1–90*) *hom.* 26 (PG 57:340.15–24).
106 Chrysostom, *Hom. Matt.*, *hom.* 58 (PG 58:600). Liebeschuetz 2011, 194. Kelly 1995, 96.
107 Chrysostom, *Oppugn.* (PG 47.365).
108 Chrysostom, *Hom. Eph.* (*hom. 1–24*), *Hom.* 19.
109 Chrysostom, *Hom. Matt.* (*hom. 1–90*), *Hom.* 55 (PG 58:546–48).
110 Chrysostom, *Hom. Gal.* Ch. Eʹ (PG 61:668–669); Chrysostom, *Hom. Matt.*, *Hom.* 62.
111 Chrysostom, *Hom. Matt.*, *hom.* 55; *Hom. 1 Tim.* (*1–18*): 12.
112 Chrysostom, *Hom. Gen.*¹⁻⁹ (PG 54:584–585 & 54.613.39–44); *Hom. Gen.*¹⁻⁶⁷ (PG 53:29.54); *Hom. 1 Tim.* (*1–18*): 12. Cf. Kelly 1995, 59.
113 Liebeschuetz 2011, 153, cf. pp. 21, 134, 137, 194.

3 'Manichaean' Individuals: Real or Imagined?

In some cases, patristic literature does allude that there were some latent alliances between Manichaeans and other *noble* heretics. In specific, there are in total twenty-eight references to certain individuals (six anonymous) who are designated as Manichaeans. Seventeen out of these individuals will be discussed, case by case, in the next section of this chapter in a chronological order.[114] The rest are discussed, to a lesser or greater extent in other chapters.[115] The aim of this investigation is to assess whether they were real or labelled Manichaeans. It is important to note from the outset, that the supposed Manichaeans were not first-generation Manichaean missionaries, but Roman citizens who, among a range of choices in the religious landscape of their time, possibly, opted in favour of Manichaeism.

3.1 Sebastian

According to Athanasius of Alexandria, Sebastian – a high-ranking commissioner in the army – was a merciless Manichaean who tortured Catholics to death and collaborated with Arians. Athanasius, who himself was persecuted by Sebastian, records extensively the maltreatment the catholic clergy and laity suffered by him in his *Apologia de fuga sua* and in *Historia Arianorum ad Monachos*.[116]

According to Athanasius' *Apologia*, when Sebastian was the *dux of Egypt* he acted as the right-hand man of George, the Arian bishop of Alexandria.[117] Athanasius recounts in detail one of the operations against the Catholics that George entrusted to Sebastian:

> [...] in the week after the holy Pentecost, the people, having fasted, went forth to the cemetery to pray, because all were averse to communion with George: that wickedest of men being informed of this, instigated against them Sebastian, an officer who was a Manichaean. He, accordingly, at the head of a body of troops armed with drawn swords, bows, and darts, marched out to attack the people, although it was the Lord's day: finding but few at prayers, – as the most part had retired because of the lateness

---

114 About Sebastian, Anastasius and Erythrius' wife, cf. Matsangou 2017b, 165–167.

115 See a table including all the cases at the end of the chapter.

116 Athanasius, *Fug.*, 6–7; Athanasius, *H. Ar.* §59–63, pp. 216–18 and §70.3–73.2, pp. 221–23.

117 Sebastian started his military career as a *dux of Egypt* (356–58), soon he was promoted to *Comes Rei Militaris* (363–78) and finally in 378 he was appointed by Valens *Magister Peditum Orientis* – which was the highest military rank. See Jones et al. 1971, 812–13. See also Lieu 1992, 127.

of the hour, – he performed such exploits as might be expected from them. Having kindled a fire, he set the virgins near it, in order to compel them to say that they were of the Arian faith: but seeing they stood their ground and despised the fire, he then stripped them, and so beat them on the face, that for a long time afterwards they could scarcely be recognized. Seizing also about forty men, he flogged them in an extraordinary manner: for he so lacerated their backs with rods fresh cut from the palm-tree, which still had their thorns on, that some were obliged to resort repeatedly to surgical aid in order to have the thorns extracted from their flesh, and others, unable to bear the agony, died under its infliction. All the survivors with virgins they banished to the Great Oasis. The bodies of the dead they did not so much as give up to their relatives, but denying them the rites of sepulture they concealed them as they thought fit, that the evidences of their cruelty might not appear.[118]

Both Socrates and Theodoret in their *HE* reproduce verbatim the above incidents from Athanasius' *Apologia*, highlighting that "all these facts will be best told in the words of him [Athanasius] who so suffered".[119]

In his *Apologia*, Athanasius explains that he was forced to flee his episcopal see in Alexandria in 356, because he and his presbyters were persecuted by the Arians who intended to convict them with capital punishment.[120] In the words of Theodoret, the emperor Constantius II wished "not only to expel, but also to condemn the holy Athanasius to death". To this end, he "dispatched Sebastian, a military commander, with a very large body of soldiery to slay him as if he had been a criminal".[121] Sebastian did not act alone: there was a human network in the army and administration connected to him that supported him. As a *dux* he exerted power over the Prefects (πραιποσίτοις) and the leaders of the army (στρατιωτικαῖς ἐξουσίαις).

In the *Historia Arianorum ad Monachos* Athanasius describes how Sebastian delivered the Catholic churches into Arian hands. The Arians, Athanasius says, had as assistants in their plans the *dux* Sebastian, who was an immoral young

---

118   Athanasius, *Fug.* 6–7. The translation is from Socrates' text, *HE* 2.28 (*NPNF*² 2: 150–51).

119   Theodoret, *HE* 11. Socrates, *HE* 2.28 (*NPNF*² 2): "such are the words of Athanasius in regard to the atrocities perpetrated by George at Alexandria". The same text from apologia is also found in *Menologia Imperialia* (eleventh cent.), "Vita sancti Athanasii Alexandrini".

120   Athanasius, *Fug.* 3.21–24 (SC 56: 136): καὶ ἡμᾶς, καὶ πρεσβυτέρους ἡμετέρους, οὕτως ἐποίησαν ζητηθῆναι, ὥστε, εἰ εὑρεθείημεν, κεφαλῆς ὑποστῆναι τιμωρίαν. Another similar episode where Athanasius stars, but with a good end this time for his flock and which ended in the flight of Athanasius, is the one that narrates Athanasius in *Fug.* 4.

121   Theodoret, *HE* 10 (Third exile and flight of Athanasius).

Manichaean man, the Prefect (Cataphorius), the *count/comes* (Heraclius), and the *Catholicos* (Faustinus) who acted as the master-mind.[122] When the Arian emperor Constantius II commanded that the Catholic bishops should be expelled from the churches and be replaced by the Arians, the command was executed by the general Sebastian who organized and co-ordinated the whole enterprise in collaboration with the magistrates.[123]

And the General Sebastian wrote to the governors (πραιποσίτοις) and military authorities (στρατιωτικαῖς ἐξουσίαις) in every place; and the true Bishops [the Catholic clergy of Egypt and Libya] were persecuted, and those who professed impious doctrines [Arians] were brought in their stead.[124]

From among the deposed Catholic bishops and presbyters some were banished, others were sentenced to work in the stone-quarries, others were persecuted and tortured to death, "and many others they plundered thoroughly".

> Straightway Bishops were sent off in chains, and Presbyters and Monks bound with iron, after being almost beaten to death with stripes.[125] The soldiers and General Gorgonios drove away their relatives from their homes, knocking them and grabbing the bread of the dying.[126]

Apart from the clerics, they "banished also forty of the laity, with certain virgins", who after being beaten severely with palm rods some of them succumbed to their injuries. Moreover, they destroyed monasteries, and attempted to burn monks, plundered houses, seized and stole properties, and hindered the distribution of alms to the poor and to the widows.[127] When Arian clerics realized that the poor and widows were supported by the Catholic priests, they persecuted the former and accused the Catholic priests before the *dux*. Sebastian, as Athanasius points out, being a Manichaean, was pleased, "for there is no mercy

---

122 Athanasius, *H. Ar.* 59.1–3. About the names of the officers, see Tardieu 1988, 497. Sebastian stars in chs. 59–73.

123 Athanasius, *H. Ar.* 63, 70 (*NPNF*[2] 4): "For behold, he has now again thrown into disorder all the Churches of Alexandria and of Egypt and Libya, and has publicly given orders, that the Bishops of the Catholic Church and faith be cast out of their churches, and that they be all given up to the professors of the Arian doctrines. The General began to carry this order into execution".

124 Athanasius, *H. Ar.* 72 (Opitz, 222; *NPNF*[2] 4): ὁ μὲν στρατηλάτης Σεβαστιανὸς ἔγραψε τοῖς κατὰ τόπον πραιποσίτοις (a military title) καὶ στρατιωτικαῖς ἐξουσίαις, καὶ οἱ μὲν ἀληθῶς ἐπίσκοποι ἐδιώχθησαν, οἱ δὲ τὰ τῆς ἀσεβείας φρονοῦντες ἀντ' ἐκείνων εἰσήχθησαν. καὶ ἐξώρισαν μὲν ἐπισκόπους γηράσαντας ἐν τῷ κλήρῳ καὶ πολυετεῖς ἐν τῇ ἐπισκοπῇ.

125 Athanasius, *H. Ar.* 70 (*NPNF*[2] 4).

126 Athanasius, *H. Ar.* 63 (*NPNF*[2] 4).

127 Athanasius, *H. Ar.* 72 (*NPNF*[2] 4).

in the Manichaeans; nay, it is considered a hateful thing among them to show mercy to a poor man". They also devised a "new kind of court" where "he who had showed mercy was accused" and brought to trial "and he who had received a benefit was beaten".[128]

As Athanasius constantly emphasizes, for all their cruelties against the Catholics, the Arians relied on the authority of the Manichaean *dux* Sebastian.[129] Indeed, in case Sebastian did not mistreat enough the Catholics, they did not hesitate even to threaten him that they would denounce him before the Emperor.[130] Athanasius concludes his narrative alluding, once more, that there was an alliance between the Arians and Manichaeans. As he states, the new Arian bishops were young licentious pagans; although they were not even catechumens, being rich and from well-known families, they obtained their episcopal seats by bribery. Anyone who rejected these 'mercenary' bishops was "locked up in prison by Sebastian (who did all this readily, being a Manichaean)".[131]

It has been argued that Sebastian possibly was labelled as a Manichaean by Athanasius so that the Arians, on whose behalf Sebastian acted, would be correlated to Manichaeans.[132] The argument is that: (1) pagan authors

---

128 Athanasius, *H. Ar.* 61 (*NPNF*[2] 4). Cf. Lieu 1992, 127: "It may be that Manichaeans in Egypt, as they did elsewhere, had the reputation of being uncharitable because they would refuse alms to those who were not of their sect"; Lieu 1994a, 103, fn. 333; Tardieu 1988, 498–99.

129 Athanasius, *H. Ar.* 62 (*NPNF*[2] 4): "But these men have lost even the common sentiments of humanity; and that kindness which they would have desired to meet with at the hands of others, had themselves been sufferers, they would not permit others to receive, but employed against them the severity and authority of the magistrates, and especially of the Duke".

130 Athanasius, *H. Ar.* 60 (*NPNF*[2] 4): "when they had seen that they did not die from the stripes they had received, complained of the Duke and threatened, saying, 'We will write and tell the eunuchs, that he does not flog as we wish'. Hearing this he was afraid, and was obliged to beat the men a second time".

131 Athanasius, *H. Ar.* 73 (Opitz, 223): ἀποστρεφόμενοι γὰρ τοὺς μισθωτοὺς ἐκείνων καὶ ἀλλοτρίους ἑαυτῶν ἐμαστίζοντο, ἐδημεύοντο, εἰς τὰ δεσμωτήρια κατεκλείοντο παρὰ τοῦ στρατηλάτου. ἐποίει γὰρ τοῦτο προθύμως Μανιχαῖος ὤν, ἵνα τοὺς μὲν ἰδίους μὴ ἐπιζητῶσιν, οὓς δὲ ἀπεστρέφοντο δέχωνται ἀνθρώπους τοιαῦτα πράττοντας, οἷα καὶ πρὸ τούτου ἐν τοῖς εἰδώλοις ἔπαιζον.

132 Cf. Lieu 1994a, 102–03; Lieu 1992, 127; Tardieu (1988, 498) referring to the issue concludes: "Telle est la pièce-maîtresse du dossier sur le manichéisme de Sebastianus. Elle est totalement inconsistante. Ce n'est que de la polémique de bas étage. L'évêque d'Alexandrie met dans le même sac ariens, manichéens, juifs, autorités civiles". Whereas Sundermann (2009) seems cautious arguing: "We can only state that by that time [330 CE] Manichaeism was already present there, more or less tolerated until the end of the 4th century and even supported by adherents and sympathizers in the ruling class, such as the *dux*, *comes*, and *magister peditum* Sebastianus (d. 378) who was supposed to be a Manichean *auditor* (which was, however, sheer

(e.g. Ammianus Marcellinus, Libanius, Eunapius and Zosimus), who *à propos* appreciated Sebastian, do not report that Sebastian was a Manichaean,[133] and (2) it is unlikely for a doctrine that was against the taking of life, even that of animals, to have appealed to military officers.[134]

Regarding the former, it is known that Ammianus Marcellinus had a rather negative view of Christianity, and a confused idea about its variant dogmas and parties.[135] It seems probable therefore, that either the issue did not interest him, or that he did not want to reveal the personal religious beliefs of Sebastian as he thought highly of him. The same can be said for Libanius, who, in addition to his friendly relationship with Sebastian, was the one who pleaded with the authorities for religious tolerance towards Palestinian Manichaeans.[136] Regarding the latter, it seems reasonable to guess that a Roman citizen, who became a Manichaean hearer, would not have any reservation for serving in the army, regardless of how high-ranked he was. In addition, the view that there were indeed Manichaeans in the imperial military service is further supported by Roman imperial legislation. According to the Cod. justin., officials in the army were asked "to investigate whether anyone among them" was a Manichaean, "and to reveal him when found" to the authorities.[137]

---

calumny, according to Tardieu, 1988, pp. 494–500)", http://www.iranicaonline.org/articles/manicheism-iv-missionary-activity-and-technique- Cf. Matsangou 2017b, 166. In any case, the fact that, according to Cyril's of Jerusalem testimony (*Catechesis 18*), Manichaeans during the reign of the Arian emperor Constantius II had churches which they called *Kyriaka*, reflects some kind of tolerance.

133   Lieu 1992, 127; Cf. Tardieu 1988, 494–95. Lieu (1994, 102–03, fn. 334) noting that "Sebastianus is labelled as a Manichaean only in Christian sources" remarks: "According to Ammianus he was later nearly declared Emperor by his troops [...] However, he was not called a Manichaean in pagan sources and it is just possible that we are here witnessing a derogatory use of the title of the sect by Athanasius in return for the wrongs he endured at the hands of Sebastianus and his troops". The pagan authors Eunapius and Libanius also praised highly Sebastian for his military qualifications/skills and his incorruptibility (contempt for wealth); indeed, Sebastian and Libanius were friends, cf. Libanius, *Epistles* (318, 350, 454, 520, 596 & 912), Eunapius, *Fragmenta historica* 1:243–244. About Sebastian's military enterprises/campaigns, see also: Zosimus, *Historia nova* (3.12.5–13.1, 4.4.2 & 4.22.4); Magnus Hist., *Fragmentum* 1.16 (apud Malalas *Chronographia*, ch. 3); Ammianus Marcellinus, *Res Gestae* 31.11.2–5. See also Jones et al. 1971, PLRE 1:812–13.

134   Lieu 1994a, 102–03: "It strikes one as odd that a cult which strictly forbade the taking of any form of animal life should find a follower in a commanding officer"; However, on other occasions Lieu seems more open to accept Athanasius' claim that Sebastian was a Manichaean. See for example, Lieu 1992, 127: "The official tolerance of the sect may also be deduced from the high rank of one of its better known converts, Sebastianus".

135   Cf. Woods 2001, 258–59, 264.

136   Libanius, *Ep.* 1253.

137   Cod. justin. 1.5.16.1.

3.2   *Hierax (or Hieracas)*

A person with the name Hierax appears in the anti-Manichaean *AFs* and in the later sources which reproduce the *AFs* (Peter of Sicily and Photius). According to the *sc*, the converted Manichaeans had to anathematize (after Mani's first disciples and parents) a certain Hierax, as "the author of the Manichaean atheism".[138] In the rest of the sources, Hierax is anathematized alongside with Heracleides and Aphthonius as "commentators and exegetes" of Mani's works.

> In addition to this, I anathematize and curse together with all those stated above, Hierax and Heracleides and Aphthonius, the expositors and commentators of this lawless and profane Mani [...].[139]

Both Photius and Peter, in addition, include all three in the list of the twelve first disciples of Mani.[140] Hierax of the *AFs* has been identified by many researchers with the famous Egyptian ascetic of the fourth century, Hierax of Leontopolis, a city located in the Nile Delta.[141] Epiphanius provides us with a detailed report about him in his *Panarion*.[142] As he begins his chapter on the Hieracites which follows the chapter on Manichaeans, "After the savage onset of this rotten, poisonous teaching of Mani, the worst of all heresies and like that of a snake, there arose a man named Hieracas, the founder of the Hieracites".[143]

According to Epiphanius, Hierax was a very talented and learned person.

> [...] he was proficient in Greek and other literary studies, and well acquainted with medicine and the other subjects of Greek and Egyptian learning, and perhaps he had dabbled in astrology and magic. For he was very well versed in many subjects and, as his works show, ⟨an extremely scholarly⟩ expositor of scripture. He knew Coptic very well – the man was Egyptian – and was also quite clear in Greek, for he was quick in every

---

138   See ch.[2], 5.3.1. *sc*, ch. 2 (Lieu 1994a, 236, 238, 252 & 2010, 118): Ἀναθεματίζω τοὺς Μανιχαίου μαθητάς, [...] καὶ Παττίκιον τὸν πατέρα [...] καὶ Καρῶσαν τὴν αὐτοῦ μητέρα καὶ τὸν συγγραφέα τῆς μανιχαϊκῆς ἀθείας Ἱέρακα.

139   *SAF* 36.8 (Goar: 696, Barb. 148.17) (Lieu 2010, 132–133). *LAF* (PG 1:1468b, Lieu 2010, 141).

140   Photius, *c. Manichaeos* 50: Ἐξηγηταὶ δὲ αὐτοῦ καὶ οἷον ὑπομνηματισταὶ γεγόνασιν Ἱέραξ τε καὶ Ἡρακλείδης καὶ Ἀφθόνιος. Peter of Sicily, *Hist. ref. Man.* 67. As Lieu (1994, 267–8) comments: "the claim by Peter of Sicily and Photius that he was a disciple of Mani must be disregarded unless they have a different Hierax in mind".

141   Lieu 1994a, 267–68; cf. Stroumsa 1986b, 310–11.

142   Epiphanius, *Pan.* 67.1.1–8.3.

143   Epiphanius, *Pan.* 67.1.1 (Williams, 316). As Lieu (1994, 267–8) points out, the same order is also followed by Augustine.

way. [...] He wrote in Greek and in Coptic, expositions he had composed ⟨of⟩ the six days of creation, fabricating some legends and pompous allegories. But he wrote on any number of other scriptural subjects and composed many latter-day psalms [...] He practiced calligraphy.[144]

Another basic characteristic of Hierax was his extreme asceticism. As Epiphanius remarks, "he was awesome in his asceticism, and able to win souls to himself; for example, many Egyptian ascetics were convinced by him". Hierax, like the Manichaeans, abstained from meat and "all sorts of foods" and "denied himself wine as well". He also did not "countenance matrimony" because as he said, "since Christ's coming marriage is no longer accept⟨able⟩, and cannot inherit the kingdom of heaven". His main 'heretical' belief, as Epiphanius highlights, was the denial of the resurrection of the bodies. He claimed: "the flesh never rises, only the soul [...] And he collected whatever texts he could ⟨find⟩ in the sacred scripture to support his position." Hierax died at a very old age (over 90).[145]

What seems to worry primarily Epiphanius was the influence that Hierax exerted on the Christian ascetic milieu, "for Hieracas [...] mimics the church's virginity but without a clear conscience".[146] Epiphanius highlights the dissemination of the extreme ascetic practices of the Hieracites to the ascetics of Egypt and Thebaid (and not only) also in his *Ancoratus*.[147] In addition, in the same work he correlates the fact that Hieracites did not believe in the resurrection with the docetic perceptions of the Manichaeans.[148] Chrysostom too, as we have seen, considered that the rejection of the resurrection of the bodies was of Manichaean origin.[149]

The appeal that Hierax had in the ascetic milieu is also illustrated in the work *Vita Sancti Epiphanii* (fifth-sixth cent.). According to the account, Epiphanius, attracted by the fame of Hierax, decided to visit him. "Entering in his monastery" he was impressed as he "found many crowds of people taught by him" (ch. 27).

---

144 Epiphanius, *Pan.* 67.1.2–3; 3.7, 9 (Williams 316, 319).
145 Epiphanius, *Pan.* 67.1.5–9, 67.3.8 (Williams 316–19).
146 Epiphanius, *Pan.* 67.8.1 (Williams 323): "For Hieracas is a winged snake and scorpion which has wings of many kinds, and flies, and mimics the church's virginity but without a clear conscience"; 67.3.8 (Williams 319): "many of those who believe in his doctrines abstain from meat".
147 Epiphanius, *Ancoratus* 82.3.4.
148 Epiphanius, *Ancoratus* 86.1.
149 Chrysostom, *Hom. 1 Cor. 38 & 39.*

Another author referring to Hierax of Leontopolis is the author of the *Sermo contra omnes haereses*, which is falsely attributed to Athanasius. Klein dates the work around 360 and argues that its "similarities to the work of Didymus" and the "dependencies on the writings of Athanasios" "suggests Egypt, perhaps even Alexandria, as the place of origin".[150] The author (Pseudo-Athanasius) appears well aware of the basic tenets of the Manichaeans, whom he calls "dregs of evils and of heresies" (τρυγίους τῶν κακῶν). In his work he discusses the issues of dualism, Docetism, and the rejection of the OT. He also combats Marcion, Valentinus, Basilides, and a certain Hierax who, as he comments, was against marriage and supported virginity.[151]

From what has been said above, it stands to reason that Hierax the ascetic might well have been the same one as in the AFs. The skills of Hierax as described by Epiphanius fit perfectly with the status of authorship and commentator attributed to the Hierax of the AFs. Furthermore, as Lieu remarks, "a person with his qualifications would have been ideal as a translator and copyist of the Manichaean texts". If this was the case, it is not improbable, as Wisse suggested, that he could have used the Manichaean books he translated in order to support his extreme asceticism, since during his day, orthopraxy was more important than orthodoxy.[152] The latter explains why he could have later been labelled as Manichaean.

3.3   *Aphthonius and Heracleides*

As noted above, in both the short and long AFs, as well as in the writings of Photius and Peter of Sicily, two other persons in addition to Hierax, namely Aphthonius and Heracleides, are anathematized as expositors and commentators of Mani's writings.

We first hear about Aphthonius from the church historian Philostorgius. Philostorgius portrays Aphthonius as a leader (προεστώς) of the Manichaeans and very famous for his wisdom and eloquence. According to the account, the famous Arian theologian and orator Aetius, drawn by the fame of Aphthonius, went from Antioch to Alexandria in order to compete against him in a debate. The debate took place during the reign of Constantius II. The victory of Aetius was so great that, as Philostorgius says, Aphthonius after a few days died of his deep grief.

---

150   Klein 1991, 33–34. Cf. Pedersen 2004, 134.
151   Pseudo-Athanasius, *Sermo contra omnes haereses* (PG 28:516).
152   Lieu 1994a, 90, 94, fn. 302. As Wisse (1978, 438–440) argues, by considering encratism as the essence of Christianity, Hierax became indiscriminately open to outside influences.

Shortly thereafter, in fact, one Aphthonius, a leader of the Manichaeans (Manichaean madness) who was held in high renown by many for his wisdom and prowess in speech, debated with him in Alexandria in Egypt, for Aetius, drawn by his reputation, came from Antioch to meet him. When they came to grips with each other, no lengthy debate ensued, for Aetius reduced Aphthonius to silence and brought him down from great fame to great shame. So dejected was he by his unexpected defeat that he fell gravely ill and in the end died; his body did not survive the blow more than seven days. Aetius for his part defeated his opponents in debate thoroughly wherever he went and won a brilliant victory.[153]

The title 'leader' (προεστώς) in the quotation above most likely means a Manichaean teacher or a bishop, rather than the one at the top of the hierarchical pyramid, the *archegos*. According to later sources (*SAF*, *LAF*, Peter of Sicily and Photius), Aphthonius was a commentator and expositor of Mani's writings, a task which looks more like the work of a teacher.[154] It is important to keep in mind that the office of the teacher in the Manichaean church was very important and different from that of an ordinary teacher. There were only twelve teachers who held the second position in the pyramid of the hierarchy after the Manichaean *archegos*.[155]

Regarding the identity of Heracleides we do not know anything. According to Lieu "he may have been the author of the "Psalms of Heracleides" in the Coptic Manichaean *Psalm-Book*".[156]

3.4 A Converted Manichaean Woman in Alexandria

Socrates the Scholastic narrates an incident which he dates to the mid-380s, when Theophilus was bishop of Alexandria, and Damasus I was bishop

---

153 Philostorgius, *HE* 3.15.50–60 (Bidez, 46–47; Amidon 2007, 54, modified): μετ' οὐ πολὺ γοῦν Ἀφθόνιός τις, τῆς Μανιχαίων λύσσης προεστὼς καὶ μεγάλην παρὰ πολλοῖς ἐπὶ σοφίᾳ καὶ δεινό-τητι λόγων φέρων τὴν δόξαν, ἐν τῇ κατ' Αἴγυπτον αὐτῷ Ἀλεξανδρείᾳ συμπλέκεται. καὶ γὰρ ἦκε πρὸς αὐτὸν ἐξ Ἀντιοχείας ὁ Ἀέτιος, ὑπὸ τῆς περὶ αὐτὸν φήμης ἑλκόμενος. ὡς δ' εἰς ἅμιλλαν ἀλλή-λοις κατέστησαν, οὐδὲ πολλῆς καταναλωθείσης διελέγξεως, εἰς ἀφωνίαν συνελάσας ὁ Ἀέτιος τὸν Ἀφθόνιον ἐκ μεγάλης δόξης εἰς μεγάλην αἰσχύνην κατήνεγκεν. διὸ καὶ τῷ ἀπροσδοκήτῳ βαρυθυμήσας τῆς ἥττης, νόσον τε ἐπεσπάσατο χαλεπὴν καὶ τῇ νόσῳ πέρας ὁ θάνατος ἦν οὐδὲ περαιτέρω τῶν ἑπτὰ ἡμερῶν διαρκέσαντος τοῦ σώματος ἀπὸ τῆς πληγῆς.

154 *LAF*, ch. 3 (PG 1:1461/1472A).

155 The office of the Teacher, as well as its significance for the Manichaean community, is recorded in the Manichaean letters from Kellis. Cf. Gardner 2006, 317–23 and Brand 2019, 141–42.

156 Lieu 1994a, 268.

of Rome.[157] Theophilus, as he states, being irritated with Petrus, the arch-presbyter of the Alexandrian church, invented the following way in order to expel him from the church. He accused him of having admitted a Manichaean woman "to participate in the sacred mysteries before she had abjured her former heresy".[158]

Although during the inquisitional procedure it appeared that "the woman was received by consent of the bishop", moreover, that the bishop "himself had administered the sacrament to her", the presbyter Peter was expelled from the Alexandrian church.

The historicity of the specific incident, obviously, cannot be supported, since the author himself presents it as a plot in the context of inter-ecclesiastical disputes and confrontations. The value of this piece of information, however, rests first on that it reflects the demonization of Manichaeism, and second on that it confirms the presence of Manichaeans in Alexandria. Indeed, it indicates that there were Manichaeans who wished to convert to Christianity, since it was just after the first wave of laws against Manichaeans that were promulgated by Theodosius I. The same story is reproduced by Sozomenus.[159]

3.5   Anonymous Manichaean Presbyter Converted to Christianity

A testimony for the rank of Manichaean presbyter is preserved in one of the *sayings* of the fathers (*Apophthegmata partum*, "regarding hospitality"). According to the scenery that this text captures from the ascetic milieu (fourth cent.), apart from the wandering Christian ascetics, Manichaean presbyters also travelled across the Egyptian desert to visit with each other.

> An old man in Egypt lived in a desert place. And far away lived a Manichaean who was a presbyter, at least was one of those whom Manichaeans call presbyters. While the Manichaean was on a journey to visit another of that erroneous sect, he was caught by nightfall in the place where lived this orthodox and holy man. He wanted to knock and go in and ask for shelter; but was afraid to do so, for he knew that he would be refused hospitality. Still, driven by his plight, he put the thought aside, and knocked.
>
> The old man opened the door and recognised him; and he welcomed him joyfully, made him pray with him, gave him supper and a bed. The

---

157   Socrates, *HE* 6.1.
158   Socrates, *HE* 6.9 (SC 505: 298): γυναῖκά τινα Μανιχαίαν τὴν θρησκείαν εἰς τὰ ἱερὰ μυστήρια προσδεξάμενος, μὴ πρότερον τῆς Μανιχαϊκῆς αἱρέσεως ἀποστήσας αὐτήν.
159   Sozomenus, *HE*, 8.12.

Manichaean lay thinking in the night, and marvelling: 'Why was he not hostile to me? He is a true servant of God.' And at break of day he rose, and fell at his feet, saying: 'Henceforth I am orthodox, and shall not leave you.' And so he stayed with him.[160]

3.6 Agapius

Agapius and his book the *Heptalogue* (Ἑπτάλογον Ἀγαπίου) appear only in the Byzantine sources written after the fifth-sixth centuries and are both "unattested in extant genuine Manichaean sources".[161] The *sc*, *saf*, and Timothy the Presbyter refer to him as the author of the *Heptalogue*, without any further comment. While, according to Photius, Peter of Sicily and the *laf*, Agapius was one of Mani's disciples and author of the *Heptalogue*.

> I anathematize [...] and the so-called *Heptalogue* of Agapius and Agapius himself.[162]
>
> I anathematize [...] and the book of Agapius which is called the *Heptalogue* [...] (I anathematize) all his remaining disciples, Sisinnios the successor of his madness, Thomas [...] Agapius, [...].[163]

All that we know about Agapius (who may have been a mid-fourth century figure)[164] and his book derives from Photius' *Bibliotheca*.[165] There, Photius speaks of a work, which he does not name, of a certain Agapius, composed of twenty-three short speeches (λογύδρια) and 102 other chapters; it was addressed to a 'fellow-philosopher' of Agapius, a woman named Urania. According to Photius, Agapius pretended to be a Christian, but his work proves

---

160 *Apophthegmata patrum* (*collectio systematica*) 13 (trans. by Gardner and Lieu 2004, 120): Ἦν τις γέρων οἰκῶν ἐν ἐρήμῳ τόπῳ. Ἦν δὲ ἄλλος μηκόθεν αὐτοῦ μανιχαῖος καὶ αὐτὸς πρεσβύτερος, ἐκ τῶν λεγομένων παρ᾽ αὐτοῖς πρεσβυτέρων. Καὶ ὡς ἦλθεν παραβαλεῖν τινι τῶν ὁμοδόξων αὐτοῦ. [...].

161 Lieu 1994a, 270–1.

162 *sc*, ch. 2 (Lieu 2010, 118): Ἀναθεματίζω [...] καὶ τὴν λεγομένην Ἑπτάλογον Ἀγαπίου καὶ αὐτὸν Ἀγάπιον. *saf* 36.8 (Goar): "I anathematize [...] and the so-called Heptalogus of Agapios and Agapios himself".

163 *laf* (PG 1:1468, Lieu 2010, 139, 141); Photius, *c. Manichaeos* 50: Ἡριθμοῦντο δὲ τῷ χορῷ τῶν μαθητευθέντων αὐτῷ καὶ Ἀγάπιος ὁ τὴν Ἑπτάλογον καλουμένην συντάξας καὶ Ζαρούας καὶ Γαυριάβιος. Peter of Sicily, *Hist. ref. Man* 67–68: Ὑπῆρχον δὲ αὐτῷ καὶ ἕτεροι μαθηταὶ τρεῖς Ἀγάπιος ὁ τὴν Ἑπτάλογον συντάξας, καὶ Ζαρούας καὶ Γαβριάβιος. Μηδεὶς ἀναγινωσκέτω τὸ κατὰ Θωμᾶν εὐαγγέλιον [...] μήτε τὴν Ἑπτάλογον Ἀγαπίου.

164 Lieu (1994, 270–71) says that if Eunomius whom Agapius attacked was the "famous Arian leader and the Bishop of Cyzicus, Agapius would have been a mid-fourth century figure". Cf. Lieu 1992, 138–40.

165 Photius, *Bibl.* 179 (124a.17–125a.28)-180.

that he hated Christ more than any other man (μισόχριστος). From the summary of his work provided by Photius, it becomes evident that he shared many common positions with Manichaeism. This enables us to assume that this is the same Agapius condemned by the abjuration formulas and that the work to which Photius is referring is the *Heptalogue*.[166] The main tenets of Agapius as presented by Photius are the following:

(1) He supports the existence of an evil first principle opposing God, which is self-subsisting and eternal; he calls it sometimes 'nature', sometimes 'matter', sometimes 'Satan', or 'devil', or 'master of the world', or 'god of the age', and he gives it various other names.

(2) "He speaks [...] of the sun and the moon as divinities (gods), which he proclaims as consubstantial with God".

(3) He worships and hymns the air (as god), calling it a column and a man, recalling the Manichaean *Column of Glory* which was also called the *Perfect Man or Air*.

(4) He places fire and earth in the domain of evil.

(5) He adopts the Manichaean thesis that Christ was the tree of Paradise (see *AA* 11.1). Agapius claims that he honours Christ, but according to Photius [only] with his lips. This is because although he speaks about Christ's incarnation, baptism, crucifixion, and his resurrection, as Photius comments, he means it differently than what Christians believe.

(6) He maintains that the body belongs to the evil portion, but the soul to the divine, the latter being consubstantial with God.

(7) He claims "that men sin" "by necessity, and in spite of themselves".

(8) He preaches strict asceticism: to abstain from meat, wine and sexual relationships.

(9) He supports the transmigration of souls: Virtuous men are dissolved in God, vicious persons are brought down to fire and darkness, while those in-between had to reincarnate.

(10) He rejects the OT while he uses selectively the Holy Gospel and the letters of Paul, which he perverts. He also relies upon apocryphal works, like the so-called *Acts of the Twelve Apostles*, especially those of Andrew.

(11) He has many loans from pagan superstition. He calls Plato (and other pagan philosophers) divine and holy just like Christ.

In contrast to *Contra Manichaeos*, where Photius says that Agapius was a disciple of Mani, in his *Bibliotheca* he nowhere explicitly says that Agapius was a Manichaean. Indeed, stating that his work could be used for both the refutation of the Manichaeans and of Agapius' disciples, he seems to distinguish the former from the latter, giving the impression that they were two different

---

166   Lieu 1994a, 270–71.

movements, although he does recognize a strong spiritual affinity, and many shared practices. This strikes one as odd, since ten out of the eleven tenets are typically Manichaean theses. Especially the view that the air is a god, which he calls a column and a man, is exclusively a Manichaean idea. So, if we rely on what Photius says, Agapius' Manichaeanness is unquestionable.[167]

3.7 Simplicius the City Prefect of Constantinople (403/6)

Theophanes records that sometime in 403, when Chrysostom was archbishop of Constantinople, the City's Prefect Simplicius, "a Manichaean and a supporter of paganism", erected a silver statue on a pillar of porphyry in honour of the empress Eudoxia. "In front of" this statue, which was located "near St Eirene" (or near St Sophia, according to Socrates), Simplicius "organized noisy choirs and dancing" and raised "a commotion, which distressed John since it did not allow him to celebrate the holy liturgy in peace. For it frequently interrupted the psalm-singing".[168]

3.8 Presbyter Philip

As recorded in Cyril of Alexandria's *Memorandum* (one of the documents of the Acts of the Ecumenical Synod at Ephesus in 431), Nestorius accused the catholic presbyter Philip of Manichaeism, and condemned him as such in a synod he convened, because he was fighting his (Nestorius') heresy.[169]

3.9 Anastasius et al.

3.9.1 Anastasius and His Mother

As Theodorus Anagnostes and Theophanes report, during the reign of the Monophysite Emperor Anastasius (491–518), Manichaeans rejoiced and had a lot of παρρησία (impudence), because they were supported by his mother, Anastasia-Constantina, who was "a zealous devotee of theirs".[170] It was also

---

167   This interpretation differs from that of Lieu (1994, 270–71) who argues: "However, it is just as possible that Agapius was a Christian whose belief in a strong dichotomy between flesh and spirit led to a dualistic theology which was labelled 'Manichaean' by more orthodox-minded churchmen", see also p. 288. Cf. Lieu 1992, 138–40.

168   Theophanes, *Chron.* 79.4–14.

169   ACO (*Ephesenum anno 431*), 1.1.7, 171–72.

170   Theodorus Anagnostes, *HE* 4.448, 454a (GCS, N.F. 3:126, 125): Οἱ Μανιχαῖοι πολλὴν ἐν Κωνσταντινουπόλει παρρησίαν ἔσχον. Theophanes, *Chron.* (de Boor, 136.13–16; Mango and Scott, 209): Μανιχαῖοι δὲ καὶ Ἀρειανοὶ ἔχαιρον ἐπὶ Ἀναστασίῳ, Μανιχαῖοι μὲν ὡς τῆς μητρὸς τοῦ βασιλέως ζηλωτρίας οὔσης καὶ προσφιλοῦς αὐτῶν, Ἀρειανοὶ δὲ ὡς Κλέαρχον, τὸν θεῖον αὐτοῦ ἀδελφὸν τῆς αὐτῆς κακόφρονος μητρός, ὁμόδοξον ἔχοντες. The work of Theodorus is lost (except for few fragments), but this loss is replaced by an epitome (composed mid. 8th cent.) which was used thoroughly by Theophanes and by other byzantine historians. Georgius Monachus (9th cent.) *Chronicon breve*, reproduces the same text.

said that Anastasius himself was a supporter of the Manichaeans.[171] According to Evagrius, when Anastasius was proclaimed emperor, Ephemius, the bishop of Constantinople, forced him to take an oath, together with a written confession, that he would remain faithful to the faith of the Catholic Church. This was because many people maintained that Anastasius was Manichaean-minded.[172] The oath finally was taken before the successor of Ephemius, Macedonius, and Anastasius kept his promise until 507. Afterwards, he changed his stance and followed a Monophysite religious policy. During the episodes that followed the Monophysite Synod of Sidon (510/11) the furious populace, "including women and children and the abbots of the monks, gathered and [...] abused the emperor for being a Manichaean and unworthy of power". Anastasius out of fear "pretended for the time being to be at one with Macedonius".[173]

Apart from the accusations against the emperor and his mother, Anastasius is presented by the sources as having relationships with persons who were also accused of being Manichaeans.

3.9.2 The Manichaean Painter

According to the testimony of Theodorus Anagnostes and Theophanes, sometime in 507, Anastasius commissioned a Syro-Persian Manichaean painter, whom he brought from Cyzicus "in the guise of a presbyter", to decorate one of the imperial palaces and the church of St. Stephen in the district of Aurelianae. His paintings were so provocative that they caused a rebellion in Constantinople.

> Anastasios brought a Syro-Persian Manichaean painter from Cyzicus, in the guise of a presbyter, who dared to depict certain fantastic subjects, quite different from the holy images of churches, in the palace of Helenianai and in St Stephen of Aurelianai, on the instruction of the

---

171   Theodorus Anagnostes, *HE* 4.467 (GCS, N.F. 3:134): τοῦ βασιλέως χαίροντος τοῖς Μανιχαίοις; Theophanes *Chron.* (de Boor, 149–50; Mango and Scott, 229–230): τοῦ βασιλέως χαίροντος τοῖς Μανιχαίοις. Theodorus Anagnostes, *HE* 4.511a: ταῦτα ὁ παρανομώτατος μανιχαιόφρων.

172   Evagrius the Scholastic, *HE* 3.32 (Bidez and Parmentier, 130): Ἐδεδράκει δὲ ταῦτα διότι γε ὁ Ἀναστάσιος δόξαν μανιχαϊκῆς νομίσεως παρὰ τοῖς πολλοῖς εἶχεν.

173   Theodorus Anagnostes, *HE* 4.485 (GCS, N.F. 3:138): Ὁ λαὸς σὺν γυναιξὶ καὶ τέκνοις πλῆθος ὑπάρχων ἄπειρον σὺν τοῖς ἡγουμένοις τῶν μοναχῶν συναθροισθεὶς [...] ὕβριζον δὲ τὸν βασιλέα Μανιχαῖον καλοῦντες καὶ τῆς βασιλείας ἀνάξιον; Theophanes, *Chron.* (de Boor, 154.11–22; Mango and Scott, 235): τὰ δὲ πλήθη σὺν γυναιξὶ καὶ τέκνοις ἡγουμένοις τε τῶν ὀρθοδόξων μοναχῶν ἔκραζον ἀθροισθέντα [...] ὑβρίζοντες τὸν βασιλέα Μανιχαῖον καὶ τοῦ κράτους ἀνάξιον. ὁ δὲ φοβηθεὶς [...] τὰ πλήθη [...] ὑπεκρίθη πρὸς τὴν ὥραν ἐνοῦσθαι αὐτῷ.

emperor who applauded the Manichaeans. This led to a great uprising among the people.[174]

3.9.3   Xenaias or Philoxenos of Hierapolis

As some sources also report, Anastasius also had a close relationship and collaboration with another Syro-Persian 'Manichaean' named Xenaias, who taught aniconic worship.[175] Finally, the text reveals that he was none other than the active leader of the Monophysite faction and bishop of Hierapolis, Philoxenos.[176] In 507 Anastasius invited Xenaias/Philoxenos to Constantinople "as someone of his own persuasion". The crowd together with the clergy and monks, already unsettled by the innovations of the Syro-Persian painter, when they were informed of his arrival protested so violently against him, that Anastasius "was forced to slip him out of the capital secretly".[177] However, the friendly relationship between the two men did not end. Three years later, the Synod at Sidon was convened at the request of Xenaias/Philoxenos and Soterichos of Caesarea and both of them were appointed by the Emperor as

---

174 Theophanes, *Chron.* 149 (Mango and Scott, 229). Theodorus Anagnostes, *HE* 4.467 (GCS, N.F. 3:134): Μανιχαῖον δέ τινα ζωγράφον Συροπέρσην ἀπὸ Κυζίκου Ἀναστάσιος ἤγαγεν ἐν σχήματι πρεσβυτέρου, ὃς ἀλλότρια τῶν ἐκκλησιαστικῶν ἁγίων εἰκόνων ἐτόλμησε γράψαι φασματώδη ἐν τῷ παλατίῳ Ἑλενιανῶν καὶ ἐν τῷ ἁγίῳ Στεφάνῳ Αὐρηλιανῶν γνώμῃ τοῦ βασιλέως χαίροντος τοῖς Μανιχαίοις, ὅθεν καὶ στάσις τοῦ λαοῦ γέγονε μεγάλη. Cf. Charanis 1974, 60.

175 Joannes Diacrinomenus, *HE* 7 (GCS, N.F. 3:155): Ξεναῖας ὁ Φιλόξενος οὔτε Χριστοῦ τοῦ θεοῦ οὔτε ἀγγέλου εἰκόνας ἐν ἐκκλησίᾳ συνεχώρει ἀνατίθεσθαι (set up as objects of worship). Theodorus Anagnostes, *HE* 3.444 (GCS, N.F. 3:124): Ξεναῖας δὲ ὁ δοῦλος τοῦ σατανᾶ τὴν δεσποτικὴν εἰκόνα καὶ τῶν ἀγγέλων ἐδίδασκε μὴ δέχεσθαι.

176 See ch.[6], 5.1. About the activities (uprisings etc.) of Philoxenos of Hierapolis (Maggub) see: the Monophysite church historian Joannes Diacrinomenus, *HE* 7; Theodorus Anagnostes, *HE* 3.444, 4.470–472a, 497a; Theophanes, *Chron.* 149–167; Cyril of Scythopolis, *Vit. Sab.* 141; Evagrius the Scholastic, *HE* 127–130. The story that Xenaias feigned the priest while he was not even baptized, and that the Monophysite bishop of Antioch Peter Knafeus when ordained him as a bishop of Hierapolis declared that the ordination sufficed, instead of baptism, are considered by researchers a mere slander. Theodorus Anagnostes, *HE* 3.444 (GCS, N.F. 3:124): Ξεναῖας δὲ [...] Πέρσης μὲν γὰρ ἦν τῷ γένει, [...] ἐπὶ Καλανδίωνος τὰς περὶ Ἀντιόχειαν κώμας ἀνεστάτου ἀπὸ τῆς πίστεως, ἀβάπτιστος ὢν καὶ κληρικὸν ἑαυτὸν λέγων. τοῦτον Καλανδίων ἀπήλασεν, Πέτρος δὲ ὁ Κναφεὺς ἐπίσκοπον Ἱεραπόλεως αὐτὸν χειροτονήσας Φιλόξενον μετωνόμασεν. μαθὼν δὲ ὕστερον ἀβάπτιστον αὐτὸν εἶναι ἀρκεῖν αὐτῷ τὴν χειροτονίαν ἀντὶ βαπτίσματος ἔφησεν.

177 Theophanes, *Chron.* 150 (Mango and Scott, 230). Theodorus Anagnostes, *HE* 4.470 (GCS, N.F. 3:134): Ξεναῖαν τὸν μανιχαιόφρονα ἤγαγεν Ἀναστάσιος εἰς τὸ Βυζάντιον, τὸν καὶ Φιλόξενον, ὡς ὁμόφρονα. Μακεδόνιος δὲ οὕτω κοινωνίας οὔτε λόγου αὐτὸν ἠξίωσεν, τοῦ κλήρου καὶ τῶν μοναχῶν καὶ τοῦ λαοῦ κατ' αὐτοῦ ταραττομένων. ὅθεν καὶ λάθρα τῆς πόλεως αὐτὸν ἐξήγαγεν Ἀναστάσιος. Charanis 1974, 60.

presidents of the Synod.[178] Xenaias/Philoxenos was finally exiled by Justin in 518/19.[179]

Apart from Xenaias/Philoxenos, at least three other cases of well-known bishops of the Monophysite faction were labelled as Manichaeans, namely, Peter the Fuller/Cnapheus, Julian of Halicarnassus, and Severus of Antioch. The fact that both Severus and Zacharias, who was his biographer and author of the *sc*, seem to have "had a first-hand knowledge of Manichaean Literature" is worth investigating.[180]

3.9.4   John the Archdeacon

The next case associated to Anastasius and characterized by the sources as a Manichaean is John, who was the archdeacon of the bishop of Constantinople Timothy. Timothy is presented by the sources as having a weak character, willing to be in line with Anastasius' anti-Chalcedonian church policy. However, finding himself in a difficult situation under pressure, he anathematized those who rejected the Synod of Chalcedon in the presence of his archdeacon John (512/13). "But," as the sources record, "John, being a Manichee, insulted Timothy and reported the matter to the emperor [Anastasius]".[181]

We note that apart from Anastasius, there was a circle of people around him who the aforementioned authors accused of being Manichaeans. Taking into account that among them were known Monophysites, for whom the term 'Manichaean' was not used in its literal sense, one could argue that the same might have been the case for the unknown 'Manichaeans' presented above (i.e. the Syro-Persian painter/presbyter and the archdeacon John). Since it was the era of disputes over the Christological issue the use of the term 'Manichaean' as a religious abuse was at its peak. The term was "applied to anyone whose

---

178   Theophanes, *Chron.* 153 (Mango and Scott, 234). Theodorus Anagnostes, *HE* 4.472a, 497a. Cyril of Scythopolis, *Vit. Sab.* 141.

179   Theophanes, *Chron.* (de Boor, 165.21–23): Ξεναΐαν δὲ τὸν Φιλόξενον, ἐπίσκοπον Ἱεραπόλεως, μανιχαιόφρονα ὄντα, καὶ Πέτρον Ἀπαμείας ἐξώρισεν ὁ εὐσεβὴς βασιλεὺς Ἰουστῖνος σὺν πᾶσι τοῖς μετέχουσι τῆς λώβης αὐτῶν.

180   Cf. Lieu 1994a, 110.

181   Theodorus Anagnostes, *HE* 4.507 (GCS, N.F. 3:134): Ἰωάννης δέ, ὁ ἀρχιδιάκονος Τιμοθέου, Μανιχαῖος ὑπάρχων […] Τιμόθεον […] τῷ βασιλεῖ ἐμήνυσεν. Theophanes, *Chron.* 158 (Mango and Scott, 239–240): "When the abbot of the monastery of Dios died, Timothy came to appoint the new abbot. But the one who was about to be appointed said that he would not accept benediction from a man who rejected the Synod of Chalcedon. Timothy said, 'Anathema to anyone who does not accept the Synod of Chalcedon.' And so the abbot consented to being appointed by him. But Timothy's archdeacon, John, being a Manichee, insulted Timothy and reported the matter to the emperor".

Christological doctrines or ascetic practices met with disapproval".[182] Monophysites, however, were labelled as Manichaeans more than any other group, indeed by all the other groups, because Monophysite Christology was often associated with Manichaean Docetism.

During the first years of his reign, Anastasius exercised a moderate and neutral religious policy. From 507 onwards he openly supported the Monophysite party and he was in constant conflict with Macedonius, the Catholic bishop of Constantinople. That same year he invited both the Manichaean painter and Xenaias/Philoxenos to Constantinople. Both of them were Syro-Persians in origin and, according to the sources, Manichaeans. Their coming caused riots and uprising.

In current research, the 'Manichaean painter' has been treated sometimes as a Manichaean literally, and sometimes as a Monophysite.[183] Indeed, Gulácsi supports the former interpretation and argues, based on Theophanes' wording (i.e. "in the guise of a presbyter"), that he was "a leading Manichaean elect, one of the 360 presbyters of the Manichaean Church".[184] However, the above expression (ἐν σχήματι πρεσβυτέρου) could also mean that he was a presbyter only in appearance (i.e. in pretence). In any case, what is certain is that his paintings did not follow the established tradition of the Catholic Church (ἀλλότρια τῶν ἐκκλησιαστικῶν ἁγίων εἰκόνων ἐτόλμησε γράψαι φασματώδη) and that was the reason that "led to a great uprising among the people". What kind of illustrations could have triggered such riots?

Gulácsi, who supports the view that he was a Manichaean, says that his "paintings most likely included" "icons of Jesus or narratives scenes from his life" because these were the common themes in the Byzantine and Manichaean iconographic repertoire. Further, she assumes that what provoked the uprising might have been either some unorthodox iconographic details or the prejudice towards the artist's religious identity.[185] In the case he was a Monophysite, he may have introduced novelties consistent with contemporary Monophysite theses (e.g. depictions of the Triad denoting theopaschist beliefs),[186] or aniconic representations (Monophysites seem to have considered it offensive to depict the divine persons of the Godhead). The latter scenario is reinforced by the testimony that Xenaias/Philoxenos also taught not to accept icons of

---

182   Whitby 2000, 173.
183   Charanis 1974, 60. Xatziantoniou 2009, 69.
184   Gulácsi 2015, 42–44.
185   Gulácsi, 2015, 43.
186   Xatziantoniou 2009, 69–70.

Christ and angels in the churches.[187] It is worth noting that as Monophysitism and Iconoclasm were associated in the minds of the Catholics,[188] later on Xenaias, along with Severus and Peter the Fuller, were considered to be pioneers of iconoclasm. At the iconophile ecumenical synod of Nicaea in 787, all three were "included in a list of anti-Chalcedonians as iconoclasts".[189] In any case, the word φασματώδη (like a vision/phantasmal) points to painting techniques expressing the immateriality of the subjects.

Concerning Anastasius himself and whether he was a Manichaean or μανιχαιόφρων/μανιχαΐζων, probably what we witness here is the use of the term as an epithet of opprobrium, since the writers (who accused him as such) were Catholics, and therefore hostile to him. Zacharias, the then-Monophysite church historian and later Catholic bishop of Mytilene, instead claims that these stories about Anastasius' Manichaeism were a plot of the Catholic bishop of Constantinople, Macedonius.

> And when he [Macedonius] saw the mind of the king [Anastasius] he formed a plan for actually raising a rebellion against him; and he was in the habit of calling him a heretic and a Manichaean.[190]

However, the fact that a wave of polemics against Manichaeans took place after Anastasius' reign, either through legislation or through a series of anti-Manichaean texts, supports the hypothesis that Manichaeans indeed had

---

187 Joannes Diacrinomenus, *HE* 7 (GCS, N.F. 3:155): οὔτε Χριστοῦ τοῦ θεοῦ οὔτε ἀγγέλου εἰκόνας ἐν ἐκκλησίᾳ συνεχώρει ἀνατίθεσθαι; Theodorus Anagnostes, *HE* 3.444 (GCS, N.F. 3:124): Ξεναΐας [...] τὴν δεσποτικὴν εἰκόνα καὶ τῶν ἀγγέλων ἐδίδασκε μὴ δέχεσθαι.

188 Parry 2016, 138.

189 Parry 2016, 151: "We have seen that at Nicaea II Philoxenus, bishop of Mabbug in northen Syria, was included in a list of anti-Chalcedonians as iconoclasts along with Severus and Peter the Fuller".

190 *The Syriac Chronicle Known as that of Zacharia of Mytilene*, 7.7: "[...] And he [Anastasius] held a Council; and in the presence of his patricians he told of the insult which had been offered to him by Macedonius; and he was distressed, and wept, and adjured them not to be influenced by fear; but if, in truth, their king was displeasing to them, or if they knew that he was infected with the deceit of heresy, they should take his dominion from him, and he should be cast out as an unbeliever. And they fell upon their faces before him, weeping". http://www.tertullian.org/fathers/zachariah07.htm. Greatrex 2011, 258–59. On the antipode of Zacharia's aspect about Anastasius' and Macedonius' debate lies Cyril's of Scythopolis in his *Vit. Sab.* (TU 49.2:140–41): ἦν τοίνυν ὁμόνοια Μακεδονίου καὶ Ἠλία, Φλαβιανοῦ δὲ μετὰ τελευτὴν Παλλαδίου τῆς Ἀντιοχέων κρατήσαντος καὶ τούτοις ἑνωθέντος οὐκ ἤνεγκεν ὁ κατὰ μόνης τῆς εὐσεβείας θρασὺς βασιλεὺς τὴν τούτων συμφωνίαν, ἀλλ᾽ ἐμάνη ὑπερορίσαι αὐτούς. καὶ πρῶτον μὲν τὸν Μακεδόνιον συκοφαντίαις διαφόροις περιβαλὼν καὶ τῆς ἐπισκοπῆς ἐξεώσας καὶ Τιμόθεον εἰς αὐτὴν προαγαγὼν Φλαβιανὸν καὶ Ἠλίαν ἀπῄτει συνθέσθαι.

a good deal of social latitude during his reign.[191] Moreover, it should not be a coincidence that the anti-Manichaean edict attributed to Anastasius (which imposed the death penalty on Manichaeans for the first time) was issued in 510: this was the same year that the riots of Sidon took place, where the mob abused and accused Anastasius as a Manichaean.[192] The fact that the above edict remained inactive until Justinian's time supports the case that his main purpose was to dissociate his name from Manichaeism.[193]

Lastly, for Anastasius' mother, several opinions have been supported by scholars.[194] If, however, she was indeed "a zealous devotee" of Manichaeans, as our authors maintain, it would be reasonable to assume that she could have influenced positively Anastasius' stance towards Manichaeans.[195]

3.10 *Photinus*

Photinus is the second case of a Manichaean teacher (Aphthonius being the first)[196] recorded in Byzantine literature.

Indeed, Photinus too, as Aphthonius, is presented as participating in a debate, this time in Constantinople in 527. However now, things have changed for the Manichaeans. The Manichaean and Christian contestants do not compete on equal terms (as equals). Unlike Aphthonius, Photinus is not given the opportunity to show off his wisdom and eloquence, since he is presented as a captive. The office of Photinus is declared right from the outset.

> On the command of the two emperors, Justin and Justinian, a debate was held between the Manichaean Photinus and the Christian Paul the Persian, when Theodorus was prefect of the city. [...] Leader (προϊστάμε-νος) of the Manichaean doctrine was a teacher of that religion.[197]

---

191 Cf. Stroumsa and Stroumsa 1988, 56.
192 Theodorus Anagnostes, *HE* 4.485; Theophanes, *Chron.* (de Boor, 154.20–22): εἰσελθὼν [Μακεδόνιος] δὲ πρὸς Ἀναστάσιον ἤλεγξεν αὐτὸν ὡς πολέμιον τῆς ἐκκλησίας. ὁ δὲ ὑπεκρίθη πρὸς τὴν ὥραν ἑνοῦσθαι αὐτῷ.
193 See also Charanis 1974, 41.
194 Jarry (1968) and Charanis (1974, 39, 41) support the view that Anastasius mother was a Manichaean. Cf. Capizzi 1969.
195 Cf. Charanis 1974, 41.
196 Apart from the above two cases of Manichaean teachers, there is also a testimony of Simplicius (*Comm. Man. Epict.* 35.90–92), that he himself held a discussion with a Manichaean teacher in Athens, see ch.[4], section 3.
197 *Disputationes Photini Manichaei cum Paulo Christiano* (PG 88:529A–578D, 529). Cf. Lieu 1994a, 113–16. It is noteworthy that both Aphthonius and Photinus are characterized as leaders (προεστὼς, προϊστάμενος). About the identity of this Paul, see Lieu 1994a, 113–114. Since my focus is on historical information provided by the text rather than on theological

Photinus, from the beginning of the debate, declares that he is a loyal exponent of his tradition; that he knows by heart and preserves what was bestowed upon him from his ancestors. When, during the first day of the debate, Paul questioned whether Photinus was a Manichaean teacher, Photinus defended his title by stating "I am [a Manichaean teacher] and I confess that I am".[198]

The debate unfolded in three sessions, each on a different day. The subjects discussed during these sessions were respectively, the origin of the souls, the two first principles, and the two Testaments. Though at every stage of the discussion the Christian arguments bested the Manichaean, the debate ends abruptly without informing us of its final outcome and whether Photinus was finally forced to anathematize his doctrines.[199] More details on Photinus' attitude during the debate will be given in the next chapter [8].

3.11   Peter Barsymes

A Manichaean (or one labelled as such) on whom Justinian's harsh measures and laws against Manichaeans do not seem to have had an effect, was a man "named Peter, who was Syrian by birth, surnamed Barsymes".[200] According to Procopius, this was because Justinian's wife, the empress Theodora, liked and favoured this man. Barsymes assumed a very high position in the palatine administration (first officer of the State), and was involved in every kind of corruption, cruelty, and illegality. It is also said that he was a magician, "a devotee of sorcerers and demons", domains that interested Theodora since her childhood, "and was admittedly a member of the Manichaeans".[201]

3.12   Erythrius' Wife

According to Malalas (fifth-sixth cent.), among the Manichaeans who were punished during Justinian's time was the wife of Senator Erythrius (Andronica?) amongst others: "At that time many Manicheans were punished in every city.

---

accounts the theological argumentation of the two adversaries is not presented here. Further research of the content of the debate that will trace parallel Manichaean theses in other Manichaean or anti-Manichaean literature, is required.

198 *Disputationes Photini Manichaei cum Paulo Christiano* (PG 88:532, 536).

199 A text entitled "Proposition of the Manichaean Photinus. Response of Paul the Persian" is recorded just after the debate. Its content is partly identical to Zacharias of Mytilene's work *Adv. Manichaeos*. Cf. Lieu 1994a, 220.

200 Lieu 1994a, 117.

201 Procopius, *Hist. Arcana* 22.25–26 (Haury, 138): ὁ Βαρσύμης οὗτος, καὶ τοὺς καλουμένους Μανιχαίους ἐτεθήπει τε καὶ αὐτῶν προστατεῖν ἐκ τοῦ ἐμφανοῦς οὐδαμῇ ἀπηξίου. On Barsymes see also ch.[6], 5.2.

Among those punished was the wife of the senator Erythrios and other women as well".[202]

It has been argued that because Erythrius was an adherent of Mazdakism his wife must have belonged to the same religious group.[203] It is questionable why it would not be equally plausible that there was a club of Manichaean women in Byzantine aristocracy. They could have been under the patronage of Empress Theodora, given the close relationship she had with the very powerful man in the state's administration, Barsymes, who according to Procopius, admired, favoured and supported the Manichaeans openly.[204] Moreover, according to the testimony, Erythrius' wife was not the only one. The attraction Manichaeism held for women is testified to elsewhere and seems probable, given the honourable position of female Elect in the Manichaean hierarchy.[205]

4 Conclusions

4.1 Jerusalem and Antioch Compared

The sources for both cases belong to the genre of oral homilies, which could reflect the historical reality in specific times and places. The religious landscape of both Jerusalem and Antioch, despite the chronological distance, is characterized by religious diversity. In both cases, the Manichaeans constituted a major and a real problem that Cyril and Chrysostom had to confront. The references to Manichaeans constitute a significant part of their lectures. Manichaeans' misconceptions, practices, and negative influence on their listeners during social interactions, causing apostasies, are common concerns for the two pastors. Their advice on how to deal with the Manichaeans, and whether they should speak or not with and about Manichaeans are similar. The basic target of both Cyril and Chrysostom was the good preparation of their listeners for the (inevitable) encounter with the Manichaeans in their everyday lives.

---

202 Malalas, *Chron.* 17.21 (CFHBSB 35:352; Jeffreys and Scott, 243): Ἐν δὲ τῷ αὐτῷ καιρῷ κατὰ πόλιν πολλοὶ ἐτιμωρήθησαν Μανιχαῖοι, ἐν οἷς ἐτιμωρήθη καὶ ἡ γυνὴ Ἐρυθρίου τοῦ συγκλητικοῦ καὶ ἄλλαι ἅμα αὐτῇ. According to the Slavonic version of the text, among the victims of the persecution was "the wife of a patrician, whose name may have been Andronica". See Martindale 1980 (PLRE) 2:402.

203 Lieu 1994a, 116–18.

204 Procopius, *Hist. Arcana* 22.22–29. However, according to Lieu (1994, 117), "we cannot be certain how precisely Procopius [...] used the term 'Manichaeism'".

205 P.Rylands 3, Gr. 469 (Roberts 1938, 42).

However, while in Cyril's speeches one gets the impression that there were Manichaeans among his listeners, this is not true for Chrysostom's speeches. At least, they did not attend the congregation openly. The Manichaeans of Antioch, during the last two decades of the fourth century, do not seem to have had the religious freedom of their coreligionists of Jerusalem in the middle of the century. More importantly, Chrysostom makes no reference to Manichaean churches. This reinforces the view that since ca. 380 the Manichaean meetings were generally held in secret.

4.2 Alleged 'Manichaean' Individuals: Real or Imagined?

TABLE 4 Alleged 'Manichaean' individuals: real or imagined?

	Person	Century	Identity	Discussed in other chapters
1.	Sebastian	4th	Military officeholder: *dux* of Egypt & *Magister Peditum Orientis*. A Manichaean?	
2.	Hierax	"	Ascetic in Egypt	
3.	Aphthonius	"	Manichaean teacher	
4.	Heracleides	"	Ascetic philosopher?	
5.	Anonymous Manichaean woman	"	A convert to Christianity in Alexandria, Egypt	
6.	Anonymous Manichaean discussing with Didymus	"	Elect?	Ch.[5], 3.3.1
7.	Bassa	"	A Manichaean missionary (?) Elect (?) in Asia Minor & Illyria	Ch.[6], 2.3
8.	Anonymous Manichaean presbyter converted to Christianity	"	A Manichaean presbyter wandering in the Egyptian desert	

TABLE 4   Alleged 'Manichaean' individuals: real or imagined? (*cont.*)

	Person	Century	Identity	Discussed in other chapters
9.	Anonymous Manichaean in a debate with Corpes (a Christian holy man)	"	A Manichaean missionary in Hermopolis Magna, Egypt	Ch.[2], 7.3.1.2
10.	Anonymous Manichaean from Sparta converted to Christianity		A leading citizen of Sparta converted by Serapion the Sindonite	Ch.[2], 7.3.1.2
11.	Agapius	"	Ascetic philosopher? A Manichaean?	
12.	Julia of Antioch	4th–5th	A Manichaean missionary, Elect? (Antioch & Gaza)	Ch.[6], 2.3
13.	Dositheus of Cilicia	"	Ascetic in Asia Minor	Ch.[5], 3.3 Ch.[6], 3.1
14.	Presbyter Philon	"	Clergymen: Catholic (?) presbyter near the border of the Empire	Ch.[4], 2.2 Ch.[8], 6.2
15.	Simplicius	5th	Officeholder: the City Prefect of Constantinople (403/6)	
16.	Presbyter Philip	"	Clergymen: Catholic presbyter	
17.	Anastasius	5th–6th	Emperor, Monophysite	
18.	Anastasia-Constantina	"	Emperor's mother. Supporter of Manichaeans	
19.	Manichaean painter	"	Syro-Persian in origin. A Manichaean presbyter or a Monophysite?	
20.	Xenaias	"	Clergymen: the Monophysite bishop of Hierapolis, Philoxenos. Syro-Persian in origin.	

TABLE 4   Alleged 'Manichaean' individuals: real or imagined? (*cont.*)

	Person	Century	Identity	Discussed in other chapters
21.	John the archdeacon	"	Archdeacon of Timothy, bishop of Constantinople. A Manichaean?	
22.	Peter the Fuller/ Cnapheus	"	Clergymen: Monophysite	Ch.[4], 2.2
23.	Severus of Antioch	"	Clergymen: Monophysite	Ch.[4], 2.2
24.	Julian of Halicarnassus	"	Clergymen: Monophysite	
25.	Peter Barsymes	6th	Officeholder: first officer of the State. Syrian in origin. Supporter of Manichaeans	
26.	Erythrius' wife	"	The wife of a senator/ patrician. A Manichaean?	
27.	Photinus	"	Manichaean teacher	
28.	Anonymous Manichaean discussing with the philosopher Simplicius	"	Manichaean teacher	Ch.[4], 3

As depicted in the above table, these twenty-eight persons come from various social backgrounds. Among them we find both eminent and insignificant citizens, representatives of both sexes, ecclesiastical and secular leaders, intellectuals, artists, ascetics and ordinary people of everyday life. So, there is no correlation made by the authors between Manichaeans and a certain social group. What is stressed in three of our cases is their 'race', namely their Syrian/Syro-Persian origin (Manichaean painter, Xenaias/Philoxenos, Barsymes).

Apart from the cases of the Manichaean missionaries and teachers (Aphthonius, Bassa, Julia, and Photinus), and the brief anonymous references, the other cases of the alleged 'Manichaeans', indeed, could have been slander. But even in this case, there are alternative scenarios: (1) either it was malicious slander aiming to discredit Arians, Catholics, or Monophysites, identifying them as Manichaeans, or (2) that the authors actually believed that the followers of these 'sects' were more vulnerable to the threat of Manichaeism. This is because the religious pluralism that existed in the religious landscape in the eastern part of the Empire blurred the boundaries between various sects. Particularly for the simple and uneducated believers, who were the main pastoral concern of the Church Fathers, the danger grew if persons of authority such as many of the above were Manichaeans, μανιχαιόφρονες, or μανιχαΐζοντες. But we cannot discount the possibility that the above persons, at some point in their life, were charmed by Manichaeism as part of a spiritual quest, as was Augustine.

CHAPTER 8

The Dissolution of Manichaeism in the Roman East

1 Introduction

The central question addressed in this chapter is how Manichaeism disappeared from the Roman East. Although, as far as I know, there has not been thorough research addressing this question, the prevailing opinion in scholarship up to recently is that the vigorous persecutions of the religion during the sixth century led to its extinction.[1] In the words of Lieu, "the Justinianic persecutions had probably reduced the Manichaeans to small pockets".[2] Researchers are unanimous in thinking that "there was clearly no Manichaean danger in Byzantium after the sixth century",[3] and any references to Manichaeans thenceforth, do not pertain to real Manichaeans, but to later heretics like Paulicians and Bogomils, whom "Byzantine polemicists [...] regarded as Neo-Manichaeans".[4] Thus, later authors, such as John of Damascus, Peter the Higoumen, Peter of Sicily and Photius, are widely believed never to have been in contact with 'real' Manichaeans. Yet in their fight against Paulicians and Bogomils they combined information drawn from older anti-Manichaean literature with their knowledge about the new heretics, intending to "demonstrate the continuity of the Manichaean heresy".[5] Indeed, it is probable that thanks to this extensive use of the earlier anti-Manichaean work, much of it was preserved.[6]

---

1   Lieu 1992, 215; Stroumsa and Stroumsa 1988, 56; Doniger 1999, 689–90; Skjærvø 2006, 32: "Justinian continued persecuting Manicheans, and they apparently disappeared from Byzantium by the end of the 6th century. After this the term Manichean remained a disparaging name of any heretical sect that professed any degree of dualism or gnosticism"; Gardner and Lieu 2004, 111. About the importance of the question "how religions disappear" and the lack of any research studies addressing this question, see de Jong 2017, 646–64.

2   Lieu 1994a, 104; Lieu 1997, 233.

3   Stroumsa and Stroumsa 1988, 56. See also Lieu 1986b, 261; Lieu 2007, 294.

4   Lieu 1994a, 137; Lieu 1992, 215–16.

5   Lieu 1994a, 211; Garsoïan 1967/2011 and 1971; Stroumsa and Stroumsa 1988, 56; Lieu 1992, 216. See also Lieu 2007, 294; Klein 1991; Pedersen 2004, 67.

6   Lieu 1994a, 159; Lieu 1997, 234. Pedersen 2004, 68. In his *Sacra Parallela*, John of Damascus used Titus quotations that have not been saved elsewhere in Greek. Cf. Klein 1991, 26 and Pedersen 2004, 115, 193 fn. 40, 293, 316, 351.

In the same vein, according to many scholars, Justinianic laws "became fossilized" and were used by later Byzantine Emperors for the persecution of other heretics, especially Paulicians and Bogomils, "on whom the charge of Manichaeism could be more easily made to stick".[7]

In this chapter I will examine an alternative, equally (if not more) likely scenario, according to which the cause of the disappearance of Manichaeism was not the violent extinction of the Manichaeans but their gradual dissolution into Christianity.[8]

2   Persecutions, Executions, and Conversions

The fact that Justinian's persecutions led to the disappearance of the Manichaeans in the Roman East mainly means two things: executions and forced conversions. Logically, both must have happened. It is well established that the fate of the Manichaeans during the reign of Justinian took a turn for the worse. Even if there would be some truth in the claim that the Manichaeans of Constantinople rejoiced and acquired a lot of boldness during Anastasius' reign, this clearly did not last very long, because with Justinian's decree the Manichaeans were ordered to disappear from the face of the Empire; they had no right to exist anywhere in Byzantine territory. Every Manichaean, "wherever on earth appearing", was "liable to extreme punishments".[9] Manichaeans had to be identified and evicted from all the cities. Administrative and army officials were asked to detect their Manichaean colleagues and deliver them to the authorities. Anyone who demonstrably knew any Manichaeans and did not turn them in would be punished as a Manichaean, even though he was not one himself.[10]

So then, during Justinian's reign, executions and massive conversions from Manichaeism to Christianity, voluntary or forced, must have taken place. Procopius' account illustrates the whole atmosphere of Justinian's religious persecutions: "agents were sent everywhere to force any heretics they chanced

---

7   Lieu 1992, 216.
8   The discussion in this chapter builds on the main arguments of Matsangou 2017b and presents more evidence towards that direction. Similar ideas about the disappearance of Manichaeism have been expressed by de Jong 2017, 654–55.
9   Cod. justin.. 1.5.12.pr. (Coleman-Norton, 996); Cod. justin.. 1.5.16.pr. (Coleman-Norton, 1006).
10   Cod. justin. 1.5.12.3, Cod. justin. 1.5.16.1. See ch.[3], sections 3.4.2 and 4.3.

upon to renounce the faith of their fathers".[11] Barsanuphius, a monk in a monastery in Gaza, speaks about Manichaeans who were baptized as Christians in an attempt to avoid persecution.[12]

However, caution is needed when data concerning persecution is interpreted as execution. Apparently, there must have been executions, but we have no direct evidence, either by Manichaean or anti-Manichaean sources, that allows us to assess on what scale they took place. As Averil Cameron argues, the question as to whether and how often "real persecution and in particular execution" took place in Byzantium, calls for further research.[13] As shown previously, during the pre-Justinian era the laws were not implemented at least on a large scale. Persecutions had a rather occasional or local character and repressed Manichaeans mainly through financial measures and exile penalty.[14] Evidently, under Justin and Justinian the persecutions were intensified. But did this mean mass executions? Malalas and Theophanes, the two well-known chronographers, give brief reports about the impact of the Justinianic laws on the persecuted Manichaeans. According to Malalas, "at that time many Manichaeans were punished (ἐτιμωρήθησαν) in every city. Among those punished was the wife of the senator Erythrius and other women as well".[15] Justin, as Theophanes states, "carried out a great persecution of the Manichaeans and punished (ἐτιμωρήσατο) many".[16] We note that both writers use the verb 'to punish' (τιμωρέω), which does not, however, clearly determine the method of punishment. This can be interpreted as a punishment by *extreme penalties* (ταῖς ἐσχάταις τιμωρίαις), without this being the only possible interpretation. In addition, as already highlighted in ch.[3], the exact meaning of the terms *extreme penalties*, *ultimate sentence* and *capital punishment* is far from clear and does not necessarily mean the death penalty. These terms could also refer to other, particularly harsh, sentences that resemble death, such as forced

---

11 Procopius, *Hist. Arcana* 11.21 (Haury, 73): Πολλοὶ δὲ εὐθὺς πανταχόσε περιιόντες δόξης τῆς πατρίου τοὺς παραπίπτοντας ἠνάγκαζον μεταβάλλεσθαι. Procopius here refers to all heretics; previously (11.14) he mentioned specifically the Montanists, the Sabbatians, and the Arians.

12 Barsanuphius, *Ep.* 820.

13 Cameron 2003, 482. Cf. On the question whether Byzantium was a 'persecuting society' or a tolerant one, see Cameron 2007, 1–24.

14 Previous chapters, especially ch.[3]; cf. Lieu 1992, 174.

15 Malalas, *Chron.* 17.21 (CFHBSB 35:243): Ἐν δὲ τῷ αὐτῷ καιρῷ κατὰ πόλιν πολλοὶ ἐτιμωρήθησαν Μανιχαῖοι, ἐν οἷς ἐτιμωρήθη καὶ ἡ γυνὴ Ἐρυθρίου τοῦ συγκλητικοῦ καὶ ἄλλαι ἅμα αὐτῇ.

16 Theophanes, *Chron.* (de Boor, 170.24–25, 171.2–3; Mango and Scott, 260): ὁ δὲ εὐσεβὴς βασιλεὺς Ἰουστῖνος [...] ἐποίησε δὲ καὶ αὐτὸς διωγμὸν μέγαν κατὰ Μανιχαίων καὶ ἐτιμωρήσατο πολλούς.

labour in the mines, or deportation.[17] The decision of the exact penalty up to the Justinianic era was within the jurisdiction of individual governors and judges. Later, as is reflected in the versions of the same laws in the *Basilica*, the type and the method of the punishment was determined by the law: decapitation (ἀποτεμνέσθω).[18]

Yet, even if the intention of the authorities was the physical extermination of all the Manichaeans in Roman territory, their identification would not have been an easy task. As is reflected in the Justinianic laws, due to persecutions the Manichaeans were no longer a discernible religious group. Justinian's agents were not asked to detect Manichaean assemblies, but those infiltrating into the institutions of the Empire.[19]

Lastly, an argument challenging the mass-execution scenario comes from the side of the persecuted Manichaeans who, as long as it was their choice, had two alternatives: either to choose the way of martyrdom (as the first Christians did), or to convert. The latter case seems more likely, if we accept as true the claim of anti-Manichaean authors that it was not a trait of Manichaeans to be sacrificed for their faith.

3 Manichaean Views on Martyrdom (According to Anti-Manichaean Authors)

A frequently occurring accusation in anti-Manichaean literature (both Christian and pagan) is that of cowardice. The charge of cowardice was attributed by the opponents of Manichaeans to the Manichaean God (the *Father of Greatness*), to Mani, and to Manichaeans themselves.

3.1 The Cowardice of the First Principle

Archelaus, addressing Mani, criticizes the cowardice of the light principle, who built a wall in order to be isolated and protected from the evil principle, saying: "So if God, as you say, constructed the wall, he proves himself fearful and lacking in courage".[20] Simplicius' criticism is along similar lines: "What kinds

---

17 See ch.[3], 4.3.

18 B 1.1.25: Ὁ Μανιχαῖος ἐν Ῥωμαϊκῷ τόπῳ διάγων ὀφθεὶς ἀποτεμνέσθω (= Cod. justin. 1.5.11). About *Basilica* see ch.[3], fn. 263. The need for a precise determination by the Law of the kind of the sentence and of the exact way the convict was executed was an innovation of the Isaurian *Eclogae*, and can be seen as a legislative reform aiming to limit the arbitrariness of local judges (Troiannos 1997, 29).

19 Ch.[3], 4.2.5 & 4.3.

20 *AA* 27.1–4 (Vermes, 79).

of and how many blasphemies against God necessarily result from their teachings? For example, they describe him as a coward who dreaded the approach of evil to the borders lest it enters his domain".[21] Commenting on another part of the Manichaean cosmogony, Epiphanius criticizes the weakness of the Manichaean God who, like a thief, could only think of one way to save the *Soul* from *Matter*, and that was to steal it secretly with the help of the luminaries.[22]

3.2   The Cowardice of Mani

One of the key features of Mani's portrait as outlined by the AA and its echo is his cowardice. Mani fled from the Persian prison by bribing the two guards; he ran away after he was defeated by Archelaus in the first and in the second debates.[23] Cyril gets very sarcastic when commenting on the claim of the fugitive Mani, who escaped before martyrdom rather than being sacrificed, to be called 'fighter for the truth' and a Paraclete. He compares his attitude towards martyrdom with that of Jesus and of other prophets of the OT.

> And there was not only the shame of the prison, but also the flight from the prison; yea, he who said that he was the Paraclete, and the champion of Truth, fled. He was not a successor of Jesus, who readily came to the cross; he was the reverse, a runaway. Then the king of Persia ordered the keepers of the prison to be led off to capital punishment. [...] Ought he not to have followed Jesus, and said, *if you seek me, let these go their way* (John 18:8)? Ought he not to have said like Jonas, *take me, and cast me into the sea* (Jonah 1:12)?[24]

---

21   Simplicius, *Comm. Man. Epict.* 35.36–39 (Hadot, 323.36–39; Lieu 2010, 102–03): Οἷα δὲ καὶ ὅσα βλάσφημα εἰς τὸν θεὸν τοῖς ὑπ' ἐκείνων λεγομένοις ἐξ ἀνάγκης ἀκολουθεῖ. Καὶ γὰρ δειλὸν εἰσάγουσιν αὐτὸν, δεδοικότα τὸ κακὸν ἐγγὺς τῶν ὅρων αὐτοῦ γενόμενον μὴ καὶ ἐντὸς εἰσέλθῃ.

22   Epiphanius, *Pan.* 66.56.9 (GCS 37:93): ὅτι οὐκ ἰσχύει ὁ θεὸς ὁ ἀγαθὸς καὶ ζῶν καὶ δυνατὸς σῶσαι, οὐ λέγω τὴν ἑαυτοῦ δύναμιν τὴν ἐξ αὐτοῦ ἐσπασμένην, ἀλλὰ τὰ ὑπ' αὐτοῦ γεγενημένα καὶ πεπλασμένα ἐὰν μὴ δι' ἄλλου τινὸς τρόπου ἢ διὰ λῃστείας, κρυφῇ συλήσας τὴν ἀπ' αὐτοῦ ἀπεσπασμένην δύναμιν ἀπὸ τῶν ἐπουρανίων, ὡς ὁ ἀγύρτης οὗτος λέγει, οὐ δύναται [ἡμᾶς] σῶσαι.

23   AA 65.7,9 (Vermes, 147): "Manes [...] escaped from the prison [...] having bribed the guards with a large sum of gold [...] The guard of the prison who had let him escape was punished"; Lieu in Vermes 2001, 6–7: "But Mani, forewarned in a dream of the King's intentions, bribed one of the guards and fled to Castellum Arabionis [...] the prison guards were executed because of his flight' Mani fled from the threatening crowd to a village". Cyril, *Catech.* 6.30: κατέκρινε καὶ διὰ τὸν τῶν δεσμοφυλάκων φόνον. AA 43.1 ("run away"), 43.3 (Vermes, 111): "So next, after Manes had fled, he was nowhere to be seen"; AA 66.1–2 (Vermes, 148): "[...] but finding him nowhere had departed, as he was then engaged in flight. 2. So when Archelaus had revealed the story as related, at once Manes launched into flight and succeeded in escaping, while no one pursued him".

24   Cyril, *Catech.* 6.26.5–15 (Reischl and Rupp 1848, 190; LFHCC 2:73): Καὶ οὐκ ἦν γε αἰσχύνη τῆς φυλακῆς μόνον, ἀλλὰ καὶ ἡ ἐκ τῆς φυλακῆς φυγή. Ὁ γὰρ λέγων ἑαυτὸν Παράκλητον καὶ τῆς

Again he, who had fled from prison, flees from this place, too: and, having escaped his adversary, he comes to a very mean village; [...] Manes seeing his adversary [Archelaus] unexpectedly, rushed away and fled; and fled for the last time. For the guards of the king of Persia, being on the search, arrested the runaway [...].[25]

3.3   The Cowardice of the Manichaeans

Following the example of their God and of Mani, Titus of Bostra states that the Manichaeans regarded martyrdom for faith as an unnecessary sacrifice and an exaggeration; this was a very good reason for Titus not to consider them as Christians.

But the Manichaeans require no anointing for battles, since they regard virtue and vice as necessities of nature. Nor does Mani wish to see his followers persecuted to death [...] So the Manichaeans are not anointed for battle and therefore do not have the right to the name of Christ.[26]

Titus ends his fourth book with Christ's promise "that the Church will be spread throughout the world", aiming to highlight the contribution of the Christians martyrs to that very end: "Where the gates to martyrdom and confession are, there the Church of Christ is also manifest, but those who believe that martyrdom is superfluous are foreign to Christ and His Church".[27]

A brief but revealing testimony of both the presumed Manichaean cowardice and of the equally presumed secretive character of the movement is that of Gregory of Nazianzus. In a canonical letter he sent from Arianzus (381/2) speaking about the inner cycle of Apollinarians initiated into the secrets of their sect, Gregory compares them to the Elect Manichaeans who in their secret meetings did not hesitate to support their beliefs, whereas when interrogated and pressed confessed the Christian teachings, but distorted their meaning.[28]

ἀληθείας ἀγωνιστήν, ἔφευγεν. Οὐκ ἦν διάδοχος Ἰησοῦ τοῦ ἑτοίμως ἐρχομένου εἰς τὸν σταυρόν· ἀλλ' οὗτος ἐναντίος ἦν, φυγάς. [...] Οὐκ ἔδει μιμήσασθαι Ἰησοῦν καὶ εἰπεῖν, Εἰ ἐμὲ ζητεῖτε, ἄφετε τούτους ὑπάγειν; Οὐκ ἔδει κατὰ τὸν Ἰωνᾶν εἰπεῖν, Ἄρατέ με καὶ βάλλετε εἰς τὴν θάλασσαν· δι' ἐμὲ γὰρ ὁ κλύδων οὗτος; Peter of Sicily, Hist. ref. Man. 55–56.

25   Cyril, Catech. 6.30.2–15 (Reischl and Rupp 1848, 196; LFHCC 2:75, modified): Φεύγει πάλιν καὶ ἐντεῦθεν, ὁ ἐκ τῆς φυλακῆς φυγών· καὶ τὸν ἀνταγωνιστὴν διαδράς, ἔρχεται ἐπὶ κώμην εὐτελεστάτην, [...] Ὁ δὲ Μάνης ἰδὼν ἐξαίφνης τὸν ἀντίδικον, ἐξεπήδησε καὶ ἔφυγεν· ἔφυγε δὲ τὴν τελευταίαν φυγήν. Οἱ γὰρ τοῦ τῶν Περσῶν βασιλέως ὑπασπισταὶ πανταχοῦ διερευνώμενοι, καταλαμβάνουσι τὸν φυγάδα.

26   Titus of Bostra, c. Manichaeos 4.10–11 (CCT 21, 391–92) summarized in Pedersen 2004, 51.

27   Titus of Bostra, c. Manichaeos 4.114 in Pedersen 2004, 64–65.

28   Gregory of Nazianzus, Epistulae theologicae (ep. 102.7–8, SC 208: 72, 74): Οὗτοι γὰρ ἡνίκα μὲν ἂν τοῖς γνησίοις αὐτῶν μαθηταῖς καὶ μύσταις τῶν ἀπορρήτων θεολογῶσιν, ὥσπερ οἱ Μανιχαῖοι

The alleged Manichaean cowardice when facing danger is best illustrated in the debate between the Manichaean teacher Photinus and the Christian Paul, the Persian. At the instigation of the Christian: "prove that it is the way you say it is" the Manichaean responds: "I am in bonds, so I am not able to do it". The Christian insists and when pressed a second time the Manichaean explains why he cannot speak: "When I have the support of the authorities I converse. But now that I have no support from anywhere, I have to remain silent".[29] This answer of the Manichaean gave his Christian opponent the opportunity to compare his stance with that of Paul, which created great difficulty for the Manichaean:

> Christian: The Manichaean teachers do suffer for the sake of truth. Or do you say something different?
> Manichaean: For the sake of truth, I reckon.
> Christian: Did the blessed apostle Paul have the support of the rulers when he was in bonds, or else, since he did not have it, did he neglect his teaching for being captive?

The Manichaean remained silent; he did not answer but feigned a sudden illness.

That Manichaeans preferred to save their lives rather than confess their faith before danger appears to be legitimized by Mani himself in later sources. According to the LAF, the last anathema that the converted Manichaean had to recite and sign was as follows:

> Anathema to those who never speak the truth under oath but always lie on purpose and swear falsely, conforming to the teaching of the thrice-accursed Mani who says: 'I am not without compassion like Christ, nor do I deny him who has denied me before men and has also lied for his own safety and I shall receive back with joy him who denied his faith through fear'.[30]

τοῖς ἐκλεκτοῖς λεγομένοις, ὅλην τὴν νόσον αὐτῶν ἐκκαλύπτοντες, μόλις καὶ τὴν σάρκα τῷ Σωτῆρι διδόασιν. Ὅταν δὲ ταῖς κοιναῖς ὑπολήψεσι περὶ τῆς ἐνανθρωπήσεως ἃς ἡ Γραφὴ παρίστησιν ἐλέγχωνται καὶ πιέζωνται, τὰς μὲν εὐσεβεῖς λέξεις ὁμολογοῦσι, περὶ δὲ τὸν νοῦν κακουργοῦσιν. Gregory's letter is quoted by Euthymius Zigabenus in his *Panoplia* 14.884.

29   *Disputationes Photini Manichaei cum Paulo Christiano* (PG 88:530–578, 533–36). See ch.[7], section 3.10; Lieu 1994a, 220.

30   *LAF* (PG 1:1469C–D.226–234, Adam 1954, 103; trans. Lieu 1994a, 298 & Lieu 2010, 142–43): Ἀνάθεμα τοῖς μηδέποτε δι' ὅρκου ἀληθεύουσιν ἀλλ' ἐξεπίτηδες ἀεὶ ψευδομένοις καὶ ἐπιορκοῦσι

Because the above anathema (1) is the last of the ten anathemas which were directed against Paulicians and (2) does not exist in the two earlier abjuration formulas (sc and saf which concerned solely Manichaeans), modern scholars have considered it to be either a slander, or as targeting Paulicians only.[31] Yet, some counter-arguments can be made that cast some doubt on the conviction with which they have come to this conclusion.

Concerning the former (1), it has to be noted, that, this particular anathema is the last one (37th) of the whole LAF; it is immediately followed by the final statement of sincere conversion that also exists in the sc.

> If I, so and so, do not believe or say these things with my whole soul, but have made these preceding anathemas hypocritically, let the anathema be on me and condemnation in the present age and in the age to come and may my soul be condemned and made to perish and perpetually be punished in hell.[32]

Thus, thematically, the correct place of the anathema is here. After the anathematization of perjury (pseudo-conversion), follows the promise and

---

κατὰ τὴν τοῦ τρικαταράτου Μάνεντος διδασκαλίαν οὕτω λέγοντος Οὐκ εἰμὶ ἄσπλαγχνος ὥσπερ ὁ Χριστὸς οὐδέ ἀρνήσομαι τὸν ἀρνησάμενόν με ἔμπροσθεν τῶν ἀνθρώπων, ἀλλά καὶ τὸν ψευδόμε-νον τὴν οἰκείαν σωτηρίαν καὶ τὸν διὰ φόβον ἀρνούμενον τὴν ἰδίαν πίστιν μετὰ χαρᾶς προσδέξομαι. The same information is provided by Photius and Peter Higumen. Photius, c. Manichaeos 24 (p. 127.24–25): καίτοιγε τοῦ διδασκάλου αὐτῶν Μάνεντος διαπρυσίως αὐτοῖς ἐμβοῶντος καὶ λέγοντος ὡς 'Οὐκ εἰμὶ ἐγὼ ἄσπλαγχνος ὡς ὁ Χριστὸς ὁ εἰπών "Ὅστις με ἀρνήσεται ἔμπροσθεν τῶν ἀνθρώπων, ἀρνήσομαι αὐτὸν κἀγώ' [...]; Petrus Hegumenus, Paulicianorum historia bre-vis 18: Οὕτως γὰρ αὐτοῖς ὁ Μάνης παρέδωκεν ὅτι 'Οὐκ εἰμὶ ἐγὼ ἄσπλαγχνος, φησίν, ὡς ὁ Χριστὸς ὁ εἰπών 'ὅστις με ἀρνήσεται ἔμπροσθεν τῶν ἀνθρώπων, ἀρνήσομαι αὐτὸν κἀγώ'· [...]. About the relationship of Petrus Hegumenus with Peter of Sicily, see Garsoïan 1967/2011, 49. Other later authors reproducing the same saying/logion attributed to Mani are: Georgius Cedrenus, hist. compend. 2.13 (Bekker 1:760) and Euthymius Zigabenus, Panoplia 24.1196. Cf. Lieu 1994a, 225.

31   As Lieu (1994a, 225) states, "More important for the historian of Byzantine Manichaeism is that the new text [sc] proves beyond doubt that the second half of the Long Formula (viz. Anathemas 27 onwards) deals exclusively with Paulicianism. Even the condemna-tions of the Manichaean proclivity to undergo false conversion to Catholicism on the advice of Mani himself [...] which some historians have regarded as genuinely pertain-ing to the Manichaeans must now be seen as Byzantine polemics against Paulicians". Cf. ch.[1], section 3.

32   LAF (PG 1: 1469D, Lieu 2010, 142–43): ἐὰν δε μὴ ἐξ ὅλης ψυχῆς ταῦτα φρονῶ, καὶ λέγω ἐγὼ ὁ δεῖνα, ἀλλά μεθ᾽ ὑποκρίσεως ἐποίησα τοὺς προκειμένους ἀναθεματισμούς, ἀνάθεμά μοι εἴη καὶ κατάθεμα, ἐν τε τῷ νῦν αἰῶνι καὶ ἐν τῷ μέλλοντι, καὶ κατακριθείη καὶ ἀπόλοιτο ἡ ψυχή μου καὶ διηνεκῶς ταρταρωθείη.

commitment of a sincere conversion. The fact that the anathemas from the twenty-seventh onwards concerned Paulicians, does not exclude the probability that the concluding anathema concerns both Manichaeans and Paulicians.

Concerning the latter (2), as noted in ch.[2], the use of anathemas was sacramental and took place in an actual situation, during the conversion of real Manichaeans, at a specific place and time. Hence, it was almost necessarily the case that there existed different contemporary versions of the AFs, which could explain the differences between the SC and SAF. Thus, the fact that the SC and SAF did not record the specific anathema does not mean that it did not exist in any other contemporary AF.[33]

In addition, there is some evidence to suggest that the anathema in question could have been addressed also against Manichaeans. (1) As said, hints concerning the presumed Manichaean cowardice that led to the avoidance of martyrdom existed much earlier. In particular, the specific anathema echoes Titus' saying "Nor does Mani wish to see his followers persecuted to death".[34] (2) Similar accusations (perjury and pseudo-conversion) were also laid against the Messalians, one of the ascetic groups with which Manichaeans had common spirituality and shared many features. Of particular interest is the information that for Messalians too, "the permission to perjure and anathematize" their own religion before danger was [...] "bestowed upon them by [...] their teachers".[35] (3) It may also be relevant that Donatists, in their polemic, put in the same basket Manichaeans and Catholics who accepted the *lapsi*, whom they considered *traditores*.[36] (4) Interestingly, among his arguments against Manichaean Docetism, Epiphanius states "if we were bought with the precious blood of Christ (1 Cor 6:20), you are not one of the purchased, oh Mani, for you deny the blood".[37] With these words, Epiphanius obviously targets the docetic views of Mani, which annulled Christ's sacrifice, but he may have hinted simultaneously at Mani's more general stance towards martyrdom. (5) Finally, regardless of whether the Manichaeans renounce and anathematize their faith on the advice of Mani, what matters is that this attitude towards danger seems to be confirmed by Manichaean sources too.

---

33   See ch.[2], 3.6 & 8.
34   Titus of Bostra, *c. Manichaeos* 4.11 in Pedersen 2004, 51.
35   See ch.[6], 3.2.3.
36   Cf. Frend 1976, 860–66.
37   Epiphanius, *Pan.* 66.79.3 (GCS 37:120–21; Williams 2013, 306): καὶ πῶς ἠγόρασεν ἡμᾶς, εὐθὺς ἐπιφέρει ὁ διδάσκαλος τῆς ἐκκλησίας φάσκων ὅτι "τιμῆς ἠγοράσθητε", "τιμίῳ αἵματι ἀμνοῦ ἀμώμου καὶ ἀσπίλου Χριστοῦ". εἰ τοίνυν τῷ αἵματι ἠγοράσθημεν, οὐχ ὑπάρχεις τῶν ἠγορασμένων, ὦ Μάνη, ἐπειδὴ τὸ αἷμα ἀρνῆσαι.

4 Manichaean Views on Martyrdom (According to Manichaean Sources)

4.1 *Prudential Secrecy*

As we have seen, anti-Manichaean writers often state that Manichaeans regarded martyrdom for faith as an unnecessary sacrifice, which they had to avoid. The same attitude towards danger is also alluded to Manichaean sources. As we read in the *CMC*: The prophet Mani declared, "[and again, when] I [am surrounded] by oppression or affliction or persecution, I might be hidden from the sight of my enemies". So, "during that great period of time" he remained "in silence" among the Baptists, and "with the greatest possible ingenuity and skill" he conformed to their Law and he "[revealed nothing] of what happened", "nor what it is that ... [he] knew to anyone", "lest someone become envious and destroy [him]".[38] The disclosure of the identity of the Elect (Mani), and "the proclamation of Truth among devotees of false dogmas" should not be done if it endangers the life of the prophet. This is the tactic of prudential secrecy, according to which the Elect "must keep silent" in a hostile environment, "until these circumstances are changed";[39] an attitude which recalls that of the Manichaean teacher Photinus.

Concealment of the beliefs, as a protective and prudential technique imposed by social circumstances, is recorded in other Manichaean texts too. According to a Sogdian source, "Lord Mar Mani said to the magus":

> I, together with my disciples and Electi, am like that child who was silent as an expedient (...) (who) did not speak and did not hear ... So we too are silent and we speak with no one and perform good deeds and pious actions as an expedient, (but) that time will come at last when I shall speak before all, like that child, and we shall demand justice for ourselves.[40]

A corresponding form of secrecy is the *taqiyya* of Shiite Islam which can be defined as the concealment of one's beliefs in times of danger.[41]

---

38 *CMC*: 4.12–13, 8.11–14, 25.2–13, 26.1, 38.1–4 (Cameron & Dewey). Cf. Gardner and Lieu 2004, 53.

39 Cf. Stroumsa 1986a, 153–58; On the protective character of secrecy in religions, see Simmel 1906, 441–98 (471–72). On secret knowledge, rituals, and identities in the ancient world, see de Jong 2006b, 37–59 and 2006a, 1050–54.

40 Sims-Williams 1981, 231–40, esp. 238.

41 According to Etan Kohlberg (2012, 269) *Taqiyya* became "an article of Imami faith" since the eighth century and "helped to preserve the Imami community in a hostile environment".

4.2   The 'Manichaean Body' in Manichaean Theology

The avoidance of blood-martyrdom by the Manichaeans has been pointed out by several researchers. As Frend highlights, the Manichaeans argued that "Not martyrdom, but a well-instructed mind, was the most acceptable sacrifice to God".[42] As Coyle comments, "The Manichaean bishop Faustus of Milevis scorned the veneration of martyrs so popular among both Catholics and Donatists of North Africa; and nowhere do the Manichaean psalms say that they *were* martyrs, let alone how they might have become such".[43] For Manichaeans like Faustus, the worship of martyrs did not differ from the worship of the idols of the pagans.[44]

The Manichaeans may have rejected the idea of the 'resurrected body', and considered the dead bodies as corpses, yet, in the present life, the 'Manichaean body', especially the bodies of the Elect, was precious, for it had a divine mission; therefore, it had to be safeguarded. Contrary to what many researchers have argued, BeDuhn says that the Manichaeans took care of their body, because without it, the soul's salvation was impossible: "Manichaeans prayed to the heavenly powers for the health and security of their bodies. 'Bright Mani, lord of fair name, life-giver, guard me in body; Jesus, lord, save my soul [...]'".[45] Particularly without the body of the Elect, the release of the *Living Self* was unattainable. Taking into consideration the above remarks, in combination with the Manichaean belief that slain animals had no *psyche* because the divine element in them was destroyed by the slaughter,[46] it is possible to imagine that the same might apply in the case of the violent death of martyrdom. The above could possibly explain why Manichaeans rejected blood-martyrdom as well as suicide as a means for the purification of the *Living Self* from Matter. According

---

Further on the phenomenon of *taqiyya*, see Kohlberg, 1975, 1995 & 2003/2016; Stroumsa 1986a, 156, 156 n.7. On other aspects of secretive attitudes among Manichaeans, see Stroumsa 1982.

42   Frend 1976, 860, 860 fn. 7; Augustine, *Faust.* 13.1 (*NPNF¹* 4:343, CSEL 25.1, 378,28).

43   Coyle 2009d, 203 (see also fn. 92 and 93 about two ambiguous references to ΜΑΡΙΑ ΘΕΟΝΑ ΜΑΡΤΥΡΕ in Ψαλμοί σαρακωτῶν 157.13 and 173.12). Cf. Augustine, *Faust.* 20.4 (p. 538.6) and *Conf.* 6.11.

44   Augustine, *Faust.* 20.4 (*NPNF¹* 4:436): "In a schism, little or no change is made from the original; as, for instance, you, in your schism from the Gentiles, have brought with you the doctrine of a single principle, for you believe that all things are of God. The sacrifices you change into love-feasts, the idols into martyrs, to whom you pray as they do to their idols. You appease the shades of the departed with wine and food". Cf. Coyle 2009d, 203 fn. 92.

45   M 311.V.10–13 in BeDuhn 2000b, 114: "It needs to be emphasized that Manichaeans were every bit as concerned with their bodies as with their 'souls.' One could say, in fact, that the salvation of the Manichaean soul absolutely necessitated a concern with the body – and not solely in negative terms".

46   See ch.[5], 2.2.1 and 2.2.3.1.

to Alexander, one of the main Manichaean tenets dictated, "One should not, by committing suicide, bring about an artificial purification of the stains inflicted upon the power by the admixture of matter".[47] Killing yourself (and therefore also seeking death via martyrdom), would harm the light encased in the body. In spite of the prophetic example of Mani, this was logically not a viable option for the Elect; it would not make sense for the Hearers either, because that would remove one more fighter for the cause of good from the earth, or one more supporter for the salvific work of the Elect.

Therefore, apart from prudential purposes, the avoidance of blood-martyrdom is fully consonant with basic Manichaean theology.

5 On the Converted Manichaeans: Sincere and False Conversions

After examining the possibility of choosing martyrdom, in this section I will focus on the second, more probable scenario for the persecuted Manichaeans: conversion.

As we saw in chapter [4], and as is reflected in the canons, the procedure for the reception into the Church of converted Manichaeans was the most strict and time-consuming.[48] Summarizing it in two words, the converted Manichaeans were received 'as pagans' (ὡς Ἕλληνες). In the present section, I will examine the whole procedure in detail. In this regard, apart from the canons discussed in ch.[4],[49] a text entitled *Ritual to be observed by those who are converted from among the Manichaeans to the pure and true faith of our Lord Jesus Christ* (RCM) is illuminating.[50] This text records the whole procedure with the words of the prayers in detail.

In brief, the stages of the ritual were as follows: Before the beginning of the procedure, the convert had to follow a preparatory programme with fasting and prayers. The first day, in the words of the canons: "we make them into Christians" (ποιοῦμεν αὐτοὺς χριστιανούς).[51] To do this, the ex-Manichaean

---

47 Alexander of Lycopolis, *Tract. Man.* 4 (Brinkmann, 7; Horst and Manfeld, 57): μὴ ἐξάγειν δὲ ἑαυτοὺς μηχανωμένους κάθαρσιν ὧν ἐλυμήνατο ἡ μῖξις τῆς ὕλης τὴν δύναμιν. Clement of Alexandria bears witness to the controversy that raged in his time over the subject of martyrdom, which some equated with suicide, see Poirier 2017, 241–53.

48 See the seventh canon of the second Ecumenical Council (381), the 95th canon of Quinisext Council (692), and the canons of Basil and Gregory.

49 Ch.[4], 2.1.3.

50 RCM (PG 100:1324c–25c, Goar 700–01): Τάξις γινομένη ἐπὶ τοῖς ἀπὸ Μανιχαίων ἐπιστρέφουσι πρὸς τὴν καθαρὰν καὶ ἀληθινὴν πίστιν ἡμῶν τῶν Χριστιανῶν. For an English translation see Lieu 1994a, 304–305.

51 Joannou 1962, 1a:54 and 232 (seventh and 95th canons).

had, first, to anathematize Mani and Manichaeism, by means of an abjuration formula, "in the presence" of "as many other believers as wish to attend" the ritual. If the convert did not speak Greek, the anathema was pronounced through an interpreter. If the convert was a child, the anathema was said by his godparent. The priest then recited a prayer over him and after the 'amen' the former Manichaean was counted as a Christian, like the un-baptized children. The second day the convert was registered in the lists of the Christian catechumens. The third day an exorcism was performed: the priest breathed three times on his face and ears pronouncing the prayers of exorcism. The next step was to remain in the class of catechumens for as long as necessary until his mentor considered that he was worthy to be baptized. During this stage, the Christian catechumen, former-Manichaean, attended the catecheses, in order to be instructed in the Christian faith and Scriptures.[52]

Thus, a prerequisite for the admission of the converted Manichaeans into the Church (in the class of believers) was their baptism, which, according to the canons, should take place after a long period during which they were instructed in the Christian teachings. Although the long period that this stage lasted is emphasized strongly (χρονίζει), its duration was not fixed by the canons. Presumably, it was left to the discretion of the cleric who was in charge of training the converts.

However, as early as the time of the First Council of Constantinople (381), there was a relevant instruction in Gregory of Nyssa's canonical letter (383/390) to Letoius, the bishop of Melitene. According to Gregory, the one who voluntarily apostatizes to Judaism or paganism or Manichaeism or any other similar kind of atheism and then reverts to the faith has to remain at the stage of penance for the rest of his life. He is neither allowed to participate in the mysteries of the Church with the believers, nor to receive the Holy Communion, unless it is at the moment of his death. If he would unexpectedly survive, he would once again be under the punishment of excommunication. Gregory accepts a shorter period of penitence only for those who were forced to apostatize by violence.[53] Thus, Gregory's canon seems to add a new category of converted,

---

52   *RCM* (PG 100:1324c–25c, Goar 701): καὶ οὕτω πάλιν κατηχούμενος, εἶτ᾽ οὖν διδασκόμενος χρονίζει εἰς τὴν ἐκκλησίαν, καὶ ἀκροᾶται τῶν γραφῶν. εἶτα τελουμένων πάντων τῶν ἐπὶ τῷ βαπτίσματι νενομισμένων, ἀξιοῦται τῆς θείας γεννήσεως.

53   Gregory of Nyssa, *Ep. Letoium* 225: Τούτων τοίνυν κατὰ τὸν εἰρημένον διακρινηθέντων τρόπον, ὅσα μὲν ἁμαρτήματα τοῦ λογιστικοῦ τῆς ψυχῆς ἅπτεται μέρους, χαλεπώτερα παρὰ τῶν Πατέρων ἐκρίθη, καὶ μείζονος καὶ διαρκεστέρας καὶ ἐπιπονωτέρας τῆς ἐπιστροφῆς ἄξια οἷον εἴ τις ἠρνήσατο τὴν εἰς Χριστὸν πίστιν, ἢ πρὸς Ἰουδαϊσμὸν, ἢ πρὸς εἰδωλολατρείαν, ἢ πρὸς Μανιχαϊσμὸν, ἢ πρὸς ἄλλο τι τοιοῦτον ἀθείας εἶδος αὐτομολήσας ἐφάνη, ὁ μὲν ἑκουσίως ἐπὶ τὸ τοιοῦτον ὁρμήσας κακὸν, εἶτα καταγνοὺς ἑαυτοῦ, χρόνον τὸν τῆς μετανοίας ἔχει, ὅλον τὸν τῆς

that of the apostates to atheism, namely, to Judaism, paganism and Manichaeism for whom the last stage of their conversion will end with the end of their life.

Summarizing the above: the converted Manichaeans, in order to be received into the Church as Christian believers (to participate in sacraments and communion), had to be baptized and their baptism would take place after a long period of training in Christian teachings. The Christian apostates to Manichaeism, who returned, constituted a separate category of converts (penitents), with a status analogous to that of the catechumens; yet, their stay on the margins of ritual life should last until the end of their life.

Observing the examined texts, it is noteworthy that both the church canons and RCM, just as the laws of the state (in their majority), do not discriminate between catechumens and Elect Manichaeans. It seems that both classes had the same treatment. The procedures for the converted Manichaeans, whether Elect or catechumens, were the same. The only text in which such a distinction exists comes from the western part of the Empire and is the *Commonitorium Sancti Augustini* (*Comm. Aug.*).[54]

According to the *Comm. Aug.*, after the converted Manichaean had anathematized Manichaeism and had "handed over a written statement of his confession and his repentance", he was given a (protective) letter by the bishop, certifying his conversion on the specific day and year, in order not to be considered guilty for his past, "either from state-laws or from Church discipline". This procedure was followed if the convert was a hearer. Of course, in case he would relapse, he would immediately be subjected to the punishments of the law and would be socially isolated from other Christians. In case the convert was an Elect, things were not so simple. While the hearers received the protective letter immediately (at the end of the ritual of the first day),[55] the Elect

---

ζωῆς αὐτοῦ. Οὐδέποτε γὰρ μυστικῆς ἐπιτελουμένης εὐχῆς, μετὰ τοῦ λαοῦ προσκυνῆσαι τὸν Θεὸν καταξιοῦται, ἀλλὰ καταμόνας μὲν εὔξεται τῆς δὲ κοινωνίας τῶν ἁγιασμάτων καθόλου ἀλλότριος ἔσται ἐν δὲ τῇ ὥρᾳ τῆς ἐξόδου αὐτοῦ, τότε τῆς τοῦ ἁγιάσματος μερίδος ἀξιωθήσεται. Εἰ δὲ συμβαίη παρ᾿ ἐλπίδας ζῆσαι αὐτόν, πάλιν ἐν τῷ αὐτῷ κρίματι διαβιώσεται, ἀμέτοχος τῶν μυστικῶν ἁγιασμάτων μέχρι τῆς ἐξόδου γινόμενος. Exception for those who were forced by violence to apostatize: Οἱ δὲ βασάνοις καὶ τιμωρίαις χαλεπαῖς αἰκισθέντες, ἐν ῥητῷ χρόνῳ ἐπετιμήθησαν, οὕτω τῶν ἁγίων Πατέρων φιλανθρωπίᾳ ἐπ᾿ αὐτῶν χρησαμένων, ὡς οὐχὶ ψυχῆς γεγενημένης ἐν πτώματι, ἀλλὰ τῆς σωματικῆς ἀσθενείας πρὸς τὰς αἰκίας οὐκ ἀντισχούσης. Διὸ τῷ μέτρῳ τῶν ἐν πορνείᾳ πλημμελησάντων, καὶ ἡ βεβιασμένη τε καὶ ἐπώδυνος παράβασις ἐν τῇ ἐπιστροφῇ συνεμετρήθη. For an English translation, see Silvas 2007, 211–25, 225. Cf. Lieu 1992, 146–47. See also ch.[4], 2.1.3, fn. 96.

54   *Comm. Aug.*, in Lieu 1994a, 301–303.
55   This can be inferred from a combination of the information in the canons, the RCM, and the *Comm. Aug.*

had to wait until the end of the instruction period, even if they had confessed, or even if they had anathematized Mani according to the abjuration formula. Moreover, as we are informed by the *Comm. Aug.*, the Elect during this process were subject to a kind of confinement, and had to remain either in a monastery or in a *xenodochium* under the supervision of a cleric or a layman, until it was sure that they had truly converted. Then and only then could they receive the protective letter and be baptized.[56]

The procedure as described in the *Comm. Aug.* does not differ from the one presented by the eastern canons, in that both classes (Elect and hearers) of converted Manichaeans have to be baptized in order to be received into the class of faithful Christians, and in that this (baptism) should take place after sufficient time to ensure their conversion.[57] So, where they are really different is that the Latin text provides some additionally illuminating information concerning when the protective letter was given to them, and the confinement of the Elect during their instruction period. Otherwise, both Elect and hearers, at the end of the stage of catechesis had to be baptized.[58]

---

56   I quote from *Comm. Aug.* (in Lieu 1994a, 303) concerning the protective letter: (1) "Since you repent that you were a Hearer of the Manichaeans, as you, yourself have confessed, anathematizing their blasphemies [...] you shall have this letter [...] (2) The letter however must not be given readily to their Elect who say they have been converted to the Catholic faith, even if they themselves have anathematised the same heresy according to the above formula, but they must remain [...] in a monastery or a guest-house for strangers, until it appears that they are completely free of that superstition [...] And, when they have received the letter, let them not move quickly elsewhere and heedless in themselves on account of the same document. They must be questioned if they know of any [other Manichaeans] so that they also may themselves be healed and thus he admitted to [the Catholic Church]".

57   I quote from *Comm. Aug.* (in Lieu 1994a, 301, 303) concerning baptism: (1) In the case the converted was a hearer: "When they have anathematized the same heresy [...] [and] handed over a written statement of his confession and his repentance, seeking a place in the church either of catechumen or penitent [...] the bishop give him a letter [...] And let them not be accepted readily for baptism if they are catechumens, nor for reconciliation if they have received the position of penitence, except under pressure of the danger of death, or if the bishop should learn that they have been approved for some considerable time, by the evidence of those to whom they were entrusted". (2) In the case the converted was an Elect: "Elect who say they have been converted to the Catholic faith, even if they themselves have anathematized the same heresy according to the above formula [...] must remain with the servants of God, either clerics or laity, in a monastery or a guest-house for strangers (xenodochium), until it appears that they are completely free of that superstition itself. And then either let them be baptized, if they have not been baptized, or let them be reconciled, if they have received the status of penitence".

58   The above interpretation is different from the one of Lieu. As Lieu (1994, 212) argues: "It is interesting to note that in the procedure for admission given in the postscript to the *Commonitorium Sanctii Augustini*, only the Elect, i.e. the priests, among the Manichaeans

So, the Greek texts actually do not differ from the *Comm. Aug.* The fact that the protective letter is not mentioned in the canons can be explained in two ways: either the custom did not exist in the East, or – perhaps more likely – since the custom mainly concerned the relationship of the convert to the State, those who drew up the church canons did not consider it necessary to include this particular aspect of the procedure.

In any case, the description of the whole process, especially the information for the protective letter just after the anathema, fits and complements what is known from the legislation. According to the law of 407 (*decrees of philanthropy*) as soon as the Manichaeans had accepted "the Catholic faith and rite" "by a simple confession" and "by a simple religious ceremony", it was decreed that they "should be absolved from all guilt".[59] A simple confession would suffice for the annulment of their penalties. Thus, once the converted hearer confessed the official faith and anathematized Manichaeism, he was named as Christian and was given the protective *epistula*, which stopped any subsequent prosecution by the law and annulled previously inflicted penalties. Afterwards, he could stay in the class of catechumens even for the rest of his life. For the converted Elect, on the other hand, persecution did not stop immediately after the anathematization and confession, since they had to wait a long time until they got the protective letter. However, the fact that they were in a mandatory restriction in the monasteries was also a kind of protection (asylum). It is noteworthy that this practice, which was a type of exile very frequent in Byzantine law, could have resulted into the infiltration of Manichaeism into monasticism. As seen in the case of Messalianism, the confinement of the suspected Messalians into monasteries was forbidden by the decision of the Council of Ephesus in 431 for that same reason (i.e. fear of Messalianism's spread among the monks).[60]

What has been pointed out from the above analysis is that it was one thing to be named Christian (which meant catechumen), and quite another to become a (faithful) Christian and member of the Church. In order to become members of the Church and participate in the mysteries, the converted Manichaeans

---

were required to be baptised before being received into the church. The Hearers would be given the protective *epistula* once they had abjured their former beliefs. This distinction was not made by Timothy, which seems to suggest that, in the Byzantine period, a Manichaean was considered as someone tainted by 'Manichaean' ideas rather than as a participant in a sect which observed a strict hierarchy of Elect and Hearer".

59   Cod. theod. 16.5.41 (407) (Coleman-Norton, 504). As *RCM* states, the first day, the Manichaean converts "anathematize Mani and Manichaeism [...] in the presence of 'as many other believers as wish to attend' the ritual". Cf. ch.[3], 3.5.

60   *ACO* (*Ephesenum anno 431*),1.1.7, 117–118.

had to be baptized. It has also been emphasized that the procedure to be baptized took a long time and that a converted Manichaean could remain in the class of catechumens for many years, even (in the case of apostasy and reconversion) for his entire life. So, it is not unreasonable to assume that many converts from Manichaeism were not baptized and remained Christian catechumens. If this was the case, however, the question in the Hippodrome "are you baptized in the one" could acquire an additional interpretation.[61] The testimony of Olympiodorus, a deacon in Alexandria in the sixth century, that the Manichaeans do not receive the baptism (as Greeks and Jews too), could be an indication that the majority of converted Manichaeans did not proceed to the last stage of their conversion; they did not get baptized.[62] Supporting the latter hypothesis is also the testimony of Barsanuphius who is particularly severe with some careless priests who ignored the canons and baptized persecuted Manichaeans without first ensuring that they have truly converted. He reminds them that in the case of Manichaeans the whole procedure has to be long-lasting.[63]

With the passage of time, the conversions logically increased due to the persecutions and the Christianization of the empire. The era favoured the Christians. The stigma of *infamia* (forfeiture of the status of *civis Romanus*) which was inflicted upon Manichaeans already from the early 380s had very real consequences in their everyday life, such as depriving them of the right to make a will or to inherit, and many other legal disabilities. The price of being openly Manichaean was too high.[64] Thus, the option of conversion must have

---

61   Cf. ch.[6], 5.2.

62   Olympiodorus, *Comm. Job.* (PTS 24:366): τοῦτο δὲ ἔστιν ἀκοῦσαι καὶ τῶν ὑπ' αὐτοῦ ἐνεργουμένων Ἑλλήνων τε καὶ Ἰουδαίων καὶ τῶν ἀνόμων Μανιχαίων οὐ προσδεχομένων τὴν διὰ τοῦ Ἰορδάνου ἀπολύτρωσιν. οὐ γὰρ βαπτίζονται Μανιχαῖοι ἀνάξιοι τυγχάνοντες. A practice that was not unusual at that time. Indeed, the law Cod. theod. 16.8.23 commanded the governors of the provinces, when they realized that any Jews were converted to Christianity for reasons of interest (i.e., not to be persecuted), to allow them to return to Judaism, if they had not been baptized.

63   Barsanuphius, *Ep.* 820 (SC 468: 290): Διὰ τοὺς ὁμολογουμένους μανιχαίους, ὀφείλεις γράψαι ὡς κωλύων καὶ δηλῶν τοῖς θέλουσιν αὐτοὺς βαπτίσαι, ὅτι τοιοῦτοί εἰσι, καὶ ἐν αὐτοῖς ἐστι τὸ βαπτίσαι αὐτοὺς ἢ μὴ βαπτίσαι, οὐ πάντες γὰρ ὡς δεῖ προσέχουσι τοῖς πράγμασι. Καὶ οὐκ οἴδασιν ὅτι πολλῆς σπουδῆς καὶ μακροῦ χρόνου, καὶ ἀκροάσεως θείων λογίων καὶ κατηχήσεως ὁσίων ἱερέων ἐπιδέονται οἱ τοιοῦτοι εἰς τὸ προσδεχθῆναι καὶ μὴ ἀφαρεὶ μηδ' ὡς ἂν ἔλθῃ.

64   As Peter Brown (1963, 291) has pointed out: "In an age in which the upper classes were especially dependent upon official privileges, titles, and their ability to protect their wealth by litigation, a penalty such as *infamia*, which prejudiced these advantages, was particularly onerous" (cf. Brown in Lieu 1994a, 155). Lieu and Lieu (1994, 155) comment: "Moreover, the opening sentence implies that Cresconius is very anxious to make a statement of some sort which would establish his conversion lest he should "depart" before the

been gradually more and more attractive; especially during Justinian's time it was the only option, because of the threat of capital punishment. We hear of similar dilemmas also among the followers of other persecuted religious groups, like the Samaritans, the Jews, and the pagans. According to Procopius, when Justinian issued a law against the Samaritans, many of them, "regarding it as a foolish thing to undergo any suffering in defence of a senseless dogma, adopted the name of Christians" in order to shake off "the danger arising from the law". Some of them, as Procopius says, once they had adopted this religion, decided to remain faithful to it. However, the majority, because they had been converted "not by their own free choice, but under compulsion of the law [...] instantly slipped away".[65] As in the case of the Samaritans so in that of the Manichaeans: some of their conversions would have been sincere and others made in pretence.[66]

A question arising at this point is: What were the practical implications for the converted Manichaeans in case they had (or opted) to stay as Christian catechumens for the whole of their life? I will investigate this question for the above two cases.

If the former Manichaean was converted sincerely, having the protective letter meant that he was no longer persecuted by the state and was discharged from all previous guilt; however, perhaps, without all the privileges (full status of *civis Romanus*) of the baptized Christians. Indeed, as indicated in a law of Justinian, a prerequisite for appointment to governmental service was that the

---

official *gesta* were properly signed. This would be important because the major disadvantage suffered by Manichaeans in the late Empire was their inability to make an effective will, which would lay it open to litigation if challenged".

65   Procopius, *Hist. Arcana*, 11.24–27 (Haury, 74–75; LCL 290, slightly modified): Νόμου δὲ τοῦ τοιούτου καὶ ἀμφὶ τοῖς Σαμαρείταις αὐτίκα τεθέντος ταραχὴ ἄκριτος τὴν Παλαιστίνην κατέλαβεν. ὅσοι μὲν οὖν ἔν τε Καισαρείᾳ τῇ ἐμῇ κἀν ταῖς ἄλλαις πόλεσιν ᾤκουν, παρὰ φαῦλον ἡγησάμενοι κακοπάθειάν τινα ὑπὲρ ἀνοήτου φέρεσθαι δόγματος, ὄνομα Χριστιανῶν τοῦ σφίσι παρόντος ἀνταλλαξάμενοι τῷ προσχήματι τούτῳ τὸν ἐκ τοῦ νόμου ἀποσείσασθαι κίνδυνον ἴσχυσαν. καὶ αὐτῶν ὅσοις μέν τι λογισμοῦ καὶ ἐπιεικείας μετῆν, πιστοὶ εἶναι τὰ ἐς δόξαν τήνδε οὐδαμῇ ἀπηξίουν, οἱ μέντοι πλεῖστοι ὥσπερ ἀγανακτοῦντες, ὅτι δὴ οὐχ ἑκούσιοι, ἀλλὰ τῷ νόμῳ ἠναγκασμένοι δόγμα τὸ πάτριον μετεβάλοντο, αὐτίκα δὴ μάλα ἐπί τε Μανιχαίους καὶ τοὺς καλουμένους Πολυθέους ἀπέκλιναν. The wording of Procopius "adopted the name of the Christians" in order to "shake off the danger arising from the law" fits perfectly with what is described above, concerning the first stage (catechumens) of conversion of the Manichaeans. The last sentence of Procopius that the falsely converted Samaritans have "instantly inclined to the Manichaeans and to the Polytheists" needs further research. I am not sure that Procopius here means the Monophysites, as has been argued, cf. Stroumsa (1985, 276) and Lieu (1994, 118).

66   See ch.[3], 3.4, 4.3.

candidate was a baptized Christian.[67] Yet, even if they had the same privileges as the faithful in theory, in practice it is probable that they faced a kind of social discrimination.[68] Concerning their relation with the Church, while they were counted as Christians, they were still not considered faithful Christians: they did not participate in the ritual life of the Church; in the congregations they could stay only during the teachings, not during the mysteries, etc.[69] In a way, they were somewhere between being Manichaeans and becoming Christians, their religious identity was blurry, under configuration.[70] Thus, the sincerely converted Manichaeans in both their relation to the state and to the Church were probably treated as second class citizens and Christians.[71] So, since they had reasons to be dissatisfied, the possibility of apostasy or crypto-Manichaeism could have been appealing.

The second case is that of the Manichaeans who converted in pretence or in an effort to save their lives; these did not want to renounce their faith, but were forced to do it by the circumstances (e.g. persecutions, legal prosecutions, harassment by the Church). Therefore, they anathematized Manichaeism and confessed the official faith in order to receive the protective letter and the name of the Christian, but actually they remained Manichaeans (i.e. they became crypto-Manichaeans). This is a common phenomenon in the history of religions when believers are forced by violence, either physical or psychological, to renounce their faith in order to save their own lives, to safeguard their properties, and to secure a more bearable everyday life.[72] It seems that

---

67   Cod. justin. 1.11.10 6–7; Cod. justin. 1.5.12.11 (527) (Frier et al., 205): "the divine certificates provided for most offices of the imperial service have as a prerequisite that the recipient must be orthodox".

68   See for example the case of converted Jews in Visigothic Spain. As Benveniste (2006, 73, 78) comments: "The Fourth Council of Toledo (633), under King Sisenand, decreed [that] [...] converts [from Judaism] could not assume public office and were to refrain from associating with ex-coreligionists. [...] the canons of the Fourth Council of Toledo dealt extensively with *relapsi*, and they also affected an innovation decreeing that "those who were formerly Jews should not seize public offices" (canon 65)".

69   Anyone to the rank of catechumen was entitled to be called a Christian, though he was not looked upon as one of the 'faithful'. "Ask a man, 'Are you a Christian?' His answer to you is, I am not, if he is a pagan or a Jew. But if he says I am; you inquire again of him, 'Are you a catechumen or a believer? (Augustine, *In Joannis* 44.2; transl. NPNF[1] 7, 403).

70   For the issue of the blurred religious identity of the converts and that they were regarded as a suspect population, see Benveniste (2006).

71   As Benveniste (2006, 74) argues, the converts from Judaism in Visigothic Spain were also treated "as a different class of Christians".

72   Cryptoreligions are a well attested interreligious and diachronic phenomenon. A known case from modern history (18th century) is that of the converted crypto-Jews in Persia, who accepted Islam superficially, whereas they privately remained faithful to their traditions, Cf. de Jong 2017, 659.

the same had happened in the case of the persecuted pagans who, according to Procopius' *Historia Arcana*, in order to avoid torture and economic plundering by Justinian, "decided to become nominal Christians, seeking thus to avert their present misfortunes", yet "not much later" "were caught performing libations and sacrifices and other unholy rites".[73]

For this second group of Manichaean converts, the prospect of a long-lasting period as Christian catechumens could probably be convenient. First, because they were not forced to be baptized (something Manichaeans abhorred). Secondly, because the rules and canons of the Church, in terms of everyday religious and social behaviour, were less stringent for the catechumens, than for the faithful (i.e. the baptized). The Church was more tolerant with the 'sins' and the 'crimes' of the catechumens since they were not yet initiated in the "legislation of Christ". As Basil explains in another letter to Amphilochius (which also became canon of the Church), "for the deeds during the stage of catechesis no responsibility is asked for", for "those who are not yet subjected under the yoke of Christ do not know the legislation of the Lord".[74] Moreover, those Manichaeans who were formerly hearers (the majority) were familiar with the idea of being catechumens for all their life.

Thus, the only option for a Manichaean who on the one hand did not want to renounce his faith, and on the other could not bear the consequences of the law, who wanted to rescue his patrimony, and to have the rights and privileges that the followers of the official religion had, was to be enlisted in the class of Christian catechumens, remaining a crypto-Manichaean.

What seems to have happened is that the laws themselves, in combination with the canons of the Church, to a certain extent contributed to the boosting of the phenomenon of crypto-Manichaeism. In both the above scenarios, the Christian catechumens, former Manichaeans, for different reasons each, were flirting with Manichaeism. In the first case (sincere conversion) the vague religious identity and the possible social marginalization could lead them to apostasy or crypto-Manichaeism; in the second case, because they were crypto-Manichaeans.

Therefore, to conclude, except for the use of the terms μανιχαῖος, μανιχαιόφρων and μανιχαΐζων as labels that the various Christian groups (Catholics, Arians, Monophysites, Nestorians, etc.) exchanged between each other as a

---

73   Procopius, *Hist. Arcana*, 11.31–33 (Haury, 75; LCL 290:139, 141; Atwater, 50–51): Ἐντεῦθεν ἐπὶ τοὺς "Ελληνας καλουμένους τὴν δίωξιν ἦγεν αἰκιζόμενός τε τὰ σώματα καὶ τὰ χρήματα ληϊζόμενος. ἀλλὰ καὶ αὐτῶν ὅσοι τοῦ Χριστιανῶν ὀνόματος δῆθεν μεταλαχεῖν ἔγνωσαν τῷ λόγῳ τὰ παρόντα σφίσιν ἐκκρούοντες, οὗτοι δὴ οὐ πολλῷ ὕστερον ἐπὶ ταῖς σπονδαῖς καὶ θυσίαις καὶ ἄλλοις οὐχ ὁσίοις ἔργοις ἐκ τοῦ ἐπὶ πλεῖστον ἡλίσκοντο. On Procopius' *Historia Arcana*, see Cameron 1985/2005, 47–65.

74   Basil of Caesarea, *Ep.* 199.

curse, and except ordinary Byzantine citizens who adopted here and there some 'Manichaean' ideas or practices, there was a group within Christianity, a part of Christian catechumens (converts from Manichaeism), who were inclined to Manichaeism (μανιχαιόφρονες and μανιχαΐζοντες). This may have been either consciously, or not knowing it distinctly (ἀνεπιγνώστως), or were considered and treated by the authorities as a population suspected of apostasy and crypto-Manichaeism. In the eyes of the leading state and church authorities, such a converted Manichaean, who was not baptized (and probably not intending to be baptized), was much easier to be considered a suspect (and accused) or be prone to apostasy and crypto-Manichaeism. Thus, it is reasonable to assume that there would be a permanent suspicion that questioned the sincerity of his conversion.

A relevant case is that of the converted Jews in Visigothic Spain, who in the eyes of the authorities were always a suspect population. For this, although they had converted to Christianity, they were still called Jews. As Benveniste states,

> Although the legislation was originally aimed against Judaic practices among Jews, willing or forced converts to Christianity soon became equally subject to controls. Converts were treated as a different class of Christians and preoccupied the Fourth, Sixth, Ninth and Sixteenth Councils. Finally, legislation against Judaic practices evolved into measures against people of Jewish origin [...] At the Seventh Council of Toledo converts were simply called Jews (646) [...]. Finally, by 694, the term "Iudaei" itself is far from clear. It refers to Christians of Jewish origin, especially those who preserved some of their ancestral rites, or to those known or suspected of defying royal and episcopal policy.[75]

This permanent suspicion is possibly the reason why Justinian's law (Cod. justin. 1.5.16) targeted the converted Manichaeans, who were suspected of both apostasy and crypto-Manichaeism. It is then probable that, for this reason, during Justinian's persecution, as Barsanuphius states, many of those revealed to be Manichaeans rushed to be baptized.[76] In particular, the status

---

75   Benveniste 2006, 74: "The 'relapsi' were a constant preoccupation (in the years 506, 633, 638, 654, 655, 681 and 693) [...] the history of laws and canons [...] are interesting on account of ideological nature and, more specifically, for the way the terms "Jew", "baptism" and "conversion" were defined in the context of Visigothic taxonomies. The sincerity of the converts may be debatable".

76   Barsanuphius, *Ep.* 820.

of 'non-baptized' was sufficient as a label for religious diversification and marginalization. A well-known case is that of an isolated community of pagans in Laconia (Greek Peloponnese); despite their Christianization during the reign of Basil I (867–886), because they had remained non-baptized for a long period, the local population in the mid-tenth century still called them 'Greeks' (which in this setting meant 'pagans').[77]

In this sense, I consider it likely that (a number of) the protestors in the Hippodrome could have been such a group, consisting of Christian catechumens, unbaptized Manichaean converts, converts who had relapsed, or converts verging or suspected of verging on Manichaeism. Similarly, this could also be true for Jews and Samaritans. "To distinguish between these categories" was impossible, because, as Benveniste observes for the case of Jews in Spain, "the fear of pollution and the blurring of the lines as a rhetorical strategy worked both ways".[78]

6   Crypto-Manichaeism Was an Old Story

Whatever the true identity of the "Manichaeans" in the Hippodrome was, the fake conversion of Manichaeans and crypto-Manichaeism were old stories which had caused problems for the Church Fathers of previous eras, before the issue of the capital punishment prevailed. Both the state and the Church were very cautious and always on high alert with the converted Manichaeans because there was the danger of fake conversions.[79] The converted Manichaeans, who were not baptized, reinforced suspicions about the phenomenon of crypto-Manichaeism. This fear is reflected at the end of the anathema formulas, where the converted ex-Manichaean promised and signed that he was not faking conversion.

---

77   Constantinus VII Porphyrogenitus, *De administrando imperio* 50.71–76: Ἰστέον, ὅτι οἱ τοῦ κάστρου Μαΐνης οἰκήτορες οὐκ εἰσὶν ἀπὸ τῆς γενεᾶς τῶν προρρηθέντων Σκλάβων, ἀλλ' ἐκ τῶν παλαιοτέρων Ῥωμαίων, οἳ καὶ μέχρι τοῦ νῦν παρὰ τῶν ἐντοπίων Ἕλληνες προσαγορεύονται διὰ τὸ ἐν τοῖς προπαλαιοῖς χρόνοις εἰδωλολάτρας εἶναι καὶ προσκυνητὰς τῶν εἰδώλων κατὰ τοὺς παλαιοὺς Ἕλληνας, οἵτινες ἐπὶ τῆς βασιλείας τοῦ ἀοιδίμου Βασιλείου βαπτισθέντες Χριστιανοὶ γεγόνασιν. Cf. Anagnostakis 1999, 25–47.

78   Benveniste 2006, 79.

79   See, for example, Serapion, *c. Manichaeos* 3.5–27, 30; Titus of Bostra, *c. Manichaeos* 3.1.13–24 (CCSG 82: 243–45); John of Caesarea, *Adv. Manichaeos, hom.* 1; Didymus the Blind, *c. Manichaeos* (PG 39:1105.49–53); Chrysostom, *Hom. Gen.*[1-9] (hom. 1) (PG 54:581–630, 585).

A signed statement must be made as follows: "I so-and-so having made these preceding anathemas have signed (below), and if I do not think, utter or speak these with the whole of my soul, but do so hypocritically, may I be anathematized and be accursed both in the present time and in future and may my soul be (destined) for destruction and perpetually be cast into (punished with) hell (ταρταρωθείη)".[80]

The same fear is also implied in John of Caesarea's and Cyril's warnings to the converted Manichaeans among their flock:

> Flee hence my beloved, from those who have received Mani's decay [...] if someone of you was previously infected/polluted by those beliefs [...] should now keep with the beliefs of the prophets and apostles.[81]
>
> Here let converts from the Manichees gain instruction, and no longer make those lights [luminaries] their gods; nor impiously think, that this sun which shall be darkened is Christ.[82]

6.1   Manichaeans: The Experts in Pretending

Regardless of the cases of false conversions, what both legal and ecclesiastical sources repeatedly stressed is the ability of Manichaeans to adapt their teachings and style of life to pretend to be Christians. Serapion begins and ends his work by emphasizing that his main aim was "to stress the danger" of "the Manichaeans, who surpass [all] previous heretics (Valentinians, Marcionites)" in passing themselves off as Christians "in order to convert those who [were] sincerely [Christians]".[83] This is also the tactic that Cyril combats, emphasizing to his catechumens that there is nothing in common between Manichaeism and Christianity.[84] In the words of Mark the Deacon, the Manichaeans are

---

80   sc, ch. 7 (Lieu 2010, 124–25): Καὶ δεῖ ὑπογράφειν οὕτως Ὁ δεῖνα ποιησάμενος τοὺς προκειμέ-νους ἀναθεματισμοὺς ὑπέγραψα, καὶ εἰ μὴ ἐξ ὅλης ψυχῆς ταῦτα φρονῶ καὶ φθέγγομαι καὶ λέγω ἀλλ' ὑποκρινόμενος, ἀνάθεμά μοι εἴη καὶ κατάθεμα καὶ ἐν τῷ νῦν αἰῶνι καὶ ἐν τῷ μέλλοντι καὶ εἰς ἀπώλειαν εἴη ἡ ψυχή μου καὶ διηνεκῶς ταρταρωθείη. The translation in English is a combination of Lieu 1994a, 254 and Lieu 2010, 125. For the same anathema in LAF, see Lieu 2010, 142–43.

81   John of Caesarea, Adv. Manichaeos hom. 1, 17.271–73 & 279–281 (Richard, 92): Φεύγετε τοί-νυν, ἀγαπητοί, τοὺς εἰσδεδεγμένους τοῦ Μάνεντος τὴν σηπεδόνα [...] εἰ δέ τις ἐν ὑμῖν πρότε-ρον τούτοις ἐρρυπωμένος τοῖς δόγμασιν, νῦν [...], φυλαττέτω τῶν προφητῶν καὶ ἀποστόλων τὰ δόγματα.

82   Cyril, Cathech. 15.3 (Reischl and Rupp 1967, 158; LFHCC, 2:185): παιδευέσθωσαν οἱ ἐκ Μανιχαίων ἐπιστρέψαντες, καὶ τοὺς φωστῆρας μηκέτι θεοποιείτωσαν, μηδὲ τὸν σκοτισθησόμε-νον τοῦτον ἥλιον τὸν Χριστὸν εἶναι δυσσεβῶς νομιζέτωσαν.

83   Serapion, c. Manichaeos 3.5–27 & 36.10–13; cf. ch.[4], 2.1.1.

84   Ch.[4], 2.1.1.

Christians only δοκήσει (in appearance, in a docetic way).[85] On every occasion it is underlined that Manichaeans pretended to be Christians for tactical reasons. According to anti-Manichaean authors, this was not a matter of ignorance, but instead was a tactic which served their missionary strategy.[86]

The biblical *topos* of the wolf in sheep's clothing was attributed also to other heretics, not solely to the Manichaeans.[87] Yet, what Church Fathers point out as a characteristic feature of the Manichaeans is that they used the same strategy in various (different) religious environments; the Manichaean adaptability resembled the tactic of a chameleon.[88] As Titus says, with Christians the Manichaeans pretend to be Christians, while with Greeks they pretend to be Greeks.[89] Epiphanius concludes his chapter *Against Manichaeans* by likening Mani with the snake *cenchritis*, whose skin changes colours following immediate environmental or social stimuli.

> this amphisbaena[90] and venomous reptile, the cenchritis, which has coils of many illustrations for the deception of those who see it, and conceals beneath it the sting and poisonous source [...] For since Mani is a pagan with the pagans [...] and [...] he knows the lore of the magi and is involved with them, and he praises astrologers and practices their mumbo jumbo. He merely mouths the name of Christ, as the cenchritis too conceals its poison, and deceives people with its tangled coils by hiding in deep woods and matching its background.[91]

---

85 Mark the Deacon, *Vit. Porph.* 86; ch.[4], 2.1.1.

86 Ch.[4], 2.1.1 and 2.1.2.3.

87 Chrysostom, *Hom. Gen.*[1-9] (hom. 1) (PG 54: 581–630, 585, 613); *Hom. Gen.*[1-67] (PG 53: 30.6–10); John of Caesarea, *Adv. Manichaeos, hom. 1*, 17.273–77; Epiphanius, *Ancoratus* 107.5.

88 Peter of Sicily, *Hist. ref. Man.* 16: Ἄλλους γὰρ ἔσχον πολὺ χείρους αὐτῶν τῆς κακίας διδασκάλους καὶ ἀρχηγέτας ὑπάρξαντας, καθὼς μετὰ μικρὸν δηλωθήσεται καὶ ἁπλῶς δίκην πολύποδος ἢ χαμαιλέοντος τῷ καιρῷ καὶ τῷ τρόπῳ καὶ τῷ προσώπῳ συμμεταβάλλονται, ὅπως τινὰ τῶν κουφοτέρων θηρεύσωσιν, καὶ ὅτε γνῶσιν αὐτὸν προσέχοντα ταῖς ματαιολογίαις αὐτῶν, τότε μικρὸν παρεκφαίνουσιν αὐτῷ καὶ τὰ παρ' αὐτοῖς μυστήρια.

89 Titus of Bostra, *c. Manichaeos* 3.1 (CCSG 82:243): Παρὰ δὲ χριστιανοῖς, τὰ χριστιανῶν δῆθεν μετιών. Titus of Bostra, *c. Manichaeos* 4.2, in Pedersen, 2004, 50 (CCSG 82, 243): "However, towards the pagan Greeks, [they] abandon the Christian material and instead set out to prove that his message accords with their traditions". See also ch.[4], 2.1.1. As Mark the Deacon (*Vit. Porph.* 85) states: "In fact the Manichaeans say that there are many gods, wishing in this way to please the Hellenes".

90 Amphisbaena is a mythological serpent which was believed to have a head at both ends, therefore it was supposed to go either forwards or backwards (TLG), cf. Levy 1996. Its name derives from the Greek words ἀμφί (on both sides) and βαίνω (walk, go).

91 Epiphanius, *Pan.* 66.88.2–3 (GCS 37:131–32; Williams, 315): ἡμεῖς δὲ πολλὴν ἐπιβεβηκότες ὁδὸν τραχεῖαν καὶ κινδυνώδεις τόπους μόλις ταυτησὶ τῆς ἀμφισβαίνης καὶ θηρὸς ὀλετηρίου τῆς κεγχρίτιδος, ἀπὸ πολλῶν ὁμοιωμάτων πεποικιλμένης πρὸς ἀπάτην τῶν ὁρώντων, ἐχούσης δὲ

6.2   Crypto-Manichaeism in the Catholic Clergy and Monasticism

As we have seen, the fear that there were crypto-Manichaeans among Christian catechumens and faithful (baptized) and, even worse, among Catholic clergy and monks, is repeatedly stressed in Greek anti-Manichaean literature. Figures such as those examined in previous chapters (e.g. presbyter Philip, presbyter/painter from Cyzicus, the archdeacon John,[92] the Alexandrian clerics of Cyril,[93] etc.) labelled as 'Manichaeans' (or μανιχαΐζοντες or μανιχαιόφρονες), are clear examples of the fear that there were Catholic clerics and monks who adopted Manichaean doctrines and practices, and thereby threatened the integrity of the church from within. Nilus of Ankara, a monk and a prolific author, in several letters addressed to clerics, monks, and state officials accuses his recipients of adopting Manichaean beliefs and practices; he stresses the responsibility they had against the Manichaean danger and expansion due to their position. Characteristic of his anxiety is his letter to Philon, a presbyter of a church in the sensitive area of the borders of the Empire, whom he reproaches in a strict and critical tone: "Stop, therefore, preaching the Manichaean myths to the people of the Lord to the church at the very outskirts of the Empire, pretending to deliver spiritual teaching".[94]

Moreover, as chapter six (and also chs. 5 and 7) argued extensively, the Christian ascetic movement "was frequently attacked as a disguised Manichee infiltration" already from the fourth century onwards.[95] The latter is clearly illustrated in the law of Theodosius in 381, according to which Encratites, Apotactites, Hydroparastates and Saccophori were regarded as camouflaged Manichaeans.[96] The fear of the diffusion of Manichaeism in ascetic environments continued to exist until the sixth century, when the 'Manichaean' label was frequently used in the Origenist controversy. According to Cyril of Scythopolis (sixth cent.), in the monastery of Holy Laura (of St. Sabbas) in

---

κεκρυμμένην κάτω τὴν κεντρώδη καὶ ἰοβόλον πηγὴν τῆς ἐκ πάντων ὁρμωμένης ἐπειδὴ γὰρ μετὰ Ἑλλήνων Ἕλλην ἐστίν, ἥλιον προσκυνῶν καὶ σελήνην καὶ τὰ ἄστρα καὶ δαίμονας, ὁ ἀνήρ, ἀγαπητοί, τυγχάνει καὶ ἡ αὐτοῦ αἵρεσις τὰ τῶν Ἑλλήνων ὑφηγεῖται, τὰ μάγων ἐπίσταται καὶ ἐν αὐτοῖς ἐγκυλινδεῖται, ἀστρονόμους ἐπαινεῖ, τὰ αὐτῶν περιεργαζόμενος, μόνον Χριστοῦ σεμνύνεται ὄνομα λόγῳ, ὡς καὶ αὐτὴ ἡ κεγχρῖτις κρύπτει μὲν τὸν ἰόν, ἀπατᾷ δὲ διὰ τῆς ποικιλίας, ἐν μέσῳ ὑλῶν πολλῶν γενομένη καὶ ἀφομοιουμένη μετὰ τῶν ὄντων.

92   See ch.[7], section 3.

93   See ch.[4], 2.2.

94   Nilus of Ankara, *Ep. 321*: Πέπαυσο τοίνυν ἐν προσποιήσει δῆθεν διδασκαλίας πνευματικῆς τὰ Μανιχαίων μυθεύματα παρατιθέμενος τῷ λαῷ τοῦ Κυρίου, ἐπὶ τῆς Ἐκκλησίας τῆς ἐν τῇ ἐσχατιᾷ. Other letters with references to Manichaeans are the following: book 1: 117, 167, 170, book 2: 8, 10, 11, 317. About the authenticity of the letters of Nilus, see Alan Cameron (1976b).

95   Chadwick 1998, 582.

96   Cod. theod. 16.5.7.

Palestine, there was a faction of monks (Origenists) that believed the Greek, Jewish, and Manichaean dogma. Finally, they seceded and established their own monastery, the New Laura.[97] Justinian's *Epistula ad synodum de Origene* speaks about monks in Jerusalem who, like Origen, became adherents of the Pythagorean, Platonic, Plotinian, and Manichaean dogmas. He claims that the misleading dogmas must be anathematized, as well as their inspirers and anyone who believes in them.[98]

6.3 Western Crypto-Manichaeans Among the Clergy and Monks in Africa & Rome

It has often been argued that those accused as "Manichaeans" in the Greek texts were not 'real' Manichaeans. If we seriously want to think through the option that some of them actually were, it will be very helpful to make a comparison with the richer dossier on this subject from the Latin West.

Augustine was terrified when he discovered that Victorinus, one of his subdeacons in Mauritania, had been for many years a crypto-Manichaean hearer and "used his position in the church as cover" to teach the Manichaean doctrine "without apparently awakening the least suspicion".[99] The anxiety of Pope Leo that "numerous Manichees who behaved outwardly as Catholic Christians" had infiltrated among the clerics of the Italian metropolises and of Rome is also recorded in his pastoral letters and sermons.[100] "Both Pope Gregory I and Gregory II issued warnings against accepting African priests entering Italy without investigation, as they might turn out to be Manichees".[101] A well-known testimony which reflects "the extent of Manichaean infiltration into the ranks of the [Egyptian] clergy and monastics", is the food-test ("the eating of meat on festive days") that Timothy the patriarch of Alexandria adopted in order to uncover crypto-Manichaeans among Christian clerics and monks.[102] In a similar fashion, clerics detected the Manichaeans (or μανιχαιόφρονες) among their flock by observing who of the "communicants at the Eucharist accepted the consecrated bread but not the cup of wine".[103]

---

97   Cyril of Scythopolis, *Vit. Sab.* (TU 49.2:124): ἀνήρ τις Παλαιστινὸς Νόννος καλούμενος, ὅστις χριστιανίζειν προσποιούμενος καὶ εὐλάβειαν ὑποκρινόμενος τὰ τῶν ἀθέων Ἑλλήνων καὶ Ἰουδαίων καὶ Μανιχαίων δόγματα ἐφρόνει.

98   Justinian, *Epistula ad synodum de Origene* 122.

99   Lieu 1992, 202–03; According to Frend (1976, 864–65), "there is evidence to suggest that a certain amount of secret Manichaeism persisted within the Catholic Church" in Numidia.

100 Lieu 1992, 205–06; Frend 1976, 865–66.

101 Lieu 1994a, 210; Frend 1976, 865.

102 Eutychius of Alexandria, *Annales* 148, in Lieu 1992, 183–84, Stroumsa 1986b, 312–15. See Gardner and Lieu 2004, 121–22 for the whole text.

103 Chadwick 2001, 171.

6.4   *Crypto-Manichaeism in Administration*

The presumed Manichaean infiltration in the imperial administration was vigorously fought by Justinian. However, measures against it appear much earlier, as is reflected in the constitution of Valentinian III in 445, according to which it was forbidden for Manichaeans to hold public office. A fine was set for the officials who allowed such appointments.

> The Manichaeans must be deprived of the dignity of governmental service [...]. The chief men of every government service or of every office staff then should be smitten by a fine of ten pounds of gold to be exacted by your apparitors, if they allow anyone polluted by this superstition to be in governmental service.[104]

Nevertheless, as can be derived from later legislation, Manichaeans had disregarded the legal ban and infiltrated governmental services and guilds.[105] Indeed, it seems that there were some Manichaeans who had come even to baptism, in order to take an office or a public position.

> 6. Those, however, who for the sake of keeping their position in the imperial service, their rank, or property, have deceitfully received or shall receive saving baptism, [...] shall also be subjected to punishment worthy of them, for it is thereby manifest that they did not receive holy baptism with pure faith. 7. We enact these provisions against the accursed pagans and Manichaeans, of which Manichaeans the Borborites are obviously part.[106]

7   The Hypothesis of *Entryism*

Feigned conversions seem to have existed even in the time of Cyril of Jerusalem, when there was still religious tolerance, before the first decree which forbade Manichaeans to assemble in churches was issued (372). Cyril of Jerusalem, in his catechetical lectures, warns his catechumens to keep aloof from converted

---

104   *NVal.* 18 (445) (Coleman-Norton, 730–31).
105   Cod. justin. 1.5. 12, Cod. justin. 1.5. 16.
106   Cod. justin. 1.11.10.6–7 (529?) (Frier et al., 247).

Manichaeans, at least until it was sure that they had truly repented.[107] Equally relevant is Gregory of Nyssa's reservation which set as the appropriate time of penitence for apostates to Manichaeism the whole of their life.[108] So, it is probable that there were crypto-Manichaeans in the Catholic Church, at a time when there was tolerance and they could have their own places of worship, as argued in ch.[7]. If this was the case, however, we can assume that, at least, for Byzantine Manichaeism, crypto-Manichaeism was not only the result of necessity, but also a missionary strategy. In this scenario, we are talking about *entryism*. This tactic is not unknown in political history. The most known modern example is Trotskyism.[109] Webber, explaining Trotskyist *entryism*, states:

> Trotsky thought that an independent Trotskyist organization would be isolated from the larger leftist movement and even destroyed. By entering larger leftist parties, Trotskyists could exert influence among the working classes with less risk of being isolated. Entryism was thus born as a pragmatic response to the local weakness of sectarian Trotskyist appeals by entering larger political organizations that offer both protection from isolation and access to the larger working class.[110]

According to a definition of *entryism*, given by John Tomlinson, a theorist of the phenomenon,

> entryism (be it Trotskyist or not) has three basic objectives for its participants: 1. To identify support for its own cause within the host group, or stimulate it; 2. To provoke and/or exploit division within that group to its

---

107 Cyril, *Catech.* 6.36.2–4 (Reischl and Rupp 1848, 206): Συναγελάζου τοῖς προβάτοις φεῦγε τοὺς λύκους τῆς Ἐκκλησίας μὴ ἀναχώρει. Μίσει καὶ τούς ποτε εἰς τὰ τοιαῦτα ὑποπτευθέντας καὶ ἐὰν μὴ χρόνῳ καταλάβῃς αὐτῶν τὴν μετάνοιαν, μὴ προπετῶς σεαυτὸν ἐμπιστεύσῃς. Παρεδόθη σοι τῆς μοναρχίας ἡ ἀλήθεια. See also Cyril, *Cath.* 6.34; *Cath.* 15.3. Cf. Lieu 1994a, 205, 212; Lieu 1992, 131.

108 Gregory of Nyssa, *Ep. Letoium* 225.

109 The term *entryism* is borrowed from modern history and political science (in particular Trotsky's strategy) in order to describe a very old tactic, cf. the 'Two Letters to the International Secretariat', 1 November and 16 December 1934, in *The Spanish Revolution 1931–39* (1973, 245–46, 251), a collection in English of Leon Trotsky's writings on the revolutionary developments in Spain. About *entryism* as a Trotskyite strategy, see Sennett 2014 (220, 280–82, 184–89, 196, 90–92, 122, 154). The idea of using the term *entryism* developed in the context of the discussions with Prof. Dimitris Kyrtatas at the University of Thessaly Late Antiquity discussion group. Cf. Matsangou 2017a, 168–69.

110 Webber 2009, 33.

own political ends and in order to achieve a degree of executive power; 3. To exert influence on the nature and direction of policy within the infiltrated group.[111]

I support that something similar could have happened with the Manichaeans. That there were crypto-Manichaeans is not a new research finding.[112] What I am arguing here, is that crypto-Manichaeism, apart from prudential purposes, also served the politics of Manichaean mission.[113] The choice of this tactic was not irrelevant to the fact that Manichaeans could not compete with the official Church on equal terms. Entering into the structures of the dominant Church became a good tool for the Manichaeans. On the one hand, it offered them protection and reduced the risk of their extinction. On the other, instead of being on the margins of politico-religious developments and in isolation, borrowing Tomlinson's and Webber's phraseology, they "could exert influence" "within the infiltrated group". In the case of Manichaeans, as in the twentieth-century case of Trotskyists, occupying positions of authority enabled them "to achieve a degree of executive power". Thus, they were able to play a role in the formation of the religious landscape. Therefore, one could argue that the policy of *entryism* was "born as a pragmatic response" to the weakness of the sectarian character of the Manichaean movement.[114]

A vivid illustration of our authors' fear regarding this presumed Manichaean *modus operandi* is the account of the missionary Julia. As Mark the Deacon recounts, Julia entered undetected (ὑπεισελθοῦσα) in the Christian Church of Gaza, and corrupted (ὑπέφθειρεν) secretly and gradually some of the Christian neophytes.[115]

---

111   Tomlinson in Webber 2009, 33–34.

112   Relevant references have been made by many scholars. See for example, Brown 1969, 100: "Secondly, Manichaeism became a problem increasingly as a form of crypto-Christianity. Mani had trumped Christ: the Manichaean missionary had to prove it by dogging the Christian community; and his converts would tend to remain prudently hidden under the shadow of the Catholic Church"; Stroumsa and Stroumsa 1988, 38: "Hence, the Christians treated Manichaeism as a threat from within, – regarding it as "the worst of all heresies," the last and most vicious trick of the Devil"; Stroumsa 1986b, 312–15, 315: "In any case, the indisputable presence of Manichaeans among Christian clerics"; Chadwick 1998, 582: Christian asceticism "was frequently attacked as a disguised Manichee infiltration"; Lieu 1992, 202–03.

113   It is for this reason that I use the term *entryism*: to differentiate it from simple infiltration that does not necessarily mean strategic infiltration.

114   Webber 2009, 33–34.

115   Mark the Deacon, *Vit. Porph.* 85 (Lieu 2010, 96–97): Ἰουλία, [...] γνοῦσά τινας νεοφωτίστους [...] ὑπεισελθοῦσα ὑπέφθειρεν αὐτοὺς διὰ τῆς γοητικῆς αὐτῆς διδασκαλίας, πολλὰ δὲ πλέον διὰ δόσεως χρημάτων.

About that time, a woman from Antioch named Julia arrived in the city [Gaza]. She belonged to the abominable sect of those known as manichaeans. Now discovering that (among Christians) there were some novices who were not yet confirmed in the holy faith, this woman [Julia] infiltrated herself among them and surreptitiously corrupted them with her bewitching doctrine, and still further by giving them money.[116]

John of Caesarea, in his first homily against the Manichaeans, targeted the same tactic (διορύττειν καὶ τοὺς τῆς ἐκκλησίας διασαλεύειν τροφίμους ἐπιχειροῦσι), as shown by the introduction and the end of his work. As John stresses, aiming to safeguard his flock (τῆς ὑμῶν ἕνεκεν ἀσφαλείας), the Manichaeans with their feigned paleness and Christ's name deceived the naive. By concealing their true self, they could 'leap in upon' (ἐπεισπηδῶσι) the Church attempting to tear her in pieces (διασπαράττειν).[117]

Of course, the fear of our sources regarding strategic Manichaean infiltration is not proof that this actually happened. Manichaean texts testifying that this was an operative missionary method do not exist. There are, however, some Manichaean features, as well as testimonies concerning Manichaean infiltration in other religious contexts which could support such a hypothesis.

8 Manichaean Features Supporting the Hypothesis of *Entryism*

8.1 *The Manichaean Concept of Sacrifice (Martyrdom): Dissolution?*
The hypothesis of *entryism* is further supported by some key features of the nature of Manichaeism, such as: (1) universality of religion precedes the theology of religion, (2) the dualistic background, and (3) eclecticism.

It is known that for the sake of universality and for the attraction of new adherents, Manichaeism had been adapting its teaching to incorporate elements of the religions of the areas where its missionary activities took

---

116   Mark the Deacon, *Vit. Porph.* 85 (Lieu 2010, 97; Lieu 1994a, 56).

117   John of Caesarea, *Adv. Manichaeos hom. 1*, 1.8–15 (Richard, 85): Ἀλλ᾽ ἐπειδή τινες τῆς τοῦ Μάνεντος ἐμφορηθέντες μανίας διορύττειν καὶ τοὺς τῆς ἐκκλησίας διασαλεύειν τροφίμους ἐπιχειροῦσι, τῷ σίτῳ παραμιγνύντες ζιζάνια καὶ τοῖς ὀρθοῖς δόγμασι τῶν ἀποστόλων ὑποσπείροντες γέλωτος πλήρεις μυθολογίας, τῆς ὑμῶν ἕνεκεν ἀσφαλείας ὡς ἐν βραχεῖ τὸν πρὸς ἐκείνους πόλεμον ἀναδέξομαι καὶ τὰς ἀκάνθας προρρίζους ἀνασπῶν ἐλεύθερον ἀσεβείας τῆς ἐκκλησίας ἀναδείξω τὸ λήϊον; ibid, 17.271–80 (Richard, 92): Φεύγετε τοίνυν, ἀγαπητοί, τοὺς εἰσδεδεγμένους τοῦ Μάνεντος τὴν σηπεδόνα, οἳ πολλάκις ὠχρότητι σώματος τὸ δοκεῖν ἐγκρατεῖς εἶναι θηρώμενοι, τῷ σχήματι καὶ τῷ βλέμματι καὶ τῇ τοῦ Χριστοῦ προσηγορίᾳ τοὺς ἁπλουστέρους ἐξαπατῶσι καὶ κῳδίῳ προβάτου τὸν ἔνδοθεν λύκον ὑποκρυπτόμενοι ἐπεισπηδῶσι καὶ τὴν Χριστοῦ ποίμνην διασπαράττειν ἐπιχειροῦσιν. Φεύγετε τοίνυν καὶ τοῖς τοιούτοις χαίρειν μὴ λέγετε· Φθείρουσιν ἤθη χρηστὰ ὁμιλίαι κακαί.

place.[118] Theoretically, such a position can be grounded in Paul's first epistle to Corinthians: 'To the Jews I became as a Jew, so that I might win Jews [...] to those who are without law, as without law [...] so that I might win those who are without law, [...]' (1 Cor. 9:19–22). The concept of sacrifice can be interpreted through the same passage.[119] The sacrifice should not be taken to mean blood-martyrdom, but as the suffering of being ὀθνεῖος (stranger) and μονήρης (solitary), in the midst of error, for the sake of truth.[120] As Mani perceives himself in the CMC,

> [I am] in multitude, but I am solitary. For these are rich, but I am poor. How then shall I, alone against all, be able to reveal this mystery in the midst of the multitude [entangled in] error? [...] and [I] became a stranger and a solitary in their midst.[121]

Behind this rationale lie the dualistic substratum and Manichaean eclecticism: "The One [elect] versus the Many, Light versus Darkness, Gnosis versus Ignorance".[122]

8.2   The 'Sacrifice' of the Primal Man (Manichaean God) in Manichaean Cosmogony

Moreover, it could be argued that some key components of the Manichaean cosmogonical myth support the above idea of sacrifice providing the necessary theological ground for the tactic of *entryism*.

Such a component is the idea that the *Father of Greatness* (light principle) voluntarily offers a portion of his substance (Primal Man), in "the guise of tempting bait" to the *King of Darkness* (evil principle), in order that he "be captured by this mingling".[123]

---

118   Lieu 1992, 250, 262: "This process of assimilation began under the guidance of Mani [...] It was continued by his disciples as the religion spread eastwards and we can tell [...] that this process developed gradually without overall control by the *archegos* in Babylonia"; "By adapting some aspects of their religion to Buddhism and Taoism the Manichaeans had succeeded in narrowing the cultural gap between China and the west".

119   Titus of Bostra, *c. Manichaeos*, 4.11 in Pedersen 2004, 51: "Nor does Mani wish to see his followers persecuted to death, but believes on the basis of 1 Cor. 9:19.22 that it is permissible to make sacrifices" (CCSG 82: 340–41).

120   CMC 44.2–12, 31.1–9.

121   CMC 31.1–9, 44.2–12, 84.12 ff (Cameron and Dewey 27, 35, 66).

122   Henrichs 1973, 27. On the "Manichaean discourse of suffering", see also Brand 2020, 112–34.

123   Severus of Antioch, *123 Cathedral Homily* (Excerpts from an untitled Manichaean Scripture), pp. 164.10–166.15 (Lieu 2010, 33): "On account of this disturbance, which was prepared out of the depths against the land of light and against the holy fruits, it was necessary that a part should come out of the light and be mingled with the evil ones, so that

Then the Primal Man offered himself [...] and his five sons as nourishment to the five sons of darkness, like one who, having an enemy, mixes a deadly poison into a cake and offers it to him. When the sons of darkness had eaten, the intelligence of the Five Shining Gods [ziwane = sons of the First Man] was toppled.[124]

The dualistic background and Manichaean eclecticism is dominant in the next act of the myth. The *Father of Greatness* dispatches a second divine power to the Land of Darkness, the *Living Spirit* and his five sons, who

found the Primal Man swallowed up by the darkness and his five sons. Then the Living Spirit called out in a loud voice. The voice of the Living Spirit was like a sharp sword, and it laid bare the form of the Primal Man and said to him: "Peace be with you, who are the good amid the wicked, the light amid the darkness, the god who dwells amid wrathful animals that know not the magnificence [of the sons of light]!".[125]

Whereas at the end of this act "the *Primal Man* was brought back [...] in the land of light", with the help of *Living Spirit* who "held out his right hand [...] and drew him out of the darkness", his five sons (his armour) remained "swallowed up" by the *Hylē* in order to act like the deadly poison in the cake; through the 'cosmic belly' of the *King of Darkness* they would work towards the salvation of *Light* and the destruction of *Matter*.[126] Thus, during the *Middle Time*, the process of purification from Matter is advancing, until the *Final Time*, when the last particle of light from the mixture will be pumped out, and the scattered Primal Man will be restored again to form the *New Man*, the *Perfect Man*. So, after his descent "into dissolution" in the Land of Darkness, the Primal Man finally "ascends reconstituted", having purged the world from the evil principle.[127]

---

the enemies would be captured by this mingling [...] And no harm comes to it; but rather this exodus or crossing-over takes place in order that, by virtue of the part which came from the light, the enemies, being scattered, might cease their attack and are captured by the mingling"; pp. 174.3–8: "this portion of light was given to Matter in the guise of tempting bait and a deception, so that after this "the mixture" – as you say – 'would be purified'. [...] 'And after the purification' [...] according to you – 'matter will be completely reduced to destruction'!".

124 Tardieu 2008, 76–78. The version of the myth transmitted by the Nestorian doctor Theodore bar Konai. See ch.[5], 2.1.

125 Tardieu 2008, 76–78, 77.

126 Tardieu, 2008, 87.

127 Gardner and Lieu 2004, 19, 12–13, 155.

The idea of Primal Man's sacrifice is echoed in a parable of the Manichaean Psalms, according to which a shepherd temporarily sacrifices one of his sheep, in order to trap the lion threatening to devour all his flock.

> Like unto a shepherd that shall see a lion coming to destroy his sheep-fold: for he uses guile and takes a lamb and sets it as a snare that he may catch him by it; for by a single lamb he saves his sheep-fold. After these things he heals the lamb that has been wounded by the lion.[128]

8.3   The 'Sacrifice' of the Manichaean God According to the Greek Anti-Manichaica

Greek anti-Manichaean authors knew and commented on the part of the myth about the 'swallowing'.[129] Some of them, such as Alexander, Titus and Simplicius, highlight that this swallowing was a sacrifice planned by the Light principle aiming for its victory over the Evil principle from within. This victory sometimes is described as the "death of matter" (Alexander), the "involuntary reformation of matter" (Titus), or as the "dominion over Evil" (John of Damascus). Yet, according to anti-Manichaean authors, this sacrifice reveals the cowardice and the nonsense of the Manichaean *King of Light*. Alexander considered it "much more reverential and in conformity to the superiority of God" to devastate Matter from the very beginning.[130] Furthermore, he criticizes as unfounded and absurd the claim that it was necessary for the two principles to be mixed:

> Therefore he [God] sent a power, which we call the soul, to confront matter, with the aim of bringing about a complete mingling with it. And its consequent separation from this power would result in the death of matter.[131]
>
> The statement "God sent down a power towards matter" is given without any proof whatsoever, and is in no way plausible. [...] As the cause of this occurrence they give what follows: "In order that nothing be bad

---

128   *2PsB* 9.3–11.32. Psalm 223 (The community sing 'the knowledge of Mani') in Gardner and Lieu 2004, 176–79, 177 (text no 56). Cf. Lieu 2010, 190.

129   In the *sc*, ch. 6: "I anathematize those who say that the human souls are consubstantial with God and, being part of (the) good (principle) were swallowed up by the *Hylē* and out of this necessity the world was created" (Lieu 2010, 123).

130   Alexander of Lycopolis, *Tract. Man.* 12 (Van der Horst and Mansfeld, 73).

131   Alexander of Lycopolis, *Tract. Man.* 3 (Lieu 2010, 39; cf. Van der Horst & Mansfeld, 54).

and all things good, the power had to mingle with matter [...] in order to vanquish matter and to stop it from being".[132]

Simplicius develops his critique in a similar vein. He additionally informs us, asserting the originality of his sources, that the Manichaeans paralleled the tactic of their God to that of a general.

What kinds of and how many blasphemies against God necessarily result from their teachings? For example, they describe him as a coward who dreaded the approach of evil to the borders lest it enters his domain. Out of fear, he unjustly and arbitrarily submitted portions and parts of himself (which were formerly innocent souls) to evil so that he might save the rest of the good souls. He acted, as they say, like a general, who sensing the approach of the enemy, sacrificed part of his army in order to save the rest. These are their own words, If not, at least the words of the reports about them.[133]

As Titus describes the goal of the project, the dispatched benevolent power acted as a lure to *Hylē/Evil*, which provoked its "involuntary reformation" (ἀκούσιον τῇ ὕλῃ σωφρονισμόν).

The good (principle) dispatches a power [...] to become a bait for the involuntary reformation of matter. That is what happened. For when Hylē saw the power sent, she longed for it as if she fell in love with the power, and grabbed her with great impetus and swallowed her; hence was bound to her like a beast.[134]

---

132 Alexander of Lycopolis, *Tract. Man.* 12 (Van der Horst and Mansfeld, 73). See also *Tract. Man.* 5 (Van der Horst and Mansfeld, 58): "their assumptions are not expressed in a generally acceptable ratiocinative form; hence a scrutiny of these assumptions is out of the question. Nor are there any proofs to be found which would be based on postulates, which renders it impossible to consider what these postulates would entail".

133 Simplicius, *Comm. Man. Epict.* 35 (Hadot, 323.36–45; Lieu 2010, 102–03): Οἷα δὲ καὶ ὅσα βλάσφημα εἰς τὸν θεὸν τοῖς ὑπ' ἐκείνων λεγομένοις ἐξ ἀνάγκης ἀκολουθεῖ. Καὶ γὰρ δειλὸν εἰσάγουσιν αὐτὸν, δεδοικότα τὸ κακὸν ἐγγὺς τῶν ὅρων αὐτοῦ γενόμενον, μὴ καὶ ἐντὸς εἰσέλθῃ. Καὶ διὰ ταύτην τὴν δειλίαν ἀδίκως καὶ ἀσυμφόρως ἑαυτῷ μέρη ἑαυτοῦ καὶ μέλη τὰς ψυχὰς οὔσας, ὥς φασι, μηδὲν ἁμαρτούσας πρότερον, ἔρριψε τῷ κακῷ, ἵνα τὰ λοιπὰ τῶν ἀγαθῶν διασώσῃ· ὥσπερ στρατηγὸς, φασί, πολεμίων ἐπιόντων, μέρος αὐτοῖς τοῦ οἰκείου στρατοῦ προΐεται, ἵνα τὸ λοιπὸν διασώσῃ. Ταῦτα γάρ ἐστιν αὐτῶν τὰ ῥήματα, εἰ καὶ μὴ ἐπ' αὐτῶν ἴσως τῶν λέξεων. Simplicius, as an honest researcher, does not conceal the possibility of his information to have been of second-hand provenance.

134 Titus of Bostra, *c. Manichaeos* 1.17.6–13 (CCSG 82:39): Ὁ δὲ ἀγαθὸς δύναμιν ἀποστέλλει τινά [...] δέλεαρ ἐσομένην εἰς ἀκούσιον τῇ ὕλῃ σωφρονισμόν. Ὃ δὴ καὶ γέγονε· θεασαμένη γὰρ ἡ ὕλη

Or in the words of John of Damascus:

> And the Light principle sent a power, and a struggle took place where the
> archons of darkness ate part of the Light. That is, the Light principle let
> them grab a part of his power, and did so to gain dominion over Evil with
> the part he let them have.[135]

Other sources, such as the *AA*, while aware of the 'swallowing', do not point out
that it was a voluntary 'sacrifice'. They do not say that Primal Man gave himself
on purpose to the *Prince of Darkness*, as a means of trapping him.[136] However,
the *AA*'s author knows and uses the parallel image that exists in the *PsB* where
a shepherd (God) temporarily offers one of his sheep (children/souls) to the
lion (Evil) in order to trap the lion, saving thereby the whole flock.[137]

8.4   *The 'Sacrifice' of the Manichaeans*

The above mythical events are of particular importance for our query, given
the relationship between the microcosm and macrocosm in Manichaean cosmological narrative. The adventure of the Primal Man in the Land of Darkness
was one of the favourite motifs of the Manichaean Psalms. The psalms that the
Manichaean believers chanted in their congregations often speak in the voice
of the *Living Self*:

> Since I went forth into the darkness I ... am in the midst of my enemies ...
> The strangers with whom I mixed ... I am the life of the world; I am the
> milk that is in all trees; I am the sweet water.[138]

The *Psalms of the Wanderers* speak of the 'long-sufferingness' and the 'endurance' of the envoys of the Land of Light to the Land of Darkness encouraging
the wandering Manichaean ascetics to imitate their divine archetypes.

τὴν ἀποσταλεῖσαν δύναμιν, προσεκίσσησε μὲν ὡς δὴ ἐρασθεῖσα, ὁρμῇ δὲ πλείονι λαβοῦσα ταύτην
κατέπιε, καὶ ἐδέθη τρόπον τινὰ ὥσπερ θηρίον.

135   John of Damascus, *c. Manichaeos* 2.17–22 (PTS 22:352–53): καὶ ἀπέστειλεν ὁ ἀγαθὸς δύναμιν παρ' αὐτοῦ, καὶ συμπλοκῆς γενομένης ἔφαγον μέρος τοῦ φωτὸς οἱ ἄρχοντες τοῦ σκότους.
Παρεχώρησε γὰρ ὁ ἀγαθὸς ἁρπαγῆναι δύναμιν ἐξ αὐτοῦ [...] Τοῦτο δὲ ἐποίησεν, ἵνα διὰ τῆς μοίρας, ἧς παρέδωκε, κατακυριεύσῃ τῆς κακίας.

136   Cf. Kaatz 2007, 103.

137   *AA* 28. Cf. *2PsB* 9.31–10.2.

138   *2PsB* 54.11 ff (Psalm 246, Allberry). A practice which, as it seems, Titus knew: Κέχρηνται γὰρ
καὶ τῷδε τῷ ὑποδείγματι, ὡς δι' ἐπῳδῆς τῆς ἀποσταλείσης δυνάμεως ἐκοιμίσθη (*c. Manichaeos*,
1.17.14–15, CCSG 82:39).

[...] spirit of endurance come to us, let endurance endure and let us bear up that we may [...] endurance [...] the First Man, he was sent out to the fight, and endurance came to him. He left his land of light behind him, he went out to the land of darkness and endurance came to him. He left also his people behind him, he went out to the field [...] and endurance came to him. [...] We also, my brethren, have our part of suffering: we shall join with them in the suffering and rest in their rest;[139]

So, the Elect Manichaeans had to act accordingly, and imitate the Primal Man, who suffered and showed patience. Thus, there are grounds to assume (without much violation of historical probability) that the sacrifice of the Manichaean God served as an exemplar for the sacrifice of Manichaeans. As the *King of Greatness* responds to the invasion of darkness not in a violent way[140] (as Alexander suggests), but wisely lets himself be partly swallowed (while simultaneously working out his salvation through the "cosmic belly of the *King of Darkness*"),[141] the Manichaean Elect instead of clashing with their religious opponents, choose the smart tactic of 'being swallowed' within their opponent's structures: the few Elect mingled within the crowd of ignorant, with a view to transform them. In Paul's words, "a little leaven leavens the whole lump" (Gal 5:9, μικρὰ ζύμη ὅλον τὸ φύραμα ζυμοῖ). The implementation of such a plan required coexistence, not conflict. Secrecy was a *sine qua non* prerequisite for its success.[142]

9 Comparative Evidence Supporting the Hypothesis of *Entryism*

The hypothesis of *entryism* is further supported by comparative evidence (from different times and places) which demonstrates that such practices were and still are actually happening. The following cases are indicative and do not aim to constitute a thorough study.

9.1 *Simon the Magus and the Gnostics*
Religious *entryism* as a tactic certainly existed before Manichaeism. Apart from the Manichaeans, various groups of heretics, especially the 'old heretics'

---

139   A psalm of endurance, 2PsB 141.1–143.34 in Gardner and Lieu 2004, 240 (no 80). Cf. Drijvers 1984, 107–10.

140   About the 'gentleness' of the Manichaean God, see Pettipiece 2007, 119.

141   Tardieu 2008, 87.

142   About the concealment of Manichaean scriptures and communities, see Lieu 2015, 130–39.

and Gnostics, were accused of entering Christian communities with subversive purposes.[143] As expected, the first instructor of this tactic was considered to have been Simon the Magus.

> Then [...] [Simon] [...] submitted, and feigned faith in Christ even to the point of baptism. It is worthy of wonder that this is still done by those who continue his most unclean heresy to the present day, for following the method of their progenitor they attach themselves to the Church like a pestilential and scurfy disease.[144]

Eusebius' view about Simon should not be taken at face value but, instead, as evidence that the method of *entryism* was not unusual.

Apparently, crypto-religions and the tactic of strategic infiltration did not stop in Late Antiquity.

9.2   The Last of the Paulicians?

An impressive testimony, revealing how resilient the secret identity of crypto-religions through time may be, is the story of Mr. Lion, "The last of the Paulicians", given by Russell.[145]

Mr. Lion, a native of Sivas (born 1901 in Sebastia, western Asia Minor), had lived in America since 1912 and was interviewed in 1995 about the communities of crypto-Paulicians in the area of Sivas in the early 20th century; in it he declared from the beginning that he was a Paulician.[146] According to him, amongst the 500 Armenian families of Sivas, there were twenty-five families of crypto-Paulicians ("Tondrakites"). He himself was raised by his grandmother, who as a faithful Paulician imparted her ideas to him. Russell repeatedly points out many beliefs and practices of Manichaean origin deriving from

---

143   However, Lieu (1992, 146) says that "for the church the Manichaeans were not like the Gnostic heretics of the second century who infiltrated the Christian communities and sought to destroy them from within. Manichaeans formed an exclusive community and strove to convert both pagan and Christian Romans to their religion. This made them rivals and competitors". However, with the gradual prevalence of Christianity, there was no such possibility.

144   Eusebius, *HE* 2.1.11–12 (LCL 153:108–09): τότε δ᾽ οὖν καὶ οὗτος τὰς ὑπὸ τοῦ Φιλίππου δυνάμει θείᾳ τελουμένας καταπλαγεὶς παραδοξοποιίας, ὑποδύεται καὶ μέχρι λουτροῦ τὴν εἰς Χριστὸν πίστιν καθυποκρίνεται ὁ καὶ θαυμάζειν ἄξιον εἰς δεῦρο γινόμενον πρὸς τῶν ἔτι καὶ νῦν τὴν ἀπ᾽ ἐκείνου μιαρωτάτην μετιόντων αἵρεσιν, οἳ τῇ τοῦ σφῶν προπάτορος μεθόδῳ τὴν ἐκκλησίαν λοιμώδους καὶ ψωραλέας νόσου δίκην ὑποδυόμενοι, τὰ μέγιστα λυμαίνονται τοὺς οἷς ἐναπομάξασθαι οἷοί τε ἂν εἶεν τὸν ἐν αὐτοῖς ἀποκεκρυμμένον δυσαλθῆ καὶ χαλεπὸν ἰόν.

145   Russell 2004, 677–91.

146   Russell 2004, 688.

Mr. Lion's interview, the most prominent of which are the following: (1) the belief that "there are two forces in the universe", (2) the "demonization of the Old Testament which Mr. Lion called an 'evil book'" and "toilet paper", and (3) that they ought not to "eat animal food, but only fruit and vegetables".[147]

Among the rest of their beliefs, he also mentions that (a) they were Docetist and disbelieved in the divinity of Christ, and (b) that they rejected: (1) the Armenian worship of the Cross, (2) infant baptism and chrismatic oil, (3) the virginity of Mary, (4) the intercession of the Saints, and (5) the various fasts. They also "had a book of doctrine [...] which the Armenian Synod confiscated. Its title was the 'Key of Truth'".[148] In his report concerning the practices of the community Mr. Lion reported that

> [his grandmother] was a humble woman, but held the Churches in contempt [...] [she] turned to the Sun in prayer every morning, and spoke, [...] of the "Children of the Sun". [...] They prayed separately and alone, but sometimes got together, some six families at a time, at various private houses, often at [...] [his] grandmother's house. These meetings were not advertised. [...] Grandmother had a scroll [...] in Armenian, and sometimes [...] a man or woman came over to read it [...] conducting a kind of ceremony.[149]

In an earlier reference to the above scroll, Mr. Leon had named it 'the key'.[150] In 1995, when Mr. Lion gave this interview, he lived in San Diego. He was an active and founding member of the Armenian church of the city, giving "occasional free sermons" in which, one can guess, he expressed "with vigor and eloquence" "his Paulician convictions", which he "never abandoned", as Russell points out.[151]

9.3 Comparative Evidence from Other Religious Contexts: Islam and China

The hypothesis of *entryism* is, moreover, supported by testimonies coming from other religious contexts, in which Manichaeans were active as missionaries, namely the early Islamic world and China.

---

147   Russell 2004, 689.
148   Russell 2004, 688.
149   Russell 2004, 689–90.
150   Russell 2004, 690.
151   Russell 2004, 691.

As Stroumsa argues, the Muslim heresiographers "dreaded the Manichaean skill to infiltrate secretly into the Muslim community in order to lure the simple people and to corrupt Islam from within, for instance by falsifying prophetic traditions."[152] According to the Mu'tazilite theologian Abd al-Jabbar (tenth cent.), the "enemies of Islam", among which he classifies the crypto-Manichaeans, were "everywhere, but above all in the Muslim community itself".[153] In a story recounted by the famous Iranian scholar Al-Biruni (tenth-eleventh cent.), the protagonists are two "notorious crypto-Manichaeans". Apart from describing their activities, Al-Biruni also identifies their "four-fold infiltration techniques across the various religious communities [in] which [they] entered".[154] Though these could be merely labelled as Manichaeans, this story is indicative of religious infiltration as a tactic during that period. It is important to note here that food-tests, similar to those mentioned previously, were also "applied to Manichaeans under Islamic rule".[155]

According to scholars who study eastern Manichaeism, similar things happened, indeed, in the context of China, where Manichaeism was increasingly 'Buddhified'. In 732 the Emperor Hsüan-tsung (also known as Xuanzong) of the Tang dynasty banned Manichaeism which he declared was a "heretic religion", and which confused peopled by claiming to be Buddhism.[156] As Lieu observes, "The primary task of the Buddhist writers, therefore, was to show that Manichaeans were not genuine Buddhists. The Taoists, too, were anxious to reject the claim that Manichaeism was a form of Taoism".[157] In South China the Manichaean "meeting-places were often disguised as Taoist temples".[158] "This find", as de Jong observes, "strongly supports a scenario for the disappearance of Manichaeism in terms of a process of gradual dissolution or dilution".[159] A famous Taoist teacher presents Mani "as a failed Taoist and Buddhist", who founded the religion of Manichaeism "after he had failed to acquire Taoist immortality or Buddhist philosophy". We have here, as Lieu observes, "an interesting parallel to the version of Mani as a rogue prophet in the Acta Archelai".[160]

---

152   Stroumsa and Stroumsa 1988, 39, fn. 7.
153   Crone 2006, 21.
154   Browder 1982, 7–8.
155   Stroumsa 1986b, 312–15.
156   Liu 1998, 182.
157   Lieu 1986b, 235–75, 260–61.
158   Lieu 1981a, 153–73.
159   De Jong 2017, 655.
160   Lieu 1986b, 260–61.

To conclude, two remarks need to be pointed out. According to scholars, "The assimilation of Manichaeism to Buddhism and Taoism was partial or even superficial".[161] The same, regarding Christianity, was repeatedly stressed by anti-Manichaean authors of the Roman Empire. A further claim in Greek anti-Manichaica, that seems to be confirmed by the Muslim, Buddhist and Chinese testimonies, is that Manichaeans used the tactic of assimilation in various (different) religious environments.

10 Conclusions

By taking into account both Manichaean and anti-Manichaean sources, as well as testimonies of relevant religious phenomena and behaviours from other religious environments, I attempted to answer the central question of this chapter. I argued that the cause of the disappearance of Manichaeans from the Eastern Roman Empire was not only their physical extinction through executions (as modern scholarship implies), but also the high numbers of conversions and their dissolution within Christianity.

The latter (dissolution), was to a great extent due to the phenomenon of crypto-Manichaeism, carried out by those Manichaeans who, when confronted with the consequences of the law and the intensification of persecutions, preferred to convert falsely and become crypto-Manichaeans: a practice common to all cases of persecuted religions. The difference that I propose here as a possible and plausible scenario, is that the phenomenon of crypto-Manichaeism existed *before* the vigorous persecutions and served as a missionary technique (*entryism*). This is an alternative interpretation that fits the known facts more harmoniously and is supported by comparative evidence showing that such practices are actually possible. The fear that the Manichaeans intruded on religious communities (both Christian and pagan) permeates Greek literature since the early fourth century. Of course, as has been said, the label 'Manichaean' came to be applied to all kinds of perceived 'heretics'. However, at the same time, the label would also apply to 'real' Manichaeans. Scholars have simply given up hope of ever being able to distinguish the one from the other. This difficulty may have been caused because the Church Fathers were correct in their assumption that (some) Manichaeans joined the Church and attempted to preserve their own religion while remaining invisible within the Church.

---

161   Lieu 1992, 261–62.

Thus, in conclusion, we can assume that the phenomenon of crypto-Manichaeism, apart from being an option of necessity, was a deliberate missionary technique and strategy. The Manichaeans did not pursue their organizational clarity and independent structure, but rather preferred to penetrate existing structures. The aim of their strategy was not to dominate the Catholic Church, but while maintaining their ideas, to infiltrate the existing structures of its power (e.g. state, clergy, monasticism), in order to spread their ideas from within. The religious pluralism that existed in the Eastern Roman Empire facilitated this procedure. Further, the hypothesis of *entryism* explains to some extent the problem we have with the patristic sources, i.e. that although the Manichaean danger was repeatedly stressed, it was scantily substantiated, and justifies the fear of the Church Fathers that behind every μανιχαΐζων and μανι-χαιόφρων could be a concealed Manichaean.

Conclusions

1 Introduction

In this concluding chapter, instead of summarizing the individual conclusions of each chapter and following the sequence of the eight thematic pillars of this book, I will attempt a horizontal scan of the study in order to answer the questions that run through the entire treatise and re-emerge steadily in all the chapters. These are: (1) the issue of reliability and interdependence of the sources, (2) the question of "real and imagined Manichaeans", (3) the question of "the silence of the sources", (4) the question of "why Manichaeans were persecuted to such an intense degree", and finally (5) the question of "the identity of East-Roman Manichaeans and its transformation over time". The above questions will act like threads that bring together the most significant findings of the study and will enable us to draw the final conclusions.

Concerning the first issue, and continuing the discussion started in the introduction, I hope that this study is a contribution to the revision of some clichés in scholarship regarding the value and importance of Greek anti-Manichaica for the reconstruction of Manichaean history in the Roman East. It is true that the difficulties and methodological problems identified by researchers regarding the Greek anti-Manichaean corpus apply to a large extent. Several scholars, trapped in the difficulties of the sources, either repeat what has already been said and which is centred around a limited number of sources, or avoid dealing with the matter altogether. Thus, an academic narrative has been created that passes from one researcher to another, a practice similar to that of some ancient writers who continue a Manichaean discourse stereotypically without having any personal experience of Manichaeans. For this reason, one of the goals of this research has been to bring to the spotlight sources that, while being very important, have received little discussion (e.g. the SC and SAF) and others that have not been studied at all. Within the voluminous Greek (Christian) corpus there are texts that have never been commented upon and translated, especially their parts concerning Manichaeans.

Examining the totality of the sources by their chronological presentation and through their comparative examination and analysis, it has been shown that:

(1) Not all Greek authors rely mainly on the AA (which is not as unreliable as initially thought); those who rely on the AA, do not always have the AA as their only source of information.

© REA MATSANGOU, 2023 | DOI:10.1163/9789004544222_011

(2)   The word 'Manichaean' in our sources is not just a term of religious abuse but also refers to real Manichaeans. A sufficient number of sources attest to the presence of real Manichaeans in the Roman East.

(3)   Beyond the theological discussion, which undoubtedly dominates and focuses on the theme of dualism and on the question of theodicy, our sources also provide information that illuminates aspects of the portrait of East-Roman Manichaeans and of their everyday life.

(4)   Regarding the reliability of the genre of the sources, we have seen that just because most authors have a religiously inspired bias against Manichaeans does not mean that everything they say is unreliable. Nor does this mean that they do not preserve historical information, although they may not have intended to do so. A comparison with the Manichaean sources that are currently known has shown that they preserve much accurate information, in some cases, indeed, drawn from original Manichaean texts.

All the literary genres of the corpus can contribute to the reconstruction of the image and history of the Manichaeans of the Roman East. Even the theological treatises, although they focus on theological argumentation and polemics, have their share in reconstructing not only Manichaean beliefs, but also Manichaean practices. The value of the live speeches (the homilies of Cyril and John Chrysostom), as well as of the letters written on the subject of the Manichaean question, lies in the fact that they substantiate the Manichaean presence at given times and places. The legal sources, first of all, present us with their own internal dynamics, and with evidence for the construction and treatment of Manichaeans. In this, they show a clear pattern of escalation. In many cases, however, they also reflect aspects of the daily life and practices of the Manichaeans. Finally, by means of the chronological and comparative examination of the sources, the importance and uniqueness of the AFs (SC and SAF) was pointed out, while a first suggestion was made regarding the question of why so much of the accurate information they provide did not find its way into contemporary and posterior anti-Manichaean sources. Certainly, further research needs to investigate thoroughly this highly interesting and intriguing issue.

It thus becomes apparent that the Greek anti-Manichaean corpus is worth studying in its own right, and not only partially and selectively, or as a complement to larger inquiries into Manichaean history. Besides, in order to reconstruct the history of Manichaeism in the Roman East, which is a part of the history of Manichaeism in general, the examination of the totality of the sources is indispensable. In the course of this study I attempted several times to highlight the differentiated context of the Roman East, which, compared to the Roman West, was religiously and culturally more pluralistic. This differentiated context must be taken into account in our interpretation, because it is a key parameter that affects the formation of the identity of East-Roman Manichaeans, as well as their representation and treatment by our anti-Manichaean authors.

2 Real and Imagined Manichaeans

One of the clichés that has dominated modern scholarship is that Greek anti-Manichaean authors did not confront real Manichaeans, and that they had neither personal experience nor contact with them, as opposed to Augustine, who did. Examining individual references to individuals designated as Manichaeans in Greek anti-Manichaica, scholars have been unanimous in their conclusion that those references did not concern real Manichaeans and that the term was rather used as a religious abuse targeting other religious groups. This has reached the point that one naturally wonders whether indeed there were any Manichaeans at all in the eastern part of the empire.

However, what more proof is needed to confirm the existence of real Manichaeans than the abjuration formulas? Such confirmation lies, on the one hand, in the ceremonial context in which these anathemas were used: the conversion ceremony of real Manichaeans. On the other, confirmation comes from the accuracy of the information they provide. Especially the sc provides the most accurate information in Greek anti-Manichaica on a number of subjects, such as the names of the first Manichaean missionaries, the titles of the books of the Manichaean canon, the grades of the Manichaean hierarchy, the Manichaean pantheon, a compendium of Manichaean beliefs on cosmology, anthropology and Christology, as well as Manichaean rituals, behaviour and ethics. Even if we had only these texts, there would be sufficient testimony for the existence of Manichaeans, indeed of so many that the need of compiling set abjuration formulas arose. As I have argued, set abjuration formulas were likely established in times of massive conversions.

The ecclesiastical function of these texts (i.e. the fact that they were not literature intended to be circulated), probably explains why so much accurate information seems to have been ignored by posterior tradition. They were circulated only in a ritual context. For this reason, it is plausible to assume that apart from the sc and saf (which, as I argue, were two contemporary and independent documents) there were other afs (with varied content) in use too. It further seems plausible that these written afs which the converted Manichaeans had to sign, and which the *chartophylax* kept in the ecclesiastical archives, were more extensive versions of the text that was read in public (εἰς ἐπήκοον πάντων) during the anathema ceremony.

Additional evidence for the existence of real Manichaeans comes from the following taxonomical classifications:

(1)   The canons for the acceptance of the converted heretics into the Church, which preserve different procedures and specific ceremonies for how to accept the converted Manichaeans.

(2)   The anti-Manichaean laws, which when speaking about Manichaeans, mean it literally. This is because, in law, Manichaeans first appear in parallel with the whole range of heretics, and more importantly, are clearly distinguished from the others.

(3)   The lists of the ecclesiastical authors, where Manichaeans are classified as a distinct category along with the other 'heretics', with whom they are compared. Indeed, Manichaeism as the 'worst heresy' *par excellence* became the metric for measuring the degree of heresy and a tool for the classification of the other 'heretics'.

Moreover, the live speeches of Cyril and John Chrysostom to their Christian catechumens and believers respectively are evidence of the presence of real Manichaeans and of a particularly strong Manichaean community and church in Palestine and Antioch. Both pastors used vivid examples to prepare their audience for the inevitable encounter they would have with Manichaeans on the streets of their city. In addition, Cyril's homilies attest to the existence of Manichaean church-buildings in the mid-fourth century. From the persistent warnings of the two men, it appears that some among their flock were in communion with or even used to visit (in the case of Cyril) Manichaean assemblies. Indeed, as is implied by Cyril's instructions, some of his catechumens could have been both Christian and Manichaean catechumens at the same time.

Apart from the above cases which concern the Manichaeans as a group, chapters [6] and [7] demonstrated that among the individuals designated as Manichaean there are certain cases that appear to have been real Manichaeans, such as the teachers Aphthonius and Photinus, and the missionary Julia and Bassa(?). It is true that the limited information we have about them neither sufficiently enables us to reconstruct their identity nor unreservedly to affirm their historicity, as is the case of the eponymous Manichaeans with whom Augustine discourses and debates, such as Felix and Fortunatus who were undoubtedly historical persons. Yet, this is not a fair comparison, because Augustine himself was a Manichaean auditor, so it makes sense that he knew them personally.

Finally, 'real' Manichaeans make their appearance occasionally in written letters (e.g. Barsanuphius, Olympiodorus, etc.) with advice and instructions on how to deal with them.

Most testimonies about Manichaeans come from the fourth century, and the picture these sources convey to us regarding real Manichaeans (in relation to subsequent ones) is more vivid. Their elderly contemporaries have seen Mani with their own eyes (Cyril) and had experienced the arrival of the first Manichaean missionaries in their provinces (Alexander, Epiphanius). Alexander points out that he had first-hand information from Manichaean missionaries who belonged to the inner circle of Mani's students. He knew that Mani accompanied Shapur, the Persian king, during his military campaigns, as well as that the Manichaeans used the form Χρηστός instead of Χριστός for Christ, which means that he had access to their books. The dynamic of the Manichaean spread from Mesopotamia to the Roman East during the fourth century is well recorded. Epiphanius dates Mani's missionary activity during the reign of Valerian and Gallienus (253–268) – as Alexander also did – whereas he dates the arrival of the second wave of Manichaean missionaries in Palestine in the time of the emperor Aurelian (270–275, i.e. just before Mani's death), which sounds very realistic. In the second half of the fourth century the Manichaeans were "found in many places"[1] and Manichaeism was "widely reported and ... talked of in many parts of the Roman world".[2] This dynamic continued at least until the end of the fourth to the beginning of the fifth century when our sources present Manichaeism as still being active, acquiring followers, and "corrupting the *oikoumene*".[3]

Yet, it is true that along with the real Manichaeans, quite early on, the term 'Manichaean' acquired the content of a term of religious abuse. This is because Christians of all factions, despite their many differences, agreed on one thing: that the Manichaeans were the worst heretics. Therefore, Christians from all parties used the *nomen Manichaeorum* in order to discredit their opponents, and not only the Catholics (as is often assumed). This clarification, which was not sufficiently noted in previous research, is very crucial for our analysis and interpretation. Characteristic of how insulting it was to call someone a 'Manichaean' is the testimony of Athanasius regarding the fear of a

---

1   Libanius, *Ep.* 1253.
2   Epiphanius, *Pan.* 66.1.3.
3   Macarius, *Apocriticus* 4.184.8–11(3).

group of Arian bishops and of the Arian Emperor Constantius II, lest they be co-classified (by the Catholics) as heretics along with the Manichaeans.[4]

However, it is important to note that the use of the term 'Manichaean' as one of abuse was not necessarily malicious (to eliminate an opponent), but also served pastoral concerns. Because the church authorities actually believed that the Manichaean beliefs and practices were dangerous and could influence the supporters of their opponent Christian factions, attributing to them the charge of Manichaeism (with all the shame that this entailed), would contribute to the 'awakening' of the 'heretics' themselves, and to the protection of their flock. "Perhaps" if we call them Manichaeans, Athanasius says, "then they will become ashamed [...] so they will be enabled to perceive into what depth of impiety they have fallen".[5] Furthermore, we saw that, in parallel with the term 'Manichaean', the terms μανιχαιόφρων (the Manichaean-minded individual) and μανιχαΐζων (the person whose specific views or statements on specific issues sound as if he were a Manichaean) were also in use. These two terms were used in the *etic* level of this study as a heuristic tool to distinguish the imagined from the real Manichaeans. However, their use at the *emic* level cannot be an absolute criterion because they are often perceived by the sources as identical and are used alternatively, or all three are assigned to the same person at the same time. Obviously, the fact that the terms Manichaean, μανιχαιόφρων and μανιχαΐζων were attributed to non-Manichaeans does not mean that there were no Manichaeans and that all the relevant references should be reflexively interpreted as examples of slander.

3   The Question of the Silence of the Sources

As the present study showed, the view that Greek anti-Manichaean authors ignored Manichaean texts and that their knowledge regarding Manichaeism was very limited is a generalization.

A number of authors claim that they derive their information from Manichaeans, converted Manichaeans, and from Manichaean books (e.g. Theonas, Alexander, Cyril, Epiphanius, Titus, compiler of sc, Simplicius, etc.). This claim, in some cases, as is deduced from the co-examination of genuine Manichaean sources, is not a rhetorical *topos*. The latter applies not only to the compilers of the AFs (the sc and saf) whose accuracy of information is confirmed, but to other authors as well. For example, the excerpts that Titus

---

4   Athanasius, *H. Ar.* 30.2.
5   Athanasius, *Ep. Adelph.* col. 1073.20–30.

quotes, as he states, verbatim ("this is exactly what they say in their book")[6] appear to be of Manichaean origin (direct or indirect), possibly coming from the *Book of Mysteries* or from the *Thesaurus*. From Cyril's testimony that his contemporary Manichaean missionaries were carrying the *Thesaurus* during their endeavours (which is correct), as well as from the fact that the *Thesaurus* is the most cited book of the Manichaean canon in Greek anti-Manichaean literature, we can infer that the *Thesaurus* must have been the most well-known and most widely circulating Manichaean book in the Roman East.

The majority of our authors know and comment on the two contradictory rationales behind Manichaean fasting, namely the materiality of food versus foods containing light particles. But it is only Alexander who explicitly points out their incompatibility. Alexander also, as well as Nemesius, point out the Manichaean qualitative distinction of foods (the former), between animate and inanimate beings (the latter), depending on whether they contain more or less light or matter. In addition, from the numerous references of our sources to the Manichaean sun and moon worship (in all probability the Manichaean daily prayers), and the accuracy of the information they provide regarding these rituals (prostrations before the sun and the moon), we can assume that (at least initially) these rituals were accessible to non-Manichaeans.

It is true, however, as noted, that our authors do not appear to know or do not discuss a number of other issues (most of them known to Augustine), concerning Manichaean organization, conduct and beliefs, such as:

(1)   They do not distinguish between Elect and catechumens. In general, in both corpora (legislation and literature), the distinction of the two classes is very rare. It is unclear whether Manichaean catechumens were considered as Manichaean as the Elect. When commenting on Manichaean ascesis, our sources do not clarify which commands apply to the Elect and which to the catechumens. There is also no distinction made between the two classes in the canons regulating the procedures for the reception of converted Manichaeans into the Church, or in the laws (with the exception of three early laws). The distinction of the two classes is clear only in the specific context of alms-giving (the Manichaean meal), and there it is only mentioned in order to emphasize the elitist division of the Manichaean community into two classes; yet even here, the distinction is not always clear, because in some cases it seems as if only the Elect were considered Manichaeans. This may have been a strategy of the anti-Manichaean authors either to take Manichaean catechumens on their side, or to equate the two classes, in the context of their

---

6   Titus of Bostra, *c. Manichaeos* 1.21.

polemic. However, we cannot rule out the probability that this was due to the vagueness of the class of Manichaean catechumens. "In practice", as BeDuhn remarks, "the boundaries of the Auditor class probably varied considerably in exclusivity of commitment from one region to the next".[7]

(2) Whereas for the Manichaean sacred meal the discussion is extensive, it is limited to the criticism of the exploitation of catechumens by the Elect, whom the former had to feed. Information about the ritual itself is non-existent, apart from the famous prayer, the Apology to the Bread, which was probably done just before the meal and which seems to be authentic, although it is not confirmed by Manichaean sources. What is striking is that both the Christian and pagan authors do not comment at all on the very purpose of the ritual, the redemptive theology that lies behind it, i.e. on the liberation of the light particles imprisoned within food by the Elect during the ritual. Comparing the representation of the Manichaean ritual meal to the Manichaean sun and moon worship, some observations could be made. The fact that the latter is well documented in the sources may be indicative of the wide circle of participants. The reverse could be argued for the sacred meal, that the absolute absence of relevant testimonies is indicative of the small circle of participants and possibly of the secrecy that surrounded the ritual.

(3) There is also silence in our sources regarding the Bema, the most important feast of the Manichaean calendar, which was celebrated during the Christian period of Easter and commemorated Mani's martyrdom. The only explicit reference to the Bema in Greek anti-Manichaica is recorded in the *sc*. A reference to the Bema could also have been Eusebius' testimony that he saw Mani's icon surrounded by the Manichaeans.

(4) The *sc* is also the only Greek anti-Manichaean source that records the structure of the Manichaean hierarchy in detail. However, none of our sources seems to know that the seat of the Manichaean leader (*archegos*) was located at Seleucia-Ctesiphon.

The fact that the focus of the Greek anti-Manichaean works is mainly on argumentative polemics rather than on Manichaean mythology has been used to support the view that the Greek anti-Manichaean authors ignored Manichaean beliefs, especially their cosmogonic narrative. If we accept ignorance as the cause of the silence of our authors, it is likely that this silence is due to the Manichaeans themselves and signifies either a process of adaptation

---

7   BeDuhn 2000b, 162. The question of the status of the Manichaean catechumens is still open to the discourse of the Manicheologists, see BeDuhn 2000b, 211ff.

into the Christianized context, or a concealment of those aspects of their rituals and beliefs that would undermine their missionary efforts and would endanger their safety. Instead of exposing the details of their complicated cosmogonic myth, they preferred to control the logical weaknesses (the 'whence evil' question) and the contradictions (e.g. in the OT versus NT) of Christianity. However, the silence of our sources does not necessarily mean that their knowledge was limited. There are also other alternative interpretations apart from interpreting silence as ignorance. As we have seen, both Epiphanius (and AA) and the SC, do record the Manichaean beliefs regarding cosmogony and anthropogony, as well as a number of technical terms used by the Manichaeans in their cosmogonic narrative. Even though the content of the SC was not known, the same does not apply in the case of the account of Turbo in the AA and Epiphanius. So, it seems that several of our authors knew the Manichaean myth, at least from AA's version. But while they had access to the AA for their information (whether they declared it or not), and used details of Manichaean cosmogony in their polemics, they avoided an in-depth discussion on Manichaean mythology and a presentation of the Manichaean pantheon. They silence Manichaean mythology and persist in dualism and its consequences in anthropology and ethics.

Thus, an alternative interpretation for the silence of our authors is that they opted for this (choice) consciously. When the heresiologists deemed that heretical knowledge could be ruinous for their flock, they restricted information. The flow of specific heretical information had to be controlled. They only said what served the needs of their *kerygma*. Our authors themselves state at least three reasons for which they choose silence and conceal information: (1) they avoid the exposition of the complex cosmogonic Manichaean system because they did not consider it appropriate to fill their audience's ears with Manichaean mythologies and scandalous words; (2) they are afraid that over-exposure of Manichaean practices and ideas will become more harmful than beneficial; (3) they conceal information lest Manichaean beliefs and conduct would seem appealing.

Of course, in some cases the above arguments (which cultivated danger and fear) may not reflect genuine fears but simply served rhetorical opportunism.[8]

---

8   Cf. Berzon 2013, 185. Lieu (1998b, 227) also questions whether the demythologized version of Manichaean theology reflects an evolving Manichaean self-identity or was "the invention of orthodox Byzantine churchmen".

4   Why Were Manichaeans Persecuted to Such an Intense Degree?

The comparison between the attitude of both the state and church authorities towards Manichaeans and their attitude towards other religious groups revealed the particularity and the gravity of the Manichaean question and shed light on the reasons why Manichaeism was persecuted to such an intense degree.

From the available data of both legislative codes (Cod. theod. and Cod. justin.) it became apparent that Manichaeans were the most harshly persecuted religious group. This is firstly reflected in the number of laws against Manichaeans which are more numerous than the respective laws against any other religious group, as well as in the whole prosecuting procedure, the persecutory rationale (kind of crime), and in the inflicted penalties. Manichaeism is the first 'heresy' that appears in the Cod. theod. (372) and remained a constant target in both codes (Cod. theod. and Cod. justin.), and not an occasional one like other heresies. In contrast to *noble* heretics, whereby only their clergy was being persecuted, in the case of Manichaeans both Elect and catechumens were persecuted. Unlike Jews and pagans who were persecuted only when infringing the law, the Manichaeans, as the Christians earlier, were persecuted in advance, just for being Manichaeans. Anti-Manichaean laws are the only case in Roman legislation in which the law is directed also against the women of a religious group.

The designation of Manichaeans as *infames* and of Manichaeism as a *public crime* constituted the tools of the imperial religious policy for imposing stricter penalties aimed at their financial (deprivation of their property rights, evaporation of real estate property), social (marginalization, exile, intra-family conflicts) and finally physical eradication (capital punishment). The escalation of the exile measure, initially aimed at the exclusion of Manichaeans from the cities, and subsequently from the *mundus*, whereby the meaning of *mundus* was broader than the 'Roman world' and signified the 'universe', and 'mankind', prefiguring likewise the death penalty.

In repressing the Manichaeans, the law proved to be surprisingly innovative by introducing for once and exclusively for the Manichaeans the concept of retroactivity of the law (381); by constituting for the first time in Roman law a specific body of inquisitors for tracking down Manichaeans (382); by establishing a collaboration between bishops and secret agents; and by inaugurating networks of cooperation between regional bishops and provincial governors. Under Justinian, the ecclesiastical authorities were empowered to act as the supreme inquisitorial body for the prosecution of Manichaeans in the service of the emperor.

However, this general observation (arising from all laws) is in actuality only relatively applied, when we focus on a local level with the help of the tool of *province wide* applicability of the laws. This enables us to observe that for a specific period of time (383–423) the most persecuted heresy in the prefecture of the East was not the Manichaeans, but the Eunomians. On the contrary, the western Manichaeans were still a steady target, and this appears to have been in part due to the increase of their number in North Africa and due to Augustine's polemics.

It should also be emphasized that generally, and for a long period of time (up to Justinian), the aim of the law was the prevention and 'correction' of the Manichaeans through their punishment and not their extermination. To a certain extent, it was due to this tactic that the laws were not always implemented and there was significant room for silent tolerance. Indeed, for the same purpose we saw that an alternative religious policy was applied: that of charity, that enabled Manichaean converts to be exempt from previous guilt and annul their penalties with a simple confession of faith. Under Justinian, however, the persecution did not end with their conversion because the converts from Manichaeism would always be suspected of crypto-Manichaeism and apostasy.

But why were Manichaeans persecuted to such an intense degree? While initially in Diocletian's rescript (302) what seemed to worry the Roman authorities was mainly the Persian origin of Manichaeism, as well as the fear of corruption of Roman citizens by the Perso-Manichaean principles and values, under the Christian emperors this dimension of the threat fades out. Apparently, this is because the Manichaean origin was no longer important since the Manichaean 'virus' was now endemic to the Roman world. Yet, a latent dimension of the national threat continued to underlie the persecutory rationale of the law and the penalties, according to which the Roman Manichaeans had to be treated as traitors (since they had succumbed to the Manichaean 'plague'). What appears to be a common denominator of both Diocletian's and Christian emperors' fears (and is also repeatedly stressed in the whole of anti-Manichaean literature) is that the Manichaeans were considered as the most dangerous corrupters of the Roman citizens. What constituted the Manichaean corruption?

The key point that has been noted in our analysis, is that the law (as Church synods too) does not even enter into a discussion about the failure of Manichaean beliefs, doctrine and teachings, as it does for other heretics. But as in the case of the persecution of pagans and Jews, it did target their bad practices. It is the Manichaean gatherings that are targeted by the law because they instigate seditious mobs and are inimical to public discipline. In the rhetoric of law, the social unrest (caused by Manichaean gatherings) that threatens public discipline is not associated with Manichaean religious beliefs (dualism), even though such political reflections exist in literary sources (as in the political theology of the era dualism meant anarchy). In the latter, dualism, as we have seen and was also expected, is a central topic, as is its implications on everyday life, behaviour, and ethics. That the Manichaean public subversion in the laws is not associated with beliefs does not mean that the religious dimension of the threat is non-existent. Social order is undermined because in the case of Manichaeans, public crime acquires the content of an additional capital crime (apart from treason), that of sacrilege. According to the law, Manichaeism was considered a public crime "because what is committed against divine religion is effected to the injury of all persons".[9] Undermining the 'correct' religion at that time was equivalent to undermining the state and its citizens.

In addition to the Manichaean gatherings that caused disturbance in civic communities, it was the very presence of Manichaean individuals, but mainly their proselytizing activity: "Manichaeans attract people and collect a multitude of followers".[10] For this reason, the goal of the law through the *infamia* and exile penalties was to deactivate the Manichaeans socially, so as not to infect the citizens through social intercourse. The Manichaeans must stop disturbing the world, the law declares.[11] That 'citizens are forbidden to talk to or about a Manichaean', is the constant advice given by almost all ecclesiastical authors.[12] What remains a latent fear in Christian legislation, while it is explicitly expressed in Christian and pagan literature, is that the Manichaeans systematically 'poison' Roman citizens in everyday life.[13] As is highlighted in a line of the law, such heretics "have nourished by long and long-lasting meditation a deep-seated evil".[14] The Manichaean issue was not a visible conflict; it was not a clash of power, a confrontation between ecclesiastical authorities that threatened the unity of the Church and of the State, as was the case with intra-Christian factions which, for a long period of time, alternated each other in imperial and episcopal thrones. Manichaeism did not threaten the unity of the Church but the Church as a whole, all its members together, and each individual member separately.

---

9   Cod. theod. 16.5.40.1.

10   Cod. theod. 16.5.9, 16.5.11.

11   Cod. theod. 16.5.18.

12   Pseudo-Didymus, *Trin.* (PG 39.989.33–34); John of Caesarea, *Adv. Manichaeos, hom. 1*, 17.271–273; cf. Cod. theod. 16.5.38.

13   The same fear is also highlighted in Diocletian's rescript: "there is danger that, in process of time, they will endeavour, as is their usual practice, to infect the innocent, orderly and tranquil Roman people, as well as the whole of our empire".

14   Cod. theod. 16.5.41 (Coleman-Norton, 504).

The rapid spread of Manichaeism and the great appeal of the Manichaean way of life to social groups prone to radicalization, such as young people and wandering urban ascetics (probably of both sexes), threatened fundamental social institutions and dominant values (marriage, procreation, labour, role of women in a male-dominated society). The problem was exacerbated by the fact that, unlike specialists, ordinary people regarded Manichaeans as Christians, since they presented themselves as the true Christians. The many external similarities (e.g. ascesis, fasting and abstinence, grades of hierarchy, form of churches, structure of sacred meal) were misleading, while the doctrinal differences, as the specialists stressed, were immense. In the eyes of the authorities, the Manichaeans were greater experts than earlier heretics (Gnostics) in pretending to be Christians, thus misleading true Christians. By presenting Manichaeism as an alternative Christianity, the collective identity of the Roman Manichaeans was not distinct like that of the Jews and pagans. Rather, it was blurred, making their boundaries as a social group indistinct, which was one factor that made them even more threatening. Moreover, the ambiguity of the boundaries of the sect was magnified because there was always a suspicion that there were crypto-Manichaeans not only among the faithful, but also among Church and state officials.

Especially their influence on the ascetic milieu was considered very critical. Because of the many similarities, it was especially difficult to distinguish between Christian ascetics and the Manichaean Elect. Groups of anarchist urban ascetics, such as Encratites et al. and Messalians, were associated by both the law and the Church with the Manichaeans, who were regarded as the mentors of their false practices and ideas. Manichaeans were also held responsible for their increase in number, and for the dissemination of their ideas in both monasteries and society. As ascetics at that time functioned as social exemplars, there was the fear that the Manichaean attitudes and ideas would be disseminated through these ascetics to the whole society. It is for this reason that both legal and ecclesiastical sources characterize the environment of anarchist asceticism as a factory producing apostates from faith. However, it is noteworthy that despite the association of these ascetics with Manichaeans, the fact that the number of anti-Manichaean laws is much higher (25) than the respective laws against Encratites (3) and Messalians (1), shows that, for the authorities, Manichaeism, was an issue of a higher order. It went beyond ecclesiastical jurisdiction and extended to the political sphere, whereas for the state the issue of Encratites and Messalians was an intra-ecclesiastical affair.

Lastly, from the data collected from Arabic and Chinese anti-Manichaean sources it appears that Manichaeans were persecuted for very similar reasons in other environments too. The "heresy of the Manichaeans", Peter of

Sicily states, "is persecuted by all the nations".[15] Probably he was referring to the persecutions of the Manichaeans in the early Islamic and in pagan world (Diocletian). Indeed, the Christian authorities did not forget this when they wanted to emphasize the seriousness of the threat: "A superstition condemned also in pagan times, inimical to public discipline [...] We speak of the Manichaeans".[16] Later Manichaeans were persecuted for the same reasons in Buddhist China too.

5   Manichaean Group Identity and Its Transformation Over Time

One of the key questions discussed repeatedly in this study is the group identity of Manichaeans and its transformation during their confrontation with the official Christian Church and Roman state. Certainly, the information provided by our sources is not sufficient and depicts a Manichaean portrait filtered through their own perspective: that of their opponents. However, although the viewpoint of our sources obviously does not coincide with that of the Manichaeans, the change that is recorded in their representation reflects a respective change in the level of reality, and possibly to the self-identity of the Manichaeans.

5.1   *National Dimension of Manichaean Group Identity*

The national dimension of the identity of the first Manichaean missionaries that dominates Diocletian's rescript fades out for later East-Roman Manichaeans (Aphthonius, Photinus, etc.). On the contrary, Mani's Persian origin and Manichaeism's Persian components are constantly emphasized throughout the Greek anti-Manichaean corpus.

It is also important to note that the use of Syriac as the language of Mani's books did not indicate to our authors that the first Manichaean missionaries in the Roman East were Syrians (and not Persians).[17]

5.2   *Social Dimension of Manichaean Group Identity*

The analysis showed that there is no correlation between social stratification and Manichaean attractiveness and that the examined individuals (designated

---

15   Peter of Sicily, *Hist. ref. Man.* 33.
16   *NVal.* 18.pr.
17   As Epiphanius (*Pan.* 66.13.4–5) clarifies, "Most Persians use the Syrian letters besides ⟨the⟩ Persian, just as, with us, many nations use the Greek letters even though nearly every nation has its own. See ch.[2], 3.4.2.

as Manichaeans) represent all social classes and both genders. However, looking at the sources as a whole, a transformation into the projected earlier and later social profile of the Manichaeans can be noticed.

In the first laws of the Cod. theod., the Manichaeans are presented as solitary ascetics on the fringes of society, and as highlighted by the law, this is the identity that the Manichaeans themselves also wished to project.[18] It was not only the state that held this perception regarding the Manichaean profile (the ascetic). Actually, the first laws against Manichaeans were the result of a long discussion that had taken place for decades between ecclesiastical authorities (culminating in the 370s–80s). Throughout this discussion, the Manichaeans were systematically affiliated with various ascetic groups.

In contrast, the social image of the Manichaeans, as captured by Justinian's first laws, after a legislative gap of 82 years, is completely different. The Manichaeans now seem to be fully integrated in society and hold public offices in the imperial civil and military structure and in other social structures (e.g. guilds). Testimonies about Manichaeans in the upper social classes at Justinian's time are also given by contemporary literary sources. For example, the chronographer Malalas talks about the wife of Senator Erythrius, and the historian Procopius informs us that the outranked officer Peter Barsymes probably even joined the sect.[19] A hint for this forthcoming evolution is reflected much earlier (445), in legislation.[20]

However, under Justinian, a further change to the Manichaean group identity must have taken place due to the persecutions. This change is reflected in the laws themselves, which instead of persecuting Manichaeans, now persecuted crypto-Manichaeans and apostates to Manichaeism. Thus, the Manichaean groupness – although blurred – remained visible through the Manichaean assemblies, churches, etc., as long as they were not persecuted (or to the extent that they were not persecuted). Yet, under Justinian this faded-out and was replaced by the group identity of crypto-Manichaeans. The possibility cannot be ruled out that crypto-Manichaeans (or Christian catechumens who were ex-Manichaean converts verging on Manichaeism) were among the members of the dēmos of the Greens; the Green faction had attracted all those dissatisfied with Justinian's policy, among whom unquestionably the two above groups belonged.

---

18   Cod. theod. 16.5.7.3, 16.5.9.
19   Malalas, *Chron.* 17.21; Procopius, *Hist. Arcana* 22.25.
20   *NVal.* 18.

5.3   *Religious Dimension of Manichaean Group Identity*

Both Christian and pagan anti-Manichaean literature often calls the Manichaeans heretics, and the Cod. theod. co-classified the Manichaeans in the same chapter with intra-Christianity heretics. These facts have led many modern scholars to support the view that Manichaeans were considered as one of the Christian parties by their contemporaries.

However, this study highlighted some basic parameters for the reconstruction of the Manichaean religious identity that have not been taken adequately into consideration in previous scholarship. As a result, it has demonstrated that this view is a generalization and misinterpretation of the data. The main weaknesses of the above position are summarized as follows:

(1)   The terms 'heresy' and 'religion' are not interpreted in context.

(2)   The Christian stance towards the issue is homogenized and identified with that of the Catholics (*etic* level). It has been argued therefore, that the distinctiveness of the Manichaean religious identity is a rhetorical construction of the Catholics.

(3)   The view concerning both: (a) Alexander's stance towards the issue and (b) the legal classification of Manichaeans in the Cod. theod., is based on the first impression that these texts give, disregarding or not examining the full material of the two sources.

Regarding the first issue, it was clarified that the concept of the term 'heresy' during the investigated period was not confined to its current meaning, as many scholars suggest. Instead it had a broader meaning that was inclusive of both the modern meanings attributed to the terms 'heresy' and 'religion' and also signified the wrong religious choice. It is for that reason that the literature of the era also called both Jews and pagans heretics. Besides, our authors, apart from the terms 'heretic'/'heresy' for Manichaeism also used the terms 'religion' and 'dogma'. Regarding the term 'religion' (θρησκεία), this study challenged the notion that the term is a modern one and that it is anachronistic to use it for the past. As was shown, the term 'religion' is used systematically by our authors with the modern meaning of the term. In brief, all three terms (αἵρεσις, θρησκεία, and δόγμα) are interchangeably attributed to Manichaeans and in most cases mean what we would today define as religion.

Concerning the second issue, it became apparent that not only the Catholics, but the Manichaean specialists of all Christian parties considered Manichaeans a distinctive religious category, different from Christianity. In addition to the arguments of the specialists, the distinction is clear in the ecclesiastical lists that co-classified and paralleled Manichaeans to Gnostics, pagans, and Jews. The non-Christian classification of Manichaeans becomes clearer in the canons that set out different procedures and rules for accepting the converted 'heretics' into the Church. For Manichaeans (as well as for Valentinians and Marcionites) the procedure (the stricter one) was the same as for the Greeks/ pagans, while for the intra-Christian heretics it was much easier. It is note-worthy that while exactly the same procedure (as that of the Manichaeans) was defined for the reception of Eunomians, Montanists and Sabellians, the latter three comprised a different set of converts. This indicates the inten-tion of the compiler of the canon to emphasize that they belonged to differ-ent (i.e. non-comparable) categories of heretics. Moreover, the fact that the Manichaean issue and doctrines had never been addressed in ecumenical or other Church synods shows that the ecclesiastical authorities in no way con-sidered Manichaeism as a form of Christianity. On the contrary, a number of synods did deal with Encratites, Messalians, Montanists, Donatists, namely the other 'heretics' with whom Manichaeans were co-classified when they were not grouped together with Gnostics, Jews and pagans. Of particular impor-tance, as a more neutral view, is the opinion of two sixth-century authors who were not ecclesiastical authorities: the historian Agathias and the geographer Cosmas. Both of them clearly regarded Manichaeism as another religion, dif-ferent from Christianity; indeed, Agathias accentuates the Zoroastrian influ-ences on Manichaeism.

The view that Alexander considered Mani as a Christian heretic and Man-ichaeism as a Christian heresy has been adopted by the majority of modern researchers and was used to support the Christian origin of Manichaeism. However, this is mainly based on the two introductory paragraphs of the text, and is in direct opposition with the rest of the work; in it, Alexander challenges the Christianness of the Manichaeans to the same degree as Christian authors do by juxtaposing and comparing Christianity and Manichaeism as two differ-ent religious categories. The core of his criticism is that whereas Manichaeans are self-identified as Christians, they differ radically from Christians on a num-ber of substantial issues. The Manichaeism that Alexander presents is more a Hellenistic than a Christian 'heresy'. It is important to note that both Alexan-der and Christian authors consistently emphasize Manichaeism's loans from Greek poetry and philosophy, as well as polytheism, and astrology. For Titus, Manichaeism is a synthesis of Persian and Greek elements, while Socrates states that the Manichaean books are Christian in voice, but pagan in ideas.[21]

Concerning the classification of Manichaeans in the Cod. theod., the com-parative examination of the treatment of Manichaeans and of other heretics revealed that the Manichaeans were regarded as a *sui generis* class of heretics, constituting their own category. The *sui generis* status of Manichaeans is also

---

21   Titus of Bostra, *c. Manichaeos* 4.16–21; Socrates the Scholastic, *HE* 1.22.5 & 8. 5.

apparent in the chapter 'De Apostatis' (Cod. theod. 16.7), where only pagans, Jews, and Manichaeans are considered as apostates. In the Cod. justin., as is reflected by the title of the corresponding chapter "*De haereticis et Manichaeis et Samaritis*", the Manichaeans are clearly distinguished from heretics.

Of course, for the illumination of the religious profile of East-Roman Manichaeans, the *ab intra* self-designation of Manichaeans is important. However, besides the fact that the Manichaean texts themselves provide contradictory testimonies regarding the use of autonyms, equally important is the opinion of the non-Manichaeans. This is because these opinions come from followers of different religious groups who were rivals of each other. The latter remark, not sufficiently emphasized by previous research, enables us to form a more comprehensive and intersubjective picture. Thus, the meaning that the terms Manichaean and Manichaeanness had during that period in the Roman East, can now be built from the individual meanings that all participants in the relevant 'language game' attributed to these terms. As Jensen notes in stressing the intersubjective character of meaning,

> ... meaning is no longer considered the property of individual subjects with privileged access to their own mental secrets [...] one of the salient features of the revised notion of meaning is that it is public, intersubjective, and translatable, and therefore it is not just 'meaning for someone' but that potentially it is meaning for all of us. [...] the meaning of a ritual is not in the informants' heads, or in their individual interpretations, but in the total network of semantic and behavioural relations, in the network of externalized intentionality, and that is more likely to be successfully analyzed by external observers.[22]

In our case, it is clear that for both Christian (of all denominations) and pagan authors the 'Manichaean Church' was not one of the many Christian Churches. The latter, however, did not apply for ordinary people, who considered Manichaeism as an alternative Christian choice. In practice, the theoretical clarity of the specialists was blurred, and this was intensified by the fact that Manichaeans in their relations with the Christianized world self-identified as Christians. The religious pluralism that existed in the eastern part of the Empire made the lines between orthodoxy and heresy, Christian and non-Christian even more obscure. Moreover, this ambiguity was magnified by crypto-Manichaeans and false conversions.

---

22   Jensen 2003, 444, 446.

The issue of crypto-Manichaeism brings our discussion to the latest and more dramatic change of the Manichaean religious identity, which took place under Justinian. This subject is directly linked to the question of the disappearance of Manichaeism in the Roman East. In the process of time, logically, due to the intensification of the persecutions the cases of pseudo-conversions and crypto-Manichaeans (prudential secrecy) would have increased. Examined testimonies of other persecuted religions in the Roman Empire and elsewhere showed that this was a common practice. Certainly, executions would have also taken place, but we cannot estimate their extent, since the evidence is inadequate, and the term 'capital/ultimate punishment' in the laws of the era did not necessarily mean the death penalty. Moreover, as appeared from the analysis, the choice of pseudo-conversion in the case of Manichaeans was more likely than that of martyrdom.

However, Manichaean pseudo-conversions had preoccupied the Church much earlier and this is reflected in the sc, where the Manichaean convert had to sign that his conversion was sincere. The reservation of the authorities was further intensified because as our sources indicate, crypto-Manichaeism could have been a missionary tactic (i.e. strategic infiltration), in addition to an option of necessity. Of course, there is no way to prove this claim as it is only the opponents' perspective. Nevertheless, I consider that it seems plausible, and it stands to reason as an alternative interpretation for the following reasons: (1) it makes sense, because by this method it was much more likely for the persecuted Manichaean minority to survive and put its missionary vision into practice; (2) some basic features of Manichaeism (e.g. importance of mission, stance towards martyrdom, meaning of sacrifice), as well as corresponding testimonies regarding this Manichaean tactic by Muslim and Buddhist writers, support the claim of our sources; (3) it provides an answer to the question of the elusiveness of the Manichaean presence in the Greek corpus.

A further suggestion of this study was that apart from prudential secrecy and the plausible strategic infiltration, the laws themselves (persecutions) in combination with the canons contributed to boost the phenomenon of crypto-Manichaeism. As I argued, there is evidence to support the hypothesis that the converted Manichaeans did not proceed to the last stage of their conversion (baptism), and remained Christian catechumens for a long period of time, or even for all their life. The Christian name was sufficient to secure their lives and property. This may have been convenient for them, as they abhorred baptism, while the majority was familiar with the idea of being catechumens for a lifetime. However, the status of unbaptized, firstly, cast on them a permanent suspicion of apostasy and crypto-Manichaeism and, secondly, rendered them second-class citizens and Christians in their relationship with the state and the Church. It is not unreasonable to assume that the ambiguity of this new group identity of the Manichaean converts, who were somewhere between being Manichaeans and becoming Christians, could actually lead them to apostasy or crypto-Manichaeism.

In conclusion, the Manichaean group identity, (at least) from Justinian's era onwards, was mainly identified with that of Christian catechumen converts from Manichaeism. To judge whether the latter were sincere converts, or converts who had relapsed, or converts verging on Manichaeism, or just suspected of verging on Manichaeism and of being crypto-Manichaeans, is rather impossible. What is highly probable though, is that the death of Manichaeism in the Eastern Roman Empire seems to have been not as violent as modern scholarship implies, but was a rather slow process of absorption, assimilation, and dissolution into Christianity.

The preceding pages have been an attempt to investigate Manichaeism through the study of Greek anti-Manichaean literature. This research aimed to illuminate aspects of the religious and social identity and daily life of East-Roman Manichaeans. Further research could explore the Greek corpus by focusing on questions that fell beyond the scope of this study, such as: Manichaean Christology in the Greek anti-Manichaean texts, biblical quotations which, according to the Greek authors, were used by the Manichaeans, the connections between Manichaeism and Hellenism, as well as the relationship between Manichaeism, Paulicianism, and Bogomilism. At the same time, more research is needed to explore in greater detail some of the issues discussed in this book, such as the interrelation of the various AFs and their source of information. Moreover, targeted research is required to shed light on the Kellis findings in terms of their comparison with patristic literature. Lastly, to continue my suggestion regarding the dissolution of Manichaeans into the Christian Church, I propose that future research could concentrate on investigating the possible Manichaean impact on theology, art, liturgical and ascetical life, and on the popular religiosity in Eastern and Orthodox Christianity.

Bibliography

The full details of the translations of ancient texts are provided in either the list of the primary or of the secondary sources. When the complete data are provided in both lists, this signifies that in addition to the translation, data from the introduction and commentary of this work have been used.

Primary Sources

Abjuration formulas. *Long Abjuration formula*. In Cotelier, J.B. 1724. ss. *Patrum qui temporibus Apostolicis floruerunt opera*, II. Amsterdam. PG 1:1461C1–1471A6; Adam 1954, 97–103. English Translation in Lieu 1994a, 235–53; Lieu 2010, 134–43.

Abjuration formulas. *Short Abjuration formula*: (1) In Goar, R.P.J. 1730. Εὐχολόγιον sive *rituale graecorum complectens ritus et ordines divinae liturgiae*. Venice: Typographia Bartholomaei Javarina (repr. Graz: Akademische Verlagsanstalt, 1960). (2) In S. Parenti and E. Velkovska. 2011. *L' eucologio Barberini gr. 336* (section 148). Omsk: Golovanov. PG 100:1321–1324; Adam 1954, 93–97. English Translation in Lieu 1994a, 299–300; Lieu 2010, 130–33.

ACO: *Concilium universale Constantinopolitanum quinisextum* (691/2). Edited by A.R. Flogaus, C.R. Kraus, and H. Ohme. 2013. *Acta conciliorum oecumenicorum*, Series 2, Vol. 2: *Concilium Constantinopolitanum a. 691/2 in Trullo habitum: (Concilium quinisextum)*, Pars 4. Berlin: De Gruyter.

ACO: *Concilium universale Ephesenum anno 431*. Edited by Schwartz, E. (1927/1929 repr. 1960/1965). *Acta conciliorum oecumenicorum*. Vol. 1. Berlin: De Gruyter.

ACO: *Synodus Constantinopolitana et Hierosolymitana anno 536*. Edited by E. Schwartz. 1940. *Acta conciliorum oecumenicorum*. Vol. 3. Berlin: De Gruyter (repr. 1965). 3–214, 217–31.

Agathias, *Historiae*. Edited by R. Keydell. 1967. *Agathiae Myrinaei historiarum libri quinque*. CFHBSB 2. Berlin: De Gruyter. Translated (*with an introduction and short explanatory notes*) by J.D. Frendo. 1975. *Agathias: The Histories*, CFHBSB 2.1. Berlin: de Gruyter.

Alexander of Lycopolis, *Tractatus de placitis Manichaeorum*. Edited by A. Brinkmann. 1895. *Alexandri Lycopolitani: Contra Manichaei opiniones disputatio*. Leipzig: Teubner. Repr. Stuttgart: Teubner, 1989. Translated by P.W. van der Horst, P. Willem, and J. Mansfeld. 1974. *An Alexandrian Platonist Against Dualism: Alexander of Lycopolis' Treatise 'Critique of the Doctrines of Manichaeus'*. Leiden: Brill. Translation by J.B.H. Hawkins in ANF 6:411–35.

Ambrosiaster, *ep. ad Tim. ii.* Translation in Gardner and Lieu 2004, 119–20.

Ammianus Marcellinus. *Res Gestae.* Translated by J. C. Rolfe. 1935. 3 vols. Cambridge. Retrieved from http://penelope.uchicago.edu/Thayer/E/Roman/Texts/Ammian /15*.html.

Ammonius Alexandrinus, *Fragmenta in Joannem.* In Reuss, J. ed. 1966. *Johannes-Kommentare aus der griechischen Kirche* (pp. 196–358). TU 89. Berlin: Akademie.

Amphilochius of Iconium, *Contra haereticos.* In Datema, C. ed. 1978. *Amphilochii Iconiensis opera: orationes, pluraque alia quae supersunt, nonnulla etiam spuria* (pp. 185–214). Turnhout: Brepols.

Anastasius of Sinai, *Hexaemeron anagogicarum contemplationum libros duodecim.* Edited and translated by C.A. Kuehn and J.D. Baggarly. 2007. *Anastasius of Sinai Hexaemeron.* OrChrAn 278. Rome: Pontificio Istituto Orientale.

Apophthegmata patrum (collectio alphabetica). (Ἀρχὴ τοῦ Λ στοιχείου. Περὶ τοῦ ἀββᾶ Λουκίου). PG 65:253.17–43 (in PG 65:72–440).

Apophthegmata patrum (*collectio systematica*). Edited by J.-C. Guy. 2003. *Les apophtegmes des pères. Collection systématique, chapitres x–xvi.* SC 474. Paris: Éditions du Cerf.

Asclepius of Tralles, *In Aristotelis metaphysicorum.* Edited by M. Hayduck. 1888. *Asclepii in Aristotelis metaphysicorum libros A–Z commentaria.* Commentaria in Aristotelem Graeca. Vol. 6.2. Berlin: Reimer.

Athanasius of Alexandria, *Apologia de fuga sua.* Edited and translated by J.M. Szymusiak. 1958. *Athanase d'Alexandrie: Apologie à l'empereur Constance: Apologie pour sa fuite.* SC 56. Paris: Éditions du Cerf. Translation in English in NPNF² 4:529–48 and in NPNF² 2 (*HE*, Socrates the Scholastic pp. 150–51 by A.C. Zenos).

Athanasius of Alexandria, *De incarnatione contra Apollinarium libri ii.* PG 26:1093–1165.

Athanasius of Alexandria, *De synodis Arimini in Italia et Seleuciae in Isauria.* Edited by H.-G. Opitz. 1940. *Athanasius Werke, vol. 2.1* (pp. 231–78). Berlin: de Gruyter.

Athanasius of Alexandria, *Epistula ad Adelphius.* PG 26:1072–1084. Translation in NPNF² 4:1380–86.

Athanasius of Alexandria, *Epistula ad episcopos Aegypti et Libyae.* Edited by K. Metzler, D.U. Hansen and K. Savvidis. 1996. *Athanasius Werke: Band 1. Die dogmatischen Schriften, Erster Teil 1, Lieferung 1* (pp. 39–64). Berlin: de Gruyter.

Athanasius of Alexandria, *Historia Arianorum.* Edited by H.-G. Opitz. 1940. *Athanasius Alexandrinus Werke, vol. 2.1* (pp. 183–230). Berlin: de Gruyter. Translation in NPNF² 4:548–607.

Athanasius of Alexandria, *Orationes contra Arianos.* Orations I, II: Edited by K. Metzler and K. Savvidis. 1998. *Athanasius Werke, Band 1. Die Dogmatischen Schriften, Teil 1, Lieferung 2* (pp. 109–75 & 177–260). Berlin: de Gruyter. Oration III: Edited by K. Metzler and K. Savvidis. 2000. *Athanasius Werke, Band 1. Die Dogmatischen Schriften, Teil 1, Lieferung 3* (pp. 305–81). Berlin: de Gruyter.

Athanasius of Alexandria, *Syntagma ad monachos*. In Batiffol, P. 1890. *Studia patristica. Études d'ancienne littérature chrétienne, fasc. 2* (pp. 121–28). Paris: Leroux.

Athanasius of Alexandria, *Vita Antonii*. Edited and translated by G. J .M. Bartelink. 2004. *Athanase d'Alexandrie: Vie d'Antoine* (pp. 124–376). SC 400. Paris: Éditions du Cerf. Translation in English by M.E. Keenan in Deferrari R.J. ed. 1952. *Early Christian Biographies*. FC 15. Washington, DC: The Catholic University of America Press.

[Athanasius of Alexandria]/Pseudo-Athanasius, *Sermo contra omnes haereses*. PG 28:501–524.

Augustine, *Confessiones*. Translated by H. Chadwick. 1991. *Saint Augustine: Confessions*. New York: Oxford University Press. Translation in Lieu 1992; Gardner and Lieu 2004; Lieu 2010.

Augustine, *Contra epistulam Manichaei quam vocant Fundamenti*. Edited by J. Zycha, CSEL 25.1, 191–248. Translation in Gardner and Lieu 2004; Lieu 2010.

Augustine, *Contra Faustum Manichaeum*. Edited by J. Zycha, CSEL 25.1, 249–797. Translation in NPNF¹ 4; BeDuhn 2000b; Gardner and Lieu 2004; Lieu 2010.

Augustine, *De duabus animabus*. Edited by J. Zycha, CSEL 25.1, 49–80. Translation in NPNF¹ 4.

Augustine, *De haeresibus*. Edited by R. Vander Plaetse and C. Beukers, CCSL 46. Translation in BeDuhn 2000b; Gardner and Lieu 2004; Lieu 2010.

Augustine, *De moribus Manichaeorum*. Edited by J.B. Bauer, CSEL 90. Translation in NPNF¹ 4; Lieu 1994a; Lieu 2010; BeDuhn 2000b.

Augustine, *De natura boni contra Manichaeos*. Edited by J. Zycha, CSEL 25.2, 853–89. Translation in NPNF¹ 4; BeDuhn 2000b.

Augustine, *De utilitate credendi*. Edited by J. Zycha, CSEL 25.1, 1–48. Translation in Vermes 2001.

Augustine, *Enarrationes in Psalmos*. Edited by E. Dekkers and J. Fraipont, CCSL 38–40. Translation in Gardner and Lieu 2004.

Augustine, *Epistulae (Ep. 236 to Deuterius)*. Edited by A. Goldbacher, CSEL 57, 523–25. Translation in BeDuhn 2000b; Gardner and Lieu 2004; Lieu 2010.

Augustine, *In Joannis evangelium tractatus*. Edited by J. Willems, CCSL 36. Translation in NPNF¹ 7.

Barsanuphius et Johannes, *Epistulae*. Edited by F. Neyt, and P. de Angelis-Noah. 2002. *Correspondance Volume III: Aux laïcs et aux évêques, Lettres 617–848*. Translated by L. Regnault. SC 468. Paris: Éditions du Cerf.

Basil of Caesarea, *Adversus Eunomium*. PG 29:497–669, 672–768.

Basil of Caesarea, *Epistulae*. Edited and translated into French by Y. Courtonne. 1961. *Saint Basile Lettres*, vol. 2. Paris: Les Belles-Lettres.

Basil of Caesarea, *Homilia in divites*. Edited by Y. Courtonne. 1935. *Saint Basile: Homélies sur la richesse*. Paris: Didot.

Basil of Caesarea, *Homiliae in Hexaemeron*. Edited and translated into French by S. Giet. 1968. *Basile de Césarée. Homélies sur l'hexaéméron, 2nd ed.* SC 26. Paris: Éditions du Cerf.

Basil of Caesarea, *Quod deus non est auctor malorum*. PG 31:329–353.

[Basil of Caesarea], *Asceticon magnum sive Quaestiones (regulae brevius tractatae)*. PG 31:1052–1305.

[Basil of Caesarea], *Asceticon magnum sive Quaestiones (regulae fusius tractatae)*. PG 31:901–1052.

Basilica. Edited by H.J. Scheltema and N. van der Wal. 1955–1988. *Basilicorum libri LX*. Series A. 8 vols. Scripta Universitatis Groninganae. Groningen: Wolters.

Church Canons. In Joannou 1962 and 1963.

Chronicon Paschale. Edited by L. Dindorf. 1832. vol. 1. CSHB. Bonn: Weber. Translated by Mich. Whitby and M. Whitby. 1989.

Codex Justinianus. Edited by P. Kruger. 1888. *Corpus Iuris Civilis II: Codex Justinianus*. Berlin: Weidmann. Reprinted 1967. Translation in Coleman-Norton, 1966; Frier et al. 2016.

Codex Theodosianus. Edited by T. Mommsen and P.M. Meyer. 1905. Berlin: Weidmann. Translation in: Coleman-Norton, 1966; Pharr et al. 1952.

Cologne Mani-Codex/Codex Manichaicus Coloniensis. (Περὶ τῆς γέννης τοῦ σώματος αὐτοῦ). Edited by L. Koenen and C. Römer. 1988. *Der Kölner Mani-Kodex: Über das Werden seines Leibes. Kritische Edition aufgrund der von A. Henrichs und L. Koenen besorgten Erstedition, herausgegeben übersetzt von L.* Koenen and C. Römer. Papyrologica Coloniensia 14. Opladen: Westdeutscher Verlag. Translated by R. Cameron and A.J. Dewey. 1979. *The Cologne Mani codex (P. Colon. inv. nr. 4780): "Concerning the Origin of his Body".* SBLTT 15. Missoula, MT: Scholars Press.

Commonitorium Sancti Augustini. Edited by J. Zycha. CSEL 25.2, 977–82. Translation in Lieu 1994a, 301–03.

Constantinus VII Porphyrogenitus, *De administrando imperio*. Edited by G. Moravcsik. 1967. 2nd ed. Corpus Fontium Historiae Byzantinae 1. Washington, DC: Dumbarton Oaks.

Constantinus VII Porphyrogenitus, *De virtutibus et vitiis*. Edited by T. Büttner-Wobst and A.G. Roos. 1906–10. *Excerpta historica iussu imp. Constantini Porphyrogeniti confecta*. Berlin: Weidmann.

Cosmas Indicopleustes, *Topographia Christiana*. Edited and translated into French by W. Wolska-Conus. 1968–73. *Cosmas Indicopleustès: Topographie chrétienne*, 3 vols. SC 141, 159, 197. Paris: Éditions du Cerf. English Translation by J.W. McCrindle. 2010. *The Christian Topography of Cosmas, an Egyptian Monk*. Cambridge: Cambridge University Press. (Original work published 1897).

Cyril of Alexandria, *Ad Calosyrium (Ep. 83)*. In Pusey, P.E., ed. 1872. *Sancti patris nostri Cyrilli archiepiscopi Alexandrini in D. Joannis evangelium*, vol. 3 (pp. 603–7). Oxford:

Clarendon Press. Translation in McEnerney, J.I. 1987. *St. Cyril of Alexandria: Letters 51–110*. FC 77. Washington DC: Catholic University of America Press, pp. 109–12.

Cyril of Alexandria, *Commentarii in Joannem*. Edited by P.E. Pusey. 1872. 3 vols. Oxford: Clarendon Press.

Cyril of Alexandria, *Commentarius in Isaiam*. PG 70:9–1449.

Cyril of Alexandria, *Contra Julianum imperatorem* (lib. 1–10). In Kinzig, W. and Th. Brüggemann, eds. 2016–17. *Kyrill von Alexandrien: Gegen Julian, Buch 1–10 und Fragmente, Teil 1–2*. GCS, N.F. 20–21. Berlin: De Gruyter.

Cyril of Alexandria, *De incarnatione Domini*. PG 75.1419–78.

Cyril of Jerusalem, *Catecheses ad illuminandos 1–18*. In Reischl, W.K. and J. Rupp, eds. 1848, 1860. *Cyrilli Hierosolymarum archiepiscopi opera quae supersunt omnia = Tou en agiois patros ēmōn Kurillou hierosolumōn archiepiskopou ta sōzomena*. 2 vols. Munich: Lentner. Repr., Olms: Hildesheim, 1967. Translation in: LFHCC 1872. *The Catechetical Lectures of S. Cyril, Archbishop of Jerusalem*. Oxford; NPNF[2] 7:104–372 translated by E.H. Gifford; Telfer ed. 1955; Yarnold 2000.

Cyril of Scythopolis, *Vita Euthymii*. Edited by E. Schwartz. 1939. *Kyrillos von Skythopolis* (pp. 3–85). TU 49.2. Leipzig: Hinrichs.

Cyril of Scythopolis, *Vita Sabae*. Edited by E. Schwartz. 1939. *Kyrillos von Skythopolis* (pp. 85–200). TU 49.2. Leipzig: Hinrichs.

De mathematicis, maleficis et Manichaeis (Diocletian's rescript). In Hyamson, M. ed. and trans. 1913. *Mosaicarum et Romanarum Legum Collatio. With Introduction, Facsimile and Transcription of the Berlin Codex* (Title 15.3, pp. 130–33). London: Oxford University Press. In Adam 1954, 82–84. English Translation in: Gardner and Lieu 2004, 116–18; Lieu 2010, 40–41.

Didymus the Blind, *Commentarii in Ecclesiasten* (*9.8–10.20*). Edited by M. Gronewald. 1979. *Didymos der Blinde. Kommentar zum Ecclesiastes, pt. 5*. Papyrologische Texte und Abhandlungen 24. Bonn: Habelt.

Didymus the Blind, *Commentarii in Zacchariam*. Doutreleau, L. 1962. *Didyme l'Aveugle sur Zacharie, 3 vols*. SC 83, 84, 85. Paris: Éditions du Cerf.

Didymus the Blind, *Contra Manichaeos*. PG 39:1085–1109. Translation in Bennett 1997.

[Didymus the Blind], *De Trinitate* (*1–7*). Edited by I. Seiler. 1975. *Didymus der Blinde: De trinitate, Buch 2, Kapitel 1–7*. Beiträge zur klassischen Philologie 52. Meisenheim am Glan: Hain. PG 39:600–769.

Disputationes Photini Manichaei cum Paulo Christiano. In PG 88:529A–578D. Edited by A. Mai. 1847. *Bibliotheca Nova Patrum*. Vol. 4.2. Rome.

Ephraim of Antioch, *Capita xii*. In Helmer, S. 1962. *Der Neuchalkedonismus: Geschichte, Berechtigung und Bedeutung eines dogmengeschichtlichen Begriffes* (pp. 262–65). Bonn.

Ephrem the Syrian, *Beati Ephraem Testamentum*. In Phrantzoles, K.G. 1998. *The Works of St. Ephrem the Syrian* (Ὁσίου Ἐφραίμ τοῦ Σύρου ἔργα) (pp. 395–432). Vol. 7. Thessaloniki: To Perivoli tis Panagias.

Ephrem the Syrian, *Hymni contra Haereses*. Edited and translated by E. Beck. 1957. *Des heiligen Ephraem des Syrers Hymnen contra haereses*. CSCO 169. Louvain: L. Durbecq. Translation in Lieu 1992; 1994a.

Ephrem the Syrian, *Prose Refutations*. In Mitchell 1912.

Epiphanius of Salamis, *De mensuris et ponderibus*. Edited by E. Moutsoulas. 1973. "Τὸ 'Περὶ μέτρων καὶ σταθμῶν' ἔργον 'Επιφανίου τοῦ Σαλαμῖνος". *Theology* (Θεολογία) 44:157–98.

Epiphanius of Salamis, *Panarion* (*Adversus haereses*). In Epiphanius I: Edited by K. Holl. 1915. *Epiphanius I: Ancoratus and Panarion, haer. 1–33* (pp. 1–149 & 150–464). GCS 25. Leipzig: Hinrichs. Epiphanius II: Edited by K. Holl and J. Dummer. 1980. *Epiphanius II: Panarion hear. 34–64*. GCS 31. Berlin: Akademie-Verlag. Epiphanius III: Edited by K. Holl and J. Dummer. 1985. *Epiphanius III: Panarion haer. 65–80: De Fide*. GCS 37. Berlin: Akademie-Verlag. Epiphanius IV: Edited by K. Holl, et al. 2006. *Register zu den Bäden I–III*. New York: de Gruyter. Translated by F. Williams. 2009. *The Panarion of Epiphanius of Salamis: Book I* (*Sects 1–46*). Rev. and enl. 2nd ed. NHMS 63. Leiden: Brill, and F. Williams. 2013. *The Panarion of Epiphanius of Salamis: Books II and III: De Fide*. Rev. 2nd ed. NHMS 79. Leiden: Brill.

[Epiphanius of Salamis], *Anacephalaeosis*. In Holl, K. 1915, 1922, 1933. *Epiphanius, Bände 1–3: Ancoratus und Panarion*. GCS 25, 31, 37. Translated by F. Williams. 2009 and 2013.

Eunapius, *Fragmenta historica*. In Dindorf, L. ed. 1870. *Historici Graeci minores*. vol. 1 (pp. 205–74). Leipzig: Teubner.

Eusebius of Caesarea, *Epistula ad Constantiam Augustam*. PG 20:1545–1549.

Eusebius of Caesarea, *Historia Ecclesiastica*. Edited by G. Bardy. 1952. *Eusèbe de Césarée: Histoire ecclésiastique*. 3 vols. SC 31, 41, 55. Paris: Éditions du Cerf. Translated by K. Lake. 1926. *Eusebius: Ecclesiastical History*. Vol. 1: Books 1–5. LCL 153. Cambridge, MA: Harvard University Press. Translated by J.E.L. Oulton. 1932. *Eusebius: The Ecclesiastical History*. Vol. 2. LCL 265. London: Heinemann. Repr. 1942.

Eusebius of Caesarea, *Vita Constantini*. Edited by F. Winkelmann. 1975. *Eusebius Caesariensis Werke: Band 1.1: Über das Leben des Kaisers Konstantin*. GCS. Berlin: Akademie Verlag. Translated by A. Cameron and S.G. Hall. 1999. *Eusebius: Life of Constantine*. Oxford: Clarendon.

Eustathius the monk, *Epistula ad Timotheum scholasticum de duabus naturis adversus Severum*. In P. Allen. 1989. *Diversorum postchalcedonensium auctorum collectanea I: Eustathii monachi opus* (pp. 413–47). CCSG 19. Turnhout: Brepols.

Eutherius of Tyana, *Confutationes quarundam propositionum*. Edited by M. Tetz. 1964. *Eine Antilogie des Eutherios von Tyana*. PTS 1. Berlin: de Gruyter.

Euthymius Zigabenus, *Panoplia dogmatica ad Alexium Comnenum*. PG 130:20–1360.

Eutychius of Alexandria, *Annales*. Edited by Breydey. Translation in Gardner and Lieu 2004, 121–22.

Evagrius the Scholastic, *Historia ecclesiastica*. Edited by J. Bidez and L. Parmentier. 1898. *The Ecclesiastical History of Evagrius with the scholia*. London: Methuen. Repr. Amsterdam, 1964. Translated by Mich. Whitby 2000.

Flavius Claudius Julianus, *Epistulae* (*Ep. 114*: "Ἰουλιανὸς Βοστρηνοῖς"). In Bidez, J. ed. 1960. *L'empereur Julien: Oeuvres complètes*. Vol. 1.2. 2nd ed. Paris: Les Belles Lettres.

Gelasius of Cyzicus, *Historia Ecclesiastica*. Edited by G.C. Hansen. 2002. *Anonyme Kirchengeschichte* (*Gelasius Cyzicenus, CPG 6034*). GCS N.F. 9. Berlin: De Gruyter.

Georgius Cedrenus, *Compendium historiarum*, 1: 455. In Bekker, I. 1838–39. *Georgius Cedrenus Ioannis Scylitzae ope.* 2 vols. CSHB. Bonn: Weber.

Georgius Monachus, *Chronicon* (*lib. 1–4*). Edited by C. de Boor. 1904. *Georgii monachi chronicon.* 2 vols. Leipzig: Teubner.

Georgius Monachus, *Chronicon breve* (*lib. 1–6*). PG 110:41–1260.

Gregory of Nazianzus, *De filio* (*orat. 29*). In Barbel, J. ed. 1963. *Gregor von Nazianz. Die fünf theologischen Reden* (pp. 128–68). Düsseldorf: Patmos.

Gregory of Nazianzus, *Epistulae theologicae* (*Ep. 102*). In Gallay, P. ed. 1974. *Grégoire de Nazianze: Lettres théologiques.* SC 208. Paris: Éditions du Cerf.

Gregory of Nazianzus, *Funebris oratio in laudem Basilii Magni Caesareae in Cappadocia episcopi* (*orat. 43*). Edited by F. Boulenger. 1908. *Grégoire de Nazianze: Discours funèbres en l'honneur de son frère Césaire et de Basile de Césarée.* Paris: Picard.

Gregory of Nyssa, *Adversus Macedonianos de spiritu sancto*. In Mueller, F. ed. 1958. *Gregorii Nysseni Opera Dogmatica Minora* (pp. 89–115). vol. 3.1. Leiden: Brill.

Gregory of Nyssa, *Contra Eunomium*. Edited by W. Jaeger. 1960. *Gregorii Nysseni opera.* 2 vols. Leiden: Brill.

Gregory of Nyssa, *Contra usurarios*. In Gebhardt, E. ed. 1967. *Gregorii Nysseni opera* (pp. 195–207). Vol. 9.1. Leiden: Brill.

Gregory of Nyssa, *Epistula canonica ad Letoium*. PG 45:221–36. Edited by E. Mühlenberg. 2008. *Gregorii Nysseni Opera: Opera dogmatica minora*. Vol. 3, pars 5. Leiden: Brill. Translation in Silvas 2007, 211–25.

[Hegemonius], *Acta Archelai*. Edited by C.H. Beeson. 1906. GCS 16. Leipzig: Hinrichs. Translated by M. Vermes with introduction and commentary by S.N.C. Lieu. 2001. *Hegemonius: Acta Archelai* (*The Acts of Archelaus*). MS 4. Turnhout: Brepols.

Herodotus, *Historiae*. N.G. Wilson. 2015. *Herodoti Historiae.* 2 vols. Oxford: Oxford University Press.

Historia Monachorum in Aegypto. Edited by A.-J. Festugière. 1971. Brussels: Société des Bollandistes.

Jerome, *Dialogus adversus Pelagianos*. Edited by C. Moreschini. 1990. CCSL 80.

Jerome, *Epistulae* (*Ep. 22 ad Eustochium*). Edited by I. Hilberg. 1910. CSEL 54, 143–211.

Joannes Diacrinomenus, *Historia ecclesiastica*. In Hansen, G.C. ed. 1995. *Theodoros Anagnostes: Kirchengeschichte* (pp. 152–57). 2nd ed. GCS N.F. 3. Berlin: Akademie Verlag.

Johannes Philoponus, *De opificio mundi*. Edited by W. Reichardt. 1897. *Joannis Philoponi de opificio mundi libri vii*. Leipzig: Teubner.

John Chrysostom, *Ad eos qui scandalizati sunt*. Edited by A.-M. Malingrey. 1961. *Jean Chrysostome: Sur la providence de Dieu*. SC 79. Paris: Éditions du Cerf.

John Chrysostom, *Adversus oppugnatores vitae monasticae*. PG 47:319–86.

John Chrysostom, *De consubstantiali* (= *Contra Anomoeos, homilia 7*). PG 48:755–68.

John Chrysostom, *De sacerdotio*. Edited by A.-M. Malingrey. 1980. *Jean Chrysostome: Sur le sacerdoce*. SC 272. Paris: Éditions du Cerf. Translation in NPNF[1] 9.

John Chrysostom, *Homiliae in epistulam ad Ephesios*. PG 62:9–176.

John Chrysostom, *Homiliae in epistulam ad Galatas commentarius*. PG 61:611–82.

John Chrysostom, *Homiliae in epistulam ad Hebraeos* (*homiliae 1–34*). PG 63:9–236.

John Chrysostom, *Homiliae in epistulam ad Romanos* (*homiliae 1–32*). PG 60:391–682.

John Chrysostom, *Homiliae in epistulam i ad Corinthios* (*homiliae 1–44*). PG 61:9–382. Translation in NPNF[1] 12.

John Chrysostom, *Homiliae in epistulam i ad Timotheum* (*hom. 1–18*). PG 62:501–600.

John Chrysostom, *Homiliae in epistulam ii ad Corinthios* (*homiliae 1–30*). PG 61:381–610.

John Chrysostom, *Homiliae in epistulam ii ad Timotheum* (homiliae 1–10). PG 62:599–662.

John Chrysostom, *Homiliae in Genesim* (*sermones 1–67*). PG 53:21–385; 54:385–580.

John Chrysostom, *Homiliae in Genesim* (*sermones 1–9*). PG 54:581–630.

John Chrysostom, *Homiliae in Joannem* (*homiliae 1–88*). PG 59:23–482.

John Chrysostom, *Homiliae in Matthaeum* (*homiliae 1–90*). PG 57:13–472; 58:471–794.

John Chrysostom, *In diem natalem*. PG 49:351–62.

John Chrysostom, *In illud: Habentes eundem spiritum*. PG 51:271–302.

John Chrysostom, *In illud: In faciem ei restiti*. PG 51:371–88.

[John Chrysostom]/Pseudo-Chrysostom, *In sancta lumina sive In baptismum et in tentationem*. In Uthemann, K.-H. ed. 1994. *Die Pseudo-Chrysostomische Predigt In Baptismum et Tentationem* (BHG 1936m; CPG 4735) (pp. 122–37). AHAW. Philosophisch-historische Klasse 3. Heidelberg: Universitätsverlag; Winter.

John of Caesarea, *Adversus Manichaeos homiliae* (1 and 2). Edited by M. Richard. 1977. *Ioannis Caesariensis: Presbyteri et Grammatice: Opera* (pp. 83–105). Turnhout: Brepols.

[John of Caesarea], *Disputatio cum Manichaeo*. Edited by M. Aubineau. 1977. In *Ioannis Caesariensis: Presbyteri et Grammatice: Opera* (pp. 107–28). Turnhout: Brepols.

John of Damascus, *Contra Manichaeos*. In Kotter, P.B. ed. 1981. *Die Schriften des Johannes von Damaskos*. vol. 4 (pp. 351–98). PTS 22. Berlin: de Gruyter.

John of Damascus, *De haeresibus*. In Kotter, P.B. ed. 1981. *Die Schriften des Johannes von Damaskos* (pp. 19–67). Vol. 4. PTS 22. Berlin: de Gruyter.

John of Damascus, *Sacra parallela*. In PG 95:1040–1588; 96:9–441 (fragmenta e cod. Berol. B.N. gr. 46).

Julianus Arianus, *Commentarius in Job*. Edited by D. Hagedorn. 1973. *Der Hiobkommentar des Arianers Julian*. PTS 14. Berlin: De Gruyter.

Justinian, *Contra monophysitas*. Edited by R. Albertella, M. Amelotti, and L. Migliardi (post E. Schwartz). 1973. *Drei dogmatische Schriften Iustinians*. 2nd ed. Legum Iustiniani imperatoris vocabularium. Subsidia 2. Milan: Giuffre.

Justinian, *Epistula ad synodum de Origene*. In M. Amelotti and L.M. Zingale, eds. 1977. *Scritti teologici ed ecclesiastici di Giustiniano* (pp. 122–24). Legum Iustiniani Imperatoris Vocabularium, 3. Milan: Giuffre.

Justinus Martyr, *Apologia prima pro Christianis ad Antoninum Pium*. Edited and translated by D. Minns and P. Parvis. 2009. *Justin, Philosopher and Martyr: Apologies* Oxford Early Christian Texts. Oxford: Oxford University Press.

Letter to Menoch. In Augustine, *Contra Julianum*. Edited by M. Zelzer, CSEL 85.1. Translation in Gardner and Lieu 2004, 172–74 (no 54); Lieu 2010, 13.

Libanius, *Epistulae* (1–1544). Edited by R. Foerster. 1921–1922. *Libanii opera*. Vols. 10–11. Leipzig: Teubner (repr. Hildesheim: Olms, 1997).

Libanius, *Orationes 1–64* (Or. 30: *Pro templis*). Edited by R. Foerster. 1903–1908. *Libanii opera*. Vols. 1–4. Leipzig: Teubner (repr. Hildesheim: Olms, 1997).

Macarius of Magnesia, *Apocriticus seu Μονογενής*. Edited and translated into French by R. Goulet. 2003. *Macarios de Magnésie: Le monogénès*. 2 vols. Textes et Traditions 7. Paris: Librairie Philosophique J. Vrin. Translation in English by T.W. Grafer. 1919. London: SPCK.

Magnus, *Fragmentum (Fragment 1.16, apud Malalas Chronographia, Ch. 3)*. In Müller, K. ed. 1841–1870. Fragmenta historicorum Graecorum (FHG) 4. Paris: Didot.

Malalas, *Chronographia*. Edited by H. Thurn. 2000. *Ioannis Malalae Chronographia*. CFHBSB 35. Berlin: De Gruyter. Translation by E. Jeffreys, M. Jeffreys and R. Scott. 1986. *The Chronicle of John Malalas*. Byzantina Australiensia 4. Melbourne: Australian Association for Byzantine Studies.

Mark the Deacon, *Vita Porphyrii episcopi Gazensis*. Edited and translated into French by M.-A. Grégoire and H. Kugener. 1930. *Marc le Diacre: Vie de Porphyre, évêque de Gaza*. Paris: Les Belles Lettres. For an English translation of chapters 85–91, see Lieu 2010, 96–101.

Menologia Imperialia. *Vita sancti Athanasii Alexandrini*. In Halkin, F. ed. 1985. *Le méno-loge impérial de Baltimore* (pp. 249–77). Subsidia hagiographica 69. Brussels: Société des Bollandistes.

Nemesius of Emesa, *De natura hominis*. Edited by M. Morani. 1987. *Nemesii Emeseni de natura hominis*. BSGRT. Leipzig: Teubner. Translation by R.W. Sharples and P.J. van Der Eijk. 2008. *Nemesius. On the Nature of Man*. Translated Texts for Historians 49. Liverpool: Liverpool University Press.

Nestorius, *Ad Cyrillum Alexandrinum 11*. In Loofs F., ed. 1905. *Nestoriana. Die Fragmente des Nestorius* (pp. 173–80). Halle: Niemeyer.

Nilus of Ankara, *Epistulae*. PG 79:82–582.

Oecumenius, *Commentarius in Apocalypsin*. Edited by H.C. Hoskier. 1928. *The Complete Commentary of Oecumenius on the Apocalypse*. Ann Arbor: University of Michigan

Press. Translated by J. Suggit. 2006. *Oecumenius: Commentary on the Apocalypse.* FC 112. Washington, D.C.: Catholic University of America Press.

Olympiodorus, *Commentarii in Job.* Edited by D. Hagedorn and U. Hagedorn. 1984. *Olympiodor Diakon von Alexandria: Kommentar zu Hiob.* PTS 24. Berlin: De Gruyter.

Ordo servanda circa eos qui a manichaeis ad puram et veram fidem nostram Christianam accedunt/Ritual to be observed by those who are converted from among the Manichaeans to the pure and true faith of our Lord Jesus Christ/Τάξις γινομένη ἐπὶ τοῖς ἀπὸ Μανιχαίων ἐπιστρέφουσι πρὸς τὴν καθαρὰν καὶ ἀληθινὴν πίστιν ἡμῶν τῶν Χριστιανῶν. In Goar, R.P.J. 1730. *Εὐχολόγιον sive rituale graecorum complectens ritus et ordines divinae liturgiae* (pp. 700–01). Venice: Typographia Bartholomaei Javarina. Repr. Graz: Akademische Verlagsanstalt, 1960; PG 100:1324c–25c. English Translation in Lieu 1994a, 304–05.

Palladius, *Historia Lausiaca.* Edited by G.J.M. Bartelink. 1974. Palladio. *La storia Lausiaca.* Verona: Fondazione Lorenzo Valla.

Peter of Sicily, *Historia utilis et refutatio Manichaeorum vel Paulicianorum.* In Papachryssanthou 1970.

Petrus Hegumenus, *Paulicianorum historia brevis.* Edited by C. Astruc. 1970. "Les sources grecques pour l'histoire des Pauliciens d'Asie Mineure II. Pierre l'Higoumène. Précis sur les Pauliciens". *Travaux et mémoires* 4: 80–92.

Philostorgius, *Historia ecclesiastica.* Edited by F. Winkelmann (post J. Bidez). 1981. *Philostorgius. Kirchengeschichte,* 3rd ed. GCS. Berlin: Akademie. Translated by P.R. Amidon. 2007. *Philostorgius: Church History.* SBL & WGRW 23. Leiden: Brill.

Photius, *Bibliotheca.* Edited and translated by R. Henry. 1959–1977. *Bibliothèque.* 8 vols. Paris: Les Belles Lettres (vols. 1, 2 & 4: 1959, 1960, 1965).

Photius, *Contra Manichaeos.* In Wolska-Conus, W. 1970. "Les sources grecques pour l'histoire des Pauliciens d'Asie Mineure. Vol. III. Photius. Récit de la réapparition des Manichéens". *Travaux et mémoires* 4:121–73.

Porphyrius, *Contra Christianos.* Edited by A. von Harnack. 1916. *Porphyrius. Gegen die Christen.* APAW Philosoph.-hist. 1. Berlin: Reimer.

Procopius, *Historia Arcana.* Edited by G. Wirth (post Jakob Haury). 1963. *Procopii Caesariensis opera Omnia,* vol. 3. Leipzig: Teubner. Translated by H.B. Dewing. 1935. *The Anecdota or Secret History.* LCL 290. Cambridge, MA: Harvard University Press. Translation by R. Atwater. 2010. *The Secret History of Procopius.* Forgotten Books (First published 1927).

Prosperi anathematismi et fidei catholicae professio. In Adam 1954, 90–93; Translation in Lieu 2010.

P.Rylands 3, Greek 469. In Roberts, C.H. ed. & trans. 1938. *Catalogue of the Greek and Latin Papyri in the John Rylands Library* (pp. 38–46). Vol. 3. Manchester: Manchester University Press. Translation in Lieu 2010, 36–37.

Pseudo-Caesarius, *Erotapokriseis/Quaestiones et responsiones*. Edited by R. Riedinger. 1989. *Pseudo-Kaisarios: Die Erotapokriseis*. GCS. Berlin: Akademie; De Gruyter.

Serapion of Thmuis, *Contra Manichaeos*. Edited by R.P. Casey. 1931. *Serapion of Thmuis: Against the Manichees*. HTS 15. Cambridge: Harvard University Press. Translated in German by K. Fitschen, 1992. *Serapion von Thmuis: echte und unechte Schriften sowie die Zeugnisse des Athanasius und anderer*. PTS 37. Berlin: De Gruyter.

Severianus of Gabala, *De Spriritu Sancto*. PG 52:813–816.

Severianus of Gabala, *In centurionem et contra Manichaeos et Apollinaristas*. Edited and translated into French by M. Aubineau. 1983. *Un traité inédit de christologie de Sévérien de Gabala: In centurionem et contra Manichaeos et Apollinaristas. Exploitation par Sévère d'Antioche (519) et le Synode du Latran (649)*. Cahiers d'Orientalisme 5. Genève: Patrick Cramer.

Severianus of Gabala, *In Genesim sermo II*. PG 56:522–526.

Severianus of Gabala, *In illud: Pater, si possibile est, transeat* (against Marcionites and Manichaeans). PG 51:31–40.

Severus of Antioch, *123 Cathedral Homily*. In Kugener, M.A. and F. Cumont. 1912. *Le Manichéisme: Extrait de la CXXIII^e homélie de Sévère d'Antioche; L'inscription de Salone*. Bruxelles: H. Lamertin.

Simplicius, *Commentarius in Epicteti enchiridion*. Edited by I. Hadot. 1996. *Simplicius: Commentaire sur le Manuel d'Épictète*. PhA 66. Leiden: Brill. Translated by T. Brennan and C. Brittain. 2002. *On Epictetus Handbook 27–53*. London: Bloomsbury.

Socrates the Scholastic, *Historia ecclesiastica*. Edited by G.C. Hansen (GCS) and translated into French by P. Maraval and P. Périchon. 2004–2007. *Socrate de Constantinople, Histoire ecclésiastique (Livres I–VII)*. SC 477, 505, 506. Paris: Éditions du Cerf. English Translation in NPNF[2] 2.

Sozomenus, *Historia ecclesiastica*. Edited by J. Bidez and G.C. Hansen. 1960. *Sozomenus. Kirchengeschichte*. GCS 50. Berlin: Akademie. English Translation in NPNF[2] 2.

Suda Lexicon. Edited by A. Adler. 1928–1935. *Suidae lexicon*, 4 vols. Leipzig: Teubner.

Theodoret of Cyrrhus, *De providentia orationes decem*. PG 83:556–773.

Theodoret of Cyrrhus, *Epistulae (Collectio Sirmondiana, ep. 1–95)*. Edited and Translated into French by Y. Azéma. 1964. *Théodoret de Cyr : Correspondance*. Vol. 2. Sources chrétiennes 98. Paris: Éditions du Cerf. English Translation in NPNF[2] 3. (Ep. 81:192–198 & 82:198–204).

Theodoret of Cyrrhus, *Eranistes*. Edited by G.H. Ettlinger. 1975. *Theodoret of Cyrus. Eranistes*. Oxford: Clarendon Press.

Theodoret of Cyrrhus. *Haereticarum fabularum compendium*. PG 83:336–556 (About Mani: 377–382, about Messalians: 429.25–432.35). English Translation in Cope 1990.

Theodoret of Cyrrhus, *Historia ecclesiastica*. Edited by L. Parmentier and F. Scheidweiler. 1954. *Theodoret. Kirchengeschichte*. 2nd ed. GCS 44. Berlin: Akademie. English Translation by Jackson in NPNF[2] 3.

Theodoret of Cyrrhus, *Historia religiosa/Philotheos historia*. Edited by P. Canivet and A. Leroy-Molinghen. 1977, 1979. *Théodoret de Cyr. L'histoire des moines de Syrie*. 2 vols. Sources chrétiennes 234, 257. Paris: Éditions du Cerf.

Theodorus Anagnostes, *Epitome historiae tripartitae*. Edited by G.C. Hansen. 1995. *Theodoros Anagnostes. Kirchengeschichte* (pp. 2–95). 2nd ed. GCS, N.F. 3. Berlin: Akademie.

Theodorus Anagnostes, *Historia ecclesiastica*. Edited by G.C. Hansen. 1995. *Theodoros Anagnostes: Kirchengeschichte* (pp. 96–151). 2nd ed. GCS, N.F. 3. Berlin: Akademie.

Theodorus Heracleensis vel Theodorus Mopsuestenus, *Fragmenta in Matthaeum (in catenis)*. In Reuss, J. 1957. *Matthäus-Kommentare aus der griechischen Kirche* (pp. 55–95). TU 61. Berlin: Akademie.

Theodorus of Raithou, *Praeparatio (= De incarnatione liber)*. In Diekamp, F. ed. 1938. *Analecta Patristica* (pp. 185–222). OrChrAn 117. Rome: Pontificum Institutum Orientalium Studiorum (repr. 1962).

Theophanes the Confessor, *Chronographia*. Edited by C. de Boor. 1883. *Theophanis: Chronographia*. Vol. 1. Leipzig: Teubner (repr. Hildesheim: Olms, 1963). Translated by C.A. Mango and R. Scott. 1997. *The chronicle of Theophanes Confessor: Byzantine and Near Eastern History, AD 284–813*. Oxford: Clarendon Press.

Timothy the Presbyter, *De Iis qui ad ecclesiam accedunt, sive, de reception haereticorum*. PG 86A: 12–73.

Titus of Bostra, *Contra Manichaeos*. Edited by A. Roman, T.S. Schmidt, P.-H. Poirier, E. Crégheur, and J.H. Declerck. 2013. *Titi Bostrensis Contra Manichaeos. Graece et Syriace Libri IV*. CCSG 82. Turnhout: Brepols. Translated into French by A. Roman, T.S. Schmidt, and P.-H. Poirier. 2015. *Titus de Bostra. Contre les manichéens*. CCT 21. Turnhout: Brepols.

Vita Sancti Epiphanii. PG 41:23–74.

Zacharias of Mytilene, *Adversus Manichaeos (Antirresis)*. In Dēmētrakopoulos, A. 1866. Ekklēsiastikē vivliothēkē (Ἐκκλησιαστικὴ Βιβλιοθήκη) (pp. 1–18). Vol. 1. Leipzig. (repr. 1965).

Zacharias of Mytilene, *Capita vii contra Manichaeos*. In Richard, M. ed. 1977. *Iohannis Caesariensis opera quae supersunt* (pp. xxxii–xxxix). CCSG 1 Turnhout: Brepols. Translated into English with a full commentary in: Lieu 1983, 152–218 & Lieu 1994a, 203–305. Further rev. trans. & comments in: Lieu 2010, 116–25, 194.

Zosimus, *Historia nova*. Edited by F. Paschoud. 1971–1989. *Zosime. Histoire nouvelle*. vols. 1–3.2. Paris: Les Belles Lettres. Translated by R.T. Ridley. 2006. *Zosimus: New History*. Austrelian Association for Byzantine Studies.

Zosimus of Panopolis, Περὶ ὀργάνων καὶ καμίνων γνήσια ὑπομνήματα περὶ τοῦ ω στοιχείου. Edited and translated by M. Mertens. 2002. *Les alchimistes grecs: Zosime e Panopolis. Memoires Authentiques*. Vol. 4.1. 2nd ed. Paris: Les Belles Lettres. Edited and translated into English by Jackson 1978.

Electronic Databases

LSJ: *The Online Liddell-Scott-Jones Greek-English Lexicon.* http://stephanus.tlg.uci .edu/lsj/#eid=1.

SEG: *Supplementum Epigraphicum Graecum.* Edited by: A. Chaniotis, T. Corsten, N. Papazarkadas, E. Stavrianopoulou and R.A. Tybout. https://referenceworks .brillonline.com/browse/supplementum-epigraphicum-graecum.

TLG: *Thesaurus Linguae Graecae.* Digital Library of Greek Literature. Edited by M.C. Pantelia. University of California, Irvine. http://www.tlg.uci.edu.

Secondary Sources

Adam, A., ed. 1954. *Texte zum Manichäismus.* Berlin: De Gruyter.

Adams, E. 2016. *The Earliest Christian Meeting Places: Almost Exclusively Houses?* Rev. ed. London: Bloomsbury T&T Clark.

Alfaric, P. 1918. *Les écritures manichéennes, leur constitution, leur historie.* Paris: E. Nourry.

Allberry, C.R.C., ed. 1938. *A Manichaean Psalm-Book: Part II* (Manichaean Manuscripts in the Chester Beatty Collection). Stuttgart: Kohlhammer.

Allen P., and W. Mayer. 1994. "Chrysostom and the Preaching of Homilies in Series: A New Approach to the Twelve Homilies in Epistulam ad Colossenses (CPG 4433)." *OCP* 60(1):21–39.

Allen, P., and W. Mayer. 1995a. "Chrysostom and the Preaching of Homilies in Series: A Re-Examination of the Fifteen Homilies in Epistulam ad Philippenses (CPG 4432)." *VC* 49(3):270–89. doi: 10.2307/1584199.

Allen, P., and W. Mayer. 1995b. "The Thirty-Four Homilies on Hebrews: The Last Series Delivered by Chrysostom in Constantinople?" *Byzantion* 65(2):309–48.

Allen, P. ed. 2013. *John Chrysostom, Homilies on Paul's Letter to the Philippians.* Atlanta: Society of Biblical Literature.

Anagnostakis, I. 1999. "The position of idolaters in Byzantium: The case of the 'Greeks' of Porphyrogenitus". In *The Marginals in Byzantium. Proceedings of Day-Conference, 9 May 1992*, edited by Ch. Maltezou, 25–47. 2nd ed. Athens: Goulandri-Horn Foundation (in Greek).

Armstrong, S.A. 2004. "The First Generation of Manichaeans and other Communities in the Egyptian Deserts: Methodology, the Available Evidence and Conclusions". *The Rose* 1:10–49.

Asmussen, J.P. 1965. *Xuāstvānīft. Studies in Manichaeism.* Copenhagen: Munksgaard.

Asmussen, J.P. 1969. "Manichaeism". In *Historia Religionum: Handbook for the History of Religions. Vol. 1: Religions of the Past*, edited by C.J. Bleeker, and G. Widengren. Leiden: Brill.

Asmussen, J.P. 1975. *Manichaean Literature: Representative Texts Chiefly from Middle Persian and Parthian Writings*. Delmar: Scholars' Facsimiles & Reprints.

Astruc, C., W. Conus-Wolska, J. Gouillard, P. Lemerle, D. Papachryssanthou, and J. Paramelle. 1970. "Les sources grecques pour l'histoire des Pauliciens d'Asie Mineure." *Travaux et Mémoires* 4:1–227.

Athanassiadi, P. 2018. *The Rise of 'Monodoxia' in Late Antiquity*. 2nd ed. History and Politics. Athens: Hestia. Institut français de Grèce. In Greek. [Original work: *Vers la pensée unique: la montée de l'intolérance dans l'Antiquité tardive*, Histoire. Vol. 102, Les Belles lettres, 2010.]

Aubert, J.-J. and B. Sirks, eds. 2002. *Speculum Iuris: Roman Law as a Reflection of Social and Economic Life in Antiquity*. Ann Arbor: University of Michigan Press.

Aubineau, M., ed. and trans. 1983. *Un traité inédit de christologie de Sévérien de Gabala: In centurionem et contra Manichaeos et Apollinaristas. Exploitation par Sévère d'Antioche (519) et le Synode du Latran (649)*. Cahiers d'Orientalisme 5. Geneva: Patrick Gramer.

Badenas, P. 2002. "Heresy, Apostasy and Different Beliefs in Byzantium: Abjuration Formulas". In *Toleration and Repression in the Middle Ages. In Memory of Lenos Mavrommatis*, edited by K. Nikolaou, 97–106. National Hellenic Research Foundation Institute for Byzantine Research. International Symposium 10. Athens.

Bagnall, R.S. ed. 1997. *The Kellis Agricultural Account Book*. Dakhleh Oasis Project: Monograph 7. Oxford: Oxbow Books.

Baker-Brian, N.J. 2006. "Biblical Traditions and their Transformation in Fourth Century Manichaeism". *Augustiniana* 56(1–2):63–80.

Baker-Brian, N.J. 2011. *Manichaeism: An Ancient Faith Rediscovered*. London: T&T Clark.

Barnard, L. 1995. "The Criminalisation of Heresy in the Later Roman Empire: A Socio-political Device?" *The Journal of Legal History* 16(2):121–46.

Barnes, T.D. 1981. *Constantine and Eusebius*. Cambridge, MA: Harvard University Press.

Barnes, T.D. 1993. "Ammianus Marcellinus and His World," review of *The Roman Empire of Ammianus, by J. Matthews and of Western Aristocracies and Imperial Court A.D. 364–425*, by J. Matthews. *Classical Philology* 88(1):55–70.

Baudrillart, A., A. Vogt, and U. Rouziès, eds. 1912. *Dictionnaire d'histoire et de géographie ecclésiastiques. Tome premier. fasc. 1–6, Aachs-Albus*. Paris: Letouzey et Ané.

Baur, F.C. 1831. *Das manichäische Religionssystem nach den Quellen neu untersucht und entwickelt*. Tübingen: Osiander.

Baviera, G., F. Contardo and G. Furlani, eds. 1940. *Fontes iuris Romani antejustiniani*. Vol. 2. Florence: Barbèra.

Beatrice, P.F. 2002. "The Word 'Homoousios' from Hellenism to Christianity." *Church History* 71(2):243–72. doi: 10.1017/S0009640700095688.

Beck, H.G. 1978. *Das byzantinische Jahrtausend*. München: Beck.

BeDuhn, J.D. 1995a. "Magical Bowls and Manichaeans." In *Ancient Magic and Ritual Power*, edited by M. Meyer and P. Mirecki, 419–34. RGRW 129. Leiden: Brill.

BeDuhn, J.D. 1995b. *The Metabolism of Salvation: The Manichaean Body in Ascesis and Ritual*. PhD diss., Department of Religious Studies, Indiana University.

BeDuhn, J.D. 1996. "The Manichaean Sacred Meal". In *Turfan, Khotan und Dunhuang: Vorträge der Tagung "Annemarie v. Gabain und die Turfanforschung", veranstaltet von der Berlin-Brandenburgischen Akademie der Wissenschaften in Berlin (9.-12.12.1994)*, edited by R.E. Emmerick, W. Sundermann, I. Warnke, and P. Zieme, 1–15. Berlin: Akademie Verlag.

BeDuhn, J.D. 2000a. "Eucharist or Yasna? Antecedents of the Manichaean Food Ritual." In *Studia Manichaica. IV. Internationaler Kongreß zum Manichäismus, Berlin, 14–18 Juli 1997*, edited by R.E. Emmerick, W. Sundermann and P. Zieme, 14–36. Berlin: Akademie Verlag.

BeDuhn, J.D. 2000b. *The Manichaean Body: In Discipline and Ritual*. Baltimore: Johns Hopkins University Press.

BeDuhn, J.D. 2001. "Introduction" In *The Light and the Darkness: Studies in Manichaeism and Its World*, edited by P.A. Mirecki and J.D. BeDuhn, 1–4. Leiden: Brill.

BeDuhn, J.D. 2007a. "A War of Words: Intertextuality and Struggle over the Legacy of Christ in the Acta Archelai." In *Frontiers of Faith: The Christian Encounter with Manichaeism in the Acts of Archelaus*, edited by J.D. BeDuhn and P.A. Mirecki, 77–102. NHMS 61. Leiden: Brill.

BeDuhn, J.D. 2007b. "Biblical Antitheses, Adda, and the Acts of Archelaus." In *Frontiers of Faith. The Christian Encounter with Manichaeism in the Acts of Archelaus*, edited by J.D. Beduhn and P.A. Mirecki, 131–47. NHMS 61. Leiden: Brill.

BeDuhn, J.D. 2008a. Review of *Demonstrative Proof in Defence of God: A Study of Titus of Bostra's Contra Manichaeos-The Work's Sources, Aims and Relation to Its Contemporary Theology*, by N.A. Pedersen. *Augustinian Studies* 39(2):301–05. doi: 10.5840/augstudies200839227.

BeDuhn, J.D. 2008b. "The Domestic Setting of Manichaean Cultic Associations in Roman Late Antiquity." *Archiv für Religionsgeschichte* 10(1):259–71. doi: 10.1515/9783110202885.2.259.

BeDuhn, J.D. 2010. *Augustine's Manichaean Dilemma 1: Conversion and Apostasy, 373–388 C.E.* Philadelphia: University of Pennsylvania Press.

BeDuhn, J.D. 2011. "Digesting the Sacrifices: Ritual Internalization in Jewish, Hindu, and Manichaean Traditions." In *Religion and Identity in South Asia and Beyond: Essays in Honor of Patrick Olivelle*, edited by S. Lindquist, 301–19. London: Anthem Press.

BeDuhn, J.D. 2013. "The Manichaean Weekly Confession Ritual." In *Practicing Gnosis: Ritual, Magic, Theurgy and Liturgy in Nag Hammadi, Manichaean and Other Ancient Literature. Essays in Honor of Birger A. Pearson*, edited by A.D. DeConick, G. Shaw and J.D. Turner, 271–99. NHMS 85. Leiden: Brill.

BeDuhn, J.D. 2015a. "Am I a Christian? The Individual at the Manichaean-Christian Interface." In *Group Identity and Religious Individuality in Late Antiquity*, edited by É. Rebillard and J. Rüpke, 31–53. Washington, D.C.: The Catholic University of America Press.

BeDuhn, J.D. 2015b. "Mani and the Crystallization of the Concept of 'Religion' in Third Century Iran." In *Mani at the Court of the Persian Kings. Studies on the Chester Beatty Kephalaia Codex*, edited by I. Gardner, J.D. BeDuhn and P. Dilley, 247–75. NHMS 87. Leiden: Brill.

BeDuhn J.D. 2021. "Augustine, Faustus, and the Jews." In *Manichaeism and Early Christianity. Selected Papers from the 2019 Pretoria Congres and Consultation*, edited by J. van Oort, 302–23. NHMS 99. Leiden: Brill.

BeDuhn, J.D., and P.A. Mirecki, eds. 2007. *Frontiers of Faith: The Christian Encounter with Manichaeism in the Acts of Archelaus*. NHMS 61. Leiden: Brill.

BeDuhn, J.D., and P.A. Mirecki. 2007. "Placing the Acts of Archelaus." In *Frontiers of Faith: The Christian Encounter with Manichaeism in the Acts of Archelaus*, edited by J.D. BeDuhn and P.A. Mirecki, 1–22. NHMS 61. Leiden: Brill.

Bennett, B.J. 1997. *The Origin of Evil: Didymus the Blind's Contra Manichaeos and its Debt to Origen's Theology and Exegesis*. PhD diss., Department of Theology, University of Saint Michael's College, Toronto School of Theology.

Bennett, B.J. 2001a. "Didymus the Blind's Knowledge of Manichaeism." In *The Light and the Darkness: Studies in Manichaeism and Its World*, edited by P.A. Mirecki and J.D. BeDuhn, 38–67. NHMS 50. Leiden: Brill.

Bennett, B.J. 2001b. "The Division of Primordial Space in Anti-Manichean Writers Descriptions of the Manichaean Cosmogony." In *The Light and the Darkness: Studies in Manichaeism and Its World*, edited by P.A. Mirecki and J.D. BeDuhn, 68–78. NHMS 50. Leiden: Brill.

Bennett, B.J. 2009. "The Conversation of John the Orthodox with a Manichaean: An Analysis of Its Sources and Its Significance for Manichaean Studies." In *New Light on Manichaeism: Papers from the Sixth International Congress on Manichaeism, Organized by the International Association of Manichaean Studies*, edited by J.D. BeDuhn, 29–44. NHMS 64. Leiden: Brill.

Benveniste, H.-R. 2006. "On the Language of Conversion: Visigothic Spain Revisited." *Historein* 6:72–87. doi: 10.12681/historein.61.

Berzon, T.S. 2013. *Classifying Christians: Ethnography, Discovery, and the Limits of Knowledge in Late Antiquity*. PhD diss., Graduate School of Arts and Sciences, Columbia University.

Berzon, T.S. 2016. *Classifying Christians: Ethnography, Heresiology, and the Limits of Knowledge in Late Antiquity*. Oakland: University of California Press.

Beskow, P. 1988. "The Theodosian Laws Against Manichaeism." In *Manichaean Studies. Proceedings of the First International Conference on Manichaeism, August 5–9,*

1987, edited by P. Bryder, 1–11. Lund Studies in African and Asian Religions 1. Lund: Plus Ultra.

Bond, S. 2014. "Altering Infamy. Status, Violence, and Civic Exclusion in Late Antiquity." *ClAnt* 33(1):1–30. doi: 10.1525/CA.2014.33.1.1.

Bowersock, G.W. 1990. *Hellenism in Late Antiquity*. Ann Arbor: University of Michigan Press.

Boyce, M. 1975. *A Reader in Manichaean Middle Persian and Parthian. Texts with Notes*. Acta Iranica 9. Leiden: Brill.

Bradshaw, P.F. 1996. *Early Christian Worship: A Basis Introduction to Ideas and Practice*. 2nd ed. Collegeville, MN: Liturgical Press.

Bradshaw, P.F. 2002. *The Search for the Origins of Christian Worship: Sources and Methods for the Study of Early Liturgy*. 2nd ed. Oxford: Oxford University Press.

Bradshaw, P.F. 2012. *Reconstructing Early Christian Worship*. London: SPCK.

Brand, M. 2017. "Speech Patterns as Indicators of Religious Identities. The Manichaean Community in Late Antique Egypt." In *Sinews of Empire: Networks in the Roman Near East and Beyond*, edited by H.F. Teigen and E.H. Seland, 105–19. Oxford: Oxbow Books.

Brand, M. 2019. *The Manichaeans of Kellis: Religion, Community, and Everyday Life*. PhD diss., Centre for the Study of Religion, Leiden University.

Brand, M. 2020. "In the Footsteps of the Apostles of Light: Persecution and the Manichaean Discourse of Suffering." In *Heirs of Roman Persecution: Studies on a Christian and Para-Christian Discourse in Late Antiquity*, edited by É. Fournier and W. Mayer, 112–34. London: Routledge.

Brand, M. 2022. *Religion and the Everyday Life of Manichaeans in Kellis: Beyond Light and Darkness*. NHMS 102. Leiden: Brill.

Browder, M.H. 1982. *Al-Biruni as a Source for Mani and Manichaeism*. PhD diss., Department of Religion, Duke University.

Brown, P.R.L. 1963. "Religious Coercion in the Later Roman Empire: the Case of North Africa." *History* 48:283–305. doi: 10.1111/j.1468-229X.1963.tb02320.x.

Brown, P.R.L. 1969. "The Diffusion of Manichaeism in the Roman Empire." *JRS* 59 (1/2):92–103.

Brown, P.R.L. 1988. *The Body and Society: Men, Women, and Sexual Renunciation in Early Christianity*. New York: Columbia University Press.

Brown, P.R.L. 2012. *Through the Eye of a Needle: Wealth, the Fall of Rome, and the Making of Christianity in the West, 350–550 AD*. Princeton: Princeton University Press.

Burkitt, F.C. 1925/2010. *The Religion of the Manichees. Donnellan Lectures for 1924*, Cambridge Library Collection – Religion. Cambridge: Cambridge University Press. (Original work published 1925). doi: 10.1017/CBO9780511710261.

Burrus, V. 1987. *Chastity as Autonomy: Women in the Stories of the Apocryphal Acts*. Studies in Women and Religion 23. Lewiston, NY: Mellen.

Bury, J.B. 1889. *A History of the Later Roman Empire. From Arcadius to Irene.* Vol. 2. London: Macmillan.

Bury, J.B. 1897. "The Nika Riot." *JHS* 17:92–119. doi: 10.2307/623820.

Bury, J.B. ed. 1899. *The Syriac Chronicle Known as that of Zacharia of Mitylene.* Translated by F.W. Hamilton and E.W. Brooks. London: Methuen.

Bury, J.B. 1958. *History of the Later Roman Empire. From the Death of Theodosius I to the Death of Justinian.* 2 vols. Vol. 2. New York: Dover Publications. (Original work published 1889).

Calder, W.M. 1929. "Two Encratite Tombstones." *ByzZ* 30(1):645–46. doi: 10.1515/bz-1929 -0110.

Cameron, Al. 1974. "Heresies and Factions." *Byzantion* 44(1):92–120.

Cameron, Al. 1976a. *Circus Factions: Blues and Greens at Rome and Byzantium.* Oxford: Clarendon Press.

Cameron, Al. 1976b. "The Authenticity of the Letters of St. Nilus of Ancyra." *GRBS* 17(2):181–96.

Cameron, Av. 1969/1970. "Agathias on the Sassanians." *DOP* 23/24:67–183. doi: 10.2307 /1291291.

Cameron, Av. 1985. *Procopius and the Sixth Century.* London: Duckworth. Reprint, Routledge 2005; Taylor & Francis e-book, 2005.

Cameron, Av. 1998. "Education and literary culture." In *The Cambridge Ancient History. Vol. 13. The Late Empire, A.D. 337–425,* edited by Av. Cameron and P. Garnsey, 665–707. Cambridge: Cambridge University Press.

Cameron, Av. 2003. "How to Read Heresiology." *Journal of Medieval and Early Modern Studies* 33(3):471–92.

Cameron, Av. 2007. "Enforcing Orthodoxy in Byzantium." In *Discipline and Diversity. Papers Read at the 2005 Summer Meeting and the 2006 Winter Meeting of the Ecclesiastical History Society,* edited by K. Cooper and J. Gregory, 1–24. SCH 43. Woodbridge: Boydell Press.

Cameron, Av. 2008. "The Violence of Orthodoxy." In *Heresy and Identity in Late Antiquity,* edited by E. Iricinschi and H.M. Zellentin, 102–14. Texts and Studies in Ancient Judaism 119. Tübingen: Mohr Siebeck.

Cameron, Av. and S.G. Hall. 1999. *Eusebius' Life of Constantine.* Translated (with Introduction and comments) by Av. Cameron and S.G. Hall. Clarendon Ancient History Series. Oxford: Clarendon Press.

Caner, D. 2002. *Wandering, Begging Monks: Spiritual Authority and the Promotion of Monasticism in Late Antiquity.* Berkeley: University of California Press.

Capizzi, C. 1969. *L'imperatore Anastasio I (491–518): studio sulla sua vita, la sua opera e la sua personalità.* OrChrAn 184. Rome: Pont. Institutum Orientalium Studiorum.

Casey, R.P., ed. 1931. *Serapion of Thmuis. Against the Manichees.* HTS 15. Cambridge, MA: Harvard University Press.

Casiday, A. 2003. Review of *Wandering, Begging Monks: Spiritual Authority and the Promotion of Monasticism in Late Antiquity*, by Daniel Caner. *JECS* 11(3):428–30. doi: 10.1353/earl.2003.0040.

Cecire, R.C. 1985. *Encratism: Early Christian Ascetic Extremism*. PhD. Diss., University of Kansas.

Chadwick, H. 1976. *Priscillian of Avila. The Occult and the Charismatic in the Early Church*. Oxford: Clarendon Press.

Chadwick, H. 1990. "The Attractions of Mani." In *Pléroma: Salus carnis: homenaje a Antonio Orbe, s.j.*, edited by E. Romero-Pose, 203–22. Santiago de Compostela: Publicationes Compostellanum.

Chadwick, H., ed. and trans. 1991. *Saint Augustine. Confessions*. Oxford: Oxford University Press.

Chadwick, H. 1998. "Orthodoxy and Heresy from the Death of Constantine to the Eve of the First Council of Ephesus." In *The Cambridge Ancient History. Vol. 13. The Late Empire, A.D. 337–425*, edited by Av. Cameron and P. Garnsey, 561–600. Cambridge: Cambridge University Press.

Chadwick, H. 2001. *The Church in Ancient Society. From Galilee to Gregory the Great*. Oxford: Oxford University Press.

Charanis, P. 1974. *Church and State in the Later Roman Empire. The Religious Policy of Anastasius the First 491–518*. 2nd ed. Thessaloniki: Kentron Byzantinōn Ereunōn.

Church, F., and G.G. Stroumsa. 1980. "Mani's Disciple Thomas and the Psalms of Thomas." *VC* 34(1):47–55. doi: 10.1163/157007280X00299.

Chuvin, P. 1990. *A Chronicle of the Last Pagans*. Translated by B.A. Archer. Revealing Antiquity 4. Cambridge, Mass.: Harvard University Press.

Clackson, S.J. 2000. *Coptic and Greek Texts Relating to the Hermopolite Monastery of Apa Apollo*. Oxford: Griffith Institute, Ashmolean Museum.

Colditz, I. 2015. "The Abstract of a Religion or: What is Manichaeism?" In *Mani in Dublin: Selected Papers from the Seventh International Conference of the International Association of Manichaean Studies in the Chester Beatty Library, Dublin, 8–12 September 2009*, edited by S.G. Richter, C. Horton and K. Ohlhafer, 47–70. NHMS 88. Leiden: Brill.

Coleman-Norton, P.R. 1966. *Roman State and Christian Church. A Collection of Legal Documents to A.D. 535*. 3 vols. London: SPCK.

Cope, G.M. 1990. *An Analysis of the Heresiological Method of Theodoret of Cyrus in the "Haereticarum Fabularum Compendium"*. PhD diss., School of Religious Studies, Catholic University of America, Washington, D.C.

Corcoran, S. 1996. *The Empire of the Tetrarchs. Imperial Pronouncements and Government, AD 284–324*, OCM. Oxford: Clarendon Press.

Corcoran, S. 2015. "From Unholy Madness to Right-Mindedness: Or How to Legislate for Religious Conformity from Decius to Justinian." In *Conversion in Late Antiquity:*

Christianity, Islam, and Beyond: Papers from the Andrew W. Mellon Foundation Sawyer Seminar, University of Oxford, 2009–2010, edited by D.L. Schwartz, N. McLynn and A. Papaconstantinou, 73–89. Burlington: Routledge.

Coyle, J.K. 2004. "Foreign and Insane: Labelling Manichaeism in the Roman Empire." *Studies in Religion/Sciences Religieuse* 33:217–34.

Coyle, J.K. 2007a. "Hesitant and Ignorant: The Portrayal of Mani in the Acts of Archelaus." In *Frontiers of Faith. The Christian Encounter with Manichaeism in the Acts of Archelaus*, edited by J.D. BeDuhn and P.A. Mirecki, 23–32. NHMS 61. Leiden: Brill.

Coyle, J.K. 2007b. "A Clash of Portraits: Contrasts Between Archelaus and Mani in the Acta Archelai." In *Frontiers of Faith. The Christian Encounter with Manichaeism in the Acts of Archelaus*, edited by J.D. BeDuhn and P.A. Mirecki, 67–76. NHMS 61. Leiden: Brill.

Coyle, J.K. 2009a. "Mary Magdalene in Manichaeism?" In *Manichaeism and Its Legacy*, 155–72. NHMS 69. Leiden: Brill.

Coyle, J.K. 2009b. "Prolegomena to a Study of Women in Manichaeism." In *Manichaeism and Its Legacy*, 141–54. NHMS 69. Leiden: Brill.

Coyle, J.K. 2009c. "Rethinking the 'Marys' of Manichaeism." In *Manichaeism and Its Legacy*, 173–86. NHMS 69. Leiden: Brill.

Coyle, J.K. 2009d. "Women and Manichaeism's Mission to the Roman Empire." In *Manichaeism and Its Legacy*, 187–205. NHMS 69. Leiden: Brill.

Crislip, A.T. 2005. *From Monastery to Hospital: Christian Monasticism and the Transformation of Health Care in Late Antiquity*. Ann Arbor: University of Michigan Press.

Crone, P. 2006. "Post-Colonialism in Tenth-Century Islam." *Der Islam* 83(1):2–38. doi: 10.1515/ISLAM.2006.002.

Cumont, F. 1908. *Recherches sur le manichéisme: I La cosmogonie manichéenne d' après Theodore Bar Khoni*. 3 vols. Bruxelles: Lamertin.

De Beausobre, I. 1734–1739. *Histoire critique de manichée et du manichéisme*. 2 vols. Amsterdam: J. Frederic Bernard.

Decret, F. 1982. "Basile le Grand et la polémique antimanichéenne en Asie Mineure au IV siècle." *Studia Patristica. Vol. XVII in Three Parts* 17(3):1060–1064.

De Jong, A.F. 1997. *Traditions of the Magi: Zoroastrianism in Greek and Latin literature*. RGRW 133. Leiden: Brill.

De Jong, A.F. 2006a. "Secrecy I: Antiquity." In *Dictionary of Gnosis and Western Esotericism*, edited by W.J. Hanegraaff, 1050–1054. Leiden: Brill.

De Jong, A.F. 2006b. "Secrets and Secrecy in the Study of Religion: Comparative Views from the Ancient World." In *The Culture of Secrecy in Japanese Religion*, edited by B. Scheid and M. Teeuwen, 37–59. London: Routledge; Taylor & Francis.

De Jong, A.F. 2008. "A *Quodam Persa Exstiterunt*: Re-Orienting Manichaean Origins." In *Empsychoi Logoi: Religious Innovations in Antiquity. Studies in Honour of Pieter*

Willem van der Horst, edited by A. Houtman, A.F. de Jong and M. Misset-van de Weg, 81–106. Leiden: Brill.

De Jong, A.F. 2017. "The Disintegration and Death of Religion." In *The Oxford Handbook of the Study of Religion*, edited by M. Stausberg and S. Engler, 646–64. Oxford: Oxford University Press.

De Stoop, E. 1909. *Essai sur la diffusion du manichéisme dans l'empire romain*. Ghent: Van Goethem.

De Wet, C.L. 2021. "Manichaeism in John Chrysostom's Heresiology." In *Manichaeism and Early Christianity. Selected Papers from the 2019 Pretoria Congres and Consultation*, edited by J. van Oort, 225–52. NHMS 99. Leiden: Brill.

Dignas, B., and E. Winter. 2007. "Rome and the Sasanian Empire: A Chronological Survey." In *Rome and Persia in Late Antiquity: Neighbours and Rivals*, edited by B. Dignas and E. Winter, 18–50. Cambridge: Cambridge University Press.

Dilley, P. 2015. "Also Schrieb Zarathustra? Mani As Interpreter of the 'Law of Zarades'." In *Mani at the Court of the Persian Kings. Studies on the Chester Beatty Kephalaia Codex*, edited by I. Gardner, J.D. BeDuhn and P. Dilley, 101–35. NHMS 87. Leiden: Brill.

Dix, G. 1932. Review of *Serapion of Thmuis Against the Manichees*, by R.P. Casey. *The Classical Review* 46(5):236.

Dix, G. 1949. *The Shape of the Liturgy*. Westminster: Dacre Press.

Dodge, B. ed. and trans. 1970. *The Fihrist of al-Nadim: A Tenth-Century Survey of Muslim Culture*. 2 vols. New York: Columbia University Press.

Doniger, W., ed. 1999. "Manichaeism." In *Merriam-Webster's Encyclopedia of World Religions*, 689–90. Massachusetts: Merriam-Webster.

Drijvers, H.J.W. 1981. "Odes of Solomon and Psalms of Mani: Christians and Manichaeans in Third-Century Syria." In *Studies in Gnosticism and Hellenistic Religions: presented to Gilles Quispel on the occasion of his 65th birthday*, edited by R. van den Broek and M.J. Vermaseren, 117–30. Leiden: Brill.

Drijvers, H.J.W. 1984. "Conflict and Alliance in Manichaeism." In *Struggles of Gods: Papers of the Groningen Work Group for the Study of the History of Religions*, edited by H.G. Kippenberg, H.J.W. Drijvers and Y. Kuiper, 99–124. Berlin: Mouton.

Drijvers, J.W. 1996. "Ammianus Marcellinus 15.13.1–2: Some Observations on the Career and Bilingualism of Strategius Musonianus." *Classical Quarterly* 46(2):532–37.

Drijvers, J.W. 2004. *Cyril of Jerusalem: Bishop and City*. VCSup 72. Leiden: Brill.

Drijvers, J.W. 2015. "The Conversion of Aelia Capitolina to Christianity in the Fourth Century." In *Conversion in Late Antiquity: Christianity, Islam, and Beyond: Papers from the Andrew W. Mellon Foundation Sawyer Seminar, University of Oxford, 2009–2010*, edited by D.L. Schwartz, N. McLynn and A. Papaconstantinou, 211–20. Burlington: Routledge.

Dubois, J.-D. 2003. "L'implantation des manichéens en Égypte." In *Les communautés religieuses dans le monde gréco-romain. Essais de définition*, edited by N. Belayche and S.C. Mimouni, 279–306. Bibliothèque de l'École des Hautes Études. Sciences Religieuses 117. Turnhout: Brepols.

Durkheim, É. 1954. *The Elementary Forms of the Religious Life*. Translated by J. Ward Swain. London: Allen & Unwin. (Original work published 1915).

Edwards, M. 1989. "A Christian Addition to Alexander of Lycopolis." *Mnemosyne* 42 (3/4):483–87. doi: 10.2307/4431859.

Edwards, M. 2015. *Religions of the Constantinian Empire*. Oxford: Oxford University Press.

Eleuteri, P., and A. Rigo. 1993. *Eretici, dissidenti, Musulmani ed Ebrei a Bisanzio: Una raccolta eresiologica del XII secolo*. Venice: Il Cardo.

Eliade, M. 1982. *A History of Religious Ideas. Vol. 2: From Gautama Buddha to the Triumph of Christianity*. Translated by W.R. Trask. Chicago: University of Chicago Press. (Original work published 1975, *Traité d'histoire des religions* Payot).

Enßlin, W. 1937. "Valentinians III. Novellen XVII und XVIII von 445." *Zeitschrift der Savigny-Stiftung für Rechtsgeschichte: Romanistische Abteilung* 57(1):367–78.

Falkenberg, R. 2021. "A Manichaean Reading of the *Gospel of Thomas*." In *Manichaeism and Early Christianity. Selected Papers from the 2019 Pretoria Congress and Consultation*, edited by J. van Oort, 98–127. NHMS 99. Leiden: Brill.

Fiey, J.M. 1968. *Assyrie Chrétienne. Bet Garmaï, Bet Aramayé et Maisan Nestoriens*. Vol. 3. Beyrouth: Imprimerie Catholique.

Fitschen, K. 1993. "Did 'Messalianism' Exist in Asia Minor after A.D. 431?" In *Biblica et Apocrypha, Orientalia, Ascetica. Papers Presented at the Eleventh International Conference on Patristic Studies Held in Oxford, 1991*. StPatr 25, edited by E.A. Livingstone, 352–55. Leuven: Peeters.

Flower, R. 2013. "'The Insanity of Heretics Must Be Restrained': Heresiology in the Theodosian Code." In *Theodosius II: Rethinking the Roman Empire in Late Antiquity*, edited by C. Kelly, 172–94. Cambridge: Cambridge University Press.

Flügel, G. 1862. *Mani, Seine Lehre und seine Schriften: Ein Beitrag zur Geschichte des Manichäismus*. Leipzig: Brockhaus. Repr., Osnabrück: Biblio-Verlag, 1969.

Foucault, M. 2005. *The Order of Things: An Archaeology of the Human Sciences*. London, New York: Routledge; Taylor & Francis. (Original work published 1966, *Les mots et les choses*. Paris: Gallimard).

Fowden, G. 1978. "Bishops and Temples in the Eastern Roman Empire A.D. 320–435." *JTS* 29(1):53–78. doi: 10.1093/jts/XXIX.1.53.

Fowden, G. 1998. "Polytheist Religion and Philosophy." In *The Cambridge Ancient History. Vol. 13. The Late Empire, A.D. 337–425*, edited by P. Garnsey and Av. Cameron, 538–60. Cambridge: Cambridge University Press.

Franzmann, M. 2017. "The Elect Cosmic Body and Manichaeism as an Exclusive Religion." In *Manichaeism East and West*, edited by S.N.C. Lieu, E.C.D. Hunter, E. Morano and N.A. Pedersen, 76–81. CFM: Analecta Manichaica 1 Turnhout: Brepols.

Franzmann, M. 2022a. "The Manichaean Women in the Greek and Coptic Letters from Kellis." In *Women in Western and Eastern Manichaeism: Selected Papers from the International Conference Les femmes dans le manichéisme occidental et oriental held in Paris, University of Paris Sorbonne, 27–28 June 2014*, edited by M. Scopello, 83–100. NHMS 101. Leiden: Brill.

Franzmann, M. 2022b. "Heavenly Mothers and Virgins and the Earthly Eve." In *Manichaica Taurinensia: Proceedings of the 9th International Conference of IAMS*, edited by S.N.C. Lieu, E. Morano, and N.A. Pedersen, 167–71. CFM: Analecta Manichaica 2. Turnhout: Brepols.

Frend, W.H.C. 1976. "Manichaeism in the Struggle between Saint Augustine and Petilian of Constantine." In *Religion, Popular and Unpopular in the Early Christian Centuries*, 859–66. London: Variorum Reprints. (Original work published 1954).

Frier, B.W., S. Connolly, S. Corcoran, M. Crawford, J.N. Dillon, D.P. Kehoe, N. Lenski, T.A.J. McGinn, C.F. Pazdernik, and B. Salway, eds. 2016. *The Codex of Justinian: A New Annotated Translation, with Parallel Latin and Greek Text. Based on a Translation by Justice F.H. Blume*. 3 vols. Cambridge: Cambridge University Press.

Frye, R.N. 1983. "The Political History of Iran Under the Sasanians." In *The Cambridge History of Iran. Vol. 3. The Seleucid, Parthian and Sasanid Periods*, edited by E. Yarshater, 116–80. Cambridge: Cambridge University Press.

Funk, W.-P. 1997. "The Reconstruction of the Manichaean Kephalaia." In *Emerging from Darkness: Studies in the Recovery of Manichaean Sources*, edited by P.A. Mirecki and J.D. BeDuhn, 143–59. NHMS 43. Leiden: Brill.

Funk, W.-P., ed. 1999–2018. *Kephalaia 1: Zweite Hälfte [Lieferung 13–14], Manichäische Handschriften der Staatlichen Museen zu Berlin*. Stuttgart: Kohlhammer.

Gardner, I., ed. 1995. *The Kephalaia of the Teacher: The Edited Coptic Manichaean Texts in Translation with Commentary*. NHMS 37. Leiden: Brill.

Gardner, I., ed. 1996. *Kellis Literary Texts*. Vol. 1. Dakhleh Oasis Project: Monograph 4. Oxford: Oxbow.

Gardner, I. 1997. "The Manichaean Community at Kellis: A Progress Report." In *Emerging from Darkness: Studies in the Recovery of Manichaean Sources*, edited by P.A. Mirecki and J.D. BeDuhn, 161–75. NHMS 43. Leiden: Brill.

Gardner, I. 2000. "He Has Gone to the Monastery. ..." In *Studia Manichaica: IV Internationaler Kongress zum Manichaismus, Berlin, 14–18 Juli 1997*, edited by R.E. Emmerick, W. Sundermann and P. Zieme, 247–57. Berlin: Akademie Verlag.

Gardner, I. 2006. "A Letter from the Teacher: Some Comments on Letter-Writing and the Manichaean Community of IVth Century Egypt." In *Coptica, Gnostica, Manichaica:*

Mélanges offerts à Wolf-Peter Funk, edited by L. Painchaud and P.H. Poirier, 317–23. Leuven: Peeters.

Gardner, I., ed. 2007a. *Kellis Literary Texts.* Vol. 2. Dakhleh Oasis Project: Monograph 15. Oxford: Oxbow.

Gardner, I. 2007b. "Mani's Letter to Marcellus: Fact and Fiction in the Acta Archelai Revisited." In *Frontiers of Faith. The Christian Encounter with Manichaeism in the Acts of Archelaus*, edited by J.D. BeDuhn and P.A. Mirecki, 33–48. NHMS 61. Leiden: Brill.

Gardner, I. 2010. "Towards an Understanding of Mani's Religious Development and the Archaeology of Manichaean Identity." In *Religion and Retributive Logic: Essays in Honour of Professor Garry W. Trompf*, edited by C. Hartney and C.M. Cusack, 147–58. SHR 126. Leiden: Brill.

Gardner, I. 2011. "Manichaean Ritual Practice at Ancient Kellis: A New Understanding of the Meaning and Function of the So-Called Prayer of the Emanations." In *'In Search of Truth': Augustine, Manichaeism and Other Gnosticism. Studies for Johannes Van Oort at Sixty*, edited by J.A. van den Berg, A. Kotzé, T. Nicklas and M. Scopello, 245–62. NHMS 74. Leiden: Brill.

Gardner, I. 2013. "Once More on Mani's Epistles and Manichaean Letter-Writing." ZAC 17(2):291–314. doi: 10.1515/zac-2013-0015.

Gardner, I., A. Alcock, and W.-P. Funk, eds. 1999. *Coptic Documentary Texts from Kellis.* Vol. 1. Dakhleh Oasis Project: Monograph 9. Oxford: Oxbow.

Gardner, I., A. Alcock, and W.-P. Funk, eds. 2014. *Coptic Documentary Texts from Kellis.* Vol. 2. Dakhleh Oasis Project: Monograph 15. Oxford: Oxbow Books.

Gardner, I., J.D. BeDuhn, and P. Dilley, eds. 2015. *Mani at the Court of the Persian Kings. Studies on the Chester Beatty Kephalaia Codex.* NHMS 87. Leiden: Brill.

Gardner, I., J.D. BeDuhn, and P. Dilley, eds. and trans. 2018. *The Chapters of the Wisdom of My Lord Mani: Part III: Pages 343–442 (Chapters 321–347).* NHMS 92. Leiden: Brill.

Gardner, I., and S.N.C. Lieu. 1996. "From Narmouthis (Medinet Madi) to Kellis (Ismant El-Kharab): Manichaean Documents from Roman Egypt." *JRS* 86:146–69. doi:10.2307/300427.

Gardner, I., and S.N.C. Lieu, eds. 2004. *Manichaean Texts from the Roman Empire.* Cambridge: Cambridge University Press.

Gardner, I., A. Nobbs, and M. Choat. 2000. "P. Harr. 107: Is This Another Greek Manichaean Letter?" *ZPE* 131:118–24.

Gardner, I., and K.A. Worp. 2018. "A Most Remarkable Fourth Century Letter in Greek, Recovered from House 4 at Ismant el-Kharab." *ZPE* 205:127–42.

Garsoïan, N.G. 1967. *The Paulician Heresy: A Study of the Origin and Development of Paulicianism in Armenia and the Eastern Provinces of the Byzantine Empire.* Publications in Near and Middle East Studies, Series A, 6. The Hague: Mouton. Repr., Pdf ed., de Gruyter, 2011.

Garsoïan, N.G. 1971. "Byzantine Heresy. A Reinterpretation." *DOP* 25:85–113. doi: 10.2307/1291305.

Gaudement, J. 1972. "Recherches sur la législation du Bas-Empire." In *Studi in onore di Gaetano Scherillo*, 693–716. Milan: Istituto editoriale Cisalpino-La Goliardica.

Gehring, R.W. 2004. *House Church and Mission: The Importance of Household Structures in Early Christianity*. Peabody, MA: Hendrickson.

Gersh, S. 1976. Review of *An Alexandrian Platonist Against Dualism: Alexander of Lycopolis' 'Critique of the Doctrines of Manichaeus'*, by P.W. van der Horst and J. Mansfeld. *JTS* 27(1):211–12. doi: 10.1093/jts/XXVII.1.211.

Giles, L. 1943. "Dated Chinese Manuscripts in the Stein Collection". *BSOAS* 11:148–219. [Text: "Mo-ni Chiao Hsia-pu Tsan. The Lower (Second?) Section of the Manichaean Hymns". Translated by Tsui, Chi, pp. 174–219].

Giversen, S., ed. 1986–88. *The Manichaean Coptic Papyri in the Chester Beatty Library. Facsimile Edition*. 4 vols. Cahiers d'Orientalisme 14–17. Genève: Cramer.

Goodrich, R. 2004. "Mendicant Monks." Review of Wandering, Begging Monks. Spiritual Authority and the Promotion of Monasticism in Late Antiquity, by D. Caner. Berkeley: University of California Press, 2002. *The Classical Review* 54(1):208–10.

Gouillard, J. 1965. "L'heresie dans l'empire byzantin des origines au XIIe siecle." *Travaux et memoires* 1:299–324.

Gouillard, J. 1967. "Le Synodikon de l'Orthodoxie: édition et commentaire." *Travaux et Mémoires* 2:1–316.

Goulet, R. 2003. "Dosithée de Cilicie." *Apocrypha* 14:55–72.

Grant, R.M. 1977. *Early Christianity and Society: Seven Studies*. San Francisco: Harper & Row.

Greatrex, G., ed. 2011. *The Chronicle of Pseudo-Zachariah Rhetor: Church and War in Late Antiquity*. Translated by R.R. Phenix and C.B. Horn (with introductory material by S.P. Brock, and W. Witakowski). *TTI* 55. Liverpool: Liverpool University Press.

Gregory, T.E. 1991. "Messalianism." In *The Oxford Dictionary of Byzantium*, edited by A.P. Kazhdan, 1349–1350. Oxford: Oxford University Press.

Gross, J. 1960. *Geschichte des Erbsündendogmas. Ein Beitrag zur Geschichte des Problems vom Ursprung des Übels. 1. Entstehungsgeschichte des Erbsündendogmas. Von der Bibel bis Augustinus*. Munich: Reinhardt.

Gulácsi, Z. 2005. *Mediaeval Manichaean Book Art: A Codicological Study of Iranian and Turkic Illuminated Book Fragments from 8th–11th Century East Central Asia*. NHMS 57. Leiden: Brill.

Gulácsi, Z. 2015. *Mani's Pictures: The Didactic Images of the Manichaeans from Sasanian Mesopotamia to Uygur Central Asia and Tang-Ming China*. NHMS 90. Leiden: Brill.

Gwynn, D.M. 2010. "Archaeology and the 'Arian Controversy' in the Fourth Century." In *Religious Diversity in Late Antiquity*, edited by D.M. Gwynn and S. Bangert, 229–63. Leiden: Brill.

Halfond, G. 2010. *The Archaeology of Frankish Church Councils, AD 511–768*. Medieval Law and its Practice 6. Leiden: Brill.

Haloun, G., and W.B. Henning. 1952. "The Compendium of the Doctrines and Styles of the Teaching of Mani, the Buddha of Light." *Asia Major* 3:184–212.

Henning, W.B. 1945. "The Manichaean Fasts." *JRAS of Great Britain and Ireland* 2:146–64. doi: 10.2307/25222029.

Henning, W.B. 1977. *Selected Papers*. Acta iranica 14–15. Deuxième série: Hommages et opera minora 5–6. Leiden: Brill.

Henrichs, A. 1973. "Mani and the Babylonian Baptists: A Historical Confrontation." *HSCP* 77:23–59.

Henrichs, A. 1979. "The Cologne Mani Codex Reconsidered." *HSCP* 83:339–67. doi: 10.2307/311105.

Henrichs, A., H. Henrichs, and L. Koenen. 1975. "Der Kölner Mani-Kodex (P. Colon. inv. nr. 4780) Περὶ τῆς γέννης τοῦ σώματος αὐτοῦ: Edition der Seiten 1–72." *ZPE* 19:1–85.

Henrichs, A., and L. Koenen. 1970. "Ein griechischer Mani-Codex (P. Colon. inv. nr. 4780)." *ZPE* 5:97–216.

Henrichs, A., and L. Koenen. 1978. "Der Kölner Mani-Kodex (P. Colon. inv. nr. 4780) Περὶ τῆς γέννης τοῦ σώματος αὐτοῦ: Edition der Seiten 72,8–99,9." *ZPE* 32:87–199.

Honoré, T. 1979. "'Imperial' Rescripts A.D. 193–305: Authorship and Authenticity." *JRS* 69:51–64. doi: 10.2307/299059.

Honoré, T. 1986. "III. The Making of the Theodosian Code." *ZSS Romanistische Abteilung* 103(1):133–222. doi: 10.7767/zrgra.1986.103.1.133.

Hunt, E.D. 2007. "Imperial Law or Councils of the Church? Theodosius I and the Imposition of Doctrinal Uniformity." In *Discipline and Diversity. Papers Read at the 2005 Summer Meeting and the 2006 Winter Meeting of the Ecclesiastical History Society*, edited by K. Cooper and J. Gregory, 57–68. SCH 43. Woodbridge: Boydell Press.

Hunt, H. 2012. *Clothed in the Body. Asceticism, the Body and the Spiritual in the Late Antique Era*. Farnham, Surrey, UK: Ashgate.

Jackson, H.M., ed. and trans. 1978. *Zosimos of Panopolis. On the Letter Omega*. Texts and Translation 14. Graeco-Roman Religion 5. Missoula, MT: Scholars Press.

Jarry, J. 1960. "Hérésies et factions à Constantinople du Vᵉ au VIIᵉ siècle." *Syria* 37(3–4):348–71.

Jarry, J. 1968. *Hérésies et factions dans l'empire byzantin du IVᵉ au VII Siècle*. Le Caire: Imprimerie de l'Institut Français d'Archéologie Orientale.

Jenkins, R.G. 1995. "The Prayer of the Emanations in Greek from Kellis (T.Kellis 22)." *Le Muséon* 108(3):243–63.

Jensen, S.J. 2003. *The Study of Religion in a New Key: Theoretical and Philosophical Soundings in the Comparative and General Study of Religion*. Aarhus: Aarhus University Press.

Jensen, S.J. 2011. "Revisiting the Insider-Outsider Debate: Dismantling a Pseudo-Problem in the Study of Religion." *MTSR* 23(1):29–47. doi: 10.1163/157006811x549689.

Joannou, P.-P., ed. 1962. *Discipline générale antique (IIᵉ–IXᵉ s.). Les canons des conciles oecuméniques.* Vol. 1.1. Grottaferrata (Rome): Tip. Italo-Orientale S. Nilo.

Joannou, P.-P., ed. 1962. *Discipline générale antique (IVᵉ–IXᵉ s.). Les canons des Synodes particuliers.* Vol. 1.2. Grottaferrata (Rome): Tip. Italo-Orientale S. Nilo.

Joannou, P.-P., ed. 1963. *Discipline générale antique (IVᵉ–IXᵉ s.). Les canons des Pères Grecs.* Vol. 2. Grottaferrata (Rome): Tip. Italo-Orientale S. Nilo.

Johnston, D. 1999. *Roman Law in Context.* Cambridge: Cambridge University Press.

Jones, A.H.M. 1959. "Were Ancient Heresies National or Social Movements in Disguise?" *JTS* 10(2):280–98. doi: 10.1093/jts/X.2.280.

Jones, A.H.M., J.R. Martindale, and J. Morris, eds. 1971. *The Prosopography of the Later Roman Empire. Vol. 1 A.D. 260–395.* Cambridge: Cambridge University Press.

Kaatz, K. 2007. "The Light and the Darkness: The Two Natures, Free Will, and the Scriptural Evidence in the Acta Archelai." In *Frontiers of Faith: The Christian Encounter with Manichaeism in the Acts of Archelaus,* edited by J.D. BeDuhn and P.A. Mirecki, 103–18. Leiden: Brill.

Kaden, E.H. 1953. "Die Edikte gegen die Manichäer von Diokletian bis Justinian". In *Festschrift Hans Lewald: bei Vollendung des vierzigsten Amtsjahres als ordentlicher Professor im Oktober 1953 überreicht von seinen Freunden und Kollegen mit Unterstützung der Basler juristischen Fakultät,* edited by H. Batiffol and H. Lewald, 55–68. Basel: Helbing & Lichtenhahn.

Karlin-Hayter, P. 1973. "Les Akta dia Kalapodion. Le contexte religieux et politique." *Byzantion* 43:84–107.

Karlin-Hayter, P., ed. 1981. *Studies in Byzantine Political History: Sources and Controversies,* 1–13. VCS 141. London: Variorum Reprints.

Kaser, M. 1971. *Das römische Privatrecht. Rechtsgeschichte Des Altertums.* 2 vols. Munich: Beck.

Kazhdan, A.P., ed. 1991. *The Oxford Dictionary of Byzantium.* 3 vols. New York: Oxford University Press.

Kazhdan, A.P., A. Cutler, and T.E. Gregory. 1991. "Heresy." In *The Oxford Dictionary of Byzantium, vol. 2,* edited by A.P. Kazhdan, 918–20. New York: Oxford University Press.

Kelly, J.N.D. 1995. *Golden Mouth: The Story of John Chrysostom – Ascetic, Preacher, Bishop.* Ithaca, NY: Cornell University Press.

Kessler, K. 1889. *Mani: Forschungen über die manichäische Religion: ein Beitrag zur vergleichenden religionsgeschichte des Orients. 1. Bd., Voruntersuchungen und Quellen.* Berlin: Reimer; de Gruyter.

Klein, W.W. 1991. *Die Argumentation in den griechisch-christlichen Antimanichaica.* StOR 19. Wiesbaden: Harrassowitz.

Klein, W.W. 2007. Review of *Demonstrative Proof in Defence of God. A Study of Titus of Bostra's Contra Manichaeos. The Work's Sources, Aims and Relation to Its Contemporary Theology,* by N.A. Pedersen. *VC* 61(1):113–15. doi: https://doi.org/10.1163/004260307X164548.

Klíma, O. 1962. *Manis Zeit und Leben.* Prague: Wissenschaften.

Knuppel, M. 2009. "'Manichaean Studies' A New Research-Project (Manichäische Studien: Ein neues Forschungs-Projekt)." *BZRGG* 61(2):179–82.

Koenen, L., and C. Römer, eds. 1988. *Der Kölner Mani-Kodex: Über das Werden seines Leibes: Kritische Edition aufgrund der von. A. Henrichs und L. Koenen besorgten Erstedition.* Papyrologica Coloniensia 14. Opladen, Köln: Westdeutscher Verlag.

Kohlberg, E. 1975. "Some Imāmī-Shīʿī Views on Taqiyya." *JAOS* 95(3):395–402. doi: 10.2307/599351.

Kohlberg, E. 1995. "Taqiyya in Shiʿi Theology and Religion." In *Secrecy and Concealment: Studies in the History of Mediterranean and Near Eastern Religions,* edited by H.H.G. Kippenberg and G.G. Stroumsa, 345–80. SHR 65. Leiden: Brill.

Kohlberg, E. 2012. "Jaʿfar al-Sadiq (702–65)." In *The Princeton Encyclopedia of Islamic Political Thought,* edited by G. Bowering, P. Crone, W. Kadi, J.S. Devin, Q. Zaman Muhammad and M. Mirza. Princeton: Princeton University Press.

Kohlberg, E., ed. 2016. *Shiʿism.* The Formation of the Classical Islamic World 33. London: Routledge (eBook. Original work published 2003).

Kraemer, R.S. 1980. "The Conversion of Women to Ascetic Forms of Christianity." *Signs* 6(2):298–307.

Krautheimer, R. 1965. *Early Christian and Byzantine Architecture.* Harmondsworth: Penguin Books. Repr., New Haven: Yale University Press, 1986.

Kristionat, J. 2013. *Zwischen Selbstverständlichkeit und Schweigen: Die Rolle der Frau im frühen Manichäismus.* Oikumene: Studien zur antiken Weltgeschichte 11. Heidelberg: Verlag Antike.

Kugener, M.A., and F. Cumont. 1912. *Recherches sur le Manichéisme: II. Extrait de la CXXIIIᵉ homélie de Sévère d'Antioche; III. L'inscription de Salone.* Bruxelles: Lamertin.

Kyrtatas, D.J. 1988. "Prophets and priests in early Christianity: Production and transmission of religious knowledge from Jesus to John Chrysostom". *International Sociology* 3(4):365–83.

Kyrtatas, D.J. 2005. "The Significance of Leadership and Organisation in the Spread of Christianity". In *The Spread of Christianity in the First Four Centuries: Essays in explanation,* edited by W.V. Harris, 53–68. Leiden: Brill.

Lampe, G.W.H., ed. 1961. *A Patristic Greek lexicon.* Oxford: Clarendon.

Le Boulluec, A. 1985. *La notion d'hérésie dans la littérature grecque, IIᵉ–IIIᵉ siècles.* 2 vols. Paris: Études augustiniennes.

Leurini, C. 2009. "The Manichaean Church between Earth and Paradise." In *New Light on Manichaeism: Papers from the Sixth International Congress on Manichaeism, Organized by the International Association of Manichaean Studies,* edited by J.D. BeDuhn, 169–79. NHMS 64. Leiden: Brill.

Leurini, C. 2013. *The Manichaean Church: An Essay Mainly Based on the Texts from Central Asia*. Orientale Roma 1. Rome: Scienze e lettere ISMEO. doi: 10.1017/S1356186315000371.

Leurini, C. 2017. *Hymns in Honour of the Hierarchy and Community, Installation Hymns and Hymns in Honour of Church Leaders and Patrons: Middle Persian and Parthian Hymns in the Berlin Turfan Collection*. Turnhout: Brepols.

Levy, S.J. 1996. "Stalking the Amphisbaena." *Journal of Consumer Research* 23(3):163–76. doi: 10.1086/209476.

Liebeschuetz, J.H.W.G. 2011. *Ambrose and John Chrysostom: Clerics Between Desert and Empire*. Oxford: Oxford University Press.

Lieu, J.M. 1998. "The Forging of Christian Identity." *Mediterranean Archaeology* 11:71–82.

Lieu, J.M. (31.05.2004). "The Synagogue and the Separation of the Christians." In *Jewish-Christian Relations: Insights and Issues in the ongoing Jewish-Christian Dialogue*/ICCJ, https://www.jcrelations.net/fr/article/the-synagogue-and-the-separation-of-the-christians.pdf.

Lieu, J.M. 2016. *Neither Jew nor Greek?: Constructing Early Christianity*. 2nd ed. Cornerstones Series. London: T&T Clark.

Lieu, S.N.C. 1981a. "Precept and Practice in Manichaean Monasticism." *JTS* 32(1):153–73. doi: 10.1093/jts/XXXII.1.153.

Lieu, S.N.C. 1981b. *The Diffusion and Persecution of Manichaeism in Rome and China: A Comparative Study*. PhD diss., University of Oxford.

Lieu, S.N.C. 1983. "An Early Byzantine Formula for the Renunciation of Manichaeism: The Capita VII contra Manichaeos of Zacharias of Mitylene. Introduction, Text, Translation and Commentary." *JAC* 26:152–218.

Lieu, S.N.C. 1985. *Manichaeism in the Later Roman Empire and Medieval China. A Historical Survey*. Manchester: Manchester University Press.

Lieu, S.N.C. 1986a. "Some Themes in Later Roman Anti-Manichaean Polemics: I." *BJRL* 68(2):434–72. doi: 10.7227/BJRL.68.2.7.

Lieu, S.N.C. 1986b. "Some Themes in Later Roman Anti-Manichaean Polemics: II." *BJRL* 69(1):235–75. doi: 10.7227/BJRL.69.1.10.

Lieu, S.N.C. 1992. *Manichaeism in the Later Roman Empire and Medieval China*. 2nd Rev. and exp. ed. WissUNT 63. Tübingen: Mohr Siebeck.

Lieu, S.N.C. 1994a. *Manichaeism in Mesopotamia and the Roman East*. RGRW 118. Leiden: Brill.

Lieu, S.N.C. 1994b. Review of *Die Argumentation in den griechisch-christlichen Antimanichaica*, by W.W. Klein. *JRAS* 4:258–59. doi: 10.1017/s1356186300005502.

Lieu, S.N.C. 1997. Manichaeism in Early Byzantium: Some Observations. In *Atti del Terzo Congresso Internazionale di Studi "Manicheismo e Oriente Cristiano Antico". Arcavacata di Rende, Amantea, 31 Agosto–5 Settembre 1993*, edited by L. Cirillo and A. van Tongerloo, 217–34. MS 3. Turnhout: Brepols.

Lieu, S.N.C. 1998a. *Manichaeism in Central Asia and China.* NHMS 45. Leiden: Brill.

Lieu, S.N.C. 1998b. "The Self-Identity of the Manichaeans in the Roman East." *Mediterranean Archaeology* 11:205–27.

Lieu, S.N.C. 2007. "Christianity and Manichaeism." In *The Cambridge History of Christianity. Volume 2: Constantine to c.600*, edited by A. Casiday and F.W. Norris, 279–95. Cambridge: Cambridge University Press.

Lieu, S.N.C., ed. 2010. *Greek and Latin Sources on Manichaean Cosmogony and Ethics.* Translated by G. Fox and J. Sheldon (with Introduction and Commentary by S.N.C. Lieu). CFM. Subsidia 6. Turnhout: Brepols & Ancient Cultures Research Centre. Macquarie University, N.S.W. Australia.

Lieu, S.N.C. 2015. "The Diffusion, Persecution and Transformation of Manichaeism in Late Antiquity and Pre-Modern China." In *Conversion in Late Antiquity: Christianity, Islam, and Beyond: Papers from the Andrew W. Mellon Foundation Sawyer Seminar, University of Oxford, 2009–2010*, edited by D.L. Schwartz, N. McLynn and A. Papaconstantinou, 123–40. Burlington: Ashgate.

Lieu, S.N.C. 2016. Review of *Mani in Dublin. Selected Papers from the Seventh International Conference of the International Association of Manichaean Studies in the Chester Beatty Library, Dublin, 8–12 September 2009*, by S.G. Richter, C. Horton and K. Ohlhafer, eds. ZAC 20(3):543–50. doi: 10.1515/zac-2016-0038.

Lieu, S.N.C. 2017. "Presidential Address: Manichaeism East and West." In *Manichaeism East and West*, edited by S.N.C. Lieu, 144–58. CFM: Analecta Manichaica 1. Turnhout: Brepols.

Lieu, S.N.C., L. Eccles, M. Franzmann, I. Gardner and K. Parry. 2012. *Medieval Christian and Manichaean Remains from Quanzhou (Zayton)*. CFM. Archaeologica et Iconographica 2. Turnhout: Brepols & Ancient Cultures Research Centre. Macquarie University, N.S.W. Australia.

Lieu, S.N.C. and J.M. Lieu. 1994. "'Felix Conversus ex Manichaeis': A Case of Mistaken Identity?" In *Manichaeism in Mesopotamia and the Roman East*, 153–55. RGRW 118. Leiden: Brill.

Lim, R. 1989. "Unity and Diversity among Western Manichaeans: A Reconsideration of Mani's Sancta Ecclesia." *Revue d'Études Augustiniennes et Patristiques* 35 (2):231–50. doi: 10.1484/j.rea.5.104599.

Lim, R. 1995. *Public Disputation, Power, and Social Order in Late Antiquity.* Berkeley: University of California Press.

Lim, R. 2001. "Christian Triumph and Controversy." In *Interpreting Late Antiquity: Essays on the Postclassical World*, edited by G.W. Bowersock, P. Brown and O. Grabar, 196–218. Cambridge, Mass.: Belknap Press of Harvard University Press.

Lim, R. 2008. "The *Nomen Manichaeorum* and Its Uses in Late Antiquity." In *Heresy and Identity in Late Antiquity*, edited by E. Iricinschi and H.M. Zellentin, 143–67. Tübingen: Mohr Siebeck.

Linder, A. 1987. *The Jews in Roman Imperial Legislation*. Detroit: Wayne State University Press; Jerusalem: The Israel Academy of Sciences and Humanities.

Liu, X. 1998. *Silk and Religion: An Exploration of Material Life and the Thought of People, AD 600–1200*: Oxford University Press.

Lössl, J. 2021. "The Religious Innovator Tatian: A Precursor of Mani in Syrian Christianity?" In *Manichaeism and Early Christianity. Selected Papers from the 2019 Pretoria Congres and Consultation*, edited by J. van Oort, 1–23. NHMS 99. Leiden: Brill.

Louth, A. 1990. "The Date of Eusebius' Historia Ecclesiastica." *JThS* 41(1):111–23. doi: 10.1093/jts/41.1.111.

Louth, A. 2007. *The Origins of the Christian Mystical Tradition: from Plato to Denys*. 2nd ed. Oxford: Oxford University Press.

Luther, A. 1999. "Die Einnahme von Birtha Asporaku durch Sapor I." *Göttinger Forum für Altertumswissenschaft* 2:77–84.

Lyman, R. 1989. "Arians and Manichees on Christ." *JThS* 40(2):493–503.

Maas, P. 1912. "Metrische Akklamationen der Byzantiner." *ByzZ* 21(1):28–51. doi: 10.1515/byzs.1912.21.1.28.

Maier, H.O. 1995a. "Religious Dissent, Heresy and Households in Late Antiquity." *VC* 49(1):49–63. doi: 10.2307/1584154.

Maier, H.O. 1995b. "The Topography of Heresy and Dissent in Late-Fourth-Century Rome." *Historia* 44(2):232–49.

Malingrey, A.-M., and S. Zincone. 2014. "John Chrysostom." In *Encyclopedia of Ancient Christianity*, edited by A. di Berardino, 429–33. Downers Grove IL: InterVarsity Press.

Mango, C.A. 1980. *Byzantium: The Empire of New Rome*. London: Weidenfeld & Nicolson.

Mango, C.A., and R. Scott, eds. 1997. *The Chronicle of Theophanes Confessor: Byzantine and Near Eastern History, AD 284–813*. Oxford: Clarendon Press.

Martindale, J.R., ed. 1980. *The Prosopography of the Later Roman Empire. Vol. II A.D. 395–527*. Cambridge: Cambridge University Press.

Matsangou, R. 2017a. "Strategius' Assignment: An Inquiry into Manichaeism and the Manichaean Churches of the Roman East, during the 4th Century." In *Zur lichten Heimat. Studien zu Manichäismus, Iranistik und Zentralasienkunde im Gedenken an Werner Sundermann*, edited by Team "Turfanforschung", 395–408. Wiesbaden: Harrassowitz.

Matsangou, R. 2017b. "Real and Imagined Manichaeans in Greek Patristic Anti-Manichaica (4th–6th Centuries)." In *Manichaeism East and West*, edited by S.N.C. Lieu, E.C.D. Hunter, E. Morano and N.A. Pedersen, 159–70. CFM: Analecta Manichaica 1. Turnhout: Brepols.

Matsangou, R. 2021. "The 'Children' of the Manichaeans: Wandering Extreme Ascetics in The Roman East Compared." In *Manichaeism and Early Christianity. Selected Papers from the 2019 Pretoria Congres and Consultation*, edited by J. van Oort, 374–400. NHMS 99. Leiden: Brill.

Matsangou, 2022. "Legal Aspects Regarding Manichaean Assembly Places in The Later Roman Empire." In *Manichaica Taurinensia: Proceedings of the 9th International Conference of IAMS*, edited by S.N.C. Lieu, E. Morano, and N.A. Pedersen, 243–52. CFM: Analecta Manichaica 2. Turnhout: Brepols.

Maxwell, J.L. 2006. *Christianization and Communication in Late Antiquity: John Chrysostom and his Congregation in Antioch*. Cambridge: Cambridge University Press.

Mayer, W. 1997. "John Chrysostom and his Audience: Distinguishing Different Congregations at Antioch and Constantinople." In *Preaching, Second Century, Tertullian to Arnobius, Egypt before Nicaea. International Conference on Patristic Studies (Oxford 1995)*, edited by E.A. Livingstone, 70–75. StPatr 31. Leuven: Peeters.

Mayer, W. 2005. *The Homilies of St John Chrysostom: Provenance, Reshaping the Foundations*. OrChrAn 273. Rome: Edizioni Orientalia Christiana.

Mertens, M., ed. and trans. 2002. *Les Alchimistes Grecs. Tome IV, 1re partie: Zosime de Panopolis – Mémoires authentiques*. 2nd ed. Paris: Les Belles Lettres.

Mikkelsen, G.B. 1997. *Bibliographia Manichaica: A Comprehensive Bibliography of Manichaeism through 1996*, CFM. Subsidia 1. Turnhout: Brepols.

Minale, V.M. 2010. "Alcune riflessioni sulla recezione della legislazione antimanichea in epoca bizantina e sulla sua applicazione, con un accenno ad un'ipotesi di ricerca." *RIDA* 57:523–61.

Minale, V.M. 2011. "Diritto bizantino ed eresia manichea: storia di un'ossessione." In *Introduzione al diritto bizantino: da Giustiniano ai Basilici*, edited by J.H.A. Lokin and B.H. Stolte, 351–78. Pavia: IUSS Press.

Minale, V.M. 2012a. "Byzantine Law and Manichaean Heresy: Some Remarks about Ekl. XVII. 52." In *Gnostica et Manichaica. Festschrift für Aloysius van Tangerloo*, edited by M. Knüppel and Luigi Cirillo, 21–41. StOR 65. Wiesbaden: Harrassowitz.

Minale, V.M. 2012b. "Byzantine Law and Manichaean Heresy: Some Considerations about Ekl. XVII. 52." In *Epetēris tou Kentrou ereunēs tēs istorias tou Ellenikou dikaiou*, 173–92. Annals of the Research Centre for the History of Greek Law 44. Athens.

Minale, V.M. 2013. *Legislazione imperiale e manicheismo da Diocleziano a Costantino: genesi di un'eresia*. Napoli: Jovene.

Minale, V.M. 2014. "Costantino, Strategio Musoniano e i Manichei: ancora su Amm. Marc. Res Gestae 15.3.2." In *Religione e diritto romano. La cogenza del rito*, edited by S. Randazzo, 333–56. Le Tricase: Libellula.

Minale, V.M. 2015. "Diritto bizantino ed eresia manichea: alcune riflessioni su sch. 3 ad Bas. 21.1. 45." *Iuris antiqui historia* 7:129–52.

Minale, V.M. 2016a. "I Valentiniani contro i Manichei: su CTh. 16.5.3 (372) e CTh. 16.7.3 (393)." *Studia et documenta historiae et iuris* 82:497–522.

Minale, V.M. 2016b. "Manichaean Women and Poena Inopiae: On the Context of Justinian's Nov. 109." *KOINΩNIA (Rivista dell'Associazione di Studi Tardoantichi)* 40:411–37.

Mirecki, P.A. 2007. "Acta Archelai 63.5–6 and PGM I. 42–195: A Rooftop Ritual for Acquiring an Aerial Spirit Assistant." In *Frontiers of Faith: The Christian Encounter with Manichaeism in the Acts of Archelaus*, edited by J.D. BeDuhn and P.A. Mirecki, 149–55. NHMS 61. Leiden: Brill.

Mirecki, P.A., and J.D. BeDuhn. 1997. "Emerging from Darkness: Manichaean Studies at the End of the 20th Century." In *Emerging from Darkness: Studies in the Recovery of Manichaean Sources*, edited by P.A. Mirecki and J.D. BeDuhn, vii–x. NHMS 43. Leiden: Brill.

Mirecki, P.A., and J.D. BeDuhn. 2001. "Introduction. The Light and the Darkness: Studies in Manichaeism and its World." In *The Light and the Darkness: Studies in Manichaeism and its World*, edited by P.A. Mirecki and J.D. BeDuhn, 1–4. Leiden: Brill.

Mitchell, C.W., ed. 1912. *S. Ephraim's Prose Refutations of Mani, Marcion and Bardaisan, of which the greater part has been transcribed from the palimpsest B.M. Add. 14623 and is now first published. Vol. 1: The Discourses Addressed to Hypatius*. London: Williams and Norgate.

Mitteis, L. 1891. *Reichsrecht und Volksrecht in den östlichen Provinzen des römischen Kaiserreichs: mit Beiträgen zur Kenntniss des griechischen Rechts und der spätrömischen Rechtsentwicklung*: Leipzig: Teubner.

Mommsen, T. 1899. *Römisches Strafrecht*: Leipzig: Duncker & Humblot.

Nawotka, K. 2017. *The Alexander Romance by Ps.-Callisthenes: A Historical Commentary*. Leiden: Brill.

Omont, H. 1918. "Fragments d'un très ancien manuscrit latin provenant de l'Afrique du Nord." *CRAI* 62(4):241–50. doi: 10.3406/crai.1918.74020.

Papachryssanthou, D. 1970. "Les sources grecques pour l'histoire des Pauliciens d'Asie Mineure I. Pierre de Sicile. Histoire des Pauliciens," *Travaux et mémoires* 4:7–67.

Parry, K. 2016. "The Doves of Antioch: Severus, Chalcedonians, Monothelites, and Iconoclasm." In *Severus of Antioch. His Life and Times*, edited by Y. Youssef and J. D' Alton, 138–59. Leiden: Brill.

Pedersen, N.A. 2004. *Demonstrative Proof in Defence of God: A Study of Titus of Bostra's Contra Manichaeos: The Work's Sources, Aims, and Relation to its Contemporary Theology*. NHMS 56. Leiden: Brill.

Pedersen, N.A., ed. 2006. *Manichaean Homilies: With a Number of Hitherto Unpublished Fragments (The Manichaean Coptic Papyri in the Chester Beatty Library)*. CFM. Series Coptica 2. Turnhout: Brepols.

Pedersen, N.A. 2012. "The Term Mysterion in Coptic-Manichaean Texts." In *Mystery and Secrecy in the Nag Hammadi Collection and Other Ancient Literature: Ideas and Practices. Studies for Einar Thomassen at Sixty*, edited by C.H. Bull, L.I. Lied and J.D. Turner, 133–43. NHMS 76. Leiden: Brill.

Pedersen, N.A. 2013a. "Manichaean Exonyms and Autonyms (Including Augustine's Writings)." *TS* 69(1):1–7. doi: 10.4102/hts.v69i1.1358.

Pedersen, N.A. 2013b. "Manichaean Self-Designators in the Western Tradition." In *Augustine and Manichaean Christianity: Selected Papers from the First South African Conference on Augustine of Hippo, University of Pretoria, 24–26 April 2012*, edited by J. van Oort, 177–96. Leiden: Brill.

Pedersen, N.A. 2015a. "Syriac Texts in Manichaean Script: New Evidence." In *Mani in Dublin. Selected Papers from the Seventh International Conference of the International Association of Manichaean Studies in the Chester Beatty Library, Dublin, 8–12 September 2009*, edited by S.G. Richter, C. Horton and K. Ohlhafer, 284–88. NHMS 88. Leiden: Brill.

Pedersen, N.A. 2015b. Review of *Titi Bostrensis Contra Manichaeos Libri IV Graece et Syriace*, by A. Roman, T.S. Smith, P.-H. Poirier and J. Declerck eds. *VC* 69(5):571–74. doi: 10.1163/15700720-12341245.

Pedersen, N.A. 2019. Review of *Biblical and Manichaean Citations in Titus of Bostra's Against the Manichaeans: An Annotated Inventory*, by P.-H. Poirier & T. Pettipiece. *VC* 73:463–71.

Pedersen, N.A, and J.M. Larsen, eds. 2013. *Manichaean Texts in Syriac: First Editions, New Editions and Studies*. CFM Syriaca 1. Turnhout: Brepols.

Pennacchietti, F.A. 1988. "Gli Acta Archelai e il viaggio di Mani nel Bet Arbaye." *Rivista di storia e letteratura religiosa* 24(3):503–14.

Perczel, I. 2004. "A Philosophical Myth in the Service of Christian Apologetics? Manichees and Origenists in the Sixth Century." In *Religious Apologetics – Philosophical Argumentation*, edited by Y. Schwartz and V. Krech, 205–36. Religion in Philosophy and Theology 10. Tübingen: Mohr Siebeck.

Peterson, E. 1935. *Der Monotheismus als politisches Problem: ein Beitrag zur Geschichte der politischen theologie im Imperium Romanum*. Leipzig: Hegner.

Pettipiece, T. 2005. "A Church to Surpass All Churches: Manichaeism as a Test Case for the Theory of Reception." *LTP* 61(2):247–60.

Pettipiece, T. 2007. "'Et sicut rex …': Competing Ideas of Kingship in the Anti-Manichaean Acta Archelai." In *Frontiers of Faith: The Christian Encounter with Manichaeism in the Acts of Archelaus*, edited by J.D. Beduhn and P.A. Mirecki, 119–29. NHMS 61. Leiden: Brill.

Pettipiece, T. 2008. "Separating Light from Darkness: Manichaean Use of Biblical Traditions in the *Kephalaia*." In *The Reception and Interpretation of the Bible in Late Antiquity: Proceedings of the Montréal Colloquium in Honour of Charles Kannengiesser, 11–13 October 2006*, edited by L. DiTommaso and L. Turcescu, 419–27. Leiden: Brill.

Pettipiece, T. 2014. "Parallel Paths. Tracing Manichaean Footprints along the Syriac Book of Steps." In *Breaking the Mind*, edited by K.S. Heal and R.A. Kitchen, 32–40. Washington, DC: Catholic University of America Press.

Pettipiece, T. 2015. "Manichaeism at the Crossroads of Jewish, Christian, and Muslim Traditions." In *Patristic Studies in the Twenty-First Century. Proceedings of an International Conference to Mark the 50th Anniversary of the International Association of Patristic Studies*, edited by C. Harrison, B. Bitton-Ashkelony and T. De Bruyn, 299–313. Turnhout: Brepols.

Pharr, C., ed. 1952. *The Theodosian Code and Novels, and the Sirmondian Constitutions. A Translation with Commentary, Glossary, and Bibliography.* Princeton: Princeton University Press.

Poirier, P.-H. 2001. "Une nouvelle hypothèse sur le titre des Psaumes Manichéens dits de Thomas." *Apocrypha* 12:9–28.

Poirier, P.-H. 2017. "Vues manichéennes sur les persécutions." *Pallas. Revue D'études Antiques* 104:241–53. doi.org/10.4000/pallas.7663.

Poirier, P.-H., & Pettipiece, T. 2017. *Biblical and Manichaean Citations in Titus of Bostra's Against the Manichaeans: An Annotated Inventory.* Instrumenta Patristica et Mediaevalia 78. Turnhout: Brepols.

Polotsky, H.J. 1934. *Manichäische Homilien*: Manichean Manuscripts in the Chester Beatty Collection. Stuttgart: Kohlhammer.

Polotsky, H.J., A. Böhlig and H. Ibscher, eds. 1935. *Kephalaia: mit einem Beitrag.* Vol. 1. Stuttgart: Kohlhammer.

Puech, H.-C. 1949. *Le manichéisme: son fondateur, sa doctrine.* Paris: Civilisations du Sud (S.A.E.P.).

Puech, H.-C. 1979. "Liturgie et pratiques rituelles dans le manichéisme (Collège de France, 1952–1972)." In *Sur le manichéisme et autres essais*, 235–394. Paris: Flammarion.

Quasten, J. 1960. *Patrology Vol. 3: The Golden Age of Greek Patristic Literature: From the Council of Nicaea to the Council of Chalcedon.* Utrecht: Spectrum.

Quispel, G. 1957. "The Gospel of Thomas and the New Testament." *VC* 11(1):189–207. doi: https://doi.org/10.1163/157007257X00196.

Quispel, G. 2008. "The Study of Encratism: A Historical Survey." In *Gnostica, Judaica, Catholica: Collected Essays of Gilles Quispel*, edited by J. van Oort, 329–63. NHMS 55. Leiden: Brill. (Original work published 1985).

Reeves, J.C. 1992. *Jewish Lore in Manichaean Cosmogony: Studies in the Book of Giants Traditions.* Cincinati: Hebrew Union College Press.

Reeves, J.C. 2011. *Prolegomena to a History of Islamicate Manichaeism.* Sheffield: Equinox.

Reitzenstein, R. 1931. *Eine wertlose und eine wertvolle überlieferung über den Manichäismus.* Berlin: Weidmann.

Richard, M., and M. Aubineau, eds. 1977. *Iohannis Caesariensis Presbyteri et Grammatici Opera Quae Supersunt.* CCSG 1. Turnhout: Brepols; Leuven: Leuven University Press.

Richter, S.G., ed. 1999. *The Manichaean Coptic Papyri in the Chester Beatty Library: Psalm Book Part II. Fasc. 2. (Die Herakleides-Psalmen)* CFM: Series Coptica 1.2. Turnhout: Brepols.

Ries, J. 1988. *Les études manichéennes: Des controverses de la réforme aux découvertes du XXᵉ siècle.* Louvain-la-Neuve: Centre d'histoire des religion.

Robinson, J.M. 2014. *The Manichaean Codices of Medinet Madi.* Havertown: James Clarke & Co.

Rohrbacher, D. 2005. "Why Didn't Constantius II Eat Fruit?" *Classical Quarterly* 55(1):323–26.

Rousseau, P. 1994. *Basil of Caesarea.* Berkeley: University of California Press.

Ruani, F. 2017. "John of Dara on Mani: Manichaean Interpretations of Genesis 2:17 in Syriac." In *Manichaeism East and West,* edited by S.N.C. Lieu, E.C.D. Hunter, E. Morano and N.A. Pedersen, 203–22. CFM: Analecta Manichaica 1. Turnhout: Brepols.

Rudolph, K. 2005. "Progress of Research since the Foundation of the I.A.M.S. in 1989." In *Il Manicheismo: Nuove Prospettive della Ricerca: Quinto Congresso Internazionale di Studi sul Manicheismo, Atti: Dipartimento di Studi Asiatici, Università degli Studi di Napoli "L'Orientale", Napoli, 2–8 Settembre 2001,* edited by A. Van Tongerloo and L. Cirillo, 1–8. MS 5. Turnhout: Brepols.

Ruffini, G.R. 2016. "Transport and Trade in Trimithis: The Texts from Area 1." In *Amheida II: A Late Romano-Egyptian House in Dakhla Oasis: Amheida House B2,* edited by A.L. Boozer, 353–67. New York: NYU Press.

Russell, J.R. 2004. "The Last of the Paulicians." In *Armenian and Iranian Studies,* edited by J.R. Russell, 677–91. Harvard Armenian Texts and Studies 9. Cambridge, Mass.: Harvard University Press.

Sachau, C.E. ed. and trans. 1879. Al-Biruni: *The chronology of Ancient Nations.* London: Minerva.

Sala, T.A. 2007. "Narrative Options in Manichaean Eschatology." In *Frontiers of Faith: The Christian Encounter with Manichaeism in the Acts of Archelaus,* edited by J.D. BeDuhn and P.A. Mirecki, 49–66. NHMS 61. Leiden: Brill.

Salzman, M.R. 1993. "The Evidence for the Conversion of the Roman Empire to Christianity in Book 16 of the "Theodosian Code"." *Historia* 42(3):362–78. doi: 10.2307/4436297.

Sandwell, I. 2008. Review of *The homilies of St John Chrysostom. Provenance. Reshaping the Foundations,* by Wendy Mayer 2005. *JEH* 59(1):99–100. doi: doi:10.1017/S0022046907003168.

Scher, A., ed. 1910–12. *Theodore Bar Kônai. Liber scholiorum.* CSCO 55, 69. Paris: Typographeo Reipublicae.

Schwartz, E. 1913. *Kaiser Constantin und die christliche kirche: fünf vorträge.* Leipzig: Teubner.

Scopello, M. 1995. "Vérités et contre-vérités: la vie de Mani selon les Acta Archelai." *Apocrypha* 6:203–34. doi: 10.1484/J.APOCRA.2.301113.

Scopello, M. 1997. "Julie, manichéenne d'Antioche (d'après la Vie de Porphyre de Marc le Diacre, ch. 85–91)." *Antiquité Tardive* 5:187–209. Repr., Leiden: Brill, 2005, NHMS 53: 237–91.

Scopello, M. 2000. "Hégémonius, les Acta Archelai et l'histoire de la controverse anti-manichéenne." In *Studia Manichaica. IV. Internationaler Kongreß zum Manichäismus, Berlin, 14–18 Juli 1997,* edited by R.E. Emmerick, W. Sundermann and P. Zieme, 528–45. Berlin: Akademie Verlag.

Scopello, M. 2001. "Femmes et propagande dans le manichéisme." *Connaissance des pères de l'église* 83:35–44.

Scopello, M. 2005a. *Femme, gnose et manichéisme: De l'espace mythique au territoire du réel,* NHMS 53. Leiden: Brill.

Scopello, M. 2005b. "Les passionarias du manichéisme: le rôle des femmes dans la propagande." *Religions et histoire* 3:44–47.

Scopello, M., ed. 2022. *Women in Western and Eastern Manichaeism: Selected Papers from the International Conference Les femmes dans le manichéisme occidental et oriental held in Paris, University of Paris Sorbonne, 27–28 June 2014.* NHMS 101. Leiden: Brill.

Sennett, A. 2014. *Revolutionary Marxism in Spain, 1930–1937.* Leiden: Brill.

Seston, W. 1940. "Authenticité et date de l'édit de Dioclétien contre les Manichéens." In *Mélanges de philologie: de littérature et d'histoire anciennes offerts à Alfred Ernout,* 345–54. Paris: Klincksieck.

Sfameni Gasparro, G. 2000. "Addas- Adimantus unus ex discipulis Manichaei: For the History of Manichaeism in the West." In *Studia Manichaica. IV Internationaler Kongress zum Manichäismus, Berlin 14–18 July 1997,* edited by R.E. Emmerick, W. Sundermann and P. Zieme, 546–59. Berlin: Akademie Verlag.

Shapira, D. 1999. "Manichaios, Jywndg Gryw and Other Manichaean Terms and Titles." In *Irano-Judaica IV: Studies Relating to Jewish Contacts with Persian Culture Throughout the Ages,* edited by S. Shaked and A. Netzer, 122–50. Jerusalem: Ben-Zvi Institute & Hebrew University of Jerusalem.

Shokri-Foumeshi, M. 2015. *Manis Living Gospel and the Ewangelyonig Hymns. Edition, Reconstruction and Commentary with a Codicological and Textological Approach Based on Manichaean Turfan Fragments in the Berlin Collection.* The University of Religions and Denominations Press.

Shokri-Foumeshi, M. 2017. "Identification of a Small Fragment of Mani's Living Gospel (Turfan Collection, Berlin, M5439)." *BSOAS* 80(3):473–83. doi: 10.1017/S0041977X17000945.

Shokri-Foumeshi, M. 2018. "I Am Alfa and Omega: A Jewish-Christian Schema in the Manichaean Context Based on the Middle Iranian Documents in the Turfan Collection." *Religious Inquiries* 7(13):35–54.

Shokri-Foumeshi, M., and Mostafa Farhoudi. 2014. "Mani's Living Gospel: A New Approach to the Arabic and Classical New Persian Testimonia." *Religious Inquiries* 3(6):53–67.

Silvas, A.M., ed. 2007. *Gregory of Nyssa: The Letters. Introduction, Translation and Commentary.* VCSup 83. Leiden: Brill.

Silvas, A.M. 2010. Review of *Gregorii Nysseni Epistula Canonica: Opera Dogmatica Minora, Pars 5 (= Gregorii Nysseni Opera vol. 3 Pars 5)*, by E. Mühlenberg. *ZAC* 14(2):462–64. doi: 10.1515/zac.2010.22.

Simmel, G. 1906. "The Sociology of Secrecy and of Secret Societies." *The American Journal of Sociology* 11(4):441–98.

Sims-Williams, N. 1981. "The Sogdian Fragments of Leningrad." *BSOAS* 44(2):231–40. doi: 10.1017/S0041977X00138935.

Sims-Williams, N. 1985. "The Manichaean Commandments: A Survey of the Sources." In *Acta Iranica. Papers in Honour of Professor Mary Boyce*, edited by J. Duchesne-Guillemin and P. Lecoq, 573–82. Leiden: Brill.

Skjærvø, P.O. 2006. *An Introduction to Manicheism.* [Electronic source]. Retrieved from https://archive.org/details/skjaervo-2006-intro-manicheism.

Smith, J.A. 1984. "The Ancient Synagogue, the Early Church and Singing." *Music & Letters* 65(1):1–16.

Spät, E. 2004. "The 'Teachers' of Mani in the Acta Archelai and Simon Magus." *VC* 58(1):1–23. doi: https://doi.org/10.1163/157007204772812313.

Stein, E., J.-R. Palanque, and E. Stein. 1949. *Histoire du Bas-Empire.* Paris: Desclée.

Stewart, C. 1991. *'Working the Earth of the Heart': The Messalian Controversy in History, Texts and Language to AD 431, Oxford Theological Monographs.* Oxford: Clarendon.

Stroumsa, G.G. 1982. "Monachisme et marranisme chez les Manichéens d'Egypte." *Numen* 29(2):184–201. doi: https://doi.org/10.1163/156852782X00024.

Stroumsa, G.G. 1984. *Another Seed: Studies in Gnostic Mythology.* NHMS 24. Leiden: Brill.

Stroumsa, G.G. 1985. "Gnostics and Manicheans in Byzantine Palestine." In *StPatr 18.1. Historica-Theologica-Gnostica-Biblica*, edited by E.A. Livingstone, 273–78. Kalamazoo, Michigan: Cistercian.

Stroumsa, G.G. 1986a. "Esotericism in Mani's Thought and Background." In *Codex Manichaicus Coloniensis: Atti del Simposio Internazionale (Rende – Amantea 3–7 settembre 1984)*, edited by L. Cirillo, 153–68. Cosenza: Marra. Repr. Leiden: Brill, 2005 (SHR 70, 63–78).

Stroumsa, G.G. 1986b. "The Manichaean Challenge to Egyptian Christianity." In *The Roots of Egyptian Christianity*, edited by B.A. Pearson and J.E. Goehring, 307–19. Philadelphia: Fortress.

Stroumsa, G.G. 1992. "Titus of Bostra and Alexander of Lycopolis: A Christian and a Platonic Refutation of Manichaean Dualism." In *Neoplatonism and Gnosticism*, edited by R.T. Wallis and J. Bregman, 337–49. Studies in Neoplatonism 6. State University of New York Press.

Stroumsa, G.G. 1999. "Purification and Its Discontents: Mani's Rejection of Baptism." In *Transformations of the Inner Self in Ancient Religions*, edited by J. Assmann and G.G. Stroumsa, 405–20. Leiden: Brill.

Stroumsa, G.G. 2000. "Isaac de Beausobre Revisited: The Birth of Manichaean Studies." In *Studia Manichaica. IV Internationaler Kongreß zum Manichäismus, Berlin, 14–18, Juli 1997*, edited by R.E. Emmerick, W. Sundermann and P. Zieme, 601–12. Berlin: Akademie-Verlag. Repr. Cambridge, MA: Harvard University Press, 2010.

Stroumsa, G.G. 2004. "Esotericism and Mysticism." In *Religions of the Ancient World: A Guide*, edited by S.I. Johnston, 640–56. Cambridge, Mass.: Belknap Press of Harvard University Press.

Stroumsa, G.G. 2010. *A New Science: The Discovery of Religion in the Age of Reason.* Cambridge, MA: Harvard University Press.

Stroumsa, S., and G.G. Stroumsa. 1988. "Aspects of Anti-Manichaean Polemics in Late Antiquity and under Early Islam." *HTR* 81(1):37–58.

Sundermann, W. 1974. "Iranische Lebensbeschreibungen Manis." *Acta Orientalia* 36:125–49.

Sundermann, W. 1986. "Studien zur kirchengeschichtlichen Literatur der iranischen Manichäer I." *AoF* 13(1):40–92.

Sundermann, W. 1986. "Studien zur kirchengeschichtlichen Literatur der iranischen Manichäer II." *AoF* 13(2):239–317.

Sundermann, W. 1987. "Studien zur kirchengeschichtlichen Literatur der iranischen Manichäer III." *AoF* 14(1):41–107.

Sundermann, W. 2008. "Zoroastrian Motifs in non-Zoroastrian Traditions." *JRAS* 18(2):155–65. doi:10.1017/S1356186307008036.

Sundermann, W. 2009. "Manicheism I. General Survey." *Encyclopaedia Iranica Online*: http://www.iranicaonline.org/articles/manicheism-1-general-survey.

Sundermann, W. 2009. "Manicheism IV. Missionary Activity and Technique." *Encyclopaedia Iranica Online*: http://www.iranicaonline.org/articles/manicheism-iv-missionary-activity-and-technique-.

Tardieu, M. 1979. "Vues nouvelles sur le manichéisme africain?" *Revue d'Études Augustiniennes* 25(3–4):249–55.

Tardieu, M. 1980. "Prātā et ād'ur chez les Manichéens." *ZDMG* 130(2):340–41.

Tardieu, M. 1986. "Archelaus." *Encyclopaedia Iranica Online*: http://www.iranica online.org/articles/archelaus-author.

Tardieu, M. 1988. "Sebastianus étiqueté comme manichéen." *Klio* 70(2):494–500.

Tardieu, M. 1991. "La nisba de Sisinnios." *Altorientalische Forschungen/AoF* 18(1):3–8.

Tardieu, M. 2008. *Manichaeism.* Translated by M.B. DeBevoise (Introduction by P.A. Mirecki). Urbana: University of Illinois Press. (Original work published 1981).

Teigen, H.F. 2021. *The Manichaean Church in Kellis: Social Networks and Religious Identity in Late Antique Egypt.* NHMS 100. Leiden: Brill.

Telfer, W., ed. 1955. *Cyril of Jerusalem and Nemesius of Emesa*. LCC 4. Louisville: Westminster John Knox.

Thomas, J.P., A. Constantinides-Hero, and G. Constable, eds. 2000. *Byzantine Monastic Foundation Documents: A Complete Translation of the Surviving Founders' Typika and Testaments*. Vol. 1, Dumbarton Oaks Studies 35. Washington, D.C.: Dumbarton Oaks Research Library and Collection.

Tolan, J. 2014. "Lex alterius: Using Law to Construct Confessional Boundaries." *History and Anthropology* 26(1):55–75.

Tolan, J. 2016. "What Do Legal Sources Tell Us about Social Practice? Possibilities and Limits" In *Law and Religious Minorities in Medieval Societies: Between Theory and Praxis*, edited by A. Echevarria, J.P. Monferrer-Sala and J. Tolan, 229–31. Turnhout: Brepols.

Troiannos, S.N. 1997. "The Punishments in Byzantine Law". In *Crime and Punishment in Byzantium*, edited by S.N. Troiannos, 13–65. Athens: Goulandris-Horn Foundation.

Trombley, F.R. 1993, 1994. *Hellenic Religion and Christianization, c. 370–529*. 2 Vols. Leiden: Brill.

Trotsky, L. 1973. *The Spanish Revolution, 1931–39*. Edited by L. Evans, N. Allen and G. Breitman. 1st ed. New York, N.Y.: Pathfinder Press.

Turpin, W. 1985. "The Law Codes and Late Roman Law". *RIDA* 32:339–53.

Tzamalikos, P. 2012. *The Real Cassian Revisited: Monastic Life, Greek Paideia, and Origenism in the Sixth Century*, VCSup 112. Leiden: Brill.

Vallas, S. 1993. *Minoan-Mycenaean Dionysus (Μινω-Μυχηναϊκός Διόνυσος/Minō-Mykinaikos Dionysos)*. Athens: Livani.

Van den Berg, J.A. 2010. *Biblical Argument in Manichaean Missionary Practice: The Case of Adimantus and Augustine*. NHMS 70. Leiden: Brill.

Van der Horst, P.W., and J. Mansfeld. 1974. *An Alexandrian Platonist Against Dualism: Alexander of Lycopolis' Treatise "Critique of the Doctrines of Manichaeus"*. Leiden: Brill.

Van Lindt, P. 1992. *The Names of Manichaean Mythological Figures: A Comparative Study on Terminology in the Coptic Sources*. StOR 26. Wiesbaden: Harrassowitz.

Van Oort, J. 1987. "Augustine and Mani on Concupiscentia Sexualis." In *Augustiniana Traiectina: Communications Présentées au Colloque International d'Utrecht, 13–14 Novembre 1986*, edited by J. den Boeft and J. van Oort, 137–52. Paris: Études Augustiniennes.

Van Oort, J. 1993. Review of *Die Argumentation in den griechisch-christlichen Antimanichaica*, by W.W. Klein *VC* 47:201–03.

Van Oort, J. 2000a. "Mani and Manichaeism in Augustine's De haeresibus. An Analysis of haer. 46,1." In *Studia Manichaica. IV. Internationaler Kongreß zum Manichäismus, Berlin, 14–18 Juli 1997*, edited by R.E. Emmerick, W. Sundermann and P. Zieme, 451–63. Berichte und Abhandlungen der Berlin-Brandenburgischen Akademie der Wissenschaften, Sonderband 4. Berlin: Akademie Verlag.

Van Oort, J. 2000b. "Würdigung Isaac de Beausobres (1659–1738)." In *Studia Manichaica. IV. Internationaler Kongreß zum Manichäismus, Berlin, 14–18 Juli 1997*, edited by R.E. Emmerick, W. Sundermann and P. Zieme, 658–66. Berichte und Abhandlungen der Berlin-Brandenburgischen Akademie der Wissenschaften, Sonderband 4. Berlin: Akademie Verlag.

Van Oort, J. 2002. "Mani". In *RGG*, Vierte Auflage, Band V, Tübingen: Mohr Siebeck, reprint Tübingen: Mohr Siebeck 2008, 731–32.

Van Oort, J. 2002. "Manichäismus". In *RGG*, Vierte Auflage, Band V, Tübingen: Mohr Siebeck, reprint Tübingen: Mohr Siebeck 2008, 732–41.

Van Oort, J. 2004. "The Paraclete Mani as the Apostle of Jesus Christ and the Origins of a New Church." In *The Apostolic Age in Patristic Thought*, edited by A. Hilhorst, 139–57. Leiden: Brill.

Van Oort, J. 2009. "Manichaeism: Its Sources and Influences on Western Christianity." *Verbum et Ecclesia* 30(2):126–30.

Van Oort, J. 2010. "Mani". In *RPP*, Vol. 8:24, Leiden: Brill.

Van Oort, J. 2010. "Manichaeism". In *RPP*, Vol. 8:25–30, Leiden: Brill.

Van Oort, J. 2013. "Alexander of Lycopolis, Manichaeism and Neoplatonism." In *Gnosticism, Platonism and the Late Ancient World: Essays in Honour of John D. Turner*, edited by K. Corrigan and T. Rasimus, 275–83. NHMS 82. Leiden: Brill.

Van Oort, J. 2016a. "'Human Semen Eucharist' Among the Manichaeans? The Testimony of Augustine Reconsidered in Context." *VC* 70(2):193–216. doi: 10.1163 /15700720-12301031.

Van Oort, J. 2016b. "Another Case of Human Semen Eucharist Among the Manichaeans? Notes on the 'Ceremony of the Fig' in Cyril of Jerusalem's Catechesis VI." *VC* 70(4):430–40. doi: 10.1163/15700720-12301031.

Van Oort, J. 2020a. "Manichaean Women in a Pseudo-Augustinian Testimony: An Analysis of the North African Testimonium de Manichaeis sectatoribus." In *Mani and Augustine: Collected Essays on Mani, Manichaeism and Augustine*, edited by J. van Oort, 433–42. NHMS 97. Leiden: Brill.

Van Oort, J. 2020b. "Manichaean Women in Augustine's Life and Works." In *Mani and Augustine: Collected Essays on Mani, Manichaeism and Augustine*, edited by J. van Oort, 418–32. NHMS 97. Leiden: Brill.

Van Oort, J. 2020c. "The Role of Women in Manichaeism." In *Mani and Augustine: Collected Essays on Mani, Manichaeism and Augustine*, edited by J. van Oort, 498–502. NHMS 97. Leiden: Brill.

Van Oort, J. 2020d. "Manichaean Eschatology: Gnostic-Christian Thinking about the Last Things." In *Mani and Augustine: Collected Essays on Mani, Manichaeism and Augustine*, edited by J. van Oort, 111–21. NHMS 97. Leiden: Brill.

Van Tongerloo, A. 1982. "La structure de la communauté manichéenne dans le Turkestan chinois à la lumière des emprunts Moyen-Iraniens en Ouigour." *Central Asiatic Journal* 26(3/4):262–88.

Vermes, M., and S.N.C. Lieu. 2001. *Hegemonius. Acta Archelai (The Acts of Archelaus)*. Translated by Mark Vermes with introduction and commentary by Samuel N.C. Lieu. MS 4. Turnhout: Brepols.

Wearring, A. 2008. "Manichaean Studies in the 21st Century." *Sydney Studies in Religion (Sydney Open Journals Online)*:249–61: https://openjournals.library.sydney.edu.au/index.php/SSR/article/download/254/233.

Webber, P. 2009. "Entryism in Theory, in Practice, and in Crisis: The Trotskyist Experience in New Brunswick, 1969–1973." *Left History: An Interdisciplinary Journal of Historical Inquiry and Debate* 14(1):33–57.

Whitby, M., ed. 2000. *The Ecclesiastical History of Evagrius Scholasticus*. Translated Texts for Historians 33. Liverpool: Liverpool University Press.

Whitby, M. 2006. "Factions, Bishops, Violence and Urban Decline." In *Die Stadt in der Spätantike – Niedergang oder Wandel? Akten des internationalen Kolloquiums in München am 30. und 31. Mai 2003*, edited by J.U. Krause and C. Witschel, 441–61. Stuttgart: Steiner.

Whitby, M. 2009. "The Violence of the Circus Factions." In *Organised Crime in Antiquity*, edited by K. Hopwood, 229–54. London: Classical Press of Wales.

Whitby, M., and M. Whitby, eds. 1989. *Chronicon Paschale 284–628 AD*. Translated Texts for Historians 7. Liverpool: Liverpool University Press.

White, L.M. 1990. *The Social Origins of Christian Architecture. Vol. 1, Building God's House in the Roman World: Architectural Adaptation among Pagans' Jews, and Christians*. HTS 42. Valley Forge, PA: Trinity Press International.

White, L.M. 1997. *The Social Origins of Christian Architecture. Vol. 2, Texts and Monuments for the Christian Domus Ecclesiae in its Environment*, HTS 42. Valley Forge, PA: Trinity Press International.

Widengren, G. 1965. *Mani and Manichaeism*. Translated by C. Kessler. rev. ed. London: Weidenfeld & Nicolson. Translation of *Mani und der Manichäismus*. Stuttgart: Kohlhammer, 1961.

Widengren, G. 1985. "Alexander of Lycopolis." *Encyclopaedia Iranica Online* 1(8):830, http://www.iranicaonline.org/articles/alexander-of-lycopolis.

Willoughby, H.R. 1932. Review of *Serapion of Thmuis against the Manichees*, by R. Casey. *Church History* 1(3):173–74. doi: 10.2307/3159960.

Wisse, F. 1978. "Gnosticism and Early Monasticism in Egypt." In *Gnosis. Festschrift für Hans Jonas*, edited by B. Aland, 431–40. Göttingen: Vandenhoeck & Ruprecht.

Woods, D. 2001. "Strategious and the 'Manichaeans'." *Classical Quarterly* 51(1):255–64.

Worp, K.A. ed. 1995. *Greek Papyri from Kellis. 1: (P.Kell.G.), nos. 1–90*, Dakhleh Oasis Project: Monograph 3. Oxford: Oxbow Books.

Wurst, G., ed. 1996. *The Manichaean Coptic Papyri in the Chester Beatty Library: Psalm Book. Part II. Fasc. 1 (Die Bema-Psalmen)* CFM: Series Coptica 1.1. Turnhout: Brepols.

Xatziantoniou, E. 2009. *The Religious Policy of Anastasios I (491–518): The Emperor's Attitude towards the Monophysite Issue and the Acacian Schism*. Byzantine Research Society 20. Thessaloniki: Vanias.

Yarnold, E. 2000. *Cyril of Jerusalem*. ECF. London: Routledge.

Young, F.M. 1982. "Did Epiphanius Know what he Meant by Heresy?" In *Studia Patristica, vol. 17, pt. 1*, edited by E.A. Livingstone, 199–205. Berlin: Akademie-Verlag.

Young, K. 2006. "Epiphanius of Cyprus and the Geography of Heresy." In *Violence in Late Antiquity: Perceptions and Practices*, edited by H.A. Drake, 235–51. Burlington: Ashgate.

Zangenberg, J.K. 2014. "The Functions of the Caves and the Settlement of Qumran: Reflections on a New Chapter of Qumran Research." In *The Caves of Qumran: Proceedings of the International Conference, Lugano 2014*, edited by M. Fidanzio, 195–209. Studies on the Texts of the Desert of Judah 118. Leiden: Brill.

Index of Ancient Authors and Sources

Index of Names and Subjects

Printed in the United States
by Baker & Taylor Publisher Services